1

Native Peoples of the World

An Encyclopedia of Groups, Cultures, and Contemporary Issues

Volume 3

Steven Danver, Editor

SHARPE REFERENCE

an imprint of M.E. Sharpe, Inc.

SHARPE REFERENCE

Sharpe Reference is an imprint of M.E. Sharpe, Inc.

M.E. Sharpe, Inc.
80 Business Park Drive
Armonk, NY 10504

Cover images (clockwise from top left) provided by: Pornchai Kittiwongsakul/AFP/Getty Images; Mike Goldwater/Getty Images; Alison Wright/National Geographic/Getty Images; Toshifumi Kitamura/AFP/Getty Images.

Library of Congress Cataloging-in-Publication Data

Native peoples of the world: an encyclopedia of groups, cultures, and contemporary issues / Steven Danver, editor.
   3 v. cm.
Includes bibliographical references and index.
ISBN 978-0-7656-8222-2 (cloth: alk. paper) 1. Indigenous peoples—Encyclopedias.
I. Danver, Steven Laurence.

GN380.N39 2012
305.8003—dc23   2012025160

Printed and bound in the United States

The paper used in this publication meets the minimum requirements of American National Standard for Information Sciences—Permanence of Paper for Printed Library Materials,
ANSI Z 39.48.1984.

CW (c) 10 9 8 7 6 5 4 3 2

Publisher: Myron E. Sharpe
Vice President and Director of New Product Development: Donna Sanzone
Vice President and Production Director: Carmen Chetti
Executive Development Editor: Jeff Hacker
Project Manager: Laura Brengelman
Program Coordinator: Cathleen Prisco
Editorial Assistant: Lauren LoPinto
Text Design and Cover Design: Jesse Sanchez
Typesetter: Nancy J. Connick

Contents

VOLUME 2

Europe

North America

South Asia and Middle East

VOLUME 3
Countries

Issues

viii   Contents

Native Peoples of the World

Volume 3

Countries

Countries

Argentina

Many Argentineans view their country as a melting pot of European races, with little or no recognition of the nation's native populations. This oversight ignores the significant role that both colonialism and the building of the republic after independence in 1810 played in stripping the country's indigenous populations of their land and subjugating them as a labor force. It was not until the early 1980s that Argentina's indigenous groups began to effectively protest the nation's policies of cultural repression, questioning practices that had subjugated them for so long.

During the Spanish colonial era, from the second half of the sixteenth century until 1810, authorities dealt with the native peoples in one of three ways. The *encomienda* system assigned indigenous communities to a Spanish *encomendero,* or landowner, who extracted tribute or labor in exchange for the natives' evangelization and education. Alternatively, in the central region of Pampas, along the Atlantic coast, and in the Paraná-Plate Basin, the Spanish established Catholic missions that were dedicated to the subjection of the Guaraní peoples. A third kind of relationship guaranteed separation between Hispanic and indigenous areas, while protecting the flow of commerce across them, using the indigenous areas and people as defensive buffers against possible European invasions.

After Argentina achieved independence in 1810, the emancipation processes of the River Plate provinces did not change the relationship between Creoles (people of European descent born in the Americas) and the native peoples. The Pampas and Patagonia plains and the Chaco forest remained under the sovereignty of the native peoples, who maintained commerce and diplomatic bonds with Creole authorities. During the 1870s and 1880s, however, those peoples finally were subjugated by the Argentine military. Beginning in 1878, military campaigns referred to as the "conquest of the desert" that were aimed at the extinction of native cultures led to the conquest of the Mapuche and Tehuelche peoples of Pampa and Patagonia. In the Chaco forest, these campaigns were

called "the conquest of the green desert." They concluded in 1917, completing the subjection of the Mocoví, Pilagá, Toba, and Whichí peoples. The populations conquered in these campaigns were held in military camps, deported, or used as cheap labor in the Argentine provinces, working in state-run industries such as sugarcane plantations in Salta and Tucumán or vineyards in Mendoza and San Juan. Part of the state's indigenous policy was the destruction of families and the distribution of children to households as domestic servants, measures aimed at crushing indigenous culture and identity.

Since 1983, with the return of democracy, indigenous peoples began to question the relationship between state and society. In this context, the mobilization of native organizations and communities put indigenous demands on the human rights agenda. As a result, indigenous groups succeeded in gaining a voice on the national level, evidenced by their role in the constitutional reforms of 1994, when they were able to ensure that international treaties on indigenous rights were given equal standing with the rest of the constitution.

Today, native peoples work in organizations such as the Indigenous Association of Argentina (AIRA) at the national and provincial levels and in positions that specifically serve indigenous Argentineans. They continue to demand recognition as indigenous peoples and denounce the government's policies that define "community" and "indigenous rights" in such ways that they really are aimed at protecting companies with interests in the extractive resources located on indigenous lands and backing nonindigenous landholders who dispute indigenous land claims.

Ana Ramos

See also: *Groups: Central and South America*—Mapuche. *Issues*—Land Rights.

Further Reading

Briones, Claudia, and Walter Delrio. "The 'Conquest of the Desert' as Trope and Enactment of Argentina's Manifest Destiny." In *Manifest Destinies and Indigenous Peoples,* ed. David Maybury-Lewis, Theodore MacDonald, and Biorn Maybury-Lewis. Cambridge, MA: Harvard University Press, 2009.

Briones, Claudia, and Jose Luis Lanata, eds. *Living on the Edge: Contemporary Perspectives on the Native Peoples of Pampa, Patagonia, and Tierra del Fuego.* Westport, CT: Bergin & Garvey, 2002.

Curtoni, Rafael, Axel Lazzari, and Marisa Lazzari. "Middle of Nowhere: A Place of War Memories, Commemoration, and Aboriginal Re-Emergence (La Pampa, Argentina)." *World Archaeology* 35:1 (June 2003): 61–78.

Gordillo, Gastón. *Landscapes of Devils: Tensions of Place and Memory in the Argentinean Chaco.* Durham, NC: Duke University Press, 2004.

Australia

Australia is the world's smallest continent and its sixth-largest country by area. The nation encompasses the Australian mainland and the island of Tasmania, as well as many smaller islands in the Indian and Pacific oceans.

Australia is among the world's most culturally diverse nations, with approximately 7 million immigrants from some 200 countries settling on the continent since 1945, augmenting the largely British and Aboriginal population already occupying the island. As a result, nearly half of the Australian population today is foreign born or has at least one parent who was born overseas. The country also is home to more than 350 groups of Australian Aborigines and Torres Strait Islanders, each of which has its own distinct language, laws, customs, and cultural and religious practices.

History

Australia has been inhabited by groups of Aborigines and Torres Strait Islanders for at least 40,000 years and possibly as long as 60,000 years. Before the British arrived, the continent was home to more than 400 groups of indigenous peoples, numbering approximately 315,000 altogether. At that time, these peoples lived in some 200 small countries, organized into clans that were defined by kinship.

In 1770, Captain James Cook claimed Australia's eastern coast for Great Britain. But even before the establishment of the first British colony in Australia at Sydney Cove in 1788, European diseases had begun to decimate native populations, just as they had in other colonial locations around the world. Much of the Aboriginal population of the region surrounding Sydney was killed off, leaving the region open for colonization. Additional epidemics followed, and by 1830, Australia's Aboriginal population had been reduced by somewhere between 40 and 60 percent.

Under the doctrine of *terra nullius,* which denied the presence of any ownership over the land, British settlers took possession of the land without any consideration of the indigenous peoples' land rights. From the 1800s through the 1830s, when Australians sought to colonize what they called Van Diemen's Land (Tasmania) and have the native peoples removed to the Bass Strait islands, the natives resisted. This resulted in the Black War, in which mass killings of Aborigines living on the island took place, reducing their population from approximately 4,000 in 1803 to only 250 by 1833.

Following these and other atrocities, the Australian government established the office of the Protector of Aborigines in 1838, in order to prevent further violence toward the Aboriginal peoples, to oversee their conversion to Christianity, and to ensure their assimilation into non-native Australian culture. But even when they did assimilate, the Aborigines could not hope to enjoy the full rights of other Australians, being denied both citizenship and voting rights until the 1940s–1960s. In addition, as non-natives continued to encroach on Aboriginal lands, many indigenous peoples were left to the perils of poverty and starvation. Nevertheless, the Aboriginal population increased. By the 1930s, they numbered approximately 20 percent of their population before European contact.

One of the most egregious violations of the indigenous peoples began in the late nineteenth century and was carried out as a matter of official policy between 1910 and 1970. Some 10 to 30 percent of indigenous children were removed from their families by force under state and federal child welfare and protection laws, becoming known as the "Stolen Generation." This had the effect of wreaking profound misery on many indigenous Australians and resulted in a cultural breakdown in many indigenous communities.

Some hesitant first moves toward guaranteeing Aboriginal rights were made during the late 1950s and early 1960s, when native peoples were deemed eligible for pensions and maternity rights, and the last of Australia's provinces, Queensland, finally allowed Aboriginals to vote. Native peoples were granted the rights of citizens in 1967, and a Council for Aboriginal Affairs was established.

By 1971, Neville Bonner of Queensland became the first Aboriginal appointed to Parliament; he was reelected until he retired in 1983. In 1976, the Aboriginal Land Rights Act was passed, beginning the process of recognizing the land rights that had been taken away from Australia's native people.

Current Status and Government Indigenous Policy

Australia's indigenous population today is estimated at 483,000. The largest sovereign groups of Australian Aborigines are the Anangu Pitjantjatjara, who live in the area around Uluru (Ayers Rock) and south into the autonomous Anangu Pitjantjatjara Yankunytjatjara Lands, followed by the Arrernte and the Anangu Luritja. The Aboriginal languages and dialects Pitjantjatjara, Arrernte, and Warlpiri have the greatest numbers of speakers.

Australian Aborigines have made significant cultural contributions, enriching Australian life in business, art, cooking, comedy, science, and sports. Overall, they have adapted to and become an integral part of Australia's open-minded, comfortable, and broadly egalitarian society. Australian society has no formal or deep-rooted class distinctions, as in other countries. Thus, every Australian, including Aborigines, is considered equal under the law and has the right to be appreciated, respected, and treated in a fair manner. Aborigines are actively claiming their rights to equal-

ity, freedom of speech, and participation in mainstream Australian society.

During the 1990s and 2000s, Australia began the long and difficult process of coming to terms with the drastic ramifications that its policies have had on its native populations. In 1992, the Australian High Court, in *Mabo and Others v. Queensland* (No. 2), recognized the unique status of Australian Aborigines and guaranteed their land rights. The Australian government, beginning with the *Bringing them Home* report presented to Parliament in May 1997, has recognized past injustices and discrimination against its native population and continues to seek settlement. The report gave fifty-four recommendations for addressing and ending injustices toward Australia's native peoples that include human rights, language rights, land and water rights, and strategies for the development of a permanently viable life for the Aborigines.

Beginning in 1998, the National Day of Healing, popularly known as National Sorry Day, has been observed each May 26, in expression of regret over the systematic cultural repression, denial of land and water rights, and specifically the forced removal of Ab-

ULURU (AYERS ROCK)

Uluru is the Australian Aboriginal word for a huge red monolith in the central Australian desert, located approximately 300 miles (480 kilometers) southwest of Alice Springs in the Northern Territory. Rising out of the desert, Ayers Rock towers to a height of 1,142 feet (348 meters) and has a circumference of approximately 5.5 miles (9 kilometers).

Considered sacred to the indigenous people, Uluru provided a traditional meeting place for the Anangu Pitjantjatjara people, as it is able to support hundreds of people in a comfortable fortress amid the otherwise harsh desert environment. Pools found at the base of Uluru provided a permanent water supply, while numerous caves offered shelter from the desert winds and summer heat. Rich in wallabies, lizards, birds, vegetables, and fruits, the area near Uluru provided reliable sources of food. In fact, Uluru was ecologically vital to the traditional people of the central Australian desert.

The imposing physical presence of Uluru has given rise to a rich oral history reflecting the local indigenous cosmology. Myriad ochre paintings and rock engravings are found in the caves and along the rock faces. For instance, on the north side of Uluru are depicted stories of Kulpunya, a devil dog sent as a curse to harm the Mala people. A related wealth of oral traditions and creation

stories is expressed by the indigenous people in song, dance, dot paintings, and rock art.

Elders use these methods to educate young people about their culture and environment. Indigenous youth hear stories about Lira (poisonous snake men) and Kunina (carpet snake men) and their epic contests on the south side of Uluru. The Lira stand today as desert oaks in the plains surrounding Uluru. Tales of Kulikkudgeri, the leader of the Lira men; Linga the lizard man; and Tjinderi-tjinderiba, the Willy wagtail woman, are among other legends told at Uluru.

Colonial explorer William Gosse was the first European to observe Uluru on July 19, 1873. He named the site Ayers Rock, after the chief secretary of South Australia, Sir Henry Ayers. The inhospitable terrain attracted few Europeans, and at the turn of the twentieth century, the region became an Aboriginal reserve.

In 1950, the area became known as Ayers Rock National Park. In 1985, the title to the site was returned to the traditional owners, who, in turn, granted the Australian National Parks and Wildlife Service a ninety-nine-year lease on the park. In 1987, the United Nations Educational, Scientific and Cultural Organization designated Uluru-Kata Tjuta National Park as a World Heritage Site.

Greg Blyton

Uluru (Ayers Rock) is a massive, red, freestanding monolith that rises from the plains of central Australia. The formation is considered sacred by the Pitjantjatjara (Anangu), area Aborigines whose ancestral spirits are said to inhabit the site. *(Torsten Blackwood/AFP/Getty Images)*

original children from their homes to place them into mission and boarding schools. The idea also has taken hold in Australian popular culture, with expressions of reparations being put forth by the popular music group Midnight Oil, whose leader, Peter Garrett, has advocated for Aboriginal rights as a Member of Parliament since 2004.

In 2008, the government, headed by Prime Minister Kevin Rudd, officially apologized to the "Stolen Generation" of Aboriginal children removed from their homes, pledging to improve indigenous education, health care, and housing. However, some, such as Aboriginal activist and writer Noel Pearson, have expressed doubts about the sincerity of the gesture, as it was not accompanied by any form of reparation.

Despite such doubts, the Australian government has shown that it is now more committed to achieving reconciliation between indigenous and nonindigenous Australians and to remedying the inequality between them than it has been in past decades. This resolution includes a symbolic acknowledgment of the privileged place of First Australians. More important, the Australian government has incorporated effective and practical measures to eradicate the profound economic and social disadvantages experienced by numerous indigenous Australians, particularly in areas of health, education, employment, and housing. It is anticipated that these measures will have a practical, positive impact on the everyday lives of indigenous Australians in future decades.

Sweta Lal

See also: *Groups: East Asia and Oceania*—Indigenous Australians. *Issues*—Assimilation; Colonialism; Land Rights.

Further Reading

Attwood, Bain. *Telling the Truth About Aboriginal History.* Sydney, Australia: Allen & Unwin, 1994.

Broome, Richard. *Aboriginal Australians: A History Since 1788.* 4th ed. Sydney, Australia: Allen & Unwin, 2010.

———. *The Victorians: Arriving.* Sydney, Australia: Fairfax, Syme & Weldon, 1984.

Chesterman, John. *Citizens Without Rights: Aborigines and Australian Citizenship.* New York: Cambridge University Press, 1996.

Coombs, H.C. *Aboriginal Autonomy: Issues and Strategies.* New York: Cambridge University Press, 1995.

Cunneen, Chris. *Conflict, Politics and Crime: Aboriginal Communities and the Police.* Sydney, Australia: Allen & Unwin, 2001.

Flood, Josephine. *The Original Australians: Story of the Aboriginal People.* Sydney, Australia: Allen & Unwin, 2007.

Pearson, Noel. "Contradictions Cloud the Apology to the Stolen Generations." *The Australian,* February 12, 2008.

Belize

Belize is located on the northeastern coast of Central America. It is bordered by Mexico to the north, the Caribbean Sea to the east, and Guatemala to the south and the west. Covering approximately 8,800 square miles (22,800 square kilometers), the country had just over 300,000 inhabitants in 2010, the smallest population among mainland nations in the Americas. Belize is a remarkably culturally diverse region, blending Caribbean, Central American, and other cultural influences. The Maya, descendants of the original inhabitants of the Yucatán Peninsula, are the largest native group in Belize.

Much of Belize's population is multiracial. The majority of Belizeans are of English Creole or mestizo (mixed indigenous and Spanish heritage) ancestry. Approximately 11 percent of the population is categorized as Maya only, and three Maya groups are found in Belize: the Kekchi, Mopan, and Yucatec Maya. Indigenous Belizeans also include the Garinagu, who are of mixed African, Arawak, and Carib ancestry. In addition, the country is home to significant expatriate communities from China and the United States, as well as other Central American countries. Today, the majority of Maya in Belize speak distinctive Maya dialects called Kekchi and Mopan. English, however, is the country's official language.

In approximately 1500 B.C.E., the Maya spread southward from the Yucatán Peninsula into present-day Belize. They located themselves in an area with the greatest potential for agriculture, taking advantage of the long rainy season and natural resources of the dense rain forest. To grow crops, they heaped up the soil on elevated fields called terraces in order to exploit the available land. As a result, by 600 B.C.E., small villages had developed into cities, and an advanced civilization had taken hold that lasted until approximately 600 C.E. More Maya peoples arrived in Belize during the nineteenth century, refugees of the Caste War of Yucatán (1847–1901) and of slavery at the hands of business owners in Guatemala.

The indigenous Garinagu are a Creole people, descendants of African slaves and Kalinago people from the Caribbean island of St. Vincent. They were exiled to Belize by the British in 1803 and today live primarily in the southern part of the country, around the city of Punta Gorda.

Belize's government is a parliamentary democracy belonging to the British Commonwealth. Known as British Honduras until 1973, Belize was the last British colony on the American mainland, achieving independence only in 1981. The government of Belize practices no institutionalized discrimination, although the Creoles, who usually are lighter skinned, tend to dominate the country politically and economically.

The discovery of oil in the Cayo and Toledo districts, which are home to many Maya peoples, has brought land rights issues to the fore, as multinational oil companies seek to exploit the region's natural resources. The Garinagu were able to convince the government to declare a national holiday on November 19 to commemorate their arrival in Belize, a step forward in official recognition of this group. As of 2012, however, the native peoples had had little success in advocating for government protection of their land and its resources.

James E. Seelye, Jr.

See also: *Groups: Central and South America*—Garífuna; Maya. *Issues*—Colonialism; Mining.

Further Reading

Clendinnen, Inga. *Ambivalent Conquests: Maya and Spaniard in Yucatan, 1517–1570.* 2nd ed. New York: Cambridge University Press, 2003.

Sharer, Robert, and Loa Traxler. *The Ancient Maya.* Stanford, CA: Stanford University Press, 2005.

Thompson, Peter. *Belize: A Concise History.* Basingstoke, UK: Macmillan Caribbean, 2005.

Bolivia

Native peoples historically have constituted a majority of Bolivia's population, yet they have long struggled with the legacy of colonialism. Absorbed by the Spanish Empire in the sixteenth century, the Aymara, Quechua, and Uru-Chipaya peoples of the central Andes Mountains provided labor to the region's silver mining operations, which continued after independence. Starting in the 1950s, the indigenous people of the Bolivian highlands began to make steady gains in terms of their socioeconomic status.

The native people of the eastern lowlands, however, had a different historical trajectory. With lower population densities and greater linguistic diversity, the lowland peoples avoided control by outsiders for a longer time. Once regular contact was established, however, they occupied a peripheral position in national affairs.

The central Andes formed a populous quarter of the Inca Empire at the time of the Spanish conquest. The first European settlements in what is now Bolivia were established in 1538. Economic necessity resulted in the subjugation of the native peoples in a system of involuntary labor known as the *mita*. Under the mita, indigenous communities were required to send one-seventh of their male members to work in the mines annually. Economic exactions and disease took a devastating toll on the indigenous peoples, resulting in a population decline that did not taper off until the eighteenth century.

In the lowlands, the Spanish began a slower expansion. Catholic missions were established among the Chiquitano and Moxo peoples during the second half of the seventeenth century. Spanish conquistadors became landowners, bringing the hacienda system of estate ownership with them. In 1780, rebellion engulfed the central Andes. Julián Apasa, known as Túpac Katari, led the most threatening uprising. The Spanish did not completely pacify the region until 1784.

On August 6, 1825, Bolivia declared its independence from Spain. A year later, the native peoples numbered 800,000 in a country of 1.1 million. But independence failed to substantially improve their position, as a Hispanic national identity undermined the use of native languages.

The Bolivian government stepped up its attacks on native communities toward the end of the nineteenth century. In 1874, the Disentailment Law sought to break up indigenous communities. In the eastern lowlands, ranching and an ephemeral rubber boom had similar deleterious effects on native peoples. At the same time, in the Andean foothills, Franciscan friars finally established missions among the Guaraní-speaking Chiriguano.

On the eve of the twentieth century, native peoples played a decisive role in the Federalist War (1898–1899), hoping in vain to reverse their land losses. Rebellions and repression punctuated the early twentieth century. In March 1921, an uprising shook the Department of La Paz, and in July and August 1927, another rebellion broke out in the Department of Potosí. Although the latter rebellion again provoked repression, the government recognized that indigenous land losses had destabilized the countryside, and it sought to slow the process.

In the 1930s, Bolivia attempted to exert sovereignty over the Paraguay River, going to war with Paraguay in what became known as the Chaco War (1932–1935), which claimed the lives of some 52,400 Bolivians and resulted in no territorial expansion. Highland native

EVO MORALES

In 2005, Evo Morales became the first elected indigenous president of Bolivia. Although six previous Bolivian presidents were of mixed ancestry, they came to power either through military coups or as the result of military interference in elections. Supporters point out that Morales is the first native head of state in Bolivia since the Inca Empire. He first became known as the leader of the *cocaleros*, the coca leaf growers' union. Although the coca plant has been used for centuries by the region's natives in medicine and religious ceremonies, efforts by the U.S. and Bolivian governments to eliminate the plant because of its use in the cocaine drug trade had alienated the Indian majority.

As the leader of the Movimiento A Socialismo (MAS, Movement Toward Socialism), Morales is part of a group of national leaders in Latin America who have pledged to end U.S. domination of the region. Joining with controversial Venezuelan President Hugo Chavez, Nicaraguan President Daniel Ortega, Ecuadorian President Rafael Correa, and representatives of the island nations of Antigua, Cuba, Dominica, and Saint Vincent, Morales led Bolivia in the Bolivarian Alliance for the Americas, an organization that rejects capitalism, neoliberalism, and foreign intrusion, incorporating populist rhetoric and socialist ideals. Both MAS and Morales have pledged to lead the organization as an indigenous movement.

Morales is an Aymara Indian, born Juan Evo Morales Ayma on October 26, 1959, in the small town of Orinoca in the Andes highlands. While he never finished school, Morales worked first as a child in the sugarcane fields and then as a herder, bricklayer, baker, and musician as a teenager. In 1981, he joined the coca leaf growers' union and was elected general secretary in 1985 and executive secretary in 1988. Often jailed, he was nearly beaten to death by the police in 1989.

MAS was formed in 1995, and two years later, Morales was elected to the Bolivian Congress. In 2002, the Congress voted to expel him because of comments that he had made advocating farmers' self-defense; when three police officers subsequently were killed, some argued that Morales's comments had played a part in the incident. Morales ran for president the same year and came in a strong second. He ran again in 2005 and won the presidency with nearly 54 percent of the vote.

Since taking office, Morales successfully has fended off a separatist movement by mestizo racists in the eastern region of the nation. He also has passed a far more democratic constitution, has nationalized some of the gas operations in Bolivia, and has renegotiated royalties with foreign companies, allaying their fears that he would seize their assets. Morales survived a recall referendum and assassination attempt, and his support grew dramatically. He won the referendum with 67 percent and reelection to a second term in 2009 with 63 percent.

Al Carroll

communities resented and resisted conscription, but the government put down this rebellion. A side effect of the Chaco War was that it broke up the old political order in Bolivia, stimulating reform.

In 1945, the government held the First Bolivian Peasant Congress to address indigenous complaints. In 1952, a social revolution brought a new government, which extended the franchise to the native majority. The revolution also destroyed the hacienda system, which had allowed the wealthy to retain large tracts of land. After native people began seizing hacienda lands, the government approved an agrarian reform law in August 1953. When the military took control in 1964, the agrarian reform remained untouched. In fact, the military relied on an understanding with the highland people that was known as the "military–peasant pact," which allowed generals to focus military repression on urban labor unions.

The military–peasant pact collapsed in the mid-1970s. On January 29, 1974, the Bolivian military carried out the so-called Massacre of the Valley. The conflict began with a protest over government manipulation of commodity prices. In the Department of Cochabamba, indigenous farmers rebelled by blocking roads, and the military responded with gunfire. Native communities responded by beginning a new phase of radical organization.

The class-based Trade Union Confederation of Bolivian Peasant Workers was founded in June 1979. Centered around El Alto and La Paz, in areas of substantial indigenous populations, it included many native people. This proved vital, as it served as a national organization uniting the disparate local indigenous populations.

With the return of civilian government in Bolivia in 1982, the desire for self-determination continued to develop among the native people. While an ephemeral insurgency developed in the late 1980s—the Túpac Katari Guerrilla Army—most native people relied on peaceful protest. For example, in 1990, indigenous people from the eastern lowlands organized the March for Territory and Dignity, protesting the actions of hostile ranchers and timber companies.

In 1993, Víctor Hugo Cárdenas became the country's first indigenous vice president. Activists founded the National Council of Ayllus and Markas of Qullasuyu in 1997 as a confederation of traditional indigenous governments. Despite these advances, setbacks still occurred. On December 19, 1996, for example, the police and military attacked native people who were protesting the effects of a gold mine on the land in their home area near Amayapampa, Potosí.

According to the 2001 census, 62 percent of Bolivia's population identified themselves as indigenous. The native majority has led the twenty-first century assault on

free market economic reforms. In September and October 2000, an indigenous movement formed to protest the privatization of natural resources such as fresh water. The Departments of Cochabamba and La Paz saw significant conflict between protestors and government forces. In September and October 2003, a popular mobilization consisting of marches, strikes, and roadblocks led to the overthrow of President Gonzalo Sánchez de Lozada. Eventually, the country held new elections. Evo Morales won the presidency on December 18, 2005, with 53.7 percent of the vote to become the country's first indigenous head of state.

Morales's government convened a constituent assembly on August 6, 2006, to draft a new constitution that would take into consideration the demands of the country's native majority. The constitution adopted in 2009 recognized thirty-six native tongues as official languages. The reforms indicated a fundamental change among Bolivians as they came to view their country from a plurinational perspective, balancing the interests of the indigenous people and the Hispanic population.

Robert Smale

See also: *Groups: Central and South America*—Aymara; Quechua. *Issues*—Colonialism; Economic Development; Political Participation.

Further Reading

Hylton, Forrest, and Sinclair Thomson. *Revolutionary Horizons: Past and Present in Bolivian Politics*. London: Verso, 2007.

Klein, Herbert S. *Bolivia: The Evolution of a Multi-Ethnic Society*. 2nd ed. New York: Oxford University Press, 1992.

Langer, Erick D. *Expecting Pears from an Elm Tree: Franciscan Missions on the Chiriguano Frontier in the Heart of South America, 1830–1949*. Durham, NC: Duke University Press, 2009.

Murrieta, Cynthia Radding. *Landscapes of Power and Identity: Comparative Histories in the Sonoran Desert and the Forests of Amazonia from Colony to Republic*. Durham, NC: Duke University Press, 2005.

Botswana

The nation of Botswana, located just north of South Africa, shares a border with Namibia on the west and north, Zambia in the north, and Zimbabwe in the east. Dominated by the Kalahari Desert, the extreme eastern part of the country is the most suitable portion for agriculture. However, Botswana is rich in one natural resource: diamonds. The nation is the world's leading diamond producer, accounting for approximately

80 percent of gem-quality stones. Botswana is home to a number of different native groups, including the Basarwa, Kalanga, Khwe (San), Mbanderu, Mbukushu, Tswana, and Wayeyi.

Botswana declared independence from Great Britain in 1966. With an economy based primarily on diamond mining and tourism, it is a nation of contrasts. On the one hand, diamond mining has brought great wealth to those involved in the trade; on the other hand, nearly one-third of the population, including many of the nation's indigenous people, lives in poverty, and Botswana has one of the highest rates of human immunodeficiency virus (HIV) infection in the world. Although the nation has a stable government, minority rights have long been subordinated to the creation of a national Botswanan identity. In fact, the nation's laws permit discrimination against some indigenous groups in Botswana.

History and Recognition of Indigenous Peoples

Until 1966, Botswana was a British protectorate called Bechuanaland. The Chieftainship Act of 1933 recognized eight tribes, collectively referred to as Tswana: the Bakgatla, Bakwena, Balete, Bangwaketse, Bangwato, Barolong, Batawana, and Batlokwa. These groups were guaranteed a place in government and granted land and language rights. Other tribes not recognized as Tswana, however, were denied these rights.

Upon independence, the distinction between Tswana and non-Tswana peoples was transferred to Botswana's constitution. In 1970, the Tribal Land Act set up a Land Board to reinforce the right of the eight Tswana tribes to their land. Excluded from such rights were the thirty-seven smaller, non-Tswana tribes that make up just over 20 percent of the nation's population, such as the Khwe, also referred to as the San or (pejoratively) as the Kalahari Bushmen.

The Khwe, the first people to live in what is now Botswana, have struggled for many years to maintain their traditional way of life. During the 1960s, Botswana's government created the Central Kalahari Game Reserve as a haven for these indigenous peoples. Beginning in 1997, however, government officials ordered police and troops to invade Khwe villages; police demolished their homes and trucked inhabitants to bleak resettlement camps. A few hundred Khwe have resisted relocation and managed to remain on their traditional lands. Following a campaign by Survival International and other organizations to advocate for the Khwe's rights, the removals ceased for a time. By 2001, pressure was again building to remove the Khwe from their homeland.

Hunting is central to the religious and ritual lives of the Khwe. In their view, their relationship to the environment and the spiritual world is intimately connected to the animals that inhabit their land. Although the Khwe once sustained themselves by hunting and gathering, today they are forbidden by Botswana authorities from capturing more than a few animals per year. The game quotas and other changes in their lifeways have forced the Khwe to depend on governmental and international authorities to obtain the basic necessities of life, including food, water, and shelter. Even as hunting among these indigenous people has been restricted, the government has encouraged hunting for sport by tourists elsewhere in the country.

By the end of 2001, only a few bands of Khwe remained on the reserve, refusing to move from the land that contained the graves of their ancestors. The government put considerable pressure on them, using threats and intimidation to persuade the roughly 700 people who remained to leave. Government officials announced that all water and food supplies to Khwe living inside the reserve would be cut off by the end of January 2002. As a result, the Khwe were forced to go to court to maintain access to boreholes, their only source of water. The government sealed the last remaining borehole after the Khwe were evicted from their lands in 2002, forcing them to travel up to 250 miles (400 kilometers) to obtain water.

That same year, the United Nations Human Rights Commission accused the Botswana government of discrimination against the Khwe by dispossessing them of their traditional lands. The UN special rapporteur on indigenous peoples, Rodolfo Stavenhagen, submitted a report in which he argued that the Khwe's survival as a distinct people was endangered by official assimilationist policies.

As these people were taken from their homes during spring 2002, protest vigils were held in London, Madrid, Milan, Paris, Rome, and Zurich. A newspaper article by Innu Nation President Peter Penashue urged Botswana to "learn from Canada's mistakes, and end the misguided policy of trying to forcibly integrate the Bushmen into your cultural mainstream. Canada has shown the world that this doesn't work."

After years of official denials, an anonymous senior Botswanan official admitted in 2009 to author James G. Workman, in his book *Heart of Dryness,* that diamond mining was the main reason for the Khwe's eviction, as the mineral-rich land they were living on held $2.2 billion worth of diamonds. The multinational corporation De Beers (which maintains a near monopoly on world diamond mining and marketing) and the Anglo American Company engaged in mining operations in the area as most of the Khwe were removed. The companies cooperated with the government of Botswana to ensure that the indigenous peoples would have no claims to the mineral wealth underlying the Central Kalahari Game Reserve. As of 2012, all but a few Khwe had left the reserve.

Current Minority Status and Remediation Efforts

In 1967, non-Tswana people began to agitate for constitutional rights to their lands and representation in Botswana's political system. In 1988 and 1995, motions were proposed in the Botswana Parliament to amend the constitution to recognize non-Tswana rights, but both measures were defeated. In response, thirteen ethnically based associations were formed to advocate for non-Tswana rights and protection of their languages and cultures. In 2002, these groups joined to form RETENG: The Multi-Cultural Coalition of Botswana.

Other minority tribes, such as the Basarwa and Kalanga peoples, with similar experiences to the Khwe, have pursued a case against the government of Botswana with the Africa Commission on Human and Peoples' Rights and the UN Committee on the Elimination of Racial Discrimination (CERD). In 2006, CERD issued a report that noted that Botswana's stated goal of equality for all groups in the country was not being realized due to pressure on minority tribes to assimilate into the Tswana-dominated society.

In 2006, the Basarwa tribe won the right to return to their ancestral lands in the Central Kgalagadi Game Reserve, but the government has not taken this ruling as a precedent for other groups, such as the Khwe. Although past efforts to amend the Constitution failed, the 1995 motion did result in an agreement that Parliament would review the sections pertaining to non-Tswana rights. In addition, President Ian Khama, elected in 2008, stated that he is amenable to recognition of minority tribes.

Bruce E. Johansen

See also: *Groups: Africa*—San (Bushmen). *Issues*—Hunting and Fishing Rights; Mining; Relocation.

Further Reading

Issacson, Rupert. *The Healing Land: The Bushmen and the Kalahari.* New York: Grove, 2004.

Nyati-Ramahobo, Lydia. *Minority Tribes in Botswana: The Politics of Recognition.* London: Minority Rights Group International, 2008.

Penashue, Peter. "Learn from Canada's Mistakes." *Ecologist* 32:6 (July/August 2002): 9.

Van der Post, Laurens. *The Lost World of the Kalahari.* New York: Harcourt Brace Jovanovich, 1977.

Workman, James G. *Heart of Dryness: How the Last Bushmen Can Help Us Endure the Coming Age of Permanent Drought.* New York: Walker, 2009.

Brazil

Before the Portuguese arrived in present-day Brazil in 1500, more than 2,000 distinct ethnic groups resided in the region, with a total population of 2 million to 5 million. According to the official census of Brazil in 2006, the country is home to approximately 519,000 native people speaking more than 180 different languages, in addition to millions of Brazilians of mixed native and European ancestry.

Over several centuries, most of Brazil's native people either were killed by the Portuguese as a result of wars of conquest or slave labor, or they died of the diseases that the Portuguese brought with them from Europe. Many native Brazilians eventually were assimilated into the settler population. Today, a majority of Brazil's native people either live in their own home areas, usually in rural parts of the country, or in urban areas, while others remain isolated, having no contact with mainstream society. A number of Brazilian tribes also reside in neighboring countries, including the Baniwa (Venezuela), Chamacoco (Paraguay), Guaraní (Argentina, Bolivia, Paraguay, and Uruguay), and Ticuna (Colombia, Guyana, and Peru).

History of the Native People

The Portuguese already had reached India three years before they arrived in Brazil in 1500. They used the term *Indians* to refer to the people of the New World in the Portuguese language, whereas the people of India were referred to as *Indianos* to make a distinction between the two people. Pêro Vaz de Caminha, the official scribe of the commander of the discovery fleet that landed in what is now the Brazilian state of Bahia, wrote a letter to the king of Portugal describing the beauty and richness of the land. The explorers found a wide coastline that was rich in resources and home to many indigenous people.

The Indians were organized into seminomadic tribes that survived by hunting, gathering, fishing, and practicing migrant agriculture. They lived mainly along the coasts and on the banks of major rivers. Early Portuguese records make reference to two groups of natives: the Tupi-Guaraní–speaking Tupi people, who resided along the length of the Brazilian coast, and those living in the interior, called Tapuia, a collective term for all non-Tupi people. By the time the Portuguese arrived, the Tapuia already had been expelled from the coastal areas by the Tupi after a long period of conflict and war. The Portuguese favored the Tupi, preferring to communicate with the culturally and linguistically homogenous population living along the coastline.

The indigenous tribes fought with one another over the Amazonian brazilwood, a timber tree that was valuable for its red dye. Initially, the Portuguese called this region Terra de Santa Cruz, but later it was renamed Brazil, after the brazilwood.

While intertribal warfare was reported to be common among the indigenous people, after the arrival of the Portuguese, the political dynamics of these conflicts took on new dimensions. For example, when fighting against one another, the tribes often made alliances with the Portuguese. But in conflicts that set the natives in opposition to the Portuguese, the Indians made alliances among themselves and sometimes with other Europeans. For instance, the Indian Tomoio Confederation allied with France against the Portuguese during the 1560–1567 wars in France Antarctique, a French colony in Rio de Janeiro.

The Portuguese, like the Spanish in North America, introduced diseases to which the native population had no immunity, such as measles, smallpox, tuberculosis, and influenza. Tens of thousands of native people died in epidemics. Over time, the male Portuguese colonists had children with indigenous women, and people of mixed heritage, speaking Indian languages, came to form a majority of the population.

This new generation organized expeditions into the interior in search of treasures of the Amazon for the Portuguese Crown. As a by-product, they came into direct conflict with the Indians when some decided to stay and occupy the Indian territories. The land also produced sugarcane, and the sugar industry became profitable. The Portuguese forced the Indians into slave labor, resulting in the deaths of many natives. Although Portugal and the Algarves (the southernmost region of present-day Portugal) banned Indian slavery in 1570 and ordered the release of all Indian captives, bondage in Brazil continued as late as 1755.

Meanwhile, the Jesuit priests who had arrived with the first Portuguese governor general began to convert the native peoples to Catholicism. Jesuit priests such as José de Anchieta and Manuel da Nóbrega studied the indigenous languages and founded São Paulo dos Campos de Piratininga and other mixed settlements, where colonists and Indians lived together peacefully. They also established missions populated by Catholic converts and by Europeanized Indians in more remote areas throughout the country.

In the mid-1770s, however, the Jesuits were expelled from Brazil by the Portuguese Crown, causing the demise of the missions and the massacre of many Indians. By the end of the eighteenth century, only 250,000 native people remained among a total population of 3.25 million Brazilians. During this time, some non-natives used diseases such as smallpox as biological weapons to further decimate the Indian tribes. For instance, in southern Maranhão, Caxias, farmers gave infected clothing to the Timbira people to clear the natives off land they wanted to extend their cattle farms.

The worldwide demand for rubber increased after the development of the vulcanization process in the early nineteenth century. People from many different areas were brought to labor in the Amazon rain forest to harvest rubber, sparking another conflict with the Indians that continues to this day.

In the early twentieth century, the Brazilian government attempted to provide protection to the indigenous people by establishing indigenous reserves. In 1920, a Brazilian army officer of mixed Portuguese and Indian ancestry, Cândido Rondon, founded the Serviço de Proteção aos Índios (SPI, Indian Protection Service), a federal agency designed to protect the native peoples and their cultures. In 1952, he established Xingu National Park, the first Indian reservation. Rondon is regarded as a national hero in Brazil, and the state of Rondônia is named for him.

After Rondon's death in 1958, however, SPI fell into decline, resulting in the mistreatment of Indians at the hands of land speculators seeking to exploit the natural resources of the Amazon region. During the second half of the twentieth century, exploitation of these resources increased as the government sought to bolster the Brazilian economy. A huge area of forest was cleared for highways (with funding from the World Bank), hydropower projects were undertaken, and cattle ranches were established without consideration for reservation lands.

In 1967, the so-called Figueiredo Report, commissioned by the Ministry of the Interior, highlighted the maltreatment of Indians in Brazil. The government subsequently launched an investigation into SPI, uncovering corruption among the organization's officials and finding that some officials actually had supported land speculators who were responsible for spreading disease among the natives and for subjecting them to such abuses as slavery, physical torture (including sexual abuse), and even mass homicide. It was revealed that during the 1950s, more than 100,000 native people were killed, and between 1960 and 1967, some ninety-eight tribes vanished altogether. The SPI was banned and replaced by the Fundação Nacional do Índio (FUNAI, National Indian Foundation), which was charged with protecting the Indians' land, culture, and rights. Many tribes contacted by FUNAI have since been assimilated into Brazilian society.

However, unrest continues in some areas. During the 1980s, large deposits of gold were discovered in reservation lands of the Yanomami tribe. Many people rushed to the land, bringing tuberculosis, malaria, and influenza to the area and polluting the rivers with mercury, which is used for excavating deposits. As a result, the Yanomami population was reduced to just 9,000 by the end of the twentieth century, compared to 20,000 in 1977. In another example, the Tupinikim and Guaraní people in Espírito Santo continue to fight for their land, which is famous for its cellulose production.

Current Status and Government Indigenous Policy

Historically, settlers, land speculators, and others who have invaded the lands and destroyed the environments of Brazil's indigenous peoples have caused dislocation, poverty, malnutrition, disease, and death. Although the Brazilian constitution of 1988 recognized the rights of the country's native peoples to pursue their own ways of life and to possess their indigenous territories, the exploitation of the Amazon rain forest for mining, logging, cattle ranching, and other uses continues to pose a threat to those rights. As a result, many tribes remain at risk of extinction.

More than 350 indigenous areas have been registered officially, but the demarcation process is slow. In 2007, FUNAI confirmed the presence of sixty-seven uncontacted (isolated) tribes, the largest number of uncontacted peoples in the world.

Muhammad Aurang Zeb Mughal

See also: *Groups: Central and South America*—Guaraní; Ticuna. *Issues*—Colonialism; Land Rights.

Further Reading

Coimbra, Carlos E.A., Jr., Nancy M. Flowers, Francisco M. Salzano, and Ricardo V. Santos. *The Xavánte in Transition: Health, Ecology and Bioanthropology in Central Brazil.* Ann Arbor: University of Michigan Press, 2004.

Gomes, Mércio P. *The Indians and Brazil.* 3rd ed. Trans. John W. Moon. Gainesville: University Press of Florida, 2000.

Heinrichs, Ann. *The Amazon Rain Forest.* New York: Marshall Cavendish Benchmark, 2010.

Ramos, Alcida R. "Frontier Expansion and Indian Peoples in the Brazilian Amazon." In *Frontier Expansion in Amazonia,* ed. Marianne Schmink and Charles H. Wood. Gainesville: University Press of Florida, 1984.

———. *Indigenism: Ethnic Politics in Brazil.* Madison: University of Wisconsin Press, 1998.

Burundi

Burundi is a tiny and densely populated country in Central Africa that is tucked between the Democratic Republic of the Congo, Rwanda, and Tanzania. Its population of 10.2 million people occupies an area of just over 10,000 square miles (28,000 square kilometers). Burundi's population is composed of three groups: the Hutu (85 percent), Tutsi (14 percent), and Twa (1 percent).

The country's economy is primarily based on agriculture. Most Burundians subsist mainly on farming manioc, corn, bananas, sorghum, and sweet potatoes, while coffee is their main foreign export. Although the vast majority of Burundians are Hutu, a farming people, the Tutsi, traditionally herders, historically have dominated the government and military, as well as the lucrative coffee trade. Another native group, the Twa, subsists on hunting game.

Rundi (also called Kirundi) and French are the official languages of Burundi, and Swahili is spoken widely in the capital of Bujumbura. Although most Burundians practice Christianity and Islam, for many, these beliefs are integrated with their indigenous cosmology.

Precolonial and Colonial History

Burundi originally was home to the Twa, a Pygmy people that were hunter-gatherers. Sometime after 1000 C.E., Hutu farmers settled in the area; the Tutsi, traditionally cattle herders, arrived later. Early on, identification as Hutu or Tutsi was fluid—the two groups often intermarried, and both spoke the same language, Rundi.

By the sixteenth century, Burundi was ruled by a monarchy headed by a *mwami* (king), who traditionally was a Tutsi. By the eighteenth century, a patron–client relationship had developed between the Hutu and Tutsi, with the Tutsi ruling elite controlling land and production. The Hutu, however, played an important role in the rituals of governance, acting as guardians of royal tombs, religious specialists, court diviners, and seers. Hutu elders known as *abashingantahe* also served as intermediaries between the commoners and the aristocracy, sometimes functioning as judges, interpreters, and ombudsman.

The process of colonization in the second half of the nineteenth century would sow the seeds of hatred between the two peoples. Burundi, together with Rwanda and parts of present-day Mozambique and Tanzania, became part of the German Protectorate of East Africa. Colonial policies clearly favored the Tutsi, whom the Germans viewed as superior to the Hutu.

Following defeat of the Germans in World War I, the territory was administered by Belgium, beginning in 1923, as a mandate of the League of Nations. The Belgian administration continued the pro-Tutsi policies of the Germans. In 1933, Belgian colonial officials established a policy that required the native peoples to carry identification cards that classified them by ethnic group—Hutu, Tutsi, or Twa—thus formalizing any differences among them. The classifications only entrenched ethnic tensions between the Hutu and Tutsi, which culminated in violence in the 1950s and 1960s.

Postcolonial Era

Burundi would carry the baggage of ethnic conflict between the Hutu and Tutsi into the postcolonial era. Following World War II, Burundians pressed for independence from Belgium. In 1955, the political organization Parti de l'Union et du Progrès National (UPRONA, Union for National Progress) was formed, led by Louis Rwagasore (a Tutsi) and Paul Mirerekano (a Hutu), to promote an ideology of national consensus. Although the party agreed that the Hutu and Tutsi would share power in an independent Burundi, in 1959, the Tutsi mwami was installed as the country's constitutional monarch.

The first legislative elections were held in 1961, resulting in a victory for UPRONA, which won fifty-eight out of sixty-four seats; twenty-two Hutu legislators were elected. Rwagasore became prime minister and formed a government. Still, some Tutsi leaders resented the concession of power of Hutu interests. Rwagasore's assassination in October of that year only heightened tensions between the two groups, a situation that Burundi has struggled to overcome ever since.

Despite the political crisis, Burundi achieved independence in July 1962. The monarchy remained intact, with the mwami acting as the ceremonial head of state under a Tutsi-dominated government headed by André Muhiriwa. Suspicion and chicanery continued to characterize Burundi's political landscape after the elections of May 1965, in which the Hutu majority defeated the Tutsi government. In 1965 and 1972, Hutu leaders who were perceived to be a threat to Tutsi power were executed without being charged with any crime.

Burundi experienced a series of coups and countercoups aimed at strengthening Tutsi power by armed force. When Michel Micombero was chosen as prime minister in 1966, he appointed several Hutu as ministers under the guise of a power-sharing deal with the Tutsi; in fact, the appointments were meant to dilute the Hutu power base. In 1969, Hutu military officers were accused of and executed for plotting a coup against Micombero. Three years later, Hutu refugees invaded Burundi and killed some 2,000 Tutsi, giving Micombero an excuse to purge the leadership. Some 300,000 Hutu were killed in the resulting genocide.

Micombero's campaign against the Hutu notwithstanding, he became increasingly unpopular within the Tutsi military ranks, and in 1976, he was ousted in a bloodless coup by Jean-Baptiste Bagaza. In 1987, Pierre Buyoya took power, again by coup. Barely a year into his tenure, Buyoya was shaken by far-reaching division in which Hutu fought back against the Tutsi-dominated army, spurring another genocide that left 25,000 Hutu dead.

Ethnic tensions in Burundi have continued. In the multiparty elections held in 1993, Melchior Ndadaye of the Front pour la Dêmocratie au Burundi (Front for Democracy in Burundi) was chosen as prime minister with 65 percent of the vote. However, on October 21 of that year, he was murdered in a military coup, again sparking mass killings. President Cyprien Ntaryamira's death in a bizarre plane crash on April 6, 1994, only exacerbated tensions, compelling thousands of Hutu refugees to flee to Tanzania in anticipation of further ethnic cleansing campaigns. Following Ntaryamira's death, moderate Sylvestre Ntibantunganya became president; his term lasted only until July 23, 1996, when Buyoya reclaimed power.

Buyoya was forced to hand over the presidency to his Hutu vice president, Domitien Ndayizeye, on April 30, 2003, under the terms of the Arusha Agreement, a power-sharing arrangement negotiated under the leadership of former South African president Nelson Mandela. In 2005, a new constitution was promulgated with the overwhelming support of Burundians. Pierre Nkurunziza, a Hutu, was elected as Burundi's president under the new constitution in August of that year.

Today, discrimination on the part of public officials still is practiced, and many Twa have difficulties claiming their lands. Land laws in Burundi are based on permanent occupation of the land, which overtly overlooks Twa hunter-gatherer practices that have little impact on the land itself.

Hannington Ochwada

See also: *Groups: Africa*—Hutu; Rundi; Tutsi; Twa. *Issues*—Colonialism.

Further Reading

Malkki, Liisa H. *Purity and Exile: Violence, Memory, and National Cosmology Among Hutu Refugees in Tanzania.* Chicago: University of Chicago Press, 1995.

Ndarubagiye, Léonce. *Burundi: The Origins of the Hutu–Tutsi Conflict.* Nairobi, Kenya: L. Ndarubagiye, 1996.

Newbury, David. "Precolonial Burundi and Rwanda: Local Loyalties, Regional Royalties." *International Journal of African Historical Studies* 34:2 (2001): 255–313.

Ochwada, Hannington. "Rethinking East African Integration: From Economic to Political and from State to Civil Society." *Africa Development* 39:2 (2004): 53–79.

Sutton, J.E.G. "The Antecedents of the Interlacustrine Kingdoms." *Journal of African History* 34:1 (1993): 33–64.

Watt, Nigel. *Burundi: The Biography of a Small African Country.* New York: Columbia University Press, 2008.

Cameroon

The Republic of Cameroon is located in West Africa. It shares a border with Nigeria to the west, Chad to the northeast, the Central African Republic to the east, and Equatorial Guinea, Gabon, and the Republic of the Congo to the south. Occupying approximately 183,600 square miles (about 475,500 square kilometers), the country is divided into five geographic regions: the coastal plains; the South Cameroon Plateau, which rises from the coastal plains; the equatorial rain forest; the hill, mountain, and plateau regions; and the southern plateau. The rivers of Cameroon form four drainage systems: the principal rivers—the Ntem, Nyong, Sanaga, and Wouri—all flow into the Atlantic Ocean; the Benoue and its tributary, the Kébi, run into the Niger River Basin; the Logone joins the Chari and flows into Lake Chad; and the Dja and Kédéï drain into the Congo River.

The early inhabitants of Cameroon were the Baka, who were primarily hunters; the Bantu from the higher country; and the Fulani, who occupied the northern regions of the area. Most of these groups formed chiefdoms and fondoms (kingdoms). The first known contact with Europeans occurred during the sixteenth century, when Portuguese explorers reached West Africa, calling the area Rio dos Camaroes (River of Prawns). The region changed hands in 1884, when the Germans claimed it as the colony of Kamerun.

During World War I, Cameroon was occupied by Belgian, British, and French troops, who expelled the Germans. After World War I, the Treaty of Versailles divided Cameroon into two "mandates" overseen by the League of Nations (later called United Nations trusts): French Cameroun and British Cameroons. The French ruled their region from Paris, while the British ruled their portion of the territory from neighboring Nigeria. During this period, there was active resistance to colonial authority from the Union des Populations du Cameroun (Cameroon People's Union), a group composed mainly of militants from the Bamileke and Bassa tribes. Cameroon gained independence from France in 1960 and from Great Britain in 1961, and the two territories were united as the Federal Republic of Cameroon. The name was changed in 1972 to the United Republic of Cameroon and in 1984 to the Republic of Cameroon.

Cameroon has a strong central government and executive branch. The president holds the executive power to hire, appoint, and dismiss officials in the government. The country is divided into ten semi-autonomous regions, each of which has an elected regional council headed by a governor appointed by the president. These regional heads follow the directions of the president. The capital is located at Yaoundé in the southwest region. The population of Cameroon is estimated to be more than 19 million, and it is evenly divided between urban and rural remote areas. About 200 ethnic and local tribes make their home in Cameroon. Life expectancy for both men and women is estimated to be under fifty-five years of age.

The nation has two official languages, English and French. Educated Cameroonians generally speak either English or French, but a majority of the population speaks a mixture of English, French, and a pidgin tongue called Camfranglais.

Cameroon has a rich culture, encompassing many different traditions and ways of life. Many of these traditions are centered on birth, death, the harvest, and religious rights and celebrations. Religious practices are diverse, with a variety of native religions being practiced by approximately 40 percent of the population. Christians (Protestants and Catholics) make up another 40 percent of the population and are concentrated in the south and west of the country, while Muslims comprise the remaining 20 percent and live primarily in the north.

Arts and crafts are an important part of the culture in Cameroon, particularly wood carving and sculpture, however, indigenous people in southern Cameroon, such as the BaAka, are facing deforestation and government pressure to abandon their seminomadic lifeways, as they cause issues with corporations engaged in natural resource extraction. In fact, most of the economy in Cameroon is based on its natural resources. As in many African and developing countries, however, Cameroon's economy has been stagnant as a result of government corruption that led to the misappropriation of revenues from its natural resources.

In 2006, Cameroon gained control of the oil-rich northern part of the Bakassi peninsula from Nigeria after years of disputes in international courts. The peninsula is home to a number of indigenous groups, including the Annang, Calabar, Efik, Efut, and Ibibio peoples. However, since Cameroon took control, many indigenous groups have complained of mistreatment by the Cameroonian military and police forces. Some have formed a group called the Bakassi Self-Determination

Movement, which is seeking independence from both Cameroon and Nigeria.

Franklyn Taylor

See also: Issues—Colonialism; Indigenous Governments; Relocation.

Further Reading

Le Vine, Victor T. *The Cameroons from Mandate to Independence.* Berkeley: University of California Press, 1964.

Mbaku, John Mukum. *Culture and Customs of Cameroon.* Westport, CT: Greenwood, 2005.

Neba, Aaron S. *Modern Geography of the Republic of Cameroon.* Camden, NJ: Neba, 1987.

Canada

When Europeans first landed in the area that later would be called Canada in the early sixteenth century, there were indigenous people living from coast to coast with very different languages and customs. At the time of European contact, these indigenous people, referred to in Canada as First Nations, migrated with herds of animals rather than living in permanent, stationary settlements and hunted in their own territories. Their dress, language, culture, spiritual beliefs, and foods were different from place to place across the vast regions that would become Canada.

Some of the native people were welcoming, while others were combative, perhaps in response to encroachment on their lands and Europeans' failure to respect the different lifestyles of the native peoples of Canada. As time went on, more and more settlers came to Canada, and Jesuit priests worked to convert the indigenous people to Christianity, with mixed results.

Pre-Columbian Canada

There are close to 700 First Nations tribes living throughout Canada. Historians began to document tribal histories after contact, because there were no written accounts of the indigenous peoples of Canada. Today, historians and anthropologists still are piecing together the prehistory of Canada's First Nations. According to one view, called the Bering Strait theory, these early civilizations migrated to present-day Canada from regions that were covered with ice sheets, through a corridor from Asia to North America via a land passage across the Bering Strait.

The first significant European contact with Canada's indigenous people is believed to have taken place in the early sixteenth century, when explorers from France traveled up the St. Lawrence Seaway on the East Coast of North America. Later, in the seventeenth century, explorers came around the northeastern coast by way of the Hudson and James bays. Many of the first Europeans to come into contact with the indigenous people were fur traders, who were followed by Jesuit priests. They met a seemingly endless assortment of tribes.

The Montagnais and Naskapi lived in present-day Labrador and Quebec. The Montagnais occupied the heavily wooded area along the north shore of the St. Lawrence River as far east as Sept-Îles (Seven Islands) in Quebec. The snow-covered, tundra-like lands of the Naskapi extended far into northeastern Quebec. These northern tribes shared many traditions, as they all hunted, fished, used dogsleds, and wore similar clothing.

Eight main tribes lived in the northeast woodland areas. These include the now-extinct Beothuk, whose home was in the area of Newfoundland, while the Micmac (or Mi'kmaq) people lived in Nova Scotia, as they still do today. The territory of the Malecite people reached from Quebec to Prince Edward Island and southwestern New Brunswick. The Ojibwa lived in a large area stretching from the Great Lakes to the Georgian Bay. The Cree also inhabited a large area from the Hudson Bay into the region that is now Manitoba and Saskatchewan. Southern Ontario was home to the Oneida and Mohawk tribes, and in the Plains there were eight main tribes, including the Blackfoot, Blood, Gros Ventre, Piegan, and Plains Cree.

The Assiniboine lived in the territory south of the Plains Cree. The Sioux were a large tribe made up of three nations—Dakota, Lakota, and Nakota—that resided in the Great Plains in the United States and in the Canadian Prairie Provinces. Today, Sioux people still live on reserves in Manitoba and Saskatchewan. Some of them are the descendants of refugees who came to Canada under the leadership of Hunkpapa (Lakota) Sioux leader Sitting Bull after the Battle of the Little Bighorn in 1876. The Sarcee people lived northwest of the Blackfoot. Seven main tribes lived in the plateau area of British Columbia—the Kootenay, Lake, Lillooet, Okanagan, Salish, Shuswap, and Thompson—in addition to three Athabascan-speaking groups, the Carrier, Tsilhqot'in, and Wet'suwet'en. The Bella Coola, Haida, Nootka, and Tsimshian people lived on the Pacific Coast of British Columbia.

Early Explorations and European Settlement

Soon after the arrival of Christopher Columbus in the New World in 1492, European explorers began sailing northward from the East Coast of North America into present-day Canada. Among these early explorers was Italian ex-

Members of Canada's First Nations tribes march for native rights in downtown Toronto in 2010. The nation's indigenous peoples did not receive full voting rights until 1960. Other federal rights, protections, and entitlements are still contested. *(Jemal Countess/Getty Images)*

plorer Giovanni Caboto, known as John Cabot. Sailing for the English Crown, he and his crew came upon Newfoundland in 1497. Slave trader Thomas Aubert brought several Amerindians back to France from his 1508 voyage to the eastern part of Canada. In 1541, French explorer Jacques Cartier traveled up the St. Lawrence River in an unsuccessful effort to establish a new French colony. It was not until 1604 that a permanent French village would be established at Port Royal in Nova Scotia. The English continued to fish off the eastern coast of Canada, while the French journeyed up the St. Lawrence in search of furs.

Henry Hudson sailed into what is now called the Hudson Bay in 1610, claiming it for the British. He established a trading post on the southern shore of the bay and formed trade relationships with many of the native groups in the region, who eventually would become dependent on European trade for their survival. There also are accounts of Basque people who arrived before the sixteenth century to trade and established trade and fishing routes in northern Canada and Greenland and on the coast of Labrador. Long before any of these explorers came to Canada, the indigenous peoples had established such routes among themselves and with other tribes.

By 1635, the colony of New France (Quebec) was thriving and had a population of farmers, priests, and soldiers. This was a base for many Jesuit missionaries who came east to convert the First Nations people. Indigenous scouts also accompanied French fur trappers and priests to new lands in search of furs, food, and land for settlers.

Beginning with the establishment of the Hudson's Bay Company in 1670, the British also began to get into the business of fur trapping, sparking a rivalry with France. From the late seventeenth century through the eighteenth century, trappers from the Hudson Bay to the Great Lakes and beyond traded with the indigenous people for goods from Europe, setting up trading posts close to fur-trapping areas. The Hudson's Bay Company initiated an expedition and built a trading post on the Saskatchewan River in the late eighteenth century.

A series of colonial wars took place during the eighteenth century, ending with the French and Indian War in 1764, mirroring the colonial wars between Great Britain and France elsewhere on the globe. Inevitably, Canada's First Nations became involved in these wars, and often the outcomes of the wars determined which First Nations would gain prominence.

In the early nineteenth century, the Hudson's Bay Company and the Northwest Company merged, and trading posts made it possible for many indigenous people to more easily acquire European goods, such as clothing, ironware, and weaponry. First Nations peoples were able to travel to trading posts by way of kayak, birch bark canoe, snowshoe, dogsled, and toboggan, and in the Central Plains, they had horses and the more northern Athabascans had reindeer. Some First Nations peoples became stationary, building villages close to trading posts and altering their subsistence patterns to concentrate on the cultivation of agricultural crops such as beans, potatoes, pumpkins, squash, and tomatoes. At the time, many First Nations people wore clothing made from skins and fur. Later, they adorned their traditional clothing with beads obtained from fur traders. Both fur traders and the indigenous people became dependent on trade to sustain themselves, and as a result, fewer First Nations were truly self-sufficient. Increasingly, tribes wanted to trade for guns, kettles, steel knives, and cloth.

Additionally, diseases new to the indigenous peoples of Canada, such as smallpox, whooping cough, scarlet fever, diphtheria, tuberculosis, and influenza, spread through their contact with Europeans. The result was significant loss of life among the native tribes from the seventeenth through the nineteenth centuries. One tribe, the Dine, lost almost two-thirds of its people as a result of these diseases. Along with the devastating impact of disease, the depletion of game animals, which many tribes relied on for food, clothing, and shelter, caused tribes to become dependent on English and French traders. The natives' traditional lifeways were affected in other ways as well. The Cree and Nakota, for example, came to depend on the rifle to hunt buffalo and other animals and thus spent less time practicing their traditional hunting skills. As in the United States, the buffalo was hunted almost to extinction. The arrival of more and more Europeans brought settlers who pushed the First Nations farther west from their traditional homelands.

Treaties and Laws Concerning the First Nations

The indigenous people practiced a collective way of life, and therefore their views on property differed from those of the settlers. First Nations people did not believe that land could be owed by any one person or that it could be bought or sold. Tribal leaders had trouble understanding that others might make agreements regarding their territories without their consent, but time and again, that pattern was repeated in negotiations between Anglo leaders and the indigenous peoples. Often, the natives thought of treaties as a system of trade, just as they traded with the Europeans in goods and supplies. However, when the natives bargained with the settlers, their concerns often were overlooked. Treaties were written by white men with the goal of making room for settler expansion, railroads, and agriculture.

Reserve lands were set aside so that the First Nations would live within a defined area, preventing them from migrating during the seasons. Bands in southern Canada had a hard time maintaining their traditional ways of life under this system, as the depletion of the buffalo forced them to move to reserves lest they starve.

On the reserves, the native people eventually became assimilated to European and Christian ways of life. They learned how to plant crops, whereas before they had been hunters and gatherers. However, promises made to tribes in treaties consistently were broken and promised annuities often did not arrive, making it difficult for them to maintain their farms on what often was not the best land for the purpose. Some treaties also provided for farmlands outside the reserves, but few natives applied for them at the time when the treaties were made.

In 1867, the Dominion of Canada was formed as a result of the first British North America Act, creating the provinces of New Brunswick, Nova Scotia, Ontario, and Quebec. By the late 1860s, the Canadian government had bought most of the fur trading territory from the Hudson's Bay Company and made an agreement with the British government for authority over the interior of Canada. First Nations leaders were not consulted in this, nor were their wishes paramount in the negotiation of the treaties that followed.

After confederation, the new Canadian government went about crafting treaties with the First Nations to define their reserves and to open land for Anglo-Canadian settlement. Treaties 1 and 2 were made in 1871 with the Cree and Ojibwa (Anishinabek); Treaty 3 was made in 1873 with the Ojibwa in western Ontario; Treaty 4 in 1874 was made with the Assiniboine, Cree, and Ojibwa in the southern part of Saskatchewan; Treaty 5 was made with the Cree and Ojibwa in 1875–1876; Treaty 6 was made in 1876 with the Assiniboine, Chipewyan, and Cree peoples; Treaty 7 was made in 1877 with the Blackfoot (Siksika) Confederacy, made up of the Blackfoot, Blood, Piegan, and Sarcee, as well as the Assiniboine and Chipewyan; Treaty 8 was made in 1899 with the Beaver, Chipewyan, and Cree peoples; Treaty 9 was made in 1905 with the Cree and Ojibwa peoples and amended in 1929 and 1930; and Treaty 10 was made with the Chippewyan and Cree in 1906. The Northwest Treaty of 1921 included the northwestern part of the Northwest Territories and the southern portion of Yukon Territory.

The Indian Act of 1876 was intended to transfer all legislation concerning the indigenous peoples to the Canadian government, even though the land still was titled to the British Crown. This left the native peoples as wards of the Crown, with an administrator of affairs or Indian agent assigned to oversee their affairs. The Indian Act also included provisions on everything from land distribution to education. An 1884 amendment, for example, required that children be removed from their homes and families and sent to boarding schools to further their assimilation. Children placed in such institutions did not fare well; sources from the late nineteenth century to 1960 reveal that at least half of the children who were taken from their homes when these residential schools were created did not survive their education.

The Indian Act also made it illegal for indigenous people to participate in traditional religious ceremonies and to produce or sell any goods without written approval from an Indian agent. Those who did not give up their native rights in exchange for the right to vote were called "Status Indians," and it was not until 1961 that they finally were granted the right to vote.

Land Rights and the Métis

In the late nineteenth century, British law accepted that indigenous peoples had rights to their lands in Canada. Between 1871 and 1877, the Canadian government made seven treaties with tribes in western Canada. When treaties were made with the First Nations of Canada, they were signed by tribal leaders who agreed to relinquish their lands for trade, promises, goods, and commitments. However, many of these agreements were not followed through.

During this time, the French-speaking Métis (people of mixed indigenous and Western European heritage), numbering about 9,000, feared that English-speaking settlers might intrude onto their land, and so they asked for and obtained separation from Ontario, becoming the province of Manitoba in 1870. Still believing that Canada had not done enough to protect their rights and lands in Manitoba from non-native settlement, Métis leader Louis Riel led what became known as the North-West Rebellion in 1885, after which he was hanged for treason. Though the Métis demands were not immediately met, this conflict eventually resulted in the creation of the province of Saskatchewan in 1905.

The Indian Act was enacted to protect any monies generated from the sales of natural resources on native lands. In essence, Canada set up a trust relationship, similar to that between the U.S. government and Native American tribes. Under this act, the Canadian government accepted responsibility for the welfare, health, and education of indigenous peoples and granted voting rights to First Nations as long as they relinquished the claims to lands and rights made under their prior status. The act also made it illegal for Indians to possess alcohol (a provision that was done away with in 1951). In addition, it revoked any entitlement to tax-free status for natives who had a university education or the equivalent.

Economic, Ecological, and Social Difficulties

Today, First Nations tribes still are negotiating with the Canadian government for fair treatment, recogni-

tion, and human rights. Many motions and proposed legislation by First Nations tribes have been initiated since Canada's Constitution Act (1982), which recognized and affirmed existing aboriginal and treaty rights, opening the door for other issues to be addressed. However, no legislation has been proposed in the Canadian Parliament to protect the rights, cultures, services, and programs of indigenous peoples, prompting some tribes to take their complaints to the United Nations.

Economic development in First Nations territories is difficult, as many reserves are located in rural areas. Most reserves hire their own tribal members to manage education, health care programs, administration, finance, sales, retail, communications, and media, as in other communities. Still, many tribal members remain unemployed and lack the education to sustain themselves. Dependency based on government control of First Nations, racism, and cultural misunderstanding are reasons why some First Nations people choose not to seek employment outside their reserve. As a result, many indigenous people in Canada, especially those with families, depend on welfare programs.

Industrial pollution is another crucial issue affecting First Nations from Ontario to British Columbia. Pollution near and within tribal territories, along with continued treaty violations, has led to protests, litigation, and other actions involving the government of Canada and the United Nations. Industrial pollution of various kinds is a major issue for many tribes, particularly along the Great Lakes and rivers in British Columbia. In addition, Canada is the biggest producer of uranium in the world. This has affected not only First Nations lands and waters but also the general public in mining areas.

The Serpent River First Nation produced a small book about the radiation poisoning of the water surrounding their reserve. Since mines were created on their land, some 250 million tons (227 million metric tons) of tailings from twelve uranium and thorium mines and mills and a uranium refinery have continued to affect the groundwater and air around the reserves. The native people wish to tell the story of how their lands were seized in 1954 so that the government could put these mills and factories on their lands, which was a direct violation of the 1850 Robinson Huron Treaty.

Colonization, the resulting displacement and conflicts, treaty violations and other government policies, and related issues ultimately have had a negative impact on many aboriginal people's lives. The effects of residential school abuse and other historical trauma still can be seen among the native peoples today. Addiction, health care, economic development, and other social issues remain challenges for these people, as with Native Americans in the United States.

Nevertheless, the First Nations people continue to seek to preserve their traditions and cultures, as well as to obtain recognition for their inherent rights as indigenous people. Increasingly tribes are working to receive restitution for violations of their rights, though historians and social scientists maintain that it may take years for First Nations to accomplish sovereignty through litigation.

Jean Bedell-Bailey

See also: *Groups: North America*—Métis. *Issues*—Assimilation; Colonialism; Education; Land Rights; Revolts.

Further Reading

Axtell, James. *The European and the Indian: Essays in the Ethnohistory of Colonial North America*. New York: Oxford University Press, 1981.

Binda, K.P., and Sharilyn Caillou, eds. *Aboriginal Education in Canada: A Study in Decolonization*. Mississauga, Canada: Canadian Educators' Press, 2001.

Daniels, Harry W., ed. *The Forgotten People: Metis and Non-Status Indian Land Claims*. Ottawa: Native Council of Canada, 1979.

Dickason, Olive Patricia, and William Newbigging. *A Concise History of Canada's First Nations*. 2nd ed. Don Mills, Canada: Oxford University Press, 2010.

Frideres, James S. *Native Peoples in Canada: Contemporary Conflicts*. 3rd ed. Scarborough, UK: Prentice Hall, 1988.

Harding, Jim. *Aboriginal Rights and Government Wrongs: Uranium Mining and Neocolonialism in Northern Saskatchewan*. 2nd ed. Regina, Canada: Prairie Justice Research, 1992.

Lussier, Antoine S. *Aspects of Canadian Metis History*. Ottawa, Canada: Department of Indian and Northern Affairs, 1985.

McMillan, Alan D. *Native Peoples and Cultures of Canada*. Vancouver, Canada: Douglas & McIntyre, 1988.

Smith, Donald B., and Edward S. Rogers, eds. *Aboriginal Ontario: Historical Perspectives on the First Nations*. Toronto, Canada: Dundurn, 1994.

Trigger, Bruce G. *Natives and Newcomers: Canada's "Heroic Age" Reconsidered*. Montreal, Canada: McGill-Queen's University Press, 1986.

Central African Republic

The French colony of Ubangi-Shari became the Central African Republic on December 1, 1958, and achieved independence from France in 1960. The indigenous Aka forest foragers that now reside in the equatorial forest in the southern part of the country and adjacent areas have the deepest roots in this region, having emerged as a distinct group some 70,000 years ago. Speakers of Nilo-Saharan languages resided along the northern rim of the Central African Republic as early as 15,000 years ago, and between 3000 B.C.E. and 1000 C.E., speakers of Adamawa-Ubangian and Bantu languages migrated into the region and gradually displaced or assimilated most of the native inhabitants. Today, all of the forest foragers speak either Bantu or Ubangian languages. The majority of the current inhabitants of the Central African Republic speak Adamawa-Ubangian languages of the Niger-Congo family, such as Banda, Gbaya, Mbum, Ngbaka, Ngbandi, and Zande, but significant minorities speak Bantu dialects as well as various Afro-Asiatic, Indo-European, and Nilo-Saharan languages.

Although the Niger-Congo–speaking immigrants initially depended on indigenous peoples who acted as guides, teachers, ritual experts, and trading partners, Bantu and Ubangian settlers increasingly dominated the local peoples, especially with the beginning of iron production. Small groups of Aka (Pygmy) foragers retreated into the forest and retained considerable independence. In the nineteenth century, slave raiders from the region that is now Cameroon, Chad, and Sudan reached the Ubangi-Shari area, but they did not penetrate the forests where the Aka foragers lived.

In the early twentieth century, European companies and French colonial authorities forced the Ubangian peoples to collect rubber and provide them with elephant tusks, animal skins, and others forest products. These exploited laborers, in turn, pressured the Aka foragers to provide the products demanded by the Europeans. The French also attempted to attract Aka workers to their cash crop plantation at the edge of the forest, but the Aka often worked briefly for money but took off to catch caterpillars, a traditional Aka food, when they came in season.

The Aka avoided full incorporation into either European or Ubangian commercial and cultural networks until recently, when both international nongovernmental organizations and the Central African Republic government insisted that foragers reduce their hunting so as not to kill the animal populations in wildlife reserves patrolled by armed guards. Some foragers now depend on tourism for their livelihood, while others have settled on the fringe of the forest to cultivate cassava as both a subsistence and a cash crop.

The country's surviving foragers often are treated either with disdain (as uncivilized) or with awe (as practitioners of occult arts) by the Ubangian peoples. Their rights are ignored, and they frequently face discrimination and mistreatment by their neighbors. Both logging companies and wildlife protection agencies have limited the ability of Aka communities to forage and hunt as in the past.

In April 2010, the Central African Republic was the first African nation to ratify the International Labour Organization's Convention 169 on the rights of indigenous and tribal peoples. However, it remains to be seen whether that commitment to protect the rights of the Aka will have a positive impact on their lives.

Richard Bradshaw and Juan Fandos-Rius

See also: *Issues*—Colonialism; Social Discrimination.

Further Reading

Bahuchet, Serge, and Henri Guillaume. "Aka–Farmer Relations in the Northwest Congo Basin." In *Politics and History in Band Societies,* ed. Eleanor Leacock and Richard B. Lee. Cambridge, UK: Cambridge University Press.

Hewlett, Barry S. *Intimate Fathers: The Nature and Context of Aka Pygmy Paternal Infant Care.* Ann Arbor: University of Michigan Press, 1991.

Kisliuk, Michelle Robin. *Seize the Dance! BaAka Musical Life and the Ethnography of Performance.* Oxford, UK: Oxford University Press, 1999.

Roach, John. "African Pygmy Hunt Threatened by Logging, Animal Trade." *National Geographic News,* June 3, 2005.

Chile

Chile, which runs along the western coast of South America, is a narrow strip situated between the Andes Mountains and the Pacific Ocean. It shares a border with Peru in the north, Bolivia in the northeast, and Argentina in the east. The majority of the population lives in the Central Valley; the northern part of the country is mostly arid desert, and the southern part is generally wet and fertile. The Polynesian island of Rapa Nui, also known as Easter Island, which is famous for its stone head and body-shaped statues, also is a part of Chile.

An estimated 95.4 percent of the population is mestizo (of mixed native and European descent) and the remaining 4.6 percent consists primarily of the Mapuche and Aymara peoples: The 2002 census indicated that out of a population of more than 15 million in Chile, the indigenous population amounts to nearly 700,000. The Mapuche people number just over 600,000 people and constitute the largest native group in Chile, accounting for 87.2 percent of the total indigenous population. Still, the Mapuche represent only 2.5 percent of the total Chilean population. The rest of the indigenous groups in Chile amount to 2.1 percent of the total country's population.

Today, seven indigenous groups of Chile are extinct: the Aonikenk, Changos, Chonos, Cuncos, Diaguitas, Pikunches, and Selk'nam. Eight remaining groups are officially recognized by the Indigenous Law of 1993: the Atacameño, Aymara, Colla, Kawashkar or Alacalufe, Mapuche, Quechua, Rapa Nui, and Yámana or Yagán.

Chilean History and Its Native Peoples

In 1536, the first Spanish conquistador, Diego de Almagro, traveled south from modern-day Peru and declared what is today Chile to be part of the Spanish Empire. Shortly before his arrival, the Inca's Tupac Yupanqui imperial armies had engaged in a number of unsuccessful battles with the fierce indigenous Mapuche warriors of central Chile, which dominated important parts of the territory south of the Maule River and to the east across the Andes Mountains into present-day Argentina.

A few years later, in 1541, Pedro de Valdivia, the first Spanish governor of Chile, embarked on a war against the Mapuche that would last for more than 250 years, until the creation of the modern Chilean republic in 1810. Although the Mapuche never were completely subjugated to the Spanish Crown, the war had a tremendous impact on the native people and their culture and language. The conflict also resulted in the loss for Spain of significant resources as well as of battle-hardened, veteran troops of European wars, including Governor Valdivia, who was captured and executed by the Mapuche in 1554.

Although peace treaties signed at Quilín in 1641 and Negrete in 1726 and 1793 did not put an end to the war, they defined the borders and mutual areas of influence of the Mapuche and Spanish in the southern region of Araucanía. These *parlamentos* (treaties) also regulated commercial interactions between the Europeans and Mapuche, which flourished during the intermittent periods of peace.

The relative independence that the Spanish colonial administration granted to the Mapuche ended with the establishment of the Chilean republic in 1810. The lack of freedoms for indigenous people became especially evident in 1881, when the emerging republic waged an overwhelming war of conquest against the Mapuche (*pacificación de la Araucanía*). Upon their defeat and confiscation of their lands, the Mapuche were placed on reservations and pressured with renewed intensity to assimilate into the new Chilean national identity, culture, and language.

Modern Chile Comes to Terms with Its Native Peoples

Despite the proclamation of indigenous people's rights in the Indigenous Law (*Ley indígena*) of 1993 and the subsequent ratification of the International Labour Organization's Convention 169 on indigenous rights in 2003, relations between the Chilean government and the Mapuche remain problematic. Conflicts sparked by Mapuche land claims have led to state repression and to the use of antiterrorist laws created by the military dictatorship that was in power during the early 1970s and 1980s.

Subsequent government policies have continued to limit the opportunities for indigenous people to participate in decisions that affect their lands, cultures, and traditions and the allocation of their natural resources. The situation has become an international embarrassment for Chile's democratically elected governments, prompting accusations of human rights violations in their relations with the Mapuche.

According to Chile's 2002 census, 95 percent of the Aymara and 80 percent of the Mapuche populations are living in urban centers as a consequence of forced economic migration from their ancestral lands. Large segments of the indigenous populations in the country remain marginalized from mainstream Chilean society. A 2003 survey conducted by Chile's Ministry of Planning reported that indigenous people earned 26 percent less than nonindigenous citizens for similar work. The most critical areas of poverty in the country encompass large indigenous populations.

The creation in 1998 of intercultural, bilingual education programs in public schools to serve the indigenous populations and of the Indigenous Scholarship Program, which benefits 36,000 low-income indigenous students at the elementary, high school, and college levels each year, has helped close the educational gap between indigenous and mainstream Chilean students, but they have not solved the problem. Challenges remain as a result of assimilation and cultural and linguistic loss among indigenous youth who increasingly are urbanized.

A government-run participatory development program called Orígenes, which is funded by the Chilean government and international development agencies, has allocated $185 million since 2000 for indigenous development in the areas of health, education, and community development. These efforts have begun to show positive results in the lives of Chile's indigenous peoples, including lowering the rate of poverty.

Patricio R. Ortiz

See also: *Groups: Central and South America*—Aymara; Mapuche; Quechua. *Groups: East Asia and Oceania*—Polynesians. *Issues*—Colonialism; Land Rights.

Further Reading

Martínez, Javier, and Alvaro Díaz. *Chile: The Great Transformation*. Washington, DC: The Brookings Institution, 1996.

Ortiz, Patricio. *Indigenous Knowledge, Education and Ethnic Identity: An Ethnography of an Intercultural Bilingual Education Program in a Mapuche School in Chile*. Saarbrücken, Germany: VDM Verlag, 2009.

Rector, John L. *The History of Chile*. New York: Palgrave Macmillan, 2003.

Sullivan, Kathleen M. "Reorganizing Indigenous-State Relations in Chile: Programa Orígenes and Participatory Governance." *Studies in Law, Politics, and Society* 55 (2011): 101–129.

China

The People's Republic of China is the largest country in Asia, occupying nearly the entirety of East Asia, and the third largest in the world, after Canada and Russia. Home to more than 1.3 billion people, China also has the largest population of any country in the world, representing about one-fifth of the global population. Although the Chinese Communist Party has sought to stress the homogeneity and equality of the Chinese people, China is in fact one of the most ethnically diverse nations in the world.

The vast majority of Chinese are Han, who constitute more than 90 percent of the population, numbering 1.2 billion people. Han Chinese are the majority in every province in China and in eleven other province-level administrative bodies. However, the Chinese government also recognizes by law fifty-five minority ethnic groups. The largest of the minorities is the Zhuang, with a population of 16.2 million. Another seventeen minority groups have populations of more than 1 million: the Bai, Buyei, Dong, Hani, Hui, Kazakhs, Koreans, Li, Manchu, Miao, Mongolians, Tai, Tibetans, Tujia, Uighurs, Yao, and Yi.

The integration of diverse peoples and lands into the Chinese state is reflected in the variety of dialects of Mandarin (also known as Putonghua) spoken today, many of which are the result of extensive interaction with now-extinct indigenous languages. Today, people from different regions of China speak dialects that are more or less mutually unintelligible. Variations in cuisine and cultural production and practice also are indicative of these differences. The many members of the pantheon of Chinese belief also point to an expanding Chinese territory that integrated local deities and animist spirits into a larger spiritual structure.

A common theme throughout four millennia of Chinese history has been the gradual expansion of the central

Chinese state across the territory that is recognized today as China, though this has not been without ethnic tension and occasional violence. An important manifestation of this expansion has been the movement of Han Chinese into the country's outlying provinces and regions. In some cases, most notably in Xinxiang province and in contemporary Tibet, that movement has been accompanied by unrest and violence.

Xinxiang, one of China's largest provinces, is on its western frontier. About 40 percent of Xinxiang's 20 million people are Uighurs, a native people who are predominantly Muslim. China's economic boom, which has fueled the growth of numerous jobs in Xinxiang, has brought Han Chinese into the region. At the same time, the Uighurs would like to see the region declared as an independent nation of East Turkistan. The Han immigrants typically are wealthier than the Uighurs, adding to the tension. Although China claims that the socioeconomic status of the Uighurs is rising, in July 2009, riots between the Uighurs and the Han erupted in Xinxiang's capital city of Urumqi. Approximately 200 people were killed, 1,600 were injured, and 700 were imprisoned by the Chinese authorities; about twenty-five of those imprisoned were sentenced to death for their roles in the riots.

Expansion and Cultural Assimilation

For much of recorded history, the majority of China has been cooling and drying out, a gradual transition from a climate that once permitted elephants to thrive in much of the country. Chinese culture originated in the northern part of present-day China, in territory that is now climatically cool, lacking in water, and prone to desertification. The first Chinese empires were created by conquest, as the Chinese state incorporated neighboring territories and then more distant ones. The most notable of these conquests was the Chinese defeat of the Shu, based in what is now Sichuan Province, during the Qin dynasty (221–206 B.C.E.). Han Chinese moved into the region and established large majorities in the coastal states and in the provinces surrounding important river valleys.

Outlying provinces retained majorities of other ethnicities until the tenth through twelfth centuries C.E., or later. The incorporation of Yunnan into China was a result of the expansion of the Mongols of the Yuan dynasty during the thirteenth and fourteenth centuries, who imported a Muslim people, the Hui, to fill the colonial administrative and executive class. It was only

GREAT WALL OF CHINA

The Great Wall of China, which the Chinese call the "Long Wall of 10,000 Li," is the world's longest human-made structure. Stretching across northern China, the Great Wall consists of earthen and stone fortifications built over centuries, interspersed with natural barriers, such as hills and rivers. Efforts have been made to accurately determine the actual length of the Great Wall. The total structure, including its undulating sections of natural barriers and trenches, is estimated to span up to 5,500 miles (8,850 kilometers).

These fortifications originally were commissioned to be linked in the late third century by China's first emperor, the infamous Shihuangdi (r. 221–210 B.C.E.). Chinese knowledge of wall-building techniques dates back to the Spring and Autumn period (770–475 B.C.E.).

Scholars maintain that the oldest parts of the Great Wall were built in the fifth century B.C.E., during China's Warring States period (475–221 B.C.E.). During this tumultuous period of China's history, the country was divided into a number of states ruled by feudal lords who often were at war with each other. Each state built up wall fortifications using earth and wood to defend its borders.

In 221 B.C.E., Qin ruler Zhao Zheng unified China and established the Qin dynasty by defeating all of the opposition. He became known as Shihuangdi, the de facto ruler of China. To promote unity and centralized rule, Shihuangdi destroyed most of the fortifications that existed along former state borders, but he ordered the connection of the sections lining the empire's northern frontier. His intention was to create a barrier that would protect China from barbarians residing in the north.

Subsequent dynasties, including the Han, Sui, and Ming, repaired and extended the Great Wall. In particular, Ming leaders made efforts to fortify the structure, as it was key to their defense against the Mongols and Manchus. Bricks and stone were used extensively during this period to reinforce and construct the wall. Over the centuries, historians estimate that between 1 million and 3 million people perished while building the Great Wall, many of whom were buried beneath it.

Many sections of the Great Wall have eroded over time; others have been restored. The sections that remain visible today extend from Shanhaiguan in the east to Lop Lake in the west. Because of its historical and architectural significance, the Great Wall of China was designated as a World Heritage Site by the United Nations Educational, Scientific and Cultural Organization in 1987.

Janelle Teng

after the Panthay Rebellion of the 1850s, in the aftermath of the Taiping Rebellion, that a concerted effort was made to introduce a large number of Han Chinese into that region.

Sustained population growth from the Ming dynasty (1368–1644) onward, fueled by technological development and urban management, enabled the annexation of provinces farther from the core region. During the Ming period, few efforts were made to persuade non-Han Chinese to adopt Chinese culture. When efforts at assimilation were made, such as the required wearing of the topknot, these typically were enforced by foreign conquerors such as the Manchu people.

Since the beginning of recorded history, extensive Chinese records have aimed to demonstrate the superiority of the Middle Kingdom—that is, the core of the Chinese empire—over the so-called barbarians, whether these were the people of the south or the nomadic horse people of the steppe. There were few opportunities for Chinese expansion into the lands occupied by the nomads, especially after the army of the Tang dynasty was defeated by an Arab coalition at the Battle of Talas in the Tarim Basin in 751 C.E. Indeed, the building of the Great Wall and similar fortifications indicated a desire to hold on to existing territory rather than to expand further.

A major attempt to extend the Chinese territory followed the loss of Dai Viet (modern-day northern Vietnam) to independence in the tenth century, following a millennium of Chinese colonial control. Several attempts were made to reimpose control in this southern area, which offered many benefits from the fertile Hong River delta and valley. These all were resisted, as were Yuan attempts to conquer parts of Burma and northern Thailand and Laos, areas that generally were considered "beyond the pale" because of the diseases that lurked there and the alien nature of the terrain. After its defeat in the Chinese Civil War (1945–1949), Chiang Kai-shek's Nationalist Kuomintang faction migrated to Taiwan and have sought to establish the island as an independent state; this has not been accepted by those on the mainland, where Taiwan is considered an intrinsic province within China.

External polities were controlled through a complex and pragmatic web of management systems that involved the exchange of embassies, the awarding of hierarchical positions and grants, access to the tributary trade system, and the *tusi* system that used barbarians to control other outlying populations. Many of these arrangements persisted into the early twentieth century.

History and the Han Dynasties

Scholars generally agree that the Han Chinese trace their origin to two separate populations, the Yanhuang, based in the Yellow (Huang) River Valley, and the Yan people, based in the Yangtze River Valley. These peoples emerged some 7,000 years ago, creating one of the earliest and most influential cultures in human history.

Early legendary figures gave way to the Three Sovereigns and Five Emperors period (ca. 2500–2100 B.C.E.). Huangdi, known as the Yellow Emperor, is recognized as the first ruler of the Chinese state. The first-known dynasty, the extent of which still is being re-created through archaeological excavation, was the Xia dynasty (ca. 2100–1600 B.C.E.). During this time, the Chinese people began to differentiate themselves from the surrounding non-Chinese populations. Founded by the legendary Emperor Yu, the Xia used jade, bamboo, copper, silk, and pottery and planted rice and millet.

The subsequent Shang dynasty (ca. 1600–1050 B.C.E.) is regarded as a semihistorical time of magic and miracles, while also one of military endeavor. The capital city was moved to Anyang, while shamanism and animism, perhaps introduced by way of Central Asia, became influential in fostering a mystical and slightly hedonistic tradition of spirituality within a broadly feudal economic and political system.

The Shang dynasty was succeeded by the Zhou dynasty (1046–256 B.C.E.), which usually is divided into the Spring and Autumn (770–475 B.C.E.) and Warring States (475–221 B.C.E.) periods. The Shang marked the beginning of the consolidation of the Chinese state and people beyond the initial core areas of settlement. Many small city-states and regions based on a small number of urban areas with generally comparable institutions arose in competition with each other and contended for scarce resources, security, and supremacy. The work of the Chinese sage Confucius (born Gong Zu, 551–479 B.C.E.) was instrumental in shaping the ordering of populations and the assimilation of states conquered by rivals or acquired through tribute or diplomacy.

This process continued through the subsequent Qin (221–206 B.C.E.) and the more significant Han (206 B.C.E.–220 C.E.) dynasties. The Qin dynasty attempted to introduce a particularly fierce form of legalism in which all types of cultural, artistic, and social expression were brought under control of the state, which doled out severe punishments for anyone who was found guilty of breaking the numerous regulations.

The Han dynasty often is divided into the earlier Western Han period (206 B.C.E.–25 C.E.), when the capital was based at Chang'an and ending with a brief usurpation by Wang Mang, and the Eastern Han period (25–220 C.E.), when the capital was moved to Loyang. The Han emperors moderated the brutality of this system by applying Confucian ideals. Indeed, the Han dynasty witnessed such a flourishing of Chinese culture and artistic achievement, documented by the great historian Sima Qian, that it was held up as a paragon against which all subsequent dynasties judged themselves.

Subsequent periods, however, were characterized by fragmentation of the political state. Smaller states, relying primarily on large landowning families that could raise their own troops, contended with one another, but eventually they were overwhelmed by the more powerful peoples of the steppe, principally the Xiongnu, known in the West as Huns. Over the course of more than 1,000 years, the sedentary Chinese people, with their reliance on irrigation and the bureaucracy of the state, were threatened by a succession of nomadic or seminomadic people with greater mobility and maneuverability. Chinese military techniques favored the use of static defenses in warfare, whether these were bodies of troops or environmental features such as rivers, cities, and walls. The nomads preyed on the Chinese when they could, extorting payments in silks and other precious items.

The nomads' power generally waned during the subsequent Three Kingdoms period (220–265 C.E.), the Jin dynasties (265–420), and the Southern and Northern dynasties (386–589). The Chinese remained comparatively weak until the creation of the Sui (581–618) and, in particular, the Tang (618–907) dynasties. The Sui stabilized China, but the state remained essentially bankrupt. Implementing a streamlined and efficient administration, the early Tang emperors restored the country's fortunes. Under the Tang, the Chinese state reached its apogee of achievement economically and culturally.

The following Five Dynasties and Ten Kingdoms (917–960) period was chaotic, leaving the people vulnerable to predation by external and internal forces. Order was restored by the Song dynasty (960–1279), when arts and commerce again flourished in a cosmopolitan, multicultural empire to which dozens of neighbors sent tribute in order to gain access to Chinese trade centers.

This progress was interrupted by the merciless campaigns of the Mongols, who, under Kublai Khan (1215–1294), conquered the whole of China and annexed Nanzhao (modern Yunnan Province) along with other western provinces, to establish the Yuan dynasty (1279–1368). The Mongols assumed the role of brutal overlords, colonizing the Chinese, and faced much resistance as a result. Popular support facilitated the restoration of Chinese rule, prestige, and power, under the Ming dynasty, which lasted from the end of the Yuan dynasty until the mid-seventeenth century.

From 1402, China dispatched the world's strongest navy (only surpassed during World War II) to explore the globe and to establish diplomatic and tribute relationships under Zheng He. Chinese prestige was at its height across East and South Asia, Arabia, and the coast of East Africa, when the Yung Lo emperor died in 1424. His successors reversed this policy, turning the nation's focus inward.

External conquest by the nomadic and fierce northern tribe of Manchu, who established the Qing dynasty (1644–1912), coincided with the rise of European colonialism in Asia and the onset of the Opium Wars (1839–1842 and 1856–1860), unequal treaties, and extraterritoriality that caused the internal weakness and divisiveness that, in the midst of revolts and uprisings, saw the end of the imperial system. The empire was replaced from 1912 with a nationalist government, initially under Sun Yat-sen, that lasted until the Communist Revolution in 1949. In 1931, Manchuria was invaded by Japan, an action leading up to World War II.

Beginning in the mid-twentieth century, the Chinese Civil War pitted the Chinese Communist Party against the Nationalist Kuomintang of General Chiang Kai-shek and the Japanese. The victory of the Chinese Communist Party led to communist rule, which has continued into the twenty-first century. During this period, a violent crackdown on student protesters in Tiananmen Square in 1989, which took hundreds of lives, was only one example of the unwillingness of the Chinese state to tolerate any form of political dissent. Gradually, during the 1990s, the Chinese government adopted a free market capitalist regime that now offers the opportunity for millions to become rich—or at least to escape poverty—while remaining under single-party control.

Cultural and Behavioral Features

Perhaps the most influential philosophical and religious voice in Chinese history is that of Confucius. His thought has been abstracted as a belief system that legitimates the state and its leadership and provides a more efficient and orderly system of governance than earlier legalist approaches. The Confucianist approach also is a secular one, a fact that has helped prolong its importance under the enforced atheism of the Chinese Communist Party.

Confucianism posits that all human interactions take place within the context of five categories of human relationships—ruler and ruled, spouses, parents and children—in which one person or people is superior in status and the other is inferior. The superior individual has a duty to protect and nourish the inferior or junior one, who, in turn, has a responsibility to obey. This basic approach has worked in combination with the tradition of ancestor reverence, which has acted to limit mobility in society by stressing the importance of proximity to one's ancestors and descendants during life and after death. Traditionally, if a Chinese person died away from home, his or her body would be walked back home so it could be buried in the appropriate resting place.

In addition to Confucianism, Daoism, Buddhism, and animism all have been important influences on the behavior of Chinese people. Both Buddhism and Daoism focus principally on the individual's engagement with a different and higher state of being and tend toward quietism in politics. However, another strong strand of religious belief has had a millenarianist element that has helped spark some of the most potent rebellions in Chinese history.

The Taiping Rebellion of 1850–1864, for example, was a millenarian movement that combined different religious factors, leading to more than 20 million deaths. Numerous secret societies and movements throughout history have combined millenarianism with exotic religious beliefs and a strong critique of Chinese cultural traditions or, more likely, the distortion of those traditions by ill-intentioned people, especially outsiders of some sort. The Red Eyebrows, White Lotus, and Boxer rebellions are just a few of the many rebellions of this type.

The Chinese Diaspora

Many millions of ethnic Chinese have moved overseas over the course of centuries. Zhou Daguan famously noted the presence of a well-established Chinese community in the Khmer Angkor state at the end of the thirteenth century.

In some cases, the movement of Chinese overseas was associated with the colonization of outlying areas. The 1,000-year colonization of the northern part of Vietnam (111 B.C.E.–938 C.E.) is an example of the sinicization of a neighboring region. In other cases, an internal event prompted large-scale emigration. For example, the destruction of the Nanzhao state in modern Yunnan in 1259 and its incorporation into the Chinese state prompted the exit of the Tai people, who established *mueang* (city-states) across the western and southern part of the Mekong River Subregion. Many ethnic Chinese assimilated to various degrees in their host countries, taking local names and marrying local partners.

In other cases, migration was undertaken for economic reasons. The coastal cities of Southeast Asia, from Manila to Yangon, became homes for merchants who capitalized on social and familial networks with mainland communities to trade a variety of imported and exported commodities, including opium. Less wealthy Chinese were attracted to such urban areas as potential places for employment. Others were attracted to the rubber plantations of Malaya, the tin mines of Phuket, or, farther afield, the railroad construction projects of the United States. Many migrants, nearly all men, were hired as indentured labor. For self-protection and to assist in the remittance of earned money, they joined mutual assistance organizations known as *tongs* or triads, which subsequently developed a reputation for criminal activities and subversion of the state.

Because most ethnic Chinese migrants dwelled in urban locations and gravitated toward commerce, they often gained advantages over the indigenous peoples, especially in rural areas. This led to periodic outbreaks of resentment and violence against the Chinese by mobs or intimidation by government agencies. In the decades following World War II and the victory of the Chinese Communist Party, Chinese communities were under suspicion of wishing to launch communist insurrections in the countries where they lived, and, in a number of cases, the suspicion was justified. This led to additional harassment and persecution. Even when a communist revolution was successfully enacted, as in Cambodia under the Khmer Rouge, ethnic Chinese were victims as a result of suspicion of counterrevolutionary tendencies.

More recent waves of emigration took place when Hong Kong Chinese left for the United Kingdom and other Commonwealth nations, which continued the tendency for the great majority of migrants to derive from a comparatively narrow strip of the southeastern coast.

Contemporary migration has broadened the geographic origin of labor migrants as part of the massive shift of population from rural to urban areas and the creation of so-called snakehead gangs that specialize in the illegal migration of Chinese people to supposedly rich opportunities overseas, situations in which they are generally exploited by both gang members and future employers. By contrast, thousands of young, highly motivated, and educated students have moved to Western countries to further their education and have become successful in doing so. This has led to concerns in China about a "brain drain" as such students are hired by local employers for high salaries.

Significance

For most of its history, China was the largest, most advanced, and wealthiest society in the world, declining only with the strengthening of European colonialism in Asia. Some cultures rivaled China for periods—Mughal India is one noted example—yet none exceeded it consistently. Scientific advances from early periods include gunpowder, printing, paper, and the compass. In the realm of war, Chinese artillery, including biological weapons, was devised as means of successfully besieging large Chinese cities, with their substantial wars.

Delegates representing China's ethnic minorities pose at the conclusion of the 2012 People's Political Consultative Conference in Beijing. Modernization, capitalism, and, in some cases, politics threaten the authenticity and diversity of ethnic culture. *(Qian Xiaodun/Imaginechina/ AP Images)*

The Great Wall of China has been noted as the only human construction visible from space, but it represents nevertheless a significant feat not just of engineering but also of the ability to gather and deploy large bodies of Chinese people and extract work from them. The military history of China, whether internal or external enemies were fought, reveals the enormous logistical efforts involved in assembling, moving, equipping, and feeding many thousands of people, animals, and ships and indicates the depth and breadth of the bureaucracy necessary to support such efforts. It is, perhaps, in the large-scale human organization of this kind that the greatest achievements of the Chinese people may be found.

The tendency toward social conservatism in China historically was counteracted by mechanisms such as the imperial examination system, which provided opportunities for talented boys from the lower ranks of society to be admitted to the civil service and to achieve promotions, which would elevate the status of his whole family. This system helped provide upward social mobility for such individuals and their families, but their subsequent efforts were part of an enormous, occasionally ponderous but nevertheless serviceable series of intersecting offices producing knowledge, justice, and direction for the Chinese masses.

Without such support in place, it is hard to imagine that the Grand Canal and the other irrigation systems that have sustained Chinese agriculture would have been completed. Nevertheless, the state continually has faced serious outbreaks of disorder over the course of millennia in much of the territory on the basis of ethnic suppression, misrule, or poverty. Millenarianism also has regularly been influential.

The same level of prominence may be accorded to the artistic, cultural, and spiritual developments of the Chinese people. Each of these has been extremely influential throughout East Asia, but rather less so in the Western world. Some cultural products, particularly in the case of food, have become globalized successfully and Chinese techniques and tastes are found around the world. However, most aesthetic fine arts have proved less amenable to international transfer.

As the Chinese economy began to open to capitalist accumulation activities in the wake of Deng Xiaoping's 1979 open door policy, it has become the world's second- or third-largest economy (depending on which measurement system is used), and many millions of people have been lifted out of poverty on an unprecedented scale. The 2008 banking crisis revealed some of the structural strains in the Chinese economy and the need for a degree of readjustment.

Nevertheless, it is evident that China is preparing itself for a much more significant global role in the political and economic spheres. This is clear from the reconfiguration of diplomatic relationships around the world and the search to secure long-term, stable, and often exclusive access to scarce mineral resources. In addition, the Chinese government is seeking to spread knowledge of Chinese language and culture by placing its Confucius Institutes in suitable overseas locations.

John Walsh

See also: *Groups: East Asia and Oceania*—Han; Mongols. *Groups: South Asia and Middle East*—Kazakhs. *Issues*—Assimilation; Revolts.

Further Reading

Chao, Kang. *Man and Land in Chinese History: An Economic Analysis.* Stanford, CA: Stanford University Press, 1986.

Charney, Michael W., Brenda S.A. Yeoh, and Tong Chee Kiong, eds. *Chinese Migrants Abroad: Cultural, Educational and Social Dimensions of the Chinese Diaspora.* Singapore: Singapore University Press, 2003.

Daguan, Zhou. *A Record of Cambodia: The Land and Its People.* Trans. Peter Harris. Chiang Mai, Thailand: Silkworm, 2007.

Elvin, Mark. *The Retreat of the Elephants: An Environmental History of China.* New Haven, CT: Yale University Press, 2006.

Pai, Hsiao-Hung. *Chinese Whispers: The True Story Behind Britain's Hidden Army of Labour.* London: Penguin, 2008.

Yiwu, Liao. *The Corpse Walker: Real Life Stories, China from the Bottom Up.* Trans. Wen Huang. New York: Pantheon, 2008.

Zhao, Tongmao, and Tsung Dao Lee. "Gm and Km Allotypes in 74 Chinese Populations: A Hypothesis of the Origin of the Chinese People." *Human Genetics* 83:2 (September 1989): 1–10.

Colombia

Indigenous people constitute just over 3 percent of the population of Colombia, numbering approximately 1.4 million. Their cultural legacy is an integral part of Colombia's history, having survived centuries of repression and neglect, first by Spanish conquerors and then by Colombia's ruling elites.

Over the span of five centuries, Colombian natives have fought back against repression, both by force and by the use of law. Native resistance against cultural suppression and assimilation has given rise to an indigenous activist movement that is gaining momentum and recognition at the national and international levels.

Pre-Columbian Times

Humans first arrived in Colombia some 10,000 years ago, migrating there from Mesoamerica. It is estimated that by the end of the fifteenth century, the indigenous population numbered approximately 3 million inhabitants, belonging to three major groups: the Arawak, Caribs, and Chibcha.

Agriculture, particularly the cultivation of maize and potatoes, was their main form of subsistence, supplemented by fishing, hunting, and gathering. Early Colombians also made pottery, carved stone, and practiced metalworking, especially in gold and silver.

They were governed by a stratified political organization whose leaders were called *caciques,* with the *Zipa* or *Zaque* at the top of the hierarchy. Among the major groups, the Muisca and Tairona peoples achieved the highest level of intellectual and scientific development, reflected in their use of the calendar; engineering achievements, such as bridges, terraces, and irrigation systems; and moral precepts and laws, including the teachings of the legendary Bochica the Great Civilizer and his code of Nemequene, a set of social laws that were orally transmitted. The pre-Columbian native population was dispersed geographically and diverse in terms of its customs, languages, and religion, a fact that later would play a role in the native peoples' submission to the Spanish conquerors.

From the Spanish Conquest to the Colombian State

The Spanish reached Colombian territory as early as 1499, and their first major settlement was established at Santa Marta in 1525 by Rodrigo de Bastidas. Spanish expeditions in the region looked to generate economic gains from the mining of precious metals. Native traditions, such as the practice of the cacique of the Guatavita, who covered himself in gold dust during religious ceremonies and dove into the village's lagoon, fueled interest in the area. Whereas some encounters between the Spanish and the natives were amicable, others resulted in confrontation. For the most part, the Colombian natives resisted the Spanish invasion, triggering a campaign of forced submission, suppression, and even decimation of the native population.

The Spanish Crown instituted a system of land grants, or *encomiendas,* and reservations, or *resguardos,* that aided in the subjugation of the natives. These institutions were aimed at controlling the native population and providing labor in support of Spanish activities in the land, chiefly mining and plantation work.

Encomiendas were introduced during the sixteenth century to guarantee a native labor force for the conqueror or *encomendero*. In exchange, the natives received protection and a Christian education. Christianization, carried out mostly by Franciscan and Jesuit missionaries, had few positive results, and the concept of protection through the encomienda was a failure: Reports of abuses by encomenderos and even religious missionaries were common.

When the resguardos were introduced in the seventeenth century, the Spanish resettled many natives, regardless of their family or tribal ties. Though the resguardos were intended to keep a pool of native labor available, they also gave the natives a degree of independence to manage their own affairs, so long as they paid tribute to the Spanish Crown. The figure of the cacique regained importance, functioning as an intermediary between the Crown and the native people, as well as a representative of indigenous interests. For example, the cacique Don Juan Tama de Vitonco fought for the establishment of resguardos and the acquisition of land titles through direct appeals to the Crown and judicial suits. Indigenous councils called *cabildos* also were created to provide a means of native authority within the resguardos.

Despite these positive developments, the native population declined precipitously as a result of epidemic diseases, the destruction of villages and crops by the Spanish, harsh working conditions in the encomiendas, intertribal warfare, and the gradual degradation of natives' social and family life. Still, the resurgence of the cacique and the creation of cabildos represented a first step toward indigenous activism in the country.

Colombia's independence from Spain in the early nineteenth century granted the native peoples citizenship in the new nation but did little to improve their living conditions. The land base of the resguardos was diminished by the expansion of great estates, and new legislation transformed the cabildos from independent native authorities into intermediaries between the state and the native communities. Native families were split up, as many were forced to leave the resguardos to find work in the extraction of quinine in the forests.

In the twentieth century, native Colombians became increasingly involved in national politics, joining political parties, army campaigns, and even civil wars. Nasa leader Manuel Quintín Lame is perhaps the best-known native figure of this period. In his 1939 manuscript *The Thoughts of an Indian Educated in the Colombian Jungles,* he compiled the native peoples' beliefs about their place in Colombian society, in terms of their rights, their destiny, and their struggle against an oppressive society. Native leaders such as Lame helped build indigenous activism throughout the twentieth century, despite violent repression.

Modern Times

Since the 1970s, indigenous activism in Colombia has gained strength and cohesion, resulting in the creation of several indigenous advocacy organizations, such as the Indigenous Regional Council of Cauca (CRIC). CRIC's efforts have resulted in the acquisition of more than 148,000 acres (60,000 hectares) of land for native use, the revival of indigenous languages, cultures, and medicine, as well as reduced illiteracy in native communities. Indigenous activism also has succeeded in enshrining indigenous rights in the country's 1991 constitution.

In practice, however, these rights are not always upheld or secured by the government, and violent repression, murders, and displacement of indigenous activists and communities are not uncommon. A decades-old agrarian reform process has not yielded the expected results for the natives, and it is often the cause of clashes between the indigenous people and government forces. Although some resguardos have increased in size, the land is not particularly suitable for agriculture. After centuries of contributing to Colombia's economy, the country's first inhabitants still are looking for a more equitable place in society.

Juan Carlos Galindo

See also: *Issues*—Colonialism; Language; Political Participation; Social Customs.

Further Reading

Hristow, Jasmin. "Social Class and Ethnicity/Race in the Dynamics of Indigenous Peasant Movements: The Case of the CRIC in Colombia." *Latin American Perspectives* 36:4 (2009): 41–63.

Parry, J.H. *The Discovery of South America.* London: Paul Elek, 1979.

Rappaport, Joanne. *The Politics of Memory: Native Historical Representations in the Colombian Andes.* Durham, NC: Duke University Press, 1998.

Rojas, Cristina, and Judy Meltzer, eds. *Elusive Peace: International, National and Local Dimensions of Conflict in Colombia.* New York: Palgrave Macmillan, 2005.

Simons, Geoff. *Colombia: A Brutal History.* London: Saqi, 2004.

Williams, Caroline. "Resistance and Rebellion on the Spanish Frontier: Native Responses to Colonization in the Colombian Chocó, 1670–1690." *Hispanic American Historical Review* 79:3 (1999): 397–424.

Comoros

Comoros is an island nation located in the Indian Ocean off the eastern coast of Africa. It comprises three islands—Ngazidja (also known as Grande Comore), Mwali (Mohéli), and Nzwani (Anjouan). A fourth island in the Comorian archipelago, Mayotte (Maoré), remains an overseas dependency of France and is not recognized by the government of Comoros. The southernmost member state in the Arab League, its closest neighbors are Madagascar, Mozambique, the Seychelles, and Tanzania. Covering only 838 square miles (2,170 square kilometers), Comoros is among the smallest countries of the African continent, yet it has one of the highest population densities, with approximately 800,000 people.

The early population of Comoros was made up of invading peoples from Indonesia, Madagascar, and the Persian Gulf. Portuguese explorers visited the Comoros Islands in the sixteenth century. During that time, Arab merchants began trading in goods and services there, and Islam was introduced to the islands. As trade flourished, Arab cultural and religious influence also increased. In the 1840s, France established a colony in the Comoros Islands. The people of Comoros, with the exception of those living on the island of Mayotte, declared their independence from France in 1975, becoming the 143rd member of the United Nations.

The people of Comoros include the Anjouan, Grande Comore, and Mohéli. Their roots are African, Arab, and Indian, but the majority of the people are African Arab and Muslim. The people of Comoros commonly speak Shikomoro, a dialect of Swahili. Comoros is a very literate society, with more than half of the people speaking French. The nation is a member of the African Union, the Organization of the Islamic Conference, the Arab League, and the Indian Ocean Commission.

Comoros is considered one of the world's poorest countries, with little infrastructure and few natural resources. Most of the inhabitants are farmers, producing bananas, cassavas, cloves, coconuts, and vanilla. One of the main economic activities is perfume distillation, as the islands produce over 80 percent of the world's ylang ylang essence, which is an essential ingredient in most high-quality perfumes. Tourism also helps boost the economy, but unemployment is high, and the government depends heavily on aid from foreign donors.

The president of Comoros is both the head of state and the head of government. The nation's constitution, which was ratified in 2001, is based on Islamic law, as well as the French Napoleonic code and local laws. Comoros operates a small police force and national defense force. It also maintains close ties with the French government by hosting a small number of French troops at their request.

However, stability has been elusive for the country. In 2007, a separatist movement on the island of Anjouan resulted in Mohammad Bacar declaring himself president of the island, and U.S. Assistant Secretary of State Jendayi Frazer even visited the small islands in an attempt to prevent radical Islam from taking hold, encouraging popular elections throughout the Comoros.

Franklyn Taylor

See also: *Issues*—Agriculture; Colonialism.

Further Reading

Lea, David, and Annamarie Rowe. *A Political Chronology of Africa.* London: Europa Publications, 2001.
Newitt, Malyn. *Comoro Islands: Struggle Against Dependency in the Indian Ocean.* Boulder, CO: Westview Press, 1984.
Ottenheimer, Martin, and Harriet Ottenheimer. *Historical Dictionary of the Comoro Islands.* Metuchen, NJ: Scarecrow, 1994.

Cuba

Cuba is the largest island in the Caribbean at 114,524 square miles (296,616 square kilometers). It is only 90 miles (145 kilometers) off of the southern tip of Florida, and lies east of Mexico's Yucatán Peninsula. The nearest island is Hispaniola, the island shared by Haiti and the Dominican Republic. According to The World Factbook of the U.S. Central Intelligence Agency, the population of Cuba is 51 percent mulatto, 37 percent white, 11 percent black, and 1 percent Chinese.

The native population of Cuba, though small in number and once thought to have disappeared completely during the colonial era, continues to hold on to its indigenous identity today, representing a vibrant part of that nation's identity. Before the Spanish conquest, the island's population is estimated to have numbered from 50,000 to 300,000 people, comprising three main ethnic groups: the Ciboney, the Guanahatabetem, and the Taino. Within twenty years of Christopher Columbus's landing on Hispaniola in 1492, however, the native Cubans would see their society and their way of life drastically transformed.

In 1511, Diego Velásquez set off from the first Spanish colony on the island of Hispaniola (now Haiti and the Dominican Republic) to conquer neighboring Cuba. After the arrival of the Spanish, the indigenous population of Cuba declined rapidly as a result of the technological superiority of the Spanish conquistadores, as well as the rapid spread of European diseases, widespread famine, dramatically increased child mortality, and suicides precipitated by the cultural collapse that accompanied the rapid conquest. A population that once had numbered in the hundreds of thousands was reduced to fewer than 5,000 survivors.

Leading the resistance among the indigenous Cubans during the early decades of colonization was the Taino hero Hatuey. Intending to warn his fellow Taino in Cuba about the poor treatment they could expect from the Spanish, Hatuey sailed to Cuba from his home on Hispaniola. He led guerilla attacks against the Spanish for three months before he was captured and sentenced to be burned at the stake. Legend has it that a Spanish priest tried to convert Hatuey before his execution, but, upon learning that the Spanish who were baptized were believed to go to Heaven, Hatuey replied, "I do not want to be with such mean people. . . . Baptize me not. I prefer to go to hell."

Until the 1970s, most historians believed that by 1550 the indigenous Cubans either had died out or had merged with the Hispanic and African slave populations on the island. However, as early as the 1840s, a Spanish scientist named Miguel Rodriguez Ferrer traveled among and wrote about the native communities still existing in Cuba. Anecdotal evidence from others, such as Cuban revolutionary José Martí and French anthropologist Henri Dumont, supported Ferrer's assertions.

Nevertheless, the assertion that Cuba had no remaining indigenous people remained the conventional wisdom among academics and Cuban government officials until studies carried out by Cuban anthropologist Manuel Rivero de la Calle in the 1960s and 1970s revealed nearly 300 people of native ethnicity in Guantánamo Province. During the 1970s and 1980s, Cuban historian José Barreiro provided further evidence of the survival of indigenous Cuban cultures and traditions among 1,000 to 3,000 people living in the eastern part of the island.

Today, although Cuba has no official policy toward its indigenous people, the Cuban government has been supportive of the indigenous rights initiatives of international groups, including the Organization of American States and the United Nations. Policies supporting sustainable agriculture, environmental protection, and the promotion of plant-based medicine appear to be recognizing the value of and envisioning a larger role for Cuba's indigenous cultures.

Steven L. Danver

See also: *Groups: Central and South America*—Taino. *Issues*—Colonialism.

Further Reading

Barreiro, José. "Beyond the Myth of Extinction: The Hatuey Regiment." *KACIKE: The Journal of Caribbean Amerindian History and Anthropology* (July 2004).

———. "Indians in Cuba." *Cultural Survival Quarterly* 13:3 (1989): 56–60.

De la Riva, Juan Pérez. "A World Destroyed." In *The Cuba Reader: History, Culture, Politics,* ed. Aviva Chomsky, Barry Carr, and Pamela Maria Smorkaliff. Durham, NC: Duke University Press, 2004.

Staten, Clifford L. *The History of Cuba.* Westport, CT: Greenwood, 2003.

Yaremko, Jason M. "'Gente Bárbara': Indigenous Rebellion, Resistance and Persistence in Colonial Cuba, c. 1500–1800." *KACIKE: The Journal of Caribbean Amerindian History and Anthropology* (December 2006).

Democratic Republic of the Congo

Situated on the equator, the Democratic Republic of the Congo (DRC), formerly known as Zaire, is located in Central Africa. The country is bordered by the Central Africa Republic and South Sudan to the north; Burundi, Rwanda, Tanzania, and Uganda to the east; Zambia to the southeast; Angola to the south; and the Republic of the Congo to the west. The DRC has a short coastline in the west fronting the southern Atlantic Ocean.

In 2010, the DRC's population totaled more than 70 million, with Christianity as the predominant religion. Like many African countries, the DRC is a multiethnic nation comprising approximately 200 peoples, most of which are of Bantu-speaking origin. The four largest ethnic groups in the country are the Kongo, Luba, Mangbetu-Azande, and Mongo, which together make up 45 percent of the population.

Before the fifteenth century, the native Congolese had contact with outsiders, such as Arabs, Europeans, and Swahili, which allowed both short- and long-distance trade to flourish. However, the devastation caused by early contact and trade with the outside world far outweighed its gains. The wreckage included the collapse of native empires, political oppression, exploitation of natural resources, and population decline as a result of the transatlantic slave trade. The DRC is known as one of the most politically turbulent regions in the world. Violence became the hallmark of the country's history in the late nineteenth century, when it was brought under colonial rule.

Precolonial Congo

The earliest evidence of human occupation in the DRC can be found in the Congo Basin (that is, the areas around the Congo River and its tributaries). Pygmies are believed to have been the first inhabitants of the region. As early as 2250 B.C.E., their presence was mentioned in a letter from the Egyptian Pharaoh Neferkare to his commander in the southern Egyptian kingdom, who had brought back a pygmy from his expedition to the southern forest.

In 2000 B.C.E., Bantu-speaking people began migrating into the Congo Basin from the Benue River area of what is now Nigeria. Archaeological evidence indicates that these people were agriculturists who brought a tradition of iron metallurgy to the region. The introduction of iron technology enhanced the cultivation of diverse crops such as palm trees, millet, and sorghum. Although the history of the groups that peopled the region between 2000 B.C.E. and 1400 C.E. is unclear, we know that by 1500 C.E., Nilotic and Sudanic groups from the north and east of the Congo River had migrated into the basin. These migrations displaced the indigenous Pygmies in some places and pushed them to the fringes in other areas.

Migration into the Congo Basin resulted in high population density and a very heterogeneous population, factors that contributed to the formation of native kingdoms. The most populous of the city-states in Central Africa during the precolonial period were Kongo, Luba, and Luanda. The geography and environment in these areas, outside of the rain forests, with a subtropical climate that allowed for agriculture were the chief factors in the development of these states. The natural advantage of proximity to the Congo River not only provided resources nearby but also enhanced the movement of goods and ideas within and between states.

The political and economic systems of the native empires were influenced greatly by the arrival of Europeans in the fifteenth century. The first such contact took place in 1483, when Portuguese explorers sailed to the shore of the Congo River. Contact with Europeans aided in the formation of trade zones in the Congo Basin, allowing regional and long-distance trade in slaves, ivory, and other exotic materials, which became a major source of wealth. In the eastern trade zone, the native Congolese traded with Arab and Swahili merchants. By the sixteenth century, the Congo Basin and its natives had become an integral part of the worldwide economy.

Human cargo was the most important commodity in Central Africa. As early as the 1500s, Arab and Zanziba merchants engaged in slave raiding in the Congo, although the region did not become a major supply center to the Americas and Europe until 1820s and 1830s. An increase in demand for slaves led to the spread of slave hunting into the interior of the Congo and instilled fear and suspicion among the native people. The number of people traded on the slave market skyrocketed: Between 1821 and 1843, more than 156,000 native Congolese were sold as slaves to the Caribbean and the Americas, the practice only ending with the abolition of the slave trade in the mid-nineteenth century.

Colonial Era

During the colonial era, the Congo witnessed a series of administrative changes. The region first became a European holding in 1885, when it was ceded to King Leopold II of Belgium at the Berlin West Africa Conference, becoming the Congo Free State. Leopold was to administer the region on behalf of a group of European investors. His mission, as codified in the Act of Berlin, was to develop the territory in order to open it up to European trade and to civilize the indigenous inhabitants. Although some infrastructure development did take place, notably railway construction and the building of industries such as rubber manufacturing, exploitation and brutalization of the native peoples were the hallmarks of Leopold's authority in the region.

Leopold's brutal treatment of the native Congolese sparked outrage among his European partners, forcing the Belgian government to take over the administration of the Congo Free State in 1908, renaming the territory the Belgian Congo. Under the Belgian colonial authorities, the natives were regarded as children to be cared for. They were excluded from politics, as they were believed to be inferior to the colonists, and the traditional rulers were employed to collect taxes for the colonial government. The native Congolese soon came to resent these practices and began to resist the Belgian authorities by forming associations and pressure groups. By 1958, a vocal nationalist movement headed by Patrice Lumumba was calling for independence.

When Belgium finally gave in to the Congolese demand for independence, a hasty transition of power was effected by the Belgian government. In May 1960, the Mouvement National Congolais (Congolese National Movement, or MNC) won the first parliamentary election. On June 30, 1960, the Republic of Congo achieved independence from Belgium. The MNC appointed Lumumba as prime minister and Joseph Kasavubu as the nation's first president.

Postcolonial Era

The immediate postindependence period was a time of political and ethnic crisis. Political unrest began when

Lumumba sided with the Eastern bloc during the Cold War—an action that Western nations saw as opposing their political interests. With the support of the U.S. and Belgian governments, Lumumba was kidnapped and executed by a firing squad in January 1961, sparking civil upheaval.

In 1965, Colonel Joseph-Désiré Mobutu overthrew President Kasavubu in a coup d'état sponsored by Western powers in order to put a stop to the civil war in the country. Rather than settling the crisis, Mobutu's tenure worsened interethnic tensions, which escalated into unabated violence throughout the country. The violence continued under Joseph Kabila, an army officer who led a rebellion to depose Mobutu in 1997.

The effects of the civil war on the native Congolese cannot be overemphasized. There were many cases of rape and sexual exploitation, people were put into forced labor, hundreds of thousands of people were displaced, and many lives and property were lost. The Pygmy population of the DRC suffered especially, as Pygmies were hunted and eaten as game by rebels who believed that they were mysterious beings and sources of spiritual power. In Kivu Province, there also were cases of cannibalism. The civil war claimed an estimated 5.4 million casualties, the most devastating man-made calamity since World War II.

The violence devastated the country's economy as well. The natural resources of the DRC, mainly gold and diamonds, were exploited and carted away for the benefit of other nations and a few native elites. The large-scale production of copper in the DRC halted as a result of an international conspiracy to fix prices. Today, the country's economy depends primarily on trade in cotton and diamonds.

In addition to the corruption and political and ethnic unrest that marked Mobutu's administration, the regime also was known for its so-called authenticity scheme, which aimed to "re-Africanize" the DRC and reclaim the lost glory of the native Congolese culture and identity. To that end, the country was renamed the Republic of Zaire in 1971, and the names of organizations, places, and people were changed, replacing Christian names with African ones. Leading by example, Mobutu changed his name to Mobutu Sese Seko. This program, however, was not entirely embraced by Zairians.

At the end of Mobutu's long dictatorship in May 1997, Laurent-Désiré Kabila, the new military leader and an ally of the MNC, became president. Kabila did not support Mobutu's agenda and renamed the country the Democratic Republic of the Congo. Likewise, the names of organizations, places, and ministries reverted to their former colonial or early independence names. However, corruption and political unrest only were exacerbated during Kabila's time in office, which ended with his assassination by his own bodyguards in January 2001.

The international community has intervened in the DRC on several occasions, with the United Nations (UN) sending peacekeeping teams to the DRC, the most recent mission beginning in 1999. The DRC's government also has made efforts to obtain peace. In 2005, President Joseph Kabila (the son of Laurent-Désiré Kabila) successfully negotiated with the parties involved in the conflict to end the war. However, such peacekeeping efforts to halt the devastation caused by war have had mixed results. Rebel organizations still congregate in the eastern Congo, and UN troops still were in the country as of 2012. Thus, the conflict continues in the region, and thousands of native Congolese continue to fall victim.

Abidemi Babatunde Babalola

See also: *Groups: Africa*—Kongo; Luba. *Issues*—Colonialism; Economic Development.

Further Reading

Duffy, Kevin. *Children of the Forest.* New York: Dodd, Mead, 1984.

Gondola, Ch. Didier. *The History of Congo.* Westport, CT: Greenwood, 2002.

Kisangani, Emizet F., and Scott F. Bobb. *Historical Dictionary of the Democratic Republic of Congo.* 3rd ed. Lanham, MD: Scarecrow, 2010.

Renton, David, David Seddon, and Leo Zeilig. *The Congo Plunder and Resistance.* New York: Zed, 2007.

Djibouti

The Republic of Djibouti, a former colony of France, occupies approximately 8,800 square miles (23,000 square kilometers) in the Horn of Africa at the southern entrance to the Red Sea. Located at the crossroads of Africa and the Middle East, it is bordered by Eritrea to the north, Somalia to the southwest, and Ethiopia to the east. Its capital also is called Djibouti. The country's name is derived from the French transcription of a local Somali expression, *jab buti,* meaning "place where the ogres were defeated," a reference to the area's harsh climatic conditions.

Djibouti's cosmopolitan population of approximately 750,000 people is made up of Somalis, who represent 60 percent of the population; Afar, making up 35 percent; and peoples of Arab, Ethiopian, French, Greek, Indian, and Italian descent, representing 5 percent. Arabic and French are the country's official languages, but Afar and Somali also are used in the media. Most

Djiboutians (94 percent) are Muslims, while 6 percent are Christians.

Djibouti's economy is primarily service oriented, a consequence of the largely desert-like conditions and the fact that the bulk of the country's population is nomadic. Approximately three-quarters of Djiboutians have migrated from the countryside to live in cities.

Djibouti's economy also has been shaped by political developments in neighboring countries in the Horn of Africa and the Middle East. For instance, as a result of Eritrea's secession from Ethiopia in 1993, goods from the latter country, such as fresh fruits and vegetables, now are exported via Djibouti, earning the tiny nation some of its foreign exchange. Moreover, Djibouti acts as a transit port in the Horn of Africa and a crucial refueling and international shipping center for vessels traveling the Suez Canal.

Precolonial and Colonial History

The area occupied by Djibouti, known as the "Land of Punt" (land of the gods), has been an important commercial corridor since antiquity. Afar and Somali nomads, inhabitants of the Abyssinian highlands, and Arab and Indian merchants across the Red Sea were involved in a brisk commerce. When Portuguese expeditions arrived in the region in the late fifteenth century, they found well-established markets and vigorous competition between the Egyptians and Turks to outdo each other in efforts to control the Indian Ocean trade. That competition notwithstanding, the Turks maintained their position as masters of the Red Sea. The Portuguese would take control of the Indian Ocean commerce after establishing various forts on the coastline of Africa during the fifteenth and sixteenth centuries.

The following century would witness a decline of commerce on the Red Sea until the invasion of Egypt (1798–1801) by France's Napoleon Bonaparte, sparking renewed European interest in the region. By 1839, the British had a base in Aden, heightening the competition with France for overseas influence. In March 1862, France signed a treaty with the Afar chiefs that gave them the harbor of Abock and much of the land between Ras Doumeira and Ras Ali. In 1885, the French signed a treaty with the chiefs of the Issa tribe that allowed them to access the Ethiopian market. Two years later, they founded the city of Djibouti, which would become known as a dependable port. In May 1896, the French christened the country the Côte Française des Somalis (also known as French Somaliland).

The French developed Djibouti as an important commercial port and a stopover en route to its other territories in Africa and Asia. Djibouti also served as a terminus of Ethiopian merchandise, courtesy of the so-called Ethiopian Imperial Railway, which was founded in 1896 by French and Swiss interests in conjunction with King Menilek II of Ethiopia. The company built a railway connecting the city of Djibouti to Dirre-Daoua, which commenced service in 1903; in 1917, it was extended to the Ethiopian capital at Addis Ababa. The railroad was crucial to Djibouti's development until the outbreak of World War II, when a blockade was imposed on goods entering the country.

During the postwar period, France attempted to turn the country into the "Hong Kong of the Red Sea" by introducing the Djibouti franc, which would be convertible into U.S. dollars. Furthermore, the French established deepwater port facilities to cater to the needs of larger vessels. Despite the upgrades, Djibouti suffered in competition with the rival port of Assab in present-day Eritrea. Moreover, the Arab–Israel conflicts of 1956, 1967, and 1975 jeopardized commercial activity on the Red Sea, causing a lasting recession in a country that relied chiefly on the port as its economic lifeline.

The mid-twentieth century marked a turning point in Africa as most countries achieved independence from their former colonial masters. But France's framework of the Union Française (French Union) under the Fourth Republic put Djibouti at a crossroads. Allowing the country's inhabitants to choose members of the local representative council as well as their representatives in the legislature in France, the French Union elicited mixed reaction among Djiboutians.

Recognizing the existing political and ethnic differences, the local French authorities in Djibouti played one faction against another in an attempt to control political developments in the country in the years to come. For instance, when France held a referendum on the proposed Communauté Française (French Community) in 1958, it played Somali politician Mahmoud Harbi (who opposed France) against Hassan Gouled Aptidon, who subsequently was elected as deputy to the French National Assembly in April 1959, creating a wedge between nationalist leaders in Djibouti for the benefit of France.

The fervor of nationalism in Djibouti picked up rapidly. Just before the official visit of French President Charles de Gaulle in 1959, two leading nationalists, Ahmed Dini and Abdallah Mohamed Kamil, forged a strategic alliance to seek independence. A referendum on self-determination held on March 19, 1967, favored independence. Consequently, the colony's name was changed to the Territoire Français de Afars et des Issas (French Territory of the Afars and the Issas).

On February 28, 1977, France called a roundtable conference in Paris to bring together nationalists associated with the Ligue Populaire Africaine pour l'Indépendance (African People's League for Independence). Djibouti achieved independence from France on June 27 of that year, and on July 2, it became a member of the Organization of African Unity. After independence, the country sought to enhance its commercial and shipping endeavors, which represented the mainstay of its economy, reduce regional inequality, and maintain national unity.

Into the Twenty-First Century

The first president of Djibouti was Hassan Gouled Aptidon, who served until 1999. He was succeeded by his nephew, Ismail Omar Guelleh, who was elected in 1999 and reelected in 2005. Both leaders tried to improve economic conditions in Djibouti, which was deeply in debt, compelling the International Monetary Fund to demand structural reforms and political liberalization to encourage foreign capital investment there. Guelleh launched several reforms, including political and economic liberalization and the creation of a free trade zone. In spite of these efforts to stimulate economic growth, the situation in Djibouti did not improve as a result of the country's reliance on diesel-generated electricity, importation of food, and lack of resources.

Today, rivalries within the government and society in Djibouti between the Afar and Issa continue. As of 2012, the government is essentially split between the two groups. But many Afar accuse the government, headed by one of their own, President Guelleh, as favoring the Issa, who outnumber the Afar in both the ruling Rassemblement Populaire pour le Progrès (People's Rally for Progress) party as well as in the civil service.

Hannington Ochwada

See also: Groups: *Africa*—Somali. *Issues*   Colonialism; Political Participation.

Further Reading

Alwan, Daoud A., and Yohanis Mibrathu. *Historical Dictionary of Djibouti.* Boston: Scarecrow, 2000.

McKenna, Amy, ed. *The Britannica Guide to Africa: The History of Central and Eastern Africa.* New York: Britannica Educational, 2011.

Thompson, Virginia, and Richard Adloff. *Djibouti and the Horn of Africa.* Stanford, CA: Stanford University Press, 1968.

Dominican Republic and Haiti

The Dominican Republic and Haiti together occupy the island of Hispaniola, located southeast of Cuba between the Caribbean Sea and the Atlantic Ocean. The Dominican Republic occupies roughly the eastern two-thirds of the island, while Haiti is situated on the western side. Although the two countries share the same natural resources, terrain, and climate, they could not be more different from one another in terms of society, politics, and economics. Whereas the Dominican Republic is economically productive and its citizens enjoy relatively high standards of living, Haiti suffers immensely in comparison, with grinding poverty, food shortages, and disease.

As a result of the rough and mountainous terrain on Hispaniola, both countries suffer periodic droughts. Sitting directly on a hurricane belt, the island is subject to severe storms from June to October. The island is also prone to earthquakes. In January 2010, a devastating earthquake struck the Haitian capital of Port-au-Prince, affecting some 2 million people.

Haiti

The native Taino people, who inhabited Hispaniola when Christopher Columbus visited there in 1492, were virtually annihilated by Spanish settlers within twenty-five years, leaving only a small population today. From the time of their arrival, the Spanish used the island as a launching point for their explorations of the Western Hemisphere.

The French occupied Hispaniola by the mid-seventeenth century and, from the western part of the island, harassed Spanish and English ships. In 1697, the Spanish ceded to France the western third of the island, which later would become Haiti; in 1795, Spain ceded the remainder of the island, which would become the Dominican Republic.

Pictographs found on a cave wall in the Dominican Republic, painted around the time of Columbus's arrival on Hispaniola in 1492, depict the mythology and history of the Taino people who greeted him. *(Charles Beeker/AP Images)*

Until 1804, Haiti was one of France's richest and most successful slave colonies, profiting from the production of sugar. In that year, a slave rebellion led by Toussaint L'Ouverture, Jean Jacques Dessalines, and Henri Christophe defeated the French army, and the colony was proclaimed the Republic of Haiti, becoming the first black republic in the Western Hemisphere. After the revolution, however, the Haitians found themselves isolated from the international community, and their hopes for a stable society dissolved into uncertainty.

From 1843 to 1915, Haiti saw twenty-two changes in government. Beginning in 1915, the U.S. military occupied Haiti for nineteen years. After the withdrawal of U.S. forces in 1934, Haiti regained sovereign rule. From 1957 to 1986, the Duvalier family ruled Haiti with an iron fist. During that time, the Haitian people saw no improvements in their living conditions. After nearly 30 years under the Duvaliers, Haiti was ruled by a series of provisional governments.

In December 1990, Jean-Bertrand Aristide won 67 percent of the vote in a presidential election that international observers deemed largely free and fair. In September of the following year, however, Aristide was ousted in a violent military coup. In 1994, under a United Nations mandate, the United States intervened to restore the constitutional government.

Since 1995, the international community has been heavily involved in Haiti. The country is classified as a republic and adopted a constitution in 1987. After the military coup and international intervention of 1994, steps were taken by the international community to make sure that the constitution was upheld. These steps included the establishment of a multinational force that ousted the military regime, the establishment of an interim government after continuous political infighting, and the creation of the United Nations Stability Mission in Haiti. International organizations still have and will continue to maintain a heavy presence in Haiti until it is able to recover from negligent governments and devastating national disasters.

Dominican Republic

After Haiti achieved independence in 1804, the Dominican Republic, which had been called Santo Domingo by the Spanish, sought to obtain its independence from France as well. However, it was ruled by Haiti until 1821, when it gained a degree of independence, but still was largely under Haitian control. In 1844, Santo Domingo finally gained its independence as the Dominican Republic. That independence, however, was short-lived, and in 1861, the Dominican Republic voluntarily rejoined the Spanish Empire. Independence was restored again in 1865.

In 1916, the United States occupied the Dominican Republic, until Horacio Vásquez was elected president in 1924. In 1930, Rafael Leónidas Trujillo seized power and ruled the republic as a dictatorship until 1961. The next year, Juan Bosch was elected president, only to be overthrown by a military coup in 1963. The United States intervened in 1965 in the midst of an uprising to restore Bosch, but three years later he was defeated in an election by Joaquín Balaguer, who held the presidency for the better part of thirty years (with an interlude from 1978 to 1986), until international pressure due to his victory in a fraudulent election in 1994 forced him to end his tenure in 1996.

Since that time, the Dominican Republic has been a democratic republic with regular elections and universal suffrage for citizens eighteen years and older; however, individuals in the armed forces and the national police cannot vote. The legislative branch is made up of the bicameral National Congress (Congreso Nacional), which consists of the 32-seat Senate (Senado) and the 178-seat House of Representatives (Camara de Diputados). Members of both houses are elected by popular vote to serve four-year terms.

The Dominican Republic enjoys an annual gross domestic product seven times that of Haiti. Only about 40 percent of the Dominican Republic's population lives below the poverty line, compared to 80 percent in Haiti. The life expectancy in the Dominican Republic is seventy-three years, while Haiti's is about sixty years. In addition, Haiti's infant mortality rate is nearly double that of the Dominican Republic, and its overall death rate is six times higher. Despite efforts by the Dominican authorities to control migration, many Haitians cross into the Dominican Republic to find work.

Abdul Karim Bangura

See also: *Issues*—Colonialism; Economic Development; Poverty.

Further Reading

Black, J.K. "Development and Dependency in the Dominican Republic." *Third World Quarterly* 8:1 (1986): 236–257.

Dubois, Laurent. *Avengers of the New World: The Story of the Haitian Revolution.* Cambridge, MA: Belknap Press of Harvard University Press, 2004.

Fatton, Robert. "Haiti: The Saturnalia of Emancipation and the Vicissitudes of Predatory Rule." *Third World Quarterly* 27:1 (2006): 115–133.

Moya Pons, F. *The Dominican Republic: A National History.* Rev. ed. Princeton, NJ: Markus Wiener, 2010.

Reisman, W. Michael. "Haiti and the Validity of International Action." *American Journal of International Law* 89:1 (1995): 82–84.

Ecuador

Ecuador is located in the northern reaches of a region that once was known as Tawantinsuyu, the ancient Inca empire. The Inca were relatively recent arrivals in Ecuador, having expanded north from their base at Cuzco in the Peruvian Andes Mountains less than 100 years before the arrival of Spanish conquistador Francisco Pizarro in 1532. Even in that short period of time, the Inca managed to homogenize what once had been a much more ethnolinguistically diverse population. The Spanish simply accelerated the processes of imperial conquest and colonization that had begun under the Inca.

At the time of the Inca and Spanish conquests, Ecuador was home to the Esmeralda, Huancavilca, Manta, and Puná indigenous groups on the tropical western coast; the Cañari, Cara, Palta, Panzaleo, Pasto, and Puruhá in the temperate highlands; and the "forest tribes" of the Cofán (A'I), Shuar (Jívaro), Kichwa (Quichua), and Zápara (Záparo) in the eastern upper Amazon Basin.

Colonial to Nineteenth-Century History

Despite stereotypes of the "passive Indian," native resistance to Spanish rule was vigorous throughout the colonial period and after independence into the nineteenth century. Repeated revolts delayed and reversed Spanish penetration into the Amazon, just as local inhabitants had resisted earlier Inca incursions. By the seventeenth century, native protests shifted to campaigns against colonial abuses, such as the confiscation of lands, tribute payments, compulsory tithes, labor drafts, censuses, and the exploitation of indigenous peoples.

Ecuadorian independence in 1822 did not lead to more rights for indigenous peoples, but rather to the entrenchment of exclusionary rule, with a small, white propertied class ruling over the majority indigenous and mestizo (mixed European and Indian heritage) populations. (Ecuador did not grant indigenous people citizenship rights until 1979, making it one of the last countries in the Americas to do so.) In response to this history of exclusion, in 1871, Fernando Daquilema, together with his wife Manuela León, led a massive uprising against elite abuses in the central highland province of Chimborazo. Although the revolt failed, it earned Chimborazo a reputation for being home to the most rebellious indigenous peoples in Ecuador.

In 1895, Eloy Alfaro led a successful liberal revolution that initially gave indigenous peoples hope that they finally would have someone in government who would listen to their demands. Alfaro promulgated a series of reforms to benefit the indigenous peoples, however, he ultimately was more interested in introducing modern systems of capitalism than in remaking state structures in ways that would benefit marginalized groups. In the eastern Amazon, the government traditionally had administered indigenous communities through the Catholic missions, whereas in the highlands, they were incorporated through systems of debt peonage into privately owned states called haciendas. Critics charged that Alfaro's goal was to break up these traditional structures so that indigenous peoples could join the wage labor pools that would benefit the emergence of export-oriented agricultural plantations on the western coast.

The 1920s was a period of increasing agitation among workers, indigenous peoples, and peasants, and the decade saw some of the worst violence in the history of popular movements in Ecuador. Declining economic conditions culminated in a general strike on November 15, 1922, in the coastal port city of Guayaquil. The resulting massacre of hundreds of workers led to the birth of new labor movements. In 1926, urban leftists included indigenous leader Jesús Gualavisí in the founding of their new Partido Socialista Ecuatoriano (Ecuadorian Socialist Party). This brought increased attention to indigenous issues.

Protests were no longer solely local affairs. Communities and regions began to work together to press for common demands, drawing on cooperation and solidarity among diverse groups across broad geographic areas. At the same time, indigenous protests moved from spontaneous reactions to immediate issues to addressing broader structural concerns, reflecting a deepening political consciousness.

Modern Life

The twentieth century witnessed a dramatic expansion of indigenous organizing efforts in Ecuador. In 1944, indigenous activists, in alliance with the Communist Party, founded the Federación Ecuatoriana de Indios (FEI, Ecuadorian Federation of Indians), which took a leading role in fighting for land reform. In 1964, the Catholic Church helped found the Shuar Federation in the Amazon, leading to additional ethnic-based organizations to counter the leftist FEI. Over time, these new organizations assumed more radical positions, eventually emerging as leading forces against neoliberal economic policies that weighed heavily on the poor.

In 1986, activists formed the Confederación de Nacionalidades Indígenas del Ecuador (CONAIE, Confederation of Indigenous Nationalities of Ecuador) in an attempt to unify all indigenous peoples under a single organization. A massive indigenous uprising in June 1990 paralyzed

Ecuador for a week but succeeded in bringing significant attention to the native peoples of the country. The emergence of CONAIE at the forefront of the protest gave Ecuador a reputation for having a well-organized indigenous movement. CONAIE presented a list of sixteen demands to the government that broadly encompassed economic, political, and social issues. The organization's demand for recognition of the presence of different indigenous nationalities in Ecuador and a revision of the first article of the country's constitution to declare it to be a plurinational state were symbolically key issues. In 1995, CONAIE helped found a political movement called Pachakutik to compete for political office.

Estimates of Ecuador's surviving native population vary widely, from a low of less than 7 percent of Ecuador's 14 million people in 2001 to a high of 40 percent, according to CONAIE. The variance is attributable to the different criteria that are used to define whether someone is indigenous, and whether it is politically advantageous for someone to self-identify as such. The largest remaining indigenous group is the Kichwa, which are divided between those living in the highlands and those in the Amazon. Seven additional indigenous nationalities survive in the Amazon, including the Achuar, Cofán, Huaorani, Secoya, Shuar, Siona, and Zápara. In addition, a 700-person group called the Andoa is struggling to reconstruct itself as a nationality. Six identifiable indigenous nationalities and peoples survive in the coastal region: the Awá, Chachi, Epera, Manta, Tsáchila, and Wancavilca. Each of these groups is small and has struggled to preserve its ethnic identity. Elsewhere on the coast, indigenous identities either have died out or have assimilated into mainstream Ecuadorian culture. The economic influence of export-oriented agribusiness has led many indigenous people to relocate to more densely populated areas, where they have increased contact with the dominant society.

Marc Becker

CONAIE

Formed in 1986, the Confederación de Nacionalidades Indígenas del Ecuador (Confederation of Indigenous Nationalities of Ecuador), known as CONAIE, is the largest indigenous organization in Ecuador, representing some thirty-one distinct groups from the coastal, Andean, and Amazonian regions. CONAIE is widely considered one of the strongest social movements in Latin America, and it is an increasingly decisive force in Ecuador's politics.

Since colonial times, indigenous communities have been among the poorest and most marginalized of Ecuadorians, even though they form a large constituency in the country; estimates range from 25 percent to 45 percent, depending on how one classifies Amerindian descendants. Founded as a coalition of existing regional federations, CONAIE's political agenda encompasses fighting for indigenous autonomy and cultural recognition, promoting solidarity and pride, securing indigenous land rights, and facilitating intercultural bilingual education.

CONAIE has served as an unprecedented model of cohesion for indigenous mobilizing efforts elsewhere on the continent. However, it also is rife with internal conflict. Tensions among ethnic groups and regional federations remain, despite the development of powerful national advocacy structures. Within the hierarchical structure of the organization, those groups that are farther from the center have expressed that they feel unevenly represented. Moreover, some social commentators contend that CONAIE's success at the national level has come at the expense of regional and local concerns.

In spite of such differences, and in the face of a hostile political environment, CONAIE has received national and international recognition for its accomplishments on behalf of indigenous rights. It has pursued an agenda of social change using a wide range of strategies, including negotiations with government representatives and formal political campaigning. Yet the organization perhaps is best known for its role in organizing popular uprisings around the country. National and regional coordinators team up with local networks of stakeholders and activists to organize marches, road blockades along major transit routes, and occupations of government buildings.

Pressure from highly publicized protests and indigenous presence has contributed to many notable political achievements since the late twentieth century. These include concessions from oil and mining industries, constitutional changes to define Ecuador as a multiethnic and multicultural state, the ousting of three presidents since 1997, and the negotiation of one of the largest land rights concessions in the continent's history.

Since the 1990s, CONAIE has shifted its focus from the defense of local autonomy toward support for inclusive democratic citizenship, and it has become directly involved in electoral politics to a greater extent. Whether this has strengthened or undermined democratic practice within the organization is contested. However, CONAIE certainly has become a key player in Ecuadorian politics, putting a face to indigenous rights on the national stage.

Emma Gaalaas Mullaney

See also: Groups: Central and South America—Cofán; Kichwa; Shuar. *Issues*—Colonialism; Political Participation.

Further Reading

Becker, Marc. *Indians and Leftists in the Making of Ecuador's Modern Indigenous Movements.* Durham, NC: Duke University Press, 2008.

Clark, A. Kim, and Marc Becker, eds. *Highland Indians and the State in Modern Ecuador.* Pittsburgh, PA: University of Pittsburgh Press, 2007.

Larson, Brooke. *Trials of Nation Making: Liberalism, Race, and Ethnicity in the Andes, 1810–1910.* New York: Cambridge University Press, 2004.

Pallares, Amalia. *From Peasant Struggles to Indian Resistance: The Ecuadorian Andes in the Late Twentieth Century.* Norman: University of Oklahoma Press, 2002.

Selverston-Scher, Melina. *Ethnopolitics in Ecuador: Indigenous Rights and the Strengthening of Democracy.* Coral Gables, FL: North-South Center Press at the University of Miami, 2001.

Whitten, Norman E., Jr., ed. *Millennial Ecuador: Critical Essays on Cultural Transformations and Social Dynamics.* Iowa City: University of Iowa Press, 2003.

El Salvador

El Salvador is the smallest and most densely populated country in Central America, with 6 million people residing in an area of just over 8,000 square miles (20,700 square kilometers). The vast majority of the Salvadoran population consists of mestizos—people of mixed Spanish and indigenous descent.

Only 1 percent of the country's inhabitants consider themselves purely indigenous, mostly Maya as well as Lenca, Pipil, and Pocomam. At the time the Spanish arrived in the early sixteenth century, a sizable indigenous population existed in El Salvador, but many of those people died during the Spanish conquest, succumbing to European diseases to which they had no immunity.

The People of El Salvador

Speaking a variety of dialects, the ancient ancestors of the Salvadoran people, the earliest Maya, transformed their environment to their advantage. They cut down trees to clear the land, dried out and drained swampland, and built villages on low stone platforms near water sources. Drainage ditches were being built by approximately 1100 B.C.E., indicating an increase in agriculture that coincided with the settlement of larger towns and cities.

Local chieftains originally ruled the Maya. However, in areas where agriculture was particularly rich, the chieftains amassed great wealth and consolidated their power in order to become kings, surrounding themselves with military forces to attain even greater power. They used that power to collect taxes, allowing their towns to grow ever larger. The kings commanded their subjects to build the first religious structures, generally rectangular platforms that rose to heights of up to 50 feet (15 meters), topped by temples and royal residences. In the tradition of animism, Maya kings took the name of an animal and a human-made object—for example, "Shield Jaguar." Heirs to the throne, usually the eldest son, used that same name with an additional suffix. Occasionally, women ruled as queens. Dead kings were believed to take their place among the Maya pantheon.

More advanced centers of Maya civilization built pyramid temples rising more than 200 feet (61 meters) into the air, with stairs leading to the top. These religious structures were the locations of sacrifices to the Maya deities. A notable trait of the Maya is their development of a writing system, which used both glyphic and syllabic scripts and contained more than 800 signs. The Maya writing system was quite complex, and historians still are deciphering their alphabet.

By the time the Spanish arrived in the early sixteenth century, the power of the Maya city-states had been declining. Hernán Cortés sent Pedro de Alvarado to search for more gold, as he had found among the Aztecs. In 1523, Alvarado left with approximately 400 Spanish soldiers and was able to conquer most of the Maya empire by 1532.

The region named El Salvador by Alvarado remained under Spanish authority, together with most of the rest of Central America, until 1786. At that time, it was made into one administrative area. This had the result of creating a sense of Salvadoran nationalism that would eventually result in independence, after a twenty-seven year struggle, in 1838.

Like many Central American countries, the lives of the native peoples were focused on the *haciendas*, large agricultural landholdings by a few wealthy families. These mostly coffee-growing families controlled the government in El Salvador, and the native peoples were landless, left to work on the haciendas through the nineteenth and much of the twentieth centuries.

Struggles for Democracy and Native Rights in the Twentieth Century

Throughout the twentieth century, El Salvador officially had no distinct native communities, as the country did not record indigenous identity in its census. The last Salvadoran census to count indigenous people, in 1930, gave a population of 80,000, or approximately 5.6 percent of the total population. However, the establishment of large coffee estates that encroached on and, ultimately, removed native land further diminished their numbers.

Additionally, in 1932, a failed uprising of Indians and peasants that was brutally suppressed by General Maximiliano Hernández Martínez. The resulting massacre, remembered today as "La Matanza" (the slaughter), resulted in the deaths of between 10,000 and 50,000 people. Those wearing indigenous clothing or thought to have an indigenous "look" were subject to abuse and even death. This persecution ultimately resulted in the forced assimilation of most of the remaining indigenous population.

During the civil war that took place in El Salvador during the 1980s and early 1990s, the various indigenous people again were the victims of treatment human rights violations. This has continued since the war ended in 1992, as ongoing land disputes continue to create tension. The Salvadoran constitution makes no accommodations for the land or cultural rights of the indigenous people.

The Salvadoran government has organized state institutions to meet the needs of the indigenous population, such as the Concultura (Center for Cultural Affairs), part of the Ministry of Education, which technically oversees indigenous affairs. Nevertheless, indigenous people are perceived to be "backward" and continue to suffer discrimination at both the personal and societal levels. Indigenous groups in El Salvador remain among the poorest in an already poor nation. The mountainous areas in which they live lack proper housing, sanitary conditions are inadequate, and they receive substandard health care as compared to the rest of the population.

Despite repression carried out by the government and by the mestizo majority, many native Salvadorans have worked to preserve their traditions and culture. Through the cooperation of groups such as the National Indigenous Coordinating Council of El Salvador, this process is continuing, and such programs are expanding in the twenty-first century.

James E. Seelye, Jr.

See also: *Groups: Central and South America*—Lenca; Maya. *Issues*—Indigenous Governments; Language.

Further Reading

Clendinnen, Inga. *Ambivalent Conquests: Maya and Spaniard in Yucatan, 1517–1570.* New York: Cambridge University Press, 2003.
Sharer, Robert, and Loa Traxler. *The Ancient Maya.* Stanford, CA: Stanford University Press, 2005.
White, Christopher. *The History of El Salvador.* Westport, CT: Greenwood, 2008.

LA MATANZA

"La Matanza," meaning "the slaughter," refers to the massacre of Indians and peasants during a failed uprising in El Salvador in 1932. Though some of the uprising's leaders were communists—anyone in the capital who voted for the communists was rounded up and shot—the overwhelming majority of those killed were not.

Salvadoran government troops, vigilantes, private militias, and police gunned down the peasants in town plazas and at meetings and demonstrations. Government orders required the execution of those carrying machetes (traditionally used by Indian peasants for clearing land and harvesting), those dressed in traditional peasant clothing, and even those judged to have Indian features.

Indian peasants in Asunción in Izalco who had not taken part in the uprising were invited to visit the military commander to receive papers clearing them of guilt. Upon their arrival, however, they were arrested, taken in groups of fifty, ordered to dig their own graves, and executed. Estimates of the number of people killed range between 10,000 and 50,000.

The most famous victim of La Matanza was rebel leader Augustín Farabundo Martí. Martí remains a martyr to Salvadoran leftists to this day. During the 1970s and 1980s, rebels took his name as their own, later establishing a political party, the Farabundo Martí National Liberation Front.

The government did its best to hide the extent of the slaughter. Most of the bodies were burned, and government files, libraries, and newspaper accounts were purged of any mention of the massacre. Still, La Matanza had a significant effect on the course of Salvadoran history and culture. At one time, the Salvadoran population was more than 80 percent Indian. But after La Matanza, most of El Salvador's Indians began to conceal their cultural identity, claiming to be mestizos (people of mixed indigenous and European heritage) or denying their Indian ancestry out of fear of further government reprisals or other discrimination.

Al Carroll

Equatorial Guinea

Equatorial Guinea is one of the smallest nations in continental Africa, with a population of approximately 700,000 people. However, with its complex colonial legacy, oppressive political regimes, diversity of ethnic groups, and abundance of natural resources—particularly oil—the history of Equatorial Guinea rivals that of any large country. The country is distinct from the West African nations of Guinea and Guinea-Bissau. Formerly known as Spanish Guinea, it was the only Spanish colony in sub-Saharan Africa and mandated Spanish as an official language. Today, French and Portuguese also are official languages.

Geographically, the nation comprises a mainland that is nestled on 186 miles (300 kilometers) of Central African coast between Cameroon and Gabon, as well as five islands; its total land area is approximately 10,830 square miles (28,050 square kilometers) or about the size of the U.S. state of Maryland. The capital of Malabo is located on the northernmost island of Bioko, which is situated off the coasts of Cameroon and Nigeria. The southernmost island, Annóbon (also called Pagalu), off the coast of Gabon, is the only part of the nation located south of the equator.

These islands, together with Corisco and Greater and Lesser Elobey, account for 20 percent of the population, although the latter islands are sparsely populated and lack freshwater. The population of Bioko consists primarily of Bubi people, followed by Fernandinos. Annóbon is home to a mixture of peoples from various parts of Africa, notably Angola. The remaining 80 percent of the population lives on the mainland, which is referred to as Mbini or Rio Muni. The majority of the people on the mainland are of Fang ethnicity, followed by the Ndewo. In all, at least twenty-five distinct ethnic groups reside in the country.

The geography of Equatorial Guinea is equally diverse. Annóbon, Bioko, and Corisco were formed by what are now inactive volcanoes. The rich volcanic soil of the islands allows for the cultivation of coffee, cocoa, and tropical fruits, as well as staples of manioc, sweet potatoes, and yams. The mainland is covered with lush tropical rain forests, rivers, and streams and supported by rich soil, allowing for the production of cash crops in cleared areas. Within the earth lie rich deposits of iron, gold, titanium, coal, and clay. In the 1990s, oil was discovered offshore. Of these resources, cocoa, timber, and oil form the basis of the economy.

History

The first inhabitants of the mainland were the forest-dwelling Bayele people. Their culture slowly was absorbed by multiple migrations of Bantu peoples beginning in the second millennium B.C.E. The earliest migrants, the Ndowe, arrived along the coast from modern-day Cameroon, followed by the Fang from the dense forest regions to the east. The migrations of these groups continued up to the eighteenth century, resulting in a complex network of related groups living throughout the country. The Bubi migrated to Bioko before the seventh century C.E. Generally speaking, these groups lived an agricultural, egalitarian lifestyle with minimal central authority.

The arrival of the Portuguese in 1472 brought changes to each group and region. The Ndowe migrated inland into Fang territory to avoid dealing with Europeans. However, the Fang sought relations with the Europeans, complicating the situation for the Ndowe. On Bioko, those who conducted trade with the Europeans emerged as leaders among the Bubi, thereby changing their internal cultural dynamics.

Initially, Bioko was not an outlet for enslaved Africans, though it was involved in other commerce with Europeans; however, in the nineteenth century, the British relocated captured Africans as part of their ban on enslavement to the island. Annóbon (the name comes from Portuguese for "good year") and Corisco developed into ports supplying Portuguese as well as British and Dutch ships with goods and enslaved Africans until the British ban took effect.

This commercial activity brought many different ethnic groups to live on the islands. On Bioko, the Fernandinos were descendants of West Africans and enslaved Africans returned from the Americas. At one point, Annóbon became home to former slaves who were too old or sick to work, as well as to Cuban freedom fighters exiled by Spain in 1898. Groups with Spanish ancestry also live in the country.

Officially, Equatorial Guinea became a Spanish colony in 1777, but active colonial rule by Spain did not commence until 1900. On Bioko, the Bubi, led by Chief Moka, fought the Spanish for ten years. On the mainland, Fang leaders put up an equally strong resistance and were not defeated until 1928, when a system of indirect rule was instituted through local leaders.

The thrust of the colonial presence was to exploit resources such as timber and cocoa. Infrastructure, such as roads, schools, and hospitals, was not developed, but Catholic missionaries were successful at converting large portions of the indigenous population. At one point during the colonial era, Equatorial Guinea had the highest number of priests per capita in Africa. Today, the country is overwhelmingly Catholic, although many people maintain traditional religious practices alongside Catholicism.

Independence came in 1968 with the election of Francisco Macías Nguema, although he was elected with the support of Spanish and French business interests. During his dictatorial eleven-year rule, the economy collapsed, and the people lived in fear, as Nguema was known to have entire families or villages executed. More than one-fourth of the population fled the country during his reign of terror. In 1979, Nguema's forces attacked members of the National Guard, resulting in a bloody struggle, Nguema's execution, and the installment of his nephew, Teodoro Obiang Nguema Mbasogo, as president.

Current Issues

President Obiang still leads the country today, and political intimidation and poverty continue. Obiang added French to the list of official languages, as Equatorial Guinea is surrounded by nations with cultural and economic ties to France. Spain and France provide much of the foreign aid entering the country.

The most pressing concerns center on poverty and the lack of economic development in Equatorial Guinea. Although the nation has a vast store of raw materials, the absence of basic infrastructure is notable, even compared to other colonized African nations. However, this situation is beginning to change, as the harvesting of oil is creating a local economy that is forcing the creation of infrastructure. Culturally, Equatorial Guineans are exploring their national identity through literature, food, and music, mostly focusing on the culture of the majority Fang population.

Denise Martin

See also: Issues—Colonialism; Missionary Activities.

Further Reading

Biko, Adolfo Obiang. *Equatorial Guinea: From Spanish Colonialism to the Discovery of Oil*. Malabo, Equatorial Guinea: Monalige, 2000.

Sundiata, Ibrahim K. *Equatorial Guinea: Colonialism, State Terror, and the Search for Stability*. Boulder, CO: Westview, 1990.

Waters, Mary-Alice, and Martin Koppel. *Capitalism and the Transformation of Africa: Notes from Equatorial Guinea*. New York: Pathfinder, 2009.

Eritrea

Eritrea is located in the Horn of Africa on the coast of the Red Sea, bordered by Djibouti to the southeast, Ethiopia to the south, and Sudan to the northwest. The country's population of approximately 5.6 million occupies an area of more than 45,000 square miles (117,000 square kilometers).

Eritrean society is ethnically, tribally, and religiously diverse. The Tigrinya people make up about half of the population, while the Tigre account for nearly one-third. The remainder of the population comprises people of the Afar, Beja, Bilen, Kunama, Nara, Rashaida, and Saho groups. The country's languages are predominantly Semitic.

Christians—mostly Orthodox and some Roman Catholics—make up slightly more than half of the population. Sunni Muslims represent 48 percent, and those that follow indigenous beliefs account for 2 percent. Most Christians live in the highlands, while Muslims and adherents of traditional beliefs tend to live in the lowland regions.

Traces of some of Africa's oldest civilizations can be found in the Eritrea–Ethiopia region, which long has been a place of movement and migration from North Africa and from the southern part of the continent. Evidence of human presence in Eritrea dates to the eighth millennium B.C.E., beginning with Cushitic (Afar), Nilotic, Pygmoid, and Semitic (Tigrinya) peoples.

During the third and fourth centuries C.E., Eritrea was a part of the kingdom of Aksum, which spread from Sudan across the Red Sea to Yemen. The capital of Aksum was located in the highlands of Tigray (now a province of Ethiopia), and the main port was Adulis, now called Zula in Eritrea. Founded by Semitic people originally from Arabia, the kingdom flourished from the trade across the Red Sea. In the early fourth century, the Aksumite king converted to Christianity and established it as the state religion. Today, the Ethiopian/Eritrean Christian Church is among the oldest Christian communities in the world.

In the sixth century C.E., Arabs arrived on the coast of what is now Eritrea in search of ivory and slaves for trade with India and Persia. Muslims destroyed Adulis, and the ancient kingdom of Aksum declined until it was reduced to a small Christian area.

Beginning in 710 C.E., and for several centuries thereafter, the region was a remote, isolated community that by the early sixteenth century was known as Abyssinia. The Abyssinian kingdom covered the Ethiopian highlands; it was ruled by kings and peopled by Christian Tigrinya.

Before Italy began to colonize the region in 1885, the area that is now Eritrea was ruled by the many powers that dominated the Red Sea area, including the Turks, Egyptians, and Mahdi forces from Sudan. The Italian colonization of Eritrea in 1890 marked the first time that Eritrean territory was ruled as a single entity. In 1936, Eritrea became a province of Italian East Africa, but following Italy's defeat in World War II, the country was placed under British military administration. In 1952, a United Nations resolution joined Eritrea with Ethiopia in a federation, ignoring Eritreans' appeal for independence.

In 1962, Ethiopian Emperor Haile Selassie unilaterally annexed Eritrea, initiating a long civil war. In Eritrea, the liberation movement was led by the Eritrean Liberation Front (ELF), which by the late 1970s dominated the fight against Ethiopian forces in Eritrea. In May 1991, the Eritrean People's Liberation Front (a faction of the original ELF) established a provisional government for Eritrea. Ethiopia subsequently recognized Eritreans' right to hold a referendum, and in April 1993, Eritreans voted for independence. Eritrea declared independence on May 24 of that year.

Many languages are spoken in Eritrea today, and the country's constitution establishes the "equality of all Eritrean languages," although Arabic and Tigrinya chiefly are used for official purposes. English also is broadly understood. The country's main ethnolinguistic groups are referred to as nationalities. They are divided into two dominant groups, Tigrinya and Tigre speakers, as well as seven small minorities.

Most Tigrinya speakers belong to the Coptic Orthodox Church. Their numbers, however, do include Catholics and Protestants, primarily as a result of nineteenth-century missionary activities in the region. Tigre speakers, whose language is of Semitic origin, mostly reside in the lowlands of the northern and western parts of the country. This group is overwhelmingly Muslim. While some are descended from Christians, others trace their origins to Arab Muslims who came from the Arabian Peninsula and married locally. Over the centuries, commerce across the Red Sea also has resulted in the spread of the Arabic language in some Tigre-speaking areas. Educated Muslims form the majority of Tigre speakers; those from Muslim minority communities frequently use Arabic, the language of the Qur'an, as a lingua franca. Until the twentieth century, Tigre-speaking tribes were divided into two castes based on a historical distinction between the ruling group of migrant conquerors and the indigenous people that were conquered.

Other native groups, residing in various regions of the Eritrea today, include speakers of Afar, Arabic, Beja, Kunama, and Nara. These peoples include Christian and Muslim groups, as well as tribes that follow traditional religions. Despite some ethnic and religious differences, Eritreans retain a tribal and communal solidarity based on their belief in a common descent, cultural identity, and linguistic orientation. This solidarity united the Eritrean people in their struggle against Ethiopia for independence.

Shak Hanish

See also: Groups: Africa—Tigrinya. *Issues*—Colonialism; Political Participation.

Further Reading

Bateman, Roy. *Eritrea: Even the Stones Are Burning.* Trenton, NJ: Red Sea, 1998.
Pool, David. *From Guerrillas to Government: The Eritrean People's Liberation Front.* Athens: Ohio University Press, 2001.

Ethiopia

Ethiopia is a northern African nation located in the northeastern extension of Africa known as the Horn. It is bordered by Djibouti and Somalia on the east, Eritrea on the north, Sudan and South Sudan in the west, and Kenya on the south. Ethiopia's geography is notable in terms of the history of Africa's native peoples, as it is the home of the Great Rift Valley, from which many native groups migrated to the south.

The modern nation of Ethiopia—officially the Federal Democratic Republic of Ethiopia—is the product of centuries of interaction among peoples from Africa, Asia, and the Arabian Peninsula. Today, the Ethiopian people, numbering 86 million, belong to more than 100 ethnic groups, speaking some seventy languages and practicing four religions. Ethiopians remain proud of their resistance to colonization when Africa was parceled among the European powers in the 1880s. In 1896, Ethiopians defeated the Italians and reclaimed their autonomy. A former monarchy, Ethiopia has a long history of international relations with many countries and peoples, including Egypt, Great Britain, India, Israel, Palestine, and Yemen. However, Ethiopia is better known for the famines, wars, and droughts that have killed millions of people since the 1970s.

Ethiopia's early inhabitants are thought to have belonged to the Afro-Asiatic language group, speakers of Cushitic, Omotic, and Semitic languages who lived in the area between the Red Sea in the region that is now Sudan and the Nile River. Sometime after 13,000 B.C.E., these groups began to migrate. Omotic speakers settled in the central and southwestern parts of what is now Ethiopia, while the Cushites occupied the area to the north, and Semitic speakers moved eastward to settle in southwestern Asia. Over time, the Cushitic and Omotic languages evolved into other tongues, including Afar, Goffa, Oromo, Somali, and Wolayta, and some of these groups played important roles in Ethiopia's later development. In fact, the two largest ethnic groups in the country today—the Oromo and the Amhara—are Afro-Asiatic in origin. Amharic is the country's official language.

As early as the first millennium B.C.E., Semitic speakers began migrating to Ethiopia. They settled in the coastal regions and intermarried with the native inhabitants, forming the foundation of what would become the Aksumite Empire in Tigray, a powerful kingdom that rose to prominence in the first century C.E. and flourished from the third to the sixth centuries. Their language, Ge'ez, was a blend of south Arabian, Cushitic, and Greek; the ancestor of Amharic, it survives today as a liturgical language.

The Aksumite kings aimed to create an empire based on a centralized system of governance. They expanded their reach throughout the region and as far as Asia, and by the middle of the fourth century, the Aksum king had converted to Christianity, forming the Ethiopian Orthodox Tewahedo Church. The Aksumite Empire was among the most powerful kingdoms in the world, expanding its influence throughout Ethiopia. In the eleventh and twelfth centuries, the Zagwe dynasty, which came from the Cushitic-speaking Agaw people, ruled Ethiopia from its base in the north. Beginning in 1270 C.E., the Solomonic dynasty ruled Ethiopia for many centuries.

In the mid-sixteenth century, the Oromo began a series of migrations that engulfed the Muslim areas to the east. They converted to Islam, but also blended their culture with those of the dominant Christian Amhara and Tigray. During this time, the people of Ethiopia faced many religious and ethnic conflicts, with the Amhara and Tigray fighting to prevent Muslim states from taking over their lands. This ended by the 1650s, and for more than two centuries, Ethiopia grew larger, with succeeding monarchies consolidating their power.

The country faced chaotic times again following the death of the last Gondar king, Yoas, in 1769. The *ras* (local chief) who took over the empire put the country in chaos, precipitating a civil war that lasted until the 1850s. Emperor Tewodros II (r. 1855–1868) sought to reunite the country, but he was unable to fully accomplish this goal, as Ethiopia faced new challenges from Egypt, the Ottoman Empire, Oromo militias, Tigrayan rebels, and Europeans. His successor, Emperor Yohannes IV (r. 1872–1889), succeeded in keeping these forces at bay, but they persisted, particularly the Italians.

Following the Berlin Conference of 1884–1885, at which the European powers negotiated their claims on Africa, an Italian company bought the port of Asseb from the sultan of Afar, which became the Italian colony of Eritrea. But Italy wanted to expand its territory into Ethiopia. In 1890, Ethiopia and Italy signed the Treaty of Uccialli; however, as it turned out, there were two different versions of the treaty. In the Amharic version, Yohannes's successor, Menilek II (r. 1889–1913), was given the right to ask Italy for assistance. But the Italian version stipulated that Ethiopia belonged to Italy.

When Menilek learned of the misunderstanding, he wrote to the rulers of France, Germany, and Great Britain, declaring that Ethiopia was an independent country. Italy disagreed, and in 1893, Menilek rejected the treaty. By 1895, Italy and Ethiopia were at war. At the Battle of Adwa (1896), Menilek's forces crushed the Italian army.

Ethiopia remained an independent nation, though under Benito Mussolini, Italy occupied the country from 1936 to 1941 during the rule of Emperor Haile Selassie I. His reign ended in 1974, when a coup led by Mengistu Haile Mariam installed a communist military regime known as the Dergue. A series of crises followed, including the Eritrean revolt and the Ogaden war against Somalia. Thousands of Ethiopians were killed under Mengistu's "Red Terror." In addition, his government deported or starved to death thousands more in response to their opposition to his policies.

In the 1980s, eight million Ethiopians suffered as a result of famine and drought; of this number, at least 1 million died. The number increased with civil wars in the north against insurgencies from Eritrea, Tigray, and other regions. Eritrea gained its independence in 1993, but the two countries started fighting again in 1998 over a border dispute. The war ended in 2000.

Ethiopia has no official policy toward its native peoples and even opened its doors to refugees from Eritrea in 2007. Three ethnic groups account for three-quarters of Ethiopia's population: the Amhara, Oromo, and Tigray. The Amhara are dominant politically, even though they are a numerical minority (27 percent). Ethiopia's 1994 constitution established a federal republic composed of nine ethnically based *killoch,* or regional states.

The country held its first democratic, multiparty elections in 1994. The constitution allows states to operate their own governments. In a continent where landownership is important, the constitution grants that right only to the state and to the people. Ethiopians can lease land from the state for ninety-nine years, or rent it for twenty years, but they cannot mortgage or sell it.

Ethnic violence has persisted, however, as the Ogaden National Liberation Front, in Ethiopia's southernmost province, has continued the sporadic attacks that began in the mid-1980s. Made up mostly of ethnic Somalis, it attacked a government-backed Chinese oil exploration effort in 2007, killing seventy-four and provoking swift retribution by the Ethiopian military. In 2011, Ethiopia had four top opposition parties, including the ethnically based Oromo People's Congress and the Oromo Federalist Democratic Movement.

Aje-Ori Agbese

See also: Groups: Africa—Amhara; Oromo. *Issues*—Colonialism; Indigenous Governments; Poverty.

Further Reading

Gish, Steve, Winnie Thay, and Zawiah Abdul Latif. *Cultures of the World: Ethiopia.* Tarrytown, NY: Marshall Cavendish, 2007.

Marcus, Harold G. *A History of Ethiopia.* Berkeley: University of California Press, 2002.

Ofcansky, Thomas P., and Berry Laverle, eds. *Ethiopia: A Country Study.* Washington, DC: U.S. Government Printing Office, 1991.

Pankhurst, Richard. *The Ethiopians: A History.* Oxford, UK: Blackwell, 2001.

Fiji

The Republic of the Fiji Islands comprises some 300 islands (of which about 100 are inhabited) and more than 500 islets in the Pacific Ocean. Its capital and main commercial center is Suva, located on the southern coast of the largest island, Viti Levu (also known as Great Fiji).

Fijian natives—sometimes called *Lapita,* after a distinctive type of local pottery—arrived in the islands as early as 3000 B.C.E. Evidence of their early settlement has been found throughout the Fiji islands, most notably near the Sigatoka Sand Dunes on Viti Levu. Melanesian peoples followed, arriving in the Fiji islands in about 500 B.C.E.

Sea-faring Fijians became well known for their *Drua,* or double-outrigger canoes, which they used for trading with peoples on other islands, most notably the Tonga. Immigrants to Fiji sought timber for building canoes that they could not obtain on their home islands. By the nineteenth century, Fiji was drawing Chinese and European traders who sought the islands' sandalwood and hardwoods. The islands also became a minor center for gold mining and trading.

Fiji achieved full independence from Great Britain in 1970, and elections were held that year under the country's new constitution. Since 1987, however, the island has seen several coups, punctuated by elections under new constitutions. Fijians elected Laisenia Qarase as prime minister in August 2001 and again in May 2006. However, he was ousted by a military coup led by Commodore Voreqe "Frank" Bainimarama in December 2006. Bainimarama appointed himself acting president and, in January 2007, interim prime minister.

In 2007 (Fiji's last census), approximately half the people on Fiji's islands, about 350,000, were indigenous, over 90 percent of whom are Fijian, with smaller Rotuman and Melanesian communities. Caucasians, Chinese, and East Indians make up the largest minorities on the islands.

An estimated 85 percent of Fiji's land still is owned by indigenous people, a result of colonial-era policies. When the islands were colonized by Great Britain in 1876, colonial governor Sir Arthur Hamilton-Gordon forbade the sale of indigenous land to non-Fijians. Hamilton-Gordon also forbade the exploitation of the native people as cheap labor, so workers emigrated from India, initially to cut sugarcane. To this day, a large number of Fiji's indigenous people farm their own lands, growing bananas, cassava, sugarcane, rice, and other crops for sustenance. Fiji's fifty-five-member Great Council of Chiefs (Bose Levu Vakaturaga), the islands' governing body since before colonization, still meets once a year to discuss issues of concern to the indigenous population in fourteen provinces.

Copper-Mining Controversy

Native peoples in Fiji's Nadroga, Namosi, Rewa, and Serua provinces opposed a 2001 proposal by the Japanese mining company Nittetsu-Nippon to pulverize the islands' copper-rich hills. The project would have endangered the ecologically fragile Coral Coast and Waisoi Valley by producing a projected 100,000 tons (90,718 metric tons) of waste rock—called "tailings" by miners—per day.

The proposed operation would have ground entire hills into rubble, making parts of Fiji's native lands largely uninhabitable as a result of the dumping of toxic waste into the waters of the Navua River Delta. An alternative dumping site was proposed at the Beqa Lagoon, dubbed the soft coral capital of the world by French oceanographer Jacques Cousteau, threatening the sea life that thrives there. The area also is one of the most seismically active areas in the world, prone to earthquakes that might disrupt the project.

The four provinces that would have been affected by the proposed mine—Nadroga, Namosi, Rewa, and Serua—are major sources of tourism income for Fiji. These areas, along with the Coral Coast and Waisoi Valley, are known for their stunning landscapes, diverse wildlife, and pristine waters, all of which would have been threatened by the proposed copper mine. The Fiji Tourism Forum, committed to keeping the area pristine for tourism purposes, formed a subcommittee to educate local people about the impact of so large a mine on the environment and traditional lifestyles.

The village of Navala, featuring traditional grass huts (*bures*), is located on the largest island in the Fijian archipelago, Viti Levu. Native culture is still very much alive on the islands of Fiji, where about half the population is indigenous. *(De Agostini/Getty Images)*

Resistance, Labor, and Economic Issues

Approximately forty small indigenous villages pooled their resources and persuaded local landowners, authorities in Namosi District, and the Fiji government to oppose the proposed mine. The mine also would have brought about 10,000 additional people to the region, inundating some traditional communities. At times, however, native leaders in Fiji have sold logging, mining, and fishing rights to foreign corporations. In the 1970s, for example, a foreign joint-venture mined copper in the Waisoi Valley, though the undertaking proved unprofitable and was soon abandoned. As is often the case, the people of the region gained no economic benefit.

Existing mines on and near Fiji have been beset by labor problems and occasional strikes. The Emperor Mine, operated by the Emperor Gold Mining Company on the Isle of Man, for example, endured a multiyear strike by the Fiji Mine Workers Union beginning in 1991. Major points of contention are pay, working conditions, and housing, which are described by the union as grossly substandard and unethical. The company refused to recognize the union, fired its 420 members, and hired nonunion labor. As of 2009, local resistance apparently had stalled the development of the copper mine on the scale that

many Fiji residents had feared. Mining in Fiji (notably of gold) continues, but on a relatively small scale.

Members of the small Melanesian population, who are descended from Solomon Islanders and New Hebrideans, have retained a distinct culture, despite much intermarriage with the Fijians. However, they are unable to own land and therefore have a lower socioeconomic status. Although the Great Council of Chiefs still meets annually, their role in the governing of the islands, as well as their opposition to the government of Frank Bainimarama, himself a Fijian, has been called into question. Many Fijians view the council as primarily symbolic in nature—a remnant of an earlier tradition based in their culture.

Bruce E. Johansen

See also: *Groups: East Asia and Oceania*—Melanesians. *Issues*—Colonialism; Political Participation.

Further Reading

Brison, Karen J. *Our Wealth Is Loving Each Other: Self and Society in Fiji*. Lanham, MD: Lexington, 2007.

Cooper, Phillip J., and Claudia María Vargas. *Implementing Sustainable Development: From Global Policy to Local Action*. Lanham, MD: Rowman & Littlefield, 2004.

Ravuvu, Asesela. *Vaka i Taukei: The Fijian Way of Life*. Suva, Fiji: University of the South Pacific, 1983.

Finland

Finland is a Nordic country located in the Scandinavian region of Northern Europe. Situated between Sweden to the west and Russia to the east, it marks the northern-most border between Western and Eastern Europe. It is among the world's most remote and most densely forested countries, characterized by a harsh Arctic climate.

The nation is home to a population of approximately 5.4 million people, who are concentrated in the southern part of the country; the far northern Arctic Lapland is sparsely populated. Finland is a relatively ethnically homogenous nation, with Finns making up most of the population, in addition to smaller numbers of Finland-Swedes (the Swedish-speaking people of Finland) and about 7,500 indigenous Sami, who live in the northern region known as Lapland; there also are about 10,000 Roma and somewhere between 2,500 and 5,000 Old Russians. Finland is a bilingual nation, with Finnish and Swedish being the official languages.

The history of Finland before the twelfth century suggests that the first settlers in Finland followed the retreating glaciers north some 10,000 years ago. These people called themselves Sumalaiset, the name that Finns still use today, and their land Suomi. Finns did not appear in the documentary record until the twelfth century, when the Sumalaiset were converted to Christianity by Swedish crusaders.

The ethnocultural history of Finland first was popularized in Finland's national epic poem, the *Kalevala*, published in 1835. Elias Lönnrot, in an effort to inspire a sense of Finnish nationalism, collected ancient songs and poetry infused with animistic and magical beliefs composed by Finnish people during the first millennium C.E. By the end of the nineteenth century, the *Kalevala* had appeared in eight languages, including English.

According to the *Kalevala,* the people that the Swedes encountered on their crusade were free-spirited backwoods folk marked by their bravery and superstition. In summer, the Finns practiced *huutu* (slash-and-burn) agriculture and plied the more than 50,000 lakes, fishing and traveling from village to village. In winter, they crossed the country on snowshoes and sledges, hunting and trapping in the vast forests and settling into crude, drafty log dwellings.

Rather than seeking to eradicate the indigenous beliefs of the Sumalaiset, the Catholic Swedish missionaries tended to overlay Christianity onto the agrarian local Finno-Ugric religion. As late as the seventeenth century, one of the primary objectives of the Lutheran bishop of Turku was the eradication of witchcraft and black magic, which he felt had been allowed to persist under the Catholics. The Finns had a reputation as magicians, believed by many to be able to slay enemies from hundreds of miles away with a *finnskolt* (magic bullet), control the winds, and read the heavens with great accuracy.

Under Swedish control, and constantly hampered by seemingly continual conflict between Russia and Sweden, Finland expanded gradually during the fourteenth and fifteenth centuries. The Swedish government encouraged Finns not only to expand into the dense forests in eastern and northern Finland, but also to colonize the Värmland, Sweden's interior wilderness, using their methods of wresting a living out of the forest. In addition, Swedish authorities encouraged Finnish settlers to move into the frontier regions of Lapland and Ostrobothnia in order to exploit the hunting and fishing resources in those regions. One group of settlers that was especially proficient at harvesting these frigid wilderness areas, the Pirkkalaiset, enjoyed a monopoly on hunting and fishing rights in its region for well over a century.

Swedish authorities turned to the enterprising Finns when they determined to set up the colony of New Sweden in North America in the seventeenth century. The Finns' methods of huutu colonization, which entailed the felling and burning of trees, the construction of simple log cabins, minimal cultivation, light livestock breeding, reliance on hunting and foraging, and relative mobility, seemed well suited to the North American wilderness. The skills fostered among the Pirkkalaiset proved invaluable in the frontier economy. Moreover, the low level of specialization involved in huutu colonization easily absorbed and adapted to more efficient Native American methods of subsistence, resulting in an effective hybrid method for hastening the development of vast amounts of wilderness land.

Finland declared independence from Russia in 1917, and Finnish and Swedish were declared national languages, though Sami was excluded. Between the 1880s and 1920s, the small Tatar population, which is Muslim, emigrated from the Volga area of Russia to the area around Helsinki.

During World War II, the two wars Finland fought against the Soviet Union mostly were fought in Sami lands in the north. These conflicts were catastrophic for the Sami, as they had the effect of obliterating much of the province, including all existing Sami houses and visible evidence of their culture. Efforts to rebuild Sami identity were delayed while the entire country rebuilt after the war. In 1973, the Parliament of Finland was established, and in 1992, February 6 was declared Sami National Day.

Finland joined the European Union in 1995. This brought with it an influx of Roma immigrants, once

Romania and Bulgaria were granted membership. In 2001, Finland established the Office of the Ombudsman for Minorities. By 2007, the nation had established a permanent regional advisory board for Roma affairs; however, discrimination against the Roma continues on an individual basis.

The main concern of the Sami today is the control of their land and its natural resources. Industries are building facilities in the midst of their traditional reindeer grazing lands; state-owned Finnish companies are foresting on Sami lands as well. In January 2011, the United Nations Special Rapporteur on Human Rights recommended that Finland take steps to clear up these land rights issues and protect Sami lands. As of 2012, such steps had not yet been taken.

Gerald Ronning

See also: *Groups: Europe*—Finns; Roma (Gypsies); Sami. *Issues*—Political Participation.

Further Reading

Niskanen, Markku. "The Origin of the Baltic-Finns from the Physical Anthropological Point of View." *Mankind Quarterly* 43:2 (Winter 2002): 121–153.

Singleton, Fred. *A Short History of Finland.* Rev. A.F. Upton. New York: Cambridge University Press, 1998.

France

France is located in northwestern Europe, bordered by Belgium and Luxembourg to the southeast; Germany, Italy, and Switzerland to the east; and Andorra and Spain to the south. The country has long coastlines on the Atlantic Ocean and the Mediterranean Sea, and the island of Corsica in the Mediterranean is a territory of France.

The French population numbers more than 63 million. A majority of people in France are described as ethnically French, referring to the descendants of the Gauls, a Celtic people of Western Europe, and speak French as their primary language. In 1992, France's constitution named French as the country's official language, recognizing the paramount place of language as a marker of cultural identity in the nation.

However, France also is home to seven indigenous minorities that together make up approximately one-fifth of the nation's population: Alsatians, Basques, Bretons, Catalans, Corsicans, Flemish, and Occitans. While some minorities have their own regions in which they reside—Alsatians, Bretons, and Corsicans—others have no region of their own but nevertheless tend to be limited to a particular territory—Basques, Catalans, and Flemish.

Occitans, perhaps the largest of the French minorities with some 10 million people, are scattered throughout the central and southern parts of the country.

Resistance to Linguistic Diversity

In 1789, the French Revolution marked the end of the monarchy and the beginning of the French Republic. Although the new regime promoted citizens' rights, it proved hostile to peoples' rights: one of the first official acts of the republic was the annexation of the island of Corsica. At the same time, regional languages other than French strongly were opposed.

The government's crackdown on minority languages reached its peak during the second half of the nineteenth century. The French Teaching Law of 1851 stated that "[i]t is strictly forbidden to speak patois during classes or breaks." In 1881, French Minister of Education Jules Ferry introduced free, compulsory primary education while implementing a series of measures aimed at weakening the influence of the regional languages. For instance, teachers were allowed to punish children for speaking in a language other than French.

The first law to authorize the teaching of regional languages, the Loi Deixonne (Deixonne Law), was passed in 1951. Four languages were included: Basque, Breton, Catalan, and Occitan. Excluded were languages spoken in neighboring countries: Alsatian (Germany), Corsican (Italy), and Flemish (Belgium). In 1975, the Loi Bas-Lauriol (Bas-Lauriol Law) made French mandatory in advertising and commerce and prohibited any foreign expression. The Toubon Law, another law aimed at promoting French against the worldwide diffusion of English, was approved in 1994. The law stipulates that all documents relating to goods and services be written in French and that the medium of education (and all educational documents) is French.

Indigenous Cultural Renaissance

During the 1960s and 1970s, several institutions promoting the teaching of minority languages were established throughout France, including Calandretas (Occitan), Diwan (Breton), and Seaska (Basque). These schools slowly gained popular support, and in 1987, a federation of minority language schools, the Fédération pour les Langues Régionales dans l'Enseignement Public (Federation for Regional Languages in Public Education), was founded. All of these organizations remain in existence today. In addition, a plethora of organizations promoting regional languages has been created since then, ranging from the Alsatian René Schickelé Society (1965) to the Corsican Parlemu Corsu (2007).

Some universities even began including these languages in their courses. A special case is on Corsica, where the only university, opened by Pasquale Paoli during the island's short-lived independence (1755–1769), was closed after its takeover by France. Two centuries later, as a result of a popular campaign, the school was reopened and became instrumental in promoting the Corsican language.

This cultural renaissance also resulted in the development of minority-language media: radios, magazines, and journals. An example of particular value is that of Radio Pays, a Paris-based private radio station founded in 1981 that broadcasts in the seven minority languages of the French Republic. TV Breizh, the first television station to broadcast some programs in Breton, was started at the beginning of the new century. Similar attempts have been made in other regions.

Indigenous Separatist Tensions

Violence emerged in the 1970s, mainly in Corsica, where the terrorist organization Front de Libération Nationale de la Corse (FLNC) was created. Named after the Algerian FLN, the movement advocated separation from France and began bombing seats of government such as post offices and military premises. Other acts of separatist violence occurred in Brittany. In 1981, the election of a Socialist president, François Mitterrand, raised new hopes for autonomy among France's minority populations. In fact, Corsica was the only region that was given new rights, resulting in special regional status in 1991. Even though this could not be called autonomy, it marked progress.

Links between France's minorities continued to strengthen, and in 1995, the Fédération Régions et Peuples Solidaires (Federation of Regions and Peoples with Solidarity) was formed as a collection of minority parties. This nonviolent, federalist, and democratic organization is not limited to Europe, as it also includes the Congres Mondial Amazigh (Berber World Council) and cooperates with non-European immigrant minorities, mainly Kurds and Tuareg.

Despite their lack of political weight at the national level, France's native minorities have been successful at the broader pan-European level. Thanks to an alliance with the French Greens political party, in 1989, Corsican autonomist Max Simeoni became a member of the European Parliament (1989), as did Francescu Alfonsi in 2009.

Alessandro Michelucci

See also: Groups: Europe—Basques; Bretons; Flemish; French; Occitans. *Issues*—Language.

Further Reading

Candea, Matei. *Corsican Fragments: Difference, Knowledge, and Fieldwork.* Bloomington: Indiana University Press, 2010.

Fischer, Christopher J. *Alsace to the Alsatians? Visions and Divisions of Alsatian Regionalism, 1870–1939.* New York: Berghahn, 2010.

Judge, Ann. *Linguistic Policies and the Survival of Regional Languages in France and Britain.* Basingstoke, UK: Palgrave Macmillan, 2007.

Zirakzadeh, Cyrus Ernesto. *A Rebellious People: Basques, Protests, and Politics.* Reno: University of Nevada Press, 1994.

Germany

Germany is Europe's most populous nation, with more than 81 million inhabitants, and the largest economy on the continent. German nationals represent more than 90 percent of the country's population; the rest is made up of foreign citizens. Today, Germany has the third-highest number of international migrants in the world (more than 10 million), according to United Nations population figures, a result of unrestricted laws on immigration and asylum in the late twentieth century.

For much of history, the territory that is now known as Germany was home to a loosely affiliated collection of Germanic tribes. The Roman historian Tacitus first described the area's inhabitants in his treatise *Germania* (98 C.E.). Though he attempted to identify three distinct groups of Germanic peoples—Hermions (or Teutons), Ingaevons, and Istaevons—with precision, the historian's limited information created some confusion about the exact composition of these three confederations.

Eventually, the Franks came to dominate the Western region, mixing with Celtic and Roman cultures in present-day France, Germany, and the Low Countries. Historical research and paleoclimatic studies indicate that in the early Middle Ages, a series of three migratory waves took place, as the Huns (in 375 C.E.), Lombards (568), and Slavic groups (577) moved into Germanic lands.

The German nation is a much more recent invention, formed when Prussian Prime Minister Otto von Bismarck united dozens of German-speaking European states to establish the German Empire in 1871. Germany became a leading power in Europe and claimed overseas colonies in Africa, Asia, and the Pacific Islands. That empire was dismantled, however, after Germany's defeat in World War I, and the economic depression that followed set the stage for the rise of the Nazi Party under Adolf Hitler.

During the Nazi domination of Germany from 1933

to 1945, the country's Jewish minority, which largely had been assimilated by the late nineteenth century and accounted for less than 1 percent of the population, was removed by the Nazis through forced emigration or destruction in ghettoes and death camps. The Roma people (also known as Gypsies) suffered a similar fate. Today, these communities have been rebuilt, albeit on a much smaller scale.

In addition, Germany once was home to an ethnic Slavic nationality, the Sorbs, living in the areas of Brandenburg and Saxony, as well as some Danish peoples in the northern realm. Another 2 million Turkish Germans live in Germany, the descendants of Turks who migrated to the country in the 1950s as the so-called German economic miracle increased the demand for guest workers and manual laborers. These Turkish Germans have been assimilated into German society, but controversy remains as to whether they should be granted German citizenship, even though members of the younger generations no longer speak Turkish.

Other German-speaking populations have lived around the world for centuries, resulting in different expressions of ethnic German self-awareness and consciousness. For instance, German-speaking minority groups in Kazakhstan, Namibia, and Russia (most of whom live in Siberia in the area of Irkutsk) consider themselves to be German. On the other hand, the German-speaking people of Austria do not identify themselves as Germans but rather as Austrians. The same is true for the Germanophone Swiss population, whose identity is Swiss. Likewise, citizens of Belgium, whose first language is German, identify as Belgians. The separation of independent territories of Germany from Austria, Belgium, and Switzerland explains the distinctive patterns of national identification.

There is a great variety in local dialects of German. Nevertheless, these variations are roofed by a common standard language that is the written and spoken medium of the mass media, the language taught in schools, and the literary language of Austria, Belgium, Germany, and Switzerland. Germans use this same language in minority communities around the world. Thus, the Germanophone Swiss, although they speak a dialectal variety of German (Schwyzerdütsch) in their daily communication, use the same written version of the language as the Germans in Germany.

A considerable number of people in Germany speak German as their second language, including Turks, émigrés from Eastern Europe who migrated to West Germany during the Cold War, and people from former German colonies in Africa and Asia. The new ethnic and linguistic minorities in Austria, Germany, and Switzerland also must adopt German in some form in

order to communicate with the majority population. In some urban communities in Germany, a German pidgin language has emerged.

Under Article 116 of the Basic Law for the Federal Republic of Germany, immigrants to Germany who can prove their German background (such as Russians whose forefathers migrated from Germany to Russia in the seventeenth century) automatically were granted citizenship. That rule changed in the early 1990s as a result of the economic challenges posed by the reunification of East and West Germany and a massive influx of immigrants into Germany, which increased from about 40,000 per year in the 1980s to more than 400,000 per year by the early 1990s. Today, the number and region of origin of immigrants are strictly controlled.

Guillaume de Syon and Harald Haarmann

See also: Groups: Europe—Germans; Jews, European; Roma (Gypsies).

Further Reading
Burns, Thomas S. *Barbarians Within the Gates of Rome: A Study of Roman Military Policy and the Barbarians (ca. 375–425).* Bloomington: Indiana University Press, 1994.

Heather, Peter J. "The Huns and the End of the Roman Empire in Western Europe." *English Historical Review* 110 (1995): 4–41.

Nathans, Eli. *The Politics of Citizenship in Germany: Ethnicity, Utility and Nationalism.* New York: Berg, 2004.

Guatemala

Guatemala is located in Central America, bordered by Mexico to the north and west, Belize to the northeast, Honduras to the east, and El Salvador to the southeast. The country has coastlines along the Pacific Ocean to the west and the Caribbean Sea to the east. With more than 42,000 square miles (109,000 square kilometers) of fertile mountains and tropical coastal lands, Guatemala's population of approximately 15 million people benefits from a productive natural resource base and a thriving export trade with the United States and Central America.

Guatemalan society is marked by significant wealth disparity between its mostly urban, Spanish-speaking Ladino population (people of mixed indigenous and European heritage) and the majority population of rural, indigenous Maya people. This is a legacy of Guatemala's history as a colony of the Spanish Empire for nearly three centuries, from 1523 to 1821. The Spanish practice of mercantilism, whereby natural resources in the colonies, including indigenous labor, were exploited for the benefit of the Crown, still defines the relationship between the Ladino minority and the indigenous Maya majority.

Guatemala is unique in world history in that its indigenous people always have outnumbered the ruling elite—first the Spanish and then the Ladinos—and yet they have struggled to play a meaningful role in the country's political affairs for almost 500 years. The great Maya civilization (highland Maya in Guatemala) was already in decline by the time of the Spanish conquest under Pedro de Alvarado in 1523–1524. The Maya long had abandoned their cities and ceremonial centers for rural farming villages, where they numbered perhaps 5 million before the so-called Columbian Exchange, a dramatic exchange of ideas and populations between the Old World and the New World beginning in the early sixteenth century. Epidemic diseases and warfare greatly reduced the Maya population in the sixteenth and seventeenth centuries—by as much as 90 percent in some areas, but a recovery was under way by the beginning of the nineteenth century.

Under the Spanish colonial administration, the Maya were classified as *Indios* and remained outside the caste system, which categorized populations by blood and by their relationship to the Spanish-born *peninsulares* (that is, individuals born in Spain but residing in the New World). The dwindling Maya population was converted to Christianity and forced to labor in the mercantile system in return for the "civilizing and Christianizing" influences of European culture. If the Maya refused, they were targeted for inquisition, violence, or even death. Such practices continue even in modern Guatemala and resulted in indigenous civil wars that only ended officially in 1996. Perhaps because the Maya possess an ancient civilization going back several thousand years, they never fully adopted Spanish and European customs, beliefs, clothing, or religion. Instead, they blended the two civilizations into a modern highland Maya civilization.

Today, more than 8 million Maya cling to their

RIGOBERTA MENCHU

Rigoberta Menchu Tum, an indigenous Quiché woman, was born in 1959 in the small village of Chimel in Uspatán, Guatemala. Her family lived in extreme poverty, as did most of her peasant neighbors in the Guatemalan northern highlands. By the age of eight, she was a farm laborer, traveling to the Pacific coast, where adults and children earned a pittance as menial workers.

Most such laborers worked on large coffee or cotton plantations with substandard working conditions, which sometimes caused the deaths of workers, including Menchu's two brothers. In Guatemala, the dominant Ladino population (Guatemalans of mixed indigenous and European ancestry) long had controlled the country's economy and politics, whereas the indigenous people, although they accounted for some 60 percent of the total population, had been the target of racism, exploitation, and oppression.

For Menchu's family, life became even more difficult in the late 1970s, when the Guatemalan government conducted a massive campaign of repression against its indigenous population. As the Indian peasants resisted another round of land grabbing carried out by the government, the Guatemalan army waged a brutal war against them. Government forces burned some 440 villages, and many native people were tortured, raped, and killed or simply disappeared.

As Menchu's family became more involved in the resistance movement, they were wanted by the government. Between 1979 and 1980, her father, mother, and brother were tortured and murdered by the Guatemalan military because of their antigovernment activities. Menchu's father, Vicente, had been active in the Committee of the Peasant Union (CUC), which sought to defend Guatemala's indigenous people against discrimination, oppression, and labor and human rights abuses. Menchu also joined the CUC in 1979 but was forced to seek exile in Mexico two years later.

In 1983, Menchu published *I, Rigoberta Menchu: An Indian Woman in Guatemala,* her personal testimonial of indigenous life in Guatemala. The book captured the world's attention, as it exposed the sufferings of the poor peasants in Guatemala, and it soon was translated into a number of languages. Menchu won the Nobel Peace Prize in 1992, becoming the youngest person (at age thirty-three) and the first indigenous person ever to be so honored.

That same year, Menchu established the Rigoberta Menchu Tum Foundation with the $1.2 million cash award that she received as part of the Nobel Peace Prize. From 1994 to 2003, Menchu served as the official spokesperson for the United Nations International Decade of Indigenous Peoples. She has gained international attention as a result of her continued efforts to fight for human rights and social justice.

Azusa Ono

Rigoberta Menchu, born to Quiché peasants in a poor Guatemalan village, was awarded the 1992 Nobel Peace Prize "in recognition of her work for social justice and ethno-cultural reconciliation based on respect for the rights of indigenous peoples." *(Orlando Sierra/ AFP/Getty Images)*

other Latin American countries ($7,169) and the world average ($8,732). According to the World Bank, more than 38 percent of Ladinos in Guatemala live below the poverty line, compared to 74 percent of indigenous Guatemalans. The majority of indigenous children still do not have access to consistent schooling, averaging only three years of education by age thirty. Corn prices rose more than 70 percent in the last few years, which has impacted the generally poorer indigenous populations. Although more indigenous people are employed than Ladinos, their wages are lower, by at least 10 percent.

Native people in Guatemala still are impacted by discrimination by Ladinos and negative portrayals in the media. The result of this social and economic discrimination, combined with the government having little money for programs to mitigate it, is that many native people are excluded from benefiting from the country's development.

Christopher Howell

See also: Groups: Central and South America—Garífuna; Maya; Quiché. *Issues*—Colonialism; Poverty.

Further Reading

Fischer, Edward F., and R. McKenna Brown, eds. *Maya Cultural Activism in Guatemala.* Austin: University of Texas Press, 1996.

Goldin, Lilliana. *Global Maya: Work and Ideology in Rural Guatemala.* Tucson: University of Arizona Press, 2011.

Grandin, Greg. *The Blood of Guatemala: A History of Race and Nation.* Durham, NC: Duke University Press, 2000.

Menchu, Rigoberta. *I, Rigoberta Menchu: An Indian Woman in Guatemala.* 1983. New York: Verso, 2010.

rural past in the highlands of Guatemala despite more than a century of military-style dictatorial rule that constantly targeted the indigenous populations. This was especially true in the twentieth century under General Jorge Ubico, whose tenure from 1931 to 1944 was followed by repeated elections and civil wars between militant right- and left-wing groups until 1996. Often both sides preyed on the indigenous people of Guatemala. The civil wars killed at least 100,000 Maya and displaced more than 1 million as refugees. Although the peace accord of 1996 led to democratic elections, Guatemala's political leadership continues to struggle to engage the indigenous Maya of the rural highlands, the country's largest population.

Guatemala's per capita income increased from less than $1,000 in 1999 to $2,600 in 2009, according to the United Nations Children's Fund, but it still lags all

Guyana

Guyana, formerly known as British Guyana, is located on the northern coast of South America. Culturally, it is related to the Caribbean nations, and it is a member state of the Caribbean Community.

Guyana's relationship with the indigenous communities that are part of the state has been characterized by tension and political negotiation concerning land title and resource rights for as long as Europeans have colonized the region. The Dutch, who established colonies in Essequibo (1616), Berbice (1627), and Demerara (1752), were the first to colonize the region, but the British assumed control in the early nineteenth century when the Dutch formally ceded the area in 1814.

Under British rule, Crown land was extended to include the ancestral homelands of Guyana's nine indigenous communities: the Akawaio, Arawak, Arekuna, Kalina/Carib, Macushi, Patamuna, Waiwai, Wapishanas, and Warrau. When Guyana achieved independence from the United Kingdom on May 26, 1966, the imperial policies that governed the treatment of indigenous people and the use of their land remained intact, simply substituting Guyanese state ownership for British authority. As a result, the indigenous communities of Guyana have had to fight a long and complicated legal and political battle to retain their rights to self-determination, to claim their traditional lands, and to control their own natural resources, such as minerals and timber.

Holding title to ancestral land has been, and continues to be, the focal point for negotiations between the Guyanese government and the elected representatives of the nine indigenous nations. Indigenous political negotiation concerning land in Guyana formally began when Stephen Campbell, the first Amerindian member of the Guyanese parliament, traveled to London to ask Queen Elizabeth II for Amerindian lands to be secured prior to independence. This resulted in the establishment of the Amerindian Lands Commission. It would be another ten years before the Amerindian Act was passed in 1976, which provided for the granting of land to Amerindian groups. That same year, sixty-four Amerindian groups received legal title to their lands.

In 1995, after consultation with indigenous leaders, the Guyanese government initiated a new policy designed to ensure legal rights to land for native groups through the establishment of title. As in the United States, however, the government retained the right to dictate the amount and location of lands given to indigenous groups. As a result, many indigenous lands that are rich in resources have been contracted for extraction to foreign companies without the consent of the communities on whose traditional lands such resources are located.

The formation of four groups dedicated to the protection and expansion of indigenous rights—the Guyana Organization of Indigenous Peoples, the Amerindian People's Association, the National Amerindian Council, and the Amerindian Action Movement of Guyana—demonstrates the continuation of indigenous agitation in Guyana toward the realization of indigenous rights. These organizations, in consultation and partnership with Amerindian Toshao, continued to demand that indigenous titles be respected and that the language related to the government's authority to demarcate the boundaries of ancestral lands be amended in the 2006 Amerindian Act. That same year, as part of the process for enacting the Amerindian Act, the government of Guyana established a comprehensive procedure and a criteria for addressing Amerindian land claims, both of which are outlined in the act.

By July 2007, seventy-one Amerindian communities had completed or were in the process of officially demarcating their titled lands, with the state bearing the cost of demarcation. As of 2012, there are ninety-six titled Amerindian villages spread across the ten administrative regions of Guyana.

Leah Stewart

See also: *Issues*—Colonialism; Land Rights; Political Participation.

Further Reading

Bulkan, Christopher Arif. *The Land Rights of Guyana's Indigenous Peoples.* Ottawa, Canada: Library and Archives of Canada, 2009.

Bulkan, Janette, and Arif Bulkan. "'These Forests Have Always Been Ours': Official and Amerindian Discourses on Guyana's Forest Estate." In *Indigenous Resurgence in the Contemporary Caribbean: Amerindian Survival and Revival,* ed. Maximilian C. Forte. New York: Peter Lang, 2006.

Chambers, Frances. *Guyana.* Santa Barbara, CA: ABC-CLIO, 1989.

Ministry of Amerindian Affairs, Guyana. www.amerindian.gov.gy.

Honduras

Honduras is located on the southern coast of the Caribbean Sea in Central America, bordered by Guatemala to the northwest, El Salvador to the southwest, and Nicaragua to the south. The nation has a rich Maya history. Native Hondurans speak six distinct languages, each with its own unique culture.

In 2012, approximately 7 percent of the population belonged to one of eight recognized indigenous groups: the Garinagu, Lenca, Maya Chortí, Mayagna, Miskito, Pech, Tawahka, and Xicaque. The Garinagu are of mixed African, Arawak, and Carib ancestry. The Lenca and Maya Chortí originated in the northern and western parts of the country, merging with Nahuatl-speaking migrants moving southward from Mexico. Other groups, such as the Mayagna, Pech, and Xicaque, migrated to Honduras from the south.

Speaking a variety of dialects, the earliest Maya transformed their environment to their advantage. They cut down trees in order to clear the land, dried out and drained swampland, and built villages on low stone platforms near sources of water. Drainage ditches appeared by approximately 1100 B.C.E., indicating an increase in agriculture that coincided with the settlement of larger towns and cities.

When the Spanish arrived in the early sixteenth century, they found large deposits of silver and set out to exploit them, employing the indigenous Hondurans as slave labor. Approximately 150,000 native Hondurans were sent to work in Spanish mines and on estates in other Spanish colonies in the Americas. Many thousands of these native peoples died.

After achieving independence in 1821, Honduras concentrated on constructing a singular national identity that emphasized the country's mestizo heritage (mixed indigenous and Spanish ancestry). As a result, indigenous groups were marginalized and discriminated against. During the 1980s, however, Honduras officially recognized its indigenous peoples as partners in the country and granted them the full protection of the law in matters of human and civil rights.

In the early 1990s, President Rafael Leonardo Callejas promised to secure land titles for the indigenous peoples, but the agreements made never were honored, prompting indigenous protests against the government starting in July 1994. Approximately 3,000 indigenous Hondurans protested outside the legislative assembly in Tegucigalpa for five days, demanding civil rights, land rights, environmental protection, and the release of some of their jailed leaders. President Carlos Roberto Reina promised to address their demands and set aside land for some of the Maya groups. However, progress in transferring the land from individual landholders, and from the Honduran government to the indigenous groups, has been very slow.

Violence and discrimination over land rights has continued into the twenty-first century, as agreements to protect and augment indigenous lands and to investigate the killing of indigenous leaders over land disputes have not made sufficient progress. The Honduran Institute of Anthropology and History has undertaken a project to conduct an ethnographic survey of Honduran indigenous groups, not only counting them but also collecting data on their lifeways.

James E. Seelye, Jr. and Steven L. Danver

See also: *Groups: Central and South America*—Garífuna; Lenca; Maya; Miskito. *Issues*—Colonialism; Revolts.

Further Reading

Clendinnen, Inga. *Ambivalent Conquests: Maya and Spaniard in Yucatan, 1517–1570.* New York: Cambridge University Press, 2003.

Leonard, Thomas. *The History of Honduras.* Westport, CT: Greenwood, 2011.

Sharer, Robert, and Loa Traxler. *The Ancient Maya.* Stanford, CA: Stanford University Press, 2005.

India

India occupies most of South Asia, a region that also is referred to as the Indian Subcontinent. It is the seventh-largest nation in the world by land area, encompassing nearly 1.3 million square miles (3.3 million square kilometers), and the second-most-populous nation, with a population of approximately 1.2 billion in 2011. India is a country of considerable religious and ethnic diversity, with eighteen officially recognized languages and some 1,600 dialects.

Officially, India is a secular country; the Indian constitution of 1950 proclaimed the country a "sovereign socialist secular democratic republic." Hindus make up approximately 83 percent of the total population. India has the second-largest number of Muslims (after Indonesia), constituting nearly 14 percent of the population. Buddhists, Christians, Jains, Parsis (Zoroastrians), and Sikhs compose the rest of the population.

India is home to the largest indigenous population in the world, representing approximately one-quarter of all indigenous people. The country's tribal peoples, officially designated as Scheduled Tribes under the Indian constitution, represent approximately 8 percent of India's total population. These tribes also are referred to as *adivasi* (original inhabitant), aborigines, *vanavasi* (forest dwellers), and *girijan* (hill people).

Generally, the tribes reside in geographically isolated areas and maintain their own distinctive cultures. The vast majority (95 percent) of the Scheduled Tribes reside in rural areas. Their livelihood is based on primitive agriculture and the sale of forest products. Although the tribes are undergoing transformation as a result of modernization and development programs created by the state, poverty levels remain high and literacy levels remain low.

The Indian constitution formally recognizes 645 Scheduled Tribes; however, the actual number is thought to be lower, as some tribes are counted more than once in the different provinces. Scholars and historians estimate that 450 tribal groups reside in the country. Among these, seventy-five are categorized by the government as "primitive tribal groups" that employ a low level of technology in agriculture, hunt to supplement their livelihood, and are backward socially and economically because of their isolation from mainstream society.

According to 2011 census statistics, the numbers of Scheduled Tribes vary in the states of India. The state of Mizoram lists nearly 95 percent of its total population as Scheduled Tribes. In the Serchhip district of the state, tribal peoples account for 98 percent of the population.

The lowest share of scheduled tribes, 0.04 percent, is found in the state of Goa. In states such as Arunachal Pradesh, Meghalaya, Mizoram, and Nagaland, tribal people constitute more than half of the total population.

In the southern provinces of India, such as Andhra Pradesh, Karnataka, Kerala, and Tamil Nadu, the main tribes are the Chenchu, Irula, Kadar, Kota, Lambadi, and Toda; they belong mainly to the Negrito and Proto-Australoid groups. In states such as Bihar, Chhattisgarh, Jharkhand, Madhya Pradesh, Orissa, and West Bengal, tribes belong to Proto-Australoid racial stock. They include the Bhutia, Bhuyan, Gadaba, Gond, Ho, Khond, Kol, Munda, Paroja, Santal, Saora, and others. The Bhil of the Proto-Australoid group are the dominant tribe in western India. The Mongoloid Lepcha, Rabha, and Tharu tribes reside in Haryana, Himachal Pradesh, Jammu and Kashmir, Punjab, Sikkim, and Uttar Pradesh. In northeastern India, the majority of tribes belong to the Mongoloid race. They include the Garo, Khasi, Kuki, Meitei, Naga, and others. In the Andaman and Nicobar islands, tribes are of Negrito and Mongoloid racial stock. These tribes include the Great Andamanese, Jarawa, Onge, Nicobarese, and others.

Religious life, economic conditions, social practices, language, level of education, and occupations vary widely from tribe to tribe, as well from region to region. Each tribe has its own culture, tradition, language, and lifestyle. The main occupations of the tribal peoples are shifting cultivation, hunting, selling forest products, and working in the agricultural and industrial labor sectors. Those who are educated may hold professional jobs in the private or public sector. The labor force participation rate among tribal peoples is about 50 percent.

Many tribes of India are organized into clans. The tribal family typically is patriarchal, with the eldest male serving as the head of the household. In some cases, sons and daughters may establish separate households after marriage. Within the Garo, Kadar, and Khasi tribal societies, the family is matrilineal and matriarchal, divided into exogamous clans.

Marriage among tribal peoples usually is monogamous; levirate and sororate marriages (remarriage to the brother or sister, respectively, of a deceased spouse) also are allowed. Polyandry (having more than one husband) is practiced in some communities, such as the Khasa, Kinnar, Kota, Kurumba, Ladkhai, Lahauli, Spitti, and Toda. The majority of the tribal population practices Hinduism and also worships innumerable deities, spirits, and objects of nature. Festivals and dances are integral parts of social life.

India's native tribes are fiercely independent, and throughout history, they generally have resisted domination by the nontribal ruling elite. Notable dynasties such as the Maurya, Gupta, and Mughal empires in the ancient and medieval periods were unsuccessful in bringing the tribes under their subjugation. Since at least the beginning of the British period in the 1600s, the tribal populations of India have suffered the loss of their lands, exploitation, and relative impoverishment. British colonial rulers gathered information about tribal peoples in an effort to consolidate their regime, increase revenue, and identify resources that could be exploited.

British encroachment on tribal land was met with rebellion, and the tribes rose up against their colonial masters. Some of the major resistance movements include the Chamka Rebellion (1776–1787), the Chuar Rebellion (1795–1800), the Khurda Rebellion (1817), the Bhil Rebellion (1822–1857), the tribal resistance movement in western Orissa (1827–1861), the Koi Revolt (1859), and the rebellions of Rani Gaidinliu (1878–1882), Madro Kalo of Gangpur (1897), Bhumkal (1910), and Nirmal Munda (1939).

India achieved independence from Great Britain in 1947. Since then, the apathetic attitude of the government toward its native peoples has fueled insurgencies, particularly in northeastern India. Many tribal peoples joined the Naxalite movement that formed in Naxalbari village in West Bengal on May 25, 1967. The Naxalite cadres swelled with bright students who joined the movement to agitate for the rights of tribal peoples and landless laborers. Since the 1980s, these activists have become known as Maoists. The extreme left movement continues to expand its areas of operation.

The Mizo and Naga people espoused secession from India during the 1970s and early 1980s, and the granting of statehood for Mizoram in 1987 brought comparative peace. In Manipur, many tribal women became involved in the Meira Paibi (woman torchbearer) movement, which was established by Ima Ramani and Ima Taruni in 1980, seeking to end violence and establish a peaceful civil society in the region. Human rights activists and various women's groups protested the actions of state security forces in the wake of agitation against the proposed Mapithel Dam in November 2008. In response to these movements, the Indian government often has used force rather than attempting a negotiated settlement.

The social condition of India's tribal groups gradually is improving as a result of social mobility, economic opportunities, and a government policy of "reservations" (set-asides for admission to colleges, jobs, political offices, and promotions), as well as state welfare measures. Although major transformations are taking place in social, political, and economic life, many age-old tribal practices continue to be practiced.

Patit Paban Mishra

See also: Issues—Colonialism; Land Rights; Language; Poverty; Revolts.

Further Reading

Anthropological Survey of India. *India, Scheduled Tribes*. Kolkata, India: National Government, 2000.

Bhengra, Ratnaker, C.R. Bijoy, and Shimreichon Luithui. *The Adivasis of India*. London: Minority Rights Group International, 1999.

Chandra, Bipan, Aditya Mukherjee, and Mridula Mukherjee. *India After Independence, 1947–2000*. New Delhi, India: Penguin, 2000.

Ghurye, G.S. *The Scheduled Tribes of India*. New Brunswick, NJ: Transaction, 1980.

Rao, Mopidevi S., and Majji Sankara Reddi. *Human Resources Development in Tribal Areas*. Ambala Cantt, India: Associated, 2006.

Rupavath, Ramdas. *Tribal Land Alienation and Political Movements: Socio-Economic Patterns from South India*. Newcastle, UK: Cambridge Scholars, 2009.

Rycroft, Daniel J., and Sangeeta Dasgupta, eds. *The Politics of Belonging in India: Becoming Adivasi*. New York: Routledge, 2011.

Sen, Sarbani. *The Constitution of India: Popular Sovereignty and Democratic Transformations*. New Delhi, India: Oxford University Press, 2007.

Singh, K. Suresh, ed. *People of India*. Kolkata, India: Anthropological Survey of India, 2008.

Indonesia

The Southeast Asian nation of Indonesia comprises an archipelago of more than 13,000 islands, including thirty provinces, two special regions, and one special capital city district. The country is home to between 35 million and 120 million *warganegara pribumi* (native Indonesians) out of a total population of more than 237 million. Approximately 45 million to 60 million native Indonesians live in what formally are classified as public forests.

Since the country declared its political independence from the Netherlands in 1945, subsequent Indonesian governments have viewed the native peoples as obstacles impeding access to a rich natural resource base required for national economic development. Successive waves of development followed, compromising local indigenous knowledge while threatening the natives' cultural and physical survival.

Seeking to rectify this historical wrongdoing, recent national policies, in particular the Draft Law on the Protection and Recognition of Indigenous Peoples in the National Legislative Programme, under discussion in 2011–2012, have made monumental advances toward improving the political, social, and economic status of native Indonesians. However, pressures from outside interests that seek to extract the mineral wealth of native lands continue to undermine efforts at cultural heritage protection. The intersection of these varied and powerful forces has led government officials to largely discount the rights of native Indonesians in order to promote national development strategies driven by the need to bolster the nation's economy.

Colonial Indonesia

Asian immigrants began to intermarry with the indigenous peoples of the Indonesian archipelago as early as 5000 B.C.E. During the first centuries of the Common Era, immigrants from Gujarat in southeast India introduced the Sanskrit language and the Pallawa script, both of which were adapted to the indigenous Kawi language. Trade partnerships followed, and the islands of Java and Sumatra emerged as the two key economic centers, engaging groups of Arabs and Chinese, as well as indigenous groups of traders and entrepreneurs. Local and regional trade augmented regional economic activity, which was characterized by subsistence agriculture.

The Hindu religion also was introduced by Indian *rishis* (those to whom the sacred Vedas were revealed) and their disciples during this period, although originally its practice was restricted to the Javanese upper classes. Leading up to the colonial period in the sixteenth century, a number of influential Hindu and Islamic kingdoms formed in the archipelago.

Arriving in 1511 in search of spices, the Portuguese conquered the Islamic kingdom of Malacca on the Malay Peninsula. The Spanish soon followed, bringing Christian teachings with them, the threat of which prompted the sultans of Aceh in Sumatra, Demak in Java, and Ternate in the Maluku Islands to unite in an attempt to jettison these European intruders. The sultans' efforts were largely unsuccessful, and in 1570, the Portuguese murdered the sultan of Ternate, Khairun. His successor, Sultan Baabullah, responded by overwhelming the Portuguese forces and then allying with the Dutch in an attempt to purge his lands of the Portuguese and Spanish.

The Dutch, regrettably, were little more than a replacement colonial force, and from the time of their arrival in 1596 until 1651, they became entrenched economically and politically under the auspices of the Dutch East Company (Verenigde Oostindische Compagnie, or VOC). By the late seventeenth century, the VOC had established a small number of trading posts in an environment of growing political fragmentation.

Increasingly reliant on coffee and sugar exports, by the early eighteenth century, the Dutch, now permanently established, began to displace the Javanese rulers, in turn tightening their regional economic and political grip. Dutch imperialism grew over the next three centuries, predicated on a military-driven economic expansionism that initially was centralized in Java.

Modern Indonesia

Fully integrated into the growing global economy by the twentieth century, the Dutch colony of Indonesia boasted an export economy. The Great Depression of the 1930s, which forced the collapse of the Java sugar industry, led to the implementation of protectionist measures aimed at promoting Indonesian industries. Import restrictions were launched, leading to a brief period of self-sufficiency that stimulated domestic economic and political integration.

A declaration of political independence from the Netherlands in 1945 (officially recognized in 1949) followed, although Indonesia had trouble reviving its economy, which had been disrupted severely by both the Depression and the Japanese occupation during World War II. Political instability surfaced in the wake of diminishing economic growth rates, further challenging attempts at establishing democratic governance.

After a two-decade struggle, in 1966, General Suharto attempted to ensure political and economic stability by implementing a number of changes. Among the more contentious moves was his decision to grant the military a fundamental role in promoting national economic growth. Economic expansion now occurred through extended territorial exploration under Suharto's authoritarian regime, which lasted until his death in 1997. In particular, oil and gas production and the logging of the rain forests in order to produce plywood, pulp, and paper brought modern machinery and resource extraction methods into previously untouched native territories.

Resistant to continued exploitation in 1999, more than 200 native Indonesian representatives gathered in Jakarta to protest these conditions and to form the Aliansi Masyarakat Adat Nusantara (AMAN, Alliance of the Indigenous Peoples of the Archipelago). The group formulated a list of demands that encapsulated the issues confronting native Indonesians: (1) elimination of terms that denigrate indigenous people and their rights; (2) recognition of indigenous diversity and of the rights, knowledge, and skills of the native peoples; (3) state institutional representation; (4) restoration of land and natural resource rights; (5) dialogues with the government and private sector regarding land and resource use; (6) creation of social welfare programs that do not violate indigenous rights; (7) termination of military involvement in civil society; (8) development of a fair and equitable dispute resolution process to determine the pith and substance of self-determination; and (9) state adherence to international agreements protecting indigenous peoples' rights, including but not limited to the International Labour Organization's Convention No. 169 and the United Nations Draft Declaration on the Rights of Indigenous Peoples (UNDRIP).

AMAN remains the national indigenous peoples' organization of Indonesia, although little progress has been made in response to their demands. The organization's leaders continue to fight for state recognition of native Indonesians as formal groups of people demonstrating a historical continuity in a given geographic area, who exhibit their own values, ideologies, and economic, cultural, and social systems within those traditional territories. AMAN also remains insistent that the state fully recognize and restore indigenous rights, including those over natural resources.

Progress and development have increased native Indonesians' socioeconomic and sociocultural mobility, as many prefer urban life to that of small towns, villages, and remote islands. Those who choose urbanization often confront the forces of assimilation, which frequently leads to the loss of native traditional knowledge. Even so, many native Indonesians remain in remote or isolated places, far from the conveniences of urban life, which has led to their being dubbed *masyarakat terasing,* or "isolated people." The resultant culture clash is unwieldy, leading to political and cultural instability for native Indonesians.

In 2007, Indonesia endorsed the UNDRIP, even though officials concluded that "the rights in the Declaration accorded exclusively to indigenous people did not apply in the context of Indonesia." Indonesian president Susilo Bambang Yudhoyono has indicated that he is aware of the issues confronting the native Indonesians; however, he insists that Indonesia's larger economic needs take precedence over native rights, justifying continued expansion into outlying territories.

Despite the efforts of AMAN to contest these conditions and to fight for the formal recognition of native rights, national policy continues to encourage economic development to the detriment of native rights, a situation that does not bode well for future generations of native Indonesians. As of 2012, recognition of native rights under Indonesian law remained weak, despite national policies and legislation implemented to counter decades of political ignorance of native issues.

Yale D. Belanger

See also: Issues—Colonialism; Land Rights; Political Participation; United Nations Declaration.

Further Reading

Bertrand, Jacques. *Nationalism and Ethnic Conflict in Indonesia.* New York: Cambridge University Press, 2004.

Bresnan, John, ed. *Indonesia: The Great Transition.* Lanham, MD: Rowman & Littlefield, 2005.

Cribb, Robert, and Colin Brown. *Modern Indonesia: A History Since 1945.* New York: Longman, 1995.

Emmerson, Donald K., ed. *Indonesia Beyond Suharto: Polity, Economy, Society, Transition.* Armonk, NY: M.E. Sharpe, 1999.

Erb, Maribeth, Priyambudi Sulistiyanto, and Carole Faucher, eds. *Regionalism in Post-Suharto Indonesia.* New York: Routledge, 2005.

Taylor, Jean Gelman. *Indonesia: Peoples and Histories.* New Haven, CT: Yale University Press, 2004.

Thorbecke, Erik, and Theodore Van Der Pluijm. *Rural Indonesia: Socio-economic Development in a Changing Environment.* New York: New York University Press, 1993.

Iran

Iran is an ethnically diverse nation located in southwestern Asia. Once known as Persia, or historically as the Persian Empire, the name *Iran* is derived from the word *Iryana,* meaning "land of Aryans." Following the Iranian Revolution of 1979, the nation officially become known as the Islamic Republic of Iran. Iran is located in a politically unstable region of northern Asia, bordering Afghanistan, Azerbaijan, Iraq, and Pakistan.

Ancient Iran was home to a number of tribes that spoke a common Proto-Iranian language and shared many cultural traits. During the seventh century B.C.E., these tribes were united by the Medes (called Mada in Persian) and expanded Iran's borders into Central Asia by conquering the Assyrian Empire in 612 B.C.E. The Median Empire later was replaced by the Achaemenid dynasty (559–330 B.C.E.), which gained power by marrying Median court nobles. Cyrus the Great, the founder of the Achaemenid dynasty, started the Persian Empire by consolidating his rule by 550 B.C.E. in what is today Iran. The Persian Empire expanded far beyond Iran's borders—to Egypt in the south, Greece in the west, and Gandhara in India in the east, encompassing a diverse mix of peoples with a variety of religions, languages, and cultures—until it was annexed by Alexander the Great in 323 B.C.E.

Ancient Iranians followed Zoroastrianism, although other religions were tolerated within the Persian Empire. At this time, the empire had two capitals—a ceremonial capital at Persepolis and an administrative capital at Susa. The Persian Empire was a ceremonial state, with annual festivities held at Persepolis each year. Other significant historical empires of Iran include the Sassanid Empire (300 C.E.) and the Safavid Empire (1500 C.E.).

The Safavid Empire united Iran as a state, with borders roughly corresponding to those of modern Iran, and introduced Shia Islam to the country, establishing a theocratic state that persecuted followers of other religions, such as Zoroastrianism. Many Zoroastrians in Iran died in the ensuing religious persecution carried out under the Safavid Empire. The variety of Shia Islam promoted by the Safavids followed the Twelver tradition, according to which the twelfth imam will return in the future. This tradition persecuted not only other faiths such as Zoroastrianism, but also other Muslim sects, and completely banned Sufism.

A minority religious group founded in 1863 in Iran by Bahā' Ullā, known as the Baha'i religion, long has been persecuted in the country. The Baha'i faith spreads a message of peace and recognizes universal humanity, an ideology that is viewed as threatening by the clergy of Iran. Baha'is faced intense discrimination and persecution after the Islamic Revolution of 1979 and the subsequent cultural revolution in Iran.

Although the Safavid Empire attempted to convert all of the ethnic groups in its domain to Shia Islam, ethnic differences persist in Iran to this day. Just over half (53 percent) of all Iranians are of Persian descent, while the rest of the population comprises Azeri (16 percent), Kurds (10 percent), Lur (6 percent), and Turkic and Arab peoples (2 percent). The Azeri of Iran also are known as Azeri Turks; they live primarily in northwestern Iran and in neighboring Azerbaijan. Kurds in northwestern Iran constitute an important minority with a distinct culture and ethnicity. The Lur people of Iran, living in the remote northwestern region, are considered indigenous to the region.

Approximately 89 percent of Iranians are Shia Muslims, while 9 percent are Sunni Muslims, and people of other faiths, including Baha'is, Christians, Jews, and Zoroastrians, account for 2 percent. Ethnic diversity also is evident in the languages spoken in Iran, which include Persian (53 percent), Azeri and Turkic dialects (18 percent), Kurdish (10 percent), Luri (6 percent), and Arab and other languages (2 percent).

Since the Soviet occupation of Afghanistan in 1980, Iran has received an influx of millions of Afghani refugees, mostly Pashtun. Afghani refugees are protected under the United Nations High Commissioner for Refugees and have been granted temporary residential status by Iran, although they are barred from obtaining permanent residency or citizenship. The children of these temporary residents also cannot be recognized as citizens of Iran, even if one parent is an Iranian citizen. Since 2008, the

Iranian government has taken a tougher stance toward the Afghani refugees, deporting many of them and even persecuting some refugees for minor crimes.

The Iranian political system is dominated by Shi'a Muslims. The Islamic Republic of Iran, established by the 1979 Islamic Revolution, is led by a guardian jurist known as the Supreme Leader (the first being the Ayatollah Khomeini, and as of 2012, the Ayatollah Khamenei). The Supreme Leader serves as the absolute head of the Iranian government, ranking above all other officials, including the president. The Supreme Leader can dismiss the president at will and has the authority to prevent the implementation of any laws or decisions. Iran has a unicameral legislature with only one parliament, the Islamic Consultative Assembly; all legislation is subject to the approval of the Guardian Council.

Iran is a highly urbanized country, with 70 percent of the population living in cities. Agriculture accounts for approximately 20 percent of the gross national product and employs one-third of the labor force. The petroleum industry is Iran's economic mainstay; oil accounts for 80 percent of export revenues.

During the first decades of the twenty-first century, Iran experienced political turmoil and cultural instability. In June 2009, a presidential election was held between the incumbent and choice of the Supreme Leader, Mahmoud Ahmadinejad, and three challengers, most notably Mir-Hossein Mousavi. After Ahmadinejad claimed a sweeping victory, accusations of fraud were immediate, both from Mousavi and the Western media. Protests swept through Tehran for the better part of the next year, resulting in the death of at least 150 and the arrest and torture of thousands. Although the protests died down, the pressure for change continued, as evidenced by the sweeping defeats experienced by Ahmadinejad's Abadgaran party in the parliamentary elections of May 2012.

Lavanya Vemsani

See also: *Groups: Europe*—Azeri (Azerbaijanians). *Groups: South Asia and Middle East*—Kurds. *Issues*—Indigenous Governments; Religion (Indigenous); Social Discrimination.

Further Reading

Curzon, R. *The Iranian Peoples of the Caucasus: A Handbook.* London: Routledge, 2001.

Momeni, Jamshid A., ed. *The Population of Iran: A Selection of Readings.* Shiraz, Iran: East West Population Institute, Pahalavi University, 1997.

Naji, Kasra. *Ahmadinejad: The Secret History of Iran's Radical Leader.* Berkeley: University of California Press, 2008.

Walker, Benjamin. *Persian Pageant: A Cultural History of Iran.* Kolkata, India: Arya, 1950.

Iraq

Iraq is located in southwestern Asia, bordering Turkey on the north, Iran on the east, Kuwait, Saudi Arabia, and the Persian Gulf on the south, Jordan on the west, and Syria on the northwest. It occupies an area that corresponds to the ancient civilization of Mesopotamia, situated between the Tigris and Euphrates rivers. The region was home to the world's earliest civilization.

In Lower Mesopotamia, Sumerians were the first people to establish city-states before they were conquered by the Akkadians around 2334 B.C.E. By 2000 B.C.E. the Amorites, a Semitic people from west of the Euphrates River, controlled southern Mesopotamia and made Babylon their capital. During the reign of King Hammurabi (r. 1792–1750 B.C.E.), Babylon controlled most of Mesopotamia, from the south to Assyria in the north.

The Assyrians, a Semitic people, controlled Mesopotamia during the tenth through seventh centuries B.C.E., and created their own empire. With the decline of Assyrian power, a native governor became king of Babylon in 625 B.C.E. and inaugurated a Chaldean dynasty. In 612 B.C.E., the Chaldeans (also called Neo-Babylonians) extinguished Assyrian power, becoming heirs to the Assyrians and conquering formerly Assyrian-held lands in Palestine and Syria. The Chaldean Empire was the last national empire to rule Mesopotamia before it fell to foreign powers. In 539 B.C.E., Babylon fell to Cyrus the Great (r. 559–530 B.C.E.) of Persia.

Beginning in the second century C.E., Christianity flourished in Mesopotamia among the descendants of the ancient empires of Assyria and Chaldea. Once baptized, the people of both nations preferred to call themselves Christians, and their church was known simply as the Church of the East. They gradually were converted through the missions of Saint Addi, Saint Mari, and Saint Thomas. More than 50 percent of the Iraqi population at this time was reported to be Christian, and most of Iraq remained Christian until the introduction of Islam in the mid-seventh century C.E.

Islam became the religion of the majority of the population. As a consequence of the Arabization and Islamization policies carried out by the Muslim caliphates and other Muslim empires, such as the Ottomans, that ruled Iraq from the seventh century until the nineteenth century, the indigenous people of Iraq long have been forced to hide their identity.

Nevertheless, many Iraqi native groups have survived, including the three Syriac-speaking or Chaldo-Assyrian peoples: the Assyrians, Chaldeans, and Syriacs. These groups share a similar identity and are distinguished by their Christian denomination: Most Assyrians associate with the Assyrian Church of the East, Chaldeans identify as Catholics, and Syriacs belong to the Syriac Orthodox Church.

Despite historic persecution, Muslims and Christians typically have lived peacefully together. Christians and Jews were regarded by Muslims as "People of the Book," and they were given a degree of religious tolerance by the Muslim regimes so long as they accepted the hegemonic rule of the Muslim sovereigns.

Iraqi society today encompasses a multitude of ethnic groups and diverse religious sects. The current Iraqi constitution, approved in November 2005, declared Iraq an Arab nation but recognized other indigenous groups, including Assyrians, Chaldeans, Kurds, and Turkmen, as well as smaller religious and ethnic minorities such as

Armenians, Mandaeans, Shabaks, and Yazidis. A large Chaldean community resides in Ankawa, close to Erbil, the capital of the Iraqi Kurdistan region; they are represented in both the Kurdish regional government and the Iraqi central government. Arabs constitute about 75 percent of the population and live mainly in middle and southern Iraq. The Kurds make up approximately 20 percent of the population and live in the north.

The majority of Iraqis are Shi'ite Muslims, who constitute about 60 percent of Iraq's population. However, the situation for Christians in Iraq has deteriorated since the U.S. invasion of the country in 2003, a result of threats by terrorist groups and Islamic fundamentalists who associate Iraqi Christians with the West. As a consequence, about a quarter million Iraqi Christians have left the country.

KURDISH GENOCIDE

The Kurdish people, numbering approximately 30 million, live in the mountainous region at the intersection of four nation-states: Iran, Iraq, Syria, and Turkey. They are culturally and linguistically distinct from Arabs, Persians, and Turks and adhere to the Sunni Islam faith.

Denied their own homeland after the collapse of the Ottoman Empire in the early twentieth century, the Kurds today are ethnic minorities within larger states, where they consistently have been abused and repressed. The Kurdish genocide was a mass murder committed against the Kurdish people of northern Iraq by the regime of Saddam Hussein during the final years of the Iran-Iraq War (1980–1988).

During the war, the Kurds of northern Iraq sided with Iran. Iraqi dictator Saddam Hussein tasked his cousin, Ali Hassan al-Majid, leader of the northern bureau of the ruling Baath Party, with the job of eradicating all resistance and granted him emergency powers to do so. What began as a counterinsurgency measure during wartime resulted in genocide.

Al-Majid undertook a series of eight military campaigns against Kurdish "saboteurs" from 1987 to 1989. The Anfal campaigns occurred over a large swath of Kurdish-inhabited northern Iraq; they were divided into eight distinct military operations, all of which shared the same objective—elimination of the Kurds. As part of these campaigns, which were known collectively as Operation Al-Anfal (Arabic for "the spoils"), Al-Majid employed a variety of chemical weapons, including mustard gas, a blistering agent, and Sarin (also known as BG), a nerve agent. His penchant for this method of extermination earned him the sobriquet "Chemical Ali."

The campaigns consisted of direct attacks on Kurdish militants and civilian populations, the razing of villages, the assembly of Kurds at collection points for transit to prison camps in the desert, the separation of the Kurdish population by gender, and the execution of fighting-age males. Replacement of the Kurdish population in key cities and around oil fields by Arabs also was effectuated. By the end of the campaigns, 1.5 million Kurds had been forcibly resettled. Between 100,000 and 200,000 Kurds had died by the close of military operations.

The most dramatic act undertaken during the Anfal campaign was the gassing of the Kurdish city of Halabja. On March 13, 1988, Iranian forces began shelling Iraqi military positions in and around Halabja, and by March 15, Iranian advance forces were already in the streets of the city. Local Kurds did not resist the Iranian advance; in fact, Kurdish militants facilitated it. Saddam Hussein's forces counterattacked the next day, first with napalm—stripping away huge areas of the city and citizens with massive firestorms—then with conventional bombs and artillery, and finally with gas.

The gassing of Halabja is widely considered the single most horrific incident that occurred during this notorious period, accounting for approximately 5,000 Kurdish deaths. Another 7,000 Kurds were wounded, crippled, blinded, or suffered other injuries related to the bombings. Consequently, Halabja has become emblematic of the Kurdish genocide, as Srebrenica is for the Bosnian genocide or Auschwitz for the Jewish Holocaust.

Michael J. Kelly

Today, fewer than half of Iraqi Christians still live in Iraq, while others live in Iran, Syria, Turkey, and elsewhere throughout the world, mainly in Australia, Europe, and the United States. It is estimated that about a half million Iraqi Christians live in the United States, mainly in Chicago, Detroit, and San Diego. Historically constituting about 3 percent of Iraq's population, in 2012, they accounted for less than 2 percent, living mainly in the regions of Baqhdaida (also called Hamdaniya or Qaraqosh), Sheikhan, and Telkaif in Nineveh Province of northern Iraq. Adherents of the Mandaean and Yazidi religions in Iraq also have been the targets of extreme Islamist groups, whether Sunni or Shiite, that aim to eliminate them or destroy their places of worship, their shops, and even their homes.

The exodus of thousands of Iraqi minorities since April 2003 could mean the end of many ancient ethnic and religious communities in Iraq. Many are fearful that these minorities will face a fate similar to that of Iraqi Jews, who fled Iraq in the 1940s following the creation of the state of Israel and sentiments against Zionism. Granting autonomy to the Chaldo-Assyrians in northern Iraq might be a solution to their exodus and may offer a way for Iraq's indigenous people to endure and to help Iraq preserve its diversity.

Shak Hanish

See also: Groups: Europe—Armenians. *Groups: South Asia and Middle East*—Assyrians; Chaldeans. *Issues*—Migration.

Further Reading

Aziz, Mahir A. *The Kurds of Iraq: Ethnonationalism and National Identity in Iraqi Kurdistan.* New York: I.B. Tauris, 2011.

Lalani, Mumtaz. *Still Targeted: Continued Persecution of Iraq's Minorities.* London: Minority Rights Group International, 2010.

Morony, Michael G. *Iraq After The Muslim Conquest.* Piscataway, NJ: Gorgias, 2005.

Rear, Michael. *Intervention, Ethnic Conflict and State-Building in Iraq: A Paradigm for the Post-Colonial State.* New York: Routledge, 2008.

Tripp, Charles. *A History of Iraq.* Cambridge, UK: Cambridge University Press, 2007.

Israel

Located on the eastern shore of the Mediterranean Sea and bordering Egypt and the Gaza Strip, Jordan and the West Bank, Lebanon, and Syria, the state of Israel is home to more than 7.75 million people, the majority of which (5.8 million) are Jewish. Although Israel has been a sacred site for Jewish people for nearly 4,000 years, political instability brought on by a steady stream of foreign conquerors has been a regional norm for nearly two millennia.

As Jews returned to their homeland in the early twentieth century, thus challenging and undermining Palestinian regional claims to the region, Israel declared independence in 1948, sparking seven decades of violence and heated debates over who are the region's "true" indigenous people: Jews or Palestinians? This dispute underscores the overarching territorial clashes that continue to destabilize what many consider to be the biblical homeland.

The beginning of Israeli nationhood can be traced to 1800 B.C.E., the year of the Hebrews' entry into Canaan, a region that roughly corresponds with modern-day Israeli and Palestinian territories. Canaan was occupied by Israelite tribes again in 1200 B.C.E. upon their return from Egypt, and for the next nine centuries, various conquerors, including the Assyrians, Babylonians, Persians, Greeks, and Romans, overwhelmed the region. Many contemporary scholars argue that, despite this political instability, the Jewish state never quite disappeared, even after Jerusalem was conquered by the imperial Roman legions following the great Jewish revolt of 70 C.E.

A massive Jewish presence maintained a decades-long resistance, which ended in 135 C.E. at the hands of the Romans, who exiled most Jews after a second unsuccessful revolt at Masada. The remainder retreated to northern Israel, which eventually was overwhelmed by the Islamic Cavalry and a succession of conquerors. The newly minted province of Syria Palestine remained a Roman territory until 390, after which it was renamed Palestine.

For the Jews, the final blow came during the twelfth-century Christian Crusades, which resulted in their near eradication. During the next ten centuries, a succession of foreign conquerors entered and left the region, including the Byzantines, Persians, Arabs, Crusaders, Mongols, Turks, and Britons. Israel, however, remained the Jewish homeland in mind and spirit, despite the diaspora (dispersal) of Jews throughout the Middle East and Europe.

Enduring hopes for a return to Jerusalem led to the formation of the modern Zionist movement to reestablish a Jewish nation in the late nineteenth century. Zionist leaders' faith was bolstered when in 1917 the British government, which then controlled Palestine, pledged to support such a proposal. During the next three decades, the Jewish community in Palestine grew from 85,000 to 650,000, while incurring the wrath of Arab landowners for their haphazard settlement models. In response, British authorities attempted to restrict immigration to Palestine, but an armed Jewish resistance and the public brutality of the Holocaust during World War II led to international calls for an independent Jewish state. This eventually compelled British authorities to withdraw their immigration restrictions.

On November 29, 1947, the United Nations General Assembly adopted a plan to divide Palestine into two economically united but politically sovereign states, one Jewish and one Arab. Jerusalem would act as an international city, physically uniting the two states. Jews accepted the plan in 1948, but Arabs and their Arab League allies—Egypt, Iraq, Jordan, Lebanon, Saudi Arabia, and Syria—resisted. A subsequent war left Israel in possession of a larger territory, which, in turn, forced hundreds of thousands of Palestinians to flee. A seven-decade conflict followed—and continues to this day—leaving the region in a state of armed preparedness.

The United Nations Declaration on the Rights of Indigenous Peoples (UNDRIP), ratified in 2007, crystallized the debates over the precise nature of sovereignty in Israel that have resulted in decades of bloodshed and animosity. Although the Bedouins often are identified as Israel's indigenous people, they largely are ignored in the nation's political sphere. The UNDRIP's flexible guidelines permit both Palestinians and Israelite Jews to claim status as the region's true indigenous peoples.

On one hand, Jews cite a biblical territorial connection that embraces a common religion, heritage, and language, all linked to a historical occupancy that never ended despite diminished population numbers. One the other hand, Palestinians, more recent immigrants to the region by comparison, cite nearly two millennia of territorial occupancy and a noteworthy regional governing authority following the Jews' almost complete ouster in the twelfth century. Several UNDRIP articles detail the criteria by which indigeneity is to be acknowledged, although various articles appear to allow both the Israelite Jews and the Arabs to claim indigenous status.

The current state of Israel continues to be mired in conflict, reflecting a 2,000-year regional history of political and social discord. The UNDRIP draws these issues to fore while raising important questions about the length of occupancy needed to assert territorial sovereignty and the role of outside agents in establishing the rules guiding these processes. In Israel's case, it also compels the creation of critical and chronologically accurate histories to help shed light on and help answer these questions. Nevertheless, it appears that a resolution will not be forthcoming soon, and for now, the status quo will remain.

Yale D. Belanger

See also: *Groups: Europe*—Jews, European. *Groups: South Asia and Middle East*—Palestinians. *Issues*—International Policy; Land Rights; United Nations Declaration.

Further Reading

Beilin, Yossi. *Israel: A Concise Political History.* New York: St. Martin's, 1993.

Ben-Ami, Shlomo. *Scars of War, Wounds of Peace: The Israeli–Arab Tragedy.* New York: Oxford University Press, 2006.

Frank, Mitch. *Understanding the Holy Land: Answering Questions About the Israeli-Palestinian Conflict.* New York: Viking, 2005.

Sachar, Howard M. *A History of Israel: From the Rise of Zionism to Our Time.* 2nd ed. New York: Alfred A. Knopf, 1996.

Seddon, David. *A Political and Economic Dictionary of the Middle East.* New York: Europa, 2004.

Japan

Japan is made up of four main islands—Hokkaido, Honshu, Kyushu, and Shikoku—along with more than 7,000 smaller islands in the Japan Archipelago, stretching across some 1,900 miles (3,000 kilometers). In January 2010, 124.8 million people lived in Japan, more than 75 percent of them in urban areas.

The Japanese frequently have claimed that they are an ethnically and racially homogenous people and have emphasized the purity of their blood. In reality, however, modern Japanese are a mixture of various ethnic and racial groups. They include Southeast Asians, who arrived in the Japan Archipelago some 30,000 years ago as the first wave of migrants; East Asians, who migrated to the region later; and the Ainu, the indigenous people of Japan who originate in the northern part of the country. In addition, Japan incorporated diverse populations through its colonization of surrounding territories: Ezo (present-day Hokkaido) in 1873, Ryukyu (now Okinawa) in 1879, Taiwan in 1895, and Korea in 1910.

The current population of indigenous peoples in Japan is unknown, but it is estimated that more than 4 percent of the Japanese population is made up of minorities, including Ainu, *burakumin* (outcasts), Koreans, and migrant workers. The Ainu and Okinawans (also known as Ryukyuans) are the two indigenous groups in Japan, although the Ainu people have achieved greater recognition as an indigenous people than the Okinawans.

After the Meiji Restoration in 1868, when imperial rule was reestablished, Japan sought to expand its territory, and a period of aggressive colonization followed. Hokkaido, Japan's northern island, had been inhabited by the Ainu until the Japanese established settlements in the southwestern corner of the island during the Edo period (1600–1868). In 1873, the Meiji government declared the territory imperial land and appropriated most of the island to former samurai, who became pioneers in northern Japan. Along with the influx of Japanese settlers came diseases, deforestation, and a near depletion of deer and salmon, the traditional staples of the Ainu diet.

In 1899, the Meiji government enacted the Hokkaido Former Aborigines Protection Act. The measure, which was inspired by the 1877 Dawes Act (also called the General Allotment Act) in the United States, provided free land grants of up to 15,000 *tubo* (equivalent to approximately 12 acres/5 hectares) for Ainu who engaged in agriculture—with the provision that they had to give up their fishing and hunting rights in exchange for the land. As the traditional lifestyle of the Ainu centered on fishing and hunting instead of farming, the law was part of an assimilation policy that aimed to destroy the Ainu way of life and transform the people into farmers.

In the late 1960s, the Ainu, following the lead of international indigenous movements, began to engage in cultural revival. The Hokkaido Ainu Association, established in the 1930s by the Hokkaido prefectural government, has played a central role in Ainu activism. One example of the association's success is its protest of the building of Nibutani Dam, the construction of which would have submerged an Ainu holy site. In 1997, the Japanese District Court ruled in favor of the Ainu, claiming that the construction of the dam without regard for the impact on local indigenous people would violate the International Covenant on Civil and Political Rights, adopted by the United Nations in 1966. In the same year, the Japanese government overturned the Hokkaido Former Aborigines Protection Act and passed a law to promote the Ainu culture and tradition.

Okinawans followed the lead of the Ainu and became more active in claiming their human and indigenous rights. Okinawans demanded from the Japanese government an official apology for the forced annexation of Okinawa in 1878, recognition as an indigenous people, protection of Okinawan culture, and a revision of the U.S.–Japan Security Agreement. The most hotly debated issue is the presence of U.S. military bases, as 75 percent of the facilities are concentrated in Okinawa Prefecture. Okinawans view the U.S. military presence as a form of discrimination, which they are forced to accept due to the U.S.–Japan Security Agreement, which no other group has to do.

Since the 1990s, the Japanese government has taken steps to increase the protection of its indigenous peoples. In 1991, Japan finally recognized the Ainu as an ethnic minority, although it did not recognize them as an indigenous people. Partly in response to international criticism of its discriminatory treatment of indigenous peoples and its unwillingness to actively engage in human rights protection, the Japanese government ratified three major conventions in the 1990s: the Convention on the Elimination of All Forms of Racial Discrimina-tion, the Convention on the Rights of the Child, and the Convention against Torture. It also reformed its policy on minority groups—*burakumin* (former outcasts), Koreans, Ainu, and migrant workers—gradually adopting programs to support native cultures. One of the most significant developments was the government's recognition of the existence of indigenous people in the country. On June 6, 2008, the Japanese Diet unanimously adopted the Resolution Calling for the Recognition of the Ainu as an Indigenous People.

In spite of the policy change and increased support for indigenous peoples, there is still a broad gap between the lives of mainstream Japanese and indigenous peoples, especially in the areas of economic development and education. In 2006, for instance, the average per capita income of all Japanese was approximately 3.07 million yen (about $25,800), while that of Okinawans was about 2.09 million yen (about $17,600). As for the Ainu (23,782 people in 2006), the average household income was only 62.2 percent of the average for the total population of Hokkaido, the prefecture where the majority of Ainu live.

Azusa Ono

See also: *Groups: East Asia and Oceania*—Ainu; Okinawans. *Issues*—Land Rights.

Further Reading

Karan, Prayumna P., ed. *Japan in the 21st Century: Environment, Economy, and Society.* Lexington: University Press of Kentucky, 2005.

Lie, John. *Multiethnic Japan.* Cambridge, MA: Harvard University Press, 2001.

Siddle, Richard. *Race, Resistance and the Ainu of Japan.* London: Routledge, 1996.

Sugimoto, Yoshio. *An Introduction to Japanese Society.* 2nd ed. Cambridge, UK: Cambridge University Press, 2003.

Weiner, Michael, ed. *Japan's Minorities: The Illusion of Homogeneity.* 2nd ed. London: Routledge, 2009.

———, ed. *Race, Ethnicity, and Migration in Modern Japan: Imagined and Imaginary Minorities.* London: Routledge, 2004.

Kenya

Kenya is an East African nation that sits just south of the Horn of Africa on the Indian Ocean. It shares a border with Ethiopia and Somalia in the north, Uganda in the west, and Tanzania in the south. It contains fertile highlands, lowland plains, and some of the highest mountains in Africa—the highest, Mount Kilimanjaro, lies just south of its border with Tanzania.

Archaeologists and scholars have described Kenya—and East Africa more generally—as the birthplace of humankind. A former British colony named for Mount Kenya, the country is home to some forty-two ethnic groups that make up its population of 40 million. Though migrants from other parts of Africa were Kenya's original inhabitants, Arabs, Europeans, and Indians also lived in the country following years of trade and painful colonization. Kenyans today are a mix of African, Arabic, European, and Indian cultures.

History of the Native People of Kenya

Archaeological evidence suggests that people have inhabited the region that is now Kenya for more than 20 million years, though it is not known who the early people were. Khoisan hunters and gatherers once lived in the Rift Valley, southwest of Nairobi, but it is unclear whether they remained there. Nevertheless, according to historical records, permanent settlers—Cushitic speakers from southern Ethiopia, Bantu-speaking people from West Africa, and Nilotic peoples from Sudan—began migrating to Kenya after 500 B.C.E. These groups settled in different parts of the country, concluding their migration between the tenth and eighteenth centuries. Today, these peoples make up two-thirds of Kenya's population.

Because of Kenya's strategic location near the Indian Ocean, Arab, Indian, and Persian traders and sailors often visited the region to conduct business. One result of this trade was the introduction of Kiswahili, a language that combines Arabic and Bantu dialects. In fact, the word *swahili* comes from the Arabic *sawahil,* meaning "coasts" or "shores." Today, Swahili is one of two official languages in Kenya (the other is English). A second result of this cultural mix was the development of a rich coastal civilization. But Kenya's proximity to the Indian Ocean also brought misfortune to its native peoples, making it a stopover for explorers and colonizers from Europe and Oman.

The Portuguese were the first Europeans to arrive in Kenya in 1498, led by explorer Vasco da Gama. Initially, the Portuguese went in search of trade, but following Da Gama's successful voyage to India, they sought to control the sea routes linking Europe to Asia. Ruling East Africa from the coastal regions, they built Fort Jesus at Mombasa in 1593 to solidify their position. But the Portuguese faced opposition from other Europeans and, especially, from Omani Arabs. Following their defeat at the hands of the Omani Arabs in 1698, the Portuguese left Kenya, and the Omanis assumed control of the region's coastal areas. Slavery and trade characterized their rule from 1700 until the 1880s, when Great Britain and Germany seized several key ports and forged alliances with local leaders beyond the coast. Kenya became a colonial protectorate of Germany in 1885 before the British took over in 1888.

Kenya officially became a British protectorate in 1895. The manner in which the British assumed control created hostile relations between colonial authorities and the native people. The Kenyans simply were told that a great king who lived in a land overseas was now their ruler and the owner of their lands. Though Ke-

A woman in drought-stricken eastern Kenya bemoans the loss of her last goat. "The life of the pastoralist is over," she said. Chronic lack of rainfall, population growth, land erosion, and civil unrest are likely to deepen the food crisis across East Africa. *(Mike Goldwater/ Getty Images)*

nyans resisted, their force was no match for the British military. The colonial government showed little regard for the rights of the indigenous Kenyans, and, in a bid to raise funds to build a railway and to establish a cash crop economy, they encouraged British citizens to settle in Kenya. Greedy for land, a series of labor and land laws were implemented that gave 30,000 white settlers control of more than 8 million acres (3.2 million hectares) of productive land at the expense of the native people.

The indigenous Kikuyu and Maasai peoples bore the brunt of the British policies. Many Kenyans became squatters on their own lands, with more than 1 million Kikuyu restricted to only 2,000 square miles (5,180 square kilometers). By 1953, almost half of the Kikuyu people could not lay claim to any land at all. The British settlers also instituted a hut tax and paid little to nothing for labor. As they could no longer farm and increasingly were suffering from poverty and starvation, many Kenyans relocated to urban areas to survive.

Following years of oppression by white settlers, in 1952, the Kikuyu united with other ethnic groups to form a nationalist resistance movement known as the Mau Mau Rebellion. In October of that year, the uprising turned violent when a senior chief was shot. Governor Evelyn Baring declared a state of emergency, and two weeks later, the first European was killed.

By 1956, more than 20,000 Mau Mau fighters had been killed by British troops, in addition to those tortured and killed by white settlers and Kenyans loyal to the colonists. Today, the Kenyan government estimates the total number of Mau Mau casualties at 90,000. For their part, the Mau Mau fighters killed only twenty-six Europeans. In 2006, ten Kenyans sued the British government for the atrocities that they suffered in the hands of the British during the clampdown.

Current Status and Government Indigenous Policy in Kenya

Currently in Kenya, Bantu speakers, including the Kamba, Kikuyu, and Luhya, make up the majority of the population; Nilotic speakers, including the Maasai and Turkana, are the second-largest group; and they are followed by Cushitic speakers, including the Booran, Gabra, and Somali. While Kenya has no official policy toward its native people, the government has created programs to encourage the Maasai people, one of the oldest cultures in Kenya, to abandon their seminomadic life.

At the same time, Kenya's native peoples have had a difficult time securing their land rights, as noted in a 2007 report by the United Nations (UN) Special Rapporteur on Indigenous Issues. The country's herding, forest-dwelling, and hunter-gatherer tribes have little political power, and their lands have been repeatedly taken by the government and government-backed companies, threatening their traditional lifeways. Although the UN report resulted in the government proposing a new land policy for its native peoples, the country's largest landowners have, as of 2012, been able to derail any progress toward guaranteeing the land rights of Kenya's native peoples.

Aje-Ori Agbese

See also: Groups: Africa—Kikuyu; Luhya; Maasai; Turkana. Issues—Colonialism; Revolts.

Further Reading

Elkins, Caroline. *Imperial Reckoning: The Untold Story of Britain's Gulag in Kenya*. New York: Henry Holt, 2005.

Miller, Norman, and Rodger Yeager. *Kenya: The Quest for Prosperity*. 2nd ed. Boulder, CO: Westview, 1994.

Radcliff, B.J. "The Spelling of Kenya." *Journal of the Royal African Society* 42.166 (1943): 42–44.

Sayer, Geoff. *Kenya: Promised Land?* London: Oxfam International, 1998.

Laos

Laos is a landlocked country located in mainland Southeast Asia, sharing borders with Cambodia, China, Myanmar, Thailand, and Vietnam. It is one of the least densely populated countries in Asia, with an average of approximately 60 people per square mile (23 people per square kilometer).

Laos's population of approximately 6.4 million people comprises forty-seven ethnic groups that officially are divided into four broad groups: Lao Lum, or "lowland" Lao; Lao Tai, or "tribal" Tai; Lao Theng, or "Lao of the mountain sides"; and Lao Sung, or "Lao of the mountain tops" (who are further divided into Meo and Yao peoples).

The Lao Lum are the dominant group in Laos, making up 68 percent of the population. Of Tai stock, they reside mainly in the Mekong River Valley. Across the border in Thailand, the Lao Lum number approximately 5 million. The Lao Tai, who belong to the same linguistic group as the Lao Lum, reside mainly in the northern mountainous region between the Mekong and Red rivers; they number approximately 35,000.

The Lao Theng, a Mon-Khmer people that were among the earliest migrants to Laos, number approximately 150,000. Among the upland Lao Theng, the

Khma and Lamet reside on the mountain slopes of the north, while the Bru, Loven, and So are found in the southern part of the country.

The Lao Sung migrated to Laos from southern China in the mid-nineteenth century and settled on lands at altitudes above 3,000 feet (915 meters). The Meo of this group number approximately 60,000, and the Yao number approximately 5,000. The Meo practice shifting cultivation and reside in scattered villages atop the mountains; they are the largest producers of opium. When these people move from one village to another, terrain suitable for poppy cultivation is their criterion for selecting land.

Despite attempts by the Laotian government to estimate population statistics, there is no clear-cut ethnic demarcation among these peoples. In addition, Buddhism has been blended with elements of indigenous religious practices, Hinduism, and traditions from neighboring countries. Thus, many people identify with more than one ethnic or religious group. Approximately 2 percent of the people of Laos adhere to Christianity, Islam, and other religions.

Other ethnic minorities in Laos also inhabit the nation's mountainous region. Tribes such as the Akha, Lolo, and Luhu live close to the Burmese and Chinese borders. The Lolo-speaking mountain villagers, of Chinese descent, are called Ho in the Lao language. Numbering approximately 66,000, the Akha tribal people reside in the same areas as the Lolo, primarily in the provinces of Luang Namtha and Phong Saly in Laos, as well as in Yunnan Province in China and in adjacent parts of Vietnam. The Alak people, numbering about 4,000, live in the Saravan and Sekong provinces, while the Akeu, numbering approximately 1,000, reside in Phong Saly Province.

The tribal groups of Laos gradually are assimilating into the mainstream population. However, the nation-building process has been complicated by the presence of so many tribes. The fact that Laos's many ethnic groups are divided by language, culture, location, and political affiliations compounds the problem.

Patit Paban Mishra

See also: *Groups: East Asia and Oceania—Lao. Issues—Assimilation.*

Further Reading

Burke, Andrew, and Joe Cummings. *Laos.* London: Lonely Planet, 2007.

Mishra, Patit Paban. *A Contemporary History of Laos.* New Delhi, India: National Book Organisation, 1999.

Schliesinger, Joachim. *Ethnic Groups of Laos: Sino-Tibetan Speaking People.* Bangkok, Thailand: White Lotus, 2004.

Libya

Libya is a North African nation situated along the Mediterranean Sea, sharing borders with Algeria, Chad, Egypt, Niger, Sudan, and Tunisia. Covering an area of approximately 680,000 square miles (1.8 million square kilometers), most of the country lies within the Sahara Desert.

Since the February 2011 uprising that ousted and killed the country's leader, Muammar Qaddafi, Libya has come under sharp focus internationally for its mode of political governance, which is perceived as nondemocratic and dictatorial from the Western liberal standpoint.

In light of the secretive and authoritarian rule of the Qaddafi years and the chaos that characterized the country following his overthrow, specific demographic data for Libya are difficult to come by. In 2011, Libya had an estimated population of about 7 million people. Most Libyans (97 percent) belong to two main ethnic groups, Arabs and Berbers; the rest of the population comprises people of Egyptian, Greek, Indian, Italian, Maltese, Pakistani, Tunisian, and Turkish origin.

Berbers are the largest native group in the country, living not only in Libya but also in many nations across North Africa. Other West African minorities inhabit southern Libya, including the Tebu and Tuareg peoples. Although many of these groups have converted to Islam, they also maintain a syncretic belief system that retains many of their pre-Islamic practices.

Arabic is the country's official language, but English and Italian also are spoken in the major cities.

History

The trade that flourished on the Mediterranean Sea some 3,000 years ago brought Phoenicians, among other groups, into contact with Berbers, who already occupied the region and thus had an advantage over those wishing to establish trading cities on the coast of now. Libya. From the sixth through the fourth century B.C.E., the Greeks were eager to extend the frontiers of their empire by setting up colonies in Cyrenaica (now Libya), which was then part of the Berber kingdoms. The region also attracted the Romans, who conquered the North African kingdom of Carthage and renamed it Tripolitania, folding it into the Nova Africa province of the expansive Roman Empire. The tumultuous history of Libya did not end with the Roman incursion, however; Vandals invaded in 431 C.E., and in the sixth century, the region was taken over by the Byzantines.

The Arab conquest of most of North Africa, including Libya between 643 and 647 C.E., introduced the Arabic language and Islamic religion to the region. Northern Libya was ruled by successive Muslim dynasties, including the Omayyad, Abbasid, Aghlabid, Tulunid, and Fatimid. In 1551 C.E., the Turks invaded Libya and made it part of the Ottoman Empire, but the fortunes of the province remained the same—it remained poor, on the periphery of economic development.

Libya came under European colonial dominance following the 1911 Italian invasion, which was framed as a philanthropic gesture to free Libyans from the misrule of the Ottoman Turks. The Ottoman provinces of Cyrenaica and Tripolitania were among the last territories to be claimed in the European scramble for Africa. Libyan anticolonial resistance under the reformist Muslim brotherhood (*tariqa*) known as Sanūsīyah troubled the Italians until 1931, when Sheikh Omar al-Mukhtar, a leading figure in the opposition guerrilla movement, was captured and executed. To bring the fighters under control, Italian colonial authorities executed or forced approximately 750,000 people (half of the Libyan population) into concentration camps.

The outbreak of World War II fundamentally changed the political landscape, however, and led to the decline of Italy's fortunes in the region. The Sanūsīyah allied with the British in 1942 to drive out the Italian forces. After the war, Cyrenaica and Tripolitania were handed over to Great Britain, while the French occupied Fezzan (now southwestern Libya). Under the terms of the 1907 Hague Convention, Libya continued to be governed as an occupied enemy territory in what was generally described as a "care and maintenance" arrangement.

Independence and After

Libya attained political independence in 1951 after the United Nations (UN) established a federation of Cyrenaica, Fezzan, and Tripolitania under King Idris I. At the time, Libya ranked as one of the poorest countries in the world, with an estimated annual per capita income of $35, and it was prone to ethnic rivalries. Perhaps as a gesture of gratitude and in recognition of the need to stabilize the economy, the king signed agreements with Great Britain in 1953 and the United States in 1954 that allowed those nations to established military bases in Libya in exchange for these nations providing financial and military assistance to his regime.

Foreign companies took advantage of the strong Western presence in the country to explore oil extraction beginning in the mid-1950s. In 1961, a huge oil reserve was discovered and quickly exploited, transforming the economic outlook of the nation. Oil revenues, which amounted to $3 million in 1961, rose to $1.2 billion by 1969. Libya soon became the second-largest producer of oil among the Arab nations and the sixth-largest producer globally. Although Libya appeared to benefit from the oil boom, in reality, only the political class profited, and institutionalized corruption wreaked havoc in the country. Libyans residing in rural areas remained trapped in abject poverty.

The rise of pan-Arab nationalism across the region precipitated the overthrow of the king by the "Free Officers" movement on September 1, 1969, led by Colonel Muammar al-Qaddafi, who declared Libya an Arab republic. In what Qaddafi christened a "revolution," the government successfully negotiated with the oil companies to raise the price of oil and to reduce limits on production so as to maximize profits. The change of policy increased oil revenues, which, in turn, were invested in the improvement of infrastructure, construction, and importation of consumer goods.

During Qaddafi's rule, political parties were banned; in their place, so-called peoples' authorities were established to run the country's affairs. Although there was opposition to Qaddafi's style of leadership and his policies, such opposition was largely fragmented, because it was forced to operate from outside the country.

Within Libya, native identities were discouraged in favor of a unified Arab identity. The 1969 constitution defined Libya as an Arab state, and Libyan law prohibited the use of languages other than Arabic and even the registration of Berber names for children. Berbers were denied Libyan citizenship and access to the basic necessities of life, including clean water, adequate housing, and education.

Increasing oppression of the Berber community took place. Berber cultural organizations were banned, and the people faced physical abuse, imprisonment, and even death for asserting their Berber identity. In May 2005, Libyan Berbers asked for the assistance of the United Nations Commission on Human Rights to address the Qaddafi regime's violations of their linguistic and cultural rights. UN requests for more information on the Qaddafi regime's treatment of Berbers and other minorities went unanswered. Amnesty International brought to light discrimination against the Tebu people, who were arrested by Qaddafi's army and evicted from their homes in the city of Kufra and other regions in southern Libya.

The overthrow and execution of Qaddafi on October 20, 2011, brought the prospect of change, but Libya's future was far from clear. In 2012, the native peoples remained in limbo, uncertain as to what type of government would emerge from the chaos and what policies Libya's new leaders would implement for the country's native populations.

Hannington Ochwada

See also: Groups: Africa—Berber. *Issues*—Colonialism; International Policy; Revolts.

Further Reading

Hawting, G.R. *The First Dynasty of Islam: The Umayyad Caliphate A.D. 661–750.* 2nd ed. New York: Routledge, 2000.

Qaddafi, Muammar. *The Green Book.* Ottawa, Canada: Jerusalem International, 1983.

Vandewalle, Dirk. *A History of Modern Libya.* New York: Cambridge University Press, 2006.

Madagascar

The Republic of Madagascar is located in the Indian Ocean approximately 250 miles (400 kilometers) off the southeastern coast of Africa. It is the fourth-largest island in the world.

The island has a total landmass of approximately 227,000 square miles (587,927 square kilometers), with areas of high elevation and a number of lakes. Some of the mountains are well over 8,000 feet (2,438 meters).

The country experiences two distinct climatic seasons: The hot rainy season runs from November to April, while the dry and much cooler season runs from May to October. The southeast trade winds often bring cyclones. Madagascar boasts an abundant mixture of flora and fauna, including many unique species due to its geographic isolation. It also is known for its tropical rain forest in the eastern part of the country.

The population of Madagascar consists of Malagasy peoples of African, Arab, Indian, and European descent, along with small populations of Comorans and South East Asians. This mix results in a rich culture that combines these influences. The national languages of Madagascar include both Malagasy, a tongue of Malayo-Polynesian origin, and French. The dominant religion is Christianity, primarily Catholicism and Protestantism, although Buddhism also is practiced.

Madagascar's economy is centered on fishing, forestry, and agriculture. While the traditional food staple is rice, the country's main exports include cloves, cocoa, coffee, sugarcane, and vanilla; other common crops are bananas, beans, and cassava. Tourism, textiles, and mining also help support the economy.

The first known settlers on Madagascar were Bantu-speaking Muslim peoples from neighboring Mozambique, who arrived around 200–500 C.E. and set up trading posts there. Other early settlers included Arabs and Indians.

The Portuguese explored the island in the early sixteenth century but did not establish settlements. This prompted both England and France to stake claims to territory in Madagascar. By the nineteenth century, Madagascar was ruled by a native monarchy, but this came to an end in 1883, when French troops began to occupy the island. Madagascar became a protectorate of France in 1895, after which the native monarchy was abolished, and French was adopted as the island's official language.

Madagascar took part in World War II by sending troops to fight the Nazi regime in France, Morocco, and Syria. The Nazis briefly sent Jews from Europe to Madagascar, a project known as the "Madagascar plan." After France fell to the Nazis, Great Britain occupied Madagascar as a precaution to protect the island from German advances, but the British relinquished the island after the Allied forces freed France in 1944.

As France recovered from the war, the people of Madagascar staged a yearlong uprising against the French government, eventually gaining control of the island. The new French constitution of 1946 made Madagascar an overseas territory of France. In 1958, the island nation declared itself an autonomous republic.

Today, Madagascar is divided into six autonomous regions. Since the departure of the French, the republic has seen numerous coups and disputed elections, with power regularly changing hands from one group to the other, most recently with a coup staged by the mayor of the capital city of Antananarivo, Andry Rajoelina of the Tanora Malagasy Vonoma (Young Malagasies Determined) party.

Madagascar remains one of the poorest nations in the world, and much of the native Malagasy population lives abject poverty, often relying on food aid from international bodies, especially when cyclones hit the island. For example, when three cyclones struck the island in 2006–2007, over 78,000 people were left homeless and destitute.

The World Bank has been instrumental in implementing reforms to assist Madagascar's economic growth during the 2000s. These reforms have included privatization programs and the establishment of export processing zones, as well as the promotion of foreign aid and investment in the Madagascar economy, however, progress has been slow.

Franklyn Taylor

See also: Issues—Colonialism; Poverty.

Further Reading

Allen, Philip M. *Madagascar: Conflicts of Authority in the Great Island.* Boulder, CO: Westview, 1995.

Brown, Mervyn. *Madagascar Rediscovered: A History from Early Times to Independence.* Hamden, CT: Archon, 1979.

Malawi

Malawi is located in southeastern Africa, occupying a narrow strip of land in the Great Rift Valley along Lake Nyasa (also called Lake Malawi). Covering an area of approximately 46,000 square miles (119,000 square kilometers), the country borders Tanzania to the northeast, Mozambique to the east, south, and west, and Zambia to the northwest.

Malawi's population of 15.4 million people is made up of many different ethnic groups, including the Chewa, Lomwe, Ngonde, Ngoni, Nyanja, Sena, Tonga, Tumbuka, and Yao, as well as people of Asian and European heritage. Approximately 80 percent of Malawians are Christian, while 13 percent are Muslim, and 8 percent adhere to other religious beliefs.

Malawi is primarily an agricultural country, producing cassava, corn, cotton, macadamia nuts, peanuts, potatoes, pulses, sorghum, sugarcane, tea, and tobacco. The people also keep cattle, goats, pigs, and poultry as livestock. In addition, the country has some deposits of bauxite, coal, and uranium that remain unexploited.

Precolonial and Colonial Periods

When the British colonized the region in the late nineteenth century, they named it the Nyasaland Districts Protectorate. After independence in 1964, the country was renamed Malawi, for the Maravi Confederacy of Bantu speakers that existed in the region from approximately 1480 to the early 1700s.

The Maravi people dispersed with the arrival of Arab traders and European capital in the eighteenth century. Commercial activities intensified competition among the local polities, which sought to benefit from the lucrative trade in ivory, iron, and slaves. The Yao, living to the south and east of Lake Nyasa, began to rival the Maravi middlemen in the long-distance trade to the Indian Ocean coast as they sought direct access to the Arab and Portuguese traders on the coast.

By the beginning of the nineteenth century, slaves were the most single important trade commodity on the market. Toward the close of the 1880s, Yao chiefs became involved in the slave-hunting expeditions that depopulated the region, resulting in economic instability. It is clear from extant Christian missionary accounts that the arrival of Europeans in the region coincided with the peak of the slave trade. Missionary David Livingstone catalogued the horrific experiences of the slaves in his

travelogues, and the reports that he sent home encouraged European nations to be proactive in occupying the region and conducting "civilizing missions."

Encouraged by early Christian missionaries to come to the region, Europeans arrived in droves as evangelists and colonists. Scottish missions and their supporters lobbied the British government in 1889 to forestall Portuguese and Swahili interests there. On June 11 of that year, an Anglo-Portuguese convention was reached that established the Nyasaland Districts Protectorate as a British territory. The convention followed on the heels of an expedition led by António Maria Cardoso to the area of Lake Nyasa to explore territorial interests for Portugal in southern Africa.

Colonial rule was met with stiff resistance from the Chewa, Ngoni, and Yao people. Citing the way in which Europeans employers treated African laborers, John Chilembwe, a beneficiary of missionary education in the United States, organized an uprising against the British in 1915 during which a plantation was attacked, leaving several people dead. Chilembwe organized another uprising, but he quickly was intercepted by the colonists and killed.

The uprisings did not stop British incursion into the region. Instead, Great Britain moved with speed to consolidate colonial rule in Malawi during the 1920s and 1930s. Thereafter, numerous cash-crop plantations, including coffee, tea, and tobacco, flourished under the *thangatha* system of forced labor system and the tax systems that were put in place to compel Africans to seek employment in the colonial economy. Because of the country's strict labors laws and fiscal system, many Africans were forced to migrate elsewhere in southern African countries to find work. At the same time, migration denied European plantation owners in Malawi the labor they desired. Paradoxically, however, the money that migrants remitted to their families in Malawi became an important source of revenue for the protectorate.

After World War I, the British colonial administration changed its approach, invoking a policy of indirect rule. Because of the small number of European settlers in the protectorate, the government employed traditional local headmen and chiefs as their loyal servants in administration. African elites in Malawi seized the opportunity to form pressure groups called "native associations" to improve their conditions by engaging in a dialogue with the colonial administrators. By the 1930s, the colonial administration had become wary of these associations and tried to prevent them from getting direct access to the governor by vetting their agendas before they were forwarded.

Throughout the 1930s, the associations pressed for representation in the Legislative Council, higher wages, and a more just tax system for Africans. Thus, in their attempt to appease and pacify the associations, the colonial government encouraged Africans to produce cash crops. Toward the end of World War II, following the formation of the Nyasaland African Congress (NAC) in 1944, Africans began to talk about independence as an imminent possibility and about more far-reaching changes in the governance of the country. The return of Hastings Kamuzu Banda—who had represented the Nyasaland African Congress at the Pan African Congress in Manchester, England, in 1946—from West Africa in 1958 boosted the fortunes of the NAC.

Banda reorganized the NAC by helping it refine its program of action. For instance, he challenged the government to institute reforms in agriculture, conservation, education, health, the thangatha system, and bicycle taxes, among others. Fearing rebellion, the governor declared a state of emergency on March 3, 1959, banned the NAC, and detained Banda without trial. The commission of inquiry set up by the colonial government to investigate the incident later indicted the governor for overstepping his mandate. Banda was released from prison and appointed to lead the Malawi Congress Party, which became the fulcrum of the independence struggle.

Modern Malawi

After Malawi achieved independence on July 6, 1964, Banda became prime minster; that title was abolished in 1966, and he was made president until 1994. However, poverty continued to plague the country, as it relied chiefly on subsistence agriculture and had not yet discovered mineral deposits to boost its economy. Moreover, the cash crops were dominated by European settler farmers, and Malawi's education system and infrastructure remained underdeveloped. The international community was skeptical about the chances for Malawi's survival as an independent nation.

In the early years following independence, Malawi relied heavily on foreign aid, specifically from Great Britain. Despite this, the country's leadership under Banda sought to wean itself from British budgetary dependence by encouraging Africans to produce their own cash crops. Under Banda's leadership, the government also developed the country's infrastructure to facilitate the transportation of crops from rural areas for export. Despite these measures, Malawi's economy remained troublesome.

Banda proclaimed himself president for life in 1971 and outlawed all other political parties except his Malawi Congress Party, thus tightening his grip as dictator. During his tenure, he encouraged close associates and ministers in his government to acquire land for agriculture at the expense of the peasant farmers. In spite of his autocratic rule, Banda also was a staunch supporter of capitalist development and encouraged foreign capital investment from Great Britain, South Africa, Taiwan, and the United States. However, the eclipse of leadership came in 1992 when Catholic bishops circulated a pastoral letter that criticized Banda and his government and the international community prevailed on Banda to institute multiparty democracy in Malawi. A referendum held in 1993 gave the country a mandate to reintroduce pluralism.

In the elections held in 1994, Banda lost the presidency to Bakili Muluzi of the United Democratic Front. Muluzi ushered in an era of political and economic liberalism. However, the new government was faced with many social and economic challenges, including high consumer prices, inadequate health care, and difficulties in meeting its people's most basic needs. In 2004, after Muluzi had exhausted his two presidential terms, Bingu wa Mutharika was elected president; he still held the office as of mid-2012.

Hannington Ochwada

See also: Groups: Africa—Yao. Issues—Agriculture; Colonialism; Revolts.

Further Reading

Gilman, Lisa. *The Dance of Politics: Gender, Performance, and Democratization in Malawi*. Philadelphia: Temple University Press, 2009.

Lwanda, John Lloyd. *Kamuzu Banda of Malawi: A Study in Power, Promise, and Legacy*. Zomba, Malawi: Kachere, 2009.

Ross, Andrew C. *Colonialism to Cabinet Crisis: A Political History of Malawi*. Zomba, Malawi: Kachere, 2009.

Malaysia

The country of Malaysia is divided into two noncontiguous regions: Peninsula Malaysia, encompassing the Malay Peninsula (called Malaya), an extension of mainland Asia, and East Malaysia on the island of Borneo (also known as Borneo Malaysia), which is part of the Malay Archipelago. The Malay Peninsula is bisected by the Titiwangsa Mountains, which extend approximately 300 miles (480 kilometers) from north to south, dividing the peninsula into eastern and western coastal regions.

The eastern side of the peninsula, which faces the South China Sea, is a sparsely populated region that is home to several groups of indigenous peoples, most of whom live in remote villages in the tropical rain forests.

The western side faces the Strait of Malacca and the Indonesian island of Sumatra. With level plains that are heavily farmed, this side is home to most Malaysians, many of whom live in cities. The extreme southern tip of the peninsula is connected to the city-state of Singapore by a causeway and bridge. Borneo Malaysia comprises the states of Sabah and Sarawak, which together occupy just over one-quarter of the island. (The rest of the island is occupied by the sultanate of Brunei and the four Kalimantan provinces of Indonesia.)

There are approximately ninety-five distinct native groups in Malaysia. Many of these groups are quite small, and most reside in the Sarawak region, which is the northern region of Borneo. Together, the groups in Sarawak are known as Orang Ulu; the largest subgroups are the Kajang, Kayan, Kenyah, Penan, and Ukit. In the Sabah region, on the northeast tip of Sarawak, there are thirty-nine groups making up the native population, called the Anak Negeri.

On the Malay Peninsula, the Orang Asli are the largest indigenous group with an estimated population of 150,000. Once forest-dwelling hunter-gatherers, they are believed to be descended from the original inhabitants of the peninsula. The Orang Asli typically are divided into three groups: the Proto-Malay or aboriginal Malay are located in the southern region of the Malay Peninsula; the Negrito (Semang) usually are found in the northern region; and the Senoi reside in the central region. Many Orang Asli live in remote areas of the rain forest, following their traditional way of life, and a few have been untouched by modern civilization. Some have been converted to Christianity or Islam.

Linguists classify the languages of the Orang Asli into two families: Austro-Asiatic and Austronesian. Most Orang Asli speak Aslian languages, which belong to the Mon-Khmer branch of the Austro-Asiatic family. They are the only people in the world who speak these languages. They also are called by a variety of names, referring to eighteen ethnic subgroups that are identified by languages and customs.

Malaysia is a federal constitutional monarchy organized into thirteen states and three federal districts (Kuala Lumpur, Labuan, and Putrajaya). Nine of Malaysia's states continue to be ruled by hereditary sultans, who every five years choose from among their number a king or paramount ruler (*yag di-pertuan agong*), whose role is

Malaysian plantation workers harvest oil palm fruit, the source of palm oil—a hot export commodity. Malaysia is a major producer, but the government has promoted sustainable development to protect the interests of indigenous peoples and the environment. *(Yuli Seperi/Getty Images)*

largely ceremonial. Executive and legislative power in the government is vested in the prime minister and an elected parliament, respectively.

History of the Malaysians

The first people arrived in Malaysia approximately 40,000 years ago, evidenced by archaeological remains found in the Niah Caves of Sarawak. Small groups are believed to have migrated to Malaysia from southern China. Approximately 2,500 years ago, trade brought a number of people, particularly Indians, to the area.

Sometime after 1000 B.C.E., the ancestors of the Malays moved into Malaysia, part of a group that traveled by sea from southern China to Taiwan, the Philippines, and Borneo. They are thought to have come from Sumatra, spreading across the Malay Archipelago and into the Philippines during ancient times.

Beginning in the fifteenth century, Malays began to convert to Islam, as Arab traders in the region influenced their rulers to accept the religion. The Malay sultanates later would arise from these conversions. (Today, most Malays are Muslims.)

Europeans began to arrive not long thereafter, with the Portuguese arriving in the sixteenth century, the Dutch in the seventeenth century, and the British in the eighteenth century. By the end of the nineteenth century, the British controlled the entire peninsula. They developed Malaysia's tin mining and rubber industries and controlled the region until the Japanese occupied it during World War II. Although the British regained Malaysia after the war, support for independence began to grow. A guerilla army began to push for the British to leave, succeeding with the establishment of the Federation of Malaysia in 1957.

Despite independence, racial tensions between the native Malay majority and the economically advantaged Chinese and Indian populations continued. The conflict finally sparked a race riot on May 13, 1969, in which 200 people were killed, mostly Chinese. In the aftermath, the government implemented its New Economic Policy, which was essentially an affirmative action program aimed at providing advantages to Malays and other native groups over immigrant ethnic groups. Much of that policy remains in force today.

Malaysia's Native People Today

Out of Malaysia's total of 28.6 million people, native peoples currently represent about 12 percent of the population. Most of the nation's indigenous people reside in Borneo Malaysia, representing two-thirds of the people of Sabah and half of the population of Sarawak. Sabah and Sarawak have a combined population of about 5 million people, a great many of whom live in the capitals of Kota Kinabalu (Sabah) and Kuching (Sarawak).

Spurred by the technology boom of the late twentieth century, tens of thousands of Indonesians have immigrated to Malaysia to work in new industrial plants. The Malaysian government distinguishes migrant workers from Bumiputras, or "sons of the soil," a designation that includes both Malays and native people but excludes Chinese and Indians. The term first was used as part of the 1969 New Economic Policy.

The policy has contributed to significant economic prosperity among Malays. However, non-Malay native groups in Sarawak, Sabah, and the Malay Peninsula tend to face discrimination in such areas as religion, language, education, and employment. In both Sarawak and Sabah, the rights of the native peoples to their land are enshrined in law. But those laws are often ignored by the government in the interest of plantations and corporate interests, intent on extracting the land's natural resources.

In fact, although the Sarawak and Sabah groups have received recognition of their land rights, the Malaysian constitution does not recognize linguistic or religious differences but instead insists that all Malaysians speak Malay and are Muslim. The country's many non-Malay native groups struggle to maintain their religions and lifeways; in these efforts, they have been aided and protected by a variety of nongovernmental organizations. Since the native peoples constitute a majority of the population of Malaysian Borneo, some observers have suggested that they may grow discontent with domination from Peninsular Malaysia and seek independence.

Andrew J. Waskey

See also: *Groups: East Asia and Oceania*—Malay. *Issues*—Economic Development; Land Rights; Language.

Further Reading

Battersby, Paul. *To the Islands: White Australia and the Malay Archipelago Since 1788*. Lanham, MD: Lexington, 2010.

Heng, Derek. *Sino-Malay Trade and Diplomacy from the Tenth Through the Fourteenth Century*. Athens: Ohio University Press, 2009.

McAmis, Robert Day. *Malay Muslims: The History and Challenge of Resurgent Islam in Southeast Asia*. Grand Rapids, MI: William B. Eerdmans, 2002.

Milner, Anthony. *The Malays*. Oxford, UK: Wiley-Blackwell, 2011.

Munoz, Paul Michel. *Early Kingdoms of the Indonesian Archipelago and the Malay Peninsula*. Barrington, IL: Continental Sales, 2006.

Syukri, Ibrahim. *History of the Malay Kingdom of Patani*. Athens: Ohio University Press, 1985.

Mexico

Mexico's indigenous population comprises approximately 12.5 million people, comprising at least 11 percent of the country's total population, speaking eighty-five languages. Despite this, the country has a history of disregarding its multiethnic populace. It was not until the revision of the Mexican constitution in 1992 that the Mexican government officially recognized that "[t]he Mexican nation has a multicultural composition, stemming originally from its indigenous communities" and, further, that "the law will protect and promote the development of their languages, cultures, usages, customs, resources and specific forms of social organization."

Mexico's native population is divided unevenly between two cultural and geographic areas. The first area, Mesoamerica, encompasses central and southern Mexico and accounts for 25 percent of the total population of the area. In this area, the state of Oaxaca has the highest number of indigenous people, with 1.12 million, followed by Chiapas with 810,000, Veracruz with 634,000, Puebla with 57,000, and Yucatán with 549,500. The second area, Aridamerica in northern Mexico, is characterized by a relatively small number of indigenous people. For instance, in Aguascalientes, there are only 1,244 members of indigenous groups. In Baja California, there are 38,000, the vast majority of whom are migrants from Mesoamerica. Chihuahua and Sonora states have 50,000 and 55,600 indigenous people, respectively.

There are marked contrasts between the two populations. The indigenous people of Mesoamerica have been characterized as exemplifying persistence and cultural revitalization, whereas those in Aridamerica are thought to reflect trends toward demographic decline and cultural assimilation. However, the distinction between the two populations also can be explained as a result of the different birth rates of the agricultural and sedentary groups living in middle and southern Mexico, as compared to that of the foraging groups of northern Mexico. The birth rate among the former is three to four times higher than it is among the latter.

Almost two-thirds of the native population in Mexico live in rural areas, such as the traditional Altos de Chiapas, Huasteca, Meseta Purépecha, Mixteca, Montaña de Guerrero, and Sierra Tarahumara regions. Yet these localities also encompass agro-industrial areas to which these populations migrate periodically. This is the case with Baja California, Chihuahua, and Sonora. A minority of the population in that region lives in suburban areas (19

EMILIANO ZAPATA

Emiliano Zapata rose to national fame in Mexico during the Mexican Revolution (1910–1920). A sort of Robin Hood figure, he used deadly force to take land from the wealthy and redistribute it to the poor. Although some critics labeled Zapata a bandit, his unwavering commitment to the cause of the people solidified his legacy as a true revolutionary.

He was born on August 8, 1879, in Anenecuilco, Mexico. Orphaned at the age of seventeen, he trained horses for a living. Fluent in the native Nahuatl tongue and gifted with leadership skills, he led his neighbors in attacks on large landowners. By 1909, Zapata was recognized as a hero among the peasants.

When the Mexican Revolution broke out the following year, Zapata used his influence to propel his agenda of land reform onto the national stage. He joined forces with revolutionary leader Francisco Madero, whom Zapata believed would help his cause, to oust sitting President Porfirio Díaz in May 1911. Late in the war, Zapata teamed up with Pancho Villa to occupy Mexico City. Villa coveted power, whereas Zapata sought to institute reform from the capital. Zapata's national push for land reform was short-lived, however, as Venustiano Carranza, whom the United States had recognized as the legitimate president of Mexico and who considered Zapata a dangerous radical, staged an ambush and had him killed on April 10, 1919.

After his death, Zapata's legend spread across the nation. Peasants reported seeing a dark figure on horseback in the countryside protecting the defenseless. Rural songsmiths wrote and sang *corridos* (narrative songs) in his memory. Historians, poets, and artists crafted stories and images of Zapata. Years later, comic books, television programs, and motion pictures continued to forge his popular image.

Today, many schools, streets, parks, and cities in Mexico bear Zapata's name. Politicians, regardless of party affiliation, pay tribute to the mestizo (mixed Nahua and Spanish ancestry) peasant who is now one of Mexico's most highly regarded national heroes. His name is inscribed with gold letters on a wall in the legislature, and a day of national mourning is observed on the anniversary of his assassination. Arguably, Zapata has been even more influential in death than he was in life.

Rolando Avila

percent) and in large cities, including Cancún, Ciudad Juárez, Distrito Federal, Ensenada, Guadalajara, León, Mérida, and Tehuacán.

Of its eighty-five languages, Mexico's most widely spoken indigenous tongue is Nahuatl, with more than 1.4 million speakers, followed by Maya (796,300), Mixtec (437,900), and Zapotec (421,800). Other languages with significant speech communities are Tzotzil (287,600), Otomí (291,700), Tzeltal (284,800), and Totonac (240,000). At the same time, some native languages in northern Mexico are spoken by very small numbers of people. That is the case with Ko'al, which has no more than 10 speakers, Kiliwa with 17, and Cocopah with 178. These three languages, all spoken by inhabitants of the northern part of the Baja California Peninsula, have been officially designated as endangered languages.

Despite their differences in traditional territory (sedentary people in Mesoamerica and nomadic people in Aridamerica) and in subsistence strategies (agriculture in the former and hunting and gathering in the latter) all of the indigenous groups in Mexico today have been incorporated into the sedentary agricultural communities that were promoted by the government following the Mexican Revolution (1910–1920). These settlements were established as a kind of social property, known as *bienes ejidales* or *bienes comunales* (community property). For that reason, at least three-fourths of the indigenous male population in Mexico works in agricultural activities.

Furthermore, because of the lack of irrigation systems, desert climate, and marshy or mountainous terrain of the indigenous lands, farming in these areas is limited, seasonal, and oriented primarily toward subsistence agriculture. As a result, Indian settlements in Mexico remain mired in extreme poverty, characterized by extremely low incomes, the need to use child labor and elderly workers, and the absence of social security, health services, or any kind of labor rights.

At the same time, the native peoples of Mexico historically have been the target of discrimination and racism, having been stigmatized as backward and unproductive. In response, the indigenous population has demanded limits on land tenure and on culturally insensitive applications of the law. They also have worked to preserve their native languages and have lobbied for respect for indigenous practices and traditional customs and the end of stigmatization. In addition, they have asked for self-government and territorial autonomy.

However, the Indian movement in Mexico faces many barriers and setbacks. One is the long-standing state control of indigenous organizations, combined with government paternalism, manipulation, and corruption. Corruption became evident after the Mexican Revolution, when the government began to assimilate indigenous organizations and traditional authorities by imposing on them new forms of organization associated with the official political party. These actions led to feuds among the Indian populations and disputes among their authorities, which competed for government recognition and a larger share of economic benefits. Such conflicts at the labor, ethnic, and political levels have made it difficult for the native populations to become a solid organization and coherent movement.

Despite these difficulties, the Indian peoples of Mexico have been able to develop important organizations outside the state structure. In contrast to some traditional organizations that were absorbed by official structures, other entities that were created by the government went on to become autonomous organizations. Some seventy-three Indian organizations represent a specific ethnic group—such as the Comité de Solidaridad Triqui, or Triqui Solidarity Committee, which represents the Triqui people of western Oaxaca. Others represent several ethnic groups, specific communities, or regions. A few remarkable organizations cut across ethnic groups to provide national representation, including the Coordinadora Nacional de Mujeres Indígenas (National Coordination of Indigenous Women) and the Congreso Nacional Indígena (National Indigenous Congress). In addition, various organizations seek to voice and redress specific economic, territorial, cultural, and human rights grievances. All of these organizations and their ongoing efforts demonstrate the growth of the national indigenous movement in Mexico.

Everardo Garduño

See also: *Groups: Central and South America*—Chontal de Oaxaca; Mixtec; Nahua. *Issues*—Colonialism; Revolts; Social Discrimination.

Further Reading

Martínez-Torres, María Elena, Rosaluz Pérez Espinosa, and Aldo González Rojas. "Mexico." In *The Indigenous World 2008*, ed. Katherin Wessendorf. Copenhagen, Denmark: International Work Group for Indigenous Affairs, 2008.

Schmal, John P. *Indigenous Mexico: A State-by-State Analysis.* Austin: Texas Education Agency, 2006.

Weinberg, Bill. *Homage to Chiapas: The New Indigenous Struggles in Mexico.* New York: Verso, 2002.

Morocco

Morocco is located in North Africa, part of the Maghreb region that borders the Mediterranean Sea, together with Algeria, Libya, Mauritania, and Tunisia. It lies directly across the Strait of Gibraltar from Spain. Morocco's population includes a large number of Arab Berbers, descendants of the region's indigenous nomadic peoples.

As early as Neolithic times (8000 B.C.E.), present-day Morocco was populated by nomadic peoples collectively known as Berbers or Imazighen (singular Amazigh) that spoke an Afro-Asiatic language. The Berbers settled in the area between the Siwa Oasis (in modern western Egypt) and Morocco. The Greeks and Phoenicians had established colonies in the region by the ninth century B.C.E., and Semitic peoples began arriving there in the seventh century B.C.E.

The most important Berber tribes of the Maghreb were the Awarba, Berghwata, Houaras, Kutama, Masmouda, Sanhadja, and Zenata, all of which were independent and had the authority to make territorial decisions. As reported by the fourteenth-century Arab historian Ibn Khuldun in the *Muqaddimah* (1377), the Berbers were a powerful and numerous people. Ancient authorities such as the Roman author Apuleius, the father of the Catholic Church Saint Augustine of Hippo, and the Muslim traveler Ibn Battuta all were of Berber origin.

Islamic Conquest, Independence, and Berber Kingdoms

Before the Islamic conquest of North Africa in the seventh century C.E., Morocco was dominated, in turn, by the Romans, Vandals, Visigoths, and Byzantines. In 670, Uqba ibn Nafi, a general of the Omayyad caliphate, arrived in Morocco and occupied the region, forcing the conversion of the Berbers and introducing Arab customs and traditions.

A century later, Idrīs I (Idrīs ibn 'Abd Allāh)—a descendant of the Prophet Muhammad—founded the first independent dynasty in the region, which ruled from 789 until 921. The Idrīsid dynasty, as it was known, with its capital at Fez, stood apart from the Abbasid caliphate of Baghdad and the emirate of Al-Andalus in Moorish Spain. Morocco's strategic geographic position permitted the Idrīsid dynasty to promote the Islamization of North Africa and its Berber population, beginning after the last Amazigh uprising led by Maysara al-Haqir in 740. Battles against the province of Tlemcen gave the Idrīsid state access to the Atlas Mountains, allowing it to become the most powerful dynasty in Morocco.

Defeated by the Fatimid dynasty of North Africa, the last Idrīsid reign was dominated by the caliphate of Cordoba. However, the decline of the Idrīsid set the stage for the emergence of other Arab Berbers dynasties such as the Almoravids (1040–1147) and the Almohads (1121–1269). The Idrīsids were ousted from power by the Al-Andalus caliphate, but a crisis sparked by infighting during the first half of eleventh century saw their decline and the rise of the Almoravids of Marrakesh, who would capture Islamic Spain, though conflict would continue with the Christian kingdoms of the north. The Almoravids were a Moroccan Berber dynasty, a federation between the tribes of Lamtuna and Sanhaja that conquered Ghana, Mauritania, and Senegal and decelerated the Christian *reconquista* (reconquest) in Spain by defeating the Christian armies at the Battle of az-Zallaqah in 1086.

As the Almoravids penetrated sub-Saharan Africa, the Berber dynasty of the Almohads, born in Morocco, with their capital at Marrakesh, conquered all of North Africa, reaching Libya and occupying the southern part of Al-Andalus; Seville became the capital of the Almohad dynasty in Spain. The line originated with Ibn Tumart, a member of the Masmuda, a Berber tribe of the Atlas Mountains of Morocco. Holding heterodox religious beliefs, Ibn Tumart represented a revolt against what he perceived as anthropomorphism in the Muslim orthodoxy. It was under the Almohads that Moroccan Berbers reached a golden age of theological, juridical, and artistic achievement. It is under this dynasty that the great philosopher, Averroes, lived. Defeated by the Christian kingdoms in Spain, in 1213 they were attacked and annihilated by the Banu Marin (Marinid dynasty) in North Africa.

Contemporary Integration

The Berber tribes that still remain in Morocco are the Riffians (in the Rif Mountains), Saharians, Shilha, and Zayanes. Under the French mandate (1912–1956), the colonial government of Morocco, the Berber Dahir (decree), which was a legislative adaptation of Berber justice for the contemporary age, was promulgated. Sultan Muhammad (r. 1956–1961) and his son, King Hassan II (r. 1961–1999), used it as the basis of their rule.

Upon independence, the process of integration between the Arab intelligentsia and the Berber nation ameliorated. Today, Berbers represent 40 percent of the Moroccan population. In the early twenty-first century, the level of juridical equality between Arabs and Berbers has improved under the reign of King Mohammed VI (r. 1999–). This has included the preservation of Berber culture and dialects, and the establishment of the Equity and Reconciliation Commission (IER) mandated to investigate the nearly 10,000 alleged human rights violations during Hassan II's rule.

Marco Demichelis

See also: *Groups: Africa*—Berber. *Issues*—Colonialism; Indigenous Governments.

Further Reading

Abun-Nasr, Jamil M. *A History of the Maghrib in the Islamic Period*. New York: Cambridge University Press, 1987.

Brett, Michael, and Elizabeth Fentress. *The Berbers*. Oxford, UK: Blackwell, 1996.

Hoffman, Katherine E., and Susan Gilson Miller. *Berbers and Others: Beyond Tribe and Nation in the Maghrib*. Bloomington: Indiana University Press, 2010.

Mozambique

Mozambique, located on the eastern coast of southern Africa, is home to a number of native peoples, including the Chopi, Lomwe, Makonde, Makua, Nguni, Sena, Shona, Tongo, Tsonga, and Yao, as well as many smaller ethnic groups of southern African origin. In 2012, 99 percent of the estimated 19 million Mozambicans residing in the country claimed African ancestry; individuals of European, Euro-African, and Indian descent make up the remaining 1 percent.

Portuguese is the country's official language, although many Mozambicans also communicate in Swahili. Other languages in use include Makua, Muchope, Ronga, and Tsongan. Mozambicans practice traditional religions alongside Catholicism, Christian Zionism, and Islam. Despite a long colonial history and the adoption of syncretic religion, Mozambicans have retained many elements of their native languages and cultures.

History of Native Peoples

Early Bantu-speaking cultures likely migrated to present-day Mozambique from west-central Africa during the third century C.E. By the eleventh century, the Shona had established an empire in the area between the Limpopo and Zambezi rivers and dominated commerce until the arrival of Arab traders at the port of Sofala 100 years later.

Citizens of the Mutapa kingdom (1430–1760), a Shona Karanga state, for example, attempted to regulate trade between the sixteenth and eighteenth centuries, understanding that trade routes were a crucial element of political power in the region. The Karanga built *madzimbabwe*, or large stone houses, wherever they settled and enjoyed a high standard of living compared to the groups they conquered. However, a lack of unity among the Karanga aristocracy, as well as political pressure from the Portuguese, caused the people to fracture into smaller groups by the end of the eighteenth century.

During the eighteenth and nineteenth centuries, coastal Mozambique hosted several trading sites, from which native peoples departed en route to South Africa or Brazil, where they were sold as slaves. As ships carrying human cargo traveled from farther up the East African coast, as well as from Asia, native Mozambicans interacted with the traders, creating a diverse culture along the coastal zone. The invasion and colonization of the area by Soshangane, a Northern Nguni chief from present-day South Africa, contributed to the intermingling of peoples. Arab and European traders, initially looking for gold, remained in the area after failing to discover the mineral. They believed that Mozambique would become an important through-point, connecting coastal Africa with the interior and southern Africa with points farther north.

Portuguese traders and colonists left extensive written records, though they rarely referred to the native peoples using specific ethnic terms or vocabulary. Colonists from Portugal commonly called all Mozambicans "Karanga" rather than distinguishing among the area's diverse ethnic groups. This may have reflected the dominance of the Karanga in the sixteenth-century Shona region but also indicated an unwillingness or inability on the part of the Portuguese to understand the complexities of local ethnic identities. The use of names such as Shona or the subgroup Ndau gained currency around the late nineteenth century, as Europeans began to acknowledge the diversity of peoples in Mozambique and viewed tribal identity as a means to divide the African peoples into more governable units.

During this time, Africans, too, began to define themselves by their common culture, language, and histories rather than political identity or chieftaincy. Historians and ethnographers have argued, however, that Mozambique's many cultures evolved throughout centuries of common linguistic and cultural development. European missionaries often employed the evolving ethnic terms to set the scope of their work, limiting their activities to a particular ethnicity or residents of a particular area. As language became a more important means of categorization to Europeans, Africans increasingly used these terms as well.

Mozambique became one of the longest-ruled colonial states in Africa, remaining under Portuguese control until 1975 and serving as the important through-route that Arab and European colonizers had envisioned. After the country achieved independence, most residents of European descent left Mozambique, leaving a largely African population. The country engaged in a civil war from 1975 until 1990, its politics linked closely to the struggle against apartheid in South Africa and elsewhere in southern Africa. Mozambique again served as a nexus for liberation movements in South Africa, Rhodesia (now Zimbabwe), and Southwest Africa (now Namibia) as they swept across the region and into neighboring Tanzania.

As the process of liberation continued in southern Africa, Mozambicans developed a strong African identity and rejected their colonial past. Although ethnicity and individual cultures remain important today, the emphasis is on creating a cohesive national identity among the native peoples.

Indigenous Policy

Mozambique remains one of the world's poorest countries. Massive flooding during the early twenty-first century destroyed many homes, businesses, and cultural centers. The rise of migrant labor in southern Africa has led to more frequent intermarriage among members of different tribes and the diminishment of distinct ethnic identity in favor of a larger pan-African identity. This social transition was perpetuated during the civil war, when Mozambicans tended to align with leaders along political rather than ethnic lines.

According to the country's 1990 constitution, all Mozambicans have full legal protection, regardless of national origin. The constitution outlines the official use of Portuguese but also notes that Mozambicans may use languages that are important to their ethnic identities. Despite a lack of overt government policies in support of the country's native peoples, Mozambique's government has addressed concerns regarding the preservation of indigenous languages and cultural identities.

Myra Houser

See also: Groups: Africa—Shona; Yao. *Issues*—Colonialism; Poverty.

Further Reading

MacGonagle, Elizabeth. *Crafting Identity in Zimbabwe and Mozambique.* Rochester, NY: University of Rochester Press, 2007.

Ndege, George O. *Culture and Customs of Mozambique.* Westport, CT: Greenwood, 2007.

Newitt, M.D.D. *A History of Mozambique.* Bloomington: Indiana University Press, 1995.

Theall, George McCall. *History and Ethnography of Africa South of the Zambesi, from the Settlement of the Portuguese at Sofala in 1505 to the Conquest of the Cape Colony by the British in 1795.* Cambridge, UK: Cambridge University Press, 2010.

Myanmar

Myanmar, also known as Burma, is located in Southeast Asia on the Bay of Bengal. It shares a border with India and Bangladesh to the west, China to the north, and Laos and Thailand to the east. The country existed as an independent kingdom until Great Britain annexed the region as part of its colony of India in 1886. Burma gained Commonwealth (self-government) status in 1937. During World War II, the country was invaded and controlled by Japan for a time before being restored to the British as a Commonwealth in 1945.

Burma achieved independence in 1948. The country became known as Myanmar after a military junta known as the State Peace and Development Council took control in 1988. However, opponents of the junta (which finally relinquished power in 2011) and most of the Western nations, including the United States, do not officially recognize the name change and continue to call the country Burma.

Myanmar's population is approximately two-thirds Burman, with the remainder made up of some 135 distinct non-Burman indigenous groups. The largest non-Burman groups are the Arakan, Chin, Kachin, Karen, Karenni, Mon, and Shan.

History of Indigenous Strife

Myanmar has had difficulty establishing a stable government since it achieved independence, as many indigenous groups desire independence themselves. Ethnic conflicts precipitated military coups in 1962 and 1988, and human rights abuses and atrocities against the country's indigenous people have occurred throughout its modern history. Forced labor, forced relocation, torture, rape, and murder all were documented by the United Nations in 2004.

In addition, Myanmar is among the world's poorest nations. The civil wars that have raged between the non-Burman groups and the Myanmar Army have only exacerbated the situation, resulting in widespread death, disease, and poverty.

The Karen, numbering approximately 7 million, are among the largest indigenous groups in the country. They reside in southern Myanmar and in neighboring regions of Thailand. The mythology and history of the Karen are filled with persecution, as they have been discriminated against by powerful outsiders for most of their collective memory. Until the last decades of the twentieth century, most Karen lived as separate groups and did not recognize a common identity.

Forced Labor, Torture, and Indigenous Burmans

Like members of other native groups in Myanmar, many Karen have been forced into labor, often in one of the world's largest remaining teak forests. At one time, Myanmar was also the site of some of the largest virgin rain forests found in mainland Asia, home to such animal species as Asian rhinoceros and Asian elephants, as well as the forest-dwelling indigenous peoples. Indeed, at the beginning of the twentieth century, forests covered an estimated 80 percent of the country; by the early 1990s, the figure had shrunk to approximately 36 percent.

Despite this extensive deforestation, as of 1994, Myanmar still held 80 percent of the world's remaining natural teak; by the end of that decade, it was one of the only countries in the world that still permitted commercial-scale teak harvesting. The nation has continued to allow an average of more than 3,000 square miles (8,000 square kilometers) of forest to be destroyed annually, the third-highest rate in the world, after Brazil and Indonesia. The destruction of the teak forests, along with other environmentally harmful practices, has resulted in flooding and drought in parts of the country.

Human rights activists have also collected evidence of torture being inflicted on Myanmar's native peoples laboring in the teak forests. In March 1997, Karen in the village of Min Tha—women, children, and the elderly among them—were forced to harvest teak by soldiers from the Myanmar Army; those villagers who did not comply were beaten. According to reports by EarthRights International and the U.S. Embassy in Rangoon, slave labor also was used in the 1990s to construct a natural gas pipeline. This project was owned by a multinational consortium that included the French oil company Total, the U.S. oil company Unocal, and state-owned energy companies from both Thailand and Myanmar.

Forced labor finally was outlawed by the nation's military junta in October 2000, but the Human Rights Watch organization accused the regime of continuing the practice. Even with the end of the junta's rule in 2011, the situation facing Myanmar's indigenous groups remained dire.

Especially devastating were natural resource extraction projects and land loss at the hands of the army. Because most indigenous people in Myanmar still make their living off the land, practicing subsistence farming, hunting, or fishing, the environmental damage has caused widespread famine. Such issues have the potential to derail any progress made by the new government in overcoming the nation's history of poverty and ethnic strife.

Bruce E. Johansen

See also: *Groups: East Asia and Oceania*—Burmese. *Issues*—International Policy; Oil and Mineral Rights.

Further Reading

Brown, David. *The State and Ethnic Politics in South-East Asia.* New York: Routledge, 1994.

Miley, Misty. *An Introduction and Overview of the Situation of Indigenous Peoples in Burma.* Chiang Mai, Thailand: Indigenous Peoples Human Rights Defenders Network, 2008.

Namibia

Located in southwestern Africa, the country of Namibia is relatively large in terms of its geography—with an area equivalent to the U.S. states of Texas and Louisiana combined—but small in population, with some 2 million inhabitants. Namibia is home to a diverse mix of peoples that are differentiated along ethnic and linguistic lines.

The Ovambo people constitute the country's largest ethnic group, comprising approximately half of all Namibians. The remainder of the population includes those identifying themselves as Afrikaner, Baster, Damara, German, Herero, Himba, Kavango, Mafwe, Nama, San, Subia, and Tswana. Though some historians categorize all or most of these groups as "native" to Namibia, only the Himba and the San are, in fact, indigenous to the region.

Until the sixteenth century, most of the territory that constitutes present-day Namibia was uninhabited. In part, this was attributable to the region's extremely dry climate—the country is the driest south of the Sahara Desert—a fact that has limited human settlement. Most archaeologists and historians believe that until the end of the first millennium, Namibia was populated by small groups of San hunter-gatherers.

Approximately 500 years ago, the territory began to take shape as a point of contact for the migrating peoples of the African subcontinent. At that time, southern-migrating Oshivambo speakers settled in the far northern part of the territory, while Otjiherero-speaking pastoralists migrated to the central region. From the south, the first Khoikhoi-speaking (Nama) peoples arrived in the seventeenth century, followed in the early nineteenth century by so-called Oorlam commando groups. The Oorlam were a mixed group of people forced northward by the expansion of the Cape Colony in present-day South Africa. In the midst of all of this migration and movement, the San hunter-gatherers were forced deeper into the Kalahari Desert.

Germany occupied the region from 1884 until 1915, when South Africa established a settler colony called

South West Africa. A century of colonial and apartheid rule had a profound impact on ethnic identities and consciousness within the country, precipitating cohesion among the region's previously disparate ethnic groups. For example, in the 1890s, Otjiherero speakers were a set of dispersed and poorly connected kinship groups, but by the 1920s, they had come to form a collective identity as Herero. In the mid-twentieth century, South Africa's apartheid regime institutionalized ethnic and racial classifications as a means to divide and dominate all Namibians.

After a thirty-year armed struggle, Namibia gained independence from South Africa in 1990. Since then, a democratic Namibia has attempted to forge a national identity. In order to unite the country's many disparate ethnic groups under a "Namibian" identity, the government reorganized the state and its institutions, adopted English as the national language, created a national educational system and curriculum, and guaranteed equal rights to all Namibians.

At the same time, the government also has moved to protect the rights of individuals and groups to practice their own native customs. Thus, Namibia formally

A woman of the Himba tribe welcomes visitors for the celebration of Namibian independence in 1990. Descended from the Herero people of the region, the Himba maintain their traditional way of life, belief system, and social structure. *(Alexander Joe/AFP/Getty Images)*

recognizes the customary laws and traditional authority structures (such as chiefs and kings) of the country's different ethnic groups, so long as they do not conflict with the nation's constitution.

The difficult issue of land reform also has figured prominently in Namibian politics since independence. In this matter, the government has attempted to balance group rights to communal land with the interests of private capital and ownership, as well as to redress past injustices through policies of land restoration and redistribution.

In addition to these national concerns, Namibia's ethnic groups are contending with unique issues of their own. For example, the indigenous San communities have struggled against their ever-growing socioeconomic marginalization. Since 1990, the Namibian government and international development organizations have attempted to aid the San by focusing on land and resettlement, education, health, and the creation of economic opportunities. However, the initiatives have yielded few positive results, and the San are continuing a rapid transformation from a group of self-sufficient hunter-gatherers to a highly dependent and impoverished underclass.

In northwest Namibia, the Himba people have been at the center of a controversial proposed project to build a hydroelectric dam on the Kunene River. If constructed, the project would force a number of Himba people off their land and inundate many important ancestral gravesites. Himba leaders have been outspoken in their opposition to the project, garnering much attention and support from international indigenous rights organizations.

In the central part of the country, two other groups of Namibians have been involved in collective struggles over identity and rights. The Baster, an Afrikaans-speaking people of mixed European and African heritage, have been fighting for greater autonomy from the state; as with many other such conflicts, land is central to the debate. Finally, the Herero are pressing ahead with demands for war reparations from Germany. Their claim, which dates to the early twentieth century, alleges that Germany adopted and implemented a policy of genocide against the Herero during the Herero-German War of 1904–1907. Additionally, the Herero have brought a series of civil lawsuits against German multinational firms for allegedly utilizing Herero slave labor during the German occupation of Namibia from 1884 to 1915, when the Germans surrendered to South African troops.

South Africa controlled Namibia under a United Nations mandate, until it was revoked in 1961, and then illegally (under international law) until 1990, when Namibia gained its independence. However, the South African era, characterized by the same apartheid regime that ruled in South Africa proper, left native peoples in

Namibia distrustful of government. Since independence, the Ovambo have held a disproportionate share of power, and other smaller native groups have endured renewed discrimination.

In 2002, Namibia sought to address the problems faced by its native peoples by setting up twelve land boards that have included traditional tribal leadership in their decision making. In 2006, the government downsized a proposed dam to be constructed, after the Himba people protested the impact that it would have on their lands. Namibia appears to have turned a corner in their treatment of their native tribes, though the San peoples have yet to benefit and still face social discrimination by members of other groups.

John T. Friedman

See also: *Groups: Africa—Himba; San (Bushmen). Issues—* Colonialism; Land Rights.

Further Reading

Bollig, Michael, and Susanne Berzborn. "The Making of Local Traditions in a Global Setting: Indigenous Peoples' Organizations and Their Effects at the Local Level in Southern Africa." In *Between Resistance and Expansion: Explorations of Local Vitality in Africa,* ed. Peter Probst and Gerd Spittler. Münster, Germany: Lit, 2004.

Daniels, Clement. "Indigenous Rights in Namibia." In *Indigenous Peoples' Rights in Southern Africa,* ed. Richard Hitchcock and Diana Vinding. Copenhagen, Denmark: International Work Group for Indigenous Affairs, 2004.

Suzman, James. *Minorities in Independent Namibia.* London: Minority Rights Group International, 2002.

Werner, Wolfgang. "The Land Question in Namibia," In *Contemporary Namibia: The First Landmarks of a Post-Apartheid Society,* ed. Ingolf Diener and Olivier Graefe. Windhoek, Namibia: Gamsberg Macmillan, 2001.

New Zealand

New Zealand is an island nation in the South Pacific Ocean, situated some 1,500 miles (2,414 kilometers) southeast of Australia. The largest country in Polynesia, New Zealand consists primarily of two large islands, the North Island and the South Island. After Papua New Guinea and Australia, it has the largest total landmass and the largest population of any country in the Pacific region.

New Zealand's native people are the Maori, a Polynesian people numbering more than 600,000 in a country of 4.3 million people. Like Australia, Canada, and the United States, New Zealand was settled by immigrants from Europe who exploited the lands and resources of the indigenous people.

In the 1950s and 1960s, it appeared that the Maori were becoming assimilated into white (*pakeha*) society and culture. But Maori cultural consciousness began to awaken in the 1970s, a period that became known as the Maori renaissance. Today, Maori people are asserting their legal, political, and economic rights, as well as a remarkable cultural self-confidence. Young Maori are learning the Maori language and culture, while simultaneously preparing for full participation in the nation's economic, political, and civic life.

The Polynesian language spoken by the Maori differs in minor ways from the languages of other Polynesian groups, but it is not so different that other Polynesians cannot understand the basics of the Maori language. Captain James Cook's interpreter, Omai from Tahiti, for example, was able to translate Maori for Cook with limited difficulty, even though Tahitians and the Maori likely had not been in contact for 600 to 800 years. The Maori language, like all Polynesian tongues, is related to Indonesian and Malay, as well as to Micronesian and a large number of languages in New Guinea, Melanesia, and even Madagascar. This language family is known as Malayo-Polynesian or Austronesian.

Early Polynesian Settlement and Culture

New Zealand was the last of the major Pacific archipelagoes to be settled. The earliest settlers in Polynesia reached Fiji, Samoa, and Tonga at least 3,000 years ago. All three island groups have been in more or less constant contact with one another ever since, and together they constitute the original Polynesian homeland. Although these islanders brought their own traditional technologies with them, including the use of obsidian (a type of natural glass) as a cutting blade and the technique of making pots stamped with designs from a comb or fork (known as the Lapita style), it probably was in this part of Polynesia that descendants of these early settlers established something resembling Polynesian culture.

In these island groups, the people developed surprisingly sophisticated navigation skills. Some settlers seem to have sought out, discovered, and intentionally settled in other Polynesian archipelagoes. Historians believe that they reached Tahiti and the Society Islands in about 200 B.C.E., Easter Island about 300 C.E., Hawaii about 400 C.E., and, finally, New Zealand by at least 1000 C.E. According to Maori scholar and activist Ranganui Walker, oral tradition suggests that there were two major migrations, perhaps as early as 800 or 900 C.E., and a more recent migration around 1350 C.E. Whereas

Hawaii, Samoa, Tahiti, and Tonga have warm, tropical, or subtropical climates, New Zealand is more temperate, with much cooler winters, especially on the South Island. Early Maori settlers hunted the large, indigenous flightless bird called the moa, which seems to have been hunted to extinction by 1500.

Maori understand their early history as it is described in oral history accounts and myths that depict several waves of settlers who arrived in the original canoes. Local groups belonged to one or another tribe or *Iwi*, whose members, in theory, descended from one of the several canoe loads of early settlers, marking families as having higher status or rank. Social organization at the local level was organized around the *marae* or communal longhouse, with its carved images of ancestors on boards, posts, and cross-beams. Maori houses were more substantial than those in other parts of Polynesia, with palisaded settlements, richly carved house posts, and boards for walls. Although men on other Polynesian islands carved religious statues and figures, the Maori developed this artistic tradition well beyond other Polynesian groups.

From early times, Maori also carved greenstone (nephrite jade) blades and pendants that marked and symbolized the social status and position of the owner. Most of the greenstone comes from quarries on the South Island. More recently, such pendants also have been carved from beef bone, a material that became available only after contact with Europeans.

Impact of European Settlement

Although Captain Cook mapped and surveyed the coasts of both the North Island and the South Island in 1769, European settlement there did not begin until the 1790s, when whalers and traders began visiting New Zealand frequently. The sailors traded iron and steel tools, as well as guns and other goods, for food, fresh water, and sex with local women. European settlement picked up after 1820. Missionaries arrived soon after 1800, hoping to convert the Maori to Christianity and to control the otherwise lawless sailors and traders, but few Europeans at the time had designs on Maori lands and resources.

In 1839, English politician Edward Gibbon Wakefield helped form the New Zealand Company, whose aim was to form "a perfect English society" for English immigrants to New Zealand, one that would not have the problems and disruptions seen in the Australian colonies, which had been settled by English and Irish convicts. The Company quickly began buying up as much Maori land as possible in order to sell it to English settlers. Forests were cut down in favor of grazing pastures, completely changing the character of the regions.

Protests from the Maori that Europeans were seizing control of their land led the British government to authorize Captain William Hobson of the Royal Navy to draft a document that would protect the rights of the native peoples. With the assistance of his secretary, James Freeman, and a British resident who spoke the Maori language named William Busby, Hobson drafted a formal document that became known as the Treaty of Waitangi, to protect Maori rights. On February 6, 1840, copies of this treaty in both English and Maori were signed by English officials and hundreds of Maori.

The Maori universally understood the treaty as protecting their lands and their resources from appropriation by European settlers. However, despite the best intentions of Hobson and the Maori elders, European settlers continued to arrive, and they sought and often took possession of Maori lands. Fighting over land between Maori groups and white settlers began in 1843. The conflicts, known as the New Zealand Wars (also called the Land Wars), continued until 1872. Maori from competing tribes, often using guns, attacked and killed their rivals, causing great disruption.

During this period, the Maori continued to lose their lands and civil rights, as white settlers ignored the Waitangi Treaty's protections. One problem was that the English and Maori versions of the treaty differed in their meanings—the English version granted sovereignty to the queen of England, while the Maori version suggested more control over land and resources by the chiefs.

The Maori Renaissance

By the early 1900s, white New Zealanders assumed that the Maori eventually would die out or assimilate into white culture. A number of Maori intellectuals had received educations, but these Maori largely provided examples of Maori assimilation.

The half-Maori physician, Member of Parliament, and scholar Sir Peter Buck (Te Rangi Hiroa in Maori) was an exception in that his research helped preserve the knowledge of Maori culture. As a research fellow at the Bishop Museum in Honolulu, later the museum's director from 1936, and sometime professor of anthropology at Yale University, Buck promoted knowledge of Maori traditions, practices, and customs through his many publications, even though it would appear to most that Maori culture was gradually disappearing.

Since 1970, a remarkable transformation has swept New Zealand. Prominent Maori protested violations of the Waitangi Treaty, and in 1975, thousands of Maori participated in a march led by Maori activist Whina Cooper protesting on behalf of Maori land rights. They marched the length of the North Island to the parliament in Wellington and convinced the government to establish the Waitangi Tribunal to review cases and advise the government on ongoing land disputes.

A decade later, the government allowed the tribunal to adjudicate land claims issues. Since that time, the tribunal has helped the Maori lodge many claims against the British Crown—some successful and some not. In 1986, the New Zealand parliament enacted the State Owned Enterprises Act, which further enhanced Maori rights, giving them control over many of the natural resources on their lands, especially the remaining forests.

With these changes came a growing appreciation of Maori culture within both Maori and white society, which resulted in an extraordinary revitalization of Maori language and culture. A nationwide Maori-language education program was established for Maori youth and adults. A new way of managing collectively owned land was set out in the Resource Management Act of 1991, relying heavily on Maori customs and concepts. Today, most important government documents are written in both English and Maori.

Robert L. Welsch and Matthew Dee

See also: *Groups: East Asia and Oceania*—Maori; Moriori; Polynesians. *Issues*—Colonialism; Language.

Further Reading

Best, Elsdon. *The Maori.* Wellington, New Zealand: H.H. Tombs, 1924.

Buck, Peter. *Vikings of the Sunrise.* New York: Frederick A. Stokes, 1938.

Kirch, Patrick Vinton. *On the Road of the Winds: An Archaeological History of the Pacific Islands Before European Contact.* Berkeley: University of California Press, 2000.

Mead, Sidney Moko. *Te Maori: Maori Art from New Zealand Collections.* New York: Harry N. Abrams, 1984.

Orange, Claudia. *The Treaty of Waitangi.* Wellington, New Zealand: Allen & Unwin, 1987.

Walker, Ranganui. *Ka Whawhahi Tonu Matou: Struggle Without End.* Auckland, New Zealand: Penguin, 1990.

Nicaragua

The Central American nation of Nicaragua historically has been peopled by a diverse population encompassing indigenous communities, Amerindians who migrated to the region during precolonial times, West Africans who came to the Americas as slaves, and European settlers, mainly from the Iberian Peninsula during the Spanish colonial period and later from other countries in Europe, particularly Germany. Today, Nicaragua is a nation of approximately 5.6 million people, the overwhelming majority of whom are of mixed heritage.

Some 17 percent of Nicaraguans self-identify as Euro-American, while another 9 percent of the population, residing mostly on the eastern coast of Nicaragua, is Afro-Caribbean. Approximately 6 percent of the population is made up of indigenous peoples. The groups tend to be concentrated in the eastern half of Nicaragua, where they constitute a majority.

Ethnically distinct indigenous communities can be found throughout Nicaragua, although those in the western or Pacific zone are only subtly distinguishable from the dominant population of mestizos (people of mixed European and Indian ancestry). These western communities, descended from farmers who migrated from elsewhere in Mesoamerica, number approximately 100,000. It is difficult for non-Nicaraguans to distinguish these indigenous enclaves from the majority mestizos, as they no longer use their indigenous languages, speaking Spanish instead. However, many groups have maintained their native languages for rituals and social interaction.

The majority of Nicaragua's indigenous population resides in the eastern half of the country, particularly along the Caribbean coast—a region known as La Mosquitia or the Mosquito Coast—and the many rivers in the region. Three distinctive indigenous groups inhabit this area, all descendants of Chibcha groups that migrated there from Colombia and Venezuela in precolonial times: the Miskito, numbering around 150,000; the Sumu-Mayangna, with nearly 10,000; and the Rama, with a population of approximately 5,000 people located in southeastern Nicaragua. In the southeastern region, there are also some 3,000 Garífuna living in several fishing communities, the southernmost location of a people whose villages dot the western Caribbean coastline as far north as Belize.

As a result of the internal colonization policies of the Nicaraguan government in the era of the Somoza family dictatorship (1937–1979), which prioritized economic development above all else, landless mestizo farmers from western Nicaragua relocated to the eastern half of the country, encroaching on indigenous lands. Today, they make up about half of the population of the east.

As in the rest of the Caribbean Basin, eastern Nicaragua was contested territory for the two largest European imperialist powers, Spain and Great Britain. The present situation of the indigenous peoples of eastern Nicaragua must be understood within the context of 450 years of British and Spanish presence and subsequent dominance by the United States since the mid-nineteenth century.

The Impact of Colonialism

During the seventeenth and eighteenth centuries, conflict between Spanish and British imperial interests led to nearly constant warfare. The western Caribbean, or eastern shores of Central America, formed the frontier between the two competing powers. The indigenous peoples of the frontier region were profoundly affected and transformed by the constant warfare. They became both parties to and victims of the long-term conflict between the European powers and, later, North American dominance.

The British ruled the western Caribbean and prevented Spanish occupation and land claims through the Miskito king, with an armed Miskito population doing the actual fighting. This policy of indirect rule shifted to direct rule after the establishment of a British protectorate over the area from 1824 to 1860.

During the 1860s and 1870s, the U.S. government became intent on constructing and controlling an interoceanic canal through southern Nicaragua. This policy, articulated in the Monroe Doctrine's invective against European influence in the Americas, disputed British presence in the region and supported the formation of a unified Nicaraguan state. This unified state would include the eastern region, allowing easier access to the United States.

In 1860, the Treaty of Managua between Great Britain and the fragile Nicaraguan government transformed the region from a British protectorate into the Mosquito Reserve, giving Nicaragua sovereignty over the autonomous territory. However, the treaty also reduced the domains of Mosquitia and of the Miskito king, excluding nearly all of the traditional centers of Miskito population, including the Wanki (Coco) river, which today forms the border between Nicaragua and Honduras. As a result, much of the Miskito population came under direct Nicaraguan rule.

As in other European colonial ventures in the Americas, Christian missionaries played a large part in the history of Nicaragua. The British invited the German Moravian Church to carry out "civilizing" programs among the Miskito in 1849 as they wound down the armed competition to control the region. The missionaries introduced their own cultural norms and values and became—and remain—influential in the local leadership structure. The Moravians created villages centered on their churches to attract permanent residences. Eventually, these became fragmented communities, transforming the indigenous economy from hunting, fishing, and slash-and-burn agriculture into a large area where these methods of livelihood are no longer prominent.

Contemporary Nicaragua

In 1994, the Nicaraguan government dissolved the Mosquito Reserve and the military occupied the eastern region, calling the project the "reincorporation of the Mosquitia." This was followed by intermittent occupations of the region by U.S. Marines.

Responding to U.S. military and corporate dominance of Nicaragua, Augusto César Sandino, a former parliamentarian, led a nationalist war against the U.S. Marines and the Standard Fruit Company beginning in 1927. In 1933, Sandino was assassinated, and the U.S.-friendly Somoza family began their forty-nine-year rule of Nicaragua.

This all ended in 1979 with an armed revolt and general strike led by the Sandinista Front for National Liberation (FSLN, commonly known as the Sandinistas). The administration of U.S. President Ronald Reagan (1981–1989) trained and financed an anti-Sandinista guerrilla organization known as the Contras to overthrow the FSLN-led government, crippling the economy and causing tens of thousands of civilian deaths. In elections held in 1990, the FSLN lost the presidency, although the group retained local and parliamentary offices.

Many Miskito and even whole communities took up arms against the FSLN, with nearly half of the Miskito population in Nicaragua crossing the river border into the Honduran Mosquito Coast; they, too, were armed and trained by the United States. In the midst of the civil war, the FSLN government began to compose a constitution, inviting all sectors of the society, particularly the indigenous communities in the eastern zone, to participate. Under that constitution, autonomy for the eastern region became the basis for negotiations between the FSLN government and the Miskito insurgents in exile. Autonomy became law with the passage of the new constitution in 1986. By the end of 1988, most Miskito in Honduras had repatriated to their original villages and towns in eastern Nicaragua.

The autonomy law reflects the ethnic and linguistic complexities of the eastern region of Nicaragua. It mandates two regional assemblies in the north and south, each with forty-five members. The autonomy law has allowed the country's indigenous peoples a role in the governance of their communities and of the region—not without conflict, but no longer amid civil war. The Miskito and Sumu-Mayangna have taken their grievances directly to the Inter-American Court of Human Rights, as well as the Inter-American Commission on Human Rights, and they are active in the indigenous initiatives of the United Nations.

Roxanne Dunbar-Ortiz

See also: Groups: Central and South America—Garífuna; Maya; Miskito. Issues—Colonialism.

Further Reading

Dunbar-Ortiz, Roxanne. *Blood on the Border: A Memoir of the Contra War.* Cambridge, MA: South End, 2005.

Gould, Jeffrey L. *To Die in This Way: Nicaraguan Indians and the Myth of Mestizaje, 1880–1965.* Durham, NC: Duke University Press, 1998.

Hale, Charles R. *Resistance and Contradiction: Miskitu Indians and the Nicaraguan State, 1894–1987.* Stanford, CA: Stanford University Press, 1994.

Walker, Thomas W., and Christine J. Wade. *Nicaragua: Living in the Shadow of the Eagle.* Boulder, CO: Westview, 2011.

Nigeria

Nigeria is located on the coast of West Africa, sharing borders with Benin, Cameroon, Chad, and Niger; its southern coast lies on the Gulf of Guinea. It has a land area of 356,669 square miles (923,768 square kilometers). The country comprises thirty-six states and the federal capital territory of Abuja. It can be divided into three major geopolitical regions in the north, west, and east.

In 2009, Nigeria was the eighth-most-populous country in the world. Its population of approximately 146 million people encompasses more than 250 distinct ethnic nationalities. The most populous are the Hausa-Fulani (29 percent) in the north, the Yoruba (21 percent) in the west, and the Igbo (18 percent) in the east. Several other groups also have significant populations, including the Ijo (10 percent), Kanuri (4 percent), Ibibio (3.5 percent), and Tiv (2.5 percent).

Culture, Language, and Religion

Nigeria is notable for its cultural and linguistic diversity. Each of its 250 ethnic groups includes several linguistic subgroups, which account for no fewer than 450 distinct languages spoken within Nigeria's borders. Although English is Nigeria's official language, native-language learning is promoted in primary and secondary education. Secondary students are required to pass tests in Hausa, Igbo, or Yoruba as part of their exit exams. Pidgin English is also a lingua franca in both urban and rural areas across Nigeria.

By the eleventh century, King Hume of Kanem-Bornu (present-day northeastern Nigeria and northwestern Chad) had adopted Islam as a means to strengthen and maintain trans-Saharan trade relations. Islam gradually spread across the area and was integrated with many tra-ditional religious beliefs and practices. This also occurred with Judeo-Christianity, which was introduced along the coast during the fifteenth century by Portuguese monks. From the fifteenth to eighteenth century, some trade partners and coastal residents converted to Christianity as interactions with Europeans increased; however, Christianity did not spread significantly beyond the coast until the nineteenth century.

Within Nigeria, half of the population identify themselves as Muslims, 40 percent as Christians, and 10 percent practice traditional indigenous beliefs. However, these religions often are not entirely distinct from one another, as elements of traditional religions frequently are practiced alongside or integrated with Muslim or Christian customs. Such syncretic religions often are referred to as Africanized Islam or African Christian theology.

Nigeria's Indigenous History

Nigerian history can be divided into three periods: precolonial, colonial, and postcolonial. The precolonial period dates to the beginning of ancient civilization in the West African savannah region. As groups developed and expanded, some settled in the forest regions and along the southern coast, while others remained in the savannah and Sahel regions to the north. Major civilizations developed by the tenth century.

Among the key Nigerian empires were the Kanem-Bornu people, which began as two distinct civilizations that had merged by the thirteenth century; they controlled a major east–west route within the trans-Sarahan trade network. The Yoruba civilization appeared by the tenth century and solidified by the eleventh century. The Yoruba Empire first was centered at Ifa, which served as the spiritual capital, but by the seventeenth century, political power had shifted to Oyo. The Hausa-Fulani of the north and the Edo people of the Benin Empire also built major civilizations that remained intact throughout the colonial period. Although their political power diminished during the colonial period, their societal institutions remained as a result of the British policy of indirect rule.

When the British first made contact with the Benin in 1553, the kingdom stretched from present-day Lagos east to the Niger River Delta. The British established formal relations with the Benin Empire, which had been weakened by the abduction of many people by European slaving expeditions, in the latter part of the nineteenth century. In 1861, Great Britain invaded, capturing Lagos, but did not expand beyond the protectorate until the 1880s.

By this time, the British National African Company controlled virtually all palm oil trade out of the Niger

Delta. At the Berlin West Africa Conference of 1884–1885, the British were given the right to control the territory that would become Nigeria. They expanded the Lagos protectorate and established another protectorate in the north. After years of resistance, in 1893 the queen mother of Ibadan, the leader of the Yoruba Empire, signed a treaty with the British that subjugated the Yoruba to the British Empire. In 1897, British troops sacked Benin City. The Sokoto caliphate in Hausaland officially agreed to protectorate status by 1903.

While the fight for freedom among the indigenous population began in the 1800s, significantly, none of these groups lost their internal structure as a result of these takeovers. A dual system was developed in which nominal representation in the British colonial government was provided to these constituencies. It was not until the British outmaneuvered the Eastern Igbo groups in 1910 that Nigeria was completely under British control. The north and south were governed as two distinct protectorates until 1946, when they were merged to form the British colony of Nigeria.

Britain maintained strategic control of Nigeria's indigenous peoples and resources until after World War II. Wartime experiences along with increased British formal education in the colony provided the knowledge and opportunity for Nigerians to negotiate effectively with the British. This culminated in a mandate for what Nnamdi Azikiwe called the "African Renaissance," a call to unite Nigerians to claim their nation for themselves and develop and control their national institutions. In 1953, the transition to independence was spearheaded by three regional leaders: Ahmadu Bello in the north, Nnamdi Azikiwe in the east, and Obafemi Awolowo in the west. A national constitution was ratified and Nigeria achieved independence on October 2, 1960.

Postindependence Nigeria

Regional differences and resource conflicts precipitated the Biafra War (1967–1970). In 1966, several thousand Igbo people were killed in ethnic or religious attacks throughout parts of northern Nigeria. That same year, a military coup installed General Yakubu Gowon as the first military leader of Nigeria. In 1967, the eastern part of the country, under Igbo leadership, seceded from the republic, sparking a civil war, also known as the Nigerian-Biafran War, which caused millions of civilians to starve as a result of ravaged crops and military attacks. Estimates range from 1 million to 3 million war casualties. The eastern region eventually was reintegrated into the republic, but regional tensions continue to stress political and economic relations to this day.

The last period of military rule under Generals Ibrahim Babangida (1983–1993) and Sani Abacha (1994–1998) fostered economic and political instability across the nation, resulting in increased corruption, underdevelopment, and mismanagement of Nigeria's infrastructure. Civilian rule was reintroduced in 1999, and strategies were implemented to combat corruption and improve infrastructure. As President Goodluck Jonathan took office in 2010, he promised to support transparency in government and in the economy, while investing in the development and maintenance of Nigeria's infrastructure to ensure a sound national future.

Nigeria is a resource-rich nation whose economy is based on petroleum—together, petroleum and petroleum-based products constitute 95 percent of the nation's exports. The country's leading agricultural products are cocoa and rubber. Other important agricultural products and industries include cassava, corn, millet, palm oil, peanuts, rice, sorghum, and yams; livestock, fish, hides, and skins; cement and construction materials, chemicals, fertilizer, minerals, and steel; ceramics, footwear, printing, and textiles; and small commercial ship construction and repair.

In 2009, Nigeria's main export partner was the United States, which received 42.5 percent of the country's exports. Brazil, France, India, and Spain also were trade partners, each receiving less than 10 percent of Nigeria's exports. By contrast, Nigeria's import partners included China, leading with 15 percent, the United States with 8.2 percent, and Belize with 7.2 percent, in addition to fifteen other countries. Nigeria's primary imports are machinery and transport equipment (46.3 percent), manufactured goods (24 percent), and chemicals and related products (12.2 percent). The nation experienced a trade surplus in 2006–2012.

Jamaine M. Abidogun

See also: *Groups: Africa*—Yoruba. *Issues*—Economic Development; Indigenous Governments.

Further Reading

Connah, Graham. *African Civilizations: An Archaeological Perspective.* 2nd ed. New York: Cambridge University Press, 2001.

Davidson, Basil. *West Africa Before the Colonial Era: A History to 1850.* London: Longman, 1998.

Falola, Toyin, ed. *Africa.* Vol. 4, *The End of Colonial Rule: Nationalism and Decolonization.* Durham, NC: Carolina Academic Press, 2002.

Oyebade, Adebayo, ed. *The Foundations of Nigeria: Essays in Honor of Toyin Falola.* Trenton, NJ: Africa World Press, 2003.

Oyeneye, O.Y., and M.O. Shoremi, eds. *Nigerian Life and Culture.* Ogun, Nigeria: Ogun State University Press, 1985.

Norway

The westernmost nation on the Scandinavian Peninsula, Norway is a country of great natural beauty. Its fjords and mountains represent just two examples of the many contrasts that characterize its land and people. The indigenous Finns and Sami form an important part of the cultural and social landscape of the modern nation-state.

Cave drawings and other archaeological findings dating to 11,000 B.C.E. indicate the early presence of hunter-gatherers in Norway. The indigenous Finns and Sami are the descendants of these early Scandinavians. Taking the "way north" (Norway) in search of new territory, Germanic peoples from Europe joined them some 9,000 years later. The meeting of these two groups of people—indigenous Scandinavians and Germanic tribesman—and the eventual domination by the immigrants would set the stage for later concerns in Norwegian government over land and minority rights.

A period of state formation in the mid-nineteenth century resulted in major changes to Norwegian legislation monitoring the nomadic Sami people and their lands. The closing of the Russian border in eastern Finnmark (Nord-Norge, a county in the extreme northeast of Norway) in 1852 greatly reduced pasture lands for Sami reindeer and led to stricter control of Sami movement within Norwegian territory. Two years later, the Norwegian government granted provincial authorities in Finnmark the right to determine the boundaries of seasonal pasture lands as legislators began to codify Sami pastoral practices as part of new agricultural laws.

A series of such laws subsequently was passed, but it was not until the so-called Agreement of 1933 that the conflict between nomadic and sedentary populations became clear. Emerging in the midst of a concerted policy by the Norwegian state to assimilate the native peoples, the 1933 agreement favored the sedentary populations, who received rights of indemnification—that is, payment—for any violations of their land rights by the reindeer herders.

By the end of World War II, Norway had entered a new stage of economic, political, and social development. Earlier assimilationist policies toward the Sami changed with the discovery of oil reserves on Sami lands in the 1960s. After a period of regrouping, the Norwegian state and the Norges Reindriftsamers Landsforbund (National Association of Reindeer Pastoralists) negotiated the Reindeer Management Act of 1978, which ensured the "socially beneficial use of the reindeer pasture resources in such a way as provides economic and social security and protection of rights for those whose livelihood is reindeer pastoralism, and to preserve reindeer pastoralism as an important component of Sami culture." The agreement included government subsidies to reindeer owners for any animals slaughtered in order to limit herd sizes.

Enforcement of the agreement proved difficult, however, and a Sami Parliament was established in 1989 to address the many concerns that had not been addressed by the 1978 talks, as well as other practical issues involved in herd management. The Sami Parliament continues today, and it plays an important part in larger discussions about the Norwegian environment and political economy, particularly in its advisory role to the Norwegian Parliament. Amid the natural and political landscape, the indigenous people of Norway remain an essential part of all such dialogue in the Norwegian state.

Madia Thomson

See also: *Groups: Europe*—Finns; Norwegians; Sami. *Issues*—Land Rights; Political Participation.

Further Reading

Braun, Eric. *Norway in Pictures.* Minneapolis, MN: Lerner, 2003.

Buchen-Knapp, Gregg. *Elites, Language, and the Politics of Identity: The Norwegian Case in Comparative Perspective.* Albany: State University of New York Press, 2003.

Kagda, Sakina, and Barbara Cooke. *Cultures of the World: Norway.* New York: Marshall Cavendish, 2006.

Paine, Robert. *Herds of the Tundra: A Portrait of Saami Reindeer Pastoralism.* Washington, DC: Smithsonian Institution Press, 1994.

Zickgraf, Ralph. *Major World Nations: Norway.* Philadelphia: Chelsea House, 1999.

Panama

The Republic of Panama is located on the Isthmus of Panama in Central America, a narrow strip of land that connects North and South America. It is bordered by Costa Rica to the north and Colombia to the south; the Caribbean Sea lies to the east and the Pacific Ocean to the west. Although the origin of the name *Panama* is unknown, the indigenous Kuna people claim that it is derived from the word *pannaba,* meaning "very far."

The northern territory of Panama is mountainous, with some flat areas and grazing lands, while the southern part of the country is dense jungle. In spite of rapid deforestation during the twentieth and twenty-first centuries, some 40 percent of the country remains densely wooded. Along the Caribbean and Pacific coasts, there are a number of islands.

The Cordillera de Talamanca mountain range, originating at the Costa Rica border, runs downward to the Panama Canal Basin. The highest point in the country is Volcan Baru, at just over 11,000 feet (3,500 meters). There is little seasonal variation in Panama's humid, tropical climate. On the grazing lands and in the regions closer to the Pacific near Costa Rica, temperatures tend to be cooler, with occasional frosts in the mountains.

Panama is divided into nine provinces: Bocas del Toro, Chiriqui, Cocle, Colon, Darien, Herrea, Los Santos, Panama, and Veraguas. In addition, five semi-autonomous indigenous *comarcas,* or reservations, have been established: Kuna Yala (1938, also known as San Blas), Kuna Madugandi (1996), Ngöbe-Bugle (1997), Embera-Wounan (1998), and Kuna Wargandi (2000). The economy centers on service industries based around the Panama Canal and a free trade zone in Colón, in addition to banking and an emerging tourism industry. Subsistence farming of beans, corn, and various tubers still is practiced, and there also are banana plantations near the Costa Rica border.

In July 2009, Panama's population numbered more than 3 million, with 70 percent living in urban areas. The population is diverse, with 70 percent considered mestizo (mixed European and Native American heritage), 10 percent white, 14 percent Asian and West Indian, and 6 percent indigenous. The official language is Spanish, but many people also speak English. In addition, indigenous languages commonly are spoken.

Estimates place the indigenous population before European contact at 500,000, encompassing sixty different ethnic groups. The Kuna people lived on the Caribbean side of the country, the Guaymí near the present-day Costa Rica border, and the Chocó on the Pacific side of the Darien Province. Among these three groups, land was owned communally, and most people farmed but also were skilled potters, stonecutters, and fishermen.

Spaniard Rodrigo de Bastidas reached the region in 1501, marking the beginning of extensive contact with European explorers and traders. The following year, Christopher Columbus established the Darien colony, the first mainland settlement, though it was short-lived. During the early sixteenth century, overland trade routes were critical for transporting silver from the Americas to Spain. The region officially was ruled by the Spanish Empire from 1538 to 1821. Portobelo, on the Atlantic side of Panama, served as an important port for the export of goods to New Spain from the Andes Mountains.

During the Latin American wars of independence (1808–1826), Panamanian residents remained neutral. In 1821, the country seceded from Spanish rule and joined Gran Colombia, a federation of states that also included Colombia, Ecuador, and Venezuela. Failed attempts to break away from Gran Colombia in the 1830s and 1840s created tensions between the semi-autonomous Panamanian government and the central government in Colombia.

A railway was constructed (1850–1855) to move gold rushers and materials between the East and West coasts of the United States, leading to the establishment of a new port town, Colón. French entrepreneur Ferdinand de Lesseps finally secured Columbian permission to launch the canal project in 1880, but, bankrupt and unable to combat yellow fever and malaria, the project was abandoned in 1889.

Tensions between Panama and Colombia continued until the end of the century, when a series of rebellions led by Panama's most prominent families challenged Colombian authority. Led by José Augustin Arango, Panamanians established a revolutionary junta in 1903. The United States intervened to prevent the Colombian government from violently suppressing the rebellion and immediately recognized Panama's sovereignty.

That same year, the Hay-Banau-Varilla Treaty granted the U.S. government extensive rights to the proposed canal zone. The United States subsequently revived the project in 1904, bolstered by medical advances and new machinery. The first ship to pass through the canal was the U.S. cargo steamer *Ancon* in August 1914.

From 1903 to 1968, Panama functioned under a democratic government with a constitution in place. That government, however, was dominated by an oligarchy composed of merchants and landed aristocracy. During World War II, Panama occupied a place of strategic importance for the United States. After the war, under the leadership of General José Antonio Rémon Cantera, the National Police became much more active in regulating political and social life.

Panama's 1968 elections were marred by accusations of improprieties and fraud. The National Guard removed President Arnulfo Arias Madrid, who had ruled the country since 1931, leading to civil unrest that precipitated student protests and rioting. General Omar Torrijos emerged as leader of the National Guard and worked to forge an alliance of peasants, students, and members of the working class. He instituted land and education reform, promoted public works, and developed urban housing projects. Despite these improvements, the populist alliance proved fragile and tainted by undemocratic rule.

Torrijos died in a plane crash in July 1981, opening the door for Manuel Antonio Noriega to step in as the leader of the Panama Defense Forces. Noriega's regime participated in a number of illicit acts, including weapons and drug trafficking and money laundering. This drew the ire of the U.S. government, and under Operation Just Cause, Noriega was removed from power, indicted, and tried in the United States. The Panama Defense Forces were reduced to a National Police once again, effectively demilitarizing the country.

In 1999, Mireya Moscoso (the widow of President Arias Madrid) was elected president, and in 2004, she was succeeded by Martin Torrijos (the son of General Torrijos). President Ricardo Bertinelli was elected in 2009.

The Panama Canal was returned to Panamanian ownership, administration, and operation on January 1, 2000. Since then, the canal has continued to run smoothly. As of 2012, it was in the process of a massive expansion to create an additional lane.

María L.O. Muñoz

See also: *Groups: Central and South America*—Kuna. *Issues*—Colonialism; Economic Development.

Further Reading

Conniff, Michael. *Black Labor on a White Canal, 1904–1981.* Pittsburgh: University of Pittsburgh Press, 1985.

Dinges, John. *Our Man in Panama: The Shrewd Rise and Brutal Fall of Manuel Noriega.* New York: Random House, 1991.

Greene, Julie. *The Canal Builders: Making America's Empire at the Panama Canal.* New York: Penguin, 2009.

Lindsay-Poland, John. *Emperors in the Jungle: The Hidden History of the U.S. in Panama.* Durham, NC: Duke University Press, 2003.

McCullough, David. *The Path Between the Seas: The Creation of the Panama Canal, 1870–1914.* New York, Simon & Schuster, 1978.

Meditz, Sandra, and Dennis M. Hanratty, eds. *Panama. A Country Study.* Washington, DC: U.S. Government Printing Office, 1987.

Siu, Lok. *Memories of a Future Home: Diasporic Citizenship of Chinese in Panama.* Stanford, CA: Stanford University Press, 2005.

Papua New Guinea

Papua New Guinea occupies the eastern half of the island of New Guinea, part of the Malay Archipelago in the southwestern Pacific Ocean, situated north of Australia. It shares the island with two provinces of Indonesia, Papua and West Papua. In addition to its territories on the mainland, Papua New Guinea also encompasses a number of large islands to the east, including the Bismarck Archipelago (New Britain, New Hanover, New Ireland, Manus, and St. Mathias), Bougainville (the northernmost of the Solomon Islands group), and the many smaller islands of the Massim District off the southeastern tip of the main island.

Papua New Guinea is the largest country in Oceania in terms of both area and population. It also has the most diverse population on Earth, with more than 800 distinct, mutually unintelligible languages, each with its own unique culture. Even with this cultural and linguistic diversity, the modern state of Papua New Guinea has succeeded in establishing a national identity that accepts the country's rich cultural diversity as a strength yet, at the same time, unites its people under a shared Melanesian identity.

The population of Papua New Guinea was estimated at 6.6 million in 2009. It is an extremely young population, with more than 60 percent under the age of twenty-one and nearly half under 15 years of age. The country has one of the fastest-growing populations in the world, with a birth rate above 3 percent. Nearly all Papua New Guineans are of indigenous descent; less than 1 percent of the resident population are foreigners or citizens having nonindigenous ancestry. Although numerically insignificant, the non-native and mixed-race population—mostly of Australian, Chinese, and Polynesian ancestry—has long played a significant role in national and regional politics and commerce.

Early Settlement and Contact

Humans first reached the island of New Guinea during the Late Pleistocene epoch, when the sea level was as much as 165 feet (50 meters) lower than it is today. Archaeological excavations at Bobongara on the Huon Peninsula indicate that humans occupied Sahul at least 40,000 to 60,000 years ago.

Excavations suggest that early humans were able to cross the sea at least 50,000 years ago, probably using simple rafts. The development of indigenous pottery was a significant feature of prehistoric Papua New Guineans, dating to 5,500 to 6,000 years ago. Lapita pottery, which has a dentate-stamped design made of dots using the tines of a fine fork or small comb, was widely distributed from the north coast of Papua New Guinea and its eastern islands to sites in Vanuatu, New Caledonia, Tonga, and Samoa.

During the seventeenth through the nineteenth centuries, Chinese and Indonesian traders visited New Guinea and established peaceful contacts with local communities, mostly to trade for sea cucumbers (called *trepang* or *bêche-de-mer*), pearl and tortoise shells, and bird of paradise plumes. These Asian traders were most active in the western part of the island, now part of Indonesia, but occasionally reached the north coast of Papua New Guinea.

Establishing European Colonies

European contact with Papua New Guinea began about 1870, when representatives of the London Missionary Society started working in communities along the south coast of Papua New Guinea. In the 1880s, the Australian colonies on New Guinea comprised six separate settlements. Settlers in Queensland on the northern coast of Australia, then a British colony, who were nearest to New Guinea, were interested in capitalizing on Great Britain's claim to the region that was not taken by the Dutch. But Crown authorities in London saw no income potential in such a wild and uncivilized place as New Guinea.

At the same time, planters from Queensland were expanding their sugar plantations and needed inexpensive labor, and the Aborigines of Queensland were not able to meet their growing needs. So planters enlisted labor recruiters with ships to find workers on New Guinea for their sugar mills and cane fields. Most of the islanders who went to work on Queensland plantations never saw their home islands or families again. This form of slavery came to be known as "blackbirding," so called for the islanders' dark skin.

To sustain the labor trade, Queenslanders petitioned the Crown to annex the eastern half of New Guinea before a hostile foreign power could claim the ungoverned country. The Crown authorities made one concession to ease Queenslanders' concerns, naming the governor of Fiji as the high commissioner of the Pacific. He, in turn, appointed an assistant as the high commissioner for the Western Pacific, with authority over British subjects in New Guinea, the Solomon Islands, and Vanuatu. But the high commissioner took many months even to reach New Guinea from Fiji and proved ineffectual. Dissatisfied with the British response, the governor of Queensland took matters into his own hands, dispatching a ship to New Guinea, where the Union Jack was raised on April 3, 1883, annexing the eastern half of New Guinea as part of Queensland.

Despite the growing involvement of German traders in the Bismarck Archipelago since the early 1870s, German authorities assured the British that they had no designs on New Guinea. In 1884, a newly formed syndicate called the German New Guinea Company dispatched the respected ornithologist Otto Finsch to New Guinea. Ostensibly, Finsch was there to collect ornithological and ethnological specimens along the coasts, but he also was charged with surveying the area and proclaiming a German protectorate. In November 1884, Finsch proclaimed the protectorate by raising the German flag wherever he went.

When the British learned of Finsch's real purpose, they sent Commodore James E. Erskine to proclaim a British protectorate over the southeast quadrant of New Guinea—the territory that neither Germany nor the Netherlands had claimed. Although the Colonial Office was forced to assert the protectorate, it insisted that the Australian colonies cover the expenses of the administration of British New Guinea. Some Australians sought to recover these expenses by seizing land to create a white colony in British New Guinea, displacing natives from the best agricultural lands and using the people as laborers on their plantations.

Using armed force, the German New Guinea Company claimed large tracts of the best lands. When the local labor force proved insufficient, the company tried importing Javanese and Chinese laborers; however, most of the Javanese returned to Indonesia, and the Chinese tended to leave German employment, marrying local women and becoming traders in coastal villages. German plantations and trading stations generated profits for individual planters or traders but few for the colony, and the native people were harshly treated. By 1900, the German government recognized that the New Guinea Company model, based on the strategy used by the Dutch in Java a century earlier, was unsuited to New Guinea. It revoked the company's charter but allowed its officers to continue their economic ventures. Such changes did not, however, change the approach or harshness of the German colonial enterprise.

The situation in British New Guinea was more hands-off, as the official staff of the protectorate 1884 to 1888 consisted of only a handful of individuals, all based in Port Moresby. In 1888, the British government formally acknowledged the territory as a Crown colony, with a slightly larger stipend from London. When the chief medical officer of Fiji, Sir William MacGregor, was appointed administrator (later lieutenant governor) of British New Guinea in 1888, exploration began in earnest. MacGregor traveled to communities never before visited by foreigners, establishing positive relations with the natives. He routinely exchanged European goods such as steel tools, beads, mirrors, cloth, and tobacco for locally made artifacts such as bows, arrows, shields, tools, and ornaments. He probably was unaware that such exchanges followed local customs for dealing with hostile neighbors. In Papua New Guinea, exchanges of objects asserted equality and respect between antagonistic clans or villages, and nearly every conflict was resolved with an exchange of goods, in many places with exchanges of unmarried women as brides as well.

In 1901, the Australian colonies united as the Commonwealth of Australia under a central administration; five years later, British New Guinea was turned over to Australian control, whereupon the territory's name was

Women from one of the many native tribes of Papua New Guinea—among the most linguistically and culturally diverse countries in the world—apply face paint before a culture festival. Most inhabitants live in indigenous rural societies; poverty is rampant. *(Torsten Blackwood/AFP/Getty Images)*

changed to Papua. Two years later, Sir Hubert Murray was appointed lieutenant governor of Papua, bringing more regular contact with Papuans than earlier British officials; he also was more protective of the villagers' rights. At the same time, he patronized the villagers, forcing coastal people to plant a certain number of coconuts each year so that they could develop a cash crop—copra, or dried coconut meat—to sell for money. To further motivate villagers to participate in the cash economy, he implemented a head tax that forced villagers to sell their labor. Likewise, Murray discouraged local Papuan entrepreneurs, and the same policies limited the growth of European businesses to extractive industries, particularly gold, copra, pearls, and pearl shells.

At the beginning of World War I in August 1914, the Australian military immediately invaded German New Guinea, consolidating control within a month. After the war, the League of Nations awarded the territory to Australia as the Mandated Territory of New Guinea, with a separate administration from Murray's administration in Papua.

Postwar Development and Independence

After World War II, the former territory of German New Guinea became a United Nations Trust Territory administered by Australia, and it was joined with Papua to form the Territory of Papua and New Guinea. Colonial administrators began routine visits to nearly every village for regular village administration, court cases, agricultural programs, and routine census. The administration encouraged the development of new plantations, including those in the highlands for newly introduced crops such as coffee and tea. By the late 1960s, the administration had begun to encourage high-tech mineral extraction in addition to the small-scale alluvial gold extraction that had been the mainstay of the Papuan economy since the 1880s.

The 1980s and 1990s saw the rise of large-scale logging by Chinese, Japanese, and Malaysian firms that promised that cleared forests would be transformed into oil palm plantations, some of which were held as smallholder blocks. However, both coconut and oil palms quickly depleted whatever nutrients are in the soil, making it difficult to return the land to ordinary gardens for food or other crops. The economy has continued to emphasize intensive mineral extraction and agricultural exports as the core of its foreign exchange. Today, the manufacturing sector plays a minor role in the national economy, largely as a consequence of decisions made in the 1960s through the 1980s.

As a United Nations Trust Territory, members of the Trusteeship Council routinely monitored conditions in the former German New Guinea. In the 1960s, several African representatives on the council complained that Australia was not educating the territory's children and that young people were being given few opportunities for employment and higher education. They also complained that the Australian administration was not preparing New Guinea for independence fast enough. Most in the colonial administration imagined that it would be fifty years before the territory was ready for independence, a timeline that the Trusteeship Council found too slow.

In 1967, a group of young Papua New Guinean leaders, including Michael Somare, who later would become the first prime minister, submitted to the House of Assembly (which later would become the national parliament) a report calling for immediate independence. Many Australians objected to the proposal, but when Gough Whitlam's Australian Labour Party won the elections in 1972, his government agreed that it was time for Papuans and New Guineans to determine their own fate. Australia transferred sovereignty to the people of Papua and New Guinea in two stages, granting self-government on December 1, 1973, and full independence on September 16, 1975. The country was renamed Papua New Guinea, with a single parliament and membership in the British Commonwealth. It was admitted to the United Nations the following month.

Although formally independent of Australia, Papua New Guinea continues to have close ties with that nation, which has provided substantial annual grants and large amounts of aid to the young country. Since the 1990s, China has increased its economic involvement in the country, and most Papua New Guineans buy inexpensive Chinese goods. Only the growing middle class of government workers, teachers, and private-sector workers in the cities can afford goods imported from Australia, Europe, and the United States.

Language, Cultural Diversity, and a National Identity

Papua New Guinea's 800 or so languages can be grouped into eight or nine unrelated language families, with more than a dozen isolates that are unrelated to any other language in the country. Only one of these, Austronesian, seems to be a relative newcomer, emerging perhaps 6,000 to 8,000 years ago. In pre-European times, most of these languages were fairly small communities of no more than 500 speakers. On the coast and on the islands are a dozen or so important languages with 5,000 to 25,000 speakers. Only in the central highlands are there languages with more than 100,000 speakers, the most notable of which is Enga, with more than 250,000 speakers and several different dialects.

This linguistic diversity did not arise from isolation, but rather was a consequence of regular interaction, often involving trade, intermarriage, and political cooperation. Language distinctiveness was one way to differentiate politically autonomous groups. As a result of this dazzling array of linguistic diversity, the majority of Papua New Guineans before the colonial era were multilingual, speaking three, four, or more languages, which allowed them to interact comfortably with their neighbors. The region's large number of ethnolinguistic groups has prevented any one tribal group from dominating the political landscape, except perhaps at the provincial level, where well-positioned groups have taken advantage of education and access to markets in order to prosper over less well-situated communities.

During colonial times, two lingua franca were used. Most New Guineans quickly learned Pidgin English (Pidgin or Neo-Melanesian), and in British New Guinea, another pidgin language called Police Motu was based on one of the local languages spoken around Port Moresby. Its use spread among government employees, plantation workers, and prisoners. At the time of independence, half of the population spoke Pidgin and a quarter spoke Police Motu. Since then, Pidgin has taken over, so that few young people know Police Motu any more, while 80 percent to 90 percent of the population knows Pidgin. Both remain national languages alongside English.

The similar horticultural background shared by most Papua New Guinea cultures has longed served as a base on which people have constructed a modern Melanesian culture that amalgamates elements from most parts of the country. Certain foods introduced by Australians during the colonial period, patterns of work, typical school days, and, more recently, national radio and television broadcasts have fostered a distinctive national culture that is not found anywhere else, including the New Guinea provinces of Indonesia.

Robert L. Welsch

See also: *Groups: East Asia and Oceania*—Melanesians. *Issues*—Colonialism; International Policy; Language.

Further Reading

Connolly, Bob, and Robin Anderson. *First Contact.* New York: Penguin, 1988.

Firth, Stewart. *New Guinea Under the Germans.* Carlton, Australia: Melbourne University Press, 1987.

Foster, Robert J., ed. *Nation Making: Emergent Identities in Postcolonial Melanesia.* Ann Arbor: University of Michigan Press, 1997.

Kirch, Patrick Vinton. *On the Road of the Winds: An Archaeological History of the Pacific Islands Before European Contact.* Berkeley: University of California Press, 2000.

Nelson, Hank. *Black, White and Gold: Gold Mining in Papua New Guinea, 1878–1930.* Canberra: Australian National University Press, 1976.

Rowley, C.D. *The New Guinea Villager: The Impact of Colonial Rule on Primitive Society and Economy.* New York: Praeger, 1966.

Soutar, Gavin. *New Guinea: The Last Unknown.* New York: Taplinger, 1966.

Terrell, John Edward, and Robert L. Welsch. "Lapita and the Temporal Geography of Melanesia." *Antiquity* 71 (1997): 548–572.

Paraguay

The Republic of Paraguay is a landlocked country in the middle of South America, bordered by Bolivia to the northwest, Brazil to the northeast, and Argentina to the south and southwest. Paraguay encompasses two distinct geographic regions, the Región Oriental (Eastern Region) and the Región Occidentale (Western Region, also known as the Chaco Boreal or Gran Chaco). Most of the country's native people groups live in the western part of the country.

The country's indigenous population, which numbers approximately 85,000 people, or 1.7 percent of the total population, can be classified into five linguistic groups that comprise at least seventeen ethnic subgroups or *parcialidades*: (1) Guaraní: Aché, Chiripá, Guaraní ñandeva, Guarayo, Mbyá, Pai, Tavytera; (2) Maskoy: Angaité, Guaná, Lengua, Sanapaná, Toba Maskoy; (3) Guaicurú: Toba Qom; (4) Zamuco: Ayoreo, Chamacoco; and (5) Mataco: Nivaclé, Chorotí, Maká. However, this conventional classification is somewhat of an oversimplification, as group members typically adopt other ethnonyms or subdivide themselves according to different contexts and relations. Some of the groups are characterized by a high level of territorial mobility and create kinship ties that extend beyond the national border. Since the late twentieth century, many groups have begun migrating to urban zones in the center of the country, close to the capital city of Asunción.

From a cultural and linguistic point of view, Paraguay constitutes an uncommon case in Latin America. It is a country in which most of the population speaks the Guaraní language, without recognizing themselves as Indian, in addition to Spanish. Other Latin American countries maintain indigenous languages but are not bilingual. This paradox is understandable, however, in light of the long-term historical processes that began in colonial times.

From the beginning of the sixteenth century, Paraguay was a theater of intense processes of contact, colonization, and *mestizaje* (the cultural and biological blending of European and indigenous peoples), which led to the differentiation of two distinct populations: one that resulted from the mixture of indigenous peoples and Spanish colonizers, which formed the basis for the rural Guaraní-speaking population, and an indigenous population that resisted colonization and preserved their cultural and linguistic differences. Indians adopted diverse attitudes toward their Spanish conquerors during this period. While the *cario*—Indians from the region of Asunción—made alliances with the Spanish, the Guaycurú from the Chaco region resisted colonization as long as they could.

It is possible to distinguish two historical phases in the expansion of the Paraguayan state into indigenous lands. The first period is characterized by the installation and consolidation of a Spanish colonial regime based on the *encomienda* work system and religious missions. As the Spanish established a colonial regime, both the encomienda system and Catholic missions were put in place to assimilate the indigenous population. The encomienda labor system obliged indigenous families to pay tribute to the Spanish settlers in exchange for their spiritual "protection"—conversion so that they would be considered human.

The difficult work conditions imposed on the Indians and repeated epidemics precipitated a demographic collapse among the native population. The Spanish Crown intervened by creating religious missions that segregated the indigenous people into villages (*reducciones*). Between 1609 and 1768, the Jesuits, in collaboration with indigenous leaders, built several villages in the regions of Guayrá, Itatín, Paraná, Tape, and Uruguay, which reached a population of more than 100,000 Guaraní Indians in the mid-eighteenth century.

The second period is characterized by the decline and fall of the Spanish colonial regime and the emergence of independent states in Latin America. The expulsion of the Jesuits from the region in 1767 inaugurated a period of cultural and political homogenization. The increasing number of interactions between Indians and people of the rural areas contributed to the emergence of a peasantry that maintained the Guaraní language. This process culminated in 1848, when President Carlos Antonio López signed a decree declaring Indians "free citizens" of the republic, meaning that they could abandon the system of town communities and collective work. At the end of the nineteenth century, however, the government promoted a process of land distribution and agrarian colonization that expelled Indians from their traditional territories.

Two events from this period are especially noteworthy: the Triple Alliance War (1865–1870) against Argentina, Brazil, and Uruguay, and the Chaco War (1932–1935) against Bolivia. Indians were recruited into the Paraguayan national army during both wars, with catastrophic demographic consequences. The surviving indigenous population was expelled from their traditional lands, which immediately were divided and sold to settlers and farmers.

Beginning in 1936, military forces and the defense ministry controlled indigenous affairs. The Paraguayan state also ceded lands to Catholic and Protestant churches with the intent of civilizing and pacifying the indigenous population. Between 1954 and 1989, the dictatorship of Alfredo Stroessner continued to direct state policy toward assimilating the indigenous population into Paraguayan society.

The return of democracy to Paraguay in 1989 led to normative advances for the indigenous peoples. Yet most of the communities continue to face discrimination and poverty. Today, 50 percent of the indigenous population has no access to land titles, prompting them to migrate to urban areas.

In the late twentieth century, some groups began to mobilize in protest against official institutions such as the National Indigenous Institute. However, the nation's constitutional reform of 1992, which defines Paraguay as a multiethnic and multicultural state, the country's adoption of Convention 169 of the International Labour Organisation, and the sanction of specific laws and pressure from international human rights organizations and nongovernmental organizations, all have supported the ongoing process of the native peoples reclaiming their ancestral lands.

Guillermo Wilde

See also: *Groups: Central and South America*—Guaraní. *Issues*—Colonialism; Relocation.

Further Reading

Ganson, Barbara. *The Guaraní Under Spanish Rule in the Río de la Plata.* Stanford, CA: Stanford University Press, 2003.
Maybury-Lewis, David, and **James Howe.** *The Indian Peoples of Paraguay: Their Plight and Their Prospects.* Cambridge, MA: Cultural Survival, 1980.
Service, Elman R. *Spanish–Guarani Relations in Early Colonial Paraguay.* Westport, CT: Greenwood, 1971.
Susnik, Branislava, and Miguel Chase-Sardi. *Los Indios del Paraguay (The Indians of Paraguay).* Madrid, Spain: Mapfre, 1992.
Wessendorf, Kathrin, ed. *The Indigenous World 2008.* Copenhagen, Denmark: International Work Group for Indigenous Affairs, 2008.
Whigham, Thomas. "Paraguay's Pueblos de Indios: Echoes of a Missionary." In *The New Latin American Mission History,* ed. Erick Langer and Robert H. Jackson. Lincoln: University of Nebraska Press, 1997.

Peru

Peru is situated on the western coast of South America, sharing borders with Colombia and Ecuador to the north, Chile to the south, and Bolivia and Brazil to the east. The country is home to nearly 30 million people, of whom approximately 45 percent belong to native groups.

About two-thirds of the native people are Quechua; Peru also recognizes fifty-one other native groups, including the Achuar, Aguaruna, Asháninka, Aymara, Huambisa, and Shipibo. The Quechua live throughout the country's three regions (coastal lowlands, Andean highlands, and Amazon Rain Forest), while the Achuar, Aguaruna, Asháninka, Huambisa, and Shipibo live in the Amazon region, and the Aymara inhabit the Andean highlands in the southern part of the country. Additionally, Peruvians of African descent live along the southern coast.

The Inca were the ancestors of the modern Quechua peoples that form a majority of the indigenous population of Peru today. They were notable for their artistry and architecture, both of which are on display at the United Nations World Heritage Site at Machu Picchu, the ruins of a pre-Columbian city located in the mountains northwest of present-day Cuzco.

Native People and History

Anthropologists have dated hunting tools in Peru to as early as 10,000 B.C.E., indicating human habitation. Although many distinctive native cultures rose and fell in the millennia before written records, history recalls the Inca Empire, which spanned the entire western coast of South America and reached its peak during the fifteenth and sixteenth centuries, a period that also saw the arrival of Spanish conquistadores in the New World.

The Spanish arrived in Peru in 1531, but diseases from the Spanish settlements in Panama made their way ahead of the conquistadores, weakening the Inca and allowing Francisco Pizarro a relatively easy conquest, which was completed by 1532. Although the native people resisted Spanish domination, rising up in revolt many times over the following decade, by 1542, the Viceroyalty of Peru was established, inaugurating a period of political stability that lasted for nearly three centuries.

By the early nineteenth century, many native Quechua had intermarried with Spanish settlers. When independence movements led by Venezuela's Simón Bolívar swept across South America during the 1810s and 1820s, Peru's native people and mestizo (mixed-race) population responded with enthusiasm, establishing Peru as an independent nation on July 28, 1821.

Following independence, the mestizo population dominated national political and social life in Peru, fighting civil wars while most of the native population sought to steer clear of the strife. Most of the native lands were taken over by mestizo Peruvians and held in haciendas; many indigenous people found work on the large plantations.

By 1969, under the military regime of President Juan Velasco, the haciendas had been broken up, and many indigenous Peruvians hoped that their lands would be restored to them. Instead, Velasco had the lands organized into state-run farms. But Velasco's government, which was deposed in 1975, did take steps to reclaim Peru's native identity, recognizing Quechua as an official language, promoting bilingual education, and introducing legislation to protect the social, political, and land rights of the native population.

During the early 1980s, many native Peruvians joined the grassroots Maoist guerrilla army known as Sendero Luminoso (Shining Path). When it became clear, however, that the group's intent was to create a Peruvian communist identity rather than to allow the native peoples to retain their cultures, many natives withdrew. In more than twenty years of civil strife precipitated by Sendero Luminoso, many Quechua died or were displaced from their rural settlements.

Many native groups began to form their own move-

TÚPAC AMARU

When the Spanish arrived in present-day northern Peru in 1531, Francisco Pizarro's army captured and executed Atahualpa, the thirteenth and last emperor of the Inca, in the city of Cajamarca. In his place, Pizarro installed Manco Inca Yupanqui, a lower-class noble of the ruling family, as leader of the Inca.

The humiliation and constant abuse of his people hardened Manco's hatred for the conquistadores. Following his imprisonment in the Saxsayhuaman fortress near Cuzco and subsequent escape, he organized an Inca army and attacked the city in 1536. Soon after, Manca retreated into Vilcabamba, situated at the edge of the Amazon Rain Forest, and created an independent Inca state, openly resisting Spanish domination. So began the belated resistance of the last four Inca rulers to the Spanish conquest of South America.

In 1544, Manco was assassinated in Vilcabamba by a Spanish group. One of his three sons, Sayri Túpac, assumed power in the newly created Inca rebel state. In 1158, however, Sayri abdicated the throne, was baptized, and moved to Cuzco, where he received a special dispensation from Pope Julius III to consecrate his marriage to his sister. He died in Cuzco in 1561.

Sayri Túpac's brother, Titu Cusi Yupanqui, assumed power in Vilcabamba and renewed hostilities against Spanish rule. Nevertheless, Titu's strong resistance during his initial years faltered by 1568, as he admitted missionaries into his territory and converted to Catholicism. His testimony, *An Inca Account of the*

Conquest of Peru (1570), documented by Spanish priest Diego Ortiz, is considered the most important colonial chronicle of the rebel state in Vilcabamba and of the last days of the Inca rulers. In 1570, Titu died under mysterious circumstances—it is unclear whether he contracted pneumonia or was poisoned.

Titu's younger brother, Túpac Amaru, assumed power and revived the resistance against the Spanish Crown with increased intensity. Amaru was accused of executing a diplomatic mission sent by the Spanish viceroy to negotiate peace, executing Ortiz and other Catholic priests, and expelling all missionaries from his kingdom. After a period of fierce resistance, Amaru was captured and executed by the Spanish in 1572. Following his death—he was the last member of the Inca royal family to rule his people—and the destruction of the last Inca kingdom in Vilcabamba, Spanish domination in the region was undisputed.

Túpac Amaru became a symbol of indigenous people's resistance against Spanish colonial rule. As such, he inspired many guerrilla groups over the centuries. In 1780, his great grandson, José Gabriel Condorcanqui, adopted the name Túpac Amaru and launched a short-lived rebellion against the Spanish in Peru. The Peruvian rebel group Movimiento Revolucionario Túpac Amaru (Túpac Amaru Revolutionary Movement) was named for him, as was the 1970s Uruguayan Marxist rebel group Tupamaru.

Patricio R. Ortiz

Sacsayhuamán was an immense stone fortress outside Cuzco, Peru, the historic capital of the Inca Empire. Begun in 1438, construction coincided with Inca territorial expansion under the ruler Pachacuti but was incomplete by the Spanish conquest in 1533. *(Jim Dyson/Getty Images)*

ments to protect their cultures, such as the Coordinadora Nacional de Comunidades Afectados por la Minería (National Coordinator of Communities Affected by Mining) in the Andean region and the Asociación Inter-étnica para el Desarrollo de la Selva Peruana (Inter-Ethnic Association for Peruvian Jungle Development) in the Amazon. By the 1990s, many groups had come to recognize the benefits that could be achieved by united action, and they joined to form the Conferencia Permanente de los Pueblos Indígenas del Perú (Standing Conference of Indigenous Peoples of Peru) to put pressure on the government to protect native lifeways, land rights, and political rights.

Present Status of Peru's Native People

As in many other nations, Peruvian native peoples and African Peruvians have protested their lack of representation in the political and social life of the nation. Discrimination and stereotyping, although criminalized in 1997, remain widespread in all areas of life, from the media to hiring. The Peruvian government has opened up native lands, which contain valuable natural resources such as tropical hardwoods and oil, to development. Even on lands granted to native groups, Peruvian law guarantees only the right to the surface land, withholding the rights to the substrata, where valuable natural resources lie.

In 2002, the Peruvian government implemented a policy requiring that 15 percent of candidates for regional political office come from native groups. In 2004, Peruvian President Alejandro Toledo, of Quechua heritage, created the Instituto Nacional de Desarrollo de los Pueblos Andinos, Amazónicas y Afro Peruanos (National Institute for the Development of Andean, Amazonian and Afro-Peruvian Peoples) to act as a bridge between the native-led groups and the Peruvian government.

With this impetus, some Peruvian natives have had success in fighting against the pollution of their lands as a result of natural resource development. During 2006 and 2007, the Achuar people fought against two multinational oil companies to stop the contamination of their water and land. Although movement toward recognizing full land rights for Peru's native peoples to their lands and lifeways has been slow, it has been steady and is expected to continue.

Steven L. Danver

See also: *Groups: Central and South America*—Quechua. *Issues*—Colonialism; Indigenous Governments; Political Discrimination; Revolts.

Further Reading

García, María Elena. *Making Indigenous Citizens: Identities, Education, and Multicultural Activism in Peru.* Stanford, CA: Stanford University Press, 2005.

Starn, Orin, Carlos Iván Degregori, and Robin Kirk, eds. *The Peru Reader: History, Culture, Politics.* 2nd ed. Durham, NC: Duke University Press, 2005.

Van Cott, Donna Lee. *From Movements to Parties in Latin America: The Evolution of Ethnic Politics.* New York: Cambridge University Press, 2005.

Philippines

The Philippines is an island nation in the Pacific Ocean, situated approximately 500 miles (805 kilometers) off the coast of Vietnam. The archipelago encompasses some 7,100 islands and islets stretching 1,150 miles (1,850 kilometers) from north to south.

The country is home to more than 160 ethnic groups with distinct languages and cultures. The Tagalog are the largest ethnic group, and theirs is the country's official language. Since achieving independence from the United States in 1946, the Philippines has been ruled by a mestizo (people of mixed heritage) elite, largely Spanish but also Chinese. The national culture prizes Western ideals of assimilation, valuing the Catholicism brought by the Spanish and the commercialism brought by the Americans, both of which have been viewed as threats to the islands' indigenous cultures.

The indigenous people of the Philippines comprise three main groups: Cordilleranos reside in the northern part of Luzon, the largest island, while in the south, in Mindanao, reside almost two-thirds of the nation's aboriginal peoples, the Lumad and Visayans. To the west are the Palawano and Tagbanwa on the island of Palawan.

Scholarly evidence points to an indigenous presence on the islands at least 47,000 years ago on Palawan. At the time of the Spanish invasion in the sixteenth century, the Philippines comprised a number of disparate sultanates and rajas. Spanish colonialists classified the indigenous people of the Philippines as *infiel,* or non-Christian, relegating them to the lowest class, together with Muslims. Over time, Spanish conquest resulted in the conversation of most Filipinos to Catholicism, while some of the native peoples retained their belief systems.

When Spain ceded the Philippines to the United States in 1898, the U.S. government modeled its approach to the Filipino peoples on its policies toward American Indians, as most of the U.S. generals at that time had fought during the Indian Wars of the nineteenth century. David Barrows, an American scholar on American Indians, was appointed as head of the new colonial authority, called the Bureau for Non-Christian Tribes. During this period, American companies such as Dole often seized tribal lands for plantations.

After independence in 1946, the indigenous tribes were gradually displaced from their lands, as the nation sought to develop its industries. Under President Ferdinand Marcos, who ruled as a dictator from 1965 to 1986, indigenous lands were handed over to domestic and foreign business interests, and non-native Filipinos were resettled on indigenous lands by the national government. Both Cordilleranos and Lumads were caught between the army and uprisings led by the Moro Island Liberation Front and the New People's Army (NPA) during the 1950s. The Lumads were recruited by the NPA and by Marcos's successor, Corazon Aquino, who held office from 1986 until 1992, for the Citizen Armed Force Geographical Units, which were widely accused of human rights abuses.

However, the transition to civilian democratic rule after Aquino took office did lead to some improvements for indigenous Filipinos. In 1997, tribes successfully lobbied for passage of the Indigenous Peoples Rights Act, which granted them title to ancestral lands, the right to self-government, human rights guarantees, and the creation of the National Commission on Indigenous Peoples (NCIP). Since that time, the NCIP has been criticized for its lack of trained personnel, for corruption in the granting of titles, and for exacerbating boundary disputes. Cordillerano groups especially have been sharply critical of the NCIP.

The United Nations (UN) Special Rapporteur on Human Rights in a 2007 report noted that the efforts of the NCIP to ensure the rights of the Philippines' native peoples remain underfunded. Native-held land still is being subsumed to the national interest in terms of the construction of industrial projects. When native people have resisted, they have faced violence. The UN Special Rapporteur found that seventy people had died as a result of their resistance to the taking of native lands. As of 2012, those cases still had not been thoroughly investigated or tried in the courts.

Al Carroll

See also: Issues—Assimilation; Colonialism; Missionary Activities.

Further Reading

Schirmer, Daniel B., and Stephen Rosskamm Shalom, eds. *The Philippines Reader: A History of Colonialism, Neocolonialism, Dictatorship, and Resistance.* Cambridge, MA: South End, 1987.

Tan, Samuel K. A *History of the Philippines.* Quezon City: University of the Philippines Press, 2008.

United Nations Office of the High Commissioner for Human Rights. "Standing Its Ground: An Indigenous Community in the Philippines." May 22, 2009.

Russia

The Russian Federation covers a vast territory of more than 6.5 million square miles (16.8 million square kilometers) spanning eastern Europe and western Asia. Until 1991, Russia was the largest and most important republic in the Union of Soviet Socialist Republics. Even with the loss of its former Baltic, Caucasian, and Central Asian republics, Russia remains the world's largest nation, with nearly twice the territory of Canada. Although Russia is culturally European—that is, Russian is an Indo-European language, and the people largely hold Christian beliefs—it encompasses extensive areas of northern Asia, including Siberia, and now is home to many Muslim populations.

Russia shares borders with many European and Asian nations, including the Baltic states (Estonia, Latvia, and Lithuania), the Caucasian and Central Asian republics (including Kazakhstan), China, Japan, and Mongolia. The Arctic Ocean lies to the north of Russia and the deserts of Central Asia to the south. Large parts of northern Russia are covered by permafrost and therefore are not suitable for agriculture. From north to south, vast strips of tundra are followed by dense forests (*taiga*), and then by the black soil belt, which provides fertile land for agriculture. Russian literature reflects this diverse landscape and praises the beauty of the forests, especially the birch tree, and the steppe, also referred to as the Russian prairie.

Approximately 144 million people live in the Russian Federation. Of those, 80 percent are ethnic Russians. The remaining 20 percent comprises more than 100 European and Asian ethnic groups, including Belorussians, Buriats, Finns, Germans, Jews, Tatars, Ukrainians, Yakuts, and many others. Inside the federation, the Russian language and culture are dominant. Autonomy for non-Russians is restricted, a policy that has prompted ethnic clashes between Russia and its minority populations (for example, the Chechens).

Today, Russia west of the Ural Mountains is urbanized and industrialized. Approximately 80 percent of the population lives in European Russia, whereas Asiatic Russia—that is, Siberia—is thinly populated and still presents a frontier that is extremely rich in natural resources such as timber, natural gas, oil, furs, gold, and diamonds. The overwhelming majority of the population in European Russia works in industry or white-collar jobs.

The Russian peasantry traditionally cultivated winter wheat, rye, and potatoes; however, Russia has seen a population shift as young people increasingly migrate to urban centers. The largest cities in European Russia are Moscow, with 8.5 million people, and St. Petersburg (called Leningrad by the Soviets), with 4.65 million inhabitants; the largest city in Siberia is Novosibirsk, with 1.5 million people. Life expectancy for Russian women is approximately seventy-one years, but for men it is fifty-eight years because of rampant alcoholism.

Indigenous History

From the beginning of its history, the territory of Russia was multiethnic. Before 800 C.E., eastern Slavs in the region mixed with peoples of Baltic and Finno-Ugric origin, and the land west of the Ural Mountains became an ethnic melting pot. Following the adoption of Orthodox Christianity throughout the Byzantine Empire, which concluded when the use of Holy Icons was upheld in what became the Orthodox Church in 843, the first "Russian" state, the Kievan Rus, came into existence in about 880. It was situated at the crossroads of the European world in the West, the Byzantine Empire in the East, and the realm of nomadic peoples, mainly Turkic tribes. Until the mid-thirteenth century, the existence of this state, with its political, economic, and cultural center in Kiev—the so-called mother of Russian cities—was destined by cooperation and conflicts with the nomads of the southern steppe. Although the Orthodox Kievans viewed the nomads as barbarians, they tolerated them because the Turkic tribes controlled the lucrative trade routes to the Oriental East.

Russia's incorporation into the steppe was accelerated by the Mongol onslaught in the mid-thirteenth century. In 1240, Mongol troops from inner Asia sacked Kiev, and the Kievan state, weakened by internal strife, vanished. The Russian territory came under Mongol rule—which Russians later would refer to as the "Tatar yoke"—for the next 200 years. Some historians argue that the roots of Russian despotism can be traced to this time. Although the Russians were drawn into the steppe culture by their Mongol-Tatar rulers, they remained culturally apart from the nomads.

By 1480, Mongol rule over Russia was in decline, a process that was accelerated by tribal rivalries among the nomads. At the same time, Moscow, a small Russian principality north of the steppe, was on the rise. Two factors contributed to Moscow's ascent. The first was its cordial relationship with the Tatars. Moscow's rulers had gained autonomy from the Mongol khans insofar as they had earned the right to collect tribute from the Russian population. The second factor was economic, as the city became an emporium for the fur trade along the Eurasian routes.

This was the basis for the creation of the Muscovite state and, later, empire. In the mid-sixteenth century, Muscovite ruler Ivan IV (also known as Ivan the Terrible, r. 1533–1584) destroyed the last of the Tatar khanates, Astrachan, Kazan, and Sibir. In the south, the Russians gained access to the steppe and the Black Sea and, in the east, to Siberia. The colonization of Russia's Asian borderlands began, marking the birth of the Russian Empire. The steppe zone and Siberia were incorporated into Russian territory, becoming the core of the empire that emerged in the sixteenth century.

The Russian Empire

After Ivan IV consolidated power into the Russian Empire beginning in the sixteenth century, the process of incorporating the diverse native populations of the regions under Imperial rule began. The conquest of the Khanates of Kazan (1552) and Astrakhan (1554) brought Muslim Tatars into the empire. Russian expansion into Siberia during the sixteenth and seventeenth centuries brought many new Uralic, Turkic, and Aleut tribes under Russian control; the conquest of the Caucasus during a war that lasted from 1817 until 1864 added many more groups, including the Avars, Circassians, and Georgians.

By the time Russia's power was at a zenith in the late nineteenth century, several hundred diverse native groups were subsumed into the empire. Until the 1830s, however, inclusion in the Russian Empire did not mean very much in terms of changes to ethnic identity and lifeways. But thereafter, the immigration of Russian peoples into the lands held by the native groups, the establishment of new urban centers throughout the empire, and an increasing pressure for the population to "Russify" began to impact native peoples.

Native peoples, especially the Tatars, resisted not only assimilation into the Russian population but also conversion from Islam to Orthodox Christianity—sometimes violently. In addition, the unrest experienced in Russia during the early twentieth century, which eventually would end the Tsarist-ruled empire, encouraged many other groups to seek to form their own national identities. With the onset of the Bolshevik Revolution in 1917, many native groups cooperated with the Reds, as they were promised a degree of ethnic and regional autonomy in the years following the Revolution.

Native Groups in the Soviet Era

As the Soviet era began in the late 1920s, the promise of recognition of native peoples seemed to be materializing. Yet even though the "autonomous Soviet socialist republics," within the Russian Soviet Federative Socialist Republic (RSFSR), the central part of the Soviet Union, were loosely organized around ethnicity, native peoples' interests were never important relative to the concerns of the economic, political, and military advancement of the Soviet Union.

Communist Party leadership was put into place in both political and internal security areas to ensure that the ethnically based republics promoted ideologies based on the Soviet ideal rather than any nationalist sentiments.

Those populations that prioritized ethnic over Soviet identity faced severe recriminations. For example, peoples in the North Caucasus and Volga Tatars were deported, and many others faced death during Stalin's purges in the 1930s. At the same time, the Russian language soon replaced local languages, which disappeared from regional schools.

In the 1960s, however, the RSFSR saw the emergence of increased native and ethnic identity. More identity with indigenous culture was allowed by the Soviet regime than had been allowed under Stalin. By the time of *perestroika* and *glastnost* in the mid-to-late 1980s, shortly before the crumbling of the Soviet regime, ethnic interests began to supplant the Communist ideology as the future direction for Russian and other indigenous identities.

By the early 1990s, Russian leaders such as Boris Yeltsin were calling on ethnic leaders to assert their authority over and against the Soviet government. Greater autonomy was exercised by the native and ethnically based republics, such as Tatarstan, Bashkortostan, and Sakha-Yakutia. By the time of the Soviet Union's collapse in 1991, the indigenous populations in Russia were ready to assume control of their own affairs.

Modern Russia

Since that time, the Russian Federation has struggled to preserve its territorial integrity. Russia is home to some 20 million Muslims, accounting for approximately one-seventh of the country's population. Birth rates among the Muslim population are increasing rapidly, with 1.7 births per 100 women among ethnic Russians compared to 4.5 births per 100 women among Muslim ethnic groups. Some regions on the Asiatic frontier, such as Chechnya, have Muslim majorities that are struggling to achieve nationhood.

As Russian Muslims and others have begun to rediscover their religious and ethnic backgrounds, ethnic conflicts have resulted. Violent recriminations against non-Russian and non-Orthodox Christian ethnic groups have been widespread during the 1990s and 2000s. This ethnic strife has contributed to the political conservatism of Russians, who have continued to deny autonomous rights for non-Russian ethnicities. Russia's territorial integration and internal security are at the top of the country's political agenda.

In response, Russian leader Vladimir Putin adopted a nationalist posture. Russian authorities have been accused of racial profiling, even arresting people of native and other minority groups with no evidence of any crime being committed. As Russia has no comprehensive law or set of laws against such discrimination, most of these cases—where they are pursued—are tried at the European

Belorussian folk dancers leap over a campfire while celebrating Ivan Kupala Day, a pre-Christian Slavic fertility rite and celebration of the summer solstice. A former Soviet republic, Belarus gained independence in 1991. With it came a revival of ethnic identity. *(Viktor Drachev/ AFP/Getty Images)*

Court of Human Rights, and few people experiencing racial injustice are able to pursue the matter.

In addition to internal discrimination, military action in places such as Chechnya and Georgia showed that the assertion of Russian identity did not end with the decline of the Soviet Union. In December 1994, Russian troops invaded Chechnya, challenging Chechen independence from Russia's sphere of influence. Many Russian troops were accused of human rights violations during the twenty-one months of conflict. In 2008, the Russia government again demonstrated its agenda for controlling areas on the nation's periphery through its war with Georgia.

As in decades past, however, other voices called for more tolerance. Russia has encouraged native language use by signing the European Charter for Regional or Minority Languages in 2001. In 2010, the Russia Duma accepted and ratified Protocol 14 of the European Convention for the Protection of Human Rights.

Eva M. Stolberg and Steven L. Danver

See also: *Groups: Europe*—Russians; Tatars, Volga. *Issues*—Indigenous Governments; Land Rights; Relocation.

Further Reading

Barker, Adele, and Bruce Grant, eds. *The Russia Reader: History, Culture, Politics.* Durham, NC: Duke University Press, 2010.

Burbank, Jane. *Russian Empire: Space, People, Power, 1700–1930.* Bloomington: Indiana University Press, 2007.

Freeze, Gregory L. *Russia: A History.* 3rd ed. New York: Oxford University Press, 2009.

Service, Robert. *A History of Modern Russia: From Tsarism to the Twenty-First Century.* 3rd ed. Cambridge, MA: Harvard University Press, 2009.

Steinberg, John W., and Rex A. Wade, eds. *The Making of Russian History: Society, Culture, and the Politics of Modern Russia.* Bloomington, IN: Slavic Publishers, 2009.

Rwanda

The Republic of Rwanda is a land-locked country located in Central Africa. Unlike many African countries, whose populations are composed of hundreds of different ethnic groups, Rwanda is home to just three indigenous peoples: the Hutu, Tutsi, and Twa. The former German and later Belgian colony has a long and painful history of ethnic prejudice and violence.

Archaeological findings indicate that humans moved into the area that is now Rwanda sometime after the last ice age, between the Neolithic period and 3000 B.C.E. Archaeologists have found evidence of hunter-gatherers in the area, who likely were the ancestors of the Twa, also known as the Batwa or Abasangwabutaka, meaning "original inhabitants." The Twa are a seminomadic

Pygmy people that also reside in parts of Burundi, the Democratic Republic of the Congo, and Uganda.

Between 700 B.C.E. and 1 C.E., Bantu farmers called Hutu (also known as Kiga) migrated to Rwanda from the north, possibly the Great Rift Valley. The Hutu mixed with the Twa but soon outnumbered them, forcing the Twa to retreat into the mountain forests and claiming ownership of their land for farming. The sociopolitical structure of the Hutu was based on class. Around 1400 came the Tutsi, a group of cattle-rearing Cushitic speakers from the Horn of Africa that brought a monarchical political system in which power lay with the *mwami* (king).

Although the two groups are known today by different names, their history is somewhat complicated, as definitions of who are Hutu and who are Tutsi have changed over time and space. Apart from their social structures and some physical features, the Hutu and Tutsi speak the same language (Kinyarwanda), intermarry, and share many cultural characteristics. Before the colonial period, the native people of Rwanda lived and worked together. The process of colonization, however, sowed the seeds of hatred between the two groups.

From 1884 to 1918, Rwanda was ruled by Germany, becoming part of German East Africa, together with Burundi. The Germans clearly favored the usually lighter-skinned Tutsi, whom they believed to be less African and therefore superior to the Hutu; colonial policy allowed only Tutsi to be educated and to participate in government. Following Germany's defeat in World War I, Rwanda was administered by Belgium, beginning in 1923, as a "mandate" of the League of Nations.

In 1933, Belgian officials established a policy requiring the native peoples to carry ethnic identity cards that classified them as Hutu, Tutsi, or Twa. The classifications were based on physical appearance, occupation, and social status. When differences in skin tone among the people were indistinguishable, the Belgian authorities checked to see whether the person had a long nose or owned cattle. Those with ten or more heads of cattle were classified as members of the Tutsi aristocracy. Such ethnic classifications, exacerbated by political, economic, and social favoritism of one group over another, entrenched hostilities between the Hutu and the Tutsi, which culminated in violence during the 1950s and 1960s.

Beginning in 1990, Rwanda was entrenched in civil war; an estimated 1.17 million people died during the four-year conflict. In October 1993, a Tutsi military coup in neighboring Burundi enflamed the Hutu in Rwanda who feared a reassertion of Tutsi domination. Violence escalated in early 1994, as anti-Tutsi propaganda was put forth by the Hutu-dominated Rwandan government. The situation came to a horrific head when on April 6, 1994, an aircraft carrying Rwandan President Juvénal Habyarimana and Burundi President Cyprian Ntaryamira, both Hutus, was shot down, killing all on board. The Hutu immediately blamed the Tutsi, and over 10,000 Tutsi were killed in the next few days. Even worse followed. Over the 100 days following the crash, some 800,000 Tutsi and their sympathizers were killed.

Today, although the Rwandan government has no official policy toward its indigenous people, the country's dominant political party, the Rwandan Patriotic Front (RPF), is composed mostly of Tutsis. Although a constitutional amendment in 2004 banned political parties from classifying themselves along ethnic lines, the RPF has refused to comply. Hutu opposition leaders have been arrested or exiled, and though the constitution also asks Rwandans who lost their nationality between 1959 and 1994 because they fled the violence in their homeland to return to Rwanda, there is no call for the Hutu who fled between 1994 and 1998 to return.

Rwanda's original inhabitants, the Twa, account for 0.4 percent of the nation's 10.5 million people. These seminomadic hunter-gatherers have lived in the forests for many years, but now the forests are being cleared to make way for farms and development projects. As a result, the Twa are being forced to find homes elsewhere. The government never has recognized the Twa's ancestral land rights, nor has it compensated them for the lands they have lost.

Socially, the Twa have little access to education and almost no representation in government. They suffer from ethnic prejudice, discrimination, marginalization, and societal exclusion. Because they no longer can make a living in the forests, many have turned to pottery, an ancestral tradition, as a source of livelihood. As a result of change in land policy instituted in 2005, however, the marshland where the Twa collect clay now is being used to grow rice. In 2007, the primary source of livelihood for 40 percent of Twa men was begging.

The International Work Group for International Affairs has asserted that the Rwandan government does not recognize the Twa as an indigenous people and that it seeks to force the Twa to assimilate into the Tutsi-dominated Rwandan culture. The Rwandan government continues to dispute that assertion.

Aje-Ori Agbese

See also: *Groups: Africa*—Hutu; Rundi; Tutsi. *Issues*—Colonialism; Genocide; Political Discrimination.

Further Reading
Adekunle, Julius O. *Culture and Customs of Rwanda.* Westport, CT: Greenwood, 2007.

Ensign, Margee M. and William E. Bertrand. *Rwanda: History and Hope.* Lanham, MD: University Press of America, 2010.

Mamdani, Mahmood. *When Victims Become Killers: Colonialism, Nativism, and the Genocide in Rwanda.* Princeton, NJ: Princeton University Press, 2001.

Stidsen, Sille, ed. *The Indigenous World 2007.* Copenhagen, Denmark: International Work Group for Indigenous Affairs, 2007.

Samoa

Samoa comprises a group of Polynesian islands and islets in the South Pacific Ocean, located approximately 1,800 miles (3,000 kilometers) northeast of New Zealand and stretching about 300 miles (483 kilometers) from east to west. Nine inhabited and five uninhabited islands make up the Independent State of Samoa (formerly called Western Samoa); the largest island is Savai'i, where the capital is located at Apia. Another six islands form American Samoa, a federal territory of the United States that is administered by the Department of the Interior. Until the twentieth century, the Samoan Islands also were known as the Navigators Islands, so called for the native Samoans' superior seafaring skills.

The first Europeans arrived in the Samoan Islands during the early eighteenth century, establishing Christian missions and settlements there. In 1899, the United States annexed the eastern Samoan Islands, while Germany took possession of western islands, calling them Western Samoa. In 1914, an expeditionary force from New Zealand occupied Western Samoa. Following the German defeat in World War I, New Zealand administered the territory as a "mandate," as part of the League of Nations Mandate.

During the influenza pandemic of 1918–1919, more than 7,500 Samoans—about one-fifth of the population—died, prompting accusations of negligence against the colonial administration. The New Zealand authorities had allowed the crew and passengers of the *SS Talune* to debark at Apia, even though it was obvious that many were sick with influenza. In response to the incompetence of their colonial administrators, Samoans formed a political movement during the 1920s called the Mau, meaning "opinion," to protest colonialism on the islands.

George Richardson, the administrator for Samoa, responded to the growing strength of the Mau movement by enacting new laws that allowed for the deportation of Europeans or Samoans of mixed heritage who engaged in political agitation. On Sunday, December 28, 1929, a large demonstration in the center of Apia turned violent.

Among those killed on "Black Sunday," as the incident became known, was High Chief Tupua Tamasese Lealofi, who led the demonstration. His death gave the movement renewed strength to press for independence, which was granted on January 1, 1962.

In 1977, Western Samoa changed its name to Samoa. Until the 1990s, the legislature was elected by and made up of the *matai* (chiefs). In 1990, all Samoans, including women, were given the right to vote for their parliament, though the government still is headed by a hereditary chief of state, who is one of the two paramount chiefs.

Andrew J. Waskey

See also: Groups: East Asia and Oceania—Polynesians. *Issues*—Colonialism; Indigenous Governments.

Further Reading
Boot, Max. *The Savage Wars of Peace: Small Wars and the Rise of American Power.* New York: Basic Books, 2002.

Lawson, Stephanie. *Tradition Versus Democracy in the South Pacific: Fiji, Tonga and Western Samoa.* Cambridge, UK: Cambridge University Press, 2008.

Lay, Graeme. *Samoa: Pacific Pride.* Honolulu: University of Hawaii Press, 2000.

Somalia

Somalia occupies an important strategic location at the crossroads of Africa and the Middle East. Covering an area of approximately 246,000 square miles (638,000 square kilometers), the country is bound by the Gulf of Aden to the north and the Indian Ocean to the east and shares borders with Djibouti, Ethiopia, and Kenya to the west.

In 2011, Somalis were estimated to number 9.9 million. Between 60 percent and 70 percent of Somalis are nomads, with some practicing farming and herding. A small segment of the population lives in urban coastal communities, engaging in fishing and petty trading. Farming and pastoralist communities are found in the Juba and Shebelle river valleys. Minority groups account for roughly one-third of Somalia's population; the indigenous Bantu and Bajuni are the largest of these. Most of Somalia's native people are landless laborers.

History and Ethnic Identities

Medieval Arab geographers described the inhabitants of present-day Somalia as Berberi, a reference to the ongoing interactions of the people of Africa with those of the

Arab Peninsula and Indonesia for more than a millennium. Some linguists posit that Somalis are of Cushitic ancestry, with close links to the Afar, Beja, Oromo, and Saho peoples of the Horn of Africa.

Oral tradition suggests that the Somalis occupied their present home by 100 C.E. and adopted Islam in the seventh century, when Muslim scholars and refugees sought asylum from Arabia among the Somalis. Their easy acceptance of Islam is attributed to their monotheistic religious belief system, which centers on the worship of a central deity called *waaq* (sky god).

During the fifteenth century, conflicts between Muslims and Christians drew in the Portuguese, whose commercial interests in the Indian Ocean combined with their zeal and support for fellow Christians. The Portuguese attacked and burned the coastal cities of Barva, Berbera, Mogadishu, and Zeilah, setting in motion the decline of coastal Muslim Somali towns and establishing their dominance in a region. Despite Portuguese colonialism, Somali cities and institutions persisted, and the clan became the basic unit of administrative structure.

During the late nineteenth century, Ismail Pasha of Egypt, with the encouragement of the British, took control of parts of northeastern Africa and captured Harrar, one of the most important cities in the region, in 1875. The Egyptians vacated Harrar in 1885, and the city was besieged by Ethiopia in 1887.

In 1891, Mohammed Abdullah Hassan waged a war that reclaimed Harrar and Mogadishu. Hassan claimed that he was the *Mahdi* (the chosen one) who would unify the Muslim world to defeat the so-called Western infidels. His power and authority grew quickly, prompting him to step up his opposition to British colonial rule in Somalia. In response to the large following that Hassan had gained, the British nicknamed him the "Mad Mullah" and proceeded to mount four military expeditions to end his attacks in British Somaliland and the Ogaden region of Ethiopia. Hassan managed to evade the British, but he died of pneumonia sometime between November 1920 and January 1921.

The history of the modern state of Somalia commenced in the 1880s, when Ethiopia, France, Great Britain, and Italy all occupied what is now Somalia. The colonial administration's policy in British Somaliland emphasized law and order as opposed to developing the territory. In Italian Somalia (which lay south along Shebelle River), colonial settlement was encouraged with a view toward establishing cash-crop banana plantations for the Italian market. Italy envisioned establishing an East African empire by invading and conquering Ethiopia in 1935 and British Somaliland in 1940. The occupation was short-lived, however, as Britain invaded and conquered the Italian forces in British Somaliland, Italian Somalia, and Ethiopia in 1941.

Italian Somalia was returned to Italy as a United Nations trusteeship territory in 1949. The arrangement stipulated that Italy would oversee the territory for a period of ten years. On June 26, 1960, British Somaliland gained independence and joined with Italian Somalia to form a union on July 1 of that year, to be known as the Somali Republic. The joint parliament of the republic elected Aden Abdullah Osman Dar president, ratifying the parliamentary form of government in the constitution in 1961.

After independence, Somalia followed a democratic system and held regular elections until 1969, when the government was deposed in a coup staged by Mohamed Siad Barre, who suspended the 1961 constitution and replaced it with a socialist-leaning junta called the Supreme Revolutionary Council. Under Siad Barre's regime, personal liberties were curbed and rural development largely was ignored. His rule alienated several Somali clans, including the Hawiye, Isaaq, and Ogadeni. The Isaaq, which long had been the ruling elite in the military and civil services, were suppressed by Siad Barre, as he consolidated power among the Darood clan.

During the late 1980s, this led to civil war between the government and five opposition armies. In January 1991, the capital, Mogadishu, fell to Hawiye soldiers, causing Siad Barre to flee the country. Although the Hawiye installed Ali Mahdi Mohamed as president, this did not end the civil war, as other clan-based groups now began to fight the Hawiye.

Modern Somalia, Chaos, and Native Peoples

By the mid-1990s, Somalia was considered a failed state, requiring the intervention of the international community to restore a working government. The governments of Djibouti, Egypt, Ethiopia, Italy, Kenya, and Yemen, together with the Intergovernmental Authority on Development, Organization of African Unity, and African Union, tried to initiate peace talks among the warring factions, with little success. With the onset of the global War on Terror in 2001, many saw Somalia as a new front in the war, with its native groups, headed by so-called warlords, acting as militias.

By January 2011, more than 1.5 million people, most of them from Somalia's minority native populations, had been displaced and were living in refugee camps. The native Bajuni and Bantu peoples had their lands and possessions confiscated, and as a result, they are disproportionately represented in refugee camps. Once in the camps, groups such as the Somali terrorist organization al-Shabab have made it difficult for the United Nations and other international aid groups to provide food and access to clean water, making the situation even more intolerable for Somalia's native populations. In this context, native women often face the terrible choice between rape and survival. As there still was no stable central government as of 2012, the situation remains bleak for Somalia's native peoples.

Hannington Ochwada and Steven L. Danver

See also: *Groups: Africa*—Somali. *Issues*—Agriculture; Colonialism; Revolts.

Further Reading

Bradbury, Mark. *Becoming Somaliland.* Bloomington: Indiana University Press, 2008.

Lewis, I.M. *A Modern History of Somalia: Nation and State in the Horn of Africa.* 4th ed. Athens: Ohio University Press, 2002.

———. *Understanding Somalia and Somaliland.* New York: Columbia University Press, 2008.

South Africa

South Africa is a country in transition. Many historians and political scientists consider it the most influential country in Africa south of the Sahara Desert. South Africa has a long history of conflict, struggle, and empowerment, all of which have contributed to the development of the modern state. Now a majority ruled democratic society, the twenty-first-century South African government has inherited many challenges, including an ill-equipped education system and a misguided health care agenda. Despite these challenges, South Africa has become the international community's model of democracy and stability in the region.

South Africa is located on the southernmost tip of continental Africa, sharing land borders with Botswana, Lesotho (which is surrounded in its entirety by South Africa), Mozambique, Namibia, Swaziland, and Zimbabwe. The South African coast marks the dividing line between the Indian Ocean and the South Atlantic Ocean. Comparable in size to the U.S. state of Texas, South Africa's interior is dominated by a plateau that is surrounded by rugged hills and a narrow coastal plain. The southeast of the country is heavily forested. The majority of the country is made up of thick savannah, while in the north, the terrain becomes thinner grasslands. South Africa is rich in natural resources such as gold, diamonds, and platinum, and it is known for having long sunny days and cool nights.

People have inhabited the area that is now South Africa for thousands of years. Native speakers of the Khoisan language are the land's oldest inhabitants, though only a few of their descendants survive today. The majority of the region's black African inhabitants migrated south from the interior of the continent and settled in the area around 100 C.E. The Nguni, ancestors of the Xhosa and Zulu, occupied most of the eastern coast by 1500. During the sixteenth century, the first Europeans arrived in the area.

The Portuguese were the first to reach the Cape of Good Hope in 1488. No permanent European settlements were established there until 1652, when the Dutch East India Company developed a station at the Cape. In the years that followed, French Huguenot refugees, Dutch, and Germans settled in the area. Together, their descendants make up today's Afrikaner population in South Africa. These settlements had profound political and social influence on the indigenous groups in the region. The Afrikaners' policies of racial superiority and their right to possess the land led to the conquest of those native cultures. By 1779, European settlements had control over much of the Cape and began to spread eastward. Many frontier wars were fought between the native inhabitants and the European conquerors.

By the eighteenth century, Great Britain had gained control over the Cape, and British colonists began to settle in the area. This marked the beginning of the conflict between the Afrikaners and the English. Starting in 1836, Afrikaner farmers, also called Boers, began moving north to escape British authority. Their migration, known as the Great Trek, put the Afrikaners into conflict with many African groups, the most powerful of which were the Zulu. After much fighting, the Boers ultimately defeated the Zulu nation at the Battle of Blood River in 1838. Although the Zulu were defeated in that battle, they were not conquered until 1879.

The Boers created their own states, Transvaal and the Orange Free State, in 1852 and 1854, respectively. In response to the discovery of gold and diamonds in the newly formed states, many British citizens and other Africans migrated to the area for investment and employment opportunities. In 1880–1881 and 1899–1902, the Anglo-Boer Wars were fought in reaction to the influx of British influence in the infant states. Subsequently, Britain conquered the tiny states and incorporated them into the British Empire.

In 1910, the Union of South Africa was formed as a dominion of the British Empire; its constitution secured power for the white population. In 1912, the South African Native National Congress, later known as the African National Congress (ANC), was formed with the primary goal of ending restrictions based on race and ensuring the inclusion of blacks in the national parliament.

In 1948, the National Party won the national elections, which were restricted to white voters, and began passing strict policies to further enhance the authority of the minority white population in the country. These policies, which became known as apartheid, meaning "apartness," put into effect restrictions based on race, such as the homeland system, where blacks were forced to live apart from whites (and usually apart from where they worked), and the pass laws, which severely curtailed the movements of black people in South Africa.

In the early 1960s, following a protest at Sharpeville in which sixty-nine demonstrators were killed by the police and 180 were injured, the ANC and the Pan Africanist Congress of Azania (PAC) were banned. Activist Nelson Mandela and many others were convicted and imprisoned on charges of treason. The ANC and other anti-apartheid organizations were forced underground, where they continued to carry out guerilla warfare and sabotage.

The popular movement for the end of apartheid, which had taken shape with the press given to the Soweto Uprisings of April 1976 and June 1985, convinced many in the National Party that a new course of action was necessary to quell the racial conflicts. Although a new constitution was adopted in 1984, blacks remained effectively disenfranchised. In 1990, after secret negotiations with Mandela, President Frederik Willem de Klerk lifted the ban on the ANC, PAC, and other political organizations. Nine days later, Mandela was released from Victor Vester prison.

In May 1994, Mandela was elected president in South Africa's first-ever democratic elections open to voters of all races. Under his leadership, the ANC pursued a policy of national social reform. Mandela's goal was to correct the wrongs that had been instituted during the apartheid regime and to forge a new South African identity. The postapartheid constitution of 1997 allowed a nation

NELSON MANDELA

On May 10, 1994, Nelson Mandela was sworn into office as the president of South Africa, becoming the country's first black president and the first South African leader ever to be chosen in a fully representative democratic election. Just a few years earlier, in 1990, Mandela had been released from prison, where he had spent more than two and a half decades for his efforts to end South Africa's racist apartheid system. Mandela's election was a landmark for the African nation, signaling the beginning of a new, democratic era.

Nelson Rolihlahla Mandela was born on July 18, 1918, in Mvezo in South Africa's Eastern Cape Province. His father, Gadla Henry Mphakanyiswa, was the native Tembu chief of the town. After finishing his studies at University College of Fort Hare and the University of Witwatersand, Mandela became an attorney. He joined the African National Congress (ANC) in 1944 and embarked on a long career as an anti-apartheid activist, working to ensure the rights of the country's indigenous peoples.

Though the majority of South Africa's population was black, the country was dominated, politically and economically, by a minority white population that imposed a system of racial segregation known as apartheid on the native peoples. Following the election victory in 1948 of the Afrikaner-led National Party, which supported apartheid, Mandela became active in politics. Under his leadership, the ANC was at the forefront of a mass movement that spoke out against the treatment meted out to the blacks.

In 1962, Mandela was convicted on charges of sabotage, among other accusations, and was sentenced to life

in prison. He spent twenty-seven years behind bars, much of that time on Robben Island, which was notorious as the home of many political prisoners.

During his imprisonment, Mandela became an international symbol of the fight against apartheid, inspiring a worldwide campaign for his release. In 1985, he turned down an offer from the government for a conditional release, refusing to change or soften his position on apartheid. He finally was released on February 11, 1990, after South African President F.W. de Klerk reversed the long-standing ban on the ANC and other anti-apartheid groups.

Mandela was elected president of the ANC at its first national conference in 1991, and in 1994, the South Africans chose him to be their president in the country's first-ever multiracial elections. During his five-year presidency, Mandela emphasized national reconciliation between whites and blacks and introduced a host of economic and social reforms to modernize the country. In retirement, he has been involved in many social causes, advocating for orphaned children and patients with human immunodeficiency virus/acquired immune deficiency syndrome (HIV/AIDS), among others.

Mandela was awarded the Nobel Peace Prize in 1993, and in 2002, President George W. Bush awarded him the Presidential Medal of Freedom, the highest civilian honor in the United States. Today, Mandela's birthday, July 18, is celebrated to commemorate his contributions to world freedom and social justice.

Patit Paban Mishra

President Nelson Mandela *(left)* and Deputy President F.W. de Klerk cheer passage of South Africa's "final" constitution in 1996. The new charter established a parliamentary democracy with majority rule, included a bill of rights, and recognized nine indigenous languages. *(Mike Hutchings/AP Images)*

scarred by racial policies to reorganize and called for a parliamentary democracy with majority rule, in which power is shared between the president and parliament.

In 1997, Mandela stepped down as president of the ANC, and in 1999, he was succeeded by Thabo Mbeki as president of both the ANC and South Africa. Mbeki served two five-year terms. He refocused the ANC's agenda from reconciliation to transformation, particularly on the economic front. He was succeeded in 2009 by former deputy president of the ANC, Jacob Zuma.

Today, South Africa still has a long way to go in the area of human rights and development. Although political violence declined dramatically in the years after the abolishment of the apartheid system, members of the police have been reported for committing abuses, and deaths of blacks in police custody as a result of excessive force remain an issue. Discrimination against women and children and against those living with human immunodeficiency virus/acquired immune deficiency syndrome (HIV/AIDS) continues.

The state of South Africa's health care system is inadequate. The country is home to more HIV-positive people—more than 20 percent of the adult population—than any other country in the world. In 2008, at least 1.4 million South African children were orphaned because of HIV/AIDS. The prevalence of HIV has fueled a concurrent tuberculosis epidemic and a growing incidence of multiple and extensive drug-resistant tuberculosis. Government policies, in concert with nongovernmental organizations that administer international aid, are working to correct these problems.

South Africa has made tremendous progress in the past twenty years, transitioning from a government ruled by the minority to a government of inclusion and democratic rule with no restrictions based on race. Critics note that although there is much work to be done to advance human rights issues, with international assistance, goals for improvement can be set and met by the mid-twenty-first century. South Africa hosted the World Cup in 2010, sending a message to the world that it was poised to meet these challenges.

Abdul Karim Bangura

See also: Groups: *Africa*—Xhosa; Zulu. *Issues*—Colonialism; Political Discrimination; Revolts; Social Discrimination.

Further Reading

Bangura, Abdul Karim. *Sweden vs. Apartheid: Putting Morality Ahead of Profit.* Aldershot, UK: Ashgate, 2004.

Clark, Nancy L., and William H. Worger. *South Africa: The Rise and Fall of Apartheid.* New York: Pearson Longman, 2004.

Liebenberg, Elri. "Mapping British South Africa: The Case of G.S.G.S. 2230." *Imago Mundi* 49 (1997): 129–142.

Outwater, Anne, Naeema Abrahams, and Jacquelyn C. Campbell. "Women in South Africa: Intentional Violence and HIV/AIDS: Intersections and Prevention." *Journal of Black Studies* 35:4 (2005): 135–154.

Ross, Robert. *A Concise History of South Africa.* New York: Cambridge University Press, 1999.

Thompson, Leonard Monteath. *The History of South Africa.* 3rd ed. New Haven, CT: Yale University Press, 2001.

United States Agency for International Development. "USAID Africa: South Africa (November 2009)."

Spain

Spain is located in southwestern Europe, occupying most of the Iberian Peninsula, which it shares with its smaller neighbor Portugal. With a population of more than 47 million people, the county is geographically and culturally diverse. Castilians are the dominant ethnic group in Spain, and their language is the basis for modern Spanish.

Today, the term *Castilian* often is used interchangeably with *Spaniard.* However, modern Spain also is home to many distinct regional cultures, including Basques, Catalans, Galicians, and others, that retain their unique traditions and languages. These people often prefer to identify themselves by their regional identities rather than adopt a common Spanish identity, and some groups have lobbied aggressively for independence from Spain.

History

Present-day Spain was inhabited by peoples of Celtic and Iberian origin—known as Celtiberians—as early as the sixth century B.C.E. Romans arrived on the Iberian Peninsula in the second century B.C.E. in pursuit of their enemies, the Carthaginians and the Phoenicians, who had colonized the coast of the Mediterranean Sea between the eighth and sixth centuries B.C.E. Initially, the native peoples resisted the invaders, but eventually they assimilated into the Germanic Visigothic culture, which arrived on the peninsula in the sixth century C.E.

That fusion produced a variety of dialects of the Ibero-Romance languages, including Castilian—the basis of the Spanish language today—through the interaction of Latin and local Celtiberian tongues. Celtic imprints still survive in Spain's regional cultures, in Asturias, Basque Country, Catalonia, and Galicia. In some areas, regional languages, such as Fala, are closer to Portuguese than to Castilian. Euskara, spoken in Basque Country, remains distinct not only from other Romance languages but also from rest of the world languages; therefore, it is categorized as a language isolate.

During the eighth century, Moors occupied most of Spain and influenced the native languages there, imparting many words that still are in use today. In order to recapture those areas from the Muslim Moors—a crusade known as the Reconquista (reconquest)—the Romans began to unite their Christian kingdoms. In 1200, the Spanish areas of Basque Country joined with the kingdoms of Aragon, Castile, Catalonia, Galicia, and Valencia to form a Spanish state, which was united after the conquest of Granada in 1492. The Castilian language and culture predominated in most areas of the new Spanish Empire.

In the early sixteenth century, Basque Country was divided between France and Spain on either side of the western Pyrenees Mountains. The Statutes of Vizcaya provided autonomy to the Spanish regions, but this was abolished in 1876 after the Basque defeat in the Carlist Wars.

Following the War of the Spanish Succession (1701–1714), the Spanish state was centralized under the Bourbon kings in 1714. Still, Spain would experience many wars and conflicts in different parts of the world, especially with the United States, in the early twentieth century.

In 1931, the Second Spanish Republic offered regional autonomy to the country's Basque, Catalan, and Galician populations, though this proved to be short-lived, ending with the onset of the Spanish Civil War in 1936. In 1939, General Francisco Franco banned all languages except Castilian in an effort to create a single Spanish identity. As a consequence, separatist movements arose in Basque Country, Catalonia, and Galicia.

The Basque separatist organization Euskadi Ta Askatasuna (ETA, Basque Homeland and Freedom) formed in 1959, earning notoriety as the most violent and most strident of the regional groups. After Franco's death in 1975, Spain's 1978 constitution outlined a decentralized system of governance that granted varying degrees of autonomy to regions and communities.

A peace process was initiated with the ETA by the Socialist government of José Luis Rodriguez Zapatero, which was targeted for bomb attacks in 2005–2006. This led to a permanent ceasefire to be declared by the ETA in October 2011.

Current Status

Today, there are seventeen autonomous communities and two autonomous cities within Spain. Many regional tongues have been recognized as official languages, alongside Spanish, in the communities where they are spoken. Euskara was declared an official language in Basque Country and Navarre, Catalan in Catalonia and the Balearic Islands, Valencian in that community, and Galician in that region. Aragonese, Aranese, Asturian, Cantabrian, and Extremaduran also are spoken by small regional populations in Spain. Public education is offered in both Spanish and native languages in autonomous communities, while local electronic media and academies promote regional cultures and languages.

The Basque city of País Vasco is the second most industrialized region in Spain after Catalonia. Development there has attracted people from elsewhere in Spain to settle in the city, leaving fewer opportunities for the local population. This is true for many other towns as well, such as Navarre. On the other hand, internal mobilization for education and work purposes has increased the diffusion of populations.

Muhammad Aurang Zeb Mughal

See also: *Groups: Europe*—Basques; Castilians; Roma (Gypsies). *Issues*—Revolts.

Further Reading

Crow, John A. *Spain: The Root and the Flower: An Interpretation of Spain and Spanish People.* Berkeley: University of California Press, 2005.

Fletcher, Richard. *Moorish Spain.* Los Angeles: University of California Press, 2006.

Hume, Martin A.S. *The Spanish People: Their Origin, Growth, and Influence.* New York: D. Appleton, 1901.

Kamen, Henry. *Spain: A Society of Conflict.* 3rd ed. New York: Pearson Longman, 2005.

Sri Lanka

Sri Lanka (formerly known as Ceylon) is an island nation in South Asia, situated in the Indian Ocean off the southern coast of India. The country is home to two major ethnic groups: the Sinhalese, who dominate the southern, western, and north-central parts of the island, and the Tamils, who claim the northeast. From the 1980s until 2009, these two groups engaged in a protracted civil war. Sri Lanka also is home to smaller populations of Burghers (the descendants of European colonists) and Muslims. Thus, this small nation boasts a diversity of cultures, religious faiths, and languages.

The Buddhist Sinhalese are the dominant ethnic group in Sri Lanka, making up about 75 percent of the population. The island's mostly Hindu Tamil population can be divided into two groups: Sri Lankan Tamils, the descendants of long-settled migrants from southeastern India, and Indian Tamils, more recent immigrants that were brought to the island as migrant workers by the British during the colonial period. Sri Lankan Tamils are the largest ethnic minority in the country, representing nearly 13 percent of the population. In 1921, Indian Tamils made up more than 13 percent of the total Tamil population; however, as a result of the Ceylon Citizenship Acts of 1948 and 1949, which stripped many Indian Tamils of their citizenship, they were reduced to just over 5 percent by 1981, and today they represent only a fraction of Sri Lanka's Tamil population. Muslims, who

trace their heritage to the seafaring Arab merchants of the eighth century, account for nearly 8 percent of the island's population.

Two main languages are spoken in Sri Lanka: Sinhala, the language of the Sinhalese majority, and Tamil, which is spoken by both Muslims and Tamils. Although Sinhala and Tamil are of different origins, they share some common features and have influenced one another's linguistic evolution. Sinhala is believed to derive from one of two phases of development of the Indo-Aryan group of languages: Old Indo-Aryan (ca. 2000–800 B.C.E.), represented by the Sanskrit language, and Middle Indo-Aryan (ca. 800 B.C.E.–400 C.E.), represented by Pali, the language of Buddhist scripture. Tamil belongs to the Dravidian family of languages, spoken by the natives of the South Indian state of Tamil Nadu. Tamil was used widely as a medium of communication in trade and business along the Indian and Sri Lankan coasts. Arab traders from the Middle East also used Tamil when they traded in the region.

The majority of Sinhalese adhere to the Theravada school of Buddhism, which was introduced in Sri Lanka during the second century B.C.E. by the Venerable Mahinda, the son of the Emperor Ashoka, during the reign of Sri Lankan King Devanampiyatissa. Hinduism, the second-largest religion in Sri Lanka, is predominantly the faith of the Tamils of Sri Lanka. Although Buddhism and Hinduism are closely related ideologically, relations between Buddhists and Hindus in Sri Lanka have been tense since the escalation of the Sinhalese–Tamil ethnic civil war in the 1980s.

Buddhist *bhikkhus* (monks) play an important role in Sri Lanka's sociopolitical life and hold considerable sway over politicians and policy makers. Religious symbols and leaders dominate the country's political agenda, and Sinhalese politicians often politicize Buddhism to win the support of Sinhalese who approach Buddhist monks for guidance. Buddhist monks argue that anyone may call Sri Lanka home, so long as the Buddhist Sinhalese enjoy cultural, religious, economic, political, and linguistic hegemony. The state remains officially neutral in religious affairs, though a provision in the country's current constitution (instituted in 1978) grants a privileged place in national life for the Buddhist religion while protecting the rights of those minority groups that adhere to other religions to practice their faiths.

Sri Lanka's economy historically was based on paddy (wet rice) cultivation. During the colonial period (1796–1948), British rulers introduced commercial agriculture. Beginning in the early 1960s, Sri Lankan governments intervened directly in the country's largely free market economy. Imports and exports were tightly regulated, and the state sector expanded, especially in manufacturing and transportation. This trend was reinforced in the 1970s, when a center-left coalition government led by the socialist Sri Lanka Freedom Party nationalized large plantations on the island and imposed direct controls on internal trade.

Beginning in 1977, the conservative United National Party embarked on a massive effort to encourage private enterprise, welcome foreign investment, and relax import controls. It shifted spending away from subsidies and social welfare to investment in the nation's infrastructure, most notably through a massive irrigation project, the Mahaweli Ganga Program, which was expected to make Sri Lanka self-reliant in rice and generate enough hydroelectric power to meet the nation's requirements. These policies resulted in higher rates of economic growth in the late 1970s and early 1980s but failed to ease the economic difficulties of the poor.

Today, Sri Lanka remains a poor country. The flow of foreign aid from China, Japan, the United States, Western Europe, and international organizations has helped Sri Lanka run its economy in the midst of civil war. The deteriorating security situation lowered growth to 3.8 percent in 1996. The economy rebounded in 1997–2000, with average growth of 5.3 percent. However, in 2001, the country experienced the first recession in its history as a result of power shortages, budgetary problems, a global economic slowdown, and continuing civil strife. Signs of recovery became evident after the 2002 cease-fire.

The civil war, coupled with the emergence of extremist Sinhalese nationalist forces, have put an end to the cultural harmony that once characterized this pluralistic society. Sri Lankan political programs have recognized and allowed expressions of Sinhalese identity. However, some Sinhalese maintain that they are the "chosen people" of the island, contributing to the radicalization of some sections of this socially and economically weakened group. Sinhalese nationalists openly endorsed a war that killed, according to former United Nations spokesperson Gordon Weiss, more than 40,000 Tamil civilians between January and May 2009.

Sri Lanka's experiences indicate that modernization can result in ethnic tensions in a deeply divided society when nation building favors one group over others. However, social scientists maintain that Sri Lanka still can achieve peace and reconciliation if the Sinhalese political class adopts a broader political and social agenda to accommodate the needs of the Tamil natives and other minorities.

A.R.M. Imtiyaz

See also: *Groups: South Asia and Middle East*—Sinhalese; Tamils. *Issues*—Political Discrimination.

Further Reading

Bartholomeusz, Tessa J., and Chandra R. de Silva. *Buddhist Fundamentalism and Minority Identities in Sri Lanka.* Albany: State University of New York Press, 1998.

De Votta, Neil. *Blowback: Linguistic Nationalism, Institutional Decay, and Ethnic Conflict in Sri Lanka.* Stanford, CA: Stanford University Press, 2004.

Imtiyaz, A.R.M. "Eastern Muslims of Sri Lanka: Special Problems and Solutions." *Journal of Asian and African Studies* 44:4 (August 2009): 404–427.

———. "Politicization of Buddhism and Electoral Politics in Sri Lanka." In *Religion and Politics in South Asia,* ed. Ali Riaz. London: Routledge, 2010.

Imtiyaz, A.R.M., and Ben Stavis. "Ethno-Political Conflict in Sri Lanka." *Journal of Third World Studies* 25:2 (Fall 2008): 135–152.

Peebles, Patrick. *The History of Sri Lanka.* Westport, CT: Greenwood, 2006.

Sudan and South Sudan

The North African countries of Sudan and South Sudan have a diverse population of African and Arab peoples, a result of centuries of migration into the region from the Arab world and from central and southern Africa. Until 2011, the two countries were a single nation, the largest in Africa with a population of nearly 40 million.

The name *Sudan* derives from the Arabic phrase *bilād al-sūdān,* meaning "land of the blacks," which medieval geographers used to refer to the African territories that began at the southern edge of the Sahara Desert. The Nile River is the area's defining geographic feature, bifurcating the region and creating a dichotomy between north and south.

The region is home to more than 600 indigenous groups. These include the Danagla, Gaalien, and Shaigia in the north; the Bija in the east; the Baggara, Fur, Hamar, Kababish, and Nuba in the west; and the Dinka, Newir, and Skeluk in the south.

Early History

The region historically known as the Sudan stretched from the Atlantic Ocean in the west through the plains and savannah to the Red Sea in the east. Archaeological evidence indicates that a Paleolithic population occupied the Sudan as early as 250,000 B.C.E.

By 9000 B.C.E., proto-Sudanese groups had begun to emerge. These populations had a pre-agricultural society associated with a complex stone tool industry.

Archaeological and linguistic evidence shows that between 8000 and 7000 B.C.E., these people adopted food processing technologies and a sedentary lifestyle, and by 4000 to 3000 B.C.E., plant cultivation and animal domestication had been developed in the central Sudan.

The period after 3000 B.C.E. was marked by increasing Egyptian influence on Sudanese culture. For some 2,500 years before the common era, the relationship between dynastic Egypt and the Sudanese kingdoms of Nubia ranged from peaceful trade to conflict and, eventually, to colonization. The Egyptian conquest of the Sudanese kingdoms was not a completely successful venture, however, as it was punctuated by a series of counterconquests by the native Sudanese during times when Egypt was politically weak.

By 950 B.C.E., Napata had become a major Sudanese city. After many threats from the Egyptians and the Romans between 591 and 23 B.C.E., Napata was moved farther south to the region of Meroe. The area flourished, developing its own cultural traits and becoming a gateway for the diffusion of ideas and technology from Middle East into Africa.

Although Christianity had made inroads among the Sudanese by 550 C.E., the spread of Islam contributed to the decline of Christianity in the region. The first Muslim king reigned in the Dunqulah (or Dongola) Empire in north-central Sudan in 1315. By the sixteenth century, the last Christian Sudanese kingdom had been conquered. The Islamization of Sudan would have adverse effects on the indigenous culture of the native Sudanese, as many would be forced to abandon their beliefs and languages.

Political authority was centralized in central and northern Sudan under the Funj Sultanate. Federated states emerged in the south among the Azande and Nilotic population and in the west in the sultanate of Darfur. This federation not only eroded the native African kinship system but also introduced division and starvation among the native Sudanese, setting the stage for the Arabization of native Sudanese culture and identity in the nineteenth century.

Modern History and Quest for Independence

The nineteenth century opened a new window in Sudanese history. During this period, Sudan went through many changes in administration, eventually becoming a target for European colonialism.

In 1820, northern Sudan became an Egyptian territory under pasha and viceroy Muhammad Ali. This

DARFUR GENOCIDE

The roots of the genocide that took place in the Darfur region of Sudan beginning in April 2003 can be traced to the nineteenth century. Located in western Sudan, Darfur is a vast, hilly plateau that lies partly in the Sahara Desert and partly in the Sahel.

In 1888, Darfur was drawn into a war between the Egyptians and their British allies and the Mahdi Sudanese, known as the Mahdist Revolt. In 1898, aided by the sultan of Darfur, the British destroyed the Mahdist state. Great Britain governed Darfur and Sudan for the next fifty years, until Sudan became an independent state in 1956.

After independence, Sudan was devastated by two civil wars, in 1955–1972 and 1983–2011. The war would prove especially deadly in Darfur, where an ethnic cleansing campaign was carried out by the Janjaweed, an Arabic-speaking Bedouin militia. Coming from northern Sudan, their attacks in Darfur aimed to Arabize the region.

In 2003, the violence between the tribes in Darfur and the Sudanese government escalated. Many young women were abducted from Darfur villages, raped, and sold as sex slaves. During the ethnic cleansing, hundreds of thousands of civilians were killed, and approximately 2 million southern Sudanese were forced from their country as refugees. Many fled to neighboring Chad, where they were housed in refugee camps. By May 2004, it was known in the West that the atrocities in Darfur had risen to the level of genocide.

In summer of that year, the U.S. Congress, Secretary of State Colin Powell, and President George W. Bush all had issued statements decrying the genocide and calling on the United Nations to take action. However, it would take another two and a half years for the International Criminal Court to charge the leaders of the Sudanese government, the Sudanese army, and the Janjaweed with war crimes. Many international human rights groups have criticized Western governments for refusing to provide military support to stop the bloodshed and for allowing such a long period of time to transpire before action was taken to stop the genocide. Finally, in 2011, the Darfur Peace Agreement was signed, hopefully bringing an end to the strife.

Andrew J. Waskey

period in Sudanese history, which lasted until 1881, is referred to as the Turco-Egyptian or Turkiya regime. Under the Turkiya, Sudan was ruled by tyrants who excessively taxed the indigenous population, leading to starvation, slave raiding, and a monopoly on trade. The Turks also controlled Sudan's natural resources, such as gold. Some indigenous Sudanese—mostly former slaves from the non-Muslim region—were recruited into Muhammed Ali's army. Turco-Egyptian rule in Sudan was characterized by sixty years of hardship, division, and loss of cultural identity among the indigenous Sudanese.

In 1881, the Turkish regime was ended by the Mahdist Revolt, when the Sudanese rebelled against the tyrannical rule of the Egyptians. The rebellion, however, took on different expressions in northern and southern Sudan. While the mostly Arab Islamic population in northern Sudan regarded the revolt as an Islamic movement born out of religious enthusiasm, the southern Sudanese saw it as merely a continuation of despotic Turkish rule, as they continued to be the victims of slave raids and political marginalization—even by the northern Sudanese. Regardless, the Mahdist regime laid the groundwork for Sudanese nationalism, a movement that was truncated by the British invasion in the 1898.

The British conquest of Sudan, supported by the Egyptians, resulted in the deaths of many Sudanese. During this period, Sudan became an Anglo-Egyptian colony under the rulership of Lord Cromer of Great Britain and Ghali Pasha of Egypt, although Britain had greater control in the relationship. The situation in Sudan was much like that in other British colonies in Africa, with native Sudanese alienated from the affairs of their country as British imperial policy dominated all areas of life. Northern Sudan benefited more from Anglo-Egyptian rule compared with the south, sparking protracted resistance and civil unrest in the south.

Hostilities continued for forty years, until a few educated Sudanese formed the Graduate Congress in 1938. The Congress protested against the Anglo-Egyptian dictatorship and called for an effective nationalist movement to give the indigenous Sudanese a voice in the nation's affairs. Sudan achieved independence on January 1, 1956. Far from uniting the indigenous Sudanese, however, independence proved devastating, resulting in further racial and religious stratification.

Postindependence and the Split of Sudan

After independence, the Sudanese government focused on healing the deep divisions between the north and south. This only led to suspicion, regional conspiracies, and conflicts that claimed many lives and much property. The situation in the south became so severe that military president Gaafar Mohamed el-Nimieri, who held power from 1971 to 1985, claimed that resolving the "southern question" was the major goal of his administration. Despite the declaration of Nimieri's regime to solve the southern problem, relations between the north and south continued to deteriorate, as he began the process of transforming Sudan into an Islamic Republic in 1977. This led to civil war, political unrest, and starvation in the south. For much of the region's history after the 1970s, there was no winner in Sudan's civil war. Add to that the violence and genocide perpetrated upon the indigenous, non-Arab population of the region of Darfur, in the western part of Sudan, by the Sudanese military and Arabized militias during 2003–2009, it seemed the country would never find peace.

However, in January 2005, a comprehensive peace agreement between the Sudan People's Liberation Movement and Army and the government of Sudan was negotiated, ending more than a century of strife among the indigenous Sudanese. In January 2011, the northern-dominated government allowed a referendum on whether to permit the south to secede from the country. More than 98 percent of the people of the south voted for independence, and in July 2011, the region split into two counties, Sudan and South Sudan. That same year, the Darfur Peace Agreement was signed, bringing an end to the ethnic struggles in the western part of the country.

Abidemi Babatunde Babalola

See also: *Issues*—Colonialism; Indigenous Governments; Revolts.

Further Reading

Collins, Robert O., and James M. Burns. *A History of Sub-Saharan Africa.* New York: Cambridge University Press, 2007.

Deng, Francis Mading, ed. *New Sudan in the Making.* Trenton, NJ: Red Sea, 2010.

Edwards, David N. *The Nubian Past: An Archaeology of the Sudan.* London: Routledge, 2004.

Ehret, Christopher. "Nilo-Saharans and the Saharo-Sudanese Neolitic." In *The Archaeology of Africa: Food, Metals, and Towns,* ed. Bassey Andah, Alex Opoko, Thurstan Shaw, and Paul Sinclair. New York: Routledge, 1993.

Lobban, Richard A., Jr., Robert S. Kramer, and Carolyn Fluehr-Lobban. *Historical Dictionary of the Sudan.* 3rd ed. London: Scarecrow, 2002.

Warburg, Gabriel R. *Historical Discord in the Nile Valley.* Evanston, IL: Northwestern University Press, 1992.

Sweden

Sweden is located on the Scandinavian Peninsula in Northern Europe, sharing a border with Norway to the west and Finland to the east. Its capital, Stockholm, lies on the eastern coast on the Baltic Sea. Sweden occupies a strategic location on the Danish Straits linking the Baltic and North seas. In the southern part of the country, the climate is temperate, with cold, cloudy winters and cool, partly cloudy summers; in the northern part of the country, conditions normally are subarctic.

Aside from the Swedish people, Sweden is home to a number of other native groups, including approximately 60,000 Tornedalians (Swedish people of native Finnish descent), 40,000 Roma, and 20,000 Sami. Sweden seldom has been at the forefront of international politics. At one time a major military power in Europe, it has retained a position of armed neutrality since World War I. The nation's economy is based on the capitalist system integrated with social welfare policies.

Sweden is organized as a limited constitutional monarchy. The Swedish parliament—the 349-member unicameral (one-chamber) Riksdag, established in the fifteenth century—holds legislative authority. The monarch's power is purely symbolic, as administrative authority to run the government is vested in the prime minister, who serves as the head of government, and the ministers who run the governmental departments. As a parliamentary system, the prime minister serves as long as his or her party has a majority in the Riksdag. There is universal suffrage for citizens aged eighteen years and older; immigrants are allowed to vote in county council and municipal elections after three years of legal residence. The government is assisted in its work by the Government Offices, which comprise a number of ministries, and some 300 central government agencies and public administrations.

In 1995, Sweden became a member of the European Union (EU) and held the EU presidency from July to December 2009. Despite the country's membership in the EU, Sweden still holds firm to the practice of nonalignment and has no official political treaties with any country. Nonetheless, it can be quite critical of aggressive actors in the global arena, as evidenced by its opposition to the U.S. war in Vietnam, the Soviet Union's war in Afghanistan, and South Africa's racist apartheid system.

Sweden's strategic location was important in earlier centuries as regional monarchies vied for economic and military supremacy. During the eleventh and twelfth centuries, Sweden joined with Finland to become a united Christian kingdom. In 1397, Sweden joined the Kalmar Union, a union of Nordic lands under the control of Denmark's Queen Margaret. In the sixteenth century, Gustav Vasa (later King Gustav I) fought for an independent Sweden, and in doing so, he laid the foundation for modern Sweden. After defeating Denmark, Poland, and Russia, Sweden emerged as a great power in Europe. The kingdom's regional power, however, began to decline in the eighteenth century. Engaged in war with Russia, Swedish plans of attack proved disastrous. It suffered further territorial losses during the Napoleonic Wars (1799–1815) in Europe and was forced to cede the territory of Finland to Russia in 1809.

In 1813, Sweden joined Russia, Prussia, and Austria allied against Napoleon. In order to secure the alliance with Russia, Sweden had to give up its claims to Finland. This brought Sweden into conflict with Denmark-Norway, which had allied with France. As the troops of Sweden and her allies came against Denmark-Norway, King Frederick VI of Denmark was forced to sign the Treaty of Kiel in January 1814, which ceded Norway to Sweden. Norway and Sweden entered into a union in which the two crowns were merged; the two nations reached an agreement whereby Norway would have its own parliament and constitution. In 1905, the union formally was dissolved when Norway declared its independence.

During World War I, Sweden remained neutral, benefiting economically from the worldwide demand for Swedish steel, ball bearings, matches, and wood pulp. Postwar prosperity laid the foundation for the social welfare policies that characterize modern Sweden. During World War II, Sweden followed a policy of armed neutrality, aiming to keep the nation out of a conflict that caused so much suffering in Europe. To this day, the Swedish government holds firm to its policy of nonalignment, with much support from its citizens.

Historically, Sweden's main non-majority native group, the Sami, have faced discrimination by the Swedish government, which has paid little attention to the Sami legal, land, and natural resource rights. In reaction to legislation during the 1990s limiting traditional Sami hunting and fishing rights, Sami took their case to the European Court of Human Rights and the UN Human Rights Commission. In 2002, Sweden appointed a committee to delineate areas the Sami could use for traditional practices, including reindeer grazing.

Today, Sweden considers its native groups as essential parts of its cultural heritage. The National Minorities in Sweden Government Act, passed in 1998, allows people to use the Finnish language, Sami, or Meänkieli (the Torendalen language) in government interactions within the regions where the native populations live. Schools recognize the right of the children of these native groups, along with the Roma, to be taught in their own language.

Although the 1998 law, along with provisions in the Swedish Constitution, educational reforms, and other changes, allows for the preservation of minority cultures, racism against newly arrived groups such as the Roma and Muslims continues. In 2003, Sweden established the Centre against Racism and strengthened its laws protecting minority and native groups.

Abdul Karim Bangura

See also: *Groups: Europe*—Finns; Roma (Gypsies); Sami; Swedes. *Issues*—Land Rights; Political Participation.

Further Reading

Bangura, Abdul Karim. *Sweden vs. Apartheid: Putting Morality Ahead of Profit.* Aldershot, UK: Ashgate, 2004.

Blyth, Mark. "The Transformation of the Swedish Model: Economic Ideas, Distributional Conflict, and Institutional Change." *World Politics* 54:1 (2001): 1–26.

Jonsson, Inge. "Swedish Culture in a European Context." *Proceedings of the American Philosophical Society* 143:1 (1998): 148–156.

Rahn, Richard W. "The Swedish Model; More than Just a Saab Sister." *Washington Times*, August 19, 2009, 19.

Sundelius, Bengt. "Sweden: Secure Neutrality." *Annals of the American Academy of Political and Social Science* 512 (1990): 116–124.

U.S. Department of State. *Background Note: Sweden.* Washington, DC: Bureau of European and Eurasian Affairs, 2009.

Valocchi, Steve. "The Origins of the Swedish Welfare State: A Class Analysis of the State and Welfare Politics." *Social Problems* 39:2 (1992): 189–200.

Syria

Syria is a predominantly Arab nation located on the eastern coast of the Mediterranean Sea in southwestern Asia, bordering Iraq, Israel, Jordan, Lebanon, and Turkey. Its capital is Damascus. Syria has a population of approximately 22.5 million people, more than 90 percent of whom are Arab, with Armenians, Kurds, and other ethnicities accounting for the remaining 10 percent.

History

Syria's history is rooted in an ancient past; archaeologists have demonstrated that its civilization is among the most ancient on Earth. Near Ebla in northern Syria, a Semitic empire that traded with Akkad, Egypt, and Sumer was constructed between 3000 and 2400 B.C.E. Shortly thereafter, around 2300 B.C.E., the region was populated by

Canaanites, Arameans (Semitic tribes), and Phoenicians (a maritime trade culture probably related to the Canaanites). Syria was occupied by the Achaemenian Empire in the fifth century B.C.E., which, in turn, was conquered by the Macedonians in the fourth century B.C.E. and then defeated by the Romans during the three Macedonian-Roman Wars in the second and third centuries B.C.E.

The result of all of these conquests was that by the beginning of the common era, the region was a hybrid of many different cultures: Hellenic, Persian, Roman, and Semitic. The early Christians found fertile ground in Syria, not only in Damascus but in other urban communities as well, such as Aleppo, Antioch (Antakya), and Hama. In fact, Antioch was home to one of the most significant theological and hermeneutical schools of early Christianity. The region remained under the control of the Roman and, later, Byzantine emperors until the rise of Islam in the seventh century C.E.

The Arab-Islamic conquerors defeated the Byzantines of Constantinople in 636 and occupied the entirety of modern Syria. In 661, Muawiyah I, the governor of Syria, became the first Umayyad caliph (a Muslim ruler), making Damascus his capital. For nearly a century, Syria was the core of an Arab-Islamic process of expansion and prosperity ruled by the clan of Banu Umayyad. Arabic become the official language under Omayyad rule.

At that time, Syria was much larger than it is today, with Greater Syria divided into several districts: Filistin (Palestine), with Ramleh and, later, Jerusalem, as its capital; Urduun (Jordan), with Tiberias as its capital; Damascus, including Baalbek, Beirut, and Tripoli; Homs, including the town of Hama; and Kinnesrin, corresponding to northern Syria. During the Omayyad caliphate, the Arab-Islamic generals occupied the entire coast of North Africa (Algeria and Morocco), as well as the Spanish coast up to the Pyrenees Mountains. In the east, Syrian armies reached Afghanistan and Turkmenistan. The Omayyads attempted to conquer Constantinople twice, in 678 and 717, but failed to breach the walls both times. The Omayyad caliphate was overthrown by the Abbasid dynasty in 750.

With the end of the Omayyad caliphate, Syria entered a long period of declining power and influence; under the Abbasids, the region diminished in importance compared to other regions, such as Egypt, Khorasan, and Khwarezm. During this period, Syria was ruled by local dynasties, such as the Hamdanids and Ikhshidids, whose internal fighting allowed the Byzantines to retake parts of northern Syria during the tenth and eleventh centuries. During the Crusades that began in the eleventh century, although Syria supposedly was under the protection of the principality of Antioch, Christian armies occupied the region for a century.

A billboard of President Bashar al-Assad overlooks a street in the violence-wracked city of Homs during the Syrian Uprising in 2012. In a country dominated by Sunni Muslims, President al-Assad and much of the military belong to the small Alawite sect. *(Joseph Eid/ AFP/Getty Images)*

The Turkish Ottoman Empire took control of the area in 1516, ruling until the end of World War I. After the defeat of Germany and its Ottoman allies in that conflict, the region was divided between France and Great Britain; Syria and Lebanon were given to the French. The French territory was separated by a straight border from Britain's zone of influence.

Syrians initiated what became known as the Great Syrian Revolt, against the French, in 1925. Although Syria and France concluded a treaty of independence for Syria in 1936, and Hashim al-Atassi was elected Syria's first president under its new constitution, the treaty never was officially ratified by the French legislature.

Into the Twenty-First Century

Syria is a relatively homogenous country: approximately 90 percent of the population is Arab, with Armenians, Kurds, and other groups making up the remaining 10 percent. Sunni Islam is the predominant religion: Some 74 percent of the population are Sunnis, while other Muslim groups (including members of the Alawite and Druze sects) account for 16 percent. Christian denominations represent 10 percent of the population, and there is a small Jewish community. Other residents include some 100,000 Palestinian refugees who left their homeland and resettled in Syria after the 1949 war that established the state of Israel.

A striking feature of present-day Syria is the dominance of a minority Islamic syncretic sect, the Alawites. This group, which has lived in the region since the eleventh century, was persecuted under the Ottoman Empire and was subsumed under the French mandate until the end of World War I. Thereafter, the Alawites gained considerable power, especially in the military. Although the Alawites represent less than 20 percent of the population today, they have ruled the country since the 1970s, when the al-Assad family took power. Hafez al-Assad, the leader of the Baath Party, seized control in 1971, stifling dissent and killing thousands of members of the Muslim Brotherhood opposition. Even today, many Sunni Muslims do not consider the Alawites to be members of the Islamic *umma* (community); on the other hand, after 1979, Iran's Shi'ite ayatollahs recognized the Alawite faith as a sect of Shi'a Islam, and the political relationship between these two countries has become stronger.

Antigovernment opposition in Syria increased markedly in 2011–2012. The wave of Arab unrest that began in Egypt and Tunisia in early 2011 reached Syria in mid-March of that year. President Bashar al-Assad, who had assumed control after his father's death in 2001, initially lifted the country's long-standing state of emergency and cracked down on protestors and antigovernment opposition, using tanks and security forces to suppress them. The conflicts persisted throughout 2011 and into 2012, bringing the country to the verge of civil war. Some members of the military defected to the opposition forces. The conflict has been exacerbated by Syria's ethnic divisions, as President al-Assad and much of the nation's military elite belong to the small Alawite sect in a country that is dominated by Sunnis.

The Syrian government's crackdown has been condemned internationally. On December 14, 2011, United Nations (UN) Secretary-General Ban Ki-moon called on other countries to intervene to help end the bloodshed. The UN estimates that some 5,000 people have been killed in the conflict, with 15,000 to 40,000 others held in detention. The deepening crisis is the bloodiest since the Arab uprisings began; there are reports of sectarian "cleansing" in once ethnically mixed neighborhoods. In April 2012, former UN Secretary General Kofi Annan attempted to negotiate a ceasefire, but the fighting continued unabated as of July 2012.

Marco Demichelis

See also: *Groups: Europe*—Armenians. *Groups: South Asia and Middle East*—Kurds. *Issues*—Revolts; Social Discrimination.

Further Reading

George, Alan. *Syria: Neither Bread nor Freedom.* New York: Zed, 2003.

Hawting, G.R. *The First Dynasty of Islam: The Umayyad Caliphate, A.D. 661–750.* London: Routledge, 2000.

Nisan, Mordechai. *Minorities in the Middle East: A History of Struggle and Self-Expression.* Jefferson, NC: McFarland, 2002.

Pipes, Daniel. *Greater Syria: The History of an Ambition.* New York: Oxford University Press, 1990.

Tahiti

Tahiti is the largest of the Society Islands, an archipelago located in French Polynesia in the South Pacific Ocean. It is a high island, consisting of two ancient volcanic cones connected by an isthmus, with rich volcanic soil. Settled by Austronesian-speaking peoples as early as 200 B.C.E., Tahiti likely was a staging area for the settlement of many neighboring island groups.

In 1768, Tahiti was the first significant island in the Pacific to be "discovered" by Europeans since Dutch explorer Abel Tasman reached New Zealand in 1642. Nearly 200 years of colonial domination have robbed the Tahitians of much of their traditional culture, as the native people intermarried with Europeans and adopted many aspects of British and French culture. Today, most Tahitians speak French as well as their own Polynesian language and have accepted elements of French culture.

Tahitians had their first encounter with Europeans when British explorer Samuel Wallis arrived on the island on June 18, 1767, aboard the HMS *Dolphin.* Tahitians quickly recognized that the nails the Europeans brought with them could be turned into chisels and other cutting tools that were far superior to any of the stone or shell implements they had used for centuries.

Although traditional Tahitian culture did not sanction extramarital sexual relations, within forty-eight hours of Wallis's arrival, Tahitian husbands and fathers were encouraging their wives and daughters to swim out to the *Dolphin* and offer the sailors sex in exchange for iron nails. This practice continued when French explorer Louis-Antoine Bougainville arrived at Tahiti the following April.

Aware of the brisk trade in iron, later explorers such as Captain James Cook brought supplies of nails and hoop iron with them to barter for freshwater, fish, pork, and vegetables. Cook's visits in April 1769, August 1773, and August 1777 only heightened the islanders' desire for iron and other Western goods. Accounts of Cook's experiences on Tahiti after each of his three voyages popularized Western images of Tahitians as sexually liberated. They became the prototype for the invented Euroamerican image of the "noble savage," fitting into the romantic imagery popularized by French thinker Jean-Jacques Rousseau.

This image of Tahitian women as highly sexed fueled desire among sailors of the period to travel to the island. When the HMS *Bounty,* captained by William Bligh, arrived at Tahiti in 1788, many of the crew members lived with Tahitian women during the several months that it took to acquire a shipload of breadfruit seedlings. When Bligh was ready to leave for the Caribbean, most of the crew wished to stay behind. Soon after leaving the island, officer Christian Fletcher led the famous mutiny on the *Bounty,* returning to Tahiti and its Polynesian women. Some of the crew remained on the island, while eight men left Tahiti with their Polynesian "wives" and a few Polynesian men, later settling on the uninhabited Pitcairn Island.

Tahitian culture again changed dramatically after the arrival of Protestant missionaries from the London Missionary Society in 1797. Landing at Matavi Bay, where Cook first had set up camp, the missionaries came to Tahiti intending to transform the "primitive" culture of the islanders by converting them to Christianity. Like earlier explorers and subsequent whalers who frequented the island, the missionaries had little appreciation for the rich culture, traditional religious practices, or fine workmanship found on the island. For the next century, Tahiti would serve as a base for mission activities throughout much of Polynesia.

At first, few Tahitians converted to Christianity, as the missionaries had little to offer that was attractive to the islanders. The Tahitians practiced a complex religious tradition that recognized a ranked series of gods, lesser gods, and family spirits of deceased relatives, all of whom were believed to control the prosperity of the family and community. The missionaries began to work through a few local converts, who could translate key Christian ideas into locally meaningful concepts. After several decades in Tahiti and the Cook Islands, the London missionaries also had to compete with French Catholic missionaries. The increasing presence of French missionaries by the 1840s was a key factor that led the French to assert colonial claims over Tahiti, the Society Islands, and the other archipelagoes of French Polynesia.

Pre-European Tahitian society was organized into numerous chiefdoms known as clans, whose members were classified as high chiefs, lesser chiefs, or commoners. These social distinctions were based on the level of influence and respect that an individual held over other people, and social rank was determined by personal accomplishments, marriage choices, and prestige. This structure began to change after contact with Europeans, as some families controlled access to iron and other European goods, while families and chiefs living farther from European settlements had little access to such goods. Thus, wealth in exotic European goods became a new path to greater social status.

European explorers incorrectly interpreted the local high-ranking chiefs as kings or paramount chiefs, when in reality, they were only prominent in their local clans. But as foreigners favored one clan over others, this caused unrest among the chiefs, who sought the goods that Europeans had to offer. Skirmishes among the clans eventually led to the rise of Pomare, who, with the support of European missionaries, became the leading chief on the island. The Pomare family was dominant in local politics until 1880, when the French forced King Pomare V to cede sovereignty to France.

Tahiti remained a French protectorate until 1946, when the island was designated a French overseas territory; in 2003, the island became a French overseas community. After more than two centuries under French rule, the island has become an entirely new place, with many residents generally following Polynesian family and community lifeways, while exhibiting French tastes and styles. Tahitians remain the dominant ethnic group in the Society Islands, although they still are largely subordinate to French residents, who dominate the economy. The heavily acculturated Polynesians are active in the tourist industry, which flourishes due to the island's beautiful beaches and lush forested mountains.

Robert L. Welsch and Cory N. Atkinson

See also: Groups: East Asia and Oceania—Polynesians. *Issues*—Colonialism, Missionary Activities.

Further Reading
Howe, K.R. *Where the Waves Fall: A New South Seas Islands History from First Settlement to Colonial Rule.* Honolulu: University of Hawaii Press, 1984.
Kirch, Patrick Vinton. *On the Road of the Winds: Archaeological History of the Pacific Islands Before European Contact.* Berkeley: University of California Press, 2000.
Levy, Robert I. *Tahitians: Mind and Experience in the Society Islands.* Chicago: University of Chicago Press, 1973.
Moorehead, Alan. *The Fatal Impact: An Account of the Invasion of the South Pacific, 1767–1840.* New York: Harper & Row, 1966.
Newbury, Colin. *Tahiti Nui: Change and Survival in French Polynesia, 1767–1945.* Honolulu: University Press of Hawaii, 1980.
Oliver, Douglas L. *Ancient Tahitian Society.* Honolulu: University Press of Hawaii, 1974.

Taiwan

Taiwan, also known as the Republic of China, is a self-governing island in East Asia, located approximately 100 miles off the coast of mainland China. Exiled to the island after the communist takeover of China and the establishment of the People's Republic of China in 1949, the Republic of China government officially claims to represent all of China, including both the mainland and Taiwan. At the same time, the People's Republic of China claims sovereignty over Taiwan and has refused to recognize it as an independent state, at times even using military force to suppress the independence movement. Today, only twenty-three nations recognize the Republic of China as a sovereign state and at the same time maintain diplomatic ties with Taiwan's government.

The island is home to a population of indigenous people that belong to fourteen government recognized tribes—the Ami, Atayal, Bunun, Kavalan, Paiwan, Puyuma, Rukai, Saisiyat, Sakizaya, Sediq, Taroko, Thao, Tsou, and Yami—as well as eleven unrecognized tribes: the Babuza, Basay, Hoanya, Ketagalan, Kulon, Luilang, Pazeh/Kaxabu, Papora, Qauqaut, Siraya, and Taokas. For most of the island's history, Taiwan's people were entirely aboriginal. It was not until the seventeenth century that Han Chinese from the mainland began to have an influence on the island.

The modern state of Taiwan was established in 1949, when the Nationalist forces of the Kuomintang (KMT), led by Chiang Kai-shek, fled to the island and set up a government in exile. For the early part of the modern state's history, Taiwanese authorities emphasized the assimilation of the island's tribal peoples. That has begun to change more recently, however, as a result of a resurgence of cultural pride and the formation of a self-determination movement among Taiwan's native people. Today, a greater number of Taiwanese people embrace their mixed aboriginal and Han ancestry. Taiwan's native people number nearly half a million people, representing 2 percent of Taiwan's population.

Taiwan's aboriginal tribes have their own accounts of their creation. While some scholars argue that they migrated from mainland China some 8,000 years ago, archaeologists have uncovered tools that are as old as 15,000 years. Linguistically and genetically, they are Austronesians, related to the peoples of Indonesia, Malaysia, the Philippines, and Polynesia.

Han Chinese accounts often described Taiwan's native groups in terms of their submission or acculturation to Han rule. The Qing Empire began colonizing the lowlands of Taiwan in the seventeenth century, as did the Dutch and Spanish for a time. The Plains tribes assimilated somewhat under Han Chinese rule, but most of the island remained aboriginal territory until the 1930s. The Han empires recognized aboriginal title by treaties. Intermarriage was widespread.

From 1895 to 1945, Taiwan was ruled by the Japanese Empire. In the 1930s, Japan made a concerted effort to subdue and culturally assimilate the native population entirely. Many adopted Japanese culture and values and were recruited into the Takasago Volunteers of the Japanese Imperial Army.

As a result of the Kuomintang's loss in the Chinese Civil War in 1949, more than 1 million refugees fled to Taiwan from the mainland. Many KMT soldiers married aboriginal brides. However, KMT policies decreed that a person must be entirely aboriginal to be so considered. KMT schools replaced Japanese ones, and the native people were forced to adopt Han values and culture. Nearly half of all aboriginal languages became extinct or endangered, and discrimination against the native groups in employment, housing, education, land rights, and social interaction remains common.

The implementation of democratic rule and the end of martial law in Taiwan in 1987 led to some improvements for the native groups. An amendment to the constitution now defends aboriginal rights. The Taiwan Aboriginal People's Movement was founded in 1984. Today's tribes are represented in Taiwan's parliament, and many have moved to cities in search of jobs. Many of the Taiwanese tribes are involved in tourism, particularly ecotourism. Most adhere to Christianity, mixed with older indigenous beliefs, in contrast to the largely Buddhist and Confucian Taiwanese population.

The 2000s saw the birth of a new wave of indigenous pop music, in which native singers incorporated traditional music into modern pop. Environmental issues remain a pressing concern among the tribes, with aboriginal efforts opposing logging and nuclear power operations.

Al Carroll

See also: *Groups: East Asia and Oceania*—Taiwanese Aborigines. *Issues*—Political Participation; Revitalization.

Further Reading

Rubenstein, Murray A., ed. *Taiwan: A New History.* Armonk, NY: East Gate, 2007.
Ta-chuan, Sun. *The Struggle for Renaissance: Taiwan's Indigenous Culture.* Taipei, Taiwan: Sinorama, 1995.

Tanzania

Tanzania is situated on the coast of East Africa, bordered by Burundi, the Democratic Republic of the Congo, and Rwanda to the west; Mozambique and Zambia to the south; and Kenya and Uganda to the north. A number of offshore islands also belong to Tanzania, including Kilwa, Mafia, Pemba, and Zanzibar. Located along the so-called Swahili Coast, which stretches some 1,000 miles (1,600 kilometers) from Somalia to Mozambique, Tanzania served as a meeting point for a variety of peoples engaged in trade and exploration. Swahili is the common language of Kenya, Tanzania, and Uganda.

Modern Tanzania is an amalgamation of the former British colonies of Tanganyika and Zanzibar, which achieved independence in the 1960s. The nation has a population of approximately 38 million people, made up of Africans, Arabs, Asians, and Europeans. The African population is the largest, comprising approximately 120 different ethnic groups, the largest of which are the Hadza, Luo, Maasai, Nyamwezi, Sandawe, and Sukuma. Although the migration of peoples has been a constant throughout the history of the region, Tanzania's native peoples were not displaced but rather amalgamated through a process of assimilation, acculturation, and adaption to form the present Tanzanian population.

The Peopling of Tanzania

Archaeological evidence indicates that one of the oldest human species, *Homo habilis,* lived on the plains of Tanzania about 1.7 million years ago. Finds revealed the skeletal remains of *Homo habilis* as well as early stone tools known as Olduwan for the place they first were found, the Olduvai Gorge near the Serengeti Plains in northern Tanzania.

Evidence also points to the presence of populations during the middle and late Stone Age. Rock paintings, particularly in central Tanzania, affirm that the late Stone Age people who inhabited this region were hunter-gatherers and that they had acquired relatively sophisticated technologies and a complex religious system. This early population, however, does not have direct ties to the native Tanzanians that emerged during a later period.

The ancestors of modern Tanzanians began to people the region during the first millennium B.C.E., including Khoisan-speaking hunter-gatherers from the south, Cushitic-speaking herders and Nilotic-speaking grain producers from the north, and Bantu-speaking ironworkers and plant cultivators from the west. By the middle of the second millennium C.E., these populations had spread across the region, resulting in ethnic assimilation rather than extinction. Thus, Tanzania became a nation of diverse ethnic groups and, as a consequence, one of the most linguistically diverse areas on the African continent.

Outside Contact, Colonization, and Independence

Archaeological evidence indicates that as early as the eighth and ninth centuries C.E., native Tanzanians lived in cities and engaged in trade on the Indian Ocean—well before the colonization of the region by Arabs and, later, Europeans between the seventeenth and nineteenth centuries. Coastal cities played an important role in Tanzania's history. As early as the sixth century C.E., the natives of Tanzania's coastal cities and offshore islands already were trading with Arab, Chinese, Egyptian, Greek, Indian, and Phoenician merchants. This early long-distance trade transformed the political economy of Tanzania, and by the fourteenth century, islands such as Kilwa, Pemba, and Zanzibar had become important entrepôts, with considerable Arab influence on the natives' lifeways. This is noticeable in both the material and nonmaterial aspects of their culture, including architecture, politics, and religion.

The free and easy contact between the coastal Tanzanian cities and islands and cities on the other side of Indian Ocean was the impetus for the conquest over and eventual colonization of the native Tanzanians. Following the arrival of explorer Vasco da Gama on the East African coast in 1498, the Portuguese lunched a conquest mission along the coast of Tanzania in 1506 and soon gained control of the Indian Ocean trade.

By 1729, Omani Arabs had taken over the Tanzanian coast from European imperialists. The Arab conquest bolstered economic relations between coastal Tanzania and other countries. For example, in order to trade freely in the region, by 1837 and 1841, the United States and Great Britain, respectively, had established consulates in Zanzibar. Arab rule in Tanzania also resulted in more trade centers. However, the Arabs promoted slavery, and native Tanzanians became the victims of slave raiders in both coastal and hinterland settlements. Slaves were used primarily to work in the production of cloves, a highly valued spice.

Native Tanzanians had stable social and political systems as early as the sixteenth century. Before colonization, Tanzania had a centralized political structure in which no group or ethnicity was subjugated to another. Although political and ritual powers were in the hands of the central government, local duties were discharged to the chief of each kingdom. Historians such as Isaria Kimambo have suggested that the unity and cooperation that existed among the early natives of Tanzania laid the foundation for the realization of the contemporary Tanzanian nation.

Tanzania was not officially colonized until the last two decades of the nineteenth century. Between 1884 and 1890, Germany took control of Tanganyika—the present-day mainland of Tanzania—in successive annexations. The German administration was ruthless, prompting the natives to rise up in the Maji Maji Rebellion (1905–1907), during which thousands of native people were killed.

After World War I, Germany lost the territory, and it became a League of Nations mandate under the control of Great Britain in 1922. The region's indigenous people were segregated geographically in Tanzania's cities under both the German and British colonial regimes, and their movements outside of these areas were regulated. Like other British colonies in Africa, such as Ghana and Nigeria, Britain established indirect rule in Tanganyika, appointing Donald Cameron as the first governor of the territory. The British administration regarded the natives as an uncivilized and untamed population that needed superiors to put its disorganized institutions together.

Julius Nyerere, the country's founding leader, is a crucial figure in the history of modern Tanzania. Upon his return from a study expedition in Europe in 1954, Nyerere became an advocate for national sovereignty under the auspices of an indigenous political organization called the Tanganyika African National Union. Tanganyika subsequently gained its independence from Great Britain in 1961, with Nyerere named prime minister, achieving a peaceful transition of power.

After three years, the natives of Tanganyika and Zanzibar reached an accord to become a single state, the United Republic of Tanzania, with Nyerere as president. Nyerere's "Arusha declaration" of 1967 shifted the political ideology of the country toward a socialist policy, with a focus on creating *Ujamaa* (communal) villages. However, his twenty-four-year administration not only monopolized power but also impoverished many natives and polarized the mainland and the coast.

Current State and Government Policy

In 2006, hundreds of the pastoralist natives were asked to vacate their territory near riverbeds in Mbeya where they had more than 400,000 head of cattle. The following year, the territory of the Hadza hunter-gatherers in the Serengeti plains was leased to a safari company without the consent of the native minority.

Such policies, which the government claimed were responses to environmental degradation in these areas, have led to the indigenous population suffering a loss of income and the ability to sustain traditional lifeways, resulting in poverty, stress, and other health issues. Although nongovernmental organizations are working with the Tanzanians to improve their plight, the relationship between the government and the natives remains tense.

Abidemi Babatunde Babalola

See also: *Groups: Africa*—Luo; Maasai. *Issues*—Colonialism; Indigenous Governments; Revolts.

Further Reading

Gonzales, Rhonda, M. *Societies, Religion, and History: Central-East Tanzanians and the World They Created, c. 200 B.C.E. to 1800 C.E.* New York: Columbia University Press, 2009.

Horton, Mark, and John Middleton. *The Swahili: The Social Landscape of a Mercantile Society.* Malden, MA: Blackwell, 2000.

Kimambo, I.N., and A.J. Temu, eds. *A History of Tanzania.* Chicago: Northwestern University Press, 1969.

Rhodes, Daniel. *Historical Archaeologies of Nineteenth-Century Colonial Tanzania: A Comparative Study.* Oxford, UK: Archaeopress.

Yeager, Rodger. *Tanzania: An African Experiment.* 2nd ed. Boulder, CO: Westview, 1989.

Thailand

Thailand, whose name means "land of the free," is the third-largest nation in Southeast Asia, spanning an area of nearly 200,000 square miles (518,000 square kilometers). It is a multiethnic society with a population of more than 67 million in 2011. Approximately 68 percent of the people of Thailand live in rural areas, while the rest of the population resides in cities such as Bangkok, Chantaburi, Chiang Mai, Chiang Rai, Khon Khaen, Nakhon Ratchasima, Songhkla, and Suratthani.

The Tai, or Thai, people, who migrated to the country over a period of centuries, are the dominant ethnic group, constituting 80 percent of the population. The Chinese are the largest ethnic minority, representing about 12 percent of the population. The Lao people, numbering approximately 20 million in the northeastern part of the country, are related to the Tai ethnically. Other ethnic groups include Cambodians, Indians, Malays, Vietnamese, and refugees from Indochina.

Approximately 90 percent of the population is Buddhist, while Muslims account for some 6 million people. In the three southern provinces of Narathiwat, Patttani, and Yala, Muslims are the majority, making up about 76 percent of the population. Approximately 1 percent of the people in Thailand are Christian, and a small number are Confucianists, Hindus, Sikhs, and Daoists.

The mountains of northern Thailand are home to a number of diverse hill tribes, including the Akha, Hmong, Karen, Lahu, Lisu, and Mien, which number approximately 500,000 altogether. These hill tribes migrated from southern China as early as 2,000 years ago and retained their separate cultural identities.

The Lisu, numbering approximately 30,000, inhabit the northwestern highlands of Thailand. The men are known for wearing dark clothing, and the women wear tunics of different colors. The Mien (or Yao), numbering approximately 50,000, live in the northeastern borderlands. They are educated, speak Miao-Yao, and live in extended families; it is not unusual for a household to have as many as twenty people. About 80,000 Hmong (or Meo) live in eastern and central Thailand. Their extended family groups include parents, grandparents, great-grandparents, and children.

The Karen, numbering about 280,000, live in the mountain areas of western and southwestern Thailand along the border with Myanmar. The Karen also maintain nuclear families and are highly regarded as trainers of elephants. The Lahu (Musser), numbering about 60,000, came to Thailand during the nineteenth and twentieth centuries. Residing in the central highlands, they are divided into Black Lahu and Yellow Lahu, according to their skin complexion. Many have adopted Christianity. The Akha, numbering about 70,000, reside in the central highlands and lower southern borderlands. The so-called Akha way of life is based on animism and a close relationship with land.

Today, relations among the different ethnic groups are somewhat more harmonious in Thailand than in other Southeast Asian nations. Although minority groups have not given up their cultures or languages, sizable numbers of minorities have adopted Tai names and speak the Tai language. However, many native groups in the north of Thailand do not have citizenship, leading to a lack of demographic data on the groups and stateless status for the people.

These small groups, who generally speak northern Tai dialects that are very different from southern or *Chao Pak* Tai, have little to no access to any benefits related to the government, such as the protection of the legal system, healthcare, education, land rights, and employment. This situation has left young girls of the northern tribes especially vulnerable to trafficking for the sex trade. At the same time, the requirement of literacy in Chao Pak Tai remains a significant barrier to citizenship and improving their circumstances for many of these people.

Patit Paban Mishra

See also: *Groups: East Asia and Oceania*—Cambodians; Lao; Malay; Thai; Vietnamese. *Issues*—Language.

Further Reading

Hanks, Jane Richardson, and Lucien Mason Hanks. *Tribes of the North Thailand Frontier.* New Haven, CT: Yale University Southeast Asia Studies, 2001.

Kunstadter, Peter, ed. *Southeast Asian Tribes, Minorities, and Nations.* Princeton, NJ: Princeton University Press, 1967.

Lewis, Paul W., and Elaine Lewis. *Peoples of the Golden Triangle: Six Tribes in Thailand.* New York: Thames & Hudson, 1984.

Mishra, Patit Paban. *The Modern Nations: The History of Thailand.* Santa Barbara, CA: Greenwood, 2010.

Tarling, Nicholas, ed. *The Cambridge History of Southeast Asia.* Vols. 1–2. Cambridge, UK: Cambridge University Press, 1992.

Tonga

The island nation of Tonga, located in the South Pacific Ocean, is unique for its uninterrupted indigenous self-governance. While many neighboring island nations were or still are occupied by foreign colonial powers, Tonga successfully has resisted colonialism and foreign occupation for centuries. In fact, the Kingdom of Tonga, as the country is formally known, is the sole remaining indigenous monarchy in the Pacific.

Although many Pacific Islanders have become minorities at home as a result of colonialism, Tongans always have made up the majority of Tonga's residential population. Tongans represent 98 percent of the population and own 100 percent of their country's land and resources.

Before European contact, Tongan society was socially stratified. *Tu'i* (kings) and *hou'eiki* (ruling chiefs) governed the islands, assisted by *mātapule* (speaking chiefs) and *mu'a* (skilled artisans). *Tu'a* (commoners) and *pōpula* (slaves) made up the nonlandholding majority of the Tongan population. In the late eighteenth century, succession crises among rival tu'i dynasties led Tonga into a protracted civil war. By the 1820s, European Christian missionaries had gained substantial influence over the war-weary hou'eiki.

One early Christian convert, the *'eiki* (chief) Taufa'āhau, after attaining tu'i status in 1845, absorbed or abolished the other heredity tu'i titles in order to establish a monarchy. Under the name George Tupou, he reigned as first sovereign (r. 1845–1893) of the Kingdom of Tonga. Tupou's first legal reforms in 1850 included a ban on the sale of land to foreigners, which remains in effect today.

Tupou's legal code of 1862 abolished slavery, as well as the entire social class hierarchy, thereby granting former chiefs, commoners, and slaves near-equal legal rights. The first Tongan constitution, enacted in 1875 with substantial input from Tupou's chief advisor, British missionary Shirley Baker, established a legislative parliament composed of equal numbers of "nobles" and elected representatives. The noble class essentially was an invention of Tupou and Baker that allowed select 'eiki to retain the privileges of their chiefly status; Baker was appointed premier in 1880. In the 1880s, an antigovernment movement known as the Mu'a Parliament challenged these reforms. Composed of both *papālangi* (whites) and native Tongans, the Mu'a Parliament protested the autocratic rule of Tupou and Baker, successfully bringing about Baker's deportation in 1890.

By 1900, the kingdom owed a substantial debt to a German South Pacific trading firm. Great Britain, fearing the geopolitical intentions of Tonga's creditor, signed a treaty of friendship with Tonga in order to contain German imperialism in the Pacific. This treaty, signed by King Tupou II (r. 1893–1918) under duress, established Tonga as a British protectorate. Despite British control over foreign affairs, the kingdom continued to govern its domestic affairs with full autonomy; furthermore, the European settler population never exceeded 300.

The successor to Tupou II, Queen Sālote (r. 1918–1965), amended the treaty in 1927 to include a provision calling for the eventual removal of all papālangi from Tongan public office, a task that was accomplished by 1964. Following World War II, Sālote devoted her energy to fostering the renewal of Tongan cultural identity in government affairs and civic life; notable achievements included orthography reform (1943) and the establishment of a Tonga Traditions Committee (1950). Sālote and her successor, King Tupou IV (r. 1965–2006), continued to renegotiate Tonga's treaty with Great Britain until the nation achieved full independence in 1970.

Following independence, Tongan politics entered yet another phase, as indigenous citizen groups and political parties mounted an unprecedented opposition to the government. The prodemocracy Human Rights and Democracy Movement (HRDM), led by 'Akilisi Pohiva, has enjoyed popular support, with candidates affiliated with HRDM consistently winning a majority of the elected representative positions in Parliament since the late 1980s.

The death of Tupou IV and the succession of King Tupou V in September 2006 were followed by rioting in the capital in November of that year. In 2008, the king announced that he would relinquish most of his monarchical powers, and Tonga held its first completely democratic elections in 2010, with Pohiva's newly founded

Democratic Party of the Friendly Islands winning twelve out of the seventeen seats in the Parliament. Meanwhile, the rapid growth and dispersal of the Tongan population presents the kingdom with another dilemma.

While Tonga's population remained stable at approximately 20,000 from European contact until circa 1900, over the past century, the population has risen dramatically to more than 200,000. According to the World Health Organization, some 100,000 Tongans live overseas in Australia, New Zealand, and the United States, while another 100,000 live in Tonga. Urbanity, democracy, and the expanding Polynesian diaspora have complicated the relationships between the traditionalist Kingdom of Tonga and its modernizing indigenous citizenry.

Gregory Rosenthal

See also: Groups: East Asia and Oceania—Polynesians. *Issues*—Colonialism; Indigenous Governments; Missionary Activities.

Further Reading

Campbell, Ian C. *Island Kingdom: Tonga, Ancient and Modern.* Christchurch, New Zealand: Canterbury University Press, 1992.

Ferdon, Edwin N. *Early Tonga: As the Explorers Saw It, 1616–1810.* Tucson: University of Arizona Press, 1987.

Gailey, Christine Ward. *Kinship to Kingship: Gender Hierarchy and State Formation in the Tongan Islands.* Austin: University of Texas Press, 1987.

Rutherford, Noel. *Shirley Baker and the King of Tonga.* New York: Oxford University Press, 1971.

Tunisia

Tunisia is an Arab country located in North Africa, situated between Algeria and Libya. Because of its location along the Mediterranean Sea, it has attracted a diverse population throughout its history, while the country's proximity to the Sahara Desert has brought Tunisians into contact with the peoples of the interior of Africa.

Tunisia's indigenous Berbers (also called Amazigh) resided in the region long before the arrival of the Arabs in the seventh century. Between 60 percent to 90 percent of modern Tunisians are thought to be descendants of the indigenous Berbers or of mixed Arab and Berber ancestry. The precise number of Berbers is unknown, however, as most of the indigenous population has assimilated with the Arabs over many centuries. A small population of some 60,000 Berbers—representing less than 1 percent of the population—live in the southern part of the country, mainly in Djerba, Matmata, Tataouine, and east of Gafsa. Primarily pastoralists, they still speak the Berber language.

History

Berbers, possibly the descendants of Mauris and Numidians or of the Moors, have been living in North Africa for more than 2,500 years. Arabs arrived in the region during the seventh century under the Umayyad caliphate to wage war against the Byzantines, who already were in conflict with many of the Berber tribes. The Tunisian city of Kairouan was founded in 670 by Arab General Uqba ibn Nafi as a military post far from the sea. The mainly Christian and Jewish Berbers resisted the Arabs; however, by 702, Berber leaders such as Kusaila and Al-Kahina of Ifriqiya, as well as those living in present-day eastern Algeria, western Libya, and Tunisia, had been killed, and a mass conversion of Berbers to Islam took place.

Berbers formed a new Islamic sect, the Kharjites, which still is present in Tunisia, mainly in Djerba, and in parts of Algeria and Morocco. The Kharijite Berbers captured Kairouan in 745. Ibrahim ibn al-Aghlab, a general of Sunni Caliph Harun ar-Rashid in Baghdad, recaptured Kairouan in 800 and founded the Aghlabid dynasty, which ruled Ifriqiya for more than a century and created a local Arabic-speaking aristocracy. The majority of the leading positions were occupied by Arab and Persian settlers, but the local Berbers, who could speak Arabic, also were incorporated into the elite, and Kairouan flourished for a time.

Kutama Berbers from present-day Algeria overthrew the Aghlabids in 909. They formed the Ismaili Shiite Fatimid dynasty and left the Zirid Berbers of Algeria as their vassal in Ifriqiya, which they ruled from Kairouan. During this period, the country flourished in the arts, education, commerce, and agriculture. The relationship of the Fatimids and the Zirids was a transitional one, and the Zirids lost Kairouan in a conflict with the Fatimid alliance in 1057. Subsequent centuries saw a series of political movements led by Muslim Berbers, who formed dynasties in Ifriqiya, including the Almoravids and Almohads, both in Morocco, and the Hafsids in Tunisia. During the sixteenth century, the weakened Hafsids were bound only to Tunisia and made an alliance with Spain for trade.

Ottomans conquered Tunis in 1574, ending the Hafsid dynasty. Initially, many Ottoman legal and political reforms were introduced in Tunisia. But later rulers, such as Ahmed Bey (r. 1826–1848), even though they maintained friendly and religious ties with the Ottoman caliphate, introduced local reforms and recruited local people into the army. During the scramble to colonize Africa, Tuni-

An Amazigh (Berber) woman prepares to vote in Tunisia's first free democratic elections in October 2011. The Amazigh demanded a greater voice in the affairs of both Tunisia and Libya in the aftermath of the Arab Spring revolutions. *(Sipa Press/ AP Images)*

sia became a French protectorate in 1881. Subsequently, French was introduced as an official language, along with other colonial regulations. During the nineteenth century, Tunisian identity was a mix of Andalusian, Arab, Berber, European, Jewish, and Turkish influences.

A common Arabic-Islamic identity was leveraged to motivate the people against the French colonists in Tunisia during the independence movement of the early 1950s. After Tunisia achieved independence in 1957, most Europeans, including Jews, left the country, and the government adopted Arabic as its official language, as in other North African countries. This accelerated the Arabic influence on Tunisian culture.

Current Status and Indigenous Policy

For religious and political reasons, Berber culture and language were assimilated into the Arabic Tunisian identity. In remote areas, people continue to speak the Berber language, including varieties such as Cheninnaoui, Djerbi, Douiri, and Matmati, which together form a Tunisian Berber dialect; however, the people who speak the Berber language generally also speak Arabic.

A small revival of the Berber language and identity is under way, although it is not as radical as movements in neighboring countries such as Algeria and Morocco. Many Berbers today call themselves Amazigh and have lobbied the government to officially recognize the Berber language. The official government stance, however, emphasizes the country's cultural unity.

In recent years, the Tunisian government has promoted Berber culture as a tourist attraction. Transportation,

education, and medical facilities are provided to small Berber villages in order to encourage the local population to wear their traditional dress. Tourism has increased the prospects for the native people to earn a living.

During late 2010 and early 2011, the "Arab Spring" came to Tunisia, when a prodemocracy revolution took place, forcing an end to President Zine El Abidine Ben Ali's twenty-three-year regime. Beji Caid-Essebsi was appointed acting president in March 2011, until parliamentary and presidential elections could be held in October. In the interim, in an effort to preserve the Berber culture and promote research on Berbers, in July 2011, the government established the Tunisian Amazigh (Berber) Culture Association. The future looks brighter for Tunisia's native peoples, as well-known human rights activist Moncef Marzouki was elected president, and the nation took a more democratic turn.

Muhammad Aurang Zeb Mughal

See also: *Groups: Africa*—Berber. *Issues*—Language; Revolts.

Further Reading

Abun-Nasr, Jamil M. *A History of the Maghrib.* Cambridge, UK: Cambridge University Press, 1971.

Battenburg, John. "The Gradual Death of the Berber Language in Tunisia." *International Journal of the Sociology of Language* 137 (1999): 151–165.

Brett, Michael, and Elizabeth Fentress. *The Peoples of Africa: The Berbers.* Oxford, UK: Wiley, 1996.

Loueslati, Besma Yacoudi, et al. "Islands Inside an Island: Reproductive Isolates on Jerba Island." *American Journal Human Biology* 18:1 (2006): 149–153.

Turkey

Turkey occupies a strategic location between Asia and Europe, stretching across Asia Minor (once known as Anatolia) and Thrace (the southeastern Balkans). Two straits, the Bosporus and the Dardanelles, delineate the boundary between the two continents. The Republic of Turkey was founded in 1923 after the fall of the Ottoman Empire (1299–1914).

The country's population of 74 million, according to 2011 statistics, is dominated by people of Turkish descent, but the country also is home to smaller Armenian, Crimean Tatar, Ezidi, Kurdish, Laz, and Roma populations. Demographic data is difficult to obtain, as the Turkish census does not distinguish among people of different ethnic groups.

Native Peoples: A Bridge Between Europe and Asia

Anatolia, which makes up 97 percent of the territory of Turkey, is one of the oldest inhabited regions of the world, dating to the Neolithic period. The Hittites formed the first known state in the area, which survived from the eighteenth to the thirteenth century B.C.E. The western coast of Anatolia was settled by Greeks around the twelfth century B.C.E. The region became part of the Roman Empire in the first century C.E., and when the empire was divided into Western and Eastern branches, Anatolia became the center of the Eastern Roman Empire, with its capital at Byzantium. Emperor Constantine renamed the city Constantinople in the fourth century C.E.; after Turkish independence in 1923, it became known as Istanbul.

In the ninth century, Turkmen raids led to Turkish settlement of the region. In 1075, Turkmen established the Anatolian Seljuk state, which lasted until the Mongol invasion of 1243, after which many petty emirates were established. The Mongol invasion was followed by a wave of Turkmen tribes settling in Anatolia, which resulted in its final Turkification. A petty emirate named Ottoman was established in 1299 on the border with Byzantium and made frequent raids westward. The emirate rapidly developed into a state and, with the conquest of Constantinople in 1453, into a worldwide empire. The Ottoman Empire was a multiethnic, multilingual domain that encompassed Asia Minor, the Balkans, and North Africa, until it was broken up into independent states by the victorious Allies after World War I.

Turkey was established after a bitter struggle against the invading European powers. The Turkish people fought in the National War (1919–1922) under the leadership of Mustafa Kemal (Atatürk), and a new Turkey was established, made up of the native people of Anatolia and Turkish people who had migrated there from former Ottoman territories.

The Turks sought the assistance of the Kurds in establishing a Muslim state rather than the smaller nation-states that the Allies had in mind. Christian Armenians, however, who just had lived through a genocide at the hands of the Ottoman government, did not relish the idea of a Muslim state. In 1923, Turkey agreed to an exchange with Greece that would transfer nearly all Orthodox Christians to Greece in return for Greece's Muslim population.

In 1924–1925, Turkey forced its small Assyrian and Chaldean populations into Iraq. At the same time, a modern, secular Turkish state was established, with a conspicuous lack of delineation between the majority Turkish and minority native populations. In order to prosper in the new Turkey, one had to self-identify as Turkish rather than as a native.

When the Atatürk regime ended in 1945, Turkey adopted a multiparty political system for the first time, allowing for the expression of non-Turkish identities. The first and founding Republican People's Party was challenged by other parties, one of which, the Democratic Party, took power in 1950. The change in government also signaled a large-scale change in Turkish society. Today, however, Turkey remains a decidedly Muslim state, and those who adhere to minority religions or ethnic identities face many difficulties in public life.

Native Peoples in Modern Society

The realities of a united Europe and Turkey's desire to become a member of the European Union (EU) accelerated the pace of reform and recognition of Turkey's native peoples during the early 2000s. Turkey's application to the EU in 2004 prompted scrutiny of its policies toward its native populations.

As a result, although Turkey's constitution does not recognize native groups—only religious minorities—efforts have been made to curb discrimination against the religious and political rights of Turkey's native peoples. In order to gain acceptance to the EU, the nation passed a number of minor reforms that granted ethnic minorities some linguistic rights but left most restrictions in place.

The Turkish government's hesitations soon may be overtaken by popular feeling among the Turkish population. When the chief of staff of the Turkish army took exception to the EU's request that Turkey recognize Assyrians and Roma as minority groups, warning that the military would protect the status quo, protesters took to the streets across the nation. A law denying a place in Parliament to minority political parties winning less than 10 percent of the vote remains in place. However, elections held in 2007 demonstrated that minority candidates can succeed as independents, as twenty-two Kurds and four Alevis were elected to the Turkish Parliament. That same year, Armenian journalist Hrant Dink was murdered by a Turkish nationalist, and approximately 200,000 assembled in Istanbul to protest.

As of 2012, the majority government still was dominated by Turkish Muslims, and Turkey's minority groups still faced officially sanctioned discrimination; however, a more moderate, accommodating attitude has begun to pervade the Turkish population. Only time will tell whether further reforms can bring true rights for Turkey's native populations.

Fatma Acun and Steven L. Danver

See also: Groups: Europe—Armenians; Roma (Gypsics); Tatars, Crimean. *Groups: South Asia and Middle East*—Kurds. *Issues*—Assimilation.

Further Reading

Hughes, Edel. *Turkey's Accession to the European Union: The Politics of Exclusion.* New York: Routledge, 2011.

Ibrahim, Ferhad, and Gülistan Gürbey, eds. *The Kurdish Conflict in Turkey: Obstacles and Chances for Peace and Democracy.* New York: St. Martin's, 2000.

Mango, Andrew. *Atatürk: The Biography of the Founder of Turkey.* London: John Murray, 1999.

Zürcher, Eric. *Turkey: A Modern History.* Rev. ed. London: I.D. Tauris, 2004.

Uganda

Uganda, the landlocked East African country that Winston Churchill described during his 1908 visit there as "truly the pearl of Africa," is endowed with fertile soils, an abundance of food, and a lush vegetation cover. The country occupies an area of approximately 93,000 square miles (241,000 square kilometers), sharing borders with the Democratic Republic of the Congo, Kenya, Rwanda, South Sudan, and Tanzania.

Uganda has a population of over 35 million people, and is home to forty different Bantu- and Nilotic-speaking ethnic communities. These communities include the Baganda, the most populous group, followed (in order of population) by the Banyankole, Basoga, Bakiga, Teso, Langi, Acholi, Bagisu, Lugbara, and Banyoro.

Uganda's official languages are English and Swahili; however, Luganda also is commonly used in areas adjacent to the country's capital, Kampala. Ugandans adhere to a diversity of religions, including Christianity, Islam, and Judaism, as well as indigenous faiths.

Colonial Period

Uganda was created in the late nineteenth century as part of a deliberate action by Great Britain to control the source of the Nile River, considered the lifeline of Egyptian and British interests, and to take advantage of the country's agricultural resources and markets for British industrialists. In July 1890, Britain and Germany signed the Anglo-German Agreements, which placed Uganda under British influence and protected Germany's interests in East Africa.

That same year, Britain formally declared Uganda its colony. In 1990, Britain and the kingdom of Buganda signed the Buganda Agreement, which introduced private landownership, altering the traditional land tenure system and effectively turning most of the Baganda into peasants. Working within the provisions of the Bugunda Agreement, British colonial administrators gave the Baganda chiefs private estates with the understanding that they would compel the peasants to produce cash crops, mainly raw cotton for the textile industry, as well as coffee.

Following Britain's military deployment in Uganda, Baganda King Mwanga II realized that the British presence in the country was to be permanent. After establishing a colonial administration, Britain sent Frederick Lugard to act as its first administrator under the auspices of the Imperial British East Africa Company. But the company soon experienced financial constraints and myriad administrative problems, compelling it to relinquish the country to direct British government control in 1893.

The following year, Mwanga signed the Protectorate Agreement between the Baganda and Great Britain, formally accepting British rule over his kingdom. Thus, Buganda became a British protectorate, called Uganda in Swahili, meaning "state of the Ganda people." The country retained the name even after the communities bordering Buganda were absorbed by the British administration to create a territory known as Uganda under the Uganda Order in Council in 1902.

Mwanga closely followed the unfolding events in the hope that the alliance with Great Britain would help him preserve his position as king. He shrewdly obtained military support from Britain to fight his enemies and collect tribute from the Banyoro and Basoga. However, when Britain prevented him from collecting tribute from the Basoga—effectively ending his prerogative as the sole giver of land to his subjects—Mwanga considered this action as betrayal. In 1897, he launched an ill-advised armed resistance against the British in which he was defeated, captured, and replaced as ruler by his infant son, Daudi Chwa. Undaunted by the resistance, Britain acquired more territory from other communities and political entities in its efforts to consolidate its grip on the country.

By the end of World War I, the boundaries of the Uganda Protectorate were set. From 1900 to 1930, the colonial government transformed Uganda's economy from one based on barter to a cash-driven economy involving cash crops, taxation, and compulsory labor. In the meantime, the British colonial administration built needed infrastructure such as roads and railways to facilitate the transport of goods to and raw materials from Uganda.

During this period, agricultural plantations flourished with the production of coffee, tea, cotton, and rubber. The government encouraged Western-style education under the auspices of Christian missionaries through the grants-in-aid programs, with the aim of acculturating the local communities into British values and ways of political governance. Education institutions worked to replace Ugandan social and economic lifeways with Western ideas, even after Uganda gained independence on October 9, 1962.

Postcolonial Uganda

Political instability, stemming from deep-rooted ethnic suspicion and mistrust among communities that had been cobbled together by the colonial administration in an effort to construct a nation, dogged postcolonial Uganda. In preparation for the country's independence, Great Britain set up a constitutional committee headed by J.V. Wild to provide a road map for political governance. Following the completion of Wild's work, the British colonial secretary announced in 1960 that direct elections would be held throughout the country

The announcement was opposed vehemently by the Baganda, which favored a federal system; the Bunyoro-Kitara Kingdom, to their west, followed and endorsed the Baganda's position. Communities that traditionally had organized themselves outside the quasi-feudal system of subnational kingdoms that governed Uganda's regions (the Buganda, Bunyoro-Kitara, Busoga, and Toro kingdoms) rejected them, arguing that the troublesome political and economic imbalances were a result of that system. Exacerbating the situation, the indigenous African farmers continued to be exploited, relegated to the periphery as cash-crop producers in the postcolonial economy.

Unsurprisingly, as long as Uganda continued the colonial legacies of the Euro-American models of development, it would experience political turbulence. In 1966, Prime Minister Apollo Milton Obote abrogated Uganda's 1962 constitution and ruled the country autocratically, transforming the political landscape into one of sharp antagonism. Even when Obote tried to institute a planned and centralized system of government, ethnic and religious differences led to his being ousted in a military coup led by Idi Amin in 1971.

Notwithstanding the political crisis, Uganda's gross domestic product averaged 5.3 percent between 1963 and 1971. The economy began to experience a downturn following Amin's takeover, which was made worse by the expulsion in 1972 of the prominent Uganda-Asian entrepreneurial community and the gross mismanagement of the economy under the brutal military regime. Abductions and killings of 100,000 to 400,000 people who were perceived to be opponents of Amin drove thousands of Ugandans into exile.

The Ugandans mobilized under the Front for National Salvation (Fronasa) and succeeded in toppling the military regime in 1979; this event was aided by the unforeseen invasion of Tanzania, which took the opportunity to use its military to get rid of its bully neighbor. Thereafter, Uganda was ruled again by Obote from 1980 to 1985, when he was overthrown by the murderous military regime of Bazilio Olara-Okello. In January 1986, Yoweri Museveni, working with the National Resistance Movement, toppled Olara-Okello and assumed the presidency.

Museveni orchestrated an economic recovery for the nation, and annual growth reached 6 percent in the early 1990s and 8 percent by 1996. Although Museveni brought the country under the rule of law, he has had to grapple with the opposition of a militant guerrilla group called the Lord's Resistance Army (LRA) in the north, which has sought to remove him from office since he first came to power. The group has been difficult to track down, as it has launched attacks on Museveni's regime from the Democratic Republic of the Congo, the Central African Republic, and South Sudan.

The activities and forced recruitment of soldiers for the LRA have been especially devastating to the Acholi people, and many have been forced from their homes into refugee camps. Starting in 2007, however, peace talks have calmed the region, and many Acholi have started to return home. Additionally, climate change has made life increasingly difficult for cattle herding people such as the Karamajong, as cycles of drought and flooding have become even more extreme during the late 2000s and early 2010s.

Hannington Ochwada

See also: *Groups: Africa*—Acholi; Baganda; Teso. *Issues*—Colonialism; Revolts.

Further Reading

Mutibwa, Phares. *Uganda Since Independence: The Unfulfilled Hopes.* Trenton, NJ: Africa World, 1992.

Mwakikagile, Godfrey. *Ethnicity and National Identity in Uganda: The Land and Its People.* Scotts Valley, CA: Custom Books, 2009.

Ofcansky, Thomas P. *Uganda: Tarnished Pearl of Africa.* Boulder, CO: Westview, 1999.

Tripp, Aili Mari. *Museveni's Uganda: Paradoxes of Power in a Hybrid Regime.* Boulder, CO: Lynne Rienner, 2010.

United States

American Indians have resided in the present-day United States for at least 20,000 years. Over that time, changes in climate and the physiology of the land have led to the development and evolution of a diversity of cultures, each with its own distinct traditions and political viewpoints. Even today, after centuries of suppression, relocation, and massacre by American settlers and their descendants, there are still more than 600 American Indian groups in the United States that are officially recognized by federal or state authorities. Native Americans also include Hawaiians, or Kanaka Maoli. Descended from Polynesians, they arrived in the Hawaiian Islands more than 1,000 years ago.

From the time of the arrival of the Spanish in the early sixteenth century to the end of the nineteenth century, the Native American population in the United States declined precipitously. The reasons for the population collapse were legion, including disease and warfare. It is estimated that the American Indian population may have fallen as low as 250,000 by 1900.

Since that time, the Native American population has steadily increased. According to the 2010 U.S. Census, more than 5.2 million people identify themselves as American Indians or Alaska Natives. Of that total, some 2.9 million individuals identify themselves by that racial designation alone, while the other 2.3 million claim a multiracial background.

Native Hawaiians are grouped in the census along with other Pacific Islanders. In total, more than 1.2 million people identify themselves as a Native Hawaiian or other Pacific Islander. Of those, approximately 540,000 identify themselves using that racial category alone, while 685,000 claim a multiracial background. In 2010, American Indians and Alaska Natives made up approximately 1.7 percent of the total population of the United States, out of some 308 million, while Native Hawaiians and other Pacific Islanders accounted for 0.4 percent.

History and Colonial Legacy

Although many Native American oral histories claim that these people have resided in North America since time immemorial, archaeological evidence indicates that their ancestors arrived in the Americas at least 20,000 years ago. Some may have arrived by boat, using the shoreline to navigate. Because sea levels changed following the last ice age, most of the settlements that those fishermen established are now underwater.

Other groups migrated from Siberia, crossing the land bridge over the Bering Strait into Alaska. These were hunter-gatherers whose culture dominated throughout North America. Following the end of the ice age, their hunter-gatherer lifestyle gradually was replaced as regional cultures began to develop. Some of those cultures continued to rely on hunting and gathering, while others adopted agriculture. By the time of European contact, agriculture in the present-day Southeastern United States yielded such abundant crops that many of the region's Mississippian chiefdoms had very large populations.

In the sixteenth century, Hernando De Soto and other Spanish conquistadores led expeditions into the Southeast in search of gold and jewels for Spain. Although the Spanish did not find the wealth they sought in the Mississippian communities that they encountered, their incursion forever would change the region. The introduction of diseases to which the natives had no immunity, such as smallpox, decimated the Indian population, depopulating much of the South. Out of the remnants of the Mississippian communities emerged new political and social groups, such as the Chickasaw, Choctaw, and Creek (Muscogee). This pattern would continue to play out in other areas of North America as Europeans and their descendants pushed into new territories over the centuries.

Other European countries, most notably England and France, joined Spain in the colonization of North America. The colony of New France was established when Jacques Cartier began his exploration of the St. Lawrence River in 1534. Rather than establishing many large, permanent settlements, the French concentrated their efforts on expanding trade opportunities with the native peoples. The English established their first permanent settlement at Jamestown in present-day Virginia in 1607.

England's relentless colonization push westward brought the English into conflict with both American Indian groups and the French. From 1754 to 1763, the French and Indian War—the North American theater of the Seven Years' War—raged as England and France, together with their respective Indian allies, fought for control of North America. The English eventually prevailed, but, tired of fighting against the Indians, the

Crown issued the Royal Proclamation of 1763, which forbade white settlement past the crest of the Appalachian Mountains.

Despite such restrictions, the colonists believed that their victory over the French gave them the right to all native lands in North America—one of many demands that precipitated the American Revolution. Most Native Americans allied with the British during that conflict, recognizing that they always would be under threat if the colonists emerged victorious. Ultimately, however, it did not matter whether the Indians fought alongside or against the colonists or chose neutrality—they all were victimized after the conclusion of the Revolution.

Indian Policy and Relations

Initially, the new U.S. government worked to coexist with the major Native American groups, such as the Cherokee and the Iroquois, by negotiating treaties. That plan failed, however, as American settlers coveted the land occupied by the Indians. Settlers refused to respect American Indians' treaty rights and continued to seize whatever lands they desired. In response, Indian warriors launched a spirited defense of their homelands, especially in the Ohio Valley and Southeastern United States. Virtually every conflict between the American Indians and the U.S. military ended with a treaty that included land cessions.

The U.S. government attempted to ameliorate the constant warfare by providing a path to citizenship for Native Americans who chose to become "civilized." In the Southeast, many Cherokee, Chickasaw, Choctaw, and Creek Indians gave up their traditional cultures and assimilated into white society. Still, their lands, among the richest agricultural areas in the United States, were highly prized by Americans, and thus their civilization efforts were ignored.

On May 26, 1830, the Indian Removal Act became law, and many native nations, including the Cherokee, Chickasaw, Choctaw, Creek, and Seminole, were uprooted from their homelands and deposited on lands west of the Mississippi River in so-called Indian Territory. The removal of the Indians in the East, however, only temporarily satisfied the appetite of settlers for Indian lands. Over the rest of the nineteenth century, the United States would continue pushing west, warring with Native Americans to seize their homelands. By the end of the century, most American Indians had been removed to designated reservations—their lands thus reduced to a fraction of their traditional territories and their populations significantly reduced by epidemic disease and centuries of warfare.

TRAIL OF BROKEN TREATIES

The Trail of Broken Treaties, also known as the March on Washington or the Trail of Broken Treaties Caravan, was a cross-country protest by Native Americans that took place in fall 1972. Its goal was to bring national attention to the issues faced by American Indians, including the loss of their culture and the high rates of poverty, illiteracy, and alcoholism in their communities.

Spearheaded by Native American leaders Dennis Banks and Russell Means and organized by the American Indian Movement, the Trail of Broken Treaties started on the West Coast. Protesters began their march from cities such as San Francisco and Seattle, with caravans stopping in native communities to pick up protesters and passing through symbolic locales, such as following the route of the infamous Trail of Tears, to bring attention to their cause.

The caravans converged in St. Paul, Minnesota, in October 1972. There, they issued their demands, which became known as the "Twenty Points." Aimed at restoring American Indian sovereignty, the points included the repeal of the 1871 federal statute that had ended treaty making, the restoration of treaty-making status to American Indian governments, and the elimination of all state jurisdiction over American Indian affairs. The group then moved on to Washington, D.C., to press their demands.

The leaders of the protest assumed that officials in Washington were prepared for their arrival, but they soon discovered that most politicians were out on the campaign trail, as the presidential election was less than a week away. The White House rejected the group's request to present their demands to President Richard M. Nixon, and the federal Bureau of Indian Affairs (BIA) refused to provide the protesters with lodging or food.

In response, the protesters occupied the BIA building and held it for six days. During that time, the protesters seized a large number of confidential documents that revealed questionable government practices regarding native land rights and cooperation with industry in the exploitation of mineral rights on reservation lands. The protest succeeded in raising awareness of American Indians' plight, although the activists were criticized for damaging the BIA building and its contents.

John R. Burch, Jr.

But reservation life did not guarantee American Indians protection from the depredations of the U.S. government. In an effort to force American Indians to assimilate into mainstream society, in 1887, the federal government passed the Dawes Act (also known as the General Allotment Act). Ostensibly, the act broke up communally held tribal reservations in order to allow individual Native Americans to become landowners. In reality, it provided a mechanism for U.S. citizens to acquire Indian lands that previously had been unavailable.

The contribution that American Indians made during World War I helped them assimilate into mainstream American culture on their own terms. As a result of their military service, the U.S. government passed the Indian Citizenship Act in 1924, which granted full U.S. citizenship to the nation's indigenous peoples. It was hoped that this would accelerate the move toward the assimilation of American Indians into the American population as a whole and the end of the reservations and federal responsibility for Indian affairs.

American Indians also provided valiant service during World War II, particularly as code-talkers—Indians who communicated on behalf of the military in their native tongues, thereby frustrating enemy code breakers. Following the war, many American Indians did not return to their reservations but instead moved to other areas of the country. Off the reservations, these veterans and their families suffered civil rights violations that would lead them to demand respect for their rights.

In the 1950s, the federal government began pursuing a policy of termination, forcing American Indian groups to become self-sufficient so that they no longer would be dependent on federal funding. In this move, leaders of the U.S. government refused to recognize that virtually all of the tribes had finite resources that quickly would be depleted, leaving them with nothing to live on. By the 1960s, the termination policy had led to a recognition among Native American groups that they had a common enemy that they had to oppose together.

Pan-Indianism came to the fore in the late 1960s and early 1970s as part of the Red Power movement. Groups such as the American Indian Movement and Indians of All Nations brought public attention to the plight of native peoples across the United States. Although the Red Power movement eventually waned, it left a lasting legacy that has uplifted Native Americans across the United States.

Today, the efforts of such groups have resulted in the establishment of many museums and programs that seek to preserve tribal cultures and languages. Most important, they have encouraged the empowerment of Native Americans through education to chart their own futures,

A young Native American calls for the reburial of Ponca Indian remains held by the University of Nebraska in 1998. The Native American Graves Protection and Repatriation Act of 1990 requires the return of Indian "cultural items" and human remains. *(Lincoln Journal Star/AP Images)*

rather than being subject to the vacillations in policy implemented by different federal administrations.

Toward Self-Determination

Beginning with the administration of President Lyndon B. Johnson, the federal government made a significant shift in its policies toward Native Americans, encouraging them to become self-sufficient rather than remaining dependent on federal funding. The level of self-sufficiency was to be determined individually by each nation, which, through "self-determination," could define its relationship, if any, with the federal government. The U.S. government's new initiative necessitated that it abandon the termination policy of the past and instead empower Native American governments to administer their own affairs and to become as economically independent as possible.

One strategy pursued by American Indian groups to raise revenues was casino gaming. This brought political and legal challenges, however, as the interests of sovereign Native American tribes and federal and state governments conflicted. Although the federal government, through agencies such as the Bureau of Indian Affairs, the Small Business Administration, and the Department of Housing and Urban Development, encouraged gaming as a means to drive down appropriations to American Indians, the states sought to regulate Native American gaming establishments.

The balance between state regulation and the economic and sovereign rights of Native Americans continues to be negotiated within the legal system and the U.S. Congress. At the same time, gaming has not necessarily been the economic panacea envisioned by many Native Americans. Although some groups located near large urban areas have succeeded in generating significant revenue, most others manage only small profit margins.

Even before gaming entered Indian country, many tribes raised funds for development efforts through marketing natural resources on Indian lands. Reservation lands have considerable reserves of timber, coal, oil, natural gas, and uranium, as well as substantial water rights guaranteed by the federal government. Approximately 20 percent of coal fields are on tribal lands, and much of the Oklahoma oil boom of the 1910s and 1920s sought to exploit resources found on the state's many reservation lands. More recently, the need for uranium with the development of nuclear power and weapons placed a premium on the large deposits found on the lands of a number of tribes, including the Navajo and Hopi.

Too often, the leases with non-Indian corporations to exploit these resources were negotiated by the federal Bureau of Indian Affairs (BIA) with little input from the tribes concerned. With the beginning of the self-determination era in the 1970s, however, the situation improved, as the BIA involved tribes in the process. Yet the potential for prioritizing what the federal government determines to be the national interest above the tribes' rights still exists. For instance, this is evidenced in the objections of many Navajos to the negotiated water rights settlements regarding the rivers running through their reservation lands. These settlements include a provision that provides water to Peabody Energy, which has mined coal on the reservation for decades and has had a long and troubled relationship with the tribe.

One of the most significant pieces of legislation enacted by the U.S. Congress was the Native American Graves Protection and Repatriation Act (NAGPRA).

Passed in 1990, the NAGPRA oversees the process of returning culturally significant items and human remains from museums and academic institutions that receive money from the U.S. government to federally recognized Native American groups.

Although the NAGPRA has resulted in the repatriation of the remains of more than 30,000 individuals and 650,000 objects, the process remains mired in controversy. Academic researchers contend that the act has denied them the opportunity to scientifically study newly discovered archaeological sites, because funerary and sacred objects, as well as human remains, are quickly given to Native American nations for reburial. Native Americans contend that these items and remains are not being repatriated quickly enough, as many museums and academics still have pieces in their collections that should have been returned to them long ago.

The NAGPRA illustrates another issue of significance to native peoples in the United States, as it applies only to federally recognized Native American nations. Other nations are not recognized by federal agencies but have achieved that status at the state level. Still other groups have strived to achieve recognition as an independent nation at any level, to no avail.

Today, official recognition is essential for Native American nations to receive the financial and legal benefits of federal legislation. Without it, members of such native nations are relegated to the margins of society, and many are left in a disadvantaged state. American Indians remain among the United States' most impoverished groups.

John R. Burch, Jr.

See also: *Issues*—Assimilation; Colonialism; Land Rights; Political Participation; Relocation; Water Rights.

Further Reading

Debo, Angie. *A History of the Indians of the United States.* Norman: University of Oklahoma Press, 1970.

Deloria, Philip J., and Neal Salisbury, eds. *A Companion to American Indian History.* Malden, MA: Blackwell, 2002.

Deloria, Vine, Jr., and Clifford M. Lytle. *The Nations Within: The Past and Future of American Indian Sovereignty.* Austin: University of Texas Press, 1984.

Fixico, Donald L. *The Invasion of Indian Country in the Twentieth Century: American Capitalism and Tribal Natural Resources.* 2nd ed. Boulder: University Press of Colorado, 2012.

Pevar, Stephen L. *The Rights of Indians and Tribes: The Basic ACLU Guide to Indian and Tribal Rights.* 2nd ed. Carbondale: Southern Illinois University Press, 1992.

Philp, Kenneth R. *Indian Self-Rule: First-Hand Accounts of Indian-White Relations from Roosevelt to Reagan.* Logan: Utah State University Press, 1995.

Prucha, Francis Paul. *The Great Father: The United States Government and the American Indians.* Lincoln: University of Nebraska Press, 1984.

Silva, Noenoe K. *Aloha Betrayed: Native Hawaiian Resistance to American Colonialism.* Durham, NC: Duke University Press, 2004.

Venezuela

The first inhabitants of present-day Venezuela arrived in the country in about 15,000 B.C.E., according to archaeological researchers. These Paleo-Indian tribes from inner Asia came to the Americas across the Bering Strait, traveling south into Mesoamerica and South America, where they established seminomadic communities of hunters, gatherers, and fishers.

At the time the Spanish arrived in the Americas in 1492, the Arawak and Carib were the two most important indigenous groups in Venezuela. The Arawak established settlements along the Atlantic coast and the shores of the Amazon River, while the Carib people migrated to the northeastern coast of the country around Lake Maracaibo and the shoreline of the Orinoco River. Other native groups of Venezuela included the Guamo, Maipure, Otomaco, and Sáliva, which lived in the Llanos or Orinoco Plains, and the Allie, Ambae, Bubure, Guajiro (or Wayuu), Kirikire, Motilone, Toa, and Zápara, which occupied the western territory.

The Spanish conquistadores found that these indigenous groups lacked a centralized political structure and large urban centers such as those of the Inca or Aztec; rather, they were composed of small and unrelated tribal groups, each representing a different culture. Although some researchers have downplayed the relevance of these indigenous communities, their contribution to the country's heritage has been rich and important.

History of Native Peoples in Venezuela

By 1498, when the Spanish arrived, Venezuela's indigenous tribes were experts in hunting with traps, arrows, darts, and blowpipes. They cultivated numerous plant species such as maize, manioc, papayas, pineapples, and pumpkins, and cleared fields for agriculture by felling trees and burning vegetation. They also used methods of irrigation, terracing, and fertilization to increase crop yields.

The natives developed pottery-making skills and created cooking utensils that can be traced to 3500 to 3200 B.C.E. Some of the indigenous communities developed permanent villages, roads, and transportation and built round or rectangular collective houses where the entire community—a few hundred individuals—could live. Today, Ye'kwana, Panare, Piaroa, and Pemón communities located in the Venezuelan Amazon continue to construct these types of houses.

During the early Spanish colonial period in the sixteenth and seventeenth centuries, many of Venezuela's indigenous groups vanished without a trace as a result of their defeat in combat, capture as slaves, or assimilation into Spanish culture by Franciscan and Capuchin missionaries. Indigenous groups left behind little written information about their history and heritage; most surviving accounts were written by Spanish conquerors. However, through historical and archaeological research, scientists have uncovered patterns of subsistence, politics, settlement, and cultural practices that persist to the present day. Indigenous traditions, food, religion, and language have helped shape Venezuelan identity. For instance, the culinary tradition of Venezuelan households includes indigenous dishes such as *arepas* (a bread of maize flour), *hallacas* (a type of tamale), and *casabas* and *cachapas* (two kinds of pancakes), all of which are staples of family menus.

The 2001 Venezuelan census recognized thirty-five indigenous groups numbering more than 500,000 people, representing 2 percent of the country's population; most of the native population is concentrated in the southern and western areas of the nation. These figures vary, however, as a result of cultural assimilation and the lack of accessibility to remote communities, which generally are ignored by the official records. Only a few native communities maintain their traditional forms of housing, religion, myths, legends, and arts, and, significantly, most of the native languages have been supplanted by Spanish. According to researchers, only 30 of 100 indigenous languages that existed in the sixteenth century still are spoken today.

Among the largest indigenous groups, the Añu, Guajiro (or Wayuu), Jivi, Kariña, Pemón, Piaroa, Warao, and Yanomami have attempted to preserve their language and cultural traditions. The Guarjiro are the largest indigenous group, representing 57 percent of Venezuela's indigenous population with nearly 180,000 people. They live in the dry lands and coastal areas of the Guajira Peninsula, a territory that spans parts of Colombia and Venezuela; Guajiro generally move freely between the two countries. Although the Guajiro have been exposed to Western culture, they continue to speak their own language and have preserved their rituals, ceremonial dances, myths, and traditional medicine. One such ritual is the *yonna,* consisting of a ceremonial dance that celebrates rites of passage and special occasions. The Guajiro also are known for their folk arts and crafts.

Today, part of the indigenous population has migrated to the cities, where they live in small communities and often work as day laborers. Men usually work in the construction sector and women as domestic servants; however, a few Guajiro occupy strategic positions of power. Nohelí Pocaterra, for example, a native Wayuu leader of Venezuela's permanent commission for the protection of indigenous peoples, became vice president of Venezuela's Congress in 1999.

Historically, Venezuelan indigenous communities have been threatened severely by Western cultures. They frequently have been driven from their lands, which have been exploited and sometimes destroyed. In 1947, in order to study the human condition of indigenous communities, Venezuela's government created the Indigenous Commission, and in 1959, this commission became the official authority responsible for developing an indigenous policy. However, it was not until the end of the twentieth century that indigenous communities were organized legally. In 1989, twenty regional indigenous organizations joined to form the National Indigenous Council of Venezuela to protect their lands and demand respect for their cultures.

Venezuela's new constitution, approved in 1999, formally guaranteed the indigenous population's right to exist and the right to preserve their languages, cultures, and territories. Indigenous peoples also gained the right to hold three representative seats in the National Assembly. In addition, the state committed to helping the indigenous communities demarcate their lands and promote indigenous culture and languages through a bilingual education program. In 2002, the Indigenous Commission was responsible for the development of the Indigenous Law, which was approved as part of the national constitution. These actions represent significant progress in the preservation and development of Venezuelan indigenous communities.

Current Status

Since taking office in 1999, President Hugo Chavez has received considerable support from Venezuela's indigenous communities. With the 1999 constitution, which was shepherded to passage by Chavez's political allies, the president paved the way for the preservation of in-

GUAICAIPURO

In 1560, a group of indigenous Venezuelans from the Caracas and Teques tribes became alarmed by the arrival of unfamiliar people in the peaceful land that had been their home for centuries. The newcomers had blazed their way through the Caracas Valley and established an extravagant base camp marked with flags near the indigenous homeland. Their suits of armor, intimidating physical appearance, and strange manners attracted curiosity and concern among the native people, as the tribes had been forewarned that foreigners were desperately searching for gold and would destroy anything or anyone that stood in their way. But indigenous Chief Guaicaipuro was prepared to defy such aggression.

Little is recorded in written history about this Venezuelan Indian leader, but it is known that Guaicaipuro was born around 1530 in Suruapo or Suruapay, Venezuela, near a town now known as San José de Los Altos in the state of Miranda. It also is known that as a young warrior in his late twenties, he attacked and defeated Spanish conquistador Pedro de Miranda and his army. Guaicaipuro became leader of the Caracas and Teques peoples, and after he successfully led more battles against the Spanish colonizers, other tribes recognized him as their chief as well.

To the Spanish conquistadores, he was a vicious killer who was capable of murder without mercy and a

threat to their colonialist agenda. To the natives, he was a brave and battle-hardened chief who would protect his tribe from all threats. His crusade against the Spanish lasted approximately ten years, ending in an ambush led by Spanish Mayor Francisco Infante. Guaicaipuro was killed, and his house burned in 1568. In the years after his death, he became a legend and a symbol of indigenous resistance against Spanish domination.

In 1993, Venezuela's Parliament adopted a proposal to honor Guaicaipuro in the National Pantheon, and eight years later, on December 8, 2001, the Indian leader was formally recognized as a national hero at a ceremony led by President Hugo Chavez and attended by members of the indigenous communities in Brazil, Ecuador, Peru, and Venezuela. In a symbolic act, ashes representing Guaicaipuro's remains were placed in the National Pantheon. An indigenous Warao woman spoke at the ceremony and expressed pain for the many years of suffering of Indian community members in Venezuela, as well as her gratitude to the government for honoring Guaicaipuro and recognizing him as a national hero. In 2003, the Venezuelan government named one of its national social programs the Guaicaipuro Mission in honor of Venezuelan indigenous leaders.

Ana Servigna

digenous habitats and gave native groups representation in the legislature.

In 2003, the Venezuelan government announced the creation of a social program called the Guaicaipuro Mission to promote development among Venezuela's indigenous groups. The project—named for the Venezuelan Indian chief who fought the Spanish—includes the demarcation of aboriginal lands, community development through low-interest credit to indigenous people, and the defense of indigenous people against exploitation by business interests. This program represents a reaffirmation of constitutional rights for Venezuela's indigenous population.

Despite these measures, most indigenous people continue to live in below-average social and economic conditions, and they remain underrepresented politically. Nonetheless, indigenous groups and leaders continue to work for their rights and the development of viable social programs. Although their hopes and dreams have not yet been realized fully, their struggle for economic, social, and political power continues.

Ana Servigna

See also: Groups: Central and South America—Warao, Wayúu, Yanomami. *Issues*—Colonialism, Migration, Political Participation.

Further Reading

Fox, Geoffrey. *The Land and People of Venezuela.* New York: HarperCollins, 1991.

Hill, Jonathan. "Colonial Transformations in Venezuela." *Ethnohistory* 47:3/4 (Summer/Autumn 2000): 747–754.

Sanoja, Mario, and Iraida Arena. "Early Modes of Life of the Indigenous Population of Northeastern Venezuela." In *Archaeology in Latin America*, ed. Gustavo Politis and Benjamin Alberti. New York: Routledge, 1999.

Van Cott, Donna Lee. "Andean Indigenous Movements and Constitutional Transformation: Venezuela in Comparative Perspective." *Latin American Perspective* 30:1 (January 2003): 46–69.

Zambia

Zambia is a landlocked country that is located in southern Africa, bordered by Angola, the Democratic Republic of the Congo, Malawi, Mozambique, Namibia, Tanzania, and Zimbabwe. The country is known worldwide for copper production, which has been the economic base for the country's economy since mining first commenced during the 1930s.

Zambia occupies approximately 290,550 square miles (752,521 square kilometers), with geography consisting of hills, mountains, and plateaus. The country's major rivers are the Luangwa, Lungwebungu, and Zambezi; Zambia also is home to two scenic waterfalls—Zambezi Falls and Victoria Falls. As in most African countries, Zambia has two distinct seasons: a rainy season that runs from November to April and a dry season from April to November; otherwise, the climate varies based on geography, primarily elevation.

The population of Zambia is composed of mostly Bantu-speaking people. Linguistically, Zambians can be divided into eight groups: the Bemba, Kaonde, Lunda, Luvale, Lozi, Nyanja-Chewa, Tonga, and Tumbuka. There is a large population of Europeans in Zambia working as expatriates in Lusaka and in the Copper Belt. About 36 percent of Zambians live in urban areas; the largest cities are Kabwe, Kitwe, Lusaka (the capital), and Ndola. A majority of Zambians are Christians, but the country also has a small Muslim population, amounting to less than 5 percent of the population. There also are small Jewish and Baha'i communities.

As a result of European influence, Zambian culture blends Bantu and European elements. The different regions of the country celebrate their regional distinctness, while at the same time maintaining a national identity as Zambians. Copper and wooden crafts remain popular in rural areas. Maize is the staple crop of Zambia, complemented by vegetables. As part of the nation's European legacy, the most popular sports are soccer (football), cricket, and rugby.

Zambia's history can be traced to approximately 300 C.E., when the Khoisan people occupied the land. Bantu migrants began arriving in present-day Zambia in the twelfth and thirteenth centuries, together with other groups such as the Ngoni, Nkoya, Nsokolo, and Sotho. As it was far inland, Zambia did not experience non-African contact until the eighteenth century, when Arab traders arrived.

In the late eighteenth century, Portuguese explorer Francisco de Lacerdo visited Zambia. He was followed by Scottish missionary David Livingston. Livingstone navigated the Zambezi River and named the magnificent waterfalls at Victoria Falls after England's Queen Victoria.

Under British colonial rule, the area of present-day Zambia was called Northern Rhodesia; the territory was completely separate from Southern Rhodesia, now called Zimbabwe. In the mid-1950s, the Federation of Rhodesia and Nyasaland was formed. Between 1953 and 1962, Kenneth Launda led the movement for independence, which resulted in self-governance and the formation of the state of Zambia.

The falling price of copper, the mainstay of the

economy, and the socialist policies of the Kaunda government in the 1970s helped exacerbate poverty in Zambia. During the 1980s and 1990s, the economy was further affected by a reduction in copper sales and a prolonged drought that affected the agricultural sector. The country's one-party rule ended in 1991, and that same year the country implemented the International Monetary Fund's structural adjustment programs, in an effort to rebuild and modernize its economy. Subsequent governments have made efforts to alleviate poverty by investing in the agricultural sector and enacting agricultural reforms.

Today, Zambia is considered poor by all standards set by the United Nations, and it is plagued by low life expectancy and increasing rates of human immunodeficiency virus/acquired immune deficiency syndrome (HIV/AIDS). These issues have had a significant social and economic impact on the economy and its people, stymieing efforts to modernize the country as it is deprived of much of its talent. It is hoped that increased foreign investment, which began during the mid-2000s, will have the effect of mitigating the crisis of poverty and poor health, giving people more access to medicines and a better standard of living.

Franklyn Taylor

See also: *Groups: Africa*—Bemba. *Issues*—Colonialism; Mining.

Further Reading

Crehan, Kate A.F. *The Fractured Community: Landscapes of Power and Gender in Rural Zambia.* Berkeley: University of California Press, 1997.

Grant, William D. *Zambia, Then and Now: Colonial Rulers and Their African Successors.* New York: Routledge, 2009.

Larmer, Miles. *Rethinking African Politics: A History of Opposition in Zambia.* Burlington, VT: Ashgate, 2011.

Issues

Issues

Agriculture

Agriculture is a key source of livelihood for many indigenous peoples, as they use the resources that are located on their lands to meet their needs. Across the globe, indigenous people have developed agroforestry systems and practices for land use, soil and water management, and environmental conservation. These traditional practices encompass methods of cultivation, food collecting, and harvesting crops, all of which are essential to many native peoples' survival. Plants also remain a traditional source of medicine among many native groups.

Indigenous peoples' intimate relationship with the environment has led to the development of a body of knowledge that is valuable for human health, sustainable horticulture and food production, and continued biodiversity. Through practical application they have developed new varieties of plants and gathered valuable information on generic resources in the field of agriculture. Recently, their knowledge of environmental management and agricultural biodiversity—including the wide range of life forms related to agriculture, such as soil fauna, heirloom seed varieties, and native plants and animals—as well as about the medicinal uses of plants, has attracted considerable attention among the broader community. In fact, the importance and contribution of indigenous environmental and agricultural practices and knowledge to the development of agriculture has been recognized internationally.

Applications of biotechnology, especially in the fields of medicine and agriculture, have attracted the attention of the pharmaceutical and biotechnology industries. Such information could aid the research and scientific analysis needed to develop products and processes for drugs, cosmetics, and other commercial products, as well as improvements in food production. Indigenous peoples have cultivated numerous species of plants, and they have developed their agricultural knowledge through practice and experience for centuries; however, this knowledge of methods, processes, products, and designations with applications to agriculture has not always been subject to documentation, as indigenous knowledge traditionally is passed down orally.

Recommendations have been made for new intercultural education systems to transmit and develop indigenous knowledge about agriculture and the management of natural resources. For example, the Draft Declaration of Cusco, issued at the Eleventh International Congress of Ethnobiology in Cuzco, Peru, in 2008, takes this approach. Yet most indigenous peoples face issues of poverty, malnourishment, and hunger, and they seldom reap the rewards of the exploitation and use of their resources and knowledge.

Biodiversity and the United Nations' Role

The United Nations declared 2010 the International Year of Biodiversity, with the theme "Biodiversity Is Life—Biodiversity Is Our Life." Integral to this focus is recognizing the important role that indigenous knowledge systems play in conservation and the sustainable use and management of agricultural biological diversity.

Agenda 21, one of the outcomes of the United Nations Conference on Environment and Development, held in Rio de Janeiro in 1992, underscored the need to intensify sustainable agriculture and acknowledged the role of indigenous peoples in sustainable agriculture and rural development. It also acknowledged calls for the incorporation of indigenous ecological knowledge and practices to ensure native people's participation in and to promote human resource development for sustainable agriculture.

Agenda 21 also highlighted the existence of the problem of land degradation affecting both developed and developing countries. One of the activities that may help achieve land conservation and rehabilitation is the collection and recording of information on indigenous conservation and rehabilitation practices and farming systems as a basis for research and extension programs.

The International Treaty on Plant Genetic Resources for Food and Agriculture (PGRFA) adopted by the Food and Agriculture Organization Conference in November

2001 aims to achieve the conservation and sustainable use of PGRFA and the fair and equitable sharing of benefits derived from their use. It also seeks to attain sustainable agriculture and food security. This treaty recognizes the important contribution of indigenous peoples to the conservation and development of PGRFA, which constitutes the basis of food and agriculture production throughout the world. Documents such as the World Conservation Strategy, prepared by the International Union for the Conservation of Nature and Natural Resources in 1980, and the 1987 report of the World Commission on Environment and Development (also known as the Brundtland Commission), *Our Common Future,* also reflect the relevant role of indigenous agricultural knowledge, practices, and systems.

Indigenous peoples have carried out agricultural production for self-consumption or self-sufficiency; however, crops also have been planted and harvested on an economic outward-oriented system for commercialization. Different types of seeds, breeds, and processing techniques have been selected and developed over centuries. Today, indigenous peoples are calling on states to respect their rights to sustain their traditional agricultural systems and to plant and reproduce heirloom plant varieties.

The international Cancun Declaration of Indigenous Peoples, issued at the Fifth World Trade Organization Ministerial Conference in Cancun, Mexico, in 2003, reflects this concern. Indigenous peoples also have stressed their right to food security and their willingness to maintain their traditional practice of saving, sharing, and exchanging seeds at community seed banks.

Threats to Indigenous Food Security and Native Resistance

Deforestation, extraction of natural resources, pollution of lands and water, loss of agricultural biodiversity, and intensive agriculture all threaten food security. Indigenous peoples are concerned with the problems that are arising in agriculture at present and in the future and with the amount of land that is available for traditional agriculture in indigenous societies.

One of the major problems that indigenous peoples face is land and crop degradation, which may have a downward effect on the prices of national agricultural products, thereby affecting indigenous agricultural systems. This also may lead to the market dominance of genetically modified organisms instead of native seeds, species, and plants.

Indigenous peoples have voiced concerns about the appropriation of their lands and resources by multinational corporations, which has had a negative impact on their traditional food production. They seek to promote the establishment of local markets for their benefit and demand the right to practice traditional methods of food production as an act of self-determination. The Declaration of Indigenous Peoples for Food Sovereignty, issued on November 24, 2009, reflects these concerns. In the declaration, indigenous peoples affirmed that they offer an "alternative model of sustainable food production and protection of biodiversity."

Indigenous peoples have shown an interest in organic, ecological, biological, and sustainable use and management of agricultural biological diversity and have expressed concerns about the scarcity of traditional foods. Some indigenous peoples have implemented projects to preserve and strength traditional food systems and native agrobiodiveristy and to protect their rights to agricultural biodiversity. For example, the Potato Park project, implemented by an association of six Quechua communities in Pisaq, located in the Sacred Valley of the Incas in Cuzco, Peru, has developed a Collective Biocultural Heritage Register in an effort to preserve their food systems.

Further, practices such as assimilation and urbanization affect indigenous societies and contribute to the transformation or loss of traditional knowledge and agricultural communal practices. Indigenous knowledge of agriculture may be affected by a lack of interest among recent generations of indigenous peoples in the culture and knowledge of their ancestors and the unwillingness of young people to learn from their elders as a result of external cultural influences.

An additional factor in the decline of traditional agriculture and local food is the lack of or insufficient state support for indigenous food crops. Limited local food markets, the entry of cheap agricultural products into their communities, and the lack of market opportunities also contribute to such a decline. As a result many indigenous peoples are forced to abandon their traditional systems either in part or entirely in order to earn income outside of their communities, impacting the group's small-scale agricultural practices and traditional lifestyles and cultures. At the same time, increasing international focus on and even tourism related to studying agricultural biodiversity may create economic opportunity and help to mitigate such out-migration and interruption in traditional lifeways.

Globally, the agricultural practices of indigenous peoples also are vulnerable to the effects of climate change. Adverse climate conditions may alter traditional agricultural activities and force indigenous peoples to look for new areas that are less affected by such conditions.

Yovana Reyes Tagle

See also: *Issues*—Indigenous Peoples and the United Nations; Land Rights; Social Customs.

Further Reading

Kuhnlein, Harriet V., Bill Erasmus, and Dina Spigelski, eds. *Indigenous Peoples' Food Systems: The Many Dimensions of Culture, Diversity and Environment for Nutrition and Health.* Rome: Food and Agriculture Organization of the United Nations, 2009.

Pimbert, Michel. *Transforming Knowledge and Ways of Knowing for Food Sovereignty and Bio-cultural Diversity.* London: International Institute for Environment and Development, 2007.

Pimbert, Michel, Khanh Tran-Thanh, Estelle Deléage, Magali Reinert, Christophe Trehet, and Elizabeth Bennett, eds. *Farmers' Views on the Future of Food and Small Scale Producers.* London: International Institute for Environment and Development, 2006.

Anthropology

The word *anthropology* comes from the Greek terms *anthrōpos* (human) and *logia* (study), referring to the holistic study of humanity. As an academic discipline, anthropology covers an enormous variety of topics. It generally is construed as the broad and interdisciplinary study of people, and it is a crossroads where academic domains such as humanities, sciences, and social sciences converge. Anthropology developed in the early nineteenth to mid-twentieth century as the study of native peoples; the majority of the published literature on cultural groups in different parts of the world has been penned by anthropologists.

Disciplines

Anthropology traditionally has been divided into four subdisciplines, known as the four-field approach: archaeological anthropology, biological or physical anthropology, cultural or social anthropology, and linguistic anthropology or anthropological linguistics. It now has diversified to include a fifth field, applied or action anthropology, as well as various specializations and subdisciplines, such as ecological anthropology, economic anthropology, forensic anthropology, gay and lesbian anthropology, legal and political anthropology, media anthropology, medical anthropology, museum anthropology, and visual anthropology. Anthropology also has played a key role in the emergence of new interdisciplinary fields such as ethnic studies, human–computer interaction, global studies, and social cognition.

Cultural anthropology is the discipline's largest branch. It focuses on the detailed study of human cultural experience and social life, including topics such as customs; economic, legal, and political organization; festivals; family structure, kinship, and social organization; language; material culture; myth; mortuary rites; religion; and symbols. Cultural anthropologists address perspectives found within one cultural group or conduct comparative studies across cultures.

During the field's early development in the early twentieth century, cultural anthropology diverged in Great Britain and North America, and each region developed its own distinct traditions, approaches, and literature. American "cultural anthropology" focused on the way in which people view themselves and their culture, especially in symbolic form, whereas British "social anthropology" focused on social behaviors, groups, and institutions. By the mid-twentieth century, these two approaches had converged, and today they are known together as "sociocultural anthropology."

The development of anthropology in continental Europe was more fragmented. In France, Émile Durkheim, Robert Hertz, and Claude Lévi-Strauss played key roles. Elsewhere in Europe—in Greece, Italy, and Portugal, for example—anthropology was influenced by British anthropology but emphasized national perspectives, including variations in local cultures, rather than cross-cultural comparison.

Linguistic anthropology is the study of people through their languages, particularly the relation between anthropological issues, such as the development of individual and group social identities, ideologies, and narratives with language and sociocultural processes. It includes the description of language such as grammar, phonology, semantics, and syntax; extinct languages and language change over time; and the relations between language and society.

Archaeological anthropology explores the evolution, functioning, and organization of human societies using archaeological evidence. This evidence may include historical artifacts of human culture such as excavations and museums exhibits and contemporary artifacts and observations related to modern-day life.

Biological anthropology studies humans using biological approaches, considering, for example, variation in human physical traits around the world, usually in the context of evolution. It has close links with other biological sciences such as genetics and molecular studies; health, medicine, and nutrition; and the study of human origins. It also includes the study of nonhuman primates (primatology).

Applied anthropology is the practical application of methods and theories from all of these fields to understand and solve human problems. Applied anthropologists tend to work in nonacademic settings such as advocacy groups, businesses, development agencies, human services, governments, nongovernmental organizations, and tribal associations.

Origins and History

Anthropology has its origins in European expansion and colonization, emerging in the early nineteenth century as the study of native peoples in colonies, including their artifacts, language, and culture. Colonialism brought Europeans—who regarded themselves as "civilized," living in modern, advanced cultures—into contact with indigenous peoples whose appearance, beliefs, customs, and traditional ways of life were regarded as primitive. Early anthropological studies were based on the premise that indigenous peoples were changing and that many faced extinction, threatened by Westernization. In the United States, early anthropology was influenced by the presence of Native American societies, which were studied by scholars in residence on Indian reservations. Anthropology also has historical roots in a number of nineteenth-century academic disciplines, particularly ethnology, which is the comparative and historical study of human societies.

Franz Boas (1858–1942) is regarded as the "Father of Modern Anthropology," especially in the United States, where he helped establish anthropology as a reputable academic endeavor. He played a key role in founding the American Anthropological Association—now the largest organization of anthropologists, with members around the globe—and developed the first American doctoral program in anthropology at Columbia University.

Boas encouraged the four-field approach, and his work in all of those fields was pioneering, especially the contextualist conception of culture and cultural relativism, which argues that cultures do not evolve from less advanced to more advanced (cultural evolution), but rather are the products of diverse cultural factors that are unique to each culture. This line of thinking formed the foundation of cultural anthropology. Many of Boas's students went on to establish successful careers in anthropology and set up anthropology programs at other universities across the United States.

Boas's 1883 study of the Inuit of Cumberland Sound on Baffin Island in the Arctic Ocean contributed to the development of ethnographic research methods, a defining characteristic of cultural anthropology, which was advanced further by Bronislaw Malinowski (1884–1942),

MUSEUMS

Governments in many nations have built museums dedicated to the exhibition, analysis, and preservation of indigenous cultures. Such institutions frequently offer educational programming to encourage patrons' understanding and respect and cross-cultural learning experiences. Examples of such institutions include the National Museum of the American Indian in Washington, D.C., and the Instituto Nacional de Antropología e Historia (National Institute of Anthropology and History) in Mexico City, Mexico. Several major political and cultural concerns dominate museum professionals' work with aboriginal objects and cultures.

First, museum professionals must consider the topic of repatriation (return) of stolen, looted, black market, or otherwise illicitly obtained objects. In 1990, the U.S. government established the Native American Graves Protection and Repatriation Act (NAGPRA) to guide federally funded museums in the repatriation of Native American objects and to give the tribes a mechanism whereby they can pursue a claim to an object held by a museum. In cases where the cultural groups responsible for those objects no longer exist, museum professionals are required to manage display and long-term care of such items.

In addition, where objects are retained by museums, some may not be appropriate for public display. Thus, to display them in exhibits would be a direct violation of aboriginal values. Museums such as the National Museum of the American Indian store many works that staff may not display publicly. Consequently, institutions consider long-term storage when repatriation may not be possible.

Another concern is that the display of objects may not accurately represent the original function that those items performed. Most objects currently on display in museums today were not intended for static display as *objets d'art*—rather, they were intended as functional objects that gained additional meaning through their use in performance and ritual. In other words, objects may be displayed as fine art or scientific objects, rather than being discussed and explained primarily as functional or religious items.

This becomes problematic when viewers understand the display as a factual and representative presentation of the item and applies expectations typical of European objects of study and beauty. In other words, such display may encourage viewers to approach the object with the same expectations that one would have when viewing a conventional Western European oil painting, for example, and judge the aboriginal item as lacking in craftsmanship, quality, or value.

Danielle Roseberry

one of the best-known anthropologists of the twentieth century. Ethnography refers to both an empirical research strategy for gathering data on human societies and the final product of research, namely, a monograph or book.

Ethnographic research is the direct, firsthand observation of a particular culture, society, or community; it is more holistic than other research methods, as it includes an extensive period of fieldwork, usually lasting at least one year but sometimes much longer. In order to understand the totality of social life, anthropologists usually immerse themselves in the group that they are studying by living with the local people, learning and conversing in the local language, and participating in social and cultural events. For example, anthropologists participate in daily activities such as employment and subsistence, marriage customs, material culture, rituals, and so on. Participant observation (observation of daily behavior) is the hallmark of ethnographic research; other data-collection methods include genealogy, in-depth interviewing, longitudinal research, and questionnaires.

Anthropology developed around several classic ethnographies published during the mid-twentieth century. Malinowski's *The Argonauts of the Western Pacific* (1922), based on his fieldwork in the Trobriand Islands (now the Kiriwina Islands) in the Pacific Ocean, is regarded as one of anthropology's most skilled ethnographies. Malinowski was one of the first anthropologists to stress the importance of detailed participant observation, and he later established the theory of functionalism, which posited that culture functions to meet the needs of individuals rather than society as a whole. *The Andaman Islanders* (1922) by Alfred R. Radcliffe Brown, based on extensive fieldwork in the Andaman Islands, contributed extensively to anthropological theories on kinship, social structure, rituals, and myths. Radcliffe-Brown is well known for developing structural functionalism, a framework that describes society as composed of functionally interdependent institutions. Malinowski and Radcliffe-Brown are considered the founders of British social anthropology. Other classic ethnographies written by pioneers in early anthropology include *Coming of Age in Samoa* (1928) by Margaret Mead, *Naven* (1936) by Gregory Bateson, and *The Nuer* (1940) by E.E. Evans-Pritchard.

Anthropology Today

Anthropology is grounded in the study of exotic cultures around the world. Early anthropologists studied small-scale, relatively isolated societies with traditional lifestyles. However, anthropological studies now are conducted everywhere.

Since the late twentieth century, there has been increasing interest in high civilizations, including modern and Western civilizations, and their variation in relation to ethnicity, region, and social class. More attention also is being paid to contemporary issues such as globalization, health, indigenous rights, poverty, and virtual communities. Ethnographies of professional communities—such as the information technology sector, law firms, and scientists—are becoming popular as well. Modern ethnographies tend to be less inclusive, focus on specific topics and questions, and are more problem focused.

Some aspects of anthropology have been controversial. The fact that early anthropology derived some of its key notions from colonialism and provided colonialists with information that eased control of natives has drawn criticism. Also, critics have raised concerns about the cultural background and power status of anthropologists and their influence on the interpretation of other cultures. Anthropology also has been used for the benefit of the state—for example, during World War I, a number of American scholars were known to have participated in espionage for the U.S. government under cover as researchers. In response to such concerns, professional anthropological bodies have formulated codes of ethics or statements to uphold the ethical conduct of their members.

Gareth Davey

See also: *Groups: East Asia and Oceania*—Andaman Islanders. *Groups: North America*—Inuit. *Issues*—Repatriation.

Further Reading
Bodley, John H. *Cultural Anthropology: Tribes, States, and the Global System.* Lanham, MD: AltaMira, 2011.
DeMallie, Raymond J., and Alfonso Ortiz, eds. *North American Indian Anthropology: Essays on Society and Culture.* Norman: University of Oklahoma Press, 1996.
Ember, Carol R., and Melvin Ember. *Cultural Anthropology.* Englewood Cliffs, NJ: Prentice Hall, 2006.
Haviland, William A., Harald E.L. Prins, and Dana Walrath. *Anthropology: The Human Challenge.* Belmont, CA: Wadsworth/Cengage, 2010.
Kottak, Conrad Phillip. *Anthropology: The Exploration of Human Diversity.* Boston: McGraw-Hill, 2008.

Assimilation

Assimilation is the process by which people alter their cultural and institutional practices—such as their language, religion, governance, or economy—to align with those of another group. Assimilation occurs in a variety of historical contexts, from voluntary immigration and adoption of a dominant society's culture to the forced assimilation of peoples of conquest as enslaved or colonized groups to internal or neocolonial assimilation of indigenous groups.

There are several modes of assimilation. Assimilation may be voluntary and occur over a long period of time through consistent interaction with or voluntary immigration to another society. Assimilation also may be achieved through coercion, where one society decides that it is beneficial to adopt the cultural norms or practices of another in order to protect trade, defend territory, or survive. In such instances, the assimilating society may be responding to occupation by settlers or facing possible conquest, while attempting to limit the loss of its culture. Finally, assimilation may occur by force as a result of one society's conquest of another.

Forced assimilation may involve the establishment of various types of colonies. Forced assimilation tends to occur during colonization and may continue into the postcolonial period. Assimilation in postcolonial or neocolonial contexts may reflect voluntary, coerced, or forced assimilation experiences and does not require the presence of the conqueror society.

Creolization—the development of a hybrid culture as a result of the interaction of two or more distinct societies—is a form of cultural assimilation that occurs as an unintended consequence of settler colonization. It may be voluntary or coerced assimilation, as two societies (one of which is politically dominant) merge to create a hybrid society.

Voluntary Assimilation

The three defining characteristics of voluntary assimilation and their primary methods of occurrence are cultural transfer or exchange, voluntary immigration, and Creolization.

Cultural Transfer or Exchange

Voluntary assimilation may occur over time as a result of regular interaction through trade and the development of social and political alliances. This type of assimilation is evident in the impact that Middle Eastern cultures had on African societies along trade routes through the Sahara Desert between the eleventh and fifteenth centuries. During that time, some African societies, especially the ruling elite, voluntarily adopted Islam as their religion and Arabic writing and numeric systems in order to facilitate trade. This type of assimilation developed through consistent interaction between societies over an extended period of time.

Such cultural exchange also may stimulate forced or coerced assimilation. For example, other African societies

on Saharan trade routes later were assimilated by force in response to military conflicts over trade or territory or were coerced to assimilate in order to maintain political and trade alliances within the region.

Voluntary Immigration

In the United States, many European groups experienced voluntary assimilation as they grew accustomed to American society. Although some aspects of cultural difference were contested, and varying levels of coerced assimilation were experienced by different immigrant groups, European immigrants, especially Western European groups, experienced a comparatively high degree of voluntary assimilation. More than 200 years of successive assimilation by a variety of European immigrant groups resulted in the development of a uniquely "American" culture that is identifiable by common language use, social practices, and norms.

The development of American culture also included aspects of forced assimilation, as the societies and cultures of Native Americans and slaves brought from Africa were coerced into merging into American culture. Virtually all societies in North and South America are the result of a similar mix of voluntary and forced assimilation. Even Native American nations have experienced some assimilation with the dominant society.

Creolization

Creole societies commonly develop within shared geographic locations over time as a result of the merger of two or more societies. The resulting Creole languages, religions, and social practices are hybrid forms of the original societies' languages, religions, and social practices.

The term *Creole* originates from the Portuguese word *crioulo,* meaning "native to the locality." It originally referred to individuals of African descent who were born into slavery in Portuguese colonies. Later, it came to denote those of mixed African and European heritage who oversaw the early Portuguese colonies. This term eventually morphed into *Creole* and most commonly referred to those of mixed African and European heritage. The French Creole of Louisiana are an exception, being of French and mixed European ancestry; within Louisiana, the term *Creole* typically is used to refer to people of African and French or French Creole blood.

The Gullah people of the Gullah Islands, located off the coast of Georgia and South Carolina, may be described as African Creoles. Of mixed African heritage, they are the descendants of slaves brought from West and Central Africa. Other examples of Creole societies include the

Afro-French people of Haiti and Martinique; the Afro-Hispanic people of Cuba, Puerto Rico, and Venezuela; and the Afro-Portuguese of Brazil.

Creole languages, such as Papiamento in Aruba, emerged as a mixture of African and Spanish languages. Likewise, Creole religions, such as Vodou in Haiti, developed from the hybridization of West African (Yoruba and Dahomean or Fon) and European Catholic religious beliefs and practices.

Forced Assimilation

Many societies have experienced forced assimilation as a result of the establishment of plantation, occupation, or settler colonies. Forced assimilation may be part of a larger historical experience such as enslavement, forced immigration, or foreign conquest. Forced assimilation occurs when a society is not allowed to maintain its cultural or societal institutions and practices. This may result in full or partial assimilation.

Full assimilation (voluntary or forced) involves the cultural adaptation of another society's language, religion, and social practices, along with full acceptance into the dominant society. While partial assimilation (coerced or forced) also may include the adaptation of another society's language, religion, and social practices,

the assimilated society does not gain the same privileges as the dominant society. Such limited assimilation is reflected in the maintenance of hierarchal relationships between the dominant and the dominated societies.

Enslavement and Forced Immigration

Enslavement and forced assimilation have occurred in many societies in Africa, Asia, Europe, the Middle East, and North America. People enslaved through acts of war or through the payment of debts normally were forced to assimilate into the dominant society. While many societies struggled to maintain and transfer indigenous knowledge and culture, the realities of slavery resulted in varying degrees of cultural loss that necessitated some extent of assimilation or Creolization in order to survive in their new environments.

In some cases, as in many African and Native American societies, historically enslaved persons could and did assimilate to the point of gaining their freedom or marrying into the dominant society. In these cases, forced assimilation allowed their families to become members of the dominant society. In other cases, forced assimilation through enslavement served the purposes of the dominant society, with few or no opportunities for freedom or full integration into the dominant society.

SYNCRETISM

Syncretism is the combination of different and sometimes opposing forms of belief or practice through the use of symbols, practices, and objects. Several examples of syncretism can be found in the visual arts of the Americas during the colonial period.

For example, Roman Catholic missionaries commissioned many artworks, such as the murals at Malinalco in Mexico, containing animals, objects, and plants that conveyed different meanings, depending on the religion and identity of the viewer. Franciscan priest Jacobo de Testera relied on overlapping meanings of visual imagery to create Testerian catechisms that guided indigenous Mexicans in their conversion to Christianity.

Syncretism also was employed by missionaries who sought to convey Christian religious dogma that did not have immediate parallels in aboriginal religions. For example, scholars have discovered that some missionaries attempted to convey the significance of the devil by relating that figure to an owl, which was associated with death and the underworld in the aboriginal religions of Mesoamerica. By using the word and the image of the owl, the missionaries attempted to reference specific ideas about death and the underworld, although indigenous

audiences may have interpreted the references in ways not intended by the friars.

Identifying syncretism is a difficult endeavor, as much of the syncretic value of a symbol or activity is understood primarily through speculation, because scholars generally lack extensive firsthand accounts describing the perceptions of such symbols or activities by native peoples. Scholars frequently rely on ethnographic or anthropological studies of historical or contemporary indigenous cultures to analyze potential alternative meanings of such symbolism. Such approaches to analysis are prone to criticism, however, as these methodologies tend to assume that indigenous cultures are static in their understanding and application of symbols and traditions.

Proponents of anthropological and ethnographic methodologies argue that such approaches allow indigenous people to involve themselves in research and writing about their native cultures. It is hoped that such direct involvement may yield more nuanced and accurate studies of syncretism.

Danielle Roseberry

For example, chattel slavery as it was practiced in the Americas was coupled with forced immigration to provide labor on plantation colonies. Africans were enslaved and forced to immigrate to the Americas. Once there, they experienced forced assimilation. The combination of enslavement and forced immigration resulted in these societies' isolation or disconnection from their places of origin; this disconnection compounded the impact of forced assimilation, as they lost continuity with their home cultures.

Forced assimilation was so thorough in the United States that only remnants of African cultural practices, languages, and religions remain. In other parts of the Americas, such as the Caribbean, African societies' cultural attributes merged with those of European societies to create Creole societies.

Foreign Conquest

Settler and occupation colonization are closely related examples of foreign conquest that result in forced assimilation. Several examples of forced assimilation can be found in European settlements in various parts of the world. These settlements led to the forced assimilation of Native American societies in the Americas, Aboriginal societies in Australia and New Zealand, and African societies in southern Africa.

Examples of Forced Assimilation

Compulsory education and forced removal from indigenous land were two ways that people were forced to assimilate. Canada and the United States viewed such methods of forced assimilation as a way to decrease Native American resistance to conquest of their lands and thereby to reduce social conflict.

In these countries, native peoples were forced, even through kidnapping, into the dominant education system, where they were banned from speaking their languages and practicing their religions. The goal was to "reeducate" native children to become part of mainstream society. This forced assimilation was so thorough that even clothing styles and food choices were adapted to the dominant society's norms. Australia and New Zealand followed similar patterns of forced relocation and compulsory education to reduce resistance.

In such cases, the indigenous peoples already were reduced to minority populations through the transmission of European diseases to which they had no immunity and through organized military and civilian attacks on indigenous societies. Indigenous societies in the Americas, Australia, and New Zealand all continue to experience some level of forced assimilation in order to survive as peoples of conquest.

Australian Aborigines gather outside Parliament House in Canberra in February 2008 to hear Prime Minister Kevin Rudd's official apology to the Stolen Generations—indigenous children taken from their families for assimilation into white society. *(Jeremy Piper/Bloomberg/Getty Images)*

In southern Africa, the settler colony and the resulting forced assimilation of indigenous societies has a complex history. When the Dutch and British colonized the area, what initially were incidents of cultural exchange soon became experiences of coerced or forced assimilation. Some Khoikhoi and San people intermarried with the Dutch settlers (known as the Boers) and French Hugenots (Protestants forced out of France, to whom the Dutch gave refuge) in the late seventeenth century, creating a Creole class known as the Griquas. Others from these tribes became servants or slaves and were forced to assimilate, as were tribes whose land the colonists confiscated.

By the early nineteenth century, the presence of the British in South Africa led to the continuation of the British tradition of treaty making with native groups; however, also following patterns established in India and North America, when the treaty making efforts failed, the British simply confiscated native lands. Native African peoples were subjected to forced assimilation through forced servitude, religious conversion, and, ultimately, the introduction of what became known as Bantu education. As a result of warfare, education, and assimilation efforts, only a few African nations remained intact in southern Africa by the end of the 1800s.

After the Boer War (1899–1902), the establishment of a united South Africa under Afrikaner and British rule began to formalize forced assimilation of African indigenous nations. This led to Bantu compulsory education, which taught indigenous African peoples that they had no history or political status. Further, this education indoctrinated indigenous Africans to believe that only white Afrikaner and British societies could provide them with an acceptable cultural identity, even if this identity came with second-class citizenship. The extreme form of this forced assimilation under a settler colony in southern Africa became known as apartheid in South Africa in the late 1940s and continued until the early 1990s. This type of forced assimilation also occurred in neighboring settler colonies, such as Rhodesia (now Zimbabwe) and Northern Rhodesia (now Zambia).

Settler colonies commonly used a range of approaches to deal with what they regarded as the "native problem." By the 1800s, forced assimilation in European settler colonies became the norm, partly as a by-product of the First and Second Great Awakenings within Christian churches, which expanded their missions to Christianize and "civilize" indigenous societies, and partly to meet labor needs in settler colonies.

The Europeans were not alone in their historical experience with establishing settler colonies. China encouraged settler colonies throughout former autonomous regions in order to promote and increase assimilation to national Chinese culture following the establishment of the People's Republic of China in 1949.

Tibet is a well-known example of a planned Chinese settlement intended to force the assimilation of the Tibetan people. While this semi-autonomous region continues to protest this process, it serves as a modern example of forced assimilation through the establishment of a settler colony.

An important work that documents the varying degrees of coerced and forced assimilation within China is Mika Toyota's 2008 study, which researches ethnic and social identity formation issues among the minority peoples of the frontier zones of China, Myanmar, and Thailand. In this study, the use of Chinese cultural capital as demonstrated partial assimilation, such as the adoption of Chinese language, dress, and other cultural practices, is documented as a survival strategy for these indigenous peoples. These societies may experience assimilation in both settler and occupation colonial contexts.

Occupation

Another context in which forced assimilation occurs is through the establishment of occupation colonies. In these cases, the conquering society or nation does not settle en masse but rather occupies and controls an area as part of its sovereign territory, extracting resources and labor from the land and the indigenous people.

Some large-scale examples of occupation include European colonization from the late 1500s to the 1900s, Japanese expansion during World War II, and Chinese expansion since World War II. European occupation colonies were established throughout much of sub-Saharan Africa, the Caribbean, and South and Southeast Asia. In Africa, the majority of the land, except for that in present-day Ethiopia and Liberia, was claimed by European countries in order to access resources and labor.

Initially, the promise of a faster route to India for spices and silk lured explorers such as Vasco de Gama from Portugal around Africa. Later, gold found on the east coast of Africa attracted many explorers, but it was the transatlantic slave trade from the 1600s to the late 1800s that created a mandate to occupy Africa. This occupation began at coastal ports and slowly spread inland as the demand for slaves grew. Occupation intensified as the slave trade ended and the demand for mineral and agricultural resources grew to support sprawling urban European communities.

South Asia, while not targeted for slaves, also experienced widespread occupation as England took over its trade, natural, and labor resources. As in the majority of African occupation colonies, indigenous cultures assimilated in order to survive and possibly even to share the economic or political benefits of the colonizer.

As with many settler colonies, mission schools were early negotiators of partial assimilation in these occupation colonies. They provided literacy and some occupational training to feed the labor needs of the colonizers. As these occupation colonies developed, missionary schools were replaced with colonial government-run schools. The extent of assimilation through education varied based on the individual goals and needs of each colonizing government.

For example, the native peoples under Portuguese rule in Angola, Mozambique, and Tanzania experienced minimal assimilation through education. In Portuguese occupation colonies, forced labor was the norm; when the colonizers left, less than 10 percent of the inhabitants had participated in mission or colonial education. For the Portuguese, assimilation was not an important strategy in their colonial plans.

This contrasted significantly with the assimilation policy of the French. French occupation governments mandated full assimilation (national identity, education, language, religion, and dress) of indigenous peoples in order to qualify for French citizenship. The French assimilation policy applied to occupation colonies in Africa, the Caribbean, and Southeast Asia. In French colonies, indigenous governments were not recognized, and assimilation was the only way to access the colonial economy and government.

Whereas the French sought an assimilation policy, the British introduced a policy of indirect rule, which resulted in varying degrees of assimilation within occupation colonies. Assimilation experiences under the British ranged from adoption of the English language in order to access economic opportunities to full assimilation through mission and later colonial schools and active participation in the colonial government. This range of assimilation under the British was experienced in African, Caribbean, and South Asian colonies.

Regardless of the level of mandated assimilation, all of these former European occupation and settler colonies experienced significant assimilation to European society. This assimilation continues in postcolonial or neocolonial contexts to this day. The continued assimilation to European or Western culture is partially attributable to continued economic ties, as well as to significant loss or weakening of indigenous institutions.

Internal Colonialism

Many modern nation-states include multiple ethnic groups as part of their citizenry. Ethnic, racial, religious, social, economic, or political stratification may result in varying levels of voluntary to coerced or forced assimilation into the dominant ethnic, racial, or religious group.

This type of assimilation is experienced through a structure of internal colonialism. Most commonly, a group that is not dominant may take on the dominant group's language, education, or dress in order to move up economically or politically within society. This may result in complete assimilation or in a duality in which "assimilation" is practiced within the larger society, but not within individual homes or local communities.

On a group level, for example, many black and Latino Americans maintain culturally specific practices within their communities, while they adopt the practices of the dominant society when they are away from their communities. On an individual level, celebrities or well-known businesspeople may take on dominant group names, such as American actor Carlos Estevez, who uses Charlie Sheen as his stage name.

Jewish societies have experienced internal colonialism in Europe, the Middle East, and the former Soviet Union. Even though European, Middle Eastern, and the former Soviet countries are considered Jews' places of origin, they have experienced forced removal, enslavement, genocide, and forced assimilation throughout their histories. As late as the nineteenth and twentieth centuries, forced assimilation was imposed as the only avenue to engage in the wider community. The establishment of ghettos (segregated neighborhoods) and pogroms (organized paramilitary and civilian attacks on Jews) resulted in a dual cultural identity for many Jewish communities in order to avoid exile or even death.

In trying to address Jewish needs after the most devastating anti-Semitic event in world history, the Holocaust, a Jewish settler colony was established in the Middle East that became the nation of Israel. As a result of its establishment, Muslim Middle Eastern or Palestinian groups faced forced assimilation or removal in order to remain in Israel. At the same time, Israelis face severe limits on their personal mobility because of anti-Israeli or anti-Semitic sentiments in neighboring Islamic nations. Religious and cultural differences and land disputes together create continued cultural and political conflict in this region. Currently, Israel and its neighbors continue to debate, negotiate, and mediate in a multicultural region that, it is hoped, may experience cultural exchange without coerced or forced assimilation to maintain national sovereignty and regional peace.

Examples of forced assimilation as a result of internal colonialism include France's ban on external religious symbols, such as the Islamic veil or Christian crucifix, in schools, which serves to assimilate groups to secular education. Another example is the dominant society's enforcement of its religious calendar, which results in other religious groups' partial assimilation into the dominant society's business and education schedules. Finally, dress and language are common types of forced assimilation, as less dominant groups, such as ethnic minorities in Bangladesh, India, and Pakistan, adopt the dominant group's attire to be accepted and, in some cases, to avoid persecution.

Neocolonial Assimilation

One result of occupation and settler colonization was the loss or weakening of indigenous institutions. In particular, former government institutions were reduced or destroyed, leaving colonial government structures as the dominant ones. At the time of independence, indigenous societies found that they could gain a place at the negotiating table only through the use of colonial government structures. The result was the formation of postindependence nation-states that duplicated Western governments and, to a large extent, Western culture. Indigenous peoples had to vie for recognition and representation with the new nation-state as it introduced a new course of assimilation aimed toward national identity formation.

Many postcolonial governments, including newly independent colonies in Africa, the Caribbean, South America, and South and Southeast Asia created forced assimilation programs as part of their nationalization plans. The goal was to transition group identities from older indigenous ethnonational identities to a single national identity. This goal was supported by the newly formed governments' motivation to increase social and political cohesion among ethnonational groups. It also had practical economic aims, such as the broad use of a national language and economic trade system that was not dependent on ethnonational ties.

Another form of neocolonial assimilation was the use of "development" rhetoric closely tied to or aligned with nation building, which forced indigenous groups to assimilate into the new national culture. Globalization reinforced this process as global markets, nongovernmental organizations, and international organizations such the International Monetary Fund and the World Bank promoted so-called development programs for a variety of reasons from the 1960s to the present.

Some development programs that forced assimilation included transnational economic agreements with these nation-state governments for access to resources and trade at the expense of sustained environmental and human development, as witnessed in the Niger River Delta. Others promoted equity, the end of pov-erty, and increased education with forced or coerced assimilation as part of the development process. Such well-intentioned development occurs as continued assimilation to Westernized or Chinese global contexts, for example, through the imposition of education schemes and medical institutions and knowledge without consideration or integration of indigenous knowledge and accompanying institutions.

Ultimately, assimilation in the twenty-first century deals with at least two factors. One involves the lasting ramifications of colonialism's long history—what historian Patricia Limerick has dubbed the "legacy of conquest." The cultural prejudices entrenched by over 500 years of imperialism have yet to be fully overcome. At the same time, new pressures, completely apart from colonialism and its history, have arisen in the late twentieth and early twenty-first centuries, the results of the globalization of business, economy, and culture. This more pressing matter involves questions about what constitutes healthy exchange and change among societies versus what impact globalization has on societies as a potentially coercive agent of assimilation. Learning how to deal with the fact of globalization and still honor and create space for native cultures is the challenge faced today.

Jamaine Abidogun

See also: *Issues*—Colonialism; Education; Globalization; Indigenous Identity; Missionary Activities; Social Customs.

Further Reading

Bayly, Christopher, and Tim Harper. *Forgotten Wars: Freedom and Revolution in Southeast Asia.* Cambridge, MA: Belknap Press of Harvard University Press, 2007.

Briscoe, Gordon, and Len Smith, eds. *The Aboriginal Population Revisited: 70,000 Years to the Present.* Canberra, Australia: Aboriginal History, 2002.

Lipski, John. *A History of Afro-Hispanic Language: Five Centuries, Five Continents.* New York: Cambridge University Press, 2005.

Mayer, Ruth. *Artificial Africas: Colonial Images in the Times of Globalization.* Sudbury, MA: Dartmouth, 2002.

Rozema, Vicki. *A Guide to the Eastern Homelands of the Cherokee Nation.* 2nd ed. Winston-Salem, NC: John F. Blair, 2007.

Steward, Charles, ed. *Creolization: History, Ethnography, Theory.* Walnut Creek, CA: Left Coast, 2007.

Toyota, Mika. "Contested Chinese Identities Among Ethnic Minorities in the China, Burma and Thai Borderlands." *Ethnic and Racial Studies* 26:2 (2003): 301–320.

Zimmerman, Andrew. *Alabama in Africa: Booker T. Washington, the German Empire, and the Globalization of the New South.* Princeton, NJ: Princeton University Press, 2010.

Climate Change

Global warming—known as "infrared forcing" to scientists—is having a direct and deleterious effect on the lives of indigenous peoples. These effects are expected to accelerate in the coming decades as thermal inertia, which causes warming of the air about half a century after carbon dioxide and methane reach the atmosphere, results in swiftly rising temperatures. This process is exacerbated by greenhouse gas levels that are higher than at any time in the past 2 million years.

Because many indigenous peoples depend on subsistence agriculture, as well as hunting and fishing, they often are the first to be affected by substantial climate change. In addition, indigenous peoples in the Arctic, where temperatures are rising more quickly than anywhere else, and residents of many small islands in the Pacific will be affected by climate change most significantly.

Warming and the Inuit in the Arctic

The impact of climate change is most clearly seen in the Arctic, where average air temperatures have increased as much as 41 degrees Fahrenheit (5 degrees Celsius) over those of the twentieth century, dramatically reducing the amount of sea ice. In Inuit villages, which historically have been connected by traveling hunters but now are linked by telephone and e-mail, there is a growing body of evidence that climate change is having far-reaching effects. Weather reports from the Arctic reveal that scientists' projections of climate change, made over a period of fifteen years or more, have been realized even sooner than expected.

In 2003, residents in the Eskimo village of Kaktovik, Alaska, located some 250 miles (400 kilometers) north of the Arctic Circle, found a robin's nest—a highly unusual occurrence in a place where the native language does not even have a word for robin. Even more telling are the reductions in the habitats of Arctic animals such as the polar bear, as well as in the number and species of fish in Arctic waters, due to temperature changes.

Growing numbers of Inuit for the first time are suffering allergies from white-pine pollen that recently reached Sachs Harbour, located on Banks Island in northern Canada. As a result of thawing permafrost, Sachs Harbour slowly is sinking into a muddy mass during the summer. In 2006, officials in the Canadian territory of Nunavut authorized the installation of air conditioners in government buildings for the first time, due to increased summertime temperatures in some southern Arctic villages.

In fact, the region is experiencing weather changes in all seasons. In Iqaluit on Baffin Island, for example, thunder and lightning once were rarities; now they are much more common. Research supports ground-level observations of increasing Arctic storm frequency and intensity during the last half century, attributing the phenomenon to warming waters and changing atmospheric circulation patterns. In addition, the weather is increasingly unpredictable.

The melting of glaciers in summer now prevents the Inuit from reaching many of their traditional hunting and harvesting places. Areas that had been accessible when water was held in glaciers have become impassible due to the effects of increased melting. As a result of such changes, traveling safely in the area has become increasingly difficult. Even the most experienced Inuit hunters have gotten lost in the ice while traveling through familiar areas. The nephew of Paul Okalik, the premier of Nunavut, was swept away in a raging river that once had been a small stream.

The anecdotal accounts of Inuit hunters concerning the effects of warmer temperatures are now corroborated by sophisticated computer models, which show the amplified effects of climate change throughout the Arctic north. Addressing a hearing of the U.S. Senate Commerce Committee on global warming on August 15, 2004, Inuit elder Sheila Watt-Cloutier stated,

> The Earth is literally melting. If we can reverse the emissions of greenhouse gases in time to save the Arctic, then we can spare untold suffering. Protect the Arctic and you will save the planet. Use us as your early-warning system. Use the Inuit story as a vehicle to reconnect us all so that we can understand the people and the planet are one.

The ancient connection of the Inuit to their hunting culture may disappear within her grandson's lifetime, Watt-Cloutier said. She further stated, "My Arctic homeland is now the health barometer for the planet." U.S. Senator John McCain commented that a trip he had taken to the Arctic proved to him that the effects of climate change are real and convinced him that scientific projections of faster Arctic climate change are valid.

Island Nations and Sea-Level Rise

Rising sea levels caused by global warming could imperil more than 3,000 small isolated islands, grouped in twenty-four political entities in the Pacific Ocean, with a population of about 5 million people in 800 distinct cultures. Many coral atolls—formed as once-volcanic peaks sank below the ocean's surface, leaving rings of coral—contain permanent areas of freshwater (lagoons), which are vulnerable to salinization (an increase in the amount of salt in the water) as sea levels rise.

Scientists expect that global temperatures will rise further in coming decades, causing ever greater sea-level rise in the twenty-first century. At the same time, many low-lying islands face two compounding problems: The sea is rising, while the land slowly is sinking, as 65 million-year-old coral atolls reach the end of their life spans.

For example, global warming is an urgent issue in the Republic of Kiribati, home to about 79,000 people. Made up of a chain of coral atolls, Kiribati's thirty-three islands are scattered across 2 million square miles (5.2 million square kilometers) of ocean, encompassing three groups: the seventeen Gilbert Islands, eight Line Islands, and eight Phoenix Islands. Kiribati includes Kiritimati (formerly Christmas Island), the world's largest coral atoll.

The island of Kiritimati more than doubles its surface area at low tide, and its land area is no more than 6 feet (about 1.8 meters) above sea level at any point. Additionally, the living corals that raise the islands above sea level are threatened by warmer ocean waters. During 1997, the area was devastated by El Niño, which brought heavy rainfall, a rise in sea level of about 18 inches (46 centimeters), and extensive flooding. Not only did the overheated water kill approximately 40 percent of the coral, but it also decimated Kiritimati Island's bird population, which had been estimated at about 14 million.

By 1998, rising sea levels were already contaminat- ing drinking water and inundating some small Pacific islands. A number of smaller islands near Kiritimati and around the nation of Tuvalu have been submerged, taking with them many sacred sites, including the islet of Tebua Tarawa. Since the first tide-measuring devices were installed in 1978, the sea has risen approximately 1.2 inches (30 millimeters); according to projections, it will rise another 16 inches (41 centimeters) by the end of the twenty-first century. Kiribati already has moved some roads inland on its main island, as the rising Pacific Ocean eats into its shores. The government of Tuvalu, observing such changes on its nine inhabited islands, has concluded that, as one of the smallest and lowest-lying countries in the world, it is destined to be one of the first nations to be sunk because of a combination of erosion and rising sea levels.

Rising sea levels also are causing ocean water to seep into soils on some islands as water tables rise. Soils in some areas are becoming too salty for growing most vegetables. Many farmers in the Pacific islands are report- ing that their crops of swamp taro (pulaka), a staple food, are dying because of rising soil salinity. Another staple food, breadfruit (artocarpus altilis), also is threatened by saltwater inundation.

Ramifications for Native Peoples Worldwide

Although the Arctic and Pacific Island scenarios are the most dramatic, climate change is having an impact on many native groups in varying topographies. For exam- ple, Bangladesh, with its flat land and long coastline,

A delegate from Ecuador ad- dresses the Indigenous Peo- ples' Global Summit on Climate Change, a UN-affiliated event in 2009 attended by representatives from eighty nations. The world's indigenous peoples feel espe- cially vulnerable to the effects of climate change. *(Al Grillo/AP Images)*

could lose much of its low-lying coastal lands, totaling up to 16 percent of its land surface. Such a change would severely impact coastal native peoples' ocean-based lifeways and cause changes in their habitation patterns and foodways.

Tropical forest peoples, such as the Dayak in Borneo, Indonesia, have found that their rivers run higher in the wet season and lower in the dry season. As a result, many of the plants necessary for making their traditional medicines are no longer found.

Twa peoples in the Congo are noticing that rainfall has lessened and become more difficult to predict. This results in changing flood patterns that make traditional fish catching impossible. In addition, the drier climate has caused the region's forested areas to experience an increasing number of wildfires, further impacting the ecosystem.

In regions where the environment already was marginal for human habitation, such as the drylands of western Sudan, droughts are becoming more frequent and longer-lasting, resulting in decreased foraging grasses for many of the indigenous peoples' animal herds. Changing weather patterns are impacting many agriculture-based native peoples, such as the Miskito in Nicaragua, who have seen lower river flows as a result of less rain throughout the rainy season, as well as more intense hurricanes and other natural disasters, causing severe disruptions to their annual farming cycle.

Examples such as those presented here have analogies all over the world and demonstrate that climate change does not impact just one type of ecosystem or only a few native cultural and subsistence patterns. Climate change impacts all native people, just as it impacts everyone. The main difference is that many native groups have developed life patterns based on the characteristics of the ecosystems in which they have lived. Thus, they are more vulnerable to the changes in those ecosystems brought by climate change. The ramifications will only increase in severity, causing both cultural disruption and increased poverty, unless the factors causing climate change are addressed in a serious way around the world.

Bruce E. Johansen

See also: *Groups: North America*—Inuit. *Issues*—Ecosystem Management; Industrial Development.

Further Reading

Jans, Nick. "Living with Oil: The Real Price." In *The Last Polar Bear: Facing the Truth of a Warming World,* ed. Steven Kazlowski. Seattle: Mountaineers, 2008.

Johansen, Bruce E. "Arctic Heat Wave." *The Progressive,* October 2001, 18–20.

Macchi, Mirjam. *Indigenous and Traditional Peoples and Climate Change.* Gland, Switzerland: International Union for Conservation of Nature, 2008.

Mearns, Robin, and Andrew Norton, eds. *Social Dimensions of Climate Change: Equity and Vulnerability in a Warming World.* Washington, DC: The World Bank, 2010.

Nakashima, Douglas. *Climate Change and Arctic Sustainable Development: Scientific, Social, Cultural, and Educational Challenges.* Paris: UNESCO, 2009.

Sudetic, Chuck. "As the World Burns." *Rolling Stone,* September 2, 1999, 97–106, 129.

Wohlforth, Charles. *The Whale and the Supercomputer: On the Northern Front of Climate Change.* New York: Farrar, Straus and Giroux, 2004.

Colonialism

The intersection of native peoples with colonialism is a complex and controversial topic. In many written and oral accounts, colonialism is equated with or seen as a form of imperialism. Frequently, histories refer to the British, French, or Spanish empires—hence the conflation of colonization with imperialism.

More often, however, it is distinguished from imperialism, which has many different meanings. A simple and ancient meaning of imperialism is formerly foreign lands ruled autocratically by a conqueror. Since the nineteenth century, the term has referred to the expansion of countries with capitalist economies seeking new resources or new markets. Debate continues among historians, scholars, and politicians about whether imperialism was necessary for the growth of capitalism or only contributed to its growth. There is general but not universal agreement that imperialism was and remains detrimental to the peoples subjugated under it and to their cultures.

Distinct from imperialism, colonialism usually involves colonial officials, merchants, farmers, and/or missionaries. In some cases, as in British or Spanish colonies, it included extensive immigration from the home country. These typically are called settler colonies. In other cases, as in India and parts of Africa, there was little immigration from the home country beyond a handful of colonial administrators and merchants. These often are referred to as nonsettler colonies. Almost always, settler colonies are far more disruptive to indigenous societies than nonsettler colonies.

The settler/nonsettler distinction is significant but represents extreme points along a continuum that often changes over time. For instance, in the early phases of colonialism in the sixteenth and seventeenth centuries, French colonies in present-day Canada initially were nonsettler colonies interested in extracting furs collected by indigenous trappers. During the eighteenth century, many French settlers arrived and created what became Francophone Canada.

Five Types of Colonialism

At least five types of colonialism are germane to native peoples. The five types of colonization overlap, and they often morph into one or more of the others. These distinctions are heuristic rather than some deep "truth"; however, they are useful because they illustrate broad social, political, economic, or cultural processes. Such processes typically had different consequences for the indigenous peoples in colonized areas; however, given both the high death rate among indigenous peoples as a result of new diseases introduced by colonizers and the long time span—nearly half a millennium in many cases—many changes inevitably occurred in colonial areas.

The first type of colonialism is undertaken in the interest of acquiring land. The second, closely related, is to acquire resources such as gold, silver, furs, and other precious objects; another type of resource might be the people used to work the land in the colony, as in the Spanish *encomienda* system. In the third, new territories and their residents might serve as untapped markets in which to sell goods produced in the colonizing country.

In the fourth type, land might be sought not for its own use but because it allows access to some other destination, such as lands along the Mississippi River in North America or the Amazon River in South America. In the early centuries of colonization in North America, a supposed "Northwest Passage" that would allow naval access to the Pacific Ocean provides one example.

Finally, colonization might be preemptive—that is, a country might stake a claim to some territory before a rival does so. Sometimes preemptive colonies served as buffers between more important colonial territories and rival colonizers. For example, in the nineteenth century, Great Britain attempted to exert control over Afghanistan so as to protect the northern flank of its most important imperial holding, the Indian Subcontinent, from rival powers such as Russia.

Another key point is that colonization and the subsequent administration of colonial areas reflected a mix of practices in the home country and indigenous practices. Occasionally, indigenous resistance was sufficient to modify administrative practices. Rarely, indigenous resistance drove colonizers away, at least for a time, as with the Pueblo Revolt of 1680 in present-day New Mexico or the Zulu uprising in South Africa in 1879.

Examples and Consequences of Different Approaches

In the Americas, Australia, and New Zealand, the British primarily sought land for its agricultural potential and as a place to relocate unwanted or excess population. Religious dissenters were sent to the northeastern part of North America and convicts to Australia. Because of the rule of primogeniture—which dictated that the first-born son inherited any land and wealth—many second and later sons moved to the American colonies to seek their fortunes. This was most common for British nobility in southeastern North America and some Caribbean Islands. It also was a major motivation for colonization by the Spanish and Portuguese throughout the Americas.

Resources such as minerals, furs, and labor also drove colonization. Many Spanish explorers sought gold and silver. The French and, later, Russians in Alaska and along the northwestern coast of North America sought furs for export. In southeastern North America, deer fur was a major commodity. While beavers, otters, and other northern mammals and deer all supplied hides, they were used for different purposes. Most beaver, otter, and other northern mammals supplied the luxury trade, often substituting for declining fur-bearing animal populations in Europe and especially in Russia. Deer hides, on the other hand, were sought for industrial uses, made into pouches to hold tools, belts in newly developing machinery, and other commercial uses.

These two motives for colonization had very different consequences for the colonized regions. Where land for agricultural use and homes for surplus population were the primary goals, death or displacement of the indigenous populations was considered a success. Early writings by colonists in New England are replete with claims that the death of native populations was a sign from the creator that he intended the colonizers to possess the land. However, where indigenous peoples were sought as laborers, their death or displacement was viewed as a failure for the colonizers. This required them to find other labor sources and thus led to significant importation of indentured servants and/or slaves from Africa. When resources, either mineral or animal, were the primary motive for colonization, indigenous populations were a problem only to the degree that they impeded access to those resources. Indeed, the northern fur trade relied on indigenous peoples to gather and process pelts.

In cases where land was a primary object, treaties and other relations were viewed as a means for access to land. Even so, violations of treaties, the spread of settlements beyond treaty lines, and military expeditions also were considered proper means for acquiring and controlling land. There was little or no interest in indigenous peoples as human subjects.

When indigenous peoples served as middlemen, as in the northern fur trade, or were sought as agricultural workers, relations were more delicate, as the populations were seen as vital to the colonial enterprise. After Spain and the pope determined, at the insistence of Bartolomé de las Casas, that "Indios" were human with souls in need of spiritual salvation, conversion to Catholicism was another reason for maintaining relations with indigenous populations.

No area was shaped entirely by one colonial goal. Occasionally, northern indigenous peoples were employed—at least those that survived the many epidemics. Spanish colonists tried to make peasants out of Indios throughout the Americas—especially those that already lived in towns and practiced agriculture. Foraging groups typically were seen as obstacles to be displaced—although, again, epidemics depleted these populations. Thus, colonizers were forced to import labor from home or elsewhere. This led to a rise in indentured servitude and the migration of poor or oppressed people from the home country; tropical and semitropical regions saw massive importation of slaves from Africa.

In areas where indigenous peoples were used as agents, as in the northern American and Canadian fur trade, or where colonies served as outlets for the sons of nobles or for people of lower social status with little opportunity, immigration often was unbalanced in terms of gender, with more males arriving than females. This often led to sexual exploitation of indigenous women and, at times, cohabitation and marriage. This created a large mixed-race (mestizo or Creole) population.

While stories of women captured by native peoples abound, there are fewer accounts of those, male or female, who voluntarily joined indigenous groups. Sometimes, captured European women did not seek return, especially after they had children by indigenous fathers. Europeans often viewed such women as tainted and did not want to accept their children into European society; however, not infrequently, women from the lower classes were treated more humanely in indigenous societies than in their own society.

French fur traders provide an especially interesting example. Often, fur traders took wives from Native American communities—whenever possible, from the families of highly ranked or esteemed males. Such marriages were a common form of alliance building among many indigenous peoples, so they were not seen as exploitative. Because these marriages were arranged with a successful and powerful male—either a neighboring group or French fur traders—many indigenous women prized such unions.

Because French fur traders needed many contacts, they had native wives in a number of settlements. The practice of polygyny (having multiple wives at the same time) was seen as immoral in European society, but it was quite common for prominent indigenous men and viewed as legitimate. This practice was so common in northern French colonies that it gave rise to a distinct ethnic group, now officially recognized as such by the Canadian government as Métis. In general, however, children of mixed parentage suffered discrimination and opprobrium, more often from Europeans, but at times, too, from indigenous societies.

Indigenous Cultural Change

As a legacy of the Reconquista—the reconquest of Moorish Spain by Catholics—completed in 1492, Spanish colonists and administrators were obsessed with parentage and ancestry. They developed an elaborate classification system of ancestries and often maintained detailed information in baptismal and other records. Consequently, scholars have been able to study this process in the Spanish colonies more thoroughly than in any other colonial area.

While the Spanish colonies were assiduous in keeping track of children of mixed ancestry—and treating them differently—analogous practices occurred wherever the colonizing people and the local people were seen to be from different races. Indeed, such concerns were a significant motivation for the development of racial categories.

The fur trade gives some indication of the roles of markets and trade. Trade always involves some sort of exchange, sometimes under duress. French and other Europeans traded metal objects, pots, pans, cutting tools, and guns for furs. As trade evolved, both sides became shrewd at striking bargains. Europeans supplied goods that were intentionally inferior so that they would wear out and need to be replaced often. This was most extreme in the African slave trade, but it occurred everywhere, especially throughout the Americas. Native fur traders, in turn, bundled pelts in bales with high-quality hides on the outside and inferior hides hidden in the interior. Occasionally, they put rocks or other objects inside the bales to increase the weight.

Still, on balance, the fur trade was more advantageous for Europeans than for the indigenous people. The fur trade, especially the northern fur trade, supplied mostly luxuries, and so it was quite volatile. It also offered an outlet for surplus and inferior goods. Contrary to common assumption, however, metal goods were not attractive because they were inherently better. Rather, they were less fragile. A stone axe—typically sharper than a metal axe—that strikes a rock is ruined. A metal axe can be resharpened. Similarly, pots and baskets are often lightweight and quite serviceable but break easily.

Because most indigenous peoples did not have metalworking capabilities, they became dependent on the trade. Indeed, by the eighteenth century, one Cherokee chief lamented that young men not only could not make a bow and arrow, they did not know how to use them. Such dependence, often fostered intentionally, gave Europeans another tool to coerce indigenous compliance. Where indigenous peoples became heavily involved in trade, local economic and social practices were severely disrupted. If they became specialized in agricultural production of one kind, they became dependent on trade to acquire goods they had formerly produced themselves. In addition, European colonizers often imposed taxes that they required to be paid in cash, not in trade.

If specialization required social reorganization, as with the northern fur trade, living and marriage customs were disrupted. Men were absent for long periods, and extended families and clans broke into smaller nuclear families in order to acquire furs. Those that were more successful than others gained status and power. As the fur trade intensified, groups that had had occasional conflicts began to war for the rights to fur-gathering territories. Others capitalized on their position as middlemen between Europeans and the products of more remote hunting grounds, as was the case for the Iroquois.

Often, the social and cultural changes induced by trade were so strong that if the trade stopped, indigenous traders suffered immensely or had to resort to raiding to acquire needed goods. All of this tended to raise the level of violence, not only between Europeans and indigenous peoples, but also among the indigenous peoples.

This effect rippled well beyond the immediate frontier of contact, as did trade in various goods. Thus, the Lewis and Clark Expedition of the early 1800s encountered many groups that had never seen a European but nevertheless had acquired horses and mastered horse riding. For European intellectuals, the spread of violence often led to a false image of indigenous peoples as more violent than they had been before European contact.

In some cases, European contact and colonization had relatively mild consequences. This was most common when land was sought not for use, but for access to other areas. Besides exploration of newly acquired territory, Lewis and Clark also sought passage to the Pacific. One of many motivations behind the war between the Mexican-American

MICAELA BASTIDAS

On November 4, 1780, José Gabriel Condorcanqui—later known as Túpac Amaru—seized a corrupt Spanish official in Tinta, Peru, and oversaw his execution six days later. The act sparked a massive and widespread rebellion among the native people against Spanish colonial rule in the old Inca heartland around Cuzco and Lake Titicaca.

Túpac Amaru's wife of twenty years and the mother of his three sons, Micaela Bastidas, played a commanding role in the rebellion. Born around 1744, she came from a wealthy and privileged family in Andean rural society. Like her husband, Bastidas was of mixed ancestry.

For years, colonial officials and royal legislation had been chipping away at the position of the hereditary native chiefs, called *caciques*. Traditional Andean political arrangements emphasized the complementary roles of husbands and wives; the couple, not the individual, held community leadership. Túpac Amaru and Bastidas sat as the hereditary native authorities of Surimana, Tinta, and Tungasuca.

During the rebellion, Bastidas organized supply deliveries, marshaled political support and funding, actively recruited soldiers, dealt with prisoners, and issued military orders. She frequently criticized her husband's missteps and sought to stimulate him to more decisive action. Bastidas emphasized the necessity of laying siege to Cuzco before royal forces could reinforce the city.

"I gave you ample warning to march immediately on Cuzco, but you took it all lightly, giving the Spanish time to prepare," she told her husband. Túpac Amaru's failure to heed her advice led to defeat.

Expelled from the old Inca capital, the couple fell into Spanish hands in April 1781. Colonial authorities carried out an elaborate execution on May 18 of that year in Cuzco's central plaza. Before her own execution, Bastidas first witnessed the deaths of five others, including her brother Antonio and her oldest son Hipólito.

When it was her turn to ascend the scaffold, Bastidas stubbornly refused to allow the executioner to cut out her tongue. Royal authorities attempted to garrote her, but the apparatus was too large for her neck and only succeeded in causing her intense suffering. The executioner then strangled Bastidas with a rope and beat her to death as her husband and youngest son watched the horrifying scene. Túpac Amaru was the last to be put to death.

After the executions, the authorities cut out Bastidas's tongue and dismembered her body, burning her torso alongside her husband's and scattering their ashes into the air and the Huatanay River. Her head and limbs were put on display throughout the region—a lesson to other native people who might seek to challenge Spanish colonial rule.

Robert Smale

War of 1846–1848 was access to Pacific Coast harbors. The subsequent Gadsden Purchase (1853, in which the United States acquired the southern part of present-day Arizona) was made in an effort to acquire an all-weather route to the Pacific. Similarly, the British established administrative control over Egypt in the mid-nineteenth century in order to gain access to the Sinai Peninsula, which offered the best site for a canal connecting the Mediterranean and Red seas, thus providing a shorter route between Britain and its imperial possessions in India.

Another case of moderate colonization occurred when one European colonial power sought to protect central colonial areas from competing European powers. A notable example in North America was the maintenance of the Spanish colony of New Mexico, even after the Pueblo Revolt of 1680. Thus, Spain maintained the colony even though it was a net drain on the treasury. Mines farther south in Durango, however, were a major source of silver. Similar efforts occurred along the Spanish and Portuguese frontiers in South America, throughout the South Pacific and Southeast Asia among many European powers, and the nineteenth century "scramble for Africa."

Occasionally, this type of colonization offered some respite for indigenous peoples. If they did not hinder either access or the buffering process, their lives were not heavily disrupted. There were two major exceptions. The first was the spread of diseases along trade routes that often depopulated areas, even before the first European contact. This was more drastic in areas where people lived in dense settlements. Second, some groups found safety and protection by serving as an effective "border patrol" against intrusion by other Europeans.

The most spectacular example of the latter exception is the role of the Comanche people in protecting New Mexico. They also developed an extensive trading network among various groups, capitalizing on their peaceful relations with New Mexico after establishing peace in 1786. This collapsed as the United States expanded westward and the Comanche became a barrier to commerce between the United States and newly independent Mexico.

Ongoing Effects of Colonialism

One lesson from examining ancient instances of colonialism is that Europeans have not been the only colonizers. Since states first were developed in Mesopotamia some five millennia ago, states have colonized other areas and have displaced, destroyed, deformed, or absorbed indigenous peoples. European states achieved colonization on a global scale, often with more drastic consequences than non-European colonizers. Still, they have not been the only colonizers. Indeed, even in the Americas, groups such as the Aztec and the Inca colonized the surrounding people.

Throughout history, colonization has been a complex set of processes that varied through time and space. Each specific instance was shaped by the various motives for colonization, the various groups and classes doing the colonizing, the variety and types of societies encountered, and, most important, their very intense interactions. While there are common patterns, all such generalizations have many exceptions.

Finally, the effects of colonization are ongoing. Which religions are common among indigenous peoples is a legacy of which religious groups were able to conduct proselytization. Similarly, which languages are spoken in addition to indigenous languages, or in some cases have replaced them, is a legacy of which country maintained the colony. Often, too, the forms of relations between indigenous people and the state, and of contemporary indigenous political organizations, have roots in the colonial process.

Thomas D. Hall and James V. Fenelon

See also: *Countries*—Peru; United States. *Issues*—Assimilation; Land Rights; Religion (Indigenous); Revolts.

Further Reading

Carter, William B. *Indian Alliances and the Spanish in the Southwest, 750–1750.* Norman: University of Oklahoma Press, 2009.

Champagne, Duane. *Social Change and Cultural Continuity Among Native Nations.* Lanham, MD: AltaMira, 2007.

Cronon, William. *Changes in the Land: Indians, Colonists, and the Ecology of New England.* New York: Hill and Wang, 1983.

Farris, Nancy M. *Maya Society Under Colonial Rule: The Collective Enterprise of Survival.* Princeton, NJ: Princeton University Press, 1984.

Ferguson, R. Brian, and Neil L. Whitehead, eds. *War in the Tribal Zone: Expanding States and Indigenous Warfare.* Santa Fe, NM: School of American Research Press, 1992.

Greaves, Alan M. *The Land of Ionia: Society and Economy in the Archaic Period.* New York: Wiley-Blackwell, 2010.

Hämäläinen, Pekka. *The Comanche Empire.* New Haven, CT: Yale University Press, 2008.

Hennessy, Alistair. *The Frontier in Latin American History.* Albuquerque: University of New Mexico Press, 1978.

Jaimes, M. Annette, ed. *The State of Native America: Genocide, Colonization, and Resistance.* Boston: South End, 1992.

Lang, James. *Conquest and Commerce: Spain and England in the Americas.* New York: Academic Press, 1975.

———. *Portuguese Brazil: The King's Plantation.* New York: Academic Press, 1979.

Mörner, Magnus. *Race Mixture in the History of Latin America.* New York: Little, Brown, 1967.

Weber, David J. *The Spanish Frontier in North America.* New Haven, CT: Yale University Press, 1992.

Economic Development

Defining economic development in the context of indigenous peoples is problematic. The dilemma is how to define economic development, determine what makes it successful, and how this plays into the role of native peoples worldwide.

Perhaps the most easily understood aspect of economic development is the overwhelming concern over Africa. Famous economists such as Jeffery D. Sachs, newspaper columnists such as Nicholas Kristof, and even musicians such as U2's Bono all have become involved in promoting the economic development of Africa. Unfortunately for both Africa and other regions with smaller populations of indigenous peoples, such a broad focus on an entire continent leaves many groups and countries off the radar of an increasingly development-minded world. The People's Republic of China is a perfect example: China has achieved a stunning rate of economic development, and yet the country still has a staggering poverty rate among its ethnic minorities, a fact that often is ignored because of the speed of the nation's economic development.

Prior to World War II, the single word *development* was used, and then only in reference to large-scale economies, not generally to smaller groups. But as economic development has taken place amid a postwar concentration on self-determination for peoples around the world, related theories have been predicated on the idea of convergence: There is one economic mode or system that is more efficient than the rest, and all of the world's economic systems gradually are moving toward it. Both the communist understanding of the course of history and capitalist democratic ideas of political development are based on the notion that all peoples are striving toward the same goal, which the most powerful nation in that model exemplifies. Thus we have competing visions of what that convergence means—is it a free market system, a state-controlled system, or a nationalized economy? Regardless of the native group or the development ideology, economic development must fit into this larger geopolitical context—the worldwide mission of capitalism or communism.

At times, however, economic development also is part of something more altruistic, such as an attempt at eradicating human immunodeficiency virus/acquired immune deficiency syndrome (HIV/AIDS), relieving hunger, or improving poor water supplies. However, as economic development still is grounded in this large-scale, politically defined idea, it often fails to truly help a localized group of people.

Indigenous Economic Development

Economic development can be based simply on extractive economic forms (such as mining or production for export), or it may be focused on internal sustainability. Each method depends on the group of people that is trying to enforce, impose, or present it to the local group. This determines, in large part, the extent to which a development plan will be effective—again depending on which group is defining success.

The definition of success in economic development among indigenous groups, like the term itself, is hard to pin down. It seems that nearly every group that offers ideas about how to "do" development work, especially in a localized context, has its own definition of success. (Though people often will agree on what failure is, success generally takes more time to figure out.)

Despite the lack of agreement, there are several things that have become standard when encountering economic development ideas among native groups and examining what success looks like. Important elements may include the development of cottage industry (the production of local goods for sale to a potentially larger market), infrastructure projects (roads, wells, schools), education initiatives (village schools, mobile schools, scholarship programs), and health projects. These things sometimes occur separately, but, more often, several elements are joined together in an effort to present a holistic solution to the problems that a given community faces.

A Brief History of Economic Development

The development of what modern historians call "economic development programs" began with colonial exploration and expansion following the arrival of Europeans in the New World. A generalized view of Spanish interaction with the Aztec, Maya, and Inca cultures shows that the burgeoning Spanish Empire sought the material wealth that local peoples could provide—already-developed mineral and metal resources (gold, silver, jewels) and, later, labor in mines and on farms.

The same pattern would be followed by the French and English to different degrees. The efforts of the French in North America are typified by their engagement of tribes to aid in fur trapping and trading enterprises. The British colonies worked to establish what would become, especially after the introduction of slavery, large commercial plantations producing such crops as tobacco and cotton as well as other sources of lucrative exports.

As the great empires of Europe moved south and east, their understanding of economic development continued to emphasize a large-scale, state-focused, exporting economy. Many, but not all, of the colonies established in Africa between 1890 and 1920 focused on growing, mining, or making products to send back to London and Paris. Rubber plantations, silver mines, and livestock development programs all were instituted to this end. In East and Southeast Asia, the major world powers (Britain, Portugal, and, in time, Germany and the United States) created development programs centered on the silk trade; the growing and selling of tea, opium, and other spices; and, in the case of French-run Vietnam, rubber plantations. Such development projects generally worked to serve the interests of the master, but rarely the servant.

It was not until after World War II and the American Marshall Plan for Europe—often argued to be the first major development program in contemporary history—that the modern idea of economic development began to be implemented. The basic premises of the Marshall Plan, large-scale development and reconstruction schemes, had a lasting impact on the economic development community. However, when this system is applied to smaller, localized native groups, it is too big, too broad, and too unresponsive to do much good.

Also established during this early postwar era were the International Monetary Fund and the World Bank—financial entities that, by and large, dictate the pace and style of large-scale economic development to the present day. While this may seem far afield from economic development among native peoples, these institutions created, maintained, and continue to shape how development theory and economics are conceptualized at the macro level.

In the aftermath of World War II and the Marshall Plan and at the beginning of the Cold War, the United States became one of the driving forces of economic development in what has been called the third world, or the developing world. The other driving force, of course, was the Soviet Union. These nations' competing systems of economic thought—communism and capitalism—would carve up the world and, by and large, dictate how regions would encounter, interpret, engage, and respond to development as the last vestiges of the colonial order fell by the wayside.

JOSÉ CARLOS MARIÁTEGUI

José Carlos Mariátegui (1894–1930) was a Peruvian Marxist activist who was renowned for his defense of indigenous rights. In his essay "The Problem of the Indian" (1928), he made the materialist claim that socioeconomic changes would be necessary to end indigenous poverty and marginalization. Rather than looking to administrative or cultural changes, Mariátegui argued for a fundamental restructuring of the country's land tenure system.

In a subsequent essay on the problem of race that was presented to a meeting of South American communist parties in 1929, Mariátegui directly rejected a proposal from the Communist International organization to create an independent indigenous republic for the Quechua and Aymara people in the Andes. A separate nation, he argued, would ensure their impoverishment and do nothing to address the fundamental class contradictions in society.

Born on June 14, 1894, in Moquegua, Peru, Mariátegui experienced health and economic problems throughout his entire life. His father abandoned the family when Mariátegui was a boy, and he badly injured his leg in 1902. At the age of fifteen, he began working at a newspaper. He subsequently used his journalism skills to earn a living and as a vehicle for expressing his political views.

In 1919, Peruvian dictator Augusto B. Leguía exiled Mariátegui to Europe. There, Mariátegui developed and matured as a Marxist thinker, and when he returned to Peru in 1923, he was a "convinced and declared Marxist." Drawing on the experiences and insights that he had gained in Europe, he gave a series of lectures on the "History of the World Crisis" at the newly formed González Prada Popular University in Lima.

In 1924, Mariátegui lost his right leg; he spent the rest of his life confined to a wheelchair. In spite of his failing health, he increased the intensity of his efforts to organize a social revolution in Peru. In 1926, he founded *Amauta* (meaning "wise teacher" in Quechua), a journal that was intended to be a vanguard voice for an intellectual and spiritual movement to create a new Peru. In 1928, Mariátegui launched a less doctrinaire and more informative biweekly newspaper called *Labor* that was targeted at the working class. In addition to writing articles for various Peruvian periodicals, he also published two books during his lifetime, *The Contemporary Scene* in 1925 and *Seven Interpretive Essays on Peruvian Reality* in 1928.

Mariátegui's revolutionary activities were not only theoretical but also practical. He founded the Peruvian Socialist Party in 1928, served as its first secretary general, and brought it into alliance with Communist International. In 1929, the party launched the General Confederation of Peruvian Workers, a Marxist-oriented federation of trade unions. Although his political party and labor confederation flourished, Mariátegui's health failed. He died on April 16, 1930.

Marc Becker

What this broad picture of history shows us is that until the 1980s, development work among small groups of native people—such as the Karamojong in Uganda—still was based firmly on large-scale understandings of economic structure and used only the terms associated with large economies, such as the United States or Russia. This philosophy led to the implementation of commercial livestock and farming programs that not only destroyed the ability of native groups to maintain a minimum standard of living, but also wreaked immense ecological harm, pushing natives peoples farther into a cycle of economic deprivation.

This cycle, attributable to many poor decisions made by the colonial powers, has continued, largely unabated, until today. One ray of hope for projects currently being instituted is the growing emphasis on working with the elders of the community, with the youth, and with both men and women to determine what a community *actually* needs, how those resources should be obtained, and where the money and labor for the project should come from.

China's Role in Development

Since the Cold Ward dawned and China began to distance itself from the Soviet Union, it has maintained an intermittent relationship with countries throughout Africa. In recent years, China has begun to invest heavily in Africa to develop mineral and petroleum resources. While this has occurred largely on a national scale, it has had a large impact on native groups in several regions—most notably in the Sudan.

While many of the issues concerning China's involvement in Africa are still the subject of speculation, it is safe to say that China's method of developing Africa's resources is modeled after what it has done at home—efforts that have left its own smaller ethnic groups without access to the income generated in areas with high mining or farming activity. This issue is not simply centered on China; the United States, Great Britain, and other larger, more developed nations have enacted similar projects to gain access to the mineral resources of Africa. This process often leaves out, or forcibly removes, the native peoples that occupy the lands where the minerals are located, often causing civil war between ethnic groups.

It is easy to see that China is poised to redefine the concept of aid in developing nations. By helping African nations develop basic infrastructure—namely, roads—the Chinese have made it easier for them to succeed in their investments. China is providing the pivotal links needed to foster long-term development in places such as the Sudan or Zambia.

The question is how much this will affect, positively or negatively, smaller groups, such as Turkana herders in northern Kenya. Often large networks of roads cut through prime grazing grounds or damage sections of farmland, leaving native groups in a worse situation. In fact, this can force such groups to move farther away from access to resources needed not only to "develop," but also to survive in a rapidly changing world.

A Few Issues in Development

Issues such as gender, lack of historical context, politics, aid societies, and a so-called dependency mentality play a role in economic development.

Gender

The impact of economic development on gender roles in indigenous societies is an issue that is beginning to be examined by scholars and activists. Development can be used to restructure traditional or nontraditional gender roles in a community. Often, when Western development workers or local government forces impose projects on a subsistence agriculture or nomadic group, they inadvertently may shift the balance of power between men and women, causing a conflict in traditional cultural boundaries and understandings within the local community.

In some places, it must be acknowledged that the traditional stratification of roles is not helpful for a group to actively or efficiently take part in any sort of economic development. When development workers confront this—say, a nomadic community in Mongolia in which the women do the primary day-to-day labor and the men labor with the herds only part of the year—they tend to argue for an immediate and complete restructuring of gender-based labor. While on the surface, this may appear positive, providing more equal workloads or better access to education, it often forces native groups into a vacuum of gender-based power. Suddenly, one group is more advantaged than tradition dictates, and another group is bereft of the full measure of cultural power that they have been accustomed to having and using.

Lack of Historical Context

One significant problem, experienced particularly in African communities, is the lack of historical context for development projects. Particularly among groups that have become highly politicized, such as the Maasai of Kenya, Uganda, and Tanzania, there is a legacy of development work by the local government and international aid groups (large or small) trying the same strategies that have yielded little success in the past, often without consulting the village or community population and leadership. The result is a feeling of despondency and disenfranchisement within the local group—thus limiting their desire and ability to actively engage with the current and future development projects.

Politics and Aid Groups

Another factor in trying to foster some sort of economic development among native groups is the government and political system in which they live. When working with Tibetan nomadic herders in central China, for example, development workers—whether they are nationals or expatriates—often are confronted with the overarching demands and concerns of the Chinese central government. The same is true with other native populations worldwide. No matter the government, it will become involved in the style, pace, end goals, and measures of success involved in development, often dictating a timetable that has nothing to do with the realities of development work.

Unfortunately, international aid groups often are beset by the same political problems, coupled with the need to project sometimes false images of a region and peoples in order to raise funds. Where the national government may not need to answer to anyone for the manner in which it is attempting development work, a large aid group—such as Doctors Without Borders or the World Health Organization—must deal with the needs of the government while also trying to appease its myriad funding groups and individuals. In doing this, development groups inadvertently can become part of the very problem that they are trying to solve. Marketing a group of people as consistently "economically underdeveloped" can run the risk of pigeonholing and thus limiting the opportunities of those people.

Dependency Mentality

The "dependency mentality" is perhaps the greatest enemy of both native communities and development workers. A dependency mentality is fostered when a community, region, country, or even continent is helped in a way that does not encourage its ability to participate in development planning and actions. Money, buildings, and resources generally are provided to a place for a series of years without any conditions—for example, that the community must invest in the school that was built (provide teachers) or show accountability for how a massive grant was used to deal with erosion and poor soil.

As this process progresses, the people of the community begin to feel, often subconsciously, that they are entitled to this beneficence because of their hard lifestyle, or that they are so poor, uneducated, and ill equipped that if an outside force does not come in and do it all, they will be unable to move forward with the development process. Development workers often act in ways that, at best, foster such ideas and, at worst, permanently instill these ideas.

Two Examples

The Maasai in Tanzania and the Kham Tibetans in China provide two examples of communities that have faced challenges with regard to economic development projects.

Maasai in Tanzania

A major problem with development projects enacted by the state (or colonial power) is that they tend to ignore or misunderstand the complicated historical, cultural, and ethnic setting in which they are working. This dynamic can be seen in the experience of the Maasai in Tanzania. The policies enacted by the British colonial government not only inadvertently restructured how the Maasai viewed their herding practices (which had been refined over centuries), but also drastically impacted gender-based delineations of power within the community. As this upheaval occurred, the Maasai increasingly were marginalized economically and politically.

As development concerns shifted from ecological (how to manage farmlands and livestock) to economic (development of business interests and large ranching cooperatives), a shift in perceptions of the Maasai from "rugged pastoralist" to "uneconomic loafer with large herds" created a new definition of rangeland mismanagement and overstocking. This concept was reinforced as the Maasai were pushed onto reserves (similar to American Indian reservations), their ability to develop economically was curtailed, and their identity as a people increasingly was linked to what rapidly was becoming an outmoded method of livestock management.

After independence, the Maasai largely were left out of the nation-building process in Tanzania. For the newly emancipated elite, the Maasai groups became icons of an image of savagery and primitiveness that the nation was working to leave behind. When they were referenced in the media, they were represented by their ethnic identity: "Maasai men" or "Maasai women." Thus, the Maasai were commodified by the state to show how far development had come, but that the new state valued "traditional" or "primitive" ethnic cultures.

Since the advent of tourism as a major income generator for Africa, the Maasai have come back into the public eye—but not for economic modernization. Instead, coinciding with the rise in sustainable development and ecological awareness, the focus of development among indigenous groups—especially nomads—has been to maintain traditional methods of subsistence. The Maasai now use these constructed images of cultural authenticity to draw a link between the protection of lands and access to development schemes.

However, like nomadic groups throughout Africa and the world, the Maasai have become disenfranchised from many opportunities in the emerging nation. This is attributable, in part, to the image of the Maasai as a group that is resistant to change—the government and international aid and development organizations instead fund other groups that are more "suited" to progressive ideology.

Kham Tibetans in China

The plight of western China has received much attention from Chinese scholars and even a few Western economists. Unfortunately for the peoples and areas being subjected to economic policy from the East, there is little understanding of localized ethnic groups, cultural needs and concerns, and long-term effects on the ecological setting of the region, especially for nomadic groups on the Qinghai-Tibetan Plateau. This is a problem that is not exclusive to China, but is a symptom of all governments dealing with smaller, more mobile groups.

The nomadic groups inhabiting the Qinghai-Tibetan Plateau region have been marginalized as economic fortunes in China have risen. As this marginalization has occurred, the more "modernized" eastern China concerns have come in to help develop regions. They bring with them a fundamentally differing viewpoint, one introduced to nomadic and subsistence agriculture communities that often objectifies the environment as a tool to be exploited until it is of no further use.

Compounding these problems is the glaring absence of historical perspectives in the development initiatives from Beijing. As a result of official rewriting of history throughout much of the prereform era, a distorted understanding of how Tibetans historically lived in and on the fragile grasslands prevails in the Chinese academy. What has been lost is a detailed understanding of how traditional Tibetan lifeways on the plateau offer solutions to many of the current development issues, as indicated by the fact that the native people have successfully survived in the region for at least two millennia.

Recent Trends

While there are indeed many problems when examining economic development and its impact on native

people groups, it is safe to say that the last five years have brought a redirection in how development workers, theorists, and governments think about their work. The rise in popularity of microloan initiatives, starting in India and moving throughout the world, has had a dramatic impact on the preservation of native peoples' ethnic and cultural understandings of themselves while affording a new source of income that men and women can have access to, granting a greater chance for savings and education for their children.

There also has been a greater emphasis on understanding the historical context in which a group lives—what development programs have attempted in the past, whether those efforts worked and why, and so forth. This will help native communities in many ways—as development workers take the time to understand the groups they are working with, they are able to better engage the community in ways that the people can understand and appreciate. Development projects that include significant "buy-in" by a community have a greater rate of success and are more likely to have a longer and more successful shelf life.

Such issues are beginning to be realized by aid groups and government departments. Especially since the 1980s and the emergence of the First Peoples Congress and their efforts to join the conversation concerning ecological/environmental preservation, the rapid emergence of grassroots development groups can be seen. Such groups, noticeably appearing in Asia (China, India, and Thailand, to name a few places), are engaging their governments and international groups regarding issues of historical context as well as pragmatically effecting policies that take into account the local culture and languages and the environmental constraints they work within. This has allowed community-led microloan institutions to take root; for instance, helping village women produce local products for a wider consumption, benefiting them, their families, and their communities.

Jared Phillips

See also: *Countries*—China. *Issues*—Industrial Development; International Policy; Political Participation; Self-Determination; Women's Rights.

Further Reading

Cullather, Nick. "Development? It's History" *Diplomatic History* 24:4 (Fall 2000): 641–653.

Dowie, Mark. *Conservation Refugees: The Hundred-Year Conflict Between Global Conservation and Native Peoples.* Cambridge, MA: MIT Press, 2009.

Easterly, William. *The White Man's Burden: Why the West's Efforts to Aid the Rest Have Done So Much Ill and So Little Good.* New York: Penguin, 2006.

Ekbladh, David. *The Great American Mission: Modernization and the Construction of an American World Order.* Princeton, NJ: Princeton University Press, 2010.

Hodgson, Dorothy L. *Once Intrepid Warriors: Gender, Ethnicity, and the Cultural Politics of Maasai Development.* Bloomington: Indiana University Press, 2001.

Hopkins, A.G., ed. *Globalization in World History.* New York: W.W. Norton, 2002.

Moyo, Dambisa. *Dead Aid: Why Aid Is Not Working and How There Is a Better Way for Africa.* New York: Farrar, Straus and Giroux, 2009.

Sachs, Jeffrey D. *The End of Poverty: Economic Possibilities for Our Time.* New York: Penguin, 2005.

Scott, James C. *Seeing Like a State: How Certain Schemes to Improve the Human Condition Have Failed.* New Haven, CT: Yale University Press, 1998.

Ecosystem Management

The purpose of ecosystem management is to ensure the sustainability of the environment—not the sustainability of the products that a particular part of the environment produces. The evolution of environmental policy over the nineteenth and twentieth centuries and the results of those policies convinced many people that it was necessary to construct a new paradigm to guarantee ecological preservation for the foreseeable future. The current concept of ecosystem management emerged in the late twentieth century as a result of changing societal values, growing scientific knowledge, and professional experience in developed nations, particularly the United States, and it has spread to other regions of the world since the 1990s. Ultimately, ecosystem management is necessary for survival in a world that is dependent on the Earth's limited resources.

Briefly defined, looking at the world as ecosystems is to views regions of the world as cohesive systems of interrelated factors—waterways, weather systems, flora, fauna, people, and so on, all existing in a close relationship to one another. A change to any one of these factors invariably has an impact on all of the others. Looking at the lifeways, cultures, and religions of the native peoples of the world, one can easily deduce that this view of the interrelatedness and holistic nature of the world is closely aligned with many of their philosophies.

Although historians and anthropologists have shown that indigenous peoples have implemented changes to their environment throughout their history, most, if not all, native religions and cultural perspectives reflect a different view of environmental resources than that of dominant Western cultures. Whereas Western cultures generally have viewed environmental resources as commodities to be exploited, native religions have tended to emphasize the spiritual dimension of what most non-natives consider secular resources. Land, water, and wildlife are viewed in a more holistic way that emphasizes their interdependence and understands the need for their preservation.

As a philosophy and a practice, ecosystem management regulates the use of the world's ecosystems by accounting for all of the components of that ecosystem, and then looking for a balanced way to proceed with human habitation. It necessarily takes into account the views of all of the constituencies—human and other—that inhabit or make use of that ecosystem. In terms of the lives and lifeways of native peoples, it is a more "enlightened" approach, seeking cooperation between peoples in order to make a positive way forward via consensus rather than control.

During the late twentieth and early twenty-first centuries, proponents of ecosystem management made many claims about the possibilities of cooperative management and ecological preservation. Ecosystem management proposes that policies should be shaped by local needs, balancing the interests of many different constituencies; however, questions remain about how feasible such a power-sharing scheme can be in practice. In the case of the Western United States, the actions of federal agencies charged with development and protection of the region have had huge ramifications for its ecosystems. At the same time, the native American Indian peoples of the region have consistently sought to share power and management with the dominant society.

However, as in other nations of the world, the history of relations between the native peoples and non-native Americans over the use and management of natural resources has been very one-sided. Until the 1930s, and to varying degrees since then, the U.S. government has imposed its policies on Indian tribes. Scholars, historians, and environmental activists have asked, given the history of resource exploitation and misuse by Americans and the imposition of federal policies on Indian tribes, how can ecosystem management be made to work? And how does this model reflect similar challenges regarding ecosystem management for indigenous peoples in other parts of the world?

Stewardship Across Boundaries

There are four themes in ecosystem management: Its goals are socially defined, it advocates a holistic science, it requires adaptable institutions, and it involves collaborative decision making. Management of the environment by government often becomes necessary when the consequences of people's actions reach a scale that requires collective rather than individual action. The father of the modern-day idea of wilderness management, Aldo Leopold, stated that those who oppose government regulation often are guilty of bad stewardship; however, effective ecosystem management often depends on decentralized decision making and adaptive management. This means that management of an ecosystem should cut across ecological, governmental, and ownership boundaries.

Success also requires large-scale management, which means managing areas that are under separate sovereignties. This creates a number of paradoxes that must be solved before ecosystem management can be effectively implemented. Also, there is a paradox involved in management for both use and preservation. Because ecosystem management values both goals and theoretically involves decision making by groups that may not agree on the best balance between these goals, conflict is likely.

As it affects native peoples, ecosystem management is problematic because of its inherent need for a lack of complete sovereignty. Decision making has to be shared in order to be effective. Ecosystem management seeks to involve federal agencies, environmental interest groups, commodity interest groups, and those who live on the land in the decision-making process, but this may require considerable social and political change, such as the dismantling of old systems and even agencies. Many of the questions raised by ecosystem management cannot be answered by science alone but also may involve a mix of applicable philosophies and ethics.

Ecosystem Management Challenges Around the World

Resource agencies in the United States, such as the Bureau of Reclamation, Forest Service, National Park Service, and Army Corps of Engineers, traditionally have limited public input by restricting the outcomes about which the public is informed. Ecosystem management requires communities to become more educated about their localities.

Many current U.S. environmental policies—what environmental historian Charles Wilkinson has termed the "lords of yesterday"—are too production oriented and need to be done away with in order for ecosystem management to be implemented. Essentially, these laws allow for the private use of public lands by people and corporations, with little regard for the impact of those activities on the ecosystems concerned. Examples of this are the Hardrock Mining Law of 1872, which allows for private persons and corporations to mine on public land, essentially royalty-free; the Taylor Grazing Act of 1934, which allows free and minimally regulated grazing of livestock on public lands; and the doctrine of "prior appropriation," allowing water developers to tap into any Western stream without charge and to extract as much water as desired. By giving private citizens and corporations unmitigated and free or low-cost access to resources on public lands with limited responsibility for the environmental effects of utilizing or extracting such resources, ecosystems are damaged. At the same time, other stakeholders in those ecosystems have little or no voice in the matter.

As with most federal programs, the U.S. government has imposed environmental policy on Indian tribes with little room for tribal autonomy. Federal courts have held that both Indian and non-Indian projects on reservations must meet the standards of the National Environmental Protection Act. The fact that so much of federal policy is mandated has created innumerable gaps in trust between the tribes and the government.

Native Americans have responded to these impositions by creating their own interest groups, such as the Council of Energy Resource Tribes, which have sought to present a united native voice. However, such groups do not fit with ecosystem management's emphasis on locally directed efforts.

Tribes have fought for sovereignty for many years. Ecosystem management's emphasis on shared decision making may cause some tribal members to question whether its implementation would mean a diminution of that sovereignty. In addition, some ideas that are central to effective ecosystem management may not fit well within native cultures. It requires accommodation by all parties concerned to come to a workable agreement that places preservation above all other goals.

Ecosystem management has not just been seen as a solution in the United States, however. Native peoples around the world are parts of their ecosystems and generally demonstrate an interest in being involved in the management of their environment when given the chance. In addition, over the centuries, many native people have developed a specialized knowledge of their ecosystems, and they usually can add invaluable insights on how it can best be managed for the benefit of all.

For example, the Hausa and Fulani peoples of northern Nigeria have contributed greatly to the management of the Hadejia-Nguru Wetlands Project since the 1990s. They have implemented their native knowledge in order to reap the benefits of increased water supplies and improved farm yields. Once it was made clear how their activities were improving the ecosystem for all of its human and nonhuman inhabitants, the local communities' commitment to a coordinated program of activities substantially increased, even though the benefits would take at least five to eight years to start taking effect.

728 Issues

In Mexico's Yucatán Peninsula, the Maya peoples of the area around Sian Ka'an hunted and foraged for centuries. During the 1980s, an ecosystem management plan was developed that established a biosphere reserve. This plan recognized the Maya's traditional rights and included them as stakeholders and decision makers regarding the land use and resource management across the region. The collaboration resulted in a dramatic increase in income for the native people, as they took control of foresting in the region rather than leasing it out to timber companies. Deforestation and the expansion of cattle ranching (which results in deforestation) have stopped and a sustainable ecosystem model that capitalizes on the Mayas' knowledge of the animals and plants of the region has taken its place.

A Way Forward for Native Peoples

These solutions to the problems inherent to ecosystem management may sound simple, but they are incredibly complex in implementation. First, the goals of ecosystem management can take a long time to achieve.

Second, ecosystem management's emphasis on local supervision and priorities should overcome the mistrust that native peoples often feel toward federally implemented programs. Of course, rational decision making does not always occur, so that mistrust may be more difficult to overcome than proponents of ecosystem management are willing to admit.

Finally, ecosystem management subordinates the desires of different stakeholders—whether they be government, industry, non-native settlement, or native peoples—in order to work toward a long-term goal. Once again, natives' resistance to give up a measure of their sovereignty, which they have fought so hard and long to restore, in order to accomplish the larger goal may prove difficult to overcome.

Ultimately, however, it must be recognized that ecosystem management's priorities are much closer to most traditional views and lifeways of indigenous peoples than former policies. And in this statement lies the most appealing way to approach the conflict with the sovereignty of native peoples. It may be a difficult case to argue in some cases, but the fact that most indigenous worldviews incorporate the sanctity and holistic nature of the natural world should make it easier to convince native peoples of the wisdom of ecosystem management than it will be to convince many other communities, commercial interests, and government bureaucracies.

Steven L. Danver

See also: *Groups: Central and South America*—Maya. *Issues*—Agriculture; Industrial Development; Self-Determination; Water Rights.

Further Reading

Cortner, Hannah, and Margaret A. Moote. *The Politics of Ecosystem Management.* Washington, DC: Island Books, 1999.

Ianni, Elena. *Ecosystem Management: A Path to Sustainable and Healthy Communities.* Saarbrücken, Germany: Lambert Academic Publishing, 2012.

Meffe, Gary K., Larry A. Nielsen, Richard L. Knight, and Dennis A. Schenborn. *Ecosystem Management: Adaptive, Community-Based Conservation.* Washington, DC: Island, 2002.

Pirot, Jean-Yves, Peter-John Meynell, and Danny Elder, eds. *Ecosystem Management: Lessons from around the World: A Guide for Development and Conservation Practitioners.* Gland, Switzerland: International Union for Conservation of Nature and Natural Resources, 2000.

Wilkinson, Charles E. *Crossing the Next Meridian: Land, Water, and the Future of the West.* Washington, DC: Island, 1993.

Education

In the broadest terms, *indigenous education* refers to the education system that originates from within a society. A narrower, more commonly used definition of indigenous education is a people's original (native) education system as opposed to the formal education system imposed by their conquerors or the dominant society.

The conqueror society may or may not be present in the latter context. For example, the indigenous education system in Native American and Aboriginal ethnonational societies runs parallel to the dominant education system within their respective nation-states. In these instances, the conqueror society—North America, Australia, and New Zealand, respectively—is also the majority and thus controls the education system.

Such a dual education system also can be found in nation-states where the peoples of conquest were former or present American, Chinese, or European colonies or territories. For example, in African ethnonational, Indian ethnonational, and Tibetan societies, the colonizers, in most cases, never constituted a majority population within the geographic location of these ethnonational societies. Instead, they imposed their societal institutions, including education, on the indigenous people as a mechanism of colonial control and development.

In such cases, the indigenous education system persisted alongside the formal education system to varying degrees; however, the conqueror society's education system eventually became dominant. Although in many colonies or territories, independence provided some opportunity for integrating indigenous knowledge into the dominant education system, there was no overthrow or dismantling of the dominant system.

好 好 学 习　天 天 向 上

Throughout modern history, government and colonial authorities have used education to assimilate indigenous peoples and dilute their cultures. Here, Tibetan students at a Chinese summer school perform a song under the Chinese flag. *(China Photos/ Getty Images)*

Indigenous and Dominant Dual Education System

Aspects of indigenous education are apparent in age-grade training, apprenticeships, gendered practices and skills, and indigenous (ethnonational) government, religion, and education institutions. The indigenous education system may take several forms. For people of conquest in North and South America, New Zealand, and Australia, it often is embedded in the ethnonational community's political, religious, and social institutions. This is especially true for peoples that continue to occupy sovereign (reservation) land.

In other cases, aspects of indigenous education, such as history, language, and religion, may vie for inclusion in primary and secondary institutions (including so-called native schools and colleges on and off ethnonational sovereign land). Indigenous knowledge may be included in the dominant education system as part of "Native American" or "Aboriginal" studies curricula.

Stand-alone courses on Native American or Aboriginal history or language also may be included in the dominant education system. In such cases, whether as an interdisciplinary study or as a set of independent courses, indigenous knowledge generally is modified to fit the structure (presentation, methods, and priority level) of the dominant education system.

The indigenous education system also may continue to operate on the margin of the dominant system. Such configurations of dual indigenous and dominant education systems may exist in places where the conqueror society is dominant but not the majority.

For people of conquest in former colonies such as Angola, Côte d'Ivoire, Ghana, and India, the indigenous education system continues to function alongside the education system imposed by the former colonizers. In these instances, the conqueror society is no longer dominant and does not constitute the majority population, but the dominant education system was imposed and spread to the extent that it became an integral part of the new nation-state at the time of independence. Such dominant education systems are identified as postcolonial or neocolonial institutions; in this context, indigenous education may survive to varying degrees.

Assimilation Impact

The survival of indigenous education depends on the extent to which the former conqueror or colonizer mandated the assimilation of ethnonational societies. Where participation in the dominant educational system is considered a requirement for inclusion in society, the indigenous system is likely to be marginalized or even eliminated entirely.

For example, in Côte d'Ivoire, ethnonationals under French assimilation policy in the early twentieth century could gain representation and citizenship rights only through participation in the French formal education system, among other requirements, resulting in their separation, both physically and intellectually, from indigenous institutions, including education. In areas that were more directly under French rule, this gradual assimilation through French education resulted in the loss of indigenous education systems, as well as indigenous knowledge and other aspects of native culture.

Similarly, China maintains an assimilation policy that results in significant loss of indigenous knowledge.

For example, in Tibet, a Chinese territory, participation in the dominant education system is compulsory, and indigenous education systems are discouraged by the government. In more rural areas, indigenous education systems were marginalized but not entirely destroyed.

Impact of Indirect Rule

In contrast to assimilation policies, Great Britain followed a comparatively milder policy of indirect rule in its former colonies and territories. In 1933, Lord Lugard described indirect rule and the role of education in it: "This policy of preserving the old social system until a better one has come into being to replace it has been called 'Indirect Rule.' . . . With the spread of education they will learn the systems adopted by Europe and America and, if suitable, they can adopt them."

This policy initially was applied by Great Britain to the Northern Protectorate of Nigeria (formerly Hausaland) and gradually was implemented throughout most British colonies and territories. In Nigeria, Ghana, India, and other areas, European missionary schools and British academic and vocational schools were established beginning in the nineteenth century; however, there was no requirement that ethnonationals attend them.

In these areas, the British did not constitute a majority or a significant population. Britain also differed from France in that ethnonationals could not become full citizens of Britain, but only subjects of the Commonwealth. Nevertheless, British schools tended to dominate because of their preparatory role in accessing economic opportunities. As Britain controlled production, trade, and political representation, learning English and the skills required to participate in the colonial system motivated many ethnonationals to attend British colonial schools. By the time of independence, the British education system had become dominant.

A significant difference between assimilation and indirect rule was that the indigenous education system was better maintained under indirect rule. In India, indigenous institutions continued to exist, and upon independence, efforts were made to integrate the dominant and indigenous education systems. In fact, despite attempts by the British to close down some indigenous education systems, such as indigenous medical training in India, most indigenous education systems remained largely intact.

Despite this difference between assimilation and indirect rule, in both cases, the indigenous education systems were reduced in status, both politically and

Dolores Cacuango

Dolores Cacuango was a native Ecuadorian leader who helped organize the first indigenous federations and schools in that country. She was targeted by the military because of her activism, prompting her to go into hiding; however, her expulsion from her home community helped spread her radical influence and foster new types of leadership.

Cacuango was born in 1881 on the Pesillo hacienda in the northern canton of Cayambe. As part of the payment of her parents' debt to the hacienda, the owner sent her at age fifteen to the capital city of Quito to work in his home as a domestic servant. The contrast that she observed between the lifestyles of the privileged landholding class and the impoverished natives was eye-opening and led her to commit her life to the liberation of her people.

Although Cacuango never attended school, she fought tirelessly to ensure that others would have that opportunity. Under her guidance, the first indigenous schools were established in Cayambe. Her son, Luis Catucuamba, taught at one of the schools from 1945 until it was shut down by a military coup in 1963.

Cacuango never learned to read or write, but she memorized portions of Ecuador's 1938 Labor Code in order to fight for the rights of agricultural workers. Cacuango secretly entered haciendas at night to meet with indigenous laborers, working to organize a movement and train new leaders. This work brought her into close contact with urban communist militants, in particularly Nela Martínez and Luisa María Gómez de la Torre. They helped Cacuango in her organizing and educational endeavors in rural communities, and in exchange, Cacuango joined them on the Central Committee of the Communist Party of Ecuador. These friendships built strong alliances between militant rural indigenous movements and the urban left.

In 1943, in the midst of World War II, Cacuango formed the first rural antifascist committee. She served as a delegate to a national antifascist conference, where she was singled out as a model for her countrymen. During a revolution in May 1944, she led an assault on the army base at Cayambe. She subsequently organized the Ecuadorian Federation of Indians and served in a leadership capacity in the organization for several decades.

When Cacuango died in 1971, people came from as far away as Guayaquil on the southern coast of Ecuador to commemorate the passing of a national treasure. Today, her image commonly is used as a symbol by indigenous movements, and an indigenous women's training school bears her name.

Marc Becker

economically, as compared to the dominant education systems. Again, the end result was a continued threat to indigenous knowledge as more and more ethnonationals participated in the dominant education system.

Dismantling

The most invasive threat to indigenous education systems occurs when the conquering society not only establishes its education system as the dominant one but also systematically attempts to dismantle all forms of indigenous education. Two examples, China and South Africa, demonstrate the systematic dismantling of indigenous education systems.

The Chinese have established Chinese schools in Tibet, which the Chinese government is working to make compulsory. Currently, Tibetans continue to teach the Tibetan language and history, but this process is in flux. If the Chinese are successful in their efforts, the Chinese education system will become dominant, and Tibetan education may or may not continue.

In South Africa, Europeans—first the Dutch and then the British—conquered and populated the region. By the time modern South Africa was established in the early 1960s, the majority of indigenous ethnonationals had been displaced, and rigid controls on all aspects of life, including education, had been imposed. This resulted in significant loss of indigenous knowledge and the dismantling of many ethnonational education systems.

Some ethnonational groups in the region have maintained their indigenous education systems. Significantly, those systems that remain intact are in areas that are physically separated from South Africa as "independent" satellite states, such as Lesotho and Swaziland.

Decolonization

In the majority of the cases discussed here, the peoples of conquest have maintained, to various degrees, their indigenous education systems. But assimilation through the dominant education system continues to threaten indigenous education. The push to assimilate raises questions about what constitutes a healthy exchange of knowledge and change among societies and what impact globalization has on indigenous education.

Recommendations for protecting indigenous systems, including education, forms of tribal government, and religion, emphasize a decolonization model that aims to preserve indigenous political and cultural nations and viewpoints. The adoption of a decolonization or similar model may allow ethnonationals, especially in postindependence societies, to reclaim and integrate indigenous knowledge and education structures and practices into the dominant education system. In this manner, native peoples can ensure that such aspects of their cultures are effectively retained.

Jamaine Abidogun

See also: Countries—Nigeria; United States. *Issues*—Assimilation; Colonialism; Indigenous Identity; Missionary Activities.

Further Reading

Abdi, Ali, and Ailie Cleghorn, eds. *Issues in African Education: Sociological Perspectives.* New York: Palgrave Macmillan, 2005.

Abidogun, Jamaine. "Education Transformations and Traditional Medicine in Nsukka, Nigeria." In *Environment and Economics in Nigeria,* ed. Toyin Falola and Adam Paddock New York: Routledge, 2011.

Champagne, Duane. "In Search of Theory and Method in American Indian Studies." *American Indian Quarterly* 31:3 (Summer 2007): 353–372.

Fischer-Tine, Harald, and Michael Mann. *Colonialism as Civilizing Mission: Cultural Ideology in British India.* London: Anthem, 2004.

Lugard, Lord. "Colonial Administration." *Economica* 41 (August 1933): 248–263.

Minde, Henry, ed. *Indigenous Peoples: Self-Determination, Knowledge, Indigeneity.* Delft, Netherlands: Eburon Delft, 2008.

Rathbone, Jessica M. "Weaving Threads of a Common Identity: Non-Formal, Intergenerational Education and the Community Museum of Ollantaytambo, Peru." *Journal of Intergenerational Relationships* 4:4 (2006): 93–97.

Genocide

Genocide commonly is defined as the killing of a group of people. The Nazis' killing of 6 million Jewish people during World War II is the most frequently cited example of genocide.

In his 1944 book *Axis Rule in Occupied Europe,* Polish scholar and attorney Raphaël Lemkin, who coined the term *genocide,* offered a broader definition that included any coordinated plan of action aimed at destroying the lives of national groups combined with efforts to kill the people themselves. This might include the destruction of political and social institutions such as language, culture, national solidarity, economic livelihoods, and religion. Destroying personal security, eliminating liberty, endangering health, and disregarding dignity are part and parcel of the exercise of genocide, which destroys an oppressed group in the name of imposing the oppressor's national pattern. This definition can be interpreted as including ethnocide, the killing of a culture, through forced assimilation or ethnic cleansing.

At the Nuremberg trials of German war criminals following World War II, genocide was described as the deliberate and systematic destruction, in whole or in part, of an ethnic, racial, religious, or national group. In 1948, the United Nations Convention on the Prevention and Punishment of the Crime of Genocide provided a more limited definition than Lemkin's, describing genocide as "any of the following acts committed with intent to destroy, in whole or in part, a national, ethnical, racial or religious group, as such: killing members of the group; causing serious bodily harm to members of the group; deliberately inflicting on the group conditions of life, calculated to bring about its physical destruction in whole or in part." No mention was made of cultural genocide.

Genocide did not begin with the Germans during World War II. Examples can be found throughout history, in the Old Testament of the Bible, the Greek destruction of Troy, the Roman annihilation of Carthage, the military campaigns of Attila the Hun and Tamerlane, and the African slave trade of the seventeenth through the nineteenth centuries.

Modern technology, including gas chambers, machine guns, and bombs, has intensified the process of genocide. During the twentieth century, examples of genocide include the Turkish killing of Armenians during World War I, the killing of Tutsis in Rwanda in 1994, and the Srebrenica Massacre in Bosnia in 1995, when thousands of Bosniaks (Bosnian Muslims) were killed. Alexander Hinton, in his study of genocide, estimated that 100 million people had been killed in the modern era and that genocide is the result of modern social conditions. It is associated with socioeconomic upheaval such that it becomes easy to blame minorities for a country's problems, including rising unemployment and crime rates.

Genocide is fueled by a genocentric and ethnocentric mythology of a "master race," a "chosen people," or "manifest destiny," as well as by greed and hunger for land, often caused by population pressures in places where too many people are living on too little land to feed themselves. Lebensraum, or "living space," was part of Adolf Hitler's plan to colonize Eastern Europe with Germans, an idea fueled by racist thinking that originated in the nineteenth century and earlier.

Theodore Roosevelt articulated this thinking in his 1889 book The Winning of the West, writing, "The settler and pioneer have at bottom had justice on their side; this great continent could not have been kept as a game preserve for squalid savages." Central to genocide is such dehumanization of the targeted groups, who are portrayed as obstacles to progress. Often, comparatively powerless indigenous peoples across the globe are the targets of genocide.

In the nineteenth century, readers of Charles Darwin's landmark Origin of the Species, including many European and American scientists, distorted his findings about biology to argue that societies were evolving from savagery to civilization in a process termed "social Darwinism," whereby advanced societies would replace less civilized ones as part of a process of natural selection. Today, we know from genetic testing that the variation within races is greater than the variation between races and that skin color and differences in facial features that once were touted as badges of superiority or inferiority are the result of minor genetic differences. Still, racism and genocidal behavior persist.

Cultural genocide is much more widespread and ongoing than the simple murder of ethnic minorities. It often is associated with colonialism and with the subjugation of people of color in the Americas, Africa, Australia, and Asia, though examples also can be found in Europe, among the Sami in Scandinavia, the Basques in Spain, and the Roma in Eastern Europe, all of whom have been the victims of genocidal activity. Examples of genocide, often perpetrated against indigenous populations, can be found worldwide, including the killing of Maya Quiché in Guatemala; Zapatistas in Mexico; Kurds in Iran, Iraq, and Turkey; Igbo and Ogoni in Nigeria; Aché in Peru; Herero in southwestern Africa; Tasmanians in Australia; Tutsi in Rwanda; Timorese in Indonesia; Kulaks in the Soviet Union; Naga in India; and Chechens in Russia. Other examples include the Japanese occupation of Korea before and during World War II, when Korean language, culture, and history were suppressed, and the Chinese repression of Tibetan and Uighur people today.

From the late nineteenth into the early twentieth century, many indigenous people forcibly were removed to boarding schools in Australia, Canada, and the United States, where they were forced to speak only English and taught to live as Christians. These schools were instruments of cultural genocide. However, if indigenous people refused to assimilate or found that their skin color excluded them from real citizenship, this could become a justification for killing or further marginalizing them.

Some people believe that democracies are immune to genocide, but through the "tyranny of the majority," laws may be passed to suppress minority languages and cultures. Lemkin, in his discussion of genocide, included prohibitions against of the use of languages by the oppressed populations in German-occupied countries. Again, this kind of cultural suppression has a long history in many different settings. Thomas Babington Macaulay's famous Minute on Indian Education (1835) demonstrated the British goal of eliminating India's indigenous languages as obstacles to the literary and scientific education of the people. Similarly, the 1868 report of the U.S. Indian Peace Commission argued that boarding schools were to become places where American Indian languages would be eliminated and replaced with English. Besides suppressing indigenous languages, colonial governments also suppressed religious practices, including potlatches, sun dances, and other indigenous ceremonies in Canada and the United States.

Many United Nations declarations support basic human rights and oppose cultural genocide. The 1948 Universal Declaration of Human Rights states in Article 26 that parents have a fundamental right to choose the type of education that will serve their children best. In the United States, the passage of laws such as the Indian Self-Determination and Education Assistance Act (1975), Indian Religious Freedom and Indian Child Welfare Acts (1978), and Native American Languages Act (1990) built on the earlier United Nations human rights efforts.

Most recently, the United Nations Declaration of the Rights of Indigenous Peoples, adopted in 2007 by the United Nations, reasserted and extended these rights. This declaration, along with recent apologies to the indigenous peoples by the prime ministers of Australia and Canada, are signs of hope that all forms of genocide against the indigenous peoples of the world soon will end.

Jon Reyhner

See also: *Groups: Africa*—Tutsi. *Groups: Europe*—Armenians; Jews, European. *Countries*—Rwanda. *Issues*—Indigenous Peoples and the United Nations.

Further Reading

Hinton, Alexander Laban, ed. *Annihilating Difference: The Anthropology of Genocide.* Berkley. University of California Press, 2002.

Kiernan, Ben. *Blood and Soil: A World History of Genocide and Extermination from Sparta to Darfur.* New Haven, CT: Yale University Press, 2007.

Lemkin, Raphaël. *Axis Rule in Occupied Europe.* Washington, DC: Carnegie Endowment for International Peace, 1944.

Nersessian, David. "Rethinking Cultural Genocide Under International Law." *Human Rights Dialogue: "Cultural Rights."* 2:12 (Spring 2005).

Roosevelt, Theodore. *The Winning of the West.* Vol. 1. 1889. Lincoln: University of Nebraska Press, 1995.

Globalization

The topic of globalization—a term often used to describe the increasing speed of communication, trade, and other interactions of the late twentieth and early twenty-first centuries—is exceedingly complex with regard to indigenous populations. Globalization encompasses economic, political, and cultural facets that interact to a large degree but at times can be somewhat autonomous.

While globalization often puts intense pressure on indigenous peoples to become "modern," that is, to be like everyone else, it also has brought means to sustain their identities. The Internet provides indigenous peoples with a vehicle to discuss and express their traditions, and many have adapted modern institutions, such as higher education, to enhance and preserve their cultures through classes on culture, religion, history, and language.

Economic globalization refers to patterns of production, exchange, and consumption that take place on a transnational scale. For instance, today, a car or a computer is assembled from parts manufactured in many parts of the world. Political globalization is, in essence, the expansion of the idea that no place in the world operates in a political vacuum; rather its politics are interrelated with those of many other places.

Cultural globalization is the most subjective form of globalization. Aspects include a focus on global entrepreneurship, the expansion of Western knowledge (often to the exclusion of other forms of knowledge), and the spread of Western popular culture, as well as resistance to it. Reactions to cultural globalization include the replacement of local cultures; the coexistence of global and local cultures; the synthesis of global and local cultures, a process dubbed "glocalization"; and the rejection of global culture by local cultures.

What is new in contemporary globalization processes? This question, of course, cannot be addressed without examining older globalization processes. Answering this question is especially germane for native peoples, who have been displaced or conquered by states for thousands of years and have suffered consequences ranging from the loss of land to the loss of lives and cultures.

Still, many native peoples and their cultures have survived. Today, there are more than 300 million indigenous people organized in several thousand groups. In many areas, such as the United States, they are one of the most rapidly growing populations. This statistic indicates that some indigenous peoples have succeeded in resisting or adapting to globalization pressures more effectively than other groups.

The Globalization of "Indigenous"

The concept of globalization hinges on the idea of defining who is indigenous. The United Nations Commission on Human Rights defined indigenous people in its

Study of the Problem of Discrimination Against Indigenous Populations (1981–1983): "Indigenous communities, peoples and nations are those which, having a historical continuity with pre-invasion and pre-colonial societies that developed on their territories, consider themselves distinct from other sectors of the societies now prevailing in those territories, or parts of them."

Moreover, indigenous people seek to preserve their identity in terms that are congruent with their own cultural and institutional practices. Continuity may include such things as staying in the same place, tracing clear descent from original occupiers, and continuity in culture, religion, values, and sometimes language.

The globalization of indigenous peoples has ramifications in terms of the economic, political, and cultural power wielded by native peoples. For example, the election of Bolivian activist Evo Morales to the presidency of that country in 2005 signaled a new level of indigenous political power. Similarly, the Zapatista guerilla movement in Chiapas, Mexico, which has carried on an indigenous revolution against the Mexican government since 1994, has become a model for indigenous peoples throughout the world.

On September 13, 2007, the United Nations General Assembly voted to adopt the Declaration on the Rights of Indigenous Peoples, which defines the individual and collective rights of indigenous peoples worldwide and outlines their rights to culture, identity, language, employment, health, and education. But the globalization of nonindigenous economic, political, and cultural systems can have negative effects on indigenous peoples as well. Pressure to assimilate into a global culture can be as intense as pressure to assimilate on a national scale.

Forms of Resistance

Many forms of indigenous resistance to globalization are covert. For instance, events in Chiapas led by the Zapatistas are sometimes viewed as a regional or peasant movement rather than a resistance to globalization. The Zapatistas are seen as an indigenous Maya rebellion against the effects of the globalization of trade, as represented by the North American Free Trade Agreement, which helped spark the revolt in 1994. However, even though the Zapatista movement, like all movements of native resistance to globalization, takes localized forms and focuses on local issues impacted by globalization, it has become a model for native movements around the world.

In the United States, the American Indian Movement (AIM), a Native American activist organization that focuses on leadership and sovereignty for native peoples, is seen as a localized ethnic, urban, or racial rebellion.

However, indigenous resisters such as members of AIM connect through international nongovernmental organizations, the United Nations, a large variety of their own organizations, and the Internet. Thus, persistent traditional cultures and social organizations are resources for resistance and survival in a broader context.

These diverse movements, with their varied organizations, goals, and methods, almost defy summary. Among their commonalities, the most significant for indigenous movements are emphases on the right to maintain traditional practices, on local community, on identity politics, and on land claims. Traditional indigenous practices may include extended kinship systems, maintenance of matrilineal descent (decent through the female line), polygyny (a marriage system in which a man may legitimately have more than one wife simultaneously), communal ownership of resources (land, minerals, water), the sacred nature of some lands, nonhierarchical decision making, and indigenous knowledge, such as the use of plants for medicine. Many of these practices contradict, challenge, or threaten deeply held values in Western and other state-based systems.

The most fundamental challenge to global capitalism, however, is communal ownership of resources, because it rejects the legal emphasis on private property. Contrary to what many early explorers and missionaries thought, indigenous people did not fail to comprehend individual ownership. Rather, they maintained a belief that many environmental movements are beginning to support today—that most resources are public goods that should not be owned privately. Still, interactions between environmentalists and indigenous peoples have been somewhat mixed, though alliances are becoming more common. The point of communal ownership is that the entire community decides which resources may be used and how. In making such decisions, the benefits to the group as a whole are seen as more important than an individual's gain or loss.

Many native peoples overtly and consciously maintain that "traditional culture" is not unchanging, but rather that it changes in accord with group decisions and not as suggested or directed by outsiders. Therefore, culture building—such as efforts to maintain or revive indigenous languages and to found local schools up to the college level (tribal colleges in the United States)—is another form of resistance.

Building local institutions that conform to traditional cultural values often can be a form of resistance. The Navajo have done this in several ways. The Navajo police force, which functions like many other rural police forces in the United States, is especially sensitive to Navajo cultural traditions. The tribe's "peacemaker courts" avoid the adversarial techniques of U.S. courts by pursuing the resolution of disputes among tribe members, especially in family matters, through means that accord with native concepts of harmony. These courts have been so successful that other indigenous groups, and even some nonindigenous communities, are adopting and adapting analogous legal processes attuned to their own values. For example, local justice among Zapatistas uses a *junta del buen gobierno* (committee for good governance), which follows indigenous values and principles in reaching decisions.

Other important forms of resistance are less institutionalized. For instance, the Northern Cheyenne have adapted to their culture the conventional twelve-step programs that address alcohol abuse or spouse abuse, promoting Cheyenne family values. Chief Dull Knife College, located on the tribe's reservation in southeastern Montana, has developed culturally sensitive ways of teaching science and mathematics. These programs have been very successful.

The maintenance of matrilineal family systems, especially through the ownership of property, contradicts most European notions of jurisprudence. Missionaries and bureaucratic functionaries repeatedly have attacked matrilineality as barbaric, unchristian, or chaotic. In response, Native American feminists organize in ways that differ from mainstream feminists, sometimes eschewing politics in order to focus on issues of cultural preservation and identity, which are less visible on the global stage but no less important.

The maintenance of religious practices asserts very different approaches to the supernatural and the sacred. Claims to lands that are considered sacred and necessary for religious ceremonies challenge not only traditional world religions but also concepts of private property.

In addition, indigenous peoples typically resent those who have adopted indigenous practices such as shamanism in a piecemeal manner, as this violates the integrity of traditional belief systems. Many native scholars argue that such intrusions into "traditional culture" are an arena of conflict. They point to instances in which holistic indigenous knowledge is being exploited by Western markets for commercial purposes, such as indigenous Amazonian peoples' understanding of natural medicinal products of the rain forest.

Sometimes older traditions, such as the Sun Dance, become another form of religious resistance. Modern Maori leaders of New Zealand have evoked the Pai Marire and Ringatu syncretic religious movements of the late nineteenth century as a means to highlight contemporary resistance to modern Western culture.

Movements such as the Longhouse religion of the Iroquois, the Ghost Dance, or the Native American Church, all of which are syncretic to some degree, preserve traditional values even while adapting to and adopting some aspects of world religions. Such movements often have been successful in the context of an increasingly globalized world. For example, the Native American Church (also known as the peyote religion) is the single most successful institution for combating alcoholism among Native Americans; it has won court battles to permit members to use peyote as part of its practices.

One of the most important forms of resistance is the collective management of resources for the collective good. Such forms of collective rationality are not solely the conventional "public goods" analyzed by economists. Rather, management is a matter of stewardship and of sustaining resources for future generations. In such cases, indigenous peoples are not managing nature, but consider themselves as part of nature.

A startling instance of this is seen in the continuing efforts of the Lakota Sioux people to regain control of the Black Hills. Several court decisions, most notably the U.S. Supreme Court's ruling in *United States v. Sioux Nation of Indians* (1980), have determined that the territory of the Black Hills was taken illegally from the Lakota. Yet according to jurisprudence in the United States, any settlement of this claim should be monetary. The Lakota have refused such a commodified settlement. Rather, they insist on the return of their sacred land. In the 1980 and 1990 U.S. censuses, Shannon County, South Dakota, the location of the Lakota's Pine Ridge Reservation, was the poorest county in the entire country. Thus, the Lakota's continued resistance to a cash settlement underscores the strength of their beliefs.

Underlying these examples is the issue of sovereignty in the United States and autonomy in other countries. Treaty agreements give indigenous peoples in the United States a special relationship with the federal government. Sovereignty and autonomy focus directly on the concept of national sovereignty, which is embodied in the Peace of Westphalia, a series of peace treaties made in 1648. To reject indigenous sovereignty undermines the very concept of national sovereignty. In this, indigenous peoples share a consequence of globalization, although the latter has not been legal as much as economic and practical.

In contesting European law on its own turf—that is, in the courtroom—indigenous peoples have had to accept some of its premises. The courts have been a major arena for commodification, especially land. That is why the Lakota's rejection of the Black Hills settlement is so important: It counters that thrust. Indigenous peoples have used the legal system to resist globalization processes and forces.

However, there is an important difference between indigenous struggles in the first world or global north (rich or developed countries) and those in the third world or global south (poor, developing, or underdeveloped countries). The rule of law carries much more force in the global north, so it is often a useful tool there. While this is generally the case, there are exceptions in both directions.

Many such issues are important because they deal with places and ideas of national symbolic significance. In Australia, several national parks, such as Uluru-Kata Tjuta (the home of one of Australia's national symbols, what settlers called Ayers Rock) and Kakadu, contain sites that are not only sacred to the Aboriginal peoples of the country, but also are used for sacred rituals. In North America, the movement against the use of Native American images as mascots by sports teams, such as the National Football League's Washington Redskins, is another example. On a more positive side, the powwow circuit is a means of asserting Indian identity in a positive way, using indigenous dances and ceremonies to present American Indian cultures to a general audience.

Challenges to globalizing capitalism have been helped by international nongovernmental organizations such as Cultural Survival, the International Work Group on Indigenous Affairs, the Center for World Indigenous Studies, the United Nations Working Group on Indigenous Populations, and many indigenous organizations. There are great variations in the approaches of these organizations, the kinds of resistance that they support, and their degree of participation in political spheres, but by and large, they resist the globalization of culture through economic means by emphasizing and protecting local traditions.

This list of examples of indigenous resistances to globalization, whether overt or implicit, is long, but it is only a small sample. These movements are more than opposition to the states within which they are embedded. They also are claims by indigenous peoples to a continued right to exist as separate entities as well as the right to preserve their own cultures as they see fit. They are claims to autonomy both from the state and from the many processes of globalization. Thus, these highly localized movements also are part of a worldwide antiglobalization process. Similar movements are occurring in other parts of the world and, in some cases, have been for far longer.

Resistance Outside the Americas

In Japan, beginning in the mid-nineteenth century, the indigenous Ainu and Okinawans resisted their domination by the Japanese, Russians, and, later, Americans. During the late 1980s and early 1990s, the Sami people of Norway secured cultural rights related to language and reindeer husbandry and negotiated the establishment of the Sameting, a Sami body appointed by the Norwegian government to ensure that the country fulfilled its national and international obligations to the Sami. In the first decade of the twenty-first century, Australian Aborigines secured an official apology from the government of Australia for the seizure of their lands and the forced schooling of their children in boarding schools that taught Australian values during the nineteenth and early twentieth centuries. In New Zealand, the Maori hold special treaty rights that include the right to their cultural traditions and official representation in the national government. In China, Uighurs continue to agitate for the right to practice their traditional culture.

One of the most striking such instances involves the so-called Adevasi people, who are labeled a "Scheduled Tribe" under the constitution of India. *Adevasi* is a term much like *American Indian,* in that it is a name imposed by outsiders. Like most American Indians, the Adevasi have their own names and organizations. Two of the best known are the Gond and Warli peoples in the Indian state of Maharashtra. Collectively, the Adevasi constitute about 9 percent of the population of India. A key point is that the Gond and Warli (and others) have struggled against change forced by outside states and have struggled to retain control of their traditions and lands. These struggles have continued for millennia.

The Adevasi and the Maori form interesting and insightful contrasts with indigenous peoples in the Americas. The Adevasi people are some of the clearest cases of resistance to state encroachment from long before European states began to expand. In the case of the Maori, it is well known that they were the first settlers of New Zealand, called Aotearoa in their own language. These two cases show that the struggles between native peoples and states are not solely a result of Western democracies and capitalism or of socialism. Rather, the key struggle is between states and nonstate peoples. Thus, the struggle against contemporary globalization is, especially for the Adevasi and people like them, an age-old struggle for survival in the face of attempts at state dominance.

Globally, native peoples' struggles for continued survival take many forms. They mostly fall into three categories of struggle: over sovereignty, autonomy, and minority status. Indigenous survival and resistance to globalization is shaped by local, regional, national, and globalization forces. These levels all interact in any one situation. To ignore any one level will distort understanding of indigenous survival and resistance. All simple accounts of indigenous survival and resistance are thus fundamentally flawed. This is why studying indigenous persistence is both fascinating and very complex.

Sometimes indigenous movements are seen as a subcategory of social movements. This is not entirely accurate. Given the age of some forms of indigenous resistance, as with the Gond or Warli, indigenous movements are more fundamental. Furthermore, they often represent a more direct challenge to globalization, which seems to be moving toward a "one-size-fits-all" position.

Indigenous persistence, in and of itself, is a claim that there are other ways for human beings to organize their collective lives. This challenges any claim by any group that "they" have the one true way to organize a state, the one true religion, or the only civilized values and traditions. Indigenous peoples forcefully remind us there are many forms of social organization, many religions, many values, and many traditions.

This diversity is itself a great resource for human beings as we face an ever-changing future. Some of these other values, traditions, and practices may be of broad use to human survival. Given environmental issues of vital concern at the beginning of the twenty-first century it is worth remembering that many indigenous peoples have been remarkably resilient. They have succeeded in living in a sustained way on the same land for millennia, adopting and adjusting to "foreign" practices while maintaining their own values.

Thomas D. Hall and James V. Fenelon

See also: Issues—Economic Development; Indigenous Identity; Indigenous Peoples and the United Nations; Social Customs; United Nations Declaration.

Further Reading

Burger, Peter L., and Samuel P. Huntington, eds. *Many Globalizations: Cultural Diversity in the Contemporary World*. New York: Oxford University Press, 2003.

Champagne, Duane, Karen Torjesen, and Susan Steiner, eds. *Indigenous People and the Modern State*. Walnut Creek, CA: AltaMira, 2005.

Gedicks, Al. *Resource Rebels: Native Challenges to Mining and Oil Corporations*. Cambridge, MA: South End, 2001.

Hall, Thomas D., and James V. Fenelon. *Indigenous Peoples and Globalization: Resistance and Revitalization*. Boulder, CO: Paradigm, 2009.

Nagel, Joane. *American Indian Ethnic Renewal: Red Power and the Resurgence of Identity and Culture*. New York: Oxford University Press, 2009.

Smith, Claire, Heather Burke, and Graeme K. Ward, eds. *Indigenous Cultures in an Interconnected World*. St. Leonards, Australia: Allen & Unwin, 2000.

Wilmer, Franke. *The Indigenous Voice in World Politics*. Newbury Park, CA: Sage, 1993.

Hunting and Fishing Rights

For native peoples around the world, hunting and fishing are important survival, economic, cultural, social, and spiritual activities. Hunting and fishing are an essential part of native peoples' subsistence economies or may supplement farming and modern forms of food procurement, often as important nutritional resources. Native peoples may harvest fish and wildlife and sell the meat, fur, or other products, providing families with an important source of income. Fish and wildlife also form part of native peoples' identities and cultural traditions, helping to reinforce community belonging and solidarity.

Native hunting and fishing practices and technologies are not static. Rather, many native peoples have added new technologies to their cultural practices in order to harvest fish and wildlife more efficiently. At the same time, they seek to retain and exercise hunting and fishing rights on reserves and outside their communities in their traditional territories. These rights, though vital to many native communities, have been challenged by non-native governments, anti-native rights organizations, competing commercial interests, and other factions.

Colonialism, Settlement, Treaties, and Reserved Rights

As native peoples around the world came into contact with colonizing nations, particularly Europeans, over the last 500 years, they faced cultural domination and competition for their traditional lands and resources. As a result of colonization, native peoples were displaced and denied access to fish and wildlife as non-native settlements expanded and as economic development (such as farming, mining, and forestry) modified, replaced, or degraded natural habitats for fish and wildlife. Such changes significantly affected the indigenous peoples' ability to maintain their hunting- and fishing-based economies and cultures.

In the case of European colonizers, the uses of natural resources and the environment by native peoples were viewed as improper and wasteful. They viewed native hunter-gatherer subsistence societies as primitive in need of civilizing. The natives' traditional lands and natural resources, it was argued, could be better used for farming, mining, forestry, or other forms of civilized modern development. In order to assimilate into "civilized" society, native peoples would have to give up hunting and fishing and adopt agriculture and industrial arts.

In regions colonized by the British—for instance, in North America and New Zealand—treaties were the legal instrument that provided for the orderly, legal colonization and occupation of native lands. Treaty negotiations resulted in the sale or cession of native lands to the British Crown and, later, North American governments. In many cases, native peoples retained only a small portion of their homelands as reserves or reservations, where it was assumed that they would have a right to hunt and fish. Native peoples also reserved the right to hunt and fish on unoccupied or unsettled areas on the ceded lands and waters.

While customary rights to hunt and fish—based on cultural customs, historical tradition, and former native occupation of the land—were not afforded formal legal recognition or protection, treaties included reserved hunting and fishing rights that were legally defined and distinguished. Native leaders assumed that the lands and their resources would be shared and that hunting and fishing could continue as long as those activities did not interfere with non-native settlement. For example, treaties negotiated between the U.S. government and Native American tribes in the Pacific Northwest between 1854 and 1856 contained a clause retaining or reserving fishing rights:

> The rights of taking fish, at all usual and accustomed grounds and stations, is further secured to said Indians in common with all citizens of the Territory . . . together with the privilege of hunting, gathering roots and berries, and pasturing their horses on open and unclaimed lands.

Treaty-reserved hunting and fishing rights were not grants of rights to native peoples; rather, they were rights that were retained or reserved by native peoples when their lands or other political rights were ceded. Native negotiators viewed retaining these rights as essential to the future economic and cultural well-being of their peoples. For non-natives, however, such treaty-based hunting and fishing rights were viewed as temporary arrangements. Settlement, development, and assimilation, they believed, would make such arrangements unnecessary and unneeded at some point in the future.

By the late nineteenth century, non-native commercialization of fisheries, state conservation laws, the development of nature-based tourism, and the creation of national parks limited native peoples' ability to exercise their treaty-reserved hunting and fishing rights. Government fishing and hunting regulations were applied to native peoples, requiring the purchase of licenses and permits, restricting them from accessing traditional harvesting territories, limiting harvest seasons and the amount of harvest, and defining appropriate harvesting methods. At the same time, commercial fishers, sports fishermen, and sports hunters sought to monopolize fish and wildlife resources, and government regulations served their interests.

National parks, such as Glacier National Park in Montana, were carved out of native harvesting territories. Park managers sought to provide visitors with a wilderness experience and required natural landscapes that exhibited no human use or habitation. As a result, native occupation and hunting and fishing were prohibited in parks, even when such rights formerly were reserved by treaty. As the idea of national parks and protected areas spread from North America to other continents, including Africa and Asia, this concept impacted native hunting and fishing rights around the world.

Indigenous Resistance and Legal Activism: Reclaiming and Exercising Hunting and Fishing Rights

Native hunting- and fishing-based cultures persisted in spite of efforts to assimilate native peoples, government conservation regulations, competition from commercial enterprises, and other efforts to eliminate native hunting and fishing rights. Native peoples consistently claimed that they had not relinquished their rights. Many continued to exercise these rights, despite arrests, fines, and confiscation of their hunting and fishing equipment. During the second half of the twentieth century, native peoples in a number of nations used a combination of political activism, protest, and legal claims to achieve legal recognition of their treaty-reserved hunting and fishing rights.

In the United States, Native American tribes in the Pacific Northwest and western Great Lakes won federal court cases recognizing their rights to hunt and fish on ceded lands and waters outside their reservations. The courts examined evidence of native understandings of the treaties and the history of settlement to find, in many cases, that native hunting and fishing rights never had been extinguished by treaty or other government regulation. Defined as use or usufructuary rights, native hunting and fishing treaty rights were not restricted to the lands owned or occupied by native peoples. Such rights could be exercised on public lands and waters, and native hunters and fishermen could use both traditional and modern harvesting technologies.

Ultimately, the courts found that the tribes were entitled to a modest living and, in many cases, at least 50 percent of the harvest of fish or wild animals, which could be used for subsistence or commercial sale. The courts also ruled that if tribes created their own rules and regulations, then state government regulations did not apply to native hunters and fishermen. Thus, in the Pacific Northwest, Native American tribes formed an intertribal conservation organization called the Columbia River Inter-Tribal Fish Commission to regulate their commercial harvest of salmon and to represent tribes in the management, protection, and restoration of Columbia River fisheries.

The Ojibwa tribes of Wisconsin established the Great Lakes Indian Fish and Wildlife Commission to regulate their off-reservation hunting and fishing rights in northern Wisconsin. The Ojibwa harvest a wide variety of fish and animal species using a combination of traditional and modern practices and technologies. Most of the harvest is used by families to supplement foods bought in conventional markets. Since 1989, the Ojibwa annually have caught an average of 26,247 walleye from inland lakes in northern Wisconsin. Some Ojibwa living along the shores of Lake Superior also fish commercially for whitefish and lake trout. In addition, the Ojibwa hunt white-tailed deer, black bears, wildfowl, and other wildlife species. For example, in 2009, the Ojibwa killed 1,650 white-tailed deer and 39 black bears in the ceded territories.

Similar cases of hunting and fishing rights have been considered in Canadian courts. For example, in 1999, the Supreme Court of Canada ruled, in what is known as the Marshall Decision, that the Micmac (Mi'kmaq) and Malecite communities of New Brunswick retained a treaty right to hunt and fish in order to earn a moderate livelihood. Thus members of these communities were entitled to participate in the region's lucrative commercial lobster and snow crab fisheries free from most state regulations.

In New Zealand, the native Maori claimed that they did not relinquish their subsistence or commercial fishing rights in 1840 when they signed the Treaty of Waitangi, which gave the British Crown sovereignty over what is now New Zealand. The Maori successfully argued their commercial fishing rights claim before the Treaty of Waitangi Tribunal, which was created in 1975 to review Maori claims. As a result of the tribunal's findings in favor of the Maori, the New Zealand government and the Maori negotiated a settlement of the Maori's commercial fishing rights claims. Under the 1992 Treaty of Waitangi Fisheries Settlement, the government purchased a 50 percent share of Sea Lord Products, New Zealand's largest fishing company, on behalf of the Maori. As a result of the Sea Lord deal and more recent negotiations, the Maori now hold 27 percent of the New Zealand offshore fishing quota and have input into how the fisheries are managed.

In the Faroe Islands of the North Atlantic, the right of the Faroese to fish was a large part of the reason that they have remained outside of the European Union. In addition, the harvesting of pilot whales is both a cultural activity and provides approximately one-third of the meat consumed produced by this group. The Faroese seek to avoid what has happened to many other native groups, when their fishing rights were subsumed to the interest of national or international bodies; for instance, in Guam, the results of the imposition of governmental environmental protection on native Chamorro fishing rights can be seen.

In the late 1990s, indigenous fishing grounds also were lost by the establishment of marine preserve areas. The loss of these and other fishing grounds has negatively impacted the native peoples' ability to pass on aspects of their culture to the younger generation, and many fear that those traditions are close to being lost.

Backlash: Opposition to Native Hunting and Fishing Rights

One response to the court rulings and native exercise of hunting and fishing rights has been the rise of local and national groups that are opposed to such rights and to native political and cultural autonomy. In North America, Groups such as All Citizens Equal, Equal Rights for Everyone, the Interstate Congress for Equal Rights and Responsibilities, Protect Americans' Rights and Resources, Steelhead and Salmon Protection Action in Washington Now, and others were formed in Michigan, Montana, Ontario, Washington, and Wisconsin.

All of these groups claimed that native treaty hunting and fishing rights were special rights granted to native peoples solely because of their race. They sought to reframe and recast the issue as one of unequal individual rights, rather than rights reserved by native people in exchange for their cession of much of their homelands. In Wisconsin, Protect Americans' Rights and Resources organized mass demonstrations and protests against the Ojibwa exercise of fishing rights during the 1980s.

Today, while local anti–native rights groups still exist, they no longer organize mass rallies and demonstrations. In the United States, the Citizens Equal Rights Alliance remains active at the national level and lobbies state and federal officials to abrogate or legislatively eliminate hunting and fishing rights. Indigenous people still are fighting to regain and retain such rights and to protect and preserve their traditional lifeways.

Steven E. Silvern

See also: Countries—New Zealand; United States. *Issues*—Colonialism; Economic Development; Social Customs.

Further Reading

Duthu, Bruce N. *American Indians and the Law.* New York, Penguin, 2008.

Fleras, Augie, and John Leonard Elliott. *The "Nations Within": Aboriginal–State Relations in Canada, the United States, and New Zealand.* Toronto, Canada: Oxford University Press, 1992.

Great Lakes Indian Fish and Wildlife Commission. www.glifwc.org.

Jentoft, Svein, Henry Minde, and Rangar Nilsen. *Indigenous Peoples: Resource Management and Global Rights.* Delft, Netherlands: Eburon, 2003.

Nettheim, Garth, Gary Meyers, and Donna Craig. *Indigenous Peoples and Governance Structures: A Comparative Analysis of Land and Resource Management Rights.* Canberra, Australia: Aboriginal Studies Press, 2002.

Richardson, Benjamin J., Shin Imai, and Kent McNeil, eds. *Indigenous Peoples and the Law: Comparative and Critical Perspectives.* Portland, OR: Hart, 2009.

Indigenous Governments

Globally, indigenous peoples live within the administrative systems, rules, and legislation of nation-states that either have continued their attempts to assimilate, marginalize, or suppress indigenous societies and cultures or have recognized, to some degree, their rights to specific forms of self-determination. In turn, numerous indigenous peoples continue to assert that they are distinct political and cultural communities. Through indigenous rights movements, they seek to exert, and where necessary, regain control over their lives and lands through land claims and campaigns for self-government.

In some regions of the world, agreements have been reached between national governments and indigenous people that recognize indigenous claims and grant native communities varying degrees of self-government. No agreement yet has been so far-reaching as to give an indigenous group full political independence, but the decentralization of specific administrative functions and responsibilities to local and regional governments has given some indigenous peoples greater responsibility over their own affairs.

Arrangements in which indigenous peoples have the greatest autonomy can be found in the models of sovereignty or self-government in the United States, in self-government agreements in Canada, in the system of extensive self-government in Greenland, and in new constitutional systems such as that in Bolivia. Other forms of participation include comanagement models, which allow indigenous peoples a measure of involvement in the management of lands and resources.

Indigenous Government and Indigenous Governance

Anthropologists have written extensively about the forms and structures of leadership, government, and politics that have existed within indigenous societies, especially in hunter-gatherer societies, and in other societies in precolonial times or alongside colonial administrations. Hunter-gatherer groups, for instance, generally have been described in the anthropological literature as egalitarian societies in which status and leadership, and therefore decision-making authority, are ascribed to an individual on the basis of certain characteristics, knowledge, and experiences (for example, those recognized as "great hunters" or elders). Tribes are organized on the basis of kinship and descent groups and have some system of social rank, while chiefdoms are more stratified tribal societies led by chiefs.

The extent to which governments—and hence social, cultural, and political rights to be in positions of power—have existed in indigenous societies has been the subject of considerable debate. For example, in the Arctic, the creation of a united Greenlandic society and nation and the eventual formation of political parties and a parliamentary government were products of colonialism in a land where formal leadership had been practically absent in Inuit society.

In their influential edited volume *African Political Systems* (1940), Meyer Fortes and E.E. Evans-Pritchard classified a set of African societies into two groups. The first were peoples that had a government consisting of a central authority, effective administration, and a judiciary. These groups had adopted Western mores and, in turn, a Western view of wealth and power. Fortes and Evans-Pritchard classified the Banyankole, Bemba, Kede, Ngwato, and Zulu as fitting this model. The other group was made up of societies that lacked a government and had fewer divisions based on wealth and power, including the Logoli, Nuer, and Tallensi. In Western parlance, the former group could be considered "civilized," while the other might be called "primitive."

It is important to make a distinction between government and governance. Government refers to public and state institutions that are vested with authority by the state to make decisions on behalf of an entire community, country, or nation. Governance, although it includes institutions of government, also encompasses other social forms, practices, institutions, and nongovernmental organizations that play a role in making decisions. In a sense, governance encompasses both formal and informal aspects of decision making and involves elements of civil society.

Writing about indigenous forms of governance in

their report for the Arctic Governance Project in 2009, Gail Fondahl and Stephanie Irlbacher-Fox described governance as the exercise of authority given by society to make decisions regarding resource allocation and the coordination of individual activities for the greater good. It regulates and exerts influence over individual actions within the group and individual relationships with the outside the world. The ability to govern, and the ability to make authoritative decisions about the use and management of the environment and its resources and of social practices, relies on knowledge of the social environment and the practices that will lead to success.

Leaders of small communities, particularly in hunter-gatherer societies, were chosen for their profound and extensive knowledge and their notable success as hunters and providers. In Greenland, for example, the *piniartorssuaq* (great hunter) is someone who is respected in Inuit society for his skill, knowledge, prowess, and wisdom and often is consulted by others on decisions that need to be made that affect the community.

Anthropologist Charles Jedrej argued that in many parts of Africa, political authority and political sovereignty traditionally were expressed through idioms of meteorology and realized through institutions described as rainmaking rituals. Rainmaking thus is linked to political power and decision making. One of the best anthropological examples of this is described in Eileen Jensen Krige's *The Realms of a Rain Queen* (1943), an ethnography of the Lovedu of the Transvaal in South Africa.

Land and resources are at the heart of indigenous claims for self-government. Traditional resource use practices and the relationships between people and the environment remain important for maintaining social relationships and cultural identity in indigenous societies. These aspects of society define a sense of individual, family, and community identity and reinforce and celebrate the relationships between indigenous peoples and the resources and environment upon which they depend. Hunting, herding, fishing, and gathering activities, for example, are based on continuing interaction between people, animals, plants, and the environment. Such activities link people inextricably to their histories and to their present cultural settings, and examining such relationships provides a way of thinking about sustainable livelihoods in the future.

Comanagement and Indigenous Governance: Examples from Arctic Societies

Since the 1970s, significant political changes have taken place in the Arctic as a result of land claims in Alaska and Canada and the formation of regional governments in Greenland and Nunavut in northern Canada. Settlements include the Alaska Native Claims Settlement Act of 1971; the establishment of home rule in Greenland in 1979, followed thirty years later by self-rule; the James Bay and Northern Quebec Agreement of 1975–1977; the Inuvialuit Final Agreement of 1984; and the Nunavut Land Claims Agreement of 1993 (the federal territory of Nunavut was inaugurated in 1999).

These political shifts resulted in changes in the ways in which living and nonliving resources are managed. In addition, a greater degree of local involvement in resource use management decisions has been introduced. In some cases, this has included the actual transfer of decision-making authority to the local or regional level, thus enabling the use of indigenous knowledge in matters of governance.

Significant steps also have been taken through innovative comanagement regimes that allow for the sharing of responsibility for resource management between indigenous and other uses and the state. As self-government is primarily about the practice of autonomy, the introduction of comanagement gives indigenous peoples opportunities to improve the degree to which management and the regulation of resource use considers and incorporates indigenous views and traditional resource use systems.

Comanagement projects involve greater recognition of indigenous rights to resource use and emphasize the importance of decentralized authority, nonhierarchical institutions, and consensus decision making. This presents opportunities for collaboration between indigenous peoples, scientists, and policy makers concerned with the sustainable use of living resources. For example, new governance mechanisms in northwestern Canada through the Inuvialuit Final Agreement of 1984 have helped the Inuvialuit people negotiate and manage the effects of environmental change. The five comanagement bodies established by the agreement provide an effective means for Inuvialuit groups to communicate with regional, territorial, and federal governments and, indeed, with the Arctic Council.

Self-Determination and Self-Government in Canada

In 1973, the Canadian federal government established a policy framework for negotiation and settlement of land claims by aboriginal people. Canada's 1982 Constitution Act recognized and affirmed the aboriginal and treaty rights of the country's indigenous peoples—the Inuit, First Nations, and Métis—and the Inherent Right Policy of 1995 outlined how self-government negotiations and arrangements could be considered part of comprehensive land claims.

Despite this, the process of dealing with land claims has been extremely slow. Most agreements have been made with Inuit groups in the Arctic and with First Nations in the Northwest Territories and Yukon.

Inuit Self-Government

In response to social change and the prospects of far-reaching and large-scale economic development, Inuit political leaders in Canada have worked since the late 1960s to achieve self-determination and self-government. Faced with oil and gas development in the Mackenzie River Delta, the Inuvialuit formed the Committee of Original People's Entitlement in 1969, and in 1971, the Inuit Tapirisat of Canada (now called Inuit Tapiriit Kanatami) was founded in Ottawa as a national voice for Inuit people throughout Canada's North.

In 1975, the Inuit of northern Quebec signed a land claims agreement against the backdrop of controversy surrounding hydroelectric development in the James Bay. In 1984, the Inuvialuit Final Agreement accorded title to 35,000 square miles (90,650 square kilometers) of the Northwest Territories to the Inuvialuit, together with financial compensation and other rights, including gas, petroleum, and mineral rights for 5,000 square miles (12,950 square kilometers) as a final settlement of territorial claims. In 1993, the Tungavik Federation of Nunavut and the government of Canada signed an agreement on Inuit land claims and harvest rights that committed the federal government to establishing the territory of Nunavut (meaning "our land" in the Inuktitut language) in the Canadian eastern Arctic. The territory of Nunavut, comprising 808,185 square miles (2.09 million square kilometers) of northern Canada, was inaugurated on April 1, 1999.

The population of Nunavut is approximately 80 percent Inuit, and the government is effectively Inuit led. The settlement did not create a new ethnic Inuit state but rather a new public government. (Canadian territories and provinces have extensive public self-government within the limits defined by the Canadian constitution.) Nunavut has given the Inuit of the eastern Arctic a greater degree of autonomy and self-government than is enjoyed by any other aboriginal group in Canada.

Following ratification of the Labrador Inuit Land Claims Agreement, the government of Nunatsiavut was established in 2005 to represent the rights of Labrador Inuit. As of early 2012, the Inuit homeland of Nunavik in northern Quebec was the subject of ongoing negotiations regarding its status as a self-governing region within the province.

Self-Government and First Nations in Yukon Territory

Approximately 26 percent of the 33,000 people living in Canada's Yukon Territory are aboriginal. There are fourteen First Nations groups. The Yukon has four levels of government: federal, territorial, First Nation, and municipal. The federal government has ownership and control of the territory's public land, water, and resources. First Nation land claims settlement negotiations have been ongoing since 1973, and the Yukon territorial government has been negotiating the transfer of federal programs to local and regional control.

An example relevant to resource development and environmental protection is the devolution to the Yukon territorial government and First Nations of responsibility for environmental assessment under the Yukon Environmental and Socio-Economic and Assessment Act (YESAA). Specifically, First Nations can use YESAA in negotiations with industry and government to make them aware of aboriginal concerns about social, cultural, and health issues.

The 1990 Umbrella Final Agreement provided a framework for Yukon First Nation final and self-government agreements that subsequently have been realized for eleven First Nation governments, which now operate as self-governing jurisdictions under the federal Yukon First Nations Self-Government Act of 1995. They have responsibility for the administration of land claims rights and benefits. Three other Yukon First Nations, still negotiating their land claim settlements, operate as band councils under the federal Indian Act.

Most Yukon First Nation governments also participate in one or more regional tribal organizations. The largest regional body, the Council of Yukon First Nations, represents nine self-governing Yukon First Nations. The Kaska Tribal Council represents five member governments in southeastern Yukon and British Columbia. And the Gwich'in Tribal Council represents four communities in northern Yukon and the Mackenzie River Delta of the Northwest Territories.

Greenland: A Model for Indigenous Government?

Hans Egede, a Dano-Norwegian Lutheran priest, arrived on Greenland's west coast in 1721. He established a trade and mission station near present-day Nuuk, Greenland's capital, marking the beginning of more than 200 years of Danish colonial rule over the indigenous Inuit inhabitants.

Greenlanders campaign for expanded home rule in a 2008 referendum; over 75 percent voted "yes." The island government took control of the courts and police; Greenlanders were recognized as a separate people; and Greenlandic became the official language. *(Slim Allagui/ AFP/Getty Images)*

The Danish authorities assumed responsibility for trade in 1726, hoping to establish a viable and lucrative trade network based on marine mammal products (mainly seal and whale oil and sealskins) and the transfer of trading rights in Greenland to independent companies. In the long term, this proved unsuccessful, so the Danish government formed the Kongelige Grønlandske Handelskompagni (Royal Greenland Trade Company), thus establishing a Danish trade monopoly in Greenland that would last until after World War II.

By 1814, the majority of Greenland's indigenous Inuit were involved in a trade economy that was controlled and monopolized by Denmark. Yet some Inuit populations still were relatively isolated, having little or no contact with Europeans. The Inughuit (Polar Eskimos) were visited in northwest Greenland by John Ross in 1818, and Douglas Clavering met and traded with groups of Inuit in northeastern Greenland in 1823 (the only recorded contact between northeastern Greenlanders and Europeans in what is today an uninhabited part of Greenland). In 1884, Gustav Holm wintered with the people of Ammassalik on the east coast.

Despite the changes to Inuit society and culture that inevitably occurred as a result of Danish involvement in Greenland, the majority of the Inuit population continued their hunting and fishing lifestyle. Seals and other marine mammals provided the mainstay of the local economy, with blubber and skins underpinning the trade economy.

The concept of Greenland as a country and Greenlanders as a people with a common identity began to take shape during the nineteenth century. The establishment of a printing house in Nuuk during the 1850s was an important development for Greenlandic as a written language. The newspaper *Atuagagdliutit* was first published in 1861. Originally, *Atuagagdliutit* came out monthly, and it was significant not only as a source of news about Greenland and the outside world, but also as a medium for cultural expression and political and intellectual development. It paved the way for the beginning of a Greenlandic literary tradition and a nascent nationalist movement that argued that Greenlanders should be involved in the government of their own land.

Following World War II, Denmark ended its isolationist policy toward Greenland and began a process of modernization. Colonial status was superseded in 1953 when Greenland became an integral part of the Kingdom of Denmark, thus giving Greenlanders equal status as Danes.

The end of colonial rule marked the beginning of another era that was characterized by profound and extensive social, economic, and political changes in Greenlandic society. Improved health care resulted in population increase, and economic development now was based almost entirely on commercial fishing. During the 1960s, the Danes implemented controversial policies of centralization and urbanization: Many Inuit were moved from small, remote settlements and relocated to the growing west coast towns.

By the late 1960s and early 1970s, Greenlandic society had been transformed from one based primarily on small-scale hunting and fishing to a modern export-oriented economy based on a commercial fishing industry. The majority of the Inuit population lived in urban centers, a demographic transition that brought its own social and economic problems. These upheavals led to the politicization of Inuit culture and identity, the formation of political parties, and the beginnings of a movement for home rule.

The Danes were well aware of the dissatisfaction felt by Greenlanders and recognized that a change in the relationship between Denmark and Greenland was both necessary and desirable. A Home Rule Commission was set up in 1975, and the Home Rule Act was passed three years later. Home rule for Greenland was established by referendum in January 1979, and the first Greenlandic government was elected in April of that year. Legislative and administrative powers in a large number of areas and public institutions quickly were transferred to the home rule authorities.

Since that time, Greenlanders have embarked on a course of nation building. Greenland left the European Economic Community in January 1985 (it had joined with Denmark in 1973), but it negotiated overseas countries and territories association status, which allows favorable access to European markets.

On November 25, 2008, 75.5 percent of those who voted in a referendum on self-governance favored greater autonomy. Greenlanders thus gave their political leaders a mandate for significant and far-reaching change. Home rule ended on June 21, 2009, when the new political arrangement of self-rule was instituted. Areas falling under Greenlandic control include the justice system, police system, prison affairs, and the coast guard. Greenland also will be able to represent itself in international affairs. Greenlandic (Kalaallisut) has become the country's official language. Despite the challenges ahead, and irrespective of whether it means eventual independence, the vote for self-rule expressed the growing cultural and political confidence in a country of only 57,000 people, more than 80 percent of whom are Inuit.

Greenland often has been considered a model for indigenous self-government, but it has been a process of nation building rather than an ethnopolitical movement. Its relevance goes beyond that of self-determination for indigenous peoples and says much about the aspirations for autonomy in small political jurisdictions and stateless nations. However, Greenlanders were left with the question of how they would pay for the responsibilities that their nation eventually might take over from the Danish state.

Sixty percent of Greenland's economy is dependent on a 3.5 billion Danish krone (around 470 million euros) annual block grant that it receives from Denmark, with the balance coming from local taxes. The main challenge to securing greater self-government will be overcoming this reliance and replacing it with revenues generated from within Greenland. Oil and gas production and mining raw materials would ease this dependence, and much of the debate prior to the referendum centered on Greenland's ownership of lucrative resources.

The Danish-Greenlandic Self-Rule Commission, established in 2004 to negotiate the terms of greater self-government, considered Greenland's claim to mineral rights, its ownership of subsoil resources, and its right to the revenues from nonrenewable resource development. The commission concluded that minerals in Greenland's subsoil belong to Greenland and that the country has a right to their extraction. Under the self-rule agreement, the income generated by subsurface resource development would be administered by Greenland, and the level of the block grant from Denmark would be reduced by an amount corresponding to 50 percent of the earnings from minerals and energy extraction over and above 75 million Danish krone. Future revenues from oil and mineral resources then will be divided between Greenland and Denmark, while the annual block grant will be reduced further and eventually phased out.

Toward Self-Government

Outside the regions of the circumpolar North, the largest strides toward self-government are being taken in Bolivia, where more than 60 percent of the population is defined as indigenous. A politically divisive debate has focused on reforms that have produced policies of decentralization in the past few years.

President Evo Morales, who is of indigenous descent, expanded land reform after taking office in January 2006. Such reforms include the granting of formal collective land title to indigenous communities (known as Tierras Comunitariasde Origen), which has recognized indigenous peoples and their legal rights. Bolivia's Congress passed a constitution in January 2009 that incorporated the principles of the United Nations Declaration on the Rights of

Indigenous People. Furthermore, in Bolivia's presidential and legislative elections in December 2009, twelve of the country's 327 municipalities voted in favor of indigenous self-government.

Such measures eventually will give indigenous peoples control over natural resources on their lands and see the increasing use of indigenous customs and traditional forms of consensus decision making. Bolivia's constitution recognizes that the country is a "multinational" state comprising a diversity of peoples that have the rights to autonomy and self-government. A number of other Latin American countries recognize that they are nations with pluricultural societies, and the rights of indigenous peoples largely are guaranteed. Although land reforms are under discussion, resource development, such as mining and hydrocarbon development, and conservation continue to affect indigenous peoples throughout Latin America.

Mark Nuttall

See also: *Countries*—Canada. *Issues*—Anthropology; Colonialism; Ecosystem Management; Self-Determination.

Further Reading

Arctic Governance Project. www.arcticgovernance.org.

Faguet, Jean-Paul. "Governance from Below in Bolivia: A Theory of Local Government with Two Empirical Tests." *Latin American Politics and Society* 51:4 (2009): 29–68.

Leas, Daryn. "Self-Government in the Yukon." In *An Indigenous Parliament? Realities and Perspectives in Russia and the Circumpolar North*, ed. Kathrin Wessendorf. Copenhagen, Denmark: International Work Group for Indigenous Affairs, 2005.

Nuttall, Mark. *Arctic Homeland: Kinship, Community and Development in Northwest Greenland.* Toronto, Canada: University of Toronto Press, 1992.

———. "Greenland: Emergence of an Inuit Homeland." In *Polar Peoples: Self-Determination and Development,* ed. Minority Rights Group. London: Minority Rights Group, 1994.

———. "Self-Rule in Greenland: Towards the World's First Independent Inuit State?" *Indigenous Affairs* 3–4 (2008): 64–70.

Roddick, David. "Yukon First Nations and the Alaska Highway Gas Pipeline." *Indigenous Affairs* 2–3 (2006): 12–19.

Indigenous Identity

The concept of indigenous identity is fluid, evolving, and contested, indicating the myriad ways in which the term *indigenous* has been used to categorize people and to self-identify. The growth and activism of the global indigenous rights movement since the mid-twentieth century has brought the question of indigenous identity to the fore in local and global forums.

How the term *indigenous* is defined has strategic importance both for marginalized social and ethnic peoples asserting their indigenous identity as they struggle to claim their rights and for the states that claim jurisdiction over them. Consequently, there is no agreed-upon definition of indigenous identity, and confusion about who qualifies as indigenous is widespread.

Indigenous identity means different things to different people. Some definitions focus on the long-term occupation of a territory, while others consider cultural affiliation and participation to be paramount. Adding to the confusion, some definitions aim at universal applicability, while others are created for particular purposes—for example, to determine tribal membership or for the purposes of legal jurisdiction.

Anthropologist Francesca Merlan offers a helpful taxonomy to make sense of the multitude of definitions, dividing them into two categories: critical and relational. Critical definitions of indigenous peoples put forth a set of criteria or conditions that are inherent only in peoples who identify themselves as indigenous. Relational definitions emphasize the relationship between indigenous people and non-native peoples.

The Meaning of Indigenous

Who is considered indigenous? And what does it mean to be indigenous? The term *indigenous* long has been used to distinguish those who are "natives" from "non-native" in specific locales and with varying scope, but it also has become a global category, leading to a generalization of experience that is not always universally shared. Despite the historical usage and current internationalization of *indigenous*, there is no consensus on the definition or application of the term. Instead, there is widespread disagreement about who may be considered indigenous and who has a right to represent indigenous interests.

Such conflicts are often political in nature, pitting governments against self-ascribed indigenous groups that reside within their borders. Consequently, the precise number of indigenous peoples across the globe is unknown. However, United Nations (UN) publications assert that there are 300 million to 350 million indigenous peoples worldwide living on every continent and in more than seventy countries.

Reflecting the lack of consensus over the definition, to date, no UN body has adopted an official definition of the term *indigenous*. Initially, the Working Group on Indigenous Populations, established in 1982, asserted that four principles should be considered in crafting any definition of indigenous peoples: (1) priority in time, with respect to the occupation and use of specific territory; (2) the voluntary perpetuation of cultural distinctiveness; (3) self-identification as well as recognition by other groups and by state authorities as a distinct collectivity; and (4) an experience of subjugation, marginalization, dispossession, exclusion, or discrimination, regardless of whether these conditions persist.

However, in the Working Group on Indigenous Populations's fifteenth and final session in 1997, it concluded that a definition of indigenous peoples at the global level was not possible at that time and certainly not necessary for the adoption of the Draft Declaration on the Rights of Indigenous Peoples. Consequently, the UN Declaration on the Rights of Indigenous Peoples (2007) does not offer an explicit definition of *indigenous peoples*. Instead, the declaration elaborates a catalogue of special group rights for indigenous people. The absence of a clear definition reflects the difficulties and contentiousness of formulating a universal, far-reaching, and flexible meaning that is applicable to the diverse realities of the numerous indigenous communities throughout the world.

Likewise, in its Operations Policy 4.10 (2006), the World Bank acknowledged the lack of a universally accepted definition of "indigenous peoples," while also rejecting definitions based on the criteria of historical continuity and colonialism. Instead, the World Bank adopted a functional definition of indigenous peoples as groups with a social and cultural identity distinct from the dominant society that makes them vulnerable to being disadvantaged in the development process. According to World Bank policies, the term *indigenous peoples* "refers to a distinct, vulnerable, social and cultural group" that exhibits the following characteristics in varying degrees: (1) self-identification as members of a distinct indigenous cultural group and recognition of this identity by others; (2) collective attachment to geographically distinct habitats or ancestral territories in the project area and to the natural resources in these habitats and territories; (3) customary cultural, economic, social, or political institutions that are separate from those of the dominant society and culture; and (4) an indigenous language, often different from the official language of the country or region.

Two definitions have been widely accepted as guiding principles for the identification of indigenous people: the so-called Cobo definition and the statement of coverage contained in Convention No. 169 (Article 1) of the International Labour Organization (ILO). In his *Study of the Problem of Discrimination Against Indigenous Populations* (1981–1983), José R. Martinez Cobo, the special rapporteur for the UN Sub-Commission on Prevention of Discrimination and Protection of Minorities, defines indigenous communities, peoples, and nations as follows:

those which, having a historical continuity with preinvasion and pre-colonial societies that developed on their territories, consider themselves distinct from other sectors of the societies now prevailing on those territories, or parts of them. They form at present non-dominant sectors of society and are determined to preserve, develop and transmit to future generations their ancestral territories, and their ethnic identity, as the basis of their continued existence as peoples, in accordance with their own cultural patterns, social institutions and legal systems.

On an individual level,

an indigenous person is one who belongs to these indigenous populations through self-identification as indigenous (group consciousness) and is recognized and accepted by these populations as one of its members (acceptance by the group).

Cobo defines historical continuity as follows:

the continuation, for an extended period reaching into the present, of one or more of the following factors: (a) occupation of ancestral lands, or at least of part of them; (b) common ancestry with the original occupants of these lands; (c) culture in general, or in specific manifestations (such as religion, living under a tribal system, membership of an indigenous community, dress, means of livelihood, lifestyle, etc.); (d) language (whether used as the only language, as mother-tongue, as the habitual means of communication at home or in the family, or as the main, preferred, habitual, general or normal language); (e) residence on certain parts of the country, or in certain regions of the world; (f) other relevant factors.

This comprehensive definition focuses on the common traits found in most indigenous populations rather than the particularities of each indigenous group. It also stresses indigenous peoples' need for cultural protection and promotion, as well as their connection to their territory as original occupiers of the land.

ILO Convention No. 169 (1989) eschews an imposed definition of indigenous peoples in favor of personal or group self-ascription. Article 1(2) of the convention states that "self-identification as indigenous or tribal shall be regarded as a fundamental criterion for determining groups to which the provisions of this Convention apply." In place of a definition, a statement of coverage is provided stipulating that the convention applies to (1) tribal peoples in independent countries whose social, cultural, and economic conditions distinguish them from

A Long Neck Karen (Kayan) woman from Thailand chats on a cellphone while displaying the tribe's signature neck rings. Not least among the challenges to indigenous cultures and identity are modern communications media and other technologies. *(Pornchai Kittiwongsakul/AFP/Getty Images)*

other parts of the national community and whose status is regulated either wholly or partially by their own customs or traditions or by special laws or regulations; and (2) peoples in independent countries who are regarded as indigenous on account of their descent from the populations that inhabited the country, or a geographic region to which the country belongs, at the time of conquest or colonization or the establishment of present state boundaries and who, irrespective of their legal status, retain some or all of their own social, economic, cultural, and political institutions.

The ILO uses two terms—*indigenous peoples* and *tribal peoples*—because some tribal peoples are not considered indigenous in the literal sense, as they are not indigenous to the territories in which they now reside, but live in situations similar to indigenous peoples. One example is the case of the Garífuna, who are descendants of African tribal peoples now living in Central America or tribal peoples in Africa such as the San or Maasai that may not have lived in the region they inhabit longer than other groups. Many of these tribal peoples refer to themselves

as "indigenous" in order to be included in discussions regarding indigenous peoples that are taking place in the UN and other international bodies.

Thus, for practical purposes, the terms *indigenous* and *tribal* are used synonymously in the UN system. These definitions share six common features: (1) connections with the land and territory; (2) aspirations for autonomy and self-determination; (3) renewed interest in distinct cultures and languages; (4) the historical experience of incursions by other groups; (5) continuing consequences of dispossession and subordination and concerns over health and education, mortality, nutrition, and income levels; (6) and the shared effects of modernity.

History of the Term *Indigenous*

"Indigenous peoples" as a category and a concept is a product of the European conquest. Prior to the 1494 Treaty of Tordesillas, in which, by papal decree, the globe was divided between Spain and Portugal, there were no "indigenous peoples"—there were only peoples.

The concept of "indigenous" also plays a significant role in indigenous peoples' resistance to European domination. The indigenous peoples who first mobilized politically in the international arena were peoples currently residing in former colonies and successor states in the West: the North American Indians and Inuit, Australian Aborigines, New Zealand Maori, and Nordic Sami. These peoples share a common history of European colonization and have similar cultures. Additionally, for this particular subset of indigenous peoples, "indigenous" or "indigeneity" is linked inextricably to struggles for self-government, self-determination, and land rights, as well as to claims for restitution and reparation.

As the forerunners of the international indigenous movement, this subset of indigenous peoples and their local history and experience have shaped the core of the concept of indigenous peoples used in international bodies such as the UN. Consequently, they remain representative of the leadership of indigenous movement worldwide.

In fact, the successes sometimes experienced by indigenous groups in the United States and Canada have motivated groups in other parts of the world to self-identify as indigenous. This increase in the variety and number of peoples articulating an indigenous identity has exposed the limitations of the concept of "indigenous."

These struggles for recognition have been shaped by international understandings of "indigenous" that derive from the histories and experiences of Western imperialists. In addition, establishing a common criteria for a definition of indigenous that takes into account the diversity of cultural backgrounds and colonial histories, without being so vague that it is rendered meaningless and open to broad interpretations, has been nearly impossible. Attempts to broaden the concept of "indigenous" to capture the multifarious experiences of indigenous peoples across the globe make clear that although the concept is not as problematic when it is used in specific local contexts, it is problematic when used to generalize unrelated historical experiences into a universal theme. Its very generality makes "indigenous identity" susceptible to arguments for greater or lesser inclusiveness.

While there is a need for a more precise conception of indigeneity, the absence of a definition that is both universally acceptable and applicable has not been a significant hindrance to indigenous peoples themselves or to their political activities, nor has it significantly undermined or limited the legitimacy of indigenous claims in national and international institutional processes. Yet the lack of a universally accepted definition may allow states to delay ratifying and implementing the indigenous rights framework that is emerging in international law, as states and their legal frameworks require specificity.

Moreover, the lack of a universally accepted definition of indigenous peoples facilitates a dynamic discourse involving its various meanings, levels, and actors. So while different participants in the discussion hold different views about the meaning of "indigenous," the dialogue eventually may lead to more stable shared meanings as those entities produce, enforce, reinforce, and institutionalize their ideas through action. More important, such a process facilitates the social act of creating intersubjectivities by which those who identify themselves as indigenous create meaning out of what they understand their role to be as both participants in and subjects of international relations.

Examining Identity

Since the 1960s, the increase in identity-based claims, such as gender, ethnic, and sexual identity, has generated an upsurge of interest in identity as a concept. The word *identity* is derived from the Latin term *iden-*

SAIIC

The South American Indian Information Center (SAIIC) was established in 1983 as a project of the South American Indian Council (CISA) to provide information on and international support for CISA and the indigenous rights movement in South America. The SAIIC represented the first attempt to unify indigenous struggles across the Western Hemisphere.

The center was formed at the Second Conference of Indian Nations and Organizations of South America, held in Tiwanaku, Bolivia. Delegates at this meeting sent Nilo Cayuqueo, a Mapuche from southern Argentina and one of the founding members of CISA, to Oakland, California, to coordinate the SAIIC and its activities. Founded with the support of North American solidarity activists, SAIC became an organization led and directed by native peoples.

The SAIIC supported self-determination and the unification of the indigenous rights movement on a continental level through a series of projects and programs, including the publication of a quarterly journal, production of a radio program, an indigenous visitor and cultural exchange program, human rights and urgent action alerts, and public presentations. The center began publication of the *SAIIC Newsletter* in 1984 to broadcast information on indigenous struggles across the Americas. The newsletter grew in size and importance, and in 1993, it was renamed *Abya Yala News,* using the Kuna word for the Americas as the name of the journal.

In July 1990, together with the Confederation of

Indigenous Nationalities of Ecuador and the National Indigenous Organization of Colombia, the SAIIC sponsored the First Continental Conference on 500 Years of Indian Resistance in Ecuador. Four hundred delegates from 120 indigenous nations and organizations across the Americas joined in defense of common interests. The meeting helped galvanize unity against the upcoming quincentennial celebration of Christopher Columbus's voyage across the Atlantic Ocean. Subsequently, the SAIIC helped lead an "Indianist" or ethnic wing of international indigenous organizing efforts against a popular movement centered on Guatemalan Nobel Peace Prize winner Rigoberta Menchú.

In 1986, the SAIIC changed its name to the South and Central American Indian Information Center in order to include Mexico. In 1994, the name was changed once again to the South and Meso American Indian Rights Center, pointing to a turn toward ethnic advocacy. (However, it always retained the acronym SAIIC.) Also in 1994, the organization helped create the Abya Yala Fund, the first foundation founded and run by indigenous peoples to work on development and advocacy issues in rural communities.

In 1998, internal divisions caused the journal to cease publication and the organization's offices to close. Subsequent efforts to revive an organization with the SAIIC's political outlook and hemispheric reach have been largely unsuccessful.

Marc Becker

titas, which is formed from *idem,* meaning *"same,"* and expresses the notion of likeness or oneness. This sameness may refer either to similarities between a person or thing in all ways or to a shared origin or characteristics among members of a group.

Yet most identity theorists would argue that identities are not static. Constructivists, in particular, argue that identity is a complex, multilayered phenomenon; it is constructed, fluid, multiple, and fragmented. Thus, while people derive particular identities from their roles in society, the groups they belong to, and their personal characteristics, those roles, group identifications, and characteristics are not fixed. A person may hold a number of identities simultaneously, and over his or her lifespan, these facets of a person's identity may be inextricably linked.

For some people, ethnic identity is primary. For others, identification with a sexual orientation, gender, or religion is more meaningful. Yet even though a person may have a primary identity, he or she may present different identities in different contexts. Not only do people use identity to make sense of themselves, their activities, others, and how they differ from others, but identity also is used strategically by political entrepreneurs to organize and justify collective action. Politicians long have sought groups that identify themselves in a general sense in order to create a sense of collective identity that makes organization easier.

Constructivist theories of identity posit that identities not only fail to exist solely within individuals or categories of individuals but also do not exist a priori. Rather, they are produced historically through the recognition of difference in individuals' or groups' relationships with others. Thus, in the case of indigenous identity, there was no "indigenous identity" prior to contact with Europeans, as "indigenous" implies the existence of the opposite—the non-native European settlers.

Indigenous identity, Hillary Weaver argues, is a combination of self-identification (perception) and the perceptions of others. Self-identifying as indigenous involves internalizing the cultural experiences of a lifetime. Yet although there is some level of choice in adopting or accepting an identity, that choice often is limited by factors such as physical appearance and blood quantum (a person's percentage of indigenous heritage).

A growing consensus of scholars argues that at the most elementary level, indigenous identity is something that only can be experienced and defined by people who identify as indigenous. This became an accepted international legal practice beginning in 1977, when the second general assembly of the World Council of Indigenous Peoples passed a resolution stating that only indigenous peoples could define indigenous peoples.

The second component of indigenous identity is community identification and affirmation. Identifying as indigenous means that an individual feels inseparably linked to the sacred traditions, traditional homelands, and shared history of his or her indigenous community. However, no two individuals who identify as indigenous will experience indigeneity in the same way. Moreover, a person's identity can be confirmed only by others who share that same identity.

The third component, external identity, is fraught with conflict, as specifying who can and should define indigenousness often has been determined from a non-native perspective. Governments, in particular, often play a decisive role in shaping indigenous identity through official recognition or nonrecognition of indigenous individuals and groups. Yet government definitions of indigenous often do not reflect indigenous peoples' definition and experience of indigeneity.

Moreover, official definitions of "indigenous" have been used to construct false indigenous identities that reinforce stereotypes. Consequently, government-constructed identities limit indigenous peoples' ability and right to define themselves and often undermine indigenous self-determination. Attempts to quantify indigenous identity are also highly contentious, as this often is done for the purposes of exclusion and inclusion. Arguably, most attempts to measure an individual's cultural identity—specifically, ones based on appearance or blood quantum—are actually measures of acculturation (into the dominant society), and thus they are of questionable adequacy and accuracy.

Collective Identity, Collective Rights

Indigenous peoples, since the European conquest, have been resisting processes of severe discrimination, dispossession, and enculturation at the local and national levels. Spurred by decolonization, the civil rights struggles of the 1960s, and growing human rights law and globalization, these localized indigenous struggles over the decades have coalesced into an international movement.

Employing the politics of identity, this political movement of self-defined indigenous peoples is demanding recognition of their collective rights to self-determination and access to land and natural resources in the context of national systems that do not readily accommodate them. Thus, at its core, and despite all of the variations in local context, the international indigenous movement is a struggle for land and autonomy. This movement has mobilized around a shared collective identity as indigenous.

Therefore, in both theory and practice, the indigenous rights movement seeks to build a collective identity by rediscovering and reinforcing indigenous values of communality, solidarity, reciprocity, social justice, equality, complementarity, and harmony with nature. As a result of strength and level of indigenous mobilization in the international arena, indigenous peoples' collective rights increasingly are being recognized in international law and respected as an international norm. The goal of this mobilization in the international sphere is to establish principles from which to renegotiate their futures with national governments.

Although international organizations such as the UN have promoted what they define as the concerns of indigenous peoples, their members are states, and thus their conclusions reflect national interests that may not be in line with the interests of the international indigenous movement. For example, this movement faces resistance from liberal states that are reluctant to recognize collective rights alongside individual rights. Opponents of recognizing indigenous collective rights argue that recognizing collective rights amounts to privileging one group's rights over others, and that recognizing collective rights undermines individual rights. In response, proponents of indigenous collective rights argue that real equality requires treating some groups differently than others.

Meredith E. Staples

See also: *Groups: Central and South America*—Garífuna. *Issues*—Colonialism; Indigenous Peoples and the United Nations; International Policy.

Further Reading

Corntassel, Jeff. "Who Is Indigenous? Peoplehood and Ethnonationalist Approaches to Rearticulating Indigenous Identity." *Nationalism and Ethnic Politics* 9:1 (Spring 2003): 75–100.

de Oliveira, Godinho. "The United Nations Declaration on the Rights of Indigenous Peoples and the Protection of Indigenous Rights in Brazil." *Max Planck Yearbook of United Nations Law* 12 (2008): 247–286.

Kenrick, Justin, and Jerome Lewis. "Indigenous Peoples' Rights and the Politics of the Term 'Indigenous.'" *Anthropology Today* 20:2 (April 2004): 4–9.

Kupar, A. "The Return of the Native." *Current Anthropology* 44:3 (2003): 389–402.

Merlan, Francesca. "Indigeneity: Global and Local." *Current Anthropology* 50:3 (2009): 303–331.

Niezen, Ronald. *The Rediscovered Self: Indigenous Identity and Cultural Justice.* Montreal, Canada: McGill-Queen's University Press, 2009.

Peang-Meth, Abdulgaffar. "The Rights of Indigenous Peoples and Their Fight for Self-Determination." *World Affairs* 164:3 (Winter 2002): 101–144.

Indigenous Peoples and the United Nations

Indigenous peoples around the world are among the most impoverished, exploited, marginalized, and discriminated against, a result of centuries of colonization and domination. In particular, because of their distinct cultures, indigenous peoples often have suffered these hardships more severely, having little recourse to seek solutions at the national level. For this reason, indigenous leaders look to international organizations, such as the United Nations (UN), as promising venues in which to voice their grievances, claims, and demands and to formulate new mechanisms and laws to promote their rights.

The principal demands of indigenous peoples worldwide are for recognition of their collective rights and right to self-determination, cultural distinctiveness, and their traditional homelands, as well as their right to open, prior, and informed consent regarding changes that affect their lands and lifeways. In addition, many indigenous peoples in various locations around the world seek the fulfillment of treaties and agreements negotiated during the period of European overseas expansion.

Indigenous Concerns in the International Community

Indigenous peoples have addressed the international community since the early twentieth century, first at the League of Nations and then at the United Nations. In 1922, a Maori representative from New Zealand arrived at the newly formed League of Nations to denounce treaty violations by the British Empire and to demand that treaties with the Maori be observed. One year later, Chief Deskaheh of the Cayuga tribe of Native Americans arrived in Geneva, Switzerland, to argue the treaty rights of the Iroquois Confederacy of Six Nations and to denounce the Canadian government for taking over a Haudenosaunee (Iroquois) reserve in Ontario. These occasions marked the first time that indigenous peoples appealed to the international community to demand respect for their rights to self-government and sovereignty. Although these appeals were not successful and were turned down with the argument that the indigenous peoples were subjects of the British Crown, indigenous issues gained considerable attention and sympathy from other countries, such as Estonia, Ireland, Japan, the Netherlands, and Panama.

Thereafter, human rights violations against indigenous peoples would be raised periodically at the UN, especially to counterbalance the power of Australia, Canada, Great Britain, and the United States. Nevertheless, indigenous issues received little attention until the 1970s, when the indigenous presence began to increase in the UN, making important contributions to many of the organization's bodies and specialized agencies.

Over the UN's history, five different bodies have been constituted to deal directly and exclusively with indigenous affairs: (1) the Working Group on Indigenous Populations (WGIP), established in 1982 under the Sub-Commission on Prevention of Discrimination and Protection of Minorities, a subsidiary body of the Commission on Human Rights; (2) the Working Group on the Draft Declaration on the Rights of Indigenous Peoples, established in 1995; (3) the Permanent Forum on Indigenous Issues (PFII), an expert body of the Economic and Social Council, established in 2000; (4) the Special Rapporteur on the Situation of the Human Rights and Fundamental Freedoms of Indigenous People, appointed in 2001 by the Commission on Human Rights; and (5) the Expert Mechanism on the Rights of Indigenous Peoples, established in 2007 as a subsidiary of the Human Rights Council (which replaced the Commission on Human Rights).

In 1921, the International Labour Organization (ILO), a specialized agency within the League of Nations, became concerned with the situation of indigenous workers. This was the first specialized international agency to undertake systematic studies on the situation of indigenous peoples, primarily focusing on their economic, social, and political conditions. In 1936, the ILO approved Convention No. 64 to provide directives on the recruitment of indigenous workers by employers.

A decade later, in 1946, Belgium proposed that the UN add the protection of indigenous peoples as part of its mandate on decolonization; however, a number of nations, including the United States and China, objected, arguing that indigenous peoples should be treated as populations of their national state, not as nations in their own right. In 1949, the UN General Assembly recommended that the problems of indigenous peoples be studied, but the United States strongly opposed this proposition as well, arguing that this was a matter of national sovereignty.

In 1957, for the first time in international law, the ILO delineated the rights of indigenous peoples in Convention No. 107, recognizing the special place of tribal and indigenous peoples in society and their need for special protection. More significant, the convention validated the collective rights of indigenous peoples to their traditional lands. The preservation of cultural diversity, however, was not acknowledged in the convention; instead, the ILO called on states to implement programs to integrate indigenous peoples into their home nations.

After World War II, the United Nations took a greater interest in minorities, especially ethnic groups. In the 1960s, the idea that all peoples—not only nation-states—have the right to self-determination and therefore should be free to determine their own political, economic, social, and cultural development earned more support. As they gained a voice in the international arena, many non-Western peoples challenged the Western premise that self-determination was the exclusive prerogative of existing nation-states.

In 1970, the debates about self-determination opened up the possibility of treating concerns of indigenous peoples as a separate issue within the UN. That same year, the UN's Sub-Commission on Prevention of Discrimination and Protection of Minorities recommended that the Commission on Human Rights study discrimination against indigenous peoples, including the effects of the assimilationist policies of nation-states. José R. Martínez Cobo, a UN expert from Ecuador, was appointed to direct the study in 1971. Its results and recommendations were reported in the *Study of the Problem of Discrimination Against Indigenous Populations* (1981–1984). This study continues to be a reference in the UN for the study of indigenous issues and for the definition of "indigenous peoples" for practical purposes. One of the major conclusions outlined in the report was the need for a draft declaration on indigenous rights. However, this was done with no consultation with indigenous peoples.

In 1977, as part of the Decade for Action to Combat Racism and Racial Discrimination (1973–1982), the UN organized the International Nongovernmental Organization (NGO) Conference on Discrimination against Indigenous Populations, which was attended by representatives of indigenous peoples from fifteen countries, UN bodies and agencies, NGOs, and observers from forty member nations. The conference discussions revolved around state-based discrimination, which was denounced as a serious obstacle to the physical and cultural survival of indigenous peoples. At the conference, indigenous peoples from the Western Hemisphere demanded to be recognized as sovereign nations subject to international law. One of the outcomes of the conference was to ask the Sub-Commission on Prevention of Discrimination and Protection of Minorities to establish a Working Group on Indigenous Populations.

For some scholars, the 1977 conference signaled to the international community that indigenous peoples had the ability to organize and voice their demands. Nevertheless, by this time, indigenous struggles for rights at the international level had not yet coalesced into a global movement.

In 1981, another NGO conference on indigenous peoples and land more clearly called attention to their suffering and losses at the hands of transnational corporations, as well as the responsibilities of the international community. For some indigenous representatives from the Americas, the conference was a catalyst for the consolidation of indigenous organizations that had been working since the creation of the World Council of Indigenous Peoples (1957) to rescue indigenous cultures from the assimilationist policies and practices of nation-states.

Finally, in 1982, the UN Economic and Social Council agreed to create a five-member Working Group on Indigenous Populations. The WGIP was a unique body within the UN because it allowed indigenous representatives and those interested in indigenous issues to meet face-to-face with representatives of states and intergovernmental organizations. This UN body became one of the largest international meetings, at which indigenous men and women were introduced into the realms of human rights law and global politics. Eventually, the global indigenous movement was organized and consolidated within this group.

Another crucial step in the recognition of indigenous rights was ILO Convention No. 169 on Indigenous and Tribal Peoples (1989). Indigenous representatives participated in its deliberations, albeit in a limited way. The convention abandoned the integrationist approach of the previous convention (No. 107) and opened the door for the legal recognition of indigenous peoples' right to retain their way of life and their social, economic, political, and cultural institutions. Furthermore, for the first time in international law, the term *peoples* (plural) was used in reference to indigenous peoples instead of *populations,* recognizing their group identity and collective rights. However, the ILO continues to accept that states have authority over indigenous peoples.

UN Declaration on the Rights of Indigenous Peoples

The WGIP was established to (1) review the social, economic, juridical, and political situation and the evolution of the human rights of indigenous peoples and to (2) elaborate new international norms for the rights of these peoples. Five independent members, all experts in international law, are elected annually from among the Sub-Commission on Prevention of Discrimination and Protection of Minorities; none of the members was indigenous.

Early on, it was decided that the WGIP could not work without the participation of indigenous peoples. Unlike other UN bodies, the WGIP opened its doors to anyone who was interested in indigenous issues, regardless of their status within the UN. Over the years, during the annual weeklong meetings, indigenous peoples gave reports on issues such as self-determination, land rights, sustainable development, the role of transnational corporations in natural resource extraction, political representation, poverty, intellectual property, the Human Genome Project, education, language, children and youth, and women. Indigenous peoples also consistently denounced human rights abuses, even though the WGIP was not authorized to deal with such matters.

One of the WGIP's major accomplishments was the Draft Declaration on the Rights of Indigenous Peoples, which was approved in 1993. The declaration represented the work of UN experts with direct input from indigenous delegates around the world, who contributed to the composition of the draft from 1985–1993. A Working Group on the Draft Declaration was formed (1995–2005) so that states, UN experts, and indigenous peoples could discuss the articles contained in the document.

In 2006, the chair of the Working Group on the Draft Declaration submitted a text that collected the language that had the consensus of both states and indigenous peoples, as well as some compromises where there was no consensus. Countries such as Australia, Canada, New Zealand, and the United States, which historically had signed treaties and agreements with indigenous peoples and nations, lobbied against the approval of the draft declaration because of its central provisions on self-determination and autonomy. Other countries expressed their support for the document in its original form early on or articulated concerns about specific provisions; the problem for some countries was the recognition of collective rights. At several moments during the ten years of deliberations, the member states seemed to be a deadlock. After eight years, only two articles had been adopted, addressing the rights of indigenous peoples as individuals. However, after years of intense deliberations and negotiations, the UN Human Rights Council (which replaced the Commission on Human Rights in 2006) adopted the declaration. It was then passed on to the General Assembly, where after intense negotiations, it was adopted by the General Assembly in September 2007. It is hoped that the declaration eventually will be converted into a UN convention, giving it the strength of international law, but as of 2012, that had not occurred.

The UN Declaration on the Rights of Indigenous Peoples covers a full range of individual and collective civil, political, economic, social, cultural, and environmental rights. It recognizes these rights as inherent and not granted by states to a specific group of people. Furthermore, the declaration assigns specific responsibilities and obligations for protecting these rights to states and international organizations. The declaration marked a major step forward in state relations with indigenous peoples, and it already has been applied to indigenous policy on land and water rights in some nations, such as Peru, Chile, and South Africa.

In addition to the draft declaration and an annual review of the situation of indigenous peoples, the experts of the WGIP have produced landmark studies on the intellectual property and heritage of indigenous peoples, treaties and agreements, land rights, globalization, and transnational corporations and their relation to indigenous issues. These studies are necessary for the development of a possible convention on the rights of indigenous peoples.

Permanent Forum on Indigenous Issues

The establishment of the Permanent Forum on Indigenous Issues under the Economic and Social Council is significant because it is the only high-level UN body in which indigenous peoples have equal status with states and can participate directly in decision-making processes. The decisions of the PFII must be made by a consensus of its sixteen members—eight representatives of indigenous peoples and eight representatives of member states. As in the WGIP, observer participation is open to anyone. For indigenous peoples, the PFII represents the promise of a new partnership with the UN and an important step toward obtaining full recognition of their right to self-determination. It means that indigenous peoples are able to recommend and counsel other UN bodies and specialized agencies, monitor the application of international instruments, participate in all global UN conferences and meetings, and disseminate information to the member states on indigenous issues.

The WGIP proposed the creation of the PFII in 1993, with support for the General Assembly, which saw the importance of institutionalizing more direct indigenous participation in the UN at a higher level. At first, however, not all of the experts, indigenous representatives, and states were equally enthusiastic about the creation of the body. Nevertheless, the UN organized

PÁTZCUARO CONGRESS

The first Inter-American Indigenous Congress, also known as the Pátzcuaro Congress, served as a blueprint for a Pan-American alliance to confront the social, political, and economic inequalities that indigenous peoples faced during the first half of the twentieth century. The conference was held in Pátzcuaro in the state of Michoacán in Mexico in April 1940 and was sponsored by the government of President Lázaro Cárdenas (1934–1940).

Participants from nineteen countries throughout the Americas attended. Mexican delegates were the most numerous, but representatives from Bolivia, Guatemala, Panama, Peru, and the United States also attended. John Collier, the leading architect of federal Indian policy in the United States during the 1930s, was in attendance.

Prior to the conference, concerns about the economic, social, and political challenges that indigenous communities faced were heard at election time or debated in intellectual circles, without any practical solutions. The conference served as a platform not only for denouncing the difficult conditions that indigenous peoples lived in, but also for pushing forward reform programs that would create real change.

One of the greatest critiques of the Pátzcuaro Congress was the absence of indigenous peoples from the proceedings. Organizing officials had stipulated that indigenous peoples could attend as part of the national delegations, but Mexico was the only country to include representatives of its native groups. As a result, government officials and academics dominated the proceedings, clearly establishing a top-down approach to indigenous policy. Policies aimed to incorporate indigenous peoples into national society, with a defined national identity, failing to consider that indigenous groups across the continent were not all the same and that programs should be adjusted to suit each culture.

To carry out proposed reforms, delegates proposed the institutionalization of indigenous programs through national indigenous institutes. In Guatemala, such an organization was created in 1945, but it was short-lived. In Mexico, a body was established in 1948 that continues to exist as the National Commission for the Development of Indigenous Peoples.

The Pátzcuaro Congress led to the creation in 1942 of the Inter-American Indigenous Institute, headquartered in Mexico City and headed by its first director, Mexican anthropologist Manuel Gamio. The *indigenismo* blueprint drawn up during the conference had an uneven impact on individual countries as reforms were applied selectively or not at all.

In total, nine Inter-American Indigenous Congresses were held: in 1949 (Peru), 1954 (Bolivia), 1959 (Guatemala), 1964 (Ecuador), 1968 (Mexico), 1972 (Brazil), 1980 (Mexico), 1985 (United States), and 1992 (Argentina).

María L.O. Muñoz

several workshops to discuss its mandates, composition, and position in Copenhagen, Denmark (1995); Santiago, Chile (1997); and Geneva (1999, 2000). Indigenous organizations, in turn, held consultation meetings about the proposal in Chile, India, Panama, Switzerland, and Tanzania. Eventually, the idea of the PFII was widely accepted. In 2000, the Commission on Human Rights adopted a resolution to create the PFII that was endorsed by the Economic and Social Council. Numerous debates took place within the WGIP about the mandate, composition, and competence of the PFII. Its first meeting was held in 2002.

Quelling most fears, the second session of the PFII, held in 2003, was hailed as a success. It attracted a record number of 1,800 registered participants, with 70 states and a large number of intergovernmental organizations participating; more than 100 proposals, objectives, recommendations, and areas of future action were outlined.

Most important, throughout the meetings, the UN's promise of a new partnership with indigenous peoples became a reality. This could be observed in the promotion of a real, interactive dialogue among indigenous representatives, governments, and agencies. For instance, when World Bank policies came under scrutiny during the discussions on development, the PFII asked the World Bank to compile examples of best practices in development projects with indigenous peoples. In another instance, the UN Security Council responded to a request of the PFII to look into allegations of gross violations of human rights against indigenous peoples in the Democratic Republic of the Congo. A further example of this new partnership in practice is the UN's recognition of the diplomatic privilege of indigenous representatives.

Even if more than half of the recommendations of the nine sessions of PFII have yet to be implemented, and there still is a crucial lack of funding for the activities of the body, its existence is an indication that indigenous peoples have acquired a powerful voice within the UN system. Through the PFII, indigenous peoples can influence policy making and program design in UN bodies and specialized agencies. They also can monitor what these bodies do in relation to indigenous peoples and provide recommendations for redress.

Other UN Bodies and Indigenous Peoples

There are many other UN bodies in which indigenous peoples have been participating and contributing for years, but here, only the most significant ones will be highlighted.

The destructive impact of the World Bank's projects and programs on indigenous peoples and the international criticism they provoked led this intergovernmental organization to adopt policies regarding indigenous peoples in 1982 (Operational Manual Statement 2.34), 1991 (Operational Directive 4.20), and 2005 (Operational Directive 4.10). The last two policies require staff to undertake positive action to protect indigenous rights in order to mitigate the negative impacts of development projects. In turn, Operational Directive 4.20 recognized the possibility of the World Bank rejecting projects that could have negative impacts.

In 2000, however, the World Bank announced its intention to revise the policy to determine which provisions are obligatory and which are simply advisory. Indigenous peoples successfully demanded that the World Bank consult with them, but their concerns were not fully addressed in Operational Directive 4.10. While it made some improvements, critics noted the absence of a definition of what constitutes "broad community support" for a project. Another problem was the ambiguity of the World Bank's right to say no to a project.

After several years of indigenous engagement in their processes, the World Intellectual Property Organization and the United Nations Educational, Scientific and Cultural Organization established provisions to protect the cultural heritage and intellectual property of indigenous peoples. Other organizations such as the World Health Organization and the United Nations Development Programme have consulted with indigenous peoples regarding their concerns and ways to address them.

Indigenous peoples have been especially active in the past two decades in the United Nations Environment Programme (UNEP). Since 1992, this organization has recognized the traditional methods and knowledge of indigenous peoples in managing and protecting the environment, as outlined in the Convention on Biological Diversity. Indigenous peoples have worked with the UNEP to monitor its activities and the implementation of the convention.

The participation of indigenous peoples in the United Nations Framework Convention on Climate Change has been very important, especially as some UN programs related to climate change are seriously affecting their livelihoods and cultural survival. More significant, participation in that body has allowed indigenous peoples to network with many other non-indigenous social movements and to create alliances and networks for the furthering of their causes. Today, not only states and international organizations, but also people around the world, recognize the role that indigenous peoples could have in mitigating the effects of climate change and in creating alternative ideas for taking care of nature.

The UN and the Global Indigenous Movement

The significance of the WGIP for the creation of discourses on indigenous rights and for the formation of the global indigenous movement cannot be understated. These UN meetings were instrumental in bringing together indigenous peoples from all over the world, but transnational and international networking—of indigenous peoples and NGOs—independent of the UN, and perhaps "more grassroots" in nature, also has played an important role in the formation of such movement. However, the role of the UN in the global indigenous rights movement does not mean that indigenous organizations and individuals may not have their own interests, goals, strategies, values, and ideologies that are informed by their unique political cultures, or that they do not often have differences. However, the experiences at the WGIP and the framing of the struggle for indigenous rights under the umbrella of human rights have been instrumental for the creation of a high degree of cohesion among indigenous organizations and participants, in turn strengthening the international struggle for indigenous rights.

Despite all of the logistical and political problems of presenting a global indigenous position through teamwork, the meetings of indigenous caucuses within the UN, such as the Asian Indigenous Caucus and the International Indigenous Youth Caucus, are fundamental for indigenous organizations and the consolidation of the international indigenous movement for rights. There are few other international spaces in which debates and negotiations among indigenous peoples and between them and other individuals can take place in such a regular and intensive way. The information presented at the caucus meetings is important because it summarizes the latest happenings in international forums and establishes a foundation for conciliating a collective position on various issues, even though it sometimes is impossible to achieve this goal.

Indigenous delegates who regularly attend the UN meetings have a wide array of experiences as activists, organizers, lawyers, scholars, film producers, community elders, and officials in intergovernmental organizations or UN bodies and specialized agencies. Indigenous intellectuals and activists have used UN spaces to organize and build alliances, international networks, and coalitions with other delegations, nongovernmental organizations, academics, state officials, and the experts and representatives of the different bodies and specialized agencies within the UN system.

Sylvia Escárcega

See also: Countries—Mexico. Issues—International Policy; United Nations Declaration.

Further Reading

Alfredsson, Gudmundur. "International Discussion of the Concerns of Indigenous Peoples: The United Nations and the Rights of Indigenous Peoples." *Current Anthropology* 30:2 (1989): 255–259.

Anaya, S. James. *Indigenous Peoples and International Law.* New York: Oxford University Press, 2004.

Bratenberg, Terje, Janne Hansen, and Henry Minde, eds. *Becoming Visible: Indigenous Peoples and Self-Government.* Tromsø, Norway: University of Tromso, Centre for Sami Studies, 1995.

Charters, Claire, and Rodolfo Stavenhagen, eds. *Making the Declaration Work: The United Nations Declaration of the Rights of Indigenous Peoples.* Copenhagen, Denmark: International Work Group for Indigenous Affairs, 2009.

Dunbar-Ortiz, Roxanne. *Indians of the Americas: Human Rights and Self-Determination.* London: Zed, 1984.

Eide, Asbjørn. "Indigenous Populations and Human Rights: The United Nations Efforts at Mid-way." In *Native Power: the Quest for Autonomy and Nationhood of Indigenous Peoples,* ed. Jens Brøsted and Jens Dahl. Bergen, Norway: Universitetsforlaget AS, 1985.

García-Alix, Lola. *The Permanent Forum on Indigenous Issues.* Copenhagen, Denmark: International Work Group for Indigenous Affairs, 2003.

Làm, Maivân Clech. *At the Edge of the State: Indigenous Peoples and Self-Determination.* Ardsley, NY: Transnational Publishers, 2000.

MacKay, Fergus. "The Draft World Bank Operational Policy 4.10 on Indigenous Peoples: Progress or More of the Same?" *Arizona Journal of International and Comparative Law* 22:1 (2005): 65–73.

Niezen, Ronald. *The Origins of Indigenism: Human Rights and the Politics of Identity.* Berkeley: University of California Press, 2003.

Roulet, Florencia. *Human Rights and Indigenous Peoples: A Handbook on the UN System.* Copenhagen, Denmark: International Work Group for Indigenous Affairs, 1999.

Sanders, Douglas. "The UN Working Group on Indigenous Populations." *Human Rights Quarterly* 11:3 (1989): 406–33.

Stamatopoulou, Elsa. "Indigenous Peoples and the United Nations: Human Rights as a Developing Dynamic." *Human Rights Quarterly* 16:1 (1994): 58–81.

Wilmer, Franke. *The Indigenous Voice in World Politics.* Newbury Park, CA: Sage, 1993.

Industrial Development

Industrial development is fundamental to economic development, as evidenced by the Industrial Revolution that began in the eighteenth century. Not unlike the Industrial Revolution, contemporary industrial development is deemed a normal route to development.

But for all of the good that has resulted, and for all of industrial development's potential to improve standards of living and augment political sovereignty and governance, critics are quick to point out that industrial development continues to rely on progressively scarcer resources, located increasingly greater distances from the core production and consumptions zones. Improved technology helps facilitate access to such resources by curtailing the cost of exploration and exploitation. Often overlooked, however, is the fact that modern industrial processes both reproduce and perpetuate the methods instigated by the Industrial Revolution—methods that historically have threatened indigenous peoples living in peripheral resource zones.

The Industrial Revolution unleashed innovative approaches to economic development that forever altered human consumption patterns. With industrial development came the need to expand beyond regional confines to procure the resources needed to fuel new resource-dependent economies.

Earlier in history, the need for resources was not an issue in Great Britain, for example, because of the population's ability to establish new settlements on nearby uncultivated lands, which helped relieve overpopulation while satiating the growing thirst for resources. But the growth of even larger, permanent settlements required expansion into outlying resource zones. Eventually, this demand obliged expansion beyond Britain's borders and into indigenous territories on the African continent, in India, and in North and South America.

Historians often describe this expansion as part of the Columbian Exchange, referring to the global exchange of plants, animals, and human populations. Such simple phrasing, however, ignores the complexity of the consequent cultural interaction. Further, European interests benefited substantially from this exchange, while the introduction of destructive diseases into indigenous populations undermined their ability to resist territorial incursions.

Competing monarchs—for instance, in Belgium and France—adopted colonial development models as well, and soon global resource competition was the norm. Politics and economic development became synonymous, in turn, leading to the emergence of global colonialism and imperialism.

Four discrete development paths evolved, leading to the expansion of colonial powers into peripheral resource zones, thereby challenging indigenous predominance. First, export-driven industrialization developed from high-yield agriculture and centralized industry in Britain was replicated throughout Europe. Second, Germany, Italy, Japan, and Russia, despite their late arrival to the Industrial Revolution, focused on localized industrial development. Third, European countries such as Denmark, the Netherlands, Sweden, and Switzerland developed internally competitive industries.

Fourth and perhaps most important, resource-privileged countries such as Australia, Canada, and New Zealand—all former imperial colonies—exploited indigenous territories to impel industrial development. This was deemed permissible based on embedded European stereotypes that portrayed indigenous peoples as ignorant fools, unaware of the considerable natural resource wealth in their midst. This, combined with a lack of indigenous industrial development and land utilization directives, only confirmed the European colonial conviction (beliefs passed down to subsequent colonial governments) that accessing resource-laden territories and establishing colonies was as much an act of salvation as it was an act of economic development and imperial expansion.

Concepts such as *terra nullius* (no man's land) were fashioned to justify colonial expansion and thus indigenous territorial dispossession. Once local markets and colonies had been established, European officers and economic leaders attempted to transform native modes of production to better reflect European industrial development mores.

Industrial development internationally, and the attendant incursion into indigenous territories, rarely was questioned. Great thinkers such as John Stuart Mill and colonial officials such as Lord Cromer, Egypt's de facto leader of the late nineteenth century, and Lord Curzon, the viceroy of India, openly supported economic and political expansion's vitality and the need for localized industrial development in a growing imperial network.

Interestingly, the Geneva-based League of Nations, created after World War I in 1919 at the urging of U.S. President Woodrow Wilson "for the purpose of affording mutual guarantees of political independence and territorial integrity to great and small states alike," supported this expansionism. Member countries during this period willingly embraced political ideologies that stressed international cooperation and global economic growth, which allowed officials to set aside indigenous concerns. Taking root within this milieu was a hegemonic global political system of nations represented by states that were free from external political coercion.

The reaffirmation of the principle of noninterference in states' internal affairs followed as international leaders seized control of crafting new categorizations of nationhood, statehood, and sovereignty in order to strategically silence domestic and international concerns about the treatment of indigenous populations. These new hierarchies did not recognize indigenous peoples as bona fide or legitimate political actors—hence, indigenous leaders' attempts to define their communities as sovereign bodies with economic development rights were not recognized. Indigenous land claims were denied by the same political participants who were seeking to bolster their own territorial claims as they pursued economic reform through the extant system of recognized states and sovereignty.

Industrial development continues to threaten indigenous interests as a result of the rapid international consumption of scarce resources, demanding swift industrial expansion into outlying zones. In recent decades, however, the rights of indigenous peoples in these regions have gained recognition, and many modern political leaders have been criticized for their aggressive tactics in acquiring resources on native-held lands. Before the mid-twentieth century, these resources were deemed free and available to be exploited by the technologically advanced mainstream societies, but now native peoples are demanding that their ownership rights are respected.

Reports from Indonesia chronicle indigenous resistance to logging interests seeking territorial access, while others document the damage wrought to the Modhupur Garh in Bangladesh by industrial agricultural techniques. The United Nations Declaration on the Rights of Indigenous Peoples underscores the importance of this issue in its inclusion of several articles intended to protect indigenous peoples from economic exploitation.

For example, Article 5 seeks to ensure that indigenous peoples have "the right to maintain and strengthen their distinct political, legal, economic, social and cultural institutions." Article 17 advocates that states "take specific measures to protect indigenous children from economic exploitation." Article 20 identifies a need to ensure that "indigenous peoples deprived of their means of subsistence and development are entitled to just and fair redress." Finally, Article 32 states that efforts must be directed "to mitigate adverse environmental, economic, social, cultural or spiritual impact."

Despite these proposed safeguards, industrial development of native lands has continued. National governments and large corporations have pressured native peoples to accept the presence of these exploitive industries on their lands, just as they pressured them for their resources, and even the land itself, in the past. When pressure does not produce the desired result, often governments and businesses have simply confiscated resources, arguing that such actions are justified as being in the national interest. Thus, native lands remain a windfall to non-native industrial developers. The continued support by industries of consumer lifestyles has resulted in the continued exploitation of the resource-rich periphery that indigenous leaders call their homelands.

Yale D. Belanger

See also: *Issues*—Colonialism; Globalization; Land Rights; Oil and Mineral Rights; Water Rights.

Further Reading
Chomsky, Noam. *Year 501: The Conquest Continues.* Cambridge, MA: South End, 1993.
De Rivero, Oswaldo. *The Myth of Development: The Non Viable Economies of the 21st Century.* New York: Zed, 2001.
Ray, Arthur J. *The Canadian Fur Trade in the Industrial Age.* Toronto, Canada: University of Toronto Press, 1990.
Ray, Arthur J., and Donald Freeman. *"Give Us Good Measure": An Economic Analysis of Relations Between the Indians and the Hudson's Bay Company Before 1763.* Toronto, Canada: University of Toronto Press, 1978.
Stewart-Harawira, Makere. *The New Imperial Order: Indigenous Responses to Globalization.* London: Zed, 2005.

International Policy

Indigenous peoples' rights are an important item on the international human rights agenda, and a number of international institutions have sought to recognize the rights of indigenous peoples. However, countries traditionally have shown a reluctance to include provisions in international treaties that clearly recognize indigenous peoples' rights, and international organizations have tended to address indigenous peoples' rights and interests from their own perspectives, often acting to achieve their specific goals and targets.

One problem is that there is no common international definition of indigenous peoples in international human rights instruments. Diverse opinions exist as to whether such a definition is even needed. At the same time, one of the central issues in defining indigenous peoples is self-determination, and recognition of the right of indigenous peoples to self-determination in international law has become difficult.

Native peoples also continue to be impacted by historical legacies of disrespect and systematic rejection and devaluation of their culture. In most countries in the Americas, this situation dates to colonization, since the time of the first encounters between indigenous peoples and European colonizers. Calls for nations to respect all human rights and the fundamental freedoms of indigenous peoples have been made, such as the Vienna Declaration and Programme of Action adopted by the 1993 World Conference on Human Rights, which set out a more concrete definition of human rights, and the Durban Declaration and Programme of Action adopted in 2001 by the World Conference against Racism, Racial Discrimination, Xenophobia and Related Intolerance, which dealt specifically with the racist outcomes of European colonialism.

International organizations and government meetings, through numerous statements and documents, have acknowledged the role and contribution of indigenous peoples to sustainable management of lands and water, health, horticulture, agriculture, climate change, sustainable development, the combat of desertification, biodiversity conservation, and culture. In addition, the exploitation of indigenous peoples' knowledge and technologies has attracted considerable attention, and interest in the rights of indigenous people has increased in the international community. Despite this interest, indigenous peoples still face serious problems in meeting their basic needs.

International concern arose from the recognition of the common problems faced by many indigenous peoples, such as poverty, poor health care, attacks on their culture, and religious and linguistic suppression. Many of these problems are rooted in the application of policies such as urbanization, assimilation, and marginalization. International organizations and governments have taken steps to address these problems.

Member states of the United Nations (UN), UN agencies, and other intergovernmental organizations, along with indigenous peoples' organizations and other nongovernmental organizations, have developed numerous activities or adopted progressive policies to deal with indigenous matters. A significant achievement came in 1971 when the UN Sub-Commission on Prevention of Discrimination and Protection of Minorities commissioned Special Rapporteur José R. Martinez Cobo to conduct a comprehensive study of discrimination against indigenous peoples. In addition to examining the scope of discrimination in existence worldwide, the study called for a definition of indigenous peoples to be used by UN agencies and NGOs. Furthermore, the UN commissioned special rapporteurs (experts) on the human rights and fundamental freedoms of indigenous

INDIGENOUS SUMMITS

Indigenous peoples from around the world regularly meet to assert their rights; express their claims, concerns, and aspirations; exchange their knowledge and experience; and assess their contribution to the sustainable use and management of nature. Summits provide an opportunity for indigenous peoples to engage with a wide range of perspectives on issues of their own interest and on the growth of indigenous advocacy. These summits serve to support the recognition of indigenous rights, advance the indigenous agenda, identify basic principles, and put forward a set of proposals.

In addition, native peoples have participated in as many regional and international forums as possible to advocate respect, recognition, promotion, and protection of their human rights. This includes participation in United Nations agencies and relevant world conferences, workshops, and symposia to raise global awareness of indigenous peoples' issues, including the World Summit of Indigenous Cultures, the Continental Summit of Indigenous Peoples, and the Indigenous Peoples' Global Summit on Climate Change. Cultural rights and rights to land, water, territories, and natural resources are central, as is the right to self-determination.

Such meetings have been instrumental in expressing indigenous peoples' demand for their prior informed

consent regarding activity on their traditional lands and rejection of the unsanctioned actions of private economic interests, such as forestry and extractive industry projects, as well as in voicing environmental concerns. Further, indigenous peoples also have resisted the exploitation of their resources, knowledge, and culture, which can impact their cultural integrity, special relationship with their lands and territories, and even their survival.

To this end, indigenous people have issued numerous declarations and statements calling for the development of systems to recognize and accommodate their rights and interests. They have called for respect for their belief systems, spirituality, customary law and practices, and the development of government policies and systems consistent with their worldviews, values, needs, and traditional lifeways. And they have urged states to explore and pursue alternative means of protection and to provide adequate structural, technical, and financial support to implement their initiatives.

In recent decades, there has been a growing drive worldwide for regional, national, and international protection of indigenous peoples' rights. At the same time, indigenous peoples have been working together to set out their goals and develop solutions to ongoing issues.

Yovana Reyes Tagle

peoples to investigate obstacles to the full realization of their rights.

In 1982, the Working Group on Indigenous Populations of the UN Sub-Commission on Prevention of Discrimination and Protection of Minorities began its work of drafting the UN Declaration on the Rights of Indigenous Peoples (UNDRIP). By a vote of 143–4 (Australia, Canada, New Zealand, and the United States opposed the measure), with eleven abstentions, the UN General Assembly adopted the landmark declaration on September 13, 2007, after more than two decades of negotiations involving representatives of indigenous peoples and member states. Australia officially endorsed the declaration in 2009, Canada and New Zealand endorsed it in 2010, and the United States did so in 2011.

The declaration is a response to the current global debate on the protection of indigenous peoples. The UNDRIP protects the individual and collective rights of indigenous peoples and considers their characteristics and cultural contexts when recommending policy decisions. Although states are not legally bound by the declaration, its significance has increased, and UN agencies have expressed a willingness to use the UNDRIP as a framework for their work on indigenous peoples. In addition, the Human Rights Council, which monitors the implementation of the International Covenant on Civil and Political Rights, has requested that states report the social, economic, and political status and standing of indigenous peoples in their respective regions.

The UN proclaimed 1993 the International Year of the World's Indigenous People, with the theme "Indigenous People: A New Partnership." The need for international cooperation, technical assistance, and the implementation of programs and specific projects to address the problems of indigenous peoples in areas such as human rights, the environment, development, education, and health formed the basis for the proclamation of the first International Decade of the World's Indigenous People (1995–2004) in 1993; this was followed by the proclamation in 2004 of the Second International Decade of the World's Indigenous People (2005–2015) by the UN General Assembly. In the meantime, the Permanent Forum on Indigenous Issues, a UN body, was created on July 28, 2000, to serve as an advisory body to the Economic and Social Council, with a mandate to discuss indigenous issues related to economic and social development, culture, the environment, education, health, and human rights.

The need to protect indigenous peoples' interests has been acknowledged in a number of other international instruments. For instance, the International Labour Organization's General Conference adopted Convention no. 169 concerning indigenous and tribal peoples in independent countries on June 27, 1989. Although it became effec-

tive on September 5, 1991, as of 2012, the convention had been ratified by only twenty countries, the majority of which are Latin American nations. While this legally binding international instrument is devoted exclusively to addressing indigenous peoples' rights, it falls short in recognizing the right to self-determination.

The UNDRIP and the International Labour Organization's Convention no. 169 specifically laid out the rights of indigenous peoples. Agreements that more generally address definitions of human rights that apply to all peoples include the 1948 Universal Declaration of Human Rights; the International Covenant on Economic, Social and Cultural Rights; the UN Charter; and the International Covenant on Civil and Political Rights.

Other important international instruments that affect indigenous peoples include the 1992 Convention on Biological Diversity; the Rio Declaration on Environment and Development and Agenda 21 (chapter 26), both adopted at the 1992 Earth Summit in Rio de Janeiro; the UN Convention to Combat Desertification; the Food and Agriculture Organization's International Treaty on Plant Genetic Resources for Food and Agriculture; the UN Educational, Scientific and Cultural Organization's Convention for the Safeguarding of the Intangible Cultural Heritage; the Universal Declaration on Cultural Diversity; and the Convention on the Protection and Promotion of the Diversity of Cultural Expressions. These international instruments do not create or expressly recognize rights for indigenous peoples, but rather cite suggestions or commitments that states pursue certain actions and programs.

Some national and international policies advocate specifically for full and effective participation of indigenous peoples in matters that affect them, such as government policies, programs, and development projects. In such cases, agencies have formulated and advocated various policies for respecting indigenous peoples' culture, identity, knowledge, and other rights. For example, indigenous participation has increased considerably at the UN; some native organizations enjoy consultative status with the UN's Economic and Social Council.

To support the participation of indigenous peoples in policy formulation, some international organizations have established funds with their own resources that are open to voluntary contributions from governments and cooperative organizations. For example, the World Intellectual Property Organization established the Voluntary Fund for Accredited Indigenous and Local Communities.

Regional organizations also are concerned with the human rights of indigenous peoples and are working to address their concerns. The 1969 American Convention on Human Rights Pact of San Jose, Costa Rica, did not embrace explicit rules concerning the protection of indigenous peoples' rights. However, the 2001 Inter-American Democratic Charter, adopted by the General Assembly of the Organization of American States (OAS), issued a statement recognizing their importance and contribution to democracy and civic participation. Further, the OAS has been discussing the protection of such rights, and a Draft American Declaration on the Rights of Indigenous Peoples has been prepared.

Some countries, especially developing countries, have enacted legislation to accord some kind of protection to indigenous peoples' rights. The constitutions of Ecuador and Venezuela, for example, include provisions to protect the collective rights of indigenous peoples, such as intellectual property rights. However, most of the work done at the international level remains limited to political declarations and programs of intent. Thus, the nature of indigenous peoples' rights and the subject and scope of protection by nations worldwide have not yet been completely clarified.

Yovana Reyes Tagle

See also: Issues—Indigenous Peoples and the United Nations; United Nations Declaration.

Further Reading

Anaya, S. James. *Indigenous Peoples in International Law.* New York: Oxford University Press, 2004.

Gayim, Eyassu. *People, Minority and Indigenous: Interpretation and Application of Concepts in the Politics of Human Rights.* Helsinki, Finland: Erik Castrén Institute, 2006.

Koivurova, Timo. "From High Hopes to Disillusionment: Indigenous Peoples' Struggle to (re)Gain Their Right to Self-Determination." *International Journal on Minority and Group Rights* 15:1 (2008): 1–26.

Land Rights

The right to have access to, live on, and use ancestral and traditional lands is of fundamental importance to the cultures and livelihoods of indigenous peoples. Ancestral and traditional lands not only sustain the economies of indigenous peoples but also nourish and sustain culture, spiritual relationships, social identities, and community well-being.

Whether they hunt, herd, fish, grow subsistence crops, or practice a combination of land- and water-based activities that integrate formal and informal economies, indigenous peoples share a unique and special relationship with the environment and the animals, plants, and other resources they depend on. This relationship is essential for economic survival, social identity, and spiritual life, and it is reflected in rich mythologies, worldviews, and moral and ethical codes that guide native people in such interactions.

For herding, hunting, and fishing peoples, animals often are believed to have a spiritual essence as well as cultural and economic value. Significantly, plants, land, and water are not viewed by indigenous peoples simply as economic resources in the sense of being commodities.

The Indigenous Worldview

In the worldview of indigenous peoples, many features of the landscape in which they dwell are considered sacred—they may have significance for the origin of a community, or they may embody the essence of ancestors. Sacred places also are found along animal migration routes, especially those places where animals reveal themselves to hunters in dreams or where people encounter animal spirits while traveling.

In Alaska and Canada, for example, Athabascan oral histories describe how certain features of the landscape were originally human beings whose spirits now are embodied in aspects of the natural world. In Siberia and northern Fennoscandia, one can find places in the landscape where reindeer antlers have been left at sacred sites and adorned with gifts, or places where sacred stones have been set on mountaintops or near lakes and rivers. Sometimes, these stones are sacred in and of themselves, or they may be considered the incarnations of local spirits or deities. For the Mbendjele of Brazzaville in the Republic of the Congo, the forest connects people to the past, and different parts of the forest are related to ancestors and historical events.

From an indigenous perspective, the environment is understood to be dynamic and complex, and nature is not separate or independent from human society. As is often expressed by indigenous peoples, all human beings, animals, and all aspects of the world emanate from the same spiritual source. Such expression is found from the Arctic to the tropics—on the tundra, in forests, in deserts, and on the steppes.

A growing body of anthropological work, as well as studies by indigenous activists and scholars, shows that indigenous perceptions of the environment and people's relationships with the environment must be understood in terms of their engagement, experiences, and understanding of the land. Such engagement, experience, and knowledge also form the basis of people's social relations and interactions. Among the Inuit of Alaska, Canada, Greenland, and Siberia, for example, the souls of animals are particularly important, and ritual and ceremonial life often are devoted to ensuring that the animals hunted for food—seals, whales, walrus, polar bears, and caribou—receive proper treatment and respect.

Therefore, for indigenous communities, land is not just a historical resource but also a tie between the past and the future. Often, though, this is not understood by the state, industry, and others who seek to use and appropriate indigenous lands. For example, around the globe, indigenous communities have come into conflict with industry and government development projects related to oil, gas, mining, logging, hydropower, and other resources.

Indigenous Land and Modern Governments

In 2001, the Inter-American Court of Human Rights ruled that the Nicaraguan government had violated the property rights of the Mayangna Awas Tingni people by granting permission to a foreign company to carry out logging operations in forests on the community's traditional lands. Community leaders argued that the state had failed to demarcate the indigenous people's communal land and to take the necessary measures to protect their property rights in regard to their ancestral lands and natural resources. In its ruling, the court noted that Nicaragua's actions violated the American Convention on Human Rights, which recognizes and protects the property rights of indigenous peoples. In the court's opinion, Nicaragua had no right to grant logging concessions to a third party on the lands of the Mayangna Awas Tingni.

A similar situation occurred in northern Norway, where the government argued that a valley that was important for Sami reindeer grazing and for fishing and hunting was *terra nullius* (a Latin expression meaning "land belonging to no one") and therefore subject to the control and management of the state. The local Sami community countered that because they always had used the land, they had the right to continue occupying and using it, and that the land was theirs based on this long-established history of occupancy and cultural and economic use. The case went to the Norwegian Supreme Court, which supported the Sami position.

Local communities thus are forced to articulate the importance of the land in both traditional and contemporary ways in order to ensure the protection of important cultural and natural areas and species. In some cases, as in the foregoing examples, indigenous peoples fight such legal battles in the highest courts or international tribunals. In others, communities aim to deal directly with industry by engaging in dialogue the outsiders with commercial interests in their lands and resources.

For example, in 2005, the Gwich'in people of Canada's Northwest Territories worked to gather local indigenous knowledge about land near the route of a proposed natural gas pipeline in the Mackenzie Valley. Although they were not overwhelmingly opposed to the pipeline, their goal was to demonstrate to the project's proponents that protection of certain lands from industrial development is necessary for the continuation of Gwich'in cultural practices and traditional livelihoods. During community workshops, elders talked about a mossy area located directly on the proposed pipeline route that is known for cloudberries, an important cultural and nutritional resource. Within this area, lands that are swampy also are suitable for growing blueberries and *Ledum goelandicum,* from which the natives make muskeg tea.

For the energy companies, there was nothing significant about this marshy area, but it would be crossed by the pipeline and lay within a proposed access route for gravel development, which would be located on a high hill. This hill is known as Oo'in, meaning "look-out site" in Gwich'in. During the workshops, elders pointed out the importance of the site as a place to scan the low-lying land and keep watch for caribou, as well as its probable importance as an archaeological site. The project's proponents listened to the community's concerns, heard about local knowledge of the land, and, when possible, took such considerations into account during the planning of the pipeline route.

International Recognition

In a comment written in 1994, the United Nations (UN) Human Rights Committee stated that "the enjoyment of a particular culture may consist of a way of life that is closely associated with territory and use of its resources. This may be particularly true of members in Indigenous cultures." Further, the committee emphasized that a particular way of life may be associated with the use of—and the right to—land resources through traditional activities, such as fishing and hunting.

Article 26 of the UN Declaration on the Rights of Indigenous Peoples (UNDRIP), which was adopted by the UN General Assembly on September 13, 2007, also states the following:

> (1) indigenous peoples have the right to the lands, territories and resources which they have traditionally owned, occupied or otherwise used or acquired; (2) indigenous peoples have the right to own, use, develop and control the lands, territories and resources that they possess by reason of traditional ownership or other traditional occupation or use, as well as those which they have otherwise acquired; (3) states shall give legal recognition and protection to these lands, territories, and resources.

Such recognition shall be conducted with due respect to the customs, traditions and land tenure systems of the Indigenous peoples concerned.

The UNDRIP also acknowledges that indigenous peoples have a distinctive spiritual relationship with their traditional lands, territories, and waters. As Pedro García Hierro of the International Work Group for Indigenous Affairs put it, "Territoriality is one of the conceptual axes of the Indigenous claims platform, not only in its nature of fundamental collective right, but as an essential existential dimension of every group. Hence, its legal treatment has underlying legal repercussions on these Indigenous peoples' ability to exercise the rest of the rights they claim."

Increasingly, there is international recognition that cultural rights, including land rights, are an integral part of human rights, as expressed in Article 27 of the Universal Declaration of Human Rights and in Articles 13 and 15 of the International Covenant on Economic, Social and Cultural Rights. On October 20, 2005, the UN Educational, Scientific and Cultural Organization (UNESCO) General Conference approved the Convention on the Protection and Promotion of the Diversity of Cultural Expressions.

This convention reinforced UNESCO's Universal Declaration on Cultural Diversity (2001), a legal instrument that recognizes that cultural protection is a prerequisite for the maintenance of cultural diversity, stating that "as a source of exchange, innovation and creativity, cultural diversity is as necessary for humankind as biodiversity is for nature. In this sense, it is the common heritage of humanity and should be recognized and affirmed for the benefit of present and future generations."

In the Arctic, for example, scientific work has argued that the conservation of wildlife and ecosystems depends in part on maintaining the strength of the relationship between indigenous peoples, animals, and the environment and securing the rights of indigenous peoples to continue their customary harvesting activities. Similarly, in the Amazon region, it has been argued that, in terms of cultural and biological diversity, safeguarding traditional territories and local cultures is important for the sustainability of global ecosystems.

Land Claims

For indigenous peoples, the relationship between people and land is indissoluble, and so it follows that land rights are linked inextricably to land claims. Indigenous peoples around the globe share the historical experience of having lost, or having faced the threat of losing, their prior rights to their lands, territories, and resources as a result of colonization.

Land claims movements—and hence the assertion and reclamation of land rights—are struggles for self-determination, self-government, autonomy, and justice. Moreover, the protection of indigenous lands, the recognition of rights to lands and resources, and the settlement of land claims often are seen as essential for the survival of indigenous peoples and their cultures. Thus, the right to land is seen as inseparable from the right to life, and separation and expulsion from the land is seen as ethnocide and cultural genocide.

In the United States, cultural protection is a key policy issue for the National Congress of American Indians, illustrated by the organization's work to ensure the protection of sacred lands. For Native Americans, sacred sites are integral to the practice of indigenous religions, and thus they are inseparable from the basis of Native American culture. Concern over the destruction of sacred sites and the loss of languages and traditions is leading Native American tribes to seek to protect and preserve their cultural heritage as a part of contemporary life.

Land also is important to indigenous peoples, because it allows them to distinguish themselves from other populations within nation-states and thus to claim special legal status and legal rights by reference to their relationship to the land. This continued relationship is considered essential for the future of indigenous communities.

On occasion, and in the face of the threat of incursions by outsiders on indigenous lands and territories, some peoples have attempted to protect their culture and lands by shunning external influences completely. For instance, in remote regions of the Peruvian Amazon, a number of indigenous peoples refuse to establish sustained contact with society, although with increasing difficulty.

The Jarawa of the Andaman Islands in the Indian Ocean also are known as a people who long have avoided contact with the outside world. For the most part, their wish to remain in isolation has been recognized by India, which established the Jarawa Tribal Reserve. Current advocacy initiatives for Jarawa cultural protection, spearheaded by civil society organizations, indigenous rights groups, and scholars, are aimed at securing the Jarawa's right to territory and to choose for themselves the future they want.

Colonization processes seldom have recognized the rights of indigenous peoples to land—indeed, colonizing powers generally fail to recognize that traditional lands are homelands for indigenous communities. Land is seen as empty and thus available to be claimed by colonizers and settlers, and this leads to the violation of the territorial and cultural rights of indigenous people. For this reason, land and resource rights often are at the heart of indigenous discourses on self-determination and self-government.

Mohawk Indians in Ontario, Canada, block a road during a land claim dispute with local, provincial, and federal authorities in 2006. The Six Nations native group claimed title to a parcel of land on which a residential subdivision was planned. *(Jonathan Hayward/ AP Images)*

Recognizing Land Rights: Examples from Canada

Since the 1980s, negotiations between the Canadian government and the Inuit and First Nations (Canada's indigenous peoples) have resulted in the recognition of aboriginal rights, specifically rights to land, including, in some cases, rights to subsurface resources. The settlement of comprehensive land claims has radically altered the map in parts of Canada, particularly in the far north, where claims to aboriginal title over traditional lands remained outstanding. In most cases, these settlements and new arrangements have transformed the political, social, and economic lives of indigenous peoples, giving them an entry point into Canada's economic and social structure and yet protecting their traditional economic and social customs.

Land claims processes—in effect, modern treaties—are unique to North America in the northern circumpolar regions, and, in Canada at least, they are a first step toward self-government. Such negotiating processes have become common as the courts involved have recognized indigenous peoples' rights to traditional lands and associated resources. The Inuvialuit of the western Arctic reached a land claim in 1984, the Gwich'in did so in 1992, the Sahtu Dene in 1994, and the Inuit of Canada's Eastern Arctic were given their own self-governing territory, Nunavut, in 1999 (following a 1993 land claims agreement). In the Northwest Territories, the Tlicho (Dogrib) First Nation signed a land claims agreement with the Canadian government in 2003. Negotiations for land, resource, and self-government rights continue with the Dehcho First Nations and the Akaitcho Dene, while negotiations for self-government are in progress with the Inuvialuit, Gwich'in, and the Sahtu Dene community of Deline.

In the Yukon Territory, the Umbrella Final Agreement, reached in 1988 and finalized in 1990, is the framework for individual land claims agreements with each of the fourteen Yukon First Nations. Since then, ten First Nations have signed and ratified an agreement, two others have signed agreements that were not ratified after they were defeated in referenda, and two still are being negotiated.

In many parts of Canada's provincial North—the northern areas of Alberta, British Columbia, Manitoba, Ontario, and Saskatchewan—treaties signed between indigenous groups and the British Crown in the late nineteenth and early twentieth centuries remain in effect. The Cree and Inuit of northern Quebec signed the first modern treaty, the James Bay and Northern Quebec Agreement, with the Canadian government in 1975.

Self-determination does not mean that indigenous peoples have control over resources; rather, self-government is about being granted sufficient rights to practice autonomy effectively. For example, in the Arctic, some states have recognized the claims of indigenous peoples to land rights and self-government, and a number of significant settlements have been negotiated over the past three to four decades. Notable among these are the Alaska Native Claims Settlement Act (1971), Greenland home rule (1979), and Greenland self-rule (2009), and, in Canada, the James Bay and Northern Quebec Agreement (1975–1977), Inuvialuit Final Agreement (1984), and Nunavut Land Claims Agreement (1993). Anthropologist Jens Dahl has pointed out the importance of recognizing that, in making these claims, the Arctic's indigenous peoples, such as the Athabascans, Dene, and Inuit, are not demanding the creation of autonomous ethnic states, but rather have attempted to assert their rights as distinctive peoples within nation-states and to be recognized as having such rights.

The 1984 Inuvialuit Final Agreement extinguished Inuvialuit rights and interests in land in exchange for ownership of approximately 35,000 square miles (91,000 square kilometers) of land, cash compensation of $170 million (Canadian dollars), preferential hunting rights, participation in resource management, subsurface mineral rights to a small area of land, and a provision for future self-government. In 1992, the Gwich'in Comprehensive Claim Agreement gave the Gwich'in ownership of more than 8,600 square miles (22,000 square kilometers) of traditional lands and subsurface mineral rights to one-third of that area. Other rights and benefits include a $75 million (Canadian dollars) payment, a share of Mackenzie Valley resource royalties, participation in the planning and management of land, water and resource use, and a federal commitment to negotiate self-government. The Sahtu Dene and Métis Agreement (1994) gave beneficiaries some 16,000 square miles (41,000 square kilometers) of land and subsurface rights over 700 square miles (1,800 square kilometers), with provisions similar to those in the Gwich'in agreement. The Nunavut Final Agreement of 1993 (which preceded the establishment of the new Nunavut Territory) established fee simple title for approximately 21,000 Inuit beneficiaries to just over 18 percent of the total territory of Nunavut, which includes mineral rights to more than 14,000 square miles (36,000 square kilometers). The Inuit of Labrador signed the Labrador Inuit Land Claims Agreement in 2005, which defines the rights of the Labrador Inuit in and to their ancestral lands. The settlement area totals 27,992 square miles (72,500 square kilometers) of land in northern Labrador, including 6,100 square miles (15,800 square kilometers) of Inuit-owned lands and an adjacent ocean zone of 18,800 square miles (48,690 square kilometers).

On paper at least, these agreements have had three significant implications for aboriginal peoples in northern Canada. First, by providing cash compensation and setting resource royalty levels, they have established administrative structures and provided the financial resources to make it possible for aboriginal communities to survive and function effectively in the mainstream Canadian economy. Second, they have defined the use of lands and resources and included guarantees to aboriginal peoples for specific access to natural resources, including subsurface minerals. Third, they have initiated comanagement regimes, which are forms of shared governance, for decision making over natural resources, land use planning, wildlife management, and environmental issues. Unlike earlier agreements and treaties, which emphasized the exchange of lands for various forms of compensation, comprehensive land claims agreements in Canada's North have emphasized instead the importance of land and resource governance over land sales.

Significantly, as was the case in Alaska with the Alaska Native Claims Settlement Act of 1971, negotiation of land claims and rights to use and access to resources occurred in the midst of plans for mega-project development. While indigenous people have been misunderstood as taking an antidevelopment stance, it is true for most that their goal is to participate in and help guide development rather than prevent it from happening.

Land claims, as well as other related legislation, have meant that aboriginal title to lands and resources and the duty to consult must be recognized by those wishing to develop lands and resources in Canada's North. As a result, aboriginal rights have been defined more clearly.

Continuing Struggles

While Canada has made significant strides in negotiating land claims settlements with many of its aboriginal peoples, some groups still face persistent difficulties in gaining recognition of their land rights. One notable case is the Lubicon Cree, a First Nation of some 500 people in northern Alberta.

The Lubicon were overlooked by treaty commissioners at the end of the nineteenth century, because they did not live near the water routes that were being surveyed. Their territory later was considered Crown lands by both the federal and provincial governments, and the Lubicon have engaged in a long-standing struggle to gain recognition of their rights to land and resources. Negotiations between the Lubicon and the federal and provincial governments remain open-ended, yet the Lubicon have experienced profound social and economic changes and poverty as a result of the erosion of their traditional activities because of logging, oil and gas extraction, and related development. The Lubicon case has been raised repeatedly in UN bodies concerned with human rights.

The Lubicon have much in common with indigenous peoples elsewhere in the world who remain engaged in struggles with state governments that fail or refuse to recognize their land rights. Indigenous peoples continue to be under considerable pressure from global market forces—the demand for natural resources means increasing interest in the availability of oil, gas, and minerals, stores of which may lie under the traditional territories of indigenous peoples. Of particular concern to indigenous peoples is land dispossession. This is felt acutely in parts of central, eastern, and southern Africa, as well as in parts of South and South East Asia.

Mark Nuttall

See also: *Issues*—Industrial Development; Political Participation; Religion (Indigenous); Self-Determination.

Further Reading

Bone, Robert M. *The Canadian North: Issues and Challenges.* New York: Oxford University Press, 2009.

García Hierro, Pedro. "Indigenous Territories: Knocking at the Gates of Law." In *The Land Within: Indigenous Territory and the Perception of the Environment,* ed. Alexandre Surrallés and Pedro Garcia Hierro. Copenhagen, Denmark: International Work Group for Indigenous Affairs, 2005.

Huertos Castillo, Beatrice. *Indigenous Peoples in Isolation in the Peruvian Amazon.* Copenhagen, Denmark: International Work Group for Indigenous Affairs, 2004.

Jentoft, Svein, Henry Minde, and Ragnar Nilsen, eds. *Indigenous Peoples: Resource Management and Global Rights.* Delft, Netherlands: Eburon, 2003.

Lewis, Jerome. "Forest People or Village People: Whose Voice Will Be Heard?" In *Africa's Indigenous Peoples: "First Peoples" or "Marginalized Minorities"?* ed. Alan Barnard and Justin Kenrick. Edinburgh, UK: Centre for African Studies, University of Edinburgh, 2001.

Nuttall, Mark. *Pipeline Dreams: People, Environment, and the Arctic Energy Frontier.* Copenhagen, Denmark: International Work Group for Indigenous Affairs, 2010.

Nuttall, Mark, and Terry V. Callaghan, eds. *The Arctic: Environment, People, Policy.* Amsterdam, Netherlands: Harwood, 2000.

Language

Of the 6,909 languages spoken across the globe in 2009, 389 languages were spoken by 94 percent of the world's population, leaving the remaining 94 percent of languages spoken by only 6 percent of the world's people. The National Geographic Society's Enduring Voices Project, which seeks to preserve those endangered languages, predicts that half of them will no longer be spoken by the year 2100 as they are replaced by national languages used by the mass media.

Today, dialects of Chinese are spoken by 1.2 billion people, Spanish by 329 million, and English by 328 million, while dialects of Arabic are spoken by 221 million people. However, many indigenous languages are spoken by only a few hundred speakers.

These figures, of course, are only estimates, and both linguists and speakers do not always agree on whether two tongues are dialects of the same language or, in fact, two completely different languages. Linguists still are learning about languages spoken in remote areas of the world, and according to the National Geographic Society, every fourteen days, another language becomes a "sleeping language" as its last surviving speaker dies.

In a sense, all languages of the world are indigenous. All natural languages are rooted in the land and people of a particular place at some time in history. Although some languages have spread across the world, most remain tethered to small, isolated communities.

Military conquest is a major reason for language spread. During the colonial period, conquering nations often enforced the use of their language in the education of indigenous children and banned the use of indigenous languages. Today, language loss is accelerating as people become less isolated, a result of more rapid means of transportation and the flood of radio, movies, television, and other mass media, which drowns out the voices of indigenous peoples. In addition, many companies require their employees to speak a national or world language such as Chinese, English, or Spanish.

Different and Divergent

Languages are studied by linguists, who still are learning more about how languages work and how they differ. All languages are complex and sophisticated. Although humans can produce a wide variety of sounds, any given language uses just a fraction of those sounds, and in different ways. Languages such as French and Navajo have nasal vowels that sound to English speakers like a half-pronounced "n" at the end of the vowel. German and Navajo both use glottal stops in their word pronunciation. In East Africa and a few other places, speakers of "click" languages use a variety of clicking sounds to denote consonants.

In addition, some languages use tone or pitch to distinguish word or grammatical meaning—that is, to distinguish or inflect words. All languages may use pitch to indicate emphasis, but in tonal languages, of which Chinese is the most widely spoken, words are differentiated solely by tone. Some American Indian languages, such as Navajo, are tonal and use a writing system that notes high tones.

Linguist Noam Chomsky theorized, and most linguists accept today, that the human brain is wired from birth to speak and understand language. Language is arbitrary—that is, the meanings that make language understandable are agreed upon within a group, and over time, those meanings change to fit new situations. Linguists have documented such changes in written languages.

For example, English evolved from Geoffrey Chaucer's time, to Shakespeare's time, to today, with pronunciations changing and new words being added or changing in meaning. If an English speaker used the word *corn* before the sixteenth century, he or she actually would have been referring to wheat, but when European explorers discovered a new plant in the New World, maize, they used the old word *corn* to describe it.

Since the twentieth century, rapidly evolving technology has required the creation of whole new words or new meanings for old words. In their effort to keep their language alive, activists in Hawaii formed a language committee to coin new words so that Hawaiian could remain a living, vital language used to teach science, technology, and other subjects in schools.

Chomsky also theorized that there is an underlying commonality to the grammar of languages. However, as linguists analyze more of the world's diverse languages, it is becoming harder to find any deep structural similarity. That is not to say that most languages cannot be grouped into families and subfamilies—groups of related languages that share some common characteristics such as vocabulary, syntax, and ancestry.

Languages develop as a result of isolation. For example, when a group of people speaking a language split up and lose contact with one another, they begin to speak dialects of the original language and, eventually, new languages that become mutually unintelligible over a period of centuries. This is the case for the "linked languages" in Australia: Aborigines that are spread over 1,000 miles are able to speak with their neighbors, but the groups that are farthest apart cannot understand one another.

After several thousands of years of separation, descendant languages become very different from one another, making it hard for linguists to find any commonalities between them. In fact, linguists can estimate when languages diverged from one another based on the degree of difference between the languages. However, because some groups borrow words from their neighbors' languages more readily than others, it is difficult to precisely date these hypothesized separations.

To complicate matters, a few language isolates, such as Basque in Spain and Zuni in the United States, defy grouping into any known family of languages. There have been attempts to link some American Indian languages, including Zuni, to European and Asian languages, including Welsh and Japanese; however, most linguists find that these claims lack adequate evidence.

The Written Word

Languages appeared in human history long before writing systems were developed, and some languages today remain unwritten. Chinese, Hebrew, and Sanskrit have some of the earliest writing systems. Chinese originally was written using symbols that stood for different words; there are hints at pronunciation in these symbols today. The Japanese, with a very different language, adapted the Chinese logographs to their own language, although today, they also have two other writing systems that they can use. Alphabetic writing systems were developed in the Middle East, where different symbols or letters stood for different sounds.

Writing systems for the world's most spoken languages developed over time. But they often seemed to make writing and reading unnecessarily difficult, as the same sound or sounds could be spelled in different ways, or the same spelling could be pronounced differently in different words. For example, in English, we have "to," "too," and "two"—all homophones—and we use the same spelling of the verb *read* to indicate both its past and present tense, though the words are pronounced differently. This makes learning to read English much more difficult than if it employed a writing system with a one-to-one sound–symbol relationship.

In a few cases, indigenous peoples in modern times developed their own writing system for their language, such as the syllabary developed by Sequoyah for the Cherokee language. But for most unwritten indigenous languages today, linguists have helped develop writing systems that use a one-to-one sound–symbol relationship, making it much simpler to learn to read the language if one speaks it.

Most indigenous languages historically lacked writing systems, though the Aztec, Epi-Olmec, Maya, Mixtec, and Zapotec in Central America used hieroglyphic writing systems, as did the Egyptians in Africa. Christian missionaries developed writing systems in many languages, mostly in order to translate Christian texts. One example is John Eliot's *Indian Bible,* which was printed at Harvard University in 1663. Other missionaries produced dictionaries that still are useful today, such as Stephen Riggs's *Grammar and Dictionary of the Dakota Language* (1852) and the Catholic Franciscan Fathers' *An Ethnologic Dictionary of the Navajo Language* (1919).

Today, the faith-based nonprofit organization SIL (Summer Institute of Linguistics) International, founded in 1934 and headquartered in Dallas, Texas, is in the process of translating the Christian Bible into all the languages of the world. The organization, which is "committed to serving language communities worldwide as they build capacity for sustainable language development," also is working to develop orthographies for all of them.

The Languages of the World

The *Ethnologue* language database lists 2,110 languages spoken in Africa, 993 in the Americas, 2,322 in Asia, 234 in Europe, and 1,240 in the Pacific. It is in Africa, where scientists have found evidence of the earliest humans, that there is the most linguistic diversity. In Nigeria alone, there are 521 different languages representing most of the African language families.

The languages of Australia, Indonesia, and the many other islands of the Pacific Ocean—making up what is called Oceania—illustrate how the people who colonized the islands developed unique languages over time. Today, some 1,200 languages are spoken in the region. Seafarers some 6,000 years ago spread out across the islands of the Pacific and Indian oceans. Papua New Guinea alone has more than 800 languages. The Austronesian language family represents approximately one-quarter of the world's languages.

In Asia, the Sino-Tibetan language family includes the many Chinese dialects. Mandarin Chinese is spoken by more than 1 billion people—more than any other language in the world. However, the largest language group is the Indo-European family, with more than 2.7 billion speakers living on the Indian Subcontinent and across Europe.

Hindi, an Indo-European language of India, is a descendant of Sanskrit, the language of Buddhist and Hindu religious texts. Sanskrit has been compared to Latin, and vice versa, in terms of its influence on later languages. Indo-European languages are believed to have originated among peoples who lived somewhere in Eastern Europe; their descendants moved eastward into India and westward as far as the British Isles and, more recently, to the Americas, Australia, and New Zealand. Indo-European descendants include Latin and the Romance languages, as well as the Celtic, Germanic, Slavic, and Uralic languages.

While Old English dates back at least seven centuries to the Germanic languages, American Black English, a newer dialect, dates to the importation of African slaves to the New World. English has borrowed words from hundreds of languages, including many American Indian languages, especially the names of animals, plants, and places that were new to Europeans.

In the Americas, linguists estimate that nearly 1,000 languages, classified into more than 100 language families, were spoken when European colonists first arrived. James Estes listed 154 indigenous American languages still spoken in the United States in 1999, representing several different language families, with Navajo having more than 100,000 speakers and seven languages with only one speaker.

In Canada, the *Ethnologue* database estimates that Cree has 80,550 first-language speakers, and in Mexico, Nahuatl, the language of the Aztec, has more than 1 million speakers. Various dialects of Quechua, the language of the Inca, still are spoken by millions of people in Bolivia, Ecuador, Peru, and elsewhere in South America. The vast differences among American Indian language families indicate that speakers have lived in the Americas for many thousands of years.

Language, Culture, and Meaning

One of the interesting aspects of language that is studied by linguists and anthropologists is the tie between language and culture. Some indigenous people believe that their culture will die if their language dies. This view is supported by the Sapir-Whorf hypothesis, the linguistic theory that the semantic structure of a language shapes or limits the ways in which a speaker forms conceptions of the world, developed by Edward Sapir and Benjamin Lee Whorf.

Recent linguistic studies also indicate that different languages structure the world differently. English speakers say that an object is to their left or right, but in some Australian Aboriginal languages, position is determined by direction—objects are situated to the west, east, north, or south of the speaker. Linguist Sean O'Neill's study of the Hupa, Karuk, and Yurok languages in Northern California found that even though these groups speak languages belonging to different language families, their cultures are quite similar because of commonalities in their environment.

Many indigenous people view their language as embodying their culture. According to Jon Reyhner and Jeanne Eder in *American Indian Education: A History* (2004), this view was expressed by a Cheyenne elder, who said,

> Cheyennes who are coming toward us are being denied by us the right to acquire that central aspect of what it means to be Cheyenne because we are not teaching them to talk Cheyenne. When they reach us, when they are born, they are going to be relegated to being mere husks, empty shells. They are going to look Cheyenne, have Cheyenne parents but they won't have the language which is going to make them truly Cheyenne.

Linguist Sally Midgette uses as an example the Navajo word *hózhó* to demonstrate the difficulty of translating concepts from one language to another. This word can mean "peace," "harmony," or "beauty" in English. But it is not just the meaning of words that makes translation difficult. English also uses verbs to indicate whether an action took place in the past, present, or future, but that is not the case in many other languages, even though they certainly distinguish when an action occurred.

An Athabascan language such as Navajo uses different verbs to show whether an action is instantaneous, repeated, or takes a long time. Unlike English, which is an analytic language, Navajo is a polysynthetic language. In analytic languages, sentences are made up of relatively short and simple words; polysynthetic languages use long, complex words with roots, prefixes, and suffixes that are sequenced in a particular order. Thus, it is possible to translate a whole sentence in English into one polysynthetic word. For instance, the Navajo word *naa'ahélgo'* can be translated as "I pushed them and made them fall over one after another."

Members of the Lepcha tribe, indigenous to the northern Indian state of Sikkim, demonstrate in Kolkata for the inclusion of their language in education and government. Literally thousands of the world's native languages now face extinction. *(Deshakalyan Chowdhury/AFP/Getty Images)*

Languages such as Navajo incorporate nouns into verbs, such as "we are going berry-picking" (verb), whereas an English speaker would say, "We are going to pick berries" (verb plus noun). Different languages also vary word order. Whereas English uses a subject-verb-object order, some languages of the Amazon basin use an object-verb-subject word order.

Language Policies and Language Rights

Many indigenous people today are working to reverse the language loss caused by colonial education polices and efforts in many countries to promote national unity by privileging the national language. They blame many of the social problems that they face today on the effects of losing their indigenous languages and cultures.

As fewer and fewer children learn to speak indigenous languages, a generation gap is created in families whereby the children speak only a world language such as English, the parents are bilingual, and the grandparents

speak only the indigenous language. Besides the obvious impact on cross-generational communication within family groups, such a language gap may inhibit cultural transmission to younger generations, thus leading to a further loss of culture.

In response, efforts are being made across the world to protect and revitalize indigenous languages. For example, in the 1980s, several American Indian nations, such as the Navajo, enacted language policies that supported the teaching of native languages in schools. As Navajo Tribal Chairman Peterson Zah stated in 1984, they believed that education could produce academic achievement in modern-day subjects, as well as teach American Indians about their language, culture, and history. In 1986, Hawaiian language activists were able to get an 1896 state law barring the use of their language in schools repealed. In 1990, the U.S. Congress passed the Native American Languages Act, which made it U.S. policy to "preserve, protect, and promote the rights and freedom of Native Americans to use, practice, and develop Native American languages."

Several linguists have argued that indigenous language revitalization efforts help bring generations of people together and make elders feel valued. Among Native Americans, many who are engaged in language preservation efforts have spoken of having had a sense of rootlessness and despair that was ameliorated when they were taught to speak their native languages by their grandmothers. Often, they regained a sense of their identity and their culture. In many cases, tribal elders want to pass on their knowledge and wisdom to the younger generation, but they are unable to do so because young people do not know their native languages. Richard Littlebear, president of Chief Dull Knife College in Montana, concluded that his Northern Cheyenne language could be an antidote to the forces enticing the youth of his tribe into joining gangs.

Traditionally, indigenous peoples viewed their languages as sacred gifts from the Creator. They also can be a path to wellness as traditional values are recovered. The Maori in New Zealand and Native Hawaiians, for example, have been among the most successful groups in revitalizing their languages. Both have pre-kindergarten to higher education indigenous educational programs available that use their native languages as the medium of instruction.

The United Nations (UN) has been in the forefront of promoting human rights, including language rights. In 1948, the UN General Assembly adopted the Universal Declaration of Human Rights, which states that "[e]veryone has the right to education" and that "[p]arents have a prior right to choose the kind of education that shall be given to their children."

The UN's Convention on the Rights of the Child, which entered into force in 1990, states that education should be directed to "[t]he development of respect for the child's parents, his or her own cultural identity, language and values," as well as "for the national values of the country in which the child is living, the country from which he or she may originate, and for civilizations different from his or her own." Only Somalia and the United States have not ratified this convention.

In 1993, the UN declared 1993 the International Year of the World's Indigenous People. UN Secretary General Boutros Boutros-Ghali wrote that allowing native languages, cultures, and different traditions to perish through "nonassistance to endangered cultures" must be considered a basic violation of human rights.

In 2007, the UN adopted the Declaration on the Rights of Indigenous Peoples by a vote of 143–4, with only Australia, Canada, New Zealand, and the United States opposing the measure. All four have since have reversed their position. The declaration affirms that indigenous peoples have "the right to revitalize, use, develop and transmit to future generations their histories, languages, oral traditions, philosophies, writing systems and literatures, and to designate and retain their own names for communities, places and persons" and "the right to establish and control their education systems and institutions providing education in their own languages, in a manner appropriate to their cultural methods of teaching and learning."

In November 1999, the UN Educational, Scientific and Cultural Organization (UNESCO) proclaimed the first International Mother Language Day, and since 2000, February 21 has marked the annual celebration of linguistic and cultural diversity and multilingualism. The UN General Assembly declared 2008 the International Year of Languages, and UNESCO Director-General Koïchiro Matsuura affirmed that "[l]anguages are indeed essential to the identity of groups and individuals and to their peaceful coexistence. They constitute a strategic factor of progress towards sustainable development and a harmonious relationship between the global and local context."

As a result of globalization, many countries are becoming more tolerant of linguistic and cultural minorities within their boundaries. Thomas Hammarberg, commissioner for human rights for the Council of Europe, which includes forty-seven member countries, argued in 2010 that the use of minority languages is important for modern societies, as such usage protects the rights of minority groups and encourages bilingualism, which is an important skill in creating understanding among cultures. A shift away from the colonial and postcolonial emphasis on promoting a single national language can be seen in Kenya's new constitution, approved by its people in 2010, which obligates the state to promote and protect the linguistic diversity of its people.

Jon Reyhner

See also: *Issues*—Education; Indigenous Identity; Literature; Social Customs.

Further Reading

Boutros-Ghali, Boutros. Foreword to *Voice of Indigenous Peoples: Native People Address the United Nations,* ed. Alexander Ewen. Santa Fe, NM: Clear Light, 1994.

Campbell, Lyle. *American Indian Languages: The Historical Linguistics of Native America.* New York: Oxford University Press, 1997.

Estes, James. *How Many Indigenous American Languages Are Spoken in the United States? By How Many Speakers?* Washington, DC: National Clearinghouse for Bilingual Education, 1999.

Fishman, Joshua A., ed. *Can Threatened Languages Be Saved? Reversing Language Shift, Revisited: A 21st Century Perspective.* Clevedon, UK: Multilingual Matters, 2001.

King, Janette. "'Whaia Te Reo: Pursuing the Language': How Metaphors Describe Our Relationships with Indigenous Languages." In *Nurturing Native Languages,* ed. Jon Reyhner, Octaviana V. Trujillo, Roberto Luis Carrasco, and Louise Lockard. Flagstaff: Northern Arizona University, 2003.

Kroskrity, Paul V., and Margaret C. Field, eds. *Native American Language Ideologies: Beliefs, Practices, and Struggles in Indian Country.* Tucson: University of Arizona Press, 2009.

Lewis, M. Paul, ed. *Ethnologue: Languages of the World.* 16th ed. Dallas, TX: SIL International, 2009.

Littlebear, Dick. "Effective Language Education Practices and Native Language Survival." In *Effective Language Education Practices and Native Language Survival,* ed. Jon Reyhner. Choctaw, OK: Native American Language Issues, 1990.

Lyovin, Anatole V. *An Introduction to the Languages of the World.* New York: Oxford University Press, 1997.

Midgette, Sally. "The Native Languages of North America." In *American Indian Studies,* ed. Dane Morrison. New York: Peter Lang, 1997.

National Geographic Society. *Enduring Voices Project.* www.nationalgeographic.com/mission/enduringvoices/.

O'Neal, Sean. *Cultural Contact and Linguistic Relativity Among the Indians of Northwestern California.* Norman: University of Oklahoma Press, 2008.

Reyhner, Jon, ed. *Teaching Indigenous Languages.* Flagstaff: Northern Arizona University, 1997.

Reyhner, Jon, and Jeanne Eder. *American Indian Education: A History.* Norman: University of Oklahoma Press, 2004.

Skutnab-Kangas, Tove, and Robert Dunbar. "Indigenous Children's Education as Linguistic Genocide and a Crime Against Humanity? A Global View." *Gáldu Cála: Journal of Indigenous Peoples Rights* 1 (2010): 1–126.

Literature

The literature of native peoples, whether oral and collected or written specifically for publication and external transmission, is as diverse in form, style, and theme as the literature of immigrant populations. Before the late twentieth century, most scholars and commentators tended to regard oral literature, in particular, as largely spontaneous expressions of tribal history and culture, unrehearsed and uncomposed, or else as extraordinary feats of memory, displays of metrical and verbal skill, or renditions of the historical, spiritual, or cultural wisdom of the tribe. While these elements do play an important part in the creation and performance of the literature, such works are by no means always spontaneous. Rather, they play an important role in transmitting the ideas and values of a culture, and many demonstrate a remarkable stability over time.

The academic study of the literature of native peoples dates to the 1960s, influenced by the work of anthropologists and literary theorists such as Franz Boas, Roman Jakobson, Edward Sapir, and Benjamin Lee Whorf. Thanks to the efforts of poets and scholars in North America, such as Dell Hymes, Jerome Rothenberg, and Dennis Tedlock, scholarly work initially focused on the peoples of that continent. But the approach of these scholars—and the development of theoretical and performative frameworks such as ethnopoetics—has resulted in a broadening of the field to include the study of the literature of native peoples on every continent.

The Oral and the Written, the Sung and the Spoken

Works such as *Beowulf,* the Maya *Popol Vuh,* the Chinese classic *Tao Te Ching,* and the books that make up the canonical text of the Bible constitute cultural and historical expressions of the cultures that produced them and originally were written in the languages and scripts of those people. Travelers and missionaries tended to record the literatures of other cultures for the benefit of their own cultures, rather than for that of the authors themselves. These situations, and the various methods of recording the texts, resulted in the recording of specific types of literature.

While religious and historical texts were written down as a matter of course, poetry, narrative, and drama often were not recorded. When these oral forms of literature were preserved, it was almost exclusively by non-natives, presumably because orality implies memorization and transmission and negates the need for such recording.

In terms of oral literature, the difference between prose and poetry is in the delivery. In many cultures, there is an explicit relationship between prose and historical narrative, on the one hand, and poetry and spiritual literature, on the other. As much of this material overlaps, however, there is much evidence indicating that the shaman, the poet, the myth teller, and the historian frequently were one and the same person.

The error of seeing native literature as a literature of stasis in the past, and not of development in the present, has created a default view of orality as premodern. To view the literary endeavors of native peoples as a vibrant and contemporary art, however, necessitates an acceptance not only of modern forms and themes and styles, but also of new information technologies, such as video, computer, and cell phone, as literary media. Possibly the best modern examples of this are forms such as Jamaican dub poetry, Algerian *raï* (a type of folk music), and the poetical lyrics of hip-hop.

Africa

Precolonial African literature is marked by the centrality of a professional literary class, particularly in West Africa, such as the Zulu *imbongo* (storyteller) or the Wolof *griot* (a wandering musician and poet), whose job was to create so-called praise songs and to openly discuss their royal patron's rulership. One of the functions of this poetry—similar to the role of the fool in medieval European courts—was to keep the ruler in check. These praise songs relate to the prose forms of epic and myth, insofar as they comment on the present using historical and metaphysical elements. The performance of the mythic, then, is a socially significant avocation, one for which a person is trained and prepared and for which they must be able to select accurately and interpret creatively from a vast cache of material.

The intent of the fictional texts, which one might characterize as epic, legend, and myth, is primarily to describe the origins of the world, the origins of the people, and the nature and behavior of the world. Traditionally, it was believed that to possess knowledge about something is to have power over it. Therefore, the narratives and the lessons they present offer a combination of natural wisdom and tribal history, both educating and entertaining the listeners, while at the same time benefiting the group.

Poetic texts are primarily religious, divinatory, and incantatory prayers, used with the understanding that language—human beings' unique gift, possessing a transformative magic—has the power to shape the world. The Yoruba *ofà* is the most comprehensive and voluminous of such religious texts, being used extensively by the *ifà* (priests) in different circumstances. In addition to religious texts, poetry as song was used for ritual battle, to address arguments, to ease heavy work, to praise oneself and others, or simply for entertainment.

The colonization of Africa by Christian—Belgian, British, French, and Portuguese—and Islamic groups brought to the literature both external spiritual influences and the expansion of the written word, which previously had been restricted to small and exclusive groups (for instance, among the Kpele of Liberia and the Calabar of Nigeria). While Islam proscribes the translation of the Qur'an, vernacular poetry came to be widely used for the purposes of religious instruction, as in the development of Islamic Hausa poetry.

The influence of Christianity came not only from the Bible but also from vernacular classics such as John Bunyan's *Pilgrim's Progress*. The first works of Christian-inspired vernacular literature were composed in Sesuto—Thomas Mofolo, who wrote in Sesuto, is regarded as the first South African vernacular author—Xhosa, and Zulu.

Mofolo's novels, such as *Chaka* (1939) and *Pitseng* (1942), mixed African history with Christian mission and addressed the tension that resulted from that mix.

The development of African literature during the twentieth century focused on the themes of colonization and race and the problems inherent in independence. Drama, which grew explicitly from ritual and religious performance, was influenced during the colonial and postcolonial periods by European and American theater, reflecting the tensions between the experience of indigenous and immigrant communities.

Central and South America

The societies in pre-Columbian Central America were sedentary (rather than nomadic), and thus their literature was concerned with the preservation of social cohesion. The Aztec and Nahua peoples both used hieroglyphic writing systems, and their manuscripts include religious, scientific, and historical texts, as well as poetry.

Poetry almost exclusively was chanted, presumably to clapping or drumming, and so it exhibits a strong metrical and alliterative framework; only in the highest echelons of society was poetry divorced from music. Rulers were expected to be poets as well, and so poetry exercised a powerful, and perhaps even exclusive, social force.

Central American poetry included lyrics and epics, dramatic poetry, and riddles, proverbs, and aphoristic verse. Following the Spanish conquest, Christian themes began to appear in poetry, especially in dramatic narrative verse, but there remain explicit pre-Columbian elements in contemporary dramas about the Passion, the cult of the Virgin Mary, and the Day of the Dead festivities.

Many of the literary texts of the Central American Maya—such as the *Popol Vuh* anthology and the calendrical *Ahilabal 3ih* (*Count of the Days*)—are highly esoteric mathematical and spiritual treatises, presented principally in the form of prose, with occasional verse of poetic couplets. They appear to be records of a culture rather than the creative works of individuals.

The three principal Aztec texts—the Dresden, Paris, and Madrid codices—address divination and medicine, astronomy and astrology, and the relationship between divination and agriculture, respectively. The poetic literature, a style called "flower and song," referring to its all-consuming use of natural imagery, was practiced by warriors during times of peace. The lack of extant secular poetry suggests that poetry was exclusively religious.

The most extensive native literature in South America is that of the Inca, composed predominantly in the Quechua language. Like the Maya, Quechua texts frequently express aspects of the spiritual and the scientific through poetry. Pre-Columbian Quechua poetry can be divided into two forms—the lyrical *hauri* and the epic *haylli,* which generally were chanted to the accompaniment of musical instruments. Poetry was used to communicate with the sun god but, following the period of colonization, this form became Christianized and fell into abeyance. Dramas such as *Ollantay* record the colonization of the Inca. Modern Quechua literature retains these lyrical and dramatic styles, as in the work of Peruvian novelist José María Arguedas during the 1930s–1960s.

The literary cultures of peoples who made contact with the outside world only in the last decades of the twentieth century, especially those in the Amazon, have scarcely been studied. Of special interest, perhaps, are the Pirahã of the Amazon, who appear to have almost no oral or material culture whatsoever.

Groups such as the Shavante in Brazil exhibit ritual keening, whereby individuals are able to show joy, sadness, or pride. Keening, a nonlinguistic form, is associated with dream and with nonmundane reality and tends to blur the distinction between speech and song. The metaphorical complexity and sonic richness of such performances, similar perhaps to the Sami *joik,* indicate the individual's interaction with his or her society and with the spirit world.

East Asia and Oceania

The central focus of East Asian literature is the classical literature of China. During the Tang dynasty (618–907 C.E.), formal poetry refined the traditional lyric and romantic styles through rigid metrical and syllabic constraints. In time, the relaxation of these forms allowed for the introduction of realism and narrative techniques. The gradual stagnation of classical poetry resulted in the development of *ci,* or popular song, which has roots in Central Asia.

The Confucian and Taoist influence on Chinese literature can be seen in texts such as the *I Ching* (ca. 800 B.C.E.) and the *Classic of Poetry* (ca. tenth–seventh century B.C.E.). Such spiritual and divinatory texts, together with military works, show how traditional

JOSÉ MARÍA ARGUEDAS

Arguably the *indigenista* writer closest to Quechua culture, José María Arguedas often is considered Peru's greatest novelist, topping polls run by the journal *Hueso Húmero* in both 1979 and 2007. Arguedas stressed the tensions between the indigenous and *criollo* (locally born people of mostly Spanish heritage) cultures, writing in a lyrical prose that was built on the incorporation into Spanish of Quechua linguistic structures and, frequently, Quechua lyrics. (He wrote poetry in Quechua toward the end of his life.)

Born in the town of Andahuaylas on January 18, 1911, Arguedas spent much of his childhood among Quechua-speaking servants and members of the *ayllu* (agrarian community). His novels are rooted in his biography. *Agua* (*Water,* 1935) details the interactions of the child Ernesto with the indigenous workers in his uncle's hacienda, as well as the struggles between the local ayllu and the latifundists (owners of large estates) over water use. In *Los Ríos Profundos* (*Deep Rivers,* 1958), arguably his masterpiece, Arguedas describes the painful experiences of the protagonist, also named Ernesto, a youth clearly influenced by Quechua worldviews who is taken from Cuzco to a boarding school in Abancay, where he is a witness to growing social tensions. Arguedas's novel *El Sexto* (*The Sexto,* 1961) is loosely based on the months that he spent in prison in 1937–1938, after participating in a demonstration against the visit of an Italian fascist dignitary.

His lifelong interest in anthropology (he became a professor in 1950 and earned a doctorate in 1963) is reflected in *Yawar Fiesta* (1941), which narrates the reactions of different groups in Puquio—migrants living in Lima, local landowners and middle class, and the local indigenous population—to the banning of the indigenous bullfight, in which the animal is killed with dynamite. *Todas las Sangres* (*All Bloods,* 1964) is a portrayal of the Andes on the verge of social explosion as the struggle between latifundists and *comuneros* (joint land owners) is heightened by the presence of foreign mining corporations.

The posthumous novel *El Zorro de Arriba y el Zorro de Abajo* (*The Fox from Up Above and the Fox from Down Below,* 1971) is composed of two narrative strands. The first documents Arguedas's struggle with suicide. The second, incomplete at the time of his death in 1969, examines the lives of migrants from the Andes in the fishing boomtown of Chimbote.

In addition to his profound influence on Peruvian literature of the mid-twentieth century, Arguedas also has had a major impact on Latin American cultural theory. Contemporary ideas about hybridity and the borderlands proposed by theorists Homi Bhabha and Gloria Anzaldúa clearly are prefigured in Arguedas's rousing speech "No Soy un Aculturado" (I Am Not an Acculturated Man, 1968).

Juan E. De Castro

concerns such as self-protection and interactions between humans and gods related to the cohesion and development of society.

With the exception of the Ainu, whose epic *Kutune Shirka,* which was passed down through centuries of oral tradition, specifically reflects an Arctic tradition, the literature of Japan was influenced heavily by that of China, although earlier material probably would have covered the myth, spirituality, and tribal history of Altaic and maybe Polynesian peoples. Much the same could be said of the Korean tradition and that of the Mongols and Manchu, too, all of which were founded in Central Asia. This poetry is primarily alliterative and, even today in Mongolia, based on nomadic lifeways and concerned with nature and the ancestors.

Much as set forms defined classical Tang dynasty poetry, so traditional Japanese poetry, though religious and mythic in origin (the first recorded poetry in Japan was ascribed to the god Susanoo, younger brother to the sun goddess Ameterasu), came to be defined by such forms as *renga* (collaborative poetry) and *haiku,* which likewise deal with particular topics such as the changing seasons and romantic love.

Filipino and Indonesian literatures converge in their thematic and stylistic material, including oral epics, poetry, chant, and drama. The many indigenous Filipino groups each have their own epic narrative, and the influence of Christianity and Islam resulted in more contemporary epics. Indonesian traditions have likewise been influenced by Islam and Hinduism, such as the reworking of the ancient Sanskrit epic, *Ramayana,* in *wayang kulit* (shadow plays).

The literature of the native peoples of Oceania and Australia is concerned primarily with creation myths. For example, among the native peoples of Australia, the "dreaming" narratives of individual groups, which describe the creation of the world, are passed on according to specific rules regarding gender and age. This is literature that, through its repetition, preserves the Aboriginal conception of the world for those who recite it—told not so much for entertainment as out of necessity.

The literature of Polynesian islanders, such as the Fijians, Hawaiians, and Maori, is founded in narrative and poetry based around the feats of gods, humans, and animals. These texts, often in the form of chants, also frequently recount genealogy and the interrelationship between peoples of different islands. The development of Creole and pidgin tongues, together with the introduction of Christianity, resulted in new forms of indigenous literatures, such as hymns and the reworking of religious texts.

Europe

The classical Western canon of European literature in ancient Greek and Latin shares similarities with the writings of Semitic and Eurasian peoples that later came to be called fairy stories, or folk stories. The word *fairy* derives from a Proto-Indo-European root indicating a wild animal, and these were stories like those of the Native Americans about coyote or buffalo—tales of animals and their interaction with the human world. The classical literatures of Greece and Rome—encompassing lyric and epic poetry, drama, comedy, philosophy, and history—clearly developed to some extent out of these earlier oral forms. Texts such as Homer's *Iliad* (ca. 800–725 B.C.E.) and Virgil's *Georgics* (29 B.C.E.) indicate the influence of oral traditions on epic and nature poetry. These traditions, moreover, exercised great influence on the literature written throughout Europe until the Renaissance, which, in turn, influenced popular writers such as Cervantes, Goethe, and Shakespeare.

The development of literature throughout Europe was primarily oral until texts, such as the Anglo-Saxon *Beowulf* (ninth to eleventh century), Marie de France's *lais* (twelfth century), Snorri Sturluson's Norse *sagas* (thirteenth century), and the Old High German epic *Muspilli* (ninth century; thought to be a retelling of the Norse *Ragnarök,* about the end of the world), began to be written down. Much medieval literature was based on the growing importance of Christianity, and the tensions between the native religion and Christianity were played out in these texts, along with older themes such as transformation, dreams, laments, love, and tribal history, which are common to other native literatures.

The Celtic poets in particular, being on the edge of Europe, retained their oral traditions throughout the medieval era, and the Old Irish and Old Welsh poets were greatly esteemed for their spiritual wisdom, literary ability, and professional standing. There is a tradition in Welsh verse of praise poetry, not unlike the tradition in West Africa, and this still is presented at *eistedfoddau* (festivals), which have been reintroduced to promote traditional literature. The Sami people in the north of Scandinavia share thematic and cultural similarities with Arctic societies such as the Inuit and Yupik. The tradition of Sami chanted poetry is founded in the *joik,* which are performed without musical accompaniment and are one of their most meaningful cultural and spiritual expressions.

The effect of the presence of the individual in the composition of poetry has resulted in a highly creative tension between tradition and improvisation in many diverse cultures, from the medieval Iberian *trobador* and Germanic *Minnesänger* (a singer of lyrical songs) to the epic poets of the Balkan region and the Turkish *aşiklar* (troubadour). The simultaneous performance and composition in these poetries suggest that, throughout Europe, as perhaps in other cultures, the interplay of the oral and the written played a vital part in literary culture during the medieval period and thereafter, and that narrative storytelling, and thus drama, developed directly from lyric poetry and from the performative culture of the epic.

North America

The wide diversity of landscape and climate that defines North America, and the complex relationships among more than 600 native cultures, produced a corresponding breadth of literary themes and styles. Moreover, the locations of these different societies—some adjacent to the sea, some on the plains, some in the warm south, and some in the cold north—make what previously was thought of as one society of "Indians" a vital and nuanced set of cultures, similar to those of Australia or Europe.

Literature before European colonization depended for its thematic material on the nature of the society, whether nomadic or settled, and its geographic location. The primary material focused on creation stories and the interrelationship between humans and the natural world. The natural elements reflected an individual people's experience, so that, in the Northwest, fish feature prominently in the stories of the Kwakiutl and Tlingit, while the Plains peoples, such as the Cherokee and Kiowa, focus on animals such as the coyote and buffalo.

The Southwestern peoples, sedentary and thus sharing concerns about social cohesion, often used sung poetry within religious ceremonies, a trend that also was taken up over the border in Mexico and beyond into South America. Elsewhere on the continent, religious poetry was used to praise and entreat the gods, while secular poetry was employed for personal and communal benefit.

In the far north of the continent, the literature of the Inuit in modern-day Alaska and Canada has similarities with that of peoples to the south, to the east (Greenland), and to the west (Siberia). Much of this literature consists of historical (mythic) narratives or biographical (often first-person) narratives, and frequently (as might be expected in such a harsh climate) deals with loss (such as an orphaned child) or with revenge.

The interaction among peoples resulted in a literature of war songs, histories of battles, and biographical narratives of heroes. With the arrival of the Europeans in the seventeenth century, these texts tended toward recording individual events. Moreover, the introduction of Christianity, exposure to Western diseases such as smallpox and measles, and the gradual spread of alcohol among native peoples were recorded in the literature throughout the continent.

The traditional forms of native literature—epics, short poems, epigrams, mythic and historical narratives—also were transformed through contact with European writings, such as the Bible. This interaction produced a hybrid literature, hymnodic poetry for instance, or the reworking of biblical material.

Although contemporary native literature in North America does not explicitly blur distinctions between peoples, there is a focus on unity. The primary interest in contemporary literature is on poetry, and relatively few novels appeared until the 1970s, when writers, such as Simon Ortiz (*Fight Back: For the Sake of the People, For the Sake of the Land*, 1980) and Leslie Marmon Silko (*Ceremony*, 1977), began to publish. In the Arctic, moreover, contemporary literature frequently is exchanged at elders' conferences, and there is a growing tradition of rendering such works in English. Since the late twentieth century, radio and the Internet have become important media for the preservation and development of native literature throughout the continent.

South Asia and the Middle East

The oldest written pieces of literature thus far recorded are Sumerian texts, such as the 2700 B.C.E. *Instructions of Šurrupak*. Epic, history, and poetic (predominantly religious) texts from the same period, such as *Gilgamesh* and various Egyptian and Akkadian writings, show an unusual level of thematic and stylistic sophistication.

Such early religious and admonitory texts developed into the genre of wisdom literature, for instance, the Egyptian *sebayt* and the biblical Book of Proverbs. The fact that these bear similarities to counsel and proverbial texts from other cultures indicates an obvious societal commonality.

The rich popular oral and written literature of Hebrew and its various developments such as Ladino and Yiddish attest to the complexity of the Hebrew diaspora and to the breadth of its chronological and intercultural expression. In particular, Hebrew is remarkable for the development of its stories and folktales and for the presence of characters such as the *dybbuk*.

The earliest Indic texts, the Vedas, were primarily religious and included both metrical verse to be chanted and prose commentaries. This literature contains the earliest written exemplars of Hindu culture, from which the Sanskrit and Prakrit literatures (including Buddhist texts in Pali) developed, and it is from the language and philosophy of the Vedas that later Indic texts (such as the Upanishads and the Sūtras) developed.

The *Ramayana* (ca. 400 B.C.E.) and the *Mahabharata*

(ca. 200 B.C.E.) epics, together with the *Manu-smriti* (*Laws of Manu,* first century C.E.), illustrate the ways in which the earliest Indic societies conceived of their origins and governance and the explicit role played by the interaction of divine and human figures. Texts such as these not only suggest a preliterate tradition of such interaction within Indic society, but also reflect traditions of the north (Nepal, Tibet) and of non-Indo-Aryan cultures such as the Kannadu, Tamil, and Telugu, indicating the possibility of ethnic interaction and concomitant trade relations.

Prior to the introduction of writing from India to Southeast Asia—and the consequent influence of Hinduism and, later, Buddhism—the oral literature of peoples such as the Khmer and Mon consisted of legends, songs, poetry, and historical accounts. Some of these came to be recorded in epigraphic stone monuments.

The literary development of native peoples in Central Asia reflects the predominance of nomadism throughout the region. What came to be called the Silk Road had long before been of geopolitical importance, and the interaction between cultures as far apart as the Chinese and the Slavs resulted in a rich diversity in narrative, drama, and poetry among the peoples along this corridor. The importance of mnemonic, alliterative verse and of equine themes—in addition to those of romance, the natural world, the ancestors, and the gods (the last were considered to be physically present within the landscape)—are features vital to the literature of the Altaic and Turkic peoples. Notwithstanding both the development of printing and the forces of Soviet nationalism, such verse, and its declamatory performance, has remained a central part of the culture.

The Implications of Intercultural Contact

The broad developmental trajectory of societies and cultures between continents and between nations and their peoples seems to point to a shared literary heritage. With the exception of some isolated groups, such as the Amazonian Pirahã, mythological and epic poetry explaining the origins and history of a given people appear to be universal, as does rhythmic poetry (whether or not accompanied by music) defined by some aspect of meter, alliteration, or rhyme. Drama comes generally from ritual, and therefore it may be called shamanic (or at least religious) in origin.

With the introduction of writing, certain literatures (religious, historical, scientific) became privileged and were committed to written text, whether for their own sakes or as *aides memoire.* The destruction of indigenous texts (for instance, of Aztec texts by the Christian conquistadores in Mexico during the sixteenth century) illustrates the threat that non-Western literatures posed to Western conceptions of the world. This threat continued in various forms through the centuries, from the colonial era (sixteenth through nineteenth centuries) into the twentieth century.

During the twentieth century, the resurgence of native people's political and cultural power around the world has been felt primarily in modern media, notably radio, television, and the Internet. Today, poetry, fiction, and drama are being used to express both what is particular to a given native people and the connections that native peoples may have with other cultures with which they come into contact.

Simon Wickham-Smith

See also: Groups: Central and South America—Maya; Quechua. *Groups: East Asia and Oceania*—Indigenous Australians. *Countries*—China. *Issues*—Indigenous Identity; Language.

Further Reading
Beissinger, Margaret, Jane Tylus, and Susanne Wofford, eds. *Epic Traditions in the Contemporary World: The Poetics of Community.* Berkeley: University of California Press, 1999.
Chadwick, Nora K., and Victor Zhirmunsky. *Oral Epics of Central Asia.* Cambridge, UK: Cambridge University Press, 1969.
DeLoughery, Elizabeth M. *Routes and Roots: Navigating Caribbean and Pacific Island Literatures.* Honolulu: University of Hawaii Press, 2007.
Dunsmore, Roger. *Earth's Mind: Essays in Native Literature.* Albuquerque: University of New Mexico Press, 1997.
Finnegan, Ruth. *Literacy and Orality: Studies in the Technology of Communication.* Oxford, UK: Blackwell, 1988.
———. *Oral Poetry.* London: Cambridge University Press, 1977.
Hymes, Dell H. *Now I Know Only So Far: Essays in Ethnopoetics.* Lincoln: University of Nebraska Press, 2003.
Kroeber, Karl, ed. *Traditional Literatures of the American Indian: Texts and Interpretations.* Lincoln: University of Nebraska Press, 1981.
Lord, Albert B. *The Singer of Tales.* Cambridge, MA: Harvard University Press, 1960.
Nicholson, Irene. *Firefly in the Night: A Study of Ancient Mexican Poetry and Symbolism.* London: Faber and Faber, 1959.
Priebe, Richard K., and Thomas A. Hale. *Artist and Audience: African Literature as a Shared Experience.* Washington, DC: Three Continents, 1979.
Rothenberg, Jerome, ed. *Technicians of the Sacred: A Range of Poetries from Africa, America, Asia and Oceania.* New York: Doubleday, 1968.
Tedlock, Dennis. *The Spoken Word and the Work of Interpretation.* Philadelphia: University of Pennsylvania Press, 1983.

———. *2000 Years of Mayan Literature.* Berkeley: University of California Press, 2010.

Thompson, Stith. *The Folktale.* Berkeley: University of California Press, 1977.

Trask, Willard R., ed. *The Unwritten Song: Poetry of the Primitive and Traditional Peoples of the World.* London: Jonathan Cape, 1969.

Logging Rights

The world's forests are home to countless native peoples, and for those groups, almost invariably form an integral part of their cultural and religious orientation. Forest rights have been an issue for native peoples throughout their history, but particularly beginning with European colonization when methods of deforestation intensified. Thus, colonialism and industrial development from the seventeenth through the nineteenth centuries proved disastrous to many native groups, and that disaster was only compounded during the twentieth century.

Most of the world's 9.8 billion acres (4 billion hectares) of forests are owned and administered by governments. The logging practices of non-native peoples historically have tended to degrade and destroy the forests, while, at the same time, ignoring the natives' right to use and preserve those environments. As a result, logging in these forests has resulted in severe damage to indigenous cultures and livelihoods. Nevertheless, traditional native lifeways have continued, often reflecting wise forest management, based on the ideas and practices of ecosystem management even before it was called that.

It has only been during the late twentieth and early twenty-first centuries that nations and international bodies have begun to recognize native logging rights, although this recognition remains uneven, with many native groups, such as those in the Amazon rain forest, still being forced to flee before the onset of clear-cutting deforestation. In a number of cases, native peoples have gained and exercised logging rights themselves, sometimes as part of conservation strategies designed to empower indigenous peoples as forest stewards.

Logging Without Consent

Frequently, governments grant logging rights to large corporations. In other cases, illegal loggers operate without the permission of native peoples or trade overpriced equipment and goods in exchange for undervalued timber. In either case, natives suffer loss of access to forests, loss of the value of logged trees, depletion of game and other wildlife, destruction of sacred places, and often loss of land as colonists settle along old logging roads.

In Indonesia, for example, 70 percent to 80 percent of the land is considered state forest, where logging concessions routinely are given to influential private firms. These concessions often overlap with native people's lands, and logging destroys the natives' rattan gardens and other sources of forest products. Natives lose access to forest resources and gain, at best, poorly paid and dangerous jobs.

In Guyana and Suriname, governments in financial distress have granted extensive concessions to forests inhabited by natives to large foreign companies, including some of the same Indonesian and Malaysian firms associated with forest degradation and violations of native land rights in Asia. Similarly, the Bolivian government has allocated many forest concessions that overlap with land claimed by native peoples.

Forest Tenure Reform and Native Logging Rights

Particularly since the mid-1980s, however, native peoples have found ways of making their land claims heard in national and international venues. Governments have recognized land rights in some cases, but not in others, and have begun to devolve forest management responsibility to forest inhabitants. Between 1985 and 2002, governments transferred or recognized rights to 494 million acres (200 million hectares) of land to forest communities, many of which are indigenous.

In 2012, about 74 percent of the world's forests still was administered by governments, 2 percent was the property of governments but assigned to forest communities, 14 percent was private property, and 9 percent was the property of communities. There is substantial variation among regions, however. In the developing world, communities control about 27 percent of the forest area.

Sometimes native peoples have used their land claims to halt logging concessions. In Nicaragua, for example, the Supreme Court declared certain logging concessions unconstitutional and upheld the territorial rights of the native people. While such conflicts between logging firms and the indigenous peoples continues, native territorial rights increasingly are recognized by governments and courts. As of 2012, the countries in the Amazon River Basin had more than 2.4 million acres (1 million hectares) of forest under community ownership.

Communities exercise rights to harvest and sell timber in parts of many countries, including Bolivia, Cameroon, Chile, China, Guatemala, Honduras, India, Mexico, Nepal, Nicaragua, Senegal, Vietnam, and Zimbabwe. In the United States, 199 Indian reservations manage 10.4 million acres (4.2 million hectares) of forests, more than half of which produce timber. Small, community-operated

A native fisherman explores a destroyed mangrove forest in the Aceh region of Indonesia. Illegal logging concessions in that country routinely intrude on indigenous lands, while unfettered slash-and-burn clearing has had a devastating environmental impact. *(Heri Juanda/AP Images)*

logging businesses also operate in parts of Guyana and Papua New Guinea. In India, there are approximately 106,482 Joint Forest Management Committees covering 54 million acres (22 million hectares) of forests. In Nepal, more than 15,000 community forest user groups manage approximately 3 million acres (1.2 million hectares) of national forests. In both countries, however, forest departments play a central role in management and often claim a share of the proceeds from timber sales.

Countries such as Canada, Guatemala, and Laos are adjusting logging concession systems to include native communities. The Guatemalan government grants timber concessions to natives and long-term colonists as a strategy to stop newcomers from moving into protected areas and clearing the land for crops and cattle pasture. In Laos, although the government is unwilling to recognize local ownership, it sometimes grants fifty-year management contracts to local communities. In Canada, following intense environmental protests against conventional concessions, the province of British Columbia transferred logging rights to Iisaak Forest Resources, a joint venture between Weyerhaeuser Limited and a coalition of native peoples.

Even when native logging rights are recognized, communities continue to struggle with limited management powers, illegal logging, and competition from cheaper wood on the global markets.

Meanwhile, the area of industrial logging concessions greatly exceeds the area of forest designated for use by, or owned by, communities and indigenous peoples. As prices for biofuels and other agricultural products continue to rise, industrial claims on forest lands are increasing, often at the expense of native peoples.

Conservation and Native Rights to Use Forests

Approximately 12 percent of the world's forests are located in protected areas that severely restrict the ability of native people to log or even to enter the forests that they claim. In an effort to reduce emissions of carbon dioxide and other greenhouse gases as a result of deforestation, a new global initiative is under way, Reducing Emissions from Deforestation and Degradation in Developing Countries, under the United Nations Framework Convention on Climate Change. This program eventually may include billions of dollars of annual payments for carbon emissions avoided by forest conservation. There are concerns among both native populations and nongovernmental organizations, however, that uneven regulation and poor management of such programs may unfairly limit the uses to which native peoples are allowed to put their forests.

Shrinidhi Ambinakudige and Dan Klooster

See also: *Issues*—Ecosystem Management; Industrial Development; Land Rights.

Further Reading

Larson, Anne M., Deborah Barry, Gange Ram Dahal, and Carol J. Pierce Colfer, eds. *Forests for People: Community Rights and Forest Tenure Reform.* Sterling, VA: Earthscan, 2010.

Lindenmayer, David, and Jerry F. Franklin. *Towards Forest Sustainability.* Washington, D.C.: Island Press, 2003.

Menzies, Charles R., ed. *Traditional Ecological Knowledge and Natural Resource Management.* Lincoln: University of Nebraska Press, 2006.

Springate-Baginski, Oliver, and Piers Blaikie, eds. *Forests People and Power: The Political Ecology of Reform in South Asia.* Sterling, VA: Earthscan, 2007.

Media

Historically, the mainstream media has been unkind to native peoples, with depictions of first peoples ranging from violent brutes and noble savages to warrior tribes and vanquished peoples. Even contemporary representations often portray native groups as primitive, childlike, or preindustrialized over more realistic depictions.

Print, video, and broadcast media all have been guilty to varying degrees of presenting a stereotypical Westernized view of indigenous peoples, with little regard for how they see themselves or how they want others to view them. The struggle of native peoples to take control of their image and voice has a long history but has accelerated in recent decades with the emergence of global indigenous rights movements and broader access to computer and other digital technology.

Early Native Media

In the nineteenth and early twentieth centuries, attempts to acculturate native populations by state, religious, and commercial authorities resulted in the development of indigenous-language newspapers. Some indigenous groups advocated the use of the written word as the most efficient means of spreading information and dealing with nonindigenous authorities.

In the United States during the 1820s, for example, the Cherokee created a syllabary that associated Cherokee phonetic syllables with symbols and published the *Cherokee Phoenix,* the first Native American newspaper. Printed in Cherokee and English, the newspaper served to unite the different Cherokee townships within its range of distribution. Later, in an attempt to broaden its appeal, the newspaper changed its name to the *Cherokee Phoenix and Indians' Advocate* as it began addressing issues relevant to all native peoples, such as assimilation and forced relocation. The newspaper ceased publication in 1834, and the printing press used to produce it was removed by the Georgia National Guard the following year.

In Africa, missionaries promoted African-language newspapers that at once proselytized and provided a medium for native expression. In 1837, the Wesleyan Methodist Missionary Society founded *Umshumayeli Wendaba* (*Publisher of the News*), the first black newspaper in South Africa. The periodical ran fifteen editions in the Xhosa language until 1841. *Ikwezi* (*The Morning Star*), founded by the Glasgow Missionary Society and published in coordination with the Wesleyan Methodist Missionary Society, lasted from 1844 to 1845 and included an assortment of articles that ranged from stories about Xhosa prophets to accounts of Christian converts.

Growth of Native Media in the Twentieth Century

In Latin America, the early twentieth century saw efforts to transform the image of indigenous people through the writings of nonindigenous—usually mestizo, that is, people of mixed European and indigenous heritage—intellectuals. The *indigenista* movement was a concerted effort to celebrate Latin America's indigenous past, while calling attention to the challenges that native peoples faced in the present. In the writings of José María Arguedas and the paintings of Diego Rivera, for example, native peoples were presented in a favorable light, but indigenous social and economic advancement depended on the intervention of a benevolent state.

This period also saw the growth of the political left and the emergence of indigenous organizations as part of it. Invariably, their interests coincided and alliances were formed. Socialist and communist publications often featured articles on the plight of native peoples.

In Ecuador, from the 1930s to the 1960s, a Spanish-Quechua bilingual newspaper called *Ñucanchic Allpa* (*Our Land*) was published periodically. Created and edited by indigenous activists and nonindigenous supporters, it originated as a voice for indigenous peoples and labor unions and later became the organ for the Federación Ecuatoriano de Indios (Ecuadorian Federation of Indians). Topics in the newspaper ranged from land and water rights to the abolition of forced labor and the preservation of indigenous culture and language.

The 1930s also saw indigenous people make inroads in visual media. Most notable was the photography of Martín Chambi, who is recognized as one of the first indigenous photographers in the Americas. Chambi's work included portraits of native townspeople in the Peruvian highlands and landscapes in and around Cuzco. His prints captured images of native peoples on their own terms, often revealing a sense of pride. They found a wide audience, both in Peru and abroad, and often were converted into postcards.

In the United States, the 1960s and 1970s saw the rise of the Red Power movement and the appearance of three major Native American newspapers: *Indian Voices, Akwesasne Notes,* and *Wassaja.* These periodicals addressed issues that resonated with native peoples in the form of news stories and opinion pieces. From 1970 to 1976, the American Indian Press Association was the source of stories and news for dozens of Native American newspapers.

During this period, the American Indian Movement (AIM) rose to prominence after orchestrating a number of high-profile demonstrations that included the takeover of the Bureau of Indian Affairs building in Washington, D.C., in 1972. AIM did not have its own media organ to present its position. A central component of AIM mobilization was the use of elaborate press conferences, the staging of protests, and the threat of confrontation to persuade broadcast and print media to air its grievances and publish its desired reforms.

In Latin America, oral history and *testimonio* projects have recorded and transcribed stories, myths, and histories of communities, as well as individual renderings of collective memories of shared experiences (both indigenous and nonindigenous). Whereas the target audience of the testimonio was typically a literate Western audience, the audience of the Andean Oral History Workshops was the indigenous villagers themselves, and its aim was to empower native peoples with a greater sense of collective identity.

Radio was the first nonprint technology that provided native peoples with a media presence. In the 1960s and 1970s, local radio stations began appearing in many parts of the developing world. These stations devoted airtime to social issues and provided native peoples with an opportunity to receive and broadcast information. Support for community radio came from the United Nations, which saw it as an appropriate medium for articulating the benefits of development projects, and from religious groups, which viewed radio as a way to get their message out to distant communities while encouraging or discouraging certain types of behavior.

For example, in the 1970s, the Baha'i Radio Project was initiated in Ecuador. The project entailed creating a community radio station run by and for the community. In addition to broadcasting Baha'i prayers, the station aired development project information, public service announcements (in Spanish and Quechua), and local and national music. Similarly, stations were developed for indigenous populations in Bolivia, Chile, Panama, Peru, and the Philippines.

Native peoples also employed radio as a means for transmitting messages to family and community members when work or other responsibilities kept them at a distance. Today, peasant and indigenous organizations in Latin America, with support from nongovernmental organizations, have created their own radio stations and have organized workshops for the next generation of media activists.

In Australia, indigenous radio stations have been airing native-language programming since the 1970s. In the next decade, the Central Australian Aboriginal Media Association (CAAMA) established an FM station that became widely popular in the Northern Territory. Broadcasting fifteen hours a day in six native languages, the station plays country and western and Aboriginal rock music, as well as talk and news programs that address Aboriginal concerns. Also during the 1980s, the National Indigenous Radio Service was created; since then, it has provided radio programming and media marketing for more than 140 indigenous radio stations.

The global politics of the 1960s and 1970s and the spread of audiovisual and cinematographic technology allowed for the emergence of film as a means of articulating the class struggle. The Cuban Revolution, for example, led the way with the creation of the Instituto Cubano del Arte y la Industria Cinematográficos (Cuban Institute of Cinematographic Art and Industry), which created scores of critically acclaimed films addressing a variety of issues, from class divisions and gender equality to Cuban history and revolutionary consciousness.

In Bolivia, the Ukamau Group pointed its cameras at Aymara miners and indigenous community members who were the objects of repression by a dictatorial state and exploitation by foreign economic interests, as well as unknowing victims of social engineering by Peace Corps workers. These films, part of the so-called Third Cinema movement of this era, critiqued U.S. imperialism and internal colonialism, especially in the Andes region, and provided alternatives to the depictions of Latin America rendered by Hollywood directors. While such films found audiences in cities and international venues, they were made for consumption primarily by indigenous and peasant viewers. The film *El Coraje del Pueblo* (*The Courage of the People,* 2011), for example, which drew from stories of a mining community, featured improvised dialogues and acting by Aymara community members.

The desire by anthropologists and politicians of the 1960s to end colonialism and to advance the cause of self-determination among indigenous peoples precipitated a shift in the field of anthropology that encouraged greater direct participation of native peoples in ethnographic studies. Consequently, in some areas, scholars undertook projects that included indigenous audiovisual training, as in the Navajo community in the Southwestern United States, with the purpose of allowing native peoples to create depictions of their culture, unadulterated by the Western gaze.

Emergence of Native-Led Networks and Native Involvement in National Networks

In Australia in the early 1970s, the Labor Party worked to improve relations and collaboration between the government and the Aboriginal people. A by-product of this cooperation was an increase in native media production.

In 1982, for example, the Warlpiri Media Association was created by the Australian Institute of Aboriginal Studies. From its inception until 1984, it produced more than fifty films that highlighted indigenous concerns, presented traditional dances, recorded historical remembrances, and broadcast local sporting events. By 1985, it was operating a low-power television station, broadcasting evening news using a homemade transmitter. Around this same time, the Aboriginal Ernabella people created Ernabella Video Television. With a small satellite dish, the network has been able to broadcast a number of videos that it has created and edited, as well as community service programs authorized by a local media committee made up of elders.

After establishing a radio station in 1980, CAAMA began producing video newsletters that were distributed to communities in Central Australia that radio signals could not reach. In 1985, fearing the culturally corrosive effects of commercial satellite television, especially with respect to language retention and the promotion of Western consumer goods, CAAMA bid on and won a broadcast license for a downlink (a link between a satellite and a ground station), the first for an Aboriginal group. By 1988, CAAMA had created its own commercial television station, Imparja, and had a viewership of more than 100,000. Its programming included current events programs, news shows, language series, Aboriginal music

programs, and a late-night talk show that featured native peoples recounting their histories and dream stories.

In addition to providing employment and income to Aboriginal people, CAAMA also has provided training to native people in media production. Australia has two national media production organizations that are supported by the state. Initiated in 1989, they are the Aboriginal Productions Unit of the state-owned Australian Broadcasting Company, whose signal reaches all of Australia, and the state-funded Aboriginal Television Unit of the Special Broadcast Service, which offers cultural and linguistic programming for the country's indigenous groups.

The Aboriginal Peoples Television Network (APTV), also established in the 1980s, is a Canadian broadcast and cable television network. Judging that there was enough interest among native people in developing their own media, and accepting that the government had a responsibility to facilitate broadcast rights and technologies so that native peoples might preserve their language and cultures, the Canadian government created and funded the Northern Native Broadcast Access Programs, the forerunner of APTV. Based in Winnipeg, Manitoba, APTV broadcasts multilingual programming related to native peoples, including documentaries, news magazines, dramas, entertainment specials, and education programs.

In New Zealand, the Maori customarily have been subject to stereotyping and negative exposure by the national media. In 2003, the Maori Television Services Act was passed, allowing for the creation of the Maori Television channel the following year. The objectives of the network were to inform, educate, and entertain; to broadcast primarily in Maori; and to focus on the needs of children participating in Maori cultural immersion education and all other people learning Maori. In 2008, a second such channel, Te Reo, was established. Offering programming solely in the Maori language during prime time, its goal is to serve the fluent Maori audience and to provide more culturally specific tribal programming. Also in 2008, recognizing that part of the problem was that the Maori had little input into how they were perceived in mainstream media, Television New Zealand revised its charter to guarantee that the Maori would be present in and consulted on program planning.

In South America, under the Bolivian government of President Evo Morales, the Centro de Formación y Realización Cinematográfica (CEFREC, Center for Cinema and Filmmaking) and the Coordinadora Audiovisual Indígena de Bolivia (CAIB, Bolivian Indigenous Media Organization) regularly produce indigenous films. In addition, these organizations enjoy an hour and a half of airtime on national television during prime time.

In Africa, the African Broadcasting Network was created in 2000 to develop the commercial television industry in the sub-Saharan region. The network's goals are to provide entertainment and educational and public service programming that reflect and reinforce indigenous cultures and values. In addition to television and broadcasting, indigenous peoples also have made significant inroads in the film industry in Africa. Hundreds of films have been created by African filmmakers since the mid-1980s, with themes ranging from political unrest to everyday life. African films tend to be ignored in the European and American press, however, and generally receive little attention in the countries where they are created. The exceptions are Burkina Faso and Tunisia, where biannual pan-African film festivals regularly take place.

Native Media, Decolonization, and Self-Representation

Indigenous organizing throughout the 1980s and 1990s shook political landscapes at the local, national, and international levels. Foremost among the demands of native peoples were constitutional recognition of pluriculturalism and concomitant rights for political autonomy. To achieve this, native peoples argued, a process of decolonization had to take place.

As indigenous demonstrations attracted the attention of the mainstream media, native peoples often found themselves subject to depictions that were based on stereotypes or incomplete knowledge. By the early 1990s, native peoples had begun to make clear that they wanted to establish their own media presence through audiovisual technology.

The appearance of indigenous media was the result of the convergence of several seemingly unrelated developments. First, many intellectuals recognized the colonial nature of research and began exploring ways to decolonize representation by helping native peoples acquire audiovisual equipment, while also providing training and consultation in the filmmaking process. This was coupled with the decision of indigenous organizations to integrate independent filmmakers into the decolonization process.

At the same time, advances in digital technology lowered the cost of cameras and computers, making their acquisition by indigenous organizations possible. More indigenous youths also have had greater access to higher education, especially in the field of communications, giving them the skills required in the media for effective self-representation. Moreover, many indigenous people who have acquired degrees have utilized their training to educate younger generations, and indigenous schools and programs have developed curricula oriented toward the recuperation of histories and traditional technologies. At the same time, indigenous media activists have begun to assume positions of national and international authority in film, video, and cinematographic organizations.

The indigenous media movement is significant on several fronts. First, control over self-representation in the media is a matter of determining how audiences (both native and non-native) see indigenous peoples—it serves both to decolonize and to empower. Second, audio and video have several pedagogical functions that serve native people's desire to preserve or reinforce their culture. Third, the implementation of indigenous media facilitates interindigenous communication and understanding. Fourth, in some parts of the world, indigenous women are included among and empowered as media producers.

Indigenous media implies control over all aspects of representation. It also entails the incorporation of traditional forms of knowledge and decision making in the formulation of a project. Indigenous media producers and activists often consult communities for possible topics and ideas on how best to represent them. The exchanges that take place are instructive as filmmakers consider the comments made by the native audience. They also draw from indigenous communities as actors. Finally, they coordinate efforts with native groups in distribution locally, nationally, and internationally.

In Bolivia, for example, production groups that include indigenous activists from diverse cultures and language groups and members of CEFREC collectively discuss scripts, editing, soundtracks, and cinematic style. For native peoples, whether in Bolivia or Australia, the process of audiovisual production strengthens the core values of native culture with respect to collective participation and decision making and reinforces the tradition of shared labor.

Audiovisual media, by its nature, is more attuned to traditional indigenous knowledge than print media. It allows native peoples to represent dimensions of their cosmology that are not always rendered accurately by the written word. Likewise, dreams and circular time sequences are easier to convey digitally or on film than in text.

Audiovisual technology has empowered native peoples linguistically as well. For one, indigenous videos in Latin America tend to be spoken in a native language, with subtitles in Spanish and/or English. The presence of indigenous languages in such films strengthens native culture and puts them on an equal footing with colonial languages. Documentaries, however, usually are presented in Spanish, recognizing that it is the lingua franca of all indigenous peoples of Latin America.

Indigenous media activists have discovered that

contemporary cinema offers genres and storylines that are well suited to indigenous subjects. These productions often include native stories, re-creations that tie the past to the present, and legends and myths that offer moral lessons. They arouse introspection, forcing the viewer to address the relevance of tradition and culture in the modern world. They also create a dialogue that explores various ways to challenge the persistence of colonialism.

For Aboriginal Australians, media production and presentation must conform to social values. Traditionally, knowledge is imparted to community members through rituals that are conducted at certain times in a person's life and at certain geographic locations. In order for film or video to be an appropriate mode of instruction, it has to abide by community mores on education. Moreover, Australia's natives often take issue with standard cinematographic conventions. Aboriginal films refrain from Western close-ups and fast cuts, preferring scenes in which entire bodies are depicted and entire scenes are recorded. The Yuendumu, a Warlpiri community, prefer landscape shots in which they can explain why the geography is filled with special meaning.

In Latin America, organizations such as the Coordinadora Latinoamericana del Cine y Video de los Pueblos Indígenas (Latin American Council of Indigenous Film and Communication) have helped train a new generation of media activists in video production, acquisition of audiovisual equipment, and organization of film festivals. In addition, anthropologists and international filmmakers have served as allies to indigenous media activists by providing cameras and technical expertise to indigenous people who are eager to create native films.

In Brazil, for example, Terence Turner repaid the Kayapó people for their participation in the making of a documentary by providing them with audiovisual technology and equipment. This resulted in the creation of a Brazilian nongovernmental organization called Video in the Villages. The Kayapó have used video to protect their territorial rights from encroachment. They also have used it to unite different Amazonian communities that historically have had tense relations and to pursue greater cooperation in order to prevent the construction of a dam on the Xingu River.

In Mexico, the Chiapas Media Project, under the guidance of independent filmmaker Alexandra Halkin, has provided access to video and computer equipment and training and has created several indigenous media production centers in southern Mexico for native peoples. Such collaboration has resulted in the training of scores of indigenous people in video production and the production of hundreds of videos that have been utilized internally and dozens that have been distributed internationally.

In addition, women have discovered media production as a powerful tool in eradicating gender inequality. In Canada, unlike Latin America, most media producers are women. In Australia, Freda Glynn, an Aboriginal woman, is the director of CAAMA.

Indigenous media projects play an important role not only in presenting native perspectives and empowering native populations, but also in the indigenous rights movements in many countries. Because audiovisual production and distribution often take place in rural areas, native peoples have established networks of knowledge beyond the metropolis. These projects allow for the exchange of perspectives and open up lines of communication among indigenous groups.

Native Media and Non-Native Audiences

Central to the indigenous media movement is distribution. Generally speaking, indigenous films are small-scale, low-budget productions that are locally based and receive little national, let alone international, attention. Whereas mainstream cinema tends to be created in distant lands and shown in urban venues, indigenous media has made a point of going to the places where indigenous peoples live.

In Bolivia, CAIB facilitators share video programs through the National Communication and Exchange Network. These distributors transport everything that might be needed to show a video or film to distant communities, many of whom do not have electricity. They often transport generators, televisions, speakers, VHS or DVD players, and videos, either by small aircraft or on foot.

These media activists also create sixty-minute video packages that include video letters, video memories related to culture, video reports or news briefs (in native languages), video stories, video debates, documentaries, docudramas, and fiction shorts from Bolivia as well as from other regions. Discussions of the materials are facilitated by local activists. Such a media package was used in Bolivia in 2006 as part of the National Communication Strategy to encourage indigenous participation and support for the native rights component of the new country's constitution. Indeed, indigenous media has become so powerful and effective that for many, from Bolivia to Australia, film, video, and television are the preferred modes of communication with nonindigenous society.

In Latin America, some states and national organizations have taken the initiative in facilitating indigenous media production. In Bolivia, for example, the National Indigenous Plan for Audiovisual Communication was created in the 1990s to devise strategies and implement processes, as well as to acquire instruments of communication, to foster indigenous media production while encouraging greater participation through education and training.

In Colombia and Ecuador, indigenous organizations such as the Consejo Regional Indígena del Cauca (CRIC, Regional Indigenous Council of Cauca) and the Confederación de las Nacionalidades Indígenas del Ecuador (Confederation of Indigenous Nationalities of Ecuador) have used audiovisual technology and the Internet to advance their demands for the recuperation of ancestral lands, culture, and language and the recognition of autonomy and political rights. Colombia's CRIC documentaries and docudramas are central to that country's bilingual education program, used alongside textbooks, compact discs, and videos. For CRIC leaders, this is part of a pedagogical approach that attempts to promote experiential learning over classroom instruction. Audiovisual media is used to revitalize the use of native languages, to resurrect traditional, sustainable agriculture, and to record history. It also has been appropriated for the articulation of demands for political rights, greater autonomy, and bilingual education.

Indigenous media organizations have expanded their reach nationally and internationally, and in doing so, they have built regional and global indigenous communication networks. CEFREC and CAIB, for example, have extended their reach beyond Bolivia and now benefit from collaboration with indigenous film makers in Brazil, Chile, Colombia, Ecuador, and Mexico.

Indigenous filmmakers recognize the commonality of indigenous movements, and they are aware of each other's work. During regional and international film festivals and training workshops, they often gather to exchange materials and share ideas. Although the cultural practices depicted in indigenous media vary based on region and ethnicity, filmmakers have discovered that they nonetheless share comparable values regarding the natural world and economic equality. Media connections are spurring a process of pan-indigenous identification that transcends the limits of national boundaries.

Kenneth Kincaid

See also: *Groups: Central and South America*—Quechua. *Groups: East Asia and Oceania*—Indigenous Australians. *Groups: North America*—Cherokee. *Issues*—Education; Self-Determination.

Further Reading
Banaji, Shakuntala, ed. *South Asian Media Cultures: Audiences, Representations, Contexts.* New York: Anthem, 2010.

Columpar, Corinn. *Unsettling Sights: The Fourth World on Film.* Carbondale: Southern Illinois University Press, 2010.

Larson, Stephanie Greco. *Media and Minorities: The Politics of Race in News and Entertainment.* Lanham, MD: Rowman & Littlefield, 2006.

Leuthold, Steven. *Indigenous Aesthetics: Native Art, Media, and Identity.* Austin: University of Texas Press, 1998.

Meadows, Michael. *Voices in the Wilderness: Images of Aboriginal People in the Australian Media.* Westport, CT: Greenwood, 2001.

Njogu, Kimani, and John Middleton, eds. *Media and Identity in Africa.* Bloomington: Indiana University Press, 2009.

Schiwy, Freya. *Indianizing Film: Decolonization, the Andes, and the Question of Technology.* New Brunswick, NJ: Rutgers University Press, 2009.

Shohat, Ella, and Robert Stam. *Unthinking Eurocentrism: Multiculturalism and the Media.* London: Routledge, 1994.

Singer, Beverly R. *Wiping the War Paint Off the Lens: Native American Film and Video.* Minneapolis: University of Minnesota Press, 2001.

Wilson, Pamela, and Michelle Stewart, eds. *Global Indigenous Media. Cultures, Poetics, and Politics.* Durham, NC: Duke University Press, 2008.

Migration

Native peoples throughout the world have migration in their histories. Many, but not all, native groups have lived a seminomadic existence at times, following their food supply in a seasonal rotation throughout the year. The Sioux tribes in the United States, for example, once followed the bison herds that roamed the Great Plains. Migration also has been experienced as a relocation from one place to another, just as the ancestors of the Bantu peoples moved from Central Africa to inhabit the eastern and southern parts of the continent.

Migration also may be forced. For example, in the nineteenth century, the Cherokee people in the United States were removed from their ancestral homelands in the American Southeast and marched to Indian Territory in Oklahoma along the infamous "Trail of Tears," experiencing the loss of approximately 25 percent of the tribe along the way because of malnutrition, disease, and exposure.

The focus here is on the modern context of migration, which frequently is necessitated by warfare or the need to find employment. Often, native people that have led a primarily rural existence are forced to find new ways of life in urban settings. Among the native peoples that have migrated since the 1980s are the Maya of Guatemala, many of whom fled to North America during their country's decade-long civil war. The Maori of New Zealand have moved from primarily rural communities to the nation's cities in search of employment.

Migration is a constant reality in the lives of many native people, and all of those who migrate have different reasons for doing so, but there are some common characteristics that can be noted. Another important facet of migration is how native immigrants adjust to their new setting, how they maintain ties with their homeland, and how the displacement affects their identities. In cases where migration is accompanied by the removal of native people from homelands to which they have cultural and spiritual ties, the resulting disconnect between the people and their land can have devastating effects.

Studying native immigration is difficult, however, because data is minimal. Native immigrants often are overlooked by official censuses, and even when they are counted, they may be hesitant to claim their native identity.

Native Immigrants and Reasons for Migration

Native people may be forced to migrate for a number of reasons. Factors that prompt native migration include the loss of land, poverty, military action, natural disasters, a lack of economic opportunity, and the suppression of traditional lifeways. During the 2000s and 2010s, a small but increasing portion of the immigrant population left their homelands as their traditional lifeways were no longer viable as a result of environmental changes.

Many native people have little education or live in regions that are prone to natural disasters or civil unrest. Many also have little access to public services and health care. Because few of these factors improve by relocating to other rural areas, native immigrants increasingly are drawn to urban areas, where jobs and economic opportunities are more plentiful.

In North and Central America, the modern phenomenon of native migration began in the 1950s, when native men left their homes, often leaving their families behind, in search of work in urban areas. Examples include the Mohawk steelworkers, who were noted for their fearless, acrobatic high-altitude walking during the construction of New York City's skyscrapers in the 1950s and 1960s. In Mexico, Mixtec men immigrated to Mexico City in the 1960s to build the city's subway system. By the later decades of the twentieth century, women had joined the men there. In New Delhi, India, a large share of the Kharia, Munda, and Oraon peoples that migrated to the city were women.

Such migrations, however, are not always voluntary. The traffic in human life, especially that centered on the sex trade, has had a dramatic impact on many native communities. Also, native children have been forcibly removed from their families and countries to be placed for adoption in the West.

Migration can be either internal to a nation, as one group migrates from a rural to an urban area in search of work, or transborder, for example, the many immigrants who came to the United States in the hope of finding better opportunities for their families. Some countries have established temporary worker programs, such as the Bracero Program in the United States from the 1940s through the 1960s, which permitted Mexican agricultural and railroad laborers to enter the country. Such programs are helpful in tracking the people who cross borders and in coordinating where they work. Many native immigrants from Mexico, including the Hñañu, Mixtec, and Zapotec peoples, came to the United States under this program and have continued to do so since the end of the program.

International native migrants have relocated not only to North America. The Otavalo and Quechua peoples of Ecuador and Peru have migrated to Italy and Spain, many overstaying their tourist visas in order to find jobs. Nor do native immigrants always come from Latin America. Native peoples from Greenland have immigrated to cities in Denmark, their colonial connection, in search of economic opportunities during the 1990s and 2000s. Similarly, Tuareg people from North Africa have migrated to France looking for jobs.

Some migrations have taken the form of a headlong rush of refugees, fleeing horrific conditions in their homelands. Those fleeing warfare—such as those coming to the United States from Cuba starting in the 1960s, Montagnards and Hmong from Southeast Asia starting in the 1970s, and Maya people from El Salvador, Guatemala, and Nicaragua starting in the 1980s—are sometimes given refugee status, allowing them to stay longer or move permanently because of the unsafe situation in their homelands. In Africa, the Tutsi refugee crisis, resulting from strife in Burundi and Rwanda during the 1990s and 2000s, drew international attention, as did the movement of the Twa people from Burundi to Rwanda. Perhaps the most famous recent migration was that of the Fur, Massalit, and Zaghawa people of the Darfur region of Sudan during 2003 and 2004.

Native migration is a worldwide phenomenon. An illustrative example is the case of Mexico, which has experienced the full range of native migration involving many different native groups.

Native Migration in Focus: Mexico

Native migration in Mexico is a growing phenomenon. Since the 1990s, migration in the country has increased at a rate of 10 percent annually, transforming the ethnic and demographic landscape of the country. Some native lands have become dramatically depopulated, and at the same time, native people increasingly have populated regions formerly dominated by mestizo (people of mixed European and indigenous heritage) populations. The former case affects the poorest people, and consequently, the main areas of out-migration are located in middle and southern Mexico. The latter case involves the most developed areas, and therefore the main areas of in-migration are in the north of Mexico.

The main causes of native migration in Mexico are related to the economy; however, warfare also has played an important role. In general, many native migrants identify the poor conditions of the lands reserved for native people, as well as low income and unemployment, as reasons for migration. Particularly, in Chihuahua, Guerrero, and Oaxaca, migration has been spurred by the low productivity of land, which makes it difficult for native people to pursue their traditional lifeways. In the Sierra Norte de Puebla, the Nahua region in Veracruz, and the Chontal region in Tabasco, this phenomenon is the result of declining prices for coffee, tobacco, avocados, sugar, and other agricultural products. In the Montaña de Guerrero and Yucatán, the increase in out-migration stems from the low demand for products made of palm and henequén (an agave plant that yields a type of fiber), respectively.

In addition to economic migration, social and political factors also may spur native migration. For instance, some native people consider the lack of electricity, running water, health centers, schools, and other basic facilities a relevant condition for them to leave their towns of origin. Others migrate because of political tensions, persecution, or armed conflict resulting from land tenure instability, disputes over resources or political control, and violent uprisings. The most notable of these incidences was the Zapatista uprising of the 1990s and 2000s involving the Chiapas and Huastec peoples. During the late 2000s and 2010s, native migration was propelled in Baja California, Chihuahua, Sinaloa, and Sonora by the increasing presence of drug traffickers in native territories and the climate of fear stoked by the state's war against them.

The main areas of native out-migration in Mexico are the regions of Chiapas, Guerrero, Hidalgo, Oaxaca, Puebla, and Veracruz; migration involves many groups, including the Maya, Mazateco, Mixtec, Nahuatl, Otomí, P'urhépecha, Triqui, and Zapotec peoples. These groups together make up nearly 85 percent of the native immigrant population in Mexico. Moreover, many other small native groups have experienced a dramatic geographic dispersion that has threatened their existence as an identifiable group. This is the case for the Cakchiquel, Chichimeca Jonaz, Chocho, Cucapa, Jacalteco, Kekchi, Kiliwa, Kumiai, Lacandon, Mame, Papago, Pima, Quiché, and Tepehuan, among others.

Many of these immigrants have moved to the agricultural lands of Baja California, Sinaloa, and Sonora in the north, as well as cities such as Acapulco, Ciudad Juárez, Culiacán, Guadalajara, Mérida, Mexico City, and Tijuana. Even smaller cities such as Cancún, Chetumal, Coatzacoalcos, Ensenada, La Paz, Matamoros, Puerto Vallarta, and Tehuacán have seen large influxes of native people.

As with much native migration worldwide, migration in Mexico began as a male endeavor, continued as a shared venture with women, and developed into a family enterprise. Migration, then, has transformed some of the traditional gender roles and status at the local level, enabling, among other things, women's participation in economic activities and in the civic-religious system of the community.

Transborder Migrations, Relationships, and Challenges

Migrations across national borders may take a number of forms. Most obvious are those cases in which people move from one nation to a neighboring country in search of work or to escape an untenable situation in their homeland.

However, there also are many people that once lived in a region before the presence of national borders and later were divided when the boundaries between modern nation-states were drawn. Some notable examples are the Guayami of Panama and Costa Rica, the Maasai of Kenya and Tanzania, the Tohono O'odham in the United States and Mexico, and the Iroquois tribes of the United States and Canada. These divisions make it difficult for groups to follow indigenous lifeways that rely on the land and annual cycles or to observe religious rituals that may occur across national borders.

Unless the nations involved have negotiated treaties to allow for the movement of native peoples across borders (such as that between the United States and Canada), these groups often evolve separate identities, or, in the case of the Sami people of Scandinavia during the nineteenth and early twentieth centuries, they are forced to live on one side of a national border or the other, removing them from a part of their traditional homelands. However, many native migrants maintain strong ties to their home nations and communities. Those who are able to often travel home for important rituals and family activities. Sometimes, those who have immigrated send funds to their relatives who have not immigrated to enable them to stay in their homelands.

However, life is often difficult for native people in new lands. They face discrimination because of their lack of knowledge of the local language or simply because they are perceived as outsiders. Immigrant children often are denied enrollment in public schools because of their undocumented status. Health care usually is no better than it was in their homeland, as they often are barred from participating in the health system of their new country. Discrimination in economic opportunities and services keeps native migrants in a disadvantaged position, often little better off than when they left their homeland.

One way in which this situation might be mitigated is through the involvement of the migrants' home countries. In Mexico, for example, the government established the Instituto de los Mexicanos en el Exterior (Institute for Mexicans Abroad) to provide services to native migrants, such as legal services to Mexican citizens in American jails. Such programs can help mitigate the cultural displacement, social discrimination, economic struggle, and other challenges experienced by many native migrants.

Everardo Garduño and Steven L. Danver

See also: *Groups: Central and South America*—Maya. *Groups: East Asia and Oceania*—Maori. *Countries*—Mexico. *Issues*—Colonialism.

Further Reading

Cornelius, Wayne A., David Fitzgerald, and Pedro Lewin Fischer, eds. *Mayan Journeys: The New Migration from Yucatán to the United States.* San Diego, CA: Center for Comparative Immigration Studies, 2007.

Cornelius, Wayne A., David Fitzgerald, Jorge Hernández-Díaz, and Scott Borger, eds. *Migration from the Mexican Mixteca: A Transnational Community in Oaxaca and California.* San Diego, CA: Center for Comparative Immigration Studies, 2009.

Foner, Nancy, Rubén G. Rumbaut, and Steven J. Gold, eds. *Immigration Research for a New Century: Multidisciplinary Perspectives.* New York: Russell Sage Foundation, 2000.

Mattingly, Doreen J., and Ellen R. Hansen, eds. *Women and Change at the U.S.–Mexico Border: Mobility, Labor, and Activism.* Tucson: University of Arizona Press, 2006.

Mullick, Bosu. *Indigenous Peoples in Urban Areas.* Copenhagen, Denmark: International Work Group for Indigenous Affairs, 2002.

Yescas, Carlos. "Hidden in Plain Sight: Indigenous Migrants, Their Movements, and Their Challenges." *Migration Information Source*, March 2010. www.migrationinformation.org.

———. *Indigenous Routes: A Framework for Understanding Indigenous Migration.* Geneva, Switzerland: International Organization for Migration, 2008.

Military Service

Most of the world's native peoples have some tradition of military service, in spite of poor, hostile, or even geno-cidal treatment by the governments of the countries they live in. For some native peoples, military service is a continuation of older warrior traditions. For others, the military offers a way out of poverty. Military service also can be a way to find a place within an encroaching dominant society.

Scholars, including indigenous ones, are sharply divided over military service. Some see it as a tragic symptom of colonialism, while others concentrate on honoring war veterans. In its worst guise, military service becomes a "divide-and-conquer" strategy. Natives often use military service as a way to turn violence by the state away from certain people and against others, including other tribes and even other people within their own tribes.

Colonial powers such as Great Britain, France, and the United States saw tribal peoples as "martial races" that were inherently warlike. Some American military personnel claimed that Native Americans had distinct advantages in warfare, as they could see in the dark like cats and knew which way was north without a compass. But military service is not universal among native peoples. The degree of participation varies enormously from tribe to tribe. Tribes with strong warrior traditions, such as the Sioux in the United States, tend to have the highest rates of enlistment. Other tribes have no warrior traditions or even are pacifists, such as the Nasa people of Colombia.

Throughout history, many indigenous people were drafted or coerced into the military. At times, tribes resisted or refused to join, even mounting tribal draft resistance campaigns, as among the Goshute and Shoshone tribes in the United States during World War I. Many Goshute, Hopi, and Tohono O'odham defied the draft, while the Iroquois refused to be drafted into the Canadian or U.S. military, volunteering instead as foreign nationals.

In the United States, the Native American tradition of military service began during the War of 1812. By the war's end, the Iroquois had gone from allies of the United States to enlistees with the British. Famed Indian scouts included the Apache, Pawnee, Seminole, and Shawnee. During the Civil War, the so-called Five Civilized Tribes (Cherokee, Choctaw, Chickasaw, Creek, and Seminole) and the Iroquois, Lumbee, and Menominee served in large numbers, while in the Spanish-American War, the famed Rough Riders recruited among the Apache. The start of World War I marked the beginning of Native American service on a large scale, with many natives going through traditional ceremonies for honoring and protection, carrying traditional medicine while in the service, and joining warrior societies after the war. Native veterans were given the vote and U.S. citizenship, and suffrage soon extended to all Native Americans.

World War II had the greatest effect of any historical event on natives since Christopher Columbus landed, according to historian Gary Nash. More than half of all Native Americans left their reservations, either as enlistees or as workers in wartime industries. Disillusionment with the Vietnam War saw native enlistment begin to drop for the first time. Most Native Americans opposed the Iraq War even before it began, seeing parallels between U.S. policy in the Middle East today and the theft of native lands in North America.

In Latin America, Spain often utilized the indigenous peoples in its colonial militia, especially the Opata and Tlaxcalan in New Spain. During the 1810s and 1820s, José Antonio Páez led many *pardo* troops (mixed black and Indian ancestry), first fighting for Spain and then in Simón Bolívar's fight for independence. Guaraní troops formed the core of Paraguay's once powerful military. In Cuba, the Hatuey Regiment of natives fought for Spain and then for independence in the late nineteenth century. In the Chaco War during the 1930s, indigenous or mestizo (mixed European and Indian ancestry) soldiers made up the majority of the Bolivian and Paraguayan militaries. Bolivia has had six presidents of native ancestry, all but one brought into power by coups. The current president of Venezuela, Hugo Chavez, is part of a long tradition of pardos in the military. The former president of Panama, Omar Torrijos, is another example. In Peru, former colonel Ollanta Humala nearly won the presidency and is the leader of the Movimento Etnocacerista (Peruvian Nationalist Movement), which glorifies the loyalty of indigenous people to the nation while disparaging wealthy white elites as disloyal. Guatemala has perhaps the most violent history of using native troops. The Civic Patrollers were native rural villagers who were used to carry out genocide against other native peoples in the 1980s; the campaign killed 200,000 and forced 1 million to flee the country.

In Asia, notable examples of tribal soldiers include the Taiwanese aborigines or Atayal tribes, recruited as the Takasago Volunteers by the Japanese during World War II. Subjected to extreme assimilation campaigns, most joined out of a sense of identity as Japanese. The Montagnards or Hill Tribes of Southeast Asia first were

IWO JIMA

The flag raising on Iwo Jima is one of the most famous photographs of World War II. The image, taken by Associated Press photographer Joe Rosenthal, of six American soldiers raising the Stars and Stripes atop Mount Suribachi represented the unity of Americans of different backgrounds fighting against a common foe. War posters, stamps, and statues all bore the image.

Iwo Jima is a barren volcanic island that lies between Japan and American bases in the Mariana Islands. Because of its strategic location, the United States considered the ashy island an important base for future landings on the Japanese mainland. On February 19, 1945, the U.S. Marines landed on Iwo Jima, where the costliest battle in the history of the U.S. Marine Corps would unfold. By the time the fierce fighting ended on March 26, some 6,000 American soldiers had lost their lives—nearly all of them Marines, accounting for almost one-third of the total Marine Corps losses during World War II. The battle was even more damaging for Japan: more than 20,000 Japanese troops were killed, and several hundred were captured as prisoners.

The inspiring photograph of the flag raising became a symbol not only of the U.S. Marine Corps, but also of Native American soldiers' contributions to America's fighting forces during the war. In all, 24,521 Native Americans from reservations and approximately 20,000 off-reservation Indians served in the European and Pacific theaters during World War II. That number represented more than 10 percent of the total Native American population of 350,000.

One of those Indian soldiers was Ira Hamilton Hayes. In August 1942, at the age of 19, Hayes, a Pima from Sacaton, Arizona, joined the Marines, and he fought in the Pacific as a paratrooper. One of the flag raisers depicted in the photograph, he became one of the most famous Native American soldiers overnight.

Hayes and two other survivors of the flag raising, John Bradley and Rene Gagon, immediately were recalled to the mainland to participate in a tour to sell war bonds. Traveling across the country selling bonds and participating in parades, receptions, and parties, Hayes felt uneasy, as he saw himself as a regular American soldier, unqualified for such admiration and appreciation as a "war hero."

After the war, Hayes had difficulty readjusting to his home environment and started wandering across the country. He suffered from alcoholism and was arrested more than fifty times in thirteen years. Hayes died from alcohol and exposure in the desert in Bapchule, Arizona, on January 24, 1955, at the age of thirty-two; he was buried at Arlington National Cemetery. His life and death represented the sad story of Native American veterans: Soldiers who once were celebrated as courageous "chiefs" on the battlefield returned home only to confront poverty, discrimination, and isolation.

Azusa Ono

recruited by French colonialists to fight against the lowland Vietnamese, and then by the U.S. military and the Central Intelligence Agency to fight as mercenaries against the North Vietnamese and the National Liberation Front from the 1950s through the 1970s. The wars were a disaster for the Hill Tribes, and most were forced to flee as refugees to Thailand or the United States. The Orang Asli (original people) of Malaysia were recruited as part of the Senoi Praaq (those who fight), first against communist insurgents and then against Indonesian troops in the Konfrontasi (confrontation) between the two nations in the 1960s. Examples of veteran military traditions in the Pacific Islands include Fijians' widespread deployment as mercenaries and high numbers of Samoans and Native Hawaiians serving in the U.S. military.

Indigenous peoples show up in military history not only as victims, and not only as aggressors, but also as important players in many conflicts worldwide. Sometimes, when indigenous peoples lived in regions disputed by nations, their service was valued and much sought after by both sides of the conflict, as with the Native American allies who fought for both the British and the French during the French and Indian War in North America during the 1750s and 1760s.

Often, indigenous peoples have used military service and the camaraderie generated by the shared experience of warfare to gain social and economic standing for their people, as some American tribes such as the Navajo did during and after World War II. Generalizations are difficult, as each tribe's experience with each different conflict has within it many diverse elements and outcomes. But the immutable facts about the records of military service left by indigenous peoples around the world are that they fought just as bravely as any soldiers and died just as often.

Al Carroll

See also: *Issues*—Colonialism; Political Participation; Violence and Warfare.

Further Reading

Carroll, Al. *Medicine Bags and Dog Tags: American Indian Veterans from Colonial Times to the Second Iraq War.* Lincoln: University of Nebraska Press, 2008.

Franco, Jere Bishop. *Crossing the Pond: The Native American Effort in World War II.* Denton: University of North Texas Press, 1999.

Hickey, Gerald Cannon. *Sons of the Mountains: Ethnohistory of the Vietnamese Central Highlands to 1954.* New Haven, CT: Yale University Press, 1982.

Holm, Tom. *Strong Hearts, Wounded Souls: Native American Veterans of the Vietnam War.* Austin: University of Texas Press, 1996.

Hue Huang, Chui. "The Yamatodamashi of the Takasago Volunteers of Taiwan: A Reading of the Postcolonial Situation." In *Globalizing Japan: Ethnography of the Japanese Presence in Asia,* ed. Harumi Befu and Sylvie Guichard Anguis. London: Routledge, 2001.

Mining

People engage in mining when they deploy technology to extract minerals from the earth that are needed for subsistence or trade, or have symbolic value. Our capacity to scratch and dig at the earth reaches back to human origins. Making tools and adornments and fetishizing rare minerals as mediums of barter and trade characterize the place of mining in civilization. While people always have engaged in mining, it became a critically important activity with the development of modern economies.

Starting with the conquest of the Americas in the 1500s, and increasing dramatically with the Industrial Revolution of the 1700s and 1800s, mining became significant because it linked peoples working in the industry, many of them indigenous, and those living in colonial areas with the centers of capitalist economic development in Europe and the United States. Through these linkages, mining wrought profound changes on the world's indigenous peoples. As a mechanism for integrating indigenous people into modern life, mining has generated conflict between indigenous and Western cultures.

Europeans undertook the task of transforming minerals into one of the driving forces of the modern economy. The riches of conquest and colonization that Europeans derived from mining were immense. The Spanish, for example, ransomed 13,420 pounds (6,087 kilograms) of pure gold from the vanquished Inca Empire. The silver taken from the Potosí mine in colonial Peru and other mines in Mexico transferred great wealth to Spain during the 300 years of its colonial rule. This transfer of wealth was extracted by the forced labor of thousands of indigenous people working under brutal and dangerous conditions. The flow of wealth fueled the transition from mercantile to industrial capitalism. Europe's wealth equated to power, which stimulated new waves of colonial domination in Africa and Asia.

Three central forces defined mining in the nineteenth century. First, changes in Western colonialism defined mining. The end of colonialism in Latin America led to a decline in mining activity as newly independent nations struggled to establish governments during the first half of the century. The emergence of modern nation-states in the second half of the century allowed for the growth of institutions and companies that were favorable to mining development. The process in Africa followed a different path, as once-independent regions fell to the continent's formal colonization by European powers during the last decades of the century.

Next, mining was transformed by the growing system of industrial production. The Industrial Revolution increased demand for the minerals needed to build infrastructure and produce commodities demanded by an emerging consumer culture. The Industrial Revolution also introduced new technologies into the mining sector that made the extraction process more efficient yet also more environmentally destructive. Railroad transport and new ports significantly facilitated the transfer of minerals from peripheral areas to the industrial center.

New ways of organizing and managing capital was the third defining force. Finance capital and the birth of the multinational corporation led to mining monopolies. By the end of the nineteenth century, corporations such as Rio Tinto Zinc were extracting minerals throughout the world.

The double shocks of World War I and the Great Depression brought significant changes to the political economy of mining. While the production of war materials stimulated demand for minerals, it also disrupted relations between dominant nations and their colonial and neocolonial possessions. Latin American nations, for example, had to produce many commodities that they previously had imported. When the financial and industrial system of free trade capitalism collapsed during the Great Depression, a new economic model emerged in many European nations that gave the state control over the economy. The state now managed the economy with the goal of self-sustained growth by substituting industrial imports with domestic production. Mining played an important role as national mining companies provided subsidized mineral inputs to the nascent industries. Dra-

POTOSÍ

Located at an elevation of more than 13,000 feet (4,000 meters) in south-central Bolivia, the city of Potosí was a major supplier of silver to the Spanish Empire and remains an important domestic mining center to the present day. Potosí is a part of the Cordillera Central in the Andes Mountains and home to Cerro Rico, one of many mined mountains that sustain the Bolivian economy. The area also is home to many *huacas,* sacred objects and locations. From pre-Columbian times through the colonial era, the people of Potosí considered specific mountains, stones, natural landscape features, and special man-made items, particularly mummies, as sacred. Thus, their reverence for Cerro Rico as a sacred location is not unusual within the context of the spiritual practices of aboriginal South Americans.

Bolivians continue to respect and atone for the exploitation of sacred mountain spaces by making offerings to a red clay rendition of El Tío, a demon spirit represented at entrances to the deep core of the mines. Miners offer coca leaves, animal blood, alcoholic beverages, small cigars or cigarettes, and other items to ensure the successful mining of loads, the safety of workers, and penance for the economic exploitation of such sacred spaces.

Mining has been a substantial industry in Potosí, focusing on silver until it was largely depleted around 1800; after that time, tin became the dominant resource, although the industry has fluctuated with changing methods of production. During the colonial era, the Spanish who controlled Potosí utilized the Inca *mit'a* system, which was a system of tribute payment through goods or labor that was characterized by forced servitude, often resulting in the death of the laborer because of difficult physical labor and poor living conditions. The Spanish continued this practice in mining and in countless other economic activities.

In the twentieth century, the increase in demand for tin, due to lower European production, ushered in a resurgence in mining activities in Potosí that revived the local economy. However, the crash of the global tin market in 1985 made it less profitable, leading the Bolivian government to abandon much large-scale mining and grant rights to small miners who eke out a living on whatever tin and silver are left.

Even long after the banning of forced servitude, however, conditions did not improve much for miners. Many aboriginal miners of Potosí continued to have short life expectancies—forty years or less—because of silicosis of the lungs.

The people of Potosí have resisted exploitation, as the Aymara and Quechua peoples have engaged in widespread upheaval, uniting miners, farmers, and laborers throughout Bolivia. In October 2003, mass protests forced President Gonzalo Sánchez de Lozada from office. His successor, Carlos Mesa, was ousted in 2005 and replaced by indigenous politician Evo Morales. Nevertheless, the exploitation of the Potosí natives, many of whom are children, continues.

Yet despite economic hardship, the people of Potosí celebrate an ongoing indigenous revival. Renewed interests in aboriginal languages, traditions, spirituality, and lifeways are flourishing in Potosí and may be observed in clothing, religious rituals, and daily activities in the town.

Danielle Roseberry

An alliance of Ecuadorean indigenous groups held a cross-country march in 2012 to protest government plans for large-scale mining projects in the Amazon region. The new mines, they maintained, would contaminate water and force native people off their land. *(Edu Leon/LatinContent/ Getty Images)*

matic economic growth resulted from these policies, until the crisis of the early 1980s. At the same time, demand for minerals continued to be strong. State-run economies, such as Sweden, implemented more favorable conditions for labor, which benefited those who worked in the mines, including large numbers of indigenous people.

A combination of global economic shocks, including the dramatic increase in fuel prices during the 1970s and the great costs of the Vietnam War, converged with a cyclical stagnation of state-run economies to cause a massive debt crisis. In response, global financial institutions, state planners, and leaders from the private sector orchestrated a transition back to free trade economic policies. Starting in the early 1980s and becoming predominant in the 1990s, so-called neoliberal policies significantly adjusted the political economy of mining. State-run mining companies were privatized, taxes and royalties nearly were eliminated, labor rights were trimmed, and environmental regulations and protections were discarded.

The new policies often were spearheaded by the World Bank, which played an active part in writing mining laws favorable to multinational mining companies. The World Bank financed projects aimed at promoting mining in new regions, such as geological surveys essential for the first stages of mining exploration. The World Bank also implemented complex financial mechanisms that provided "political insurance" to protect multinational mining companies from loss as a result of regional instability. These reforms constituted major subsidies to mining companies and their financial backers, and they carried marginal benefit to the countries and communities where the mines were located.

The reforms also pushed mining further and deeper

into remote and ecologically vulnerable regions of the word, such as the Amazon rain forest and the South Pacific, which often were populated with indigenous communities far off the "grid" of modernity. This penetration intensifying the ongoing conflict between modern mining and indigenous peoples.

Throughout the nineteenth and twentieth centuries, mining intensified the scope and depth of indigenous integration into modern society. Organized around precepts of private property, mining further displaced indigenous peoples from their communal lands. Mining commodified water, animals, and forests, increasing indigenous alienation from nature. Land enclosure forced more indigenous peoples into a new economic model, where once-autonomous means of indigenous subsistence were transformed into wage labor dependence. The harshness of mine labor, workplace hazards, the indignities of racism, and exploitative relations with the mining companies exacerbated the negatives.

Industrial mining further increased the severity of violation of indigenous cultures. While indigenous peoples had dug into the earth, they did so within a distinct cultural system. Modernity's digging into the earth ruptured indigenous ways of being in the universe. The indigenous Bolivian saying, "We eat the mines, the mines eat us," reflects the gravity of the rupture: Deadly tunnel collapses were the gods' revenge for scaring the earth. The massive destruction of nature caused by industrialized mining profoundly altered the indigenous world. Mining polluted water, dammed and diverted rivers, leveled forests, and contaminated land with toxic wastes. As minerals flowed from less to more developed nations, wealth went with it. Indigenous peoples saw few benefits of this industrial transformation, while the costs to them were immense.

Mining has presented indigenous peoples with difficult choices throughout its history. Some have opted to accommodate the great changes that mining brings, either by resignation to forces larger than their ability to resist or through calculated attempts to secure the benefits of modernity. Some indigenous peoples have collaborated with mining companies to advance projects as a way to "get rich quick" or as part of political strategies against competitors. The pressure to accommodate or collaborate can be immense, especially as elders and leaders seek to advance the best interests of their people.

When faced with continued economic marginalization, embracing mining can appear a wise option for many indigenous groups. Some, however, such as the Navajo in the United States, who have protested the resumption of uranium mining on their lands, have resisted the environmental and cultural destruction that accompanies this activity. Often resistance emerges after the process of mining has begun, when indigenous peoples conclude that promises made in treaties and agreements will not be kept or when they see that the costs outweigh the benefits.

Resistance sometimes becomes violent, such as when Guatemala's Tz'ununija' Indigenous Women's Movement resisted gold mining in their communities in the 2000s, as saying no to mining means confronting powerful political and economic forces. In addition, mining companies have a long history of human rights violations against those who resist. In the case of the Bougainville mine in Papua New Guinea, during the late 1980s, resistance sparked a guerrilla movement that led to a brutal repression that merged state security forces with paramilitary squads organized by the mining company.

As mining continues to penetrate new regions, it stimulates new conflicts, and indigenous resistance still is often met with violence. With ever-increasing demand for minerals from expanding economies such as China and India, the pattern of conflict between the mining industry and indigenous groups is likely to continue into the foreseeable future.

Glen David Kuecker

See also: *Countries*—Bolivia. *Issues*—Industrial Development; Land Rights.

Further Reading

Bunker, Stephen, and Paul Ciccantell. *Globalization and the Race for Resources.* Baltimore: Johns Hopkins University Press, 2005.

Gedicks, Al. *Resource Rebels: Native Challenges to Mining and Oil Corporations.* Cambridge, MA: South End, 2001.

Kirsch, Stuart. *Reverse Anthropology: Indigenous Analysis of Social and Environmental Relations in New Guinea.* Stanford, CA: Stanford University Press, 2006.

Moody, Roger. *Rocks and Hard Places: The Globalization of Mining.* New York: Zed, 2007.

Nash, June. *We Eat the Mines, the Mines Eat Us: Dependency and Exploitation in Bolivian Tin Mines.* New York: Colombia University Press, 1979.

Missionary Activities

Missionary activities have been carried out in some form since the dawn of organized religion, and opinions have been proffered regarding their effects ever since. Academics, activists, indigenous peoples, and governments alike hotly debated the benefits and detriments of these activities with growing fervor during the twentieth century. The general conclusion is that missionary activities bring potentially irreversible changes to a society.

In this context, a missionary is defined as a proselytizer of any belief system. Missionary activities are those that attempt to engage a culture so as to convert the indigenous population to a new system or form of belief. When they enter a region, missionaries of any religion decide how and where to focus their attention—for example, on herding communities, young children, elders, or women. They strive to produce a societal shift away from what they believe are outdated or ethically incorrect beliefs to their own belief system.

The more modern or Western conception of missionary work began when the Christian apostle Paul began his first journey in 46 C.E. Thereafter, Christian groups focused their efforts worldwide, seeking to bring their new beliefs to the ends of the Earth. In the scholarship of the twentieth and twenty-first centuries, Christian missionaries are accused of warping indigenous culture—that is, attempting to eradicate local customs and beliefs in favor of those of their imported culture.

In addition, throughout world history—in the Americas with Christianity, in North Africa with Islam, and in Asia with Buddhism, Christianity, and Hinduism—missionaries often have defined success in terms that exclude mobile (nomadic) populations. To this end, missionaries frequently have worked, either wittingly or unwittingly, with the central state apparatus to encourage a sort of settled lifestyle—especially when dealing with nomadic populations. If sedentarization is not achieved, the missionaries, and thus the culture affected by their actions, often are unable to deal with or grant political enfranchisement to a mobile group that does not adhere to the new belief system. The effect of this on an indigenous group is clearly detrimental, for it does not allow members of the group to take part in either the historic or current "modernization" movement of a given region.

Age of Exploration and Mission History

The Age of Exploration, a period from the early fifteenth century to the seventeenth century during which Europeans began exploring the world by sea, brought with it the expansion of missionary activities, especially Christian, alongside those of the great explorers. Reaching back to the conversion of much of Europe by Catholics at the end of the thirteenth century (ca. sixth through fourteenth centuries) and of the New World by the Spanish in Aztec and Maya regions (1517–1521) or, later, by French Jesuits among Native Americans in New England (1610–1790), it becomes clear that Christian missions were either the forerunner or the ready partner of colonization. This would be the trend worldwide

through the eighteenth century, changing only when imperial boundaries began to solidify after the American and French revolutions at the end of the 1700s.

A notable exception to the general practices by Christian missionaries during the Age of Exploration was the Jesuit monk Ippolito Desideri, who made his way to the Tibetan capital of Lhasa in the early eighteenth century. Desideri undertook a comprehensive study of Tibetan language and culture, as many Jesuits did, in an effort to meet the culture on its own terms, rather than force the culture to meet his.

By the nineteenth century, missionaries were at the forefront of exploration in Africa and Asia, helping to pave the way for full-scale colonization by the early twentieth century (and later paving the way for the end of colonization by the mid-twentieth century). Christian missionary efforts in Africa and Asia followed the same patterns as in the New World—namely, mission schools and attempts to replace the native culture with that of the modernizing West. Activities revolved around the

BARTOLOMÉ DE LAS CASAS

Bartolomé de Las Casas, regarded as the "Apostle of the Indies," was born in Seville, Spain, in 1484. A passionate, erudite, and judicious friar, Las Casas made his first voyage to the Indies with his father as part of an expedition headed by Nicolás de Ovando in 1502, and in 1522, he joined the Dominican order. Las Casas is renowned for promoting the peaceful conversion and submission of the native population to Catholicism and the Spanish Crown. But he is equally infamous for endorsing the enslavement of African peoples, a position that he regretted later in life, stating that "they had been made slaves unjustly and tyrannically."

Las Casas first encountered the native inhabitants of the Americas in 1493, when Christopher Columbus brought back seven surviving Indians to Spain. His first voyage to the New World landed him in Hispaniola (present-day Dominican Republic and Haiti), where Las Casas witnessed firsthand the enslavement, abuse, and almost complete demise of the Taino people. His experience in the Caribbean profoundly affected the course of his life, though he did not free his own indigenous slaves until 1514.

After this conversion, Las Casas began documenting the atrocities committed by the settlers. He wrote three works about the abuse of the indigenous population—*Memorial de Remedios para Las Indias* (*Memorial Concerning Remedies for the Indies,* 1516), *Brevisima Relación de la Destrucción de Las Indias* (*A Brief Account of the Destruction of the Indies,* 1542), and *Apologética Historia Summaria de Las Gentes Destas Indias* (*Apologetic Summary History of the*

People of These Indies, 1553)—eventually using these works to support his attempts to reform Spanish laws regarding indigenous peoples.

During his time in the Americas, Las Casas made several trips back to Spain in his attempts to influence the way royal officials treated indigenous peoples. His lobbying eventually influenced the passing of laws (*Leyes Nuevas,* 1542) that favored Indians. He temporarily succeeded in influencing the king's suspension of the *encomienda* system (the way in which the Spanish acquired land and slaves) and managed to request colonization by farmers rather than soldiers; however, these two victories were short-lived.

One of Las Casas's greatest triumphs was his public challenge of Juan Ginés Sepúlveda's work, *Democrates Secundus* (*The Just Causes of War Against the Indians,* 1547), which rationalized on Aristotelian grounds war against indigenous peoples as a just means of Christianization. While the royal representatives from the Council of the Indies did not pass a verdict, Las Casas's repudiation of Sepúlveda's thesis influenced subsequent papal bulls on the method of conversion of indigenous peoples.

Las Casas became the first resident bishop of Chiapas, Mexico. At eighty-two years old, he was lucid and full of conviction when he advocated before King Philip II's ministers that Guatemalans should have their own courts. His *Brief Account of the Destruction of the Indies* remains among the most important documents on the history of colonialism in the Americas. He died in July 1566 in Madrid.

Gloria E. Chacon

translation of the Bible, the establishment of boarding schools, the equation (by missionaries and, later, by native groups) of Christian culture with Western culture, and the gradual exclusion of native peoples who did not adhere to the new religion.

Though Christian missions often were detrimental to indigenous cultures, they provided much of the earliest ethnographic information on those peoples. Starting with the *Jesuit Relations* (1610–1790), a compilation of French Jesuit communications with Paris in the early seventeenth century, Europe began learning about the Algonquian and Iroquois confederations in New England. Spanish missionaries, notably Francisco Palou (1723–1789) and Geronimo Boscano (1776–1831), provided similar information about American Indian groups in California and Mexico. Perhaps the most notable twentieth-century missionary to provide ethnographic information was Robert Ekvall (1898–1978). His work among Tibetan nomads, *Fields on the Hoof: Nexus of Tibetan Nomadic Pastoralism* (1968), remains one of the seminal ethnographic works on the people.

While examination of the influence of Christianity on indigenous cultures has dominated scholarly discussion since the mid-twentieth century, historians note that Christian missionaries were not the first, or necessarily the most virile, actors in this discourse. For centuries, Buddhist missionaries in Asian regions enacted similar schemes of indoctrination and assimilation.

The interplay in China between Buddhist, Confucian, and Daoist proponents created vying regimes and interpretations of power that resulted in varying conceptions of how indigenous groups on the fringes of the empire were dealt with from the Warring States period (ca. 475–221 B.C.E.) to the Qing dynasty (1644–1911 C.E.). Tibetan accounts of their interactions with Mongolian rulers note that Tibetans were asked to send missionaries to Mongolia to teach their form of Buddhism to the population and that the reigning Buddhist sect was supported by the Mongolian imperial army in its conflicts in Lhasa.

Modern Missionary Activities

In modern times, missionary activities have evolved. Instead of focusing on boarding schools or rapid cultural change, mission groups (most notably Buddhist, Christian, and Muslim) tend to focus on aid projects: medical clinics, construction of schools, water projects, and disease eradication. This provides local people with services that are needed and invites, but in no way requires, them to embrace the beliefs of those who provide such services.

This sort of program is seen especially in Africa, where missions have established stations and schools with the goal of serving populations uprooted by years of civil war or poverty. The World Health Organization has commended the efforts of medical missionaries, citing their long-term presence in Africa as a major reason for the gradually shrinking rates of disease and their ability to help in places that often are off-limits to other international aid groups.

There also is an increasing effort by mission groups to effect change in the area of human trafficking. Groups of missionary-oriented policy makers, lawyers, and activists of many different faiths are working among minority populations in Asia to build recovery centers, extract people from the flesh trade, and protect and educate villagers and nomadic groups about the reality of these trafficking networks.

When interacting with native peoples today, missionaries generally are more willing to meet an indigenous culture on its own terms, rather than bringing in idealized systems of belief and living. This translates into more broad-ranging development projects—education initiatives, water projects, or health programs. These allow native peoples to more strategically engage both mission groups and individuals and to create a space for a less confrontational dialogue to be established by both parties—an important change in the historical precedent set by many missionary groups.

Traditionally, the phrase "missionary activity" has carried a negative impression and legacy for native peoples, but, in some cases, it has resulted in positive gains for native groups—the eradication of disease, increased social mobility as a result of enhanced education, and the ability to engage an increasingly linked world. These positive gains often are overlooked by the academic and political community, resulting in a lopsided analysis of issues such as community health. Instead, it is helpful to see modern interactions between indigenous groups and missionaries as a dialogue in which the boundaries of power often are blurred, creating a new arena for strategic engagement by both groups.

Given the context of missionary history and current activities, it is important to appreciate that the discourse on missionary activities no longer is bounded by the traditional understanding of all missionary activity as negative. This leaves us with a paradigm that is much larger, much more complicated, and much richer than we traditionally have constructed when thinking about missionaries and their engagement with native groups.

Jared Phillips

See also: *Countries*—United States. *Issues*—Colonialism; Religion (Indigenous).

Further Reading

Anderson, Gerald H., ed. *Biographical Dictionary of Christian Missions.* New York: Macmillan, 1998.

Ballard, Martin. *White Men's God: The Extraordinary Story of Missionaries in Africa.* Westport, CT: Greenwood, 2008.

Desideri, Ippolito. *An Account of Tibet: The Travels of Ippolito Desideri of Pistoia, S.J., 1712–1727.* London: Routledge, 1932.

Wade, Maria F. *Missions, Missionaries, and Native Americans: Long-Term Processes and Daily Practices.* Gainesville: University Press of Florida, 2008.

Wessels, C. *Early Jesuit Travellers in Central Asia, 1603–1721.* The Hague, Netherlands: Nijhoff, 1924.

Native Nongovernmental Organizations

Analyzing nongovernmental organizations (NGOs) and the unequal field of power relations within and between targeted populations and government funding agencies at the local, national, and international levels is very complex. Native organizations are, by their nature, nongovernmental. These organizations exhibit some characteristics of other NGOs, such as government funding, social and advocacy service, and promotion of human rights and well-being. They also tend to be heterogeneous in their origins, conceptions, and political and organizational endeavors, while sharing the primary function of helping indigenous peoples.

In Paraguay, native organizations face many dilemmas and contradictions. For instance, Paraguayan government organizations such as the Instituto Paraguayo del Indígena (Paraguayan Institute of the Indian) and NGOs such as the Asociación Rural del Paraguay (ARP, Paraguayan Rural Association) often have been found to focus more on their own material, political, and economic interests rather than on promoting those of the indigenous Yshiro Indians. For example, landowners established the ARP to counteract and redirect indigenous land claims in response to imminent threat of land expropriations.

In El Chaco, Paraguay, both government organizations and NGOs, whether conservative or radical, provide a variety of expert knowledge on indigenous peoples while lobbying for governmental and transnational development projects. The NGOs claim that they are legitimate representatives of indigenous peoples because their projects reflect Yshiro interests. However, in 2004, Bruno Barras, a Yshiro leader, argued quite the opposite: "NGOs treat us [Indians] as if we are babies. . . . They speak for us and design projects for us. Most of the time, they are the main beneficiaries of the projects for the communities."

One solution was the establishment of a native NGO (NNGO) envisioned by five Yshiro community leaders who founded La Unión de las Comunidades Indígenas de la Nación Yshir (Yshir Nation Union of Indigenous Communities) in 1999. Through this NNGO, the Yshir Nation pursued community interests and worked to reduce the power and misrepresentations created by multiple governmental and nongovernmental Paraguayan organizations.

Since 2006, a native nongovernmental health organization, the Mapu Ñuke Centre, has served the Williche community of Chiloé, Chile. Its objective is to promote and preserve the cultural and natural heritage of the Williche indigenous community. The Mapu Ñuke health care model not only strives to promote a holistic approach to health initiatives, but it also seeks the inclusion of indigenous knowledge in medical practice and education and takes an intercultural approach to health care, productive management, and the defense of Williche territorial rights. The Williche community has accessed multiple services related to health issues, basing its health care program on previous experience, and also has created areas for learning traditional culture, forest lore, and natural remedies. The model has been recognized at the national and international levels by the Citizenship Program and Local Management, by the Foundation Azhoca, and by the Comisión Económica para América Latina y el Caribe (Economic Commission for Latin America and the Caribbean).

Since the late 1960s, off-reserve native political organizations have proliferated throughout Canada. Several NNGOs were established in the city of London, Ontario, including the Nokee Kwe Occupational Skills and Development, At Lohsa Native Family Healing Services, and the N'Amerind Friendship Centre. The Native Learning Centre at Nokee Kwe provides basic skills and literacy services to aboriginal people. Its mandate is "to learn and understand the needs of Native learners, thereby responding to their needs and respecting their heritage and culture, as well as developing their literacy and numeracy needs, all within one holistic environment." This learning initiative strives to teach English, math, and other subjects, as well as aboriginal traditions.

The N'Amerind Friendship Centre illustrates how such organizations attempt to meet the changing needs of their service community in urban areas. This organization provides services to children through the tenth grade, including such efforts as the alternative secondary, native court work, family support, child protection, drug and alcohol, urban youth, language, and prenatal programs. Other services pertain to the restorative justice system, literacy, and employment services.

In another example, the Healing of the Seven Generations in Kitchener, Ontario, was founded by Donna

Dubie, a First Nations intergenerational survivor of the residential school system. The organization strives to restore health and well-being to aboriginal and community members who suffer from negative effects of the residential school system.

Native nongovernmental organizations are flexible and shifting community entities that respond to the pressing needs of the indigenous population. At the same time, they implement government policies, programs, and projects directed at indigenous people. NNGOs represent a political force that at various times may contest or support the actions of the state, while ever engaging with it for the inclusion of aboriginal peoples' needs and interests.

María Cristina Manzano-Munguía

See also: Issues—Indigenous Peoples and the United Nations; International Policy; United Nations Declaration.

Further Reading

Blaser, Mario, Harvey A. Feit, and Glenn McRae, eds. *The Way of Development: Indigenous Peoples, Life Projects and Globalization.* London: Zed, 2004.

Fisher, William. "Doing Good? The Politics and Antipolitics of NGO Practices." *Annual Review of Anthropology* 26 (1997): 439–464.

Manzano-Munguía, María Cristina. "Conceptualizing Native Non-Government Organizations in Canada: An Ethnographic Approach." *International Journal of Interdisciplinary Social Sciences* 2:1 (2007): 449–459.

Markowitz, Lisa. "Finding the Field: Notes on the Ethnography of NGOs." *Human Organization* 60(1): 40–46.

Sassen, Saskia. *Losing Control? Sovereignty in an Age of Globalization.* New York: Columbia University Press, 1995.

Oil and Mineral Rights

The oil and mineral rights held by indigenous people worldwide have long been a point of contention in their relations with the countries they inhabit. This remains the case, as evidenced by a meeting that took place in Manila, Philippines, on March 23–25, 2009, at which representatives of indigenous peoples from around the world met at the International Conference on Extractive Industries and Indigenous Peoples.

The event highlighted that—from the Arctic to the tropics, to the rain forests of South America and Southeast Asia, and to the deserts and arid lands of Australia and Africa—oil, gas, and mining development activities are of critical importance to indigenous peoples, who increasingly are concerned about the impact of the interests of

national governments, extractive industries, and the far-reaching world market on their homelands, traditional territories, and customary resources. The Manila Declaration that was produced by the conference participants stated the indigenous position:

> We have suffered disproportionately from the impact of extractive industries as our territories are home to over sixty percent of the world's most coveted mineral resources. This has resulted in many problems to our peoples, as it has attracted extractive industry corporations to unsustainably exploit our lands, territories and recourses without our consent. This exploitation has led to the worst forms of, environmental degradation, human rights violations and land dispossession and is contributing to climate change.

Native Lands and Cultures

In Siberia and eastern Russia oil and gas extraction and mining ventures have removed large tracts of lands from indigenous use, and the transport of hydrocarbons across the lands of indigenous peoples interferes with their traditional activities. For much of the late twentieth century, hydrocarbon development in Russia took place on native lands, largely in western Siberian oil fields on Khanty and Mansi traditional territory and northwestern gas fields on Nenets homelands. During the 2000s, in the far east of Russia, controversies over the exploitation of oil reserves on Sakhalin Island have challenged the territorial rights of the Evenki, Nivkhi, and Uilta. While Russia's indigenous peoples have received some economic benefit from oil and gas development, they have no right to subsurface resources. But just as with oil development in Oklahoma during the 1920s, for some, the costs and negative effects of development on native societies, cultures, and the environment have outweighed the benefits.

Article 26 of the United Nations Declaration on the Rights of Indigenous Peoples, adopted in 2007, states that "[i]ndigenous peoples have the right to the lands, territories and resources which they have traditionally owned, occupied or otherwise used or acquired." Article 32 further goes on to assert that "[s]tates shall consult and cooperate in good faith with the indigenous peoples concerned through their own representative institutions in order to obtain their free and informed consent prior to the approval of any project affecting their lands or territories and other resources, particularly in connection with the development, utilization or exploitation of mineral, water or other resources." This principle of informed consent was emphasized during the World Bank's 2003 Extractive Industries Review, but all too often, indigenous rights are infringed on.

For instance, following its acquisition of Burlington Resources in 2006, ConocoPhillips became one of the chief developers of oil and gas resources in the Amazon River Basin—in Peru alone, it owns drilling rights in areas covering 10.5 million acres (4.3 million hectares) of tropical rain forest. In Ecuador, the Achuar, Kichwa, and Shuar peoples have been calling for the protection of the rain forest in an area that now is marked off for oil extraction. Elsewhere in the Amazon, indigenous peoples also are resisting the incursions of ConocoPhillips and other multinational companies.

In May 2008, the Peruvian government sent troops to back up police to quell protests by indigenous peoples over land, oil, and mineral rights in the Maranon River Basin. Indigenous organizations have accused the Peruvian government of selling those rights to foreign companies and point to a failure to consult with indigenous communities about plans for resource extraction. In the government's view, oil and mineral rights belong to the state.

Native Economic Development

Energy and mining development activities generally provide few long-term jobs for local residents who live on or near lands that are marked off for oil and mineral development. In Kenya's Rift Valley, for example, the Maasai are employed in gypsum, limestone, and soda ash mining, but the jobs available to natives overwhelmingly are for unskilled workers, while higher-paid skilled positions are filled by outsiders. In addition, pastoral lands have been reduced by the activities of extractive industries, forcing local Maasai communities to become dependent on corporations—which now own local water rights—for their water supplies.

It is not simply the case that traditional cultures are facing the onslaught of change and disruption brought by industry. In some parts of the world, indigenous business and community leaders are reaping the benefits of such development, and indeed, companies owned by indigenous groups now are involved in the energy sector. This is particularly the case in northern North America, where indigenous groups have negotiated subsurface rights.

The implementation of land claims in Alaska and in Canada's Yukon, Northwest, and Nunavut territories provides an institutional framework for mitigation and compensation, as well as the involvement of indigenous peoples in oil, gas, and mining activities. Furthermore, comprehensive land claims in northern Canada, such as the Inuvialuit Final Agreement (1984), the Gwich'in Comprehensive Agreement (1992), and the Sahtu Dene and Métis Agreement (1994), have granted indigenous people subsurface mineral rights for specific areas of land.

In the Northwest Territories, for example, extractive industries such as diamond mining and oil and gas exploration provide substantial income to some communities.

In Russia's northern autonomous districts, taxes from oil revenues represent a major source of revenue. While current legislation requires companies to compensate local indigenous communities on whose lands they operate, in reality, payments often are made directly to indigenous families rather than to the wider community or group. There also is a lack of community participation in regulatory processes concerned with large-scale development in Russia. The indigenous people complain that they have not had a say in oil development projects that affect their lands. They seek to ensure that such projects do not have a negative environmental impact and that they receive the economic benefits of development.

In the Danish territory of Greenland, the Inuit-led government aims to make oil, gas, and mining major drivers of the economy, and some political leaders have expressed the hope that resource extraction will generate enough revenues to help Greenland achieve full independence from Denmark. Greenland is viewed as a significant source of new mineral and petroleum development, evidenced by the opening of new mines and heightened interest in offshore exploration opportunities.

In 2008, the Danish-Greenlandic Self-Rule Commission concluded a series of negotiations on mineral rights, ownership of subsoil resources, and the administration of revenues from mining and hydrocarbon development. The commission underscored the fact that minerals located in Greenland's subsoil belong to Greenland, which therefore retains the rights to their extraction. Under the new political arrangement of self-rule, which was instituted on June 21, 2009, the government of Greenland was granted the rights to administer revenues from energy and other extractive industries.

Non-Native Economic Development and Native Rights

While political developments in Greenland mark a significant change in the relationship between indigenous people and the extractive industries, most indigenous peoples throughout the world feel increasing pressure from governments and corporations to sign off on development projects and to adapt to a changing environment driven by the activities of extractive industries. With no rights to oil, gas, and mineral resources, some indigenous peoples feel that they are losing control of their homelands and livelihoods, and they are calling for increased participation in consultation and decision-making processes. The rights of indigenous peoples to cultural sustainability; to the protection, conservation, and management of their natural resources; and to determine their own development are guaranteed within international human rights law, even if those rights are not necessarily recognized by nation-states.

In Canada, federal, provincial, and territorial governments, as well as industry, have a constitutional obligation to consult with aboriginal peoples on oil, gas, and mineral development. These obligations, however, are not always met. In Alberta, enormous deposits of oil sands (a type of petroleum deposit) lie underneath the traditional territories of the Cree and Dene peoples, as well as Métis communities. Indigenous concerns relate to environmental disturbance, air and water pollution, and habitat loss, as well as the impact of oil extraction activities on human health and community well-being.

The aboriginal people do derive some benefits from development related to oil sands resources. For example, around 1,200 aboriginal people are employed in the oil sands mines and related industries, and indigenous-owned companies have negotiated lucrative contracts with oil companies. Yet there is little consultation with aboriginal peoples about oil sands development, and environmental assessments are virtually nonexistent. The current consultation process fails to meet the high standards of conduct required by Canada's Supreme Court; in particular, it lacks a process of detailed land and resource use plans to identify the potential impacts of development on aboriginal and treaty rights. Negotiations continue between the Alberta government and five indigenous tribes regarding an aboriginal consultation process for further development in northeast Alberta.

In the same region, TransCanada is building a North Central Corridor Pipeline to take natural gas to areas of oil sands production. The pipeline will cross the traditional territory of the Lubicon Cree, a tribe of some 500 people. The Lubicon were overlooked by the Treaty 8 Commission, which guaranteed many First Nations' land rights in 1899, as they did not live near the water routes being surveyed by the treaty commissioners. Their lands later were considered British Crown lands by both the federal government and the government of Alberta, and the Lubicon have been engaged in a long-standing struggle to gain recognition of their rights to land and resources.

Negotiations between the Lubicon and the federal and provincial government remain open-ended. In the meantime, the Lubicon have experienced profound social and economic change and poverty as a result of the erosion of their traditional activities due to logging and oil and gas development. From the perspective of the Lubicon, they retain their rights to their traditional territory because they never signed a treaty. Since the early 1980s,

they have been articulating their claim to land rights, and their case has been raised repeatedly in United Nations bodies concerned with human rights.

Reports of continuing conflicts between indigenous communities and nation-states and between indigenous communities and national and multinational corporations during the twenty-first century have brought into focus concerns over the social, cultural, economic, and environmental impacts of extractive industries on indigenous peoples, while raising the question of who owns the rights to subsurface resources and their development. This is of particular concern in areas where indigenous peoples are fighting for land claims and rights to resources and in places where the ownership of subsurface rights is highly contested. But even where the rights to the oil and mineral resources are clear, the ramifications of the extraction of these resources on the native peoples concerned, on their societies, and on their ecosystems have not been uniformly positive.

Mark Nuttall

See also: Groups: North America—Cherokee. Countries—Canada; Kenya; Russia. Issues—Industrial Development; United Nations Declaration.

Further Reading

Churchill, Ward. *Struggle for the Land: Native North American Resistance to Genocide, Ecocide and Colonization.* San Francisco: City Lights, 2002.

Fjellheim, Rune S., and John B. Henriksen. "Oil and Gas Exploitation on Arctic Indigenous Peoples' Territories: Human Rights, International Law, and Corporate Social Responsibility." *Journal of Indigenous Peoples' Rights* 4 (2006): 8–52.

Fondahl, Gail, and Anna Sirina. "Oil Pipeline Development and Indigenous Rights in Eastern Siberia." *Indigenous Affairs* 1–2 (2006): 58–76.

Murashko, Olga. "Protecting Indigenous Peoples' Rights to Their Natural Resources: The Case of Russia." *Indigenous Affairs* 3–4 (2008): 48–59.

Nuttall, Mark. "Self-Rule in Greenland: Towards the World's First Independent Inuit State?" *Indigenous Affairs* 3–4 (2008): 64–70.

Passelac-Ross, Monique, and Verónica Potes. "Crown Consultation with Aboriginal Peoples in Oil Sands Development: Is It Adequate, Is It Legal?" *Occasional Paper* No. 19, Canadian Institute of Resources Law, 2007.

Soikan, Meitiaki Ole. "The Social, Environmental and Cultural Effects of Extractive Industries in Kajiado District, Rift Valley Province, Kenya: A Case Study of (Gypsum and Limestone) Cement Factories and Soda Ash Companies." Paper presented at the International Conference on Extractive Industries and Indigenous Peoples, Manila, Philippines, March 23–25, 2009.

Peyotism

When the Spanish conquistadores reached the isolated tribes of inland Mexico, they discovered the natives of the Cora tribe using an unknown substance in their nocturnal religious rites. In his *Historia del Nayarit, Sonora, Sinaloa y ambas Californias,* written in 1690 and published in 1754, Spanish historian José de Ortega described "a tray filled with *peyote* which is a diabolical root (*raiz diabolica*) that is ground up and drunk by them so that they may not become weakened by the exhausting effects of so long a function." While Ortega described peyote as a "diabolical root," the Mexican Indians called it a "divine cactus." A hallucinogenic drug containing mescaline derived from the peyote cactus, the substance has been in ritual use among the native peoples of Mexico for some 7,000 to 10,000 years.

The ritual and curative use of peyote was transmitted from Mexican tribes to Native Americans around 1870. Over the next fifty years, peyote use became diffused among the tribes of the Western United States. Although peyote was only one of many plants used in native religious ceremonies in Mexico and other parts of North and Central America, in North America its use became part of an important spiritual sacrament. The peyote faith was viewed as a means of accommodating and accepting the facts of modern life, while maintaining a connection with traditional Indian beliefs, and often achieving a higher level of religious insight and consciousness.

By 1906, the use of peyote had spread throughout the Great Plains. When Christian missionaries in the area threatened legislative action to ban the use of the drug, members of the Arapaho, Kiowa, and Oto tribes united; with the assistance of anthropologist James Mooney, they formed the Native American Church in Oklahoma in 1918. By formally organizing themselves as a church, members were exempt from criminal penalties for the ceremonial use of peyote according to federal laws at that time.

Although the Native American Church helped foster a pan-Indian identity among peyote users, it did little to dissuade whites and many Indians from attacking the movement. Many Native Americans who had been educated and favored assimilation into white culture saw the establishment of an Indian church as a step backward. In addition, many of those who remained devoted to their traditional tribal religions did not embrace the new practices.

Because peyote is a mild hallucinogen, federal, state, and local government officials opposed its use, regardless of its ceremonial function among Native Americans.

Eleven state governments and the federal government banned the use of peyote during the twentieth century. Although some overtures were made by the peyotists to explain that peyote was used as a sacrament, differentiating it from other substances such as alcohol that plagued Indian Country, most missionary groups condemned the new Indian church, blaming the use of peyote as the cause of poverty, illness, and death on Native American reservations.

Jonathan Koshiway was a founder of the Oto Church of the First-Born in 1914, which used both tobacco and peyote as sacraments, and he later helped organize the Native American Church. Influenced by different forms of Christianity, he had worked as a native evangelist for the Church of Jesus Christ of Latter-day Saints and had received some theological education in Kansas City. Koshiway's experiences and studies brought him to the conclusion that "the old native religion of his childhood was the same as the White Christianity of his maturity, with merely different phrasing and vocabulary." The ingestion of peyote and the tea made from peyote, he concluded, were roughly equivalent to the Christian sacramental use of bread and wine. He even saw symbolism in the fact that the Plains ritual number was echoed in the "four foundations" of Christianity: love, faith, hope, and charity.

The peyote faith stresses personal revelation and visions; encourages individual commitment to live a life of respect, generosity, and harmony; and places a heavy emphasis on the sacramental aspects of worship. Similar to the Arminian bent of mainstream American Protestantism, peyotists believe that each person must come to the peyote belief of their own volition through an overt decision of faith. Declaring this belief makes the communicant a part of the faith community—one that shows concern for other members.

Congress first acted to protect the ceremonial use of peyote in the Drug Abuse Control Amendments of 1965, which led American Indian scholar Vine Deloria, Jr., to call the Native American Church "the religion of the future," predicting in 1970 that it eventually would replace Christianity among Native Americans. Litigation on peyote's use and the ability of states to control a substance integral to American Indian religions (American Indian policy being the exclusive purview of the federal government) continued throughout the 1970s and 1980s.

In 1990, the U.S. Supreme Court gave the states the legal right to ban peyote in *Smith v. Oregon.* Congress acted to remedy this by enacting the Religious Freedom Restoration Act of 1993 and the American Indian Religious Freedom Act Amendments of 1994, which gives peyote special status as part of a religious sacrament.

Steven L. Danver

See also: Groups: North America—Navajo; Ute. Countries—United States. Issues—Indigenous Identity; Religion (Indigenous).

Further Reading

Anderson, Edward F. *Peyote: The Divine Cactus.* 2nd ed. Tucson: University of Arizona Press, 1996.

Deloria, Vine, Jr. *Custer Died For Your Sins: An Indian Manifesto.* Norman: University of Oklahoma Press, 1988.

LaBarre, Weston. *The Peyote Cult.* North Haven, CT: Shoe String, 1970.

Slotkin, J.S. *The Peyote Religion: A Study in Indian–White Relations.* New York: Octagon, 1975.

Smith, Huston, and Reuben Snake, eds. *One Nation Under God: The Triumph of the Native American Church.* Santa Fe, NM: Clear Light, 1996.

Stewart, Omer C. *Ute Peyotism: A Study of a Cultural Complex.* Boulder: University of Colorado Press, 1948.

Political Discrimination

Political discrimination is a form of discrimination that occurs when a country's political system limits the opportunity of social groups to participate in political activities because of their ethnicity or race, certain cultural characteristics such as language or religion, party membership, or political views.

While it is difficult to trace the origin of political discrimination, political scientists maintain that it often accompanies other forms of discrimination that develop as societies become more stratified. In a stratified society, access to certain conveniences or privileges, including political power, depends on an individual's class status. Many stratified societies in ancient times, particularly those that practiced slavery, gave little or no political rights to members of the lowest social classes. One of the oldest examples is the caste system practiced in India. Although education and other social changes gradually are diminishing the modern-day effects of this stratification, in the past, political power was reserved almost exclusively for members of the upper Brahmin and Kshatriya castes.

In Africa and Asia, many of these discriminatory systems survived during the colonial period. The existing social hierarchy was maintained by colonial powers to control and manage their extensive colonies. In the Dutch East Indies (modern-day Indonesia), for example, colonial authorities effectively employed members of the local aristocracy to rule parts of the colony as well as to collect taxes on their behalf.

Political discrimination still can be found in many parts of the world, although instances of overtly racist practices of political discrimination have declined since the second half of the twentieth century. This decline is partly attributable to the advance of democracy, which has resulted in increased political freedom, the installation of politically inclusive governments, and a growing global awareness and protection of human rights. International pressures and sanctions on governments also have played an important part in this trend. The last significant state-sponsored system of political discrimination, the racist apartheid regime in South Africa, was dismantled in 1994, and political rights were restored to the country's black citizens.

Political discrimination is motivated by a desire to prevent certain individuals or groups from changing or influencing the current political system, which is favorable to those in power. This is most obvious in the case of minority rule, as in South Africa under apartheid (1948–1994) and in Rhodesia (present-day Zimbabwe) under Prime Minister Ian Smith (1965–1979). In these countries, white-minority regimes blocked the political participation of the majority black population in order to maintain power.

Another reason for political discrimination is the potential security threat posed by certain segments of a population, which may force the state to limit the political rights of such groups. For example, the Kurdish diaspora in Central Asia has experienced political discrimination because of its separatist activities in the region. In Turkey, Kurdish political parties have been banned. Similarly, Kurds faced severe political restrictions in Iraq under Saddam Hussein until 1991.

Political discrimination also may be a result of attempts to protect indigenous rights, usually at the expense of non-native groups. Malaysia's constitution explicitly grants quotas for the *bumiputra,* the indigenous people, in civil service recruitment. This, together with other measures, eventually will have a negative effect on the political advancement of nonindigenous people. Similarly, since the end of apartheid, the South African government has implemented a series of affirmative action strategies to increase the share of black South Africans in the civil service and security forces, often at the expense of its white citizens.

The desire to maintain cultural or national identity may result in political discrimination against minorities, who are regarded as a threat to cultural homogeneity. In 1952, the Japanese government and people welcomed the decision of the Allied forces in Japan to denaturalize Korean nationals in the country. This decision marked the culmination of efforts by the Japanese government to ostracize Korean nationals in order to keep Japan a monoethnic nation-state. Although many Korean nationals finally obtained citizenship, they still are marginalized in Japanese society today.

Another example is the doctrine of Aryan racial superiority preached by Nazi leader Adolf Hitler, who believed that a strong Germany could be achieved only when those of non-Aryan ancestry were driven out of the country. This led to a series of politically and socially discriminating laws against the German Jewish population and ended with the extermination of millions of Jews at the hands of the Nazis.

There are many kinds of political discrimination. Deprivation of citizenship and the rights that come with it is paramount. Without citizenship, an individual cannot participate in elections to choose the government and parliament, cannot stand for election, and cannot work in public service or the armed forces. Noncitizens usually have limited access to government facilities and support, as well as restricted residency and legal status. Cases of forced denaturalization include the Jews in Germany in 1935, Koreans in Japan in 1952, Kurds in Syria in 1962, and black Africans in South Africa in 1971.

Another kind of political discrimination is achieved by limiting citizens' ability to exercise their political rights, such as the rights to vote, to join the armed forces, to access the civil service, to join political organizations, and to participate in judicial proceedings. For example, many authoritarian regimes disenfranchise legitimate voters during elections out of concern that they will vote for the opposition. Because of security concerns, some governments exclude certain citizens from occupying strategic posts; for example, Israeli Arab and Singaporean Malays are not permitted to serve in strategic senior military positions in their countries.

Although most political discrimination is ethnic or racial in nature, it does exist in other contexts. Under Indonesia's New Order (1966–1998), political rights were denied for millions of former members of the Communist Party. Many of the descendants of these people, who had no direct political connection with the Communist Party, also were prosecuted and barred from joining the military and public service.

Under many authoritarian regimes, membership in the ruling party is crucial. In China, for example, it is almost impossible for those who are not members of the Chinese Communist Party to occupy important leadership positions in government ministries or agencies. Similarly, Indonesia's New Order regime required all civil servants to be members of the ruling party, Golkar; members of other political parties generally were not able to occupy public office. Religion also may be a reason for discrimination. This was the case for Shiite Muslims in Iraq, whose political role was controlled under Saddam Hussein.

Sometimes political marginalization may be a product, intended or not, of other discriminatory policies. Lack of employment opportunities and access to education as a result of systemic discrimination can be politically detrimental to affected groups. Up to the early twentieth century, many African Americans were unable to vote in elections, because they could not pay the required poll tax or failed literacy tests. African Americans continued to be ostracized politically at least until the 1960s, even though their political rights were protected by the U.S. Constitution.

Severe political discrimination may spark violent ethnonationalist or separatist movements. The separation of East Pakistan (now Bangladesh) from Pakistan in 1971 was a result of political discrimination against Bengali citizens. As the majority ethnic population in East Pakistan, the Bengalis had complained about their inadequate representation in the central government administration and military. Many conflicts involving minorities in other parts of the world can be traced to unresolved grievances, many of them political.

Not all political grievances end in violence, however. Instead of inciting violence, some groups that experience political discrimination may thrive in areas other than politics. The Indonesian Chinese, for example, chose to become professionals in the private sector, including business and academia, as careers in politics, civil service, and the military are mostly closed to them. In other circumstances, marginalized people may leave their country as migrants or refugees.

Today, although many countries have outlawed discrimination in their legal systems, political discrimination still is prevalent, particularly in the developing world. Countries that continue to struggle with nation building and face minority conflicts or security threats may exercise some kind of political discrimination against segments of their population, placing restrictions or conditions on their political activities. These policies tend to be worded carefully and implemented cautiously to minimize extreme reactions from the affected population and to avoid international criticism.

Most remaining politically discriminatory policies are obscured, hidden under administrative measures and procedures. Administrative requirements that appear neutral could be used to exclude undesirable political candidates. For example, the state apparatus may require more paperwork or extra security checks for certain occupations in order to exclude foreign-born applicants. Questionnaires and tests in the civil servant recruitment process may be written in complex and sophisticated official language in order to screen out applicants with minority backgrounds. Such cases of indirect and obscure political discriminations can be difficult to monitor. The effects, however, are visible and sometimes easily shown, for example, through statistics.

Taufiq Tanasaldy

See also: *Issues*—Colonialism; Indigenous Governments; Indigenous Peoples and the United Nations; Political Participation.

Further Reading

Gurr, Ted Robert. *Minorities at Risk: A Global View of Ethnopolitical Conflicts.* Washington, DC: United States Institute of Peace Press, 1993.

———. *Peoples Versus States: Minorities at Risk in the New Century.* Washington, DC: United States Institute of Peace Press, 2000.

Midlarsky, Manus I. *The Evolution of Inequality: War, State Survival, and Democracy in Comparative Perspective.* Stanford, CA: Stanford University Press, 1999.

Peoples, Clayton D., and Tina Hsu Schweizer. "Restricting Public Life, Creating Deadly Strife: How Political Discrimination Impacts Interethnic Conflict." *Research in Social Movements, Conflicts, and Change* 28 (2010): 325–349.

Political Participation

The extent of indigenous peoples' political participation in nation-states depends partly on the existence of structures that either impede or facilitate participation and on financial resources to encourage participation.

Structural Barriers

Indigenous people that live as minority populations within larger nation-states often are precluded from meaningful political participation at the local, regional, and national levels because of structural barriers. These barriers can be simple—as in racially based legal prohibitions that were common in Asia, Australia, and Latin America into the twentieth century—or they can be historical anomalies that persist.

An example of the latter concerns the experience of Native Americans in the continental United States. Corralled onto reservations during the nineteenth century, Native American tribes came to live on remotely located and often geographically small areas of land—the Navajo tribe is a notable exception. The federal government recognized the right of tribes to govern themselves internally and, for the most part, has protected this dependent sovereign status from state government incursion. As such, the tribes enjoy internal local political sovereignty; however, their political participation at the state and national levels is curtailed significantly.

Because tribal reservations are not states within the U.S. federal system, they are not accorded representation in the U.S. Senate. And because the Native American population typically is small compared to surrounding populations, very few natives are elected to the U.S. House of Representatives. To the extent that native people serve in the U.S. Congress, it is through participation in the regular political party apparatus, which only rarely has produced successful native candidates, such as former senator Ben Nighthorse Campbell (R-CO).

Constitutional Status

Occasionally, indigenous peoples can achieve political representation through a recognized constitutional status that accords them meaningful political participation. In Spain, the Basque people control a federally recognized province. This accords them not only local and regional sovereignty, but also representation in the national parliament. Similarly, indigenous political parties have been formed to achieve focused representation.

In Canada, the Inuit people succeeded in having part of the Northwest Territories reconfigured into a new federal territory called Nunavut. Although Nunavut does not enjoy the status of a province in the Canadian federal system, the indigenous people of the Arctic have local and regional sovereignty and are represented in the federal parliament in Ottawa.

The Kurdish people of Iraq, since the establishment of a federal system in that country in 2005, have controlled a region and its governing structures, which accords them guaranteed representation in the federal parliament. The Kurdish people have two main political parties that contend with one another within the region

Officials unveil the flag of Nunavut, Canada's newest federal territory, on April 1, 1999. The creation of the territory gave the Inuit people, who constitute a vast majority of the population, local sovereignty and representation in parliament. *(Pool/AP Images)*

but cooperate on the national level. However, the Kurds of Iran, Syria, and Turkey do not enjoy this same level of political participation in their respective nation-states.

The Aboriginal people of Australia do not control regional entities within a federal system such as those in Canada, Iraq, or Spain. Nevertheless, they have requested seats in the national parliament. While this request has been rejected, state governments are considering similar requests.

Financial Resources

According to the United Nations, in 2010, indigenous people numbered 370 million, representing about 5 percent of the world's population. Yet they make up fully one-third of the world's extremely poor rural population of 900 million. Therefore, most indigenous people, like impoverished communities everywhere, have few financial resources available to influence the political discourse of the dominant societies in which they live.

In the United States, until indigenous peoples' rights movements gained momentum in the 1970s and 1980s, their political participation was marginal at best. However, once they claimed a voice in the voting franchise, organized themselves, reclaimed some of their lost lands and natural resources, and achieved some significant victories in judicial cases, the political impact of indigenous people began to be felt—despite structural and constitutional impediments.

In addition to public pressure and litigation, a key method for overcoming obstacles to greater political participation is the acquisition and targeted use of financial resources. This is especially true for the Native American tribes of the United States. With their sovereignty protected by federal law, American Indian reservations are largely exempt from state laws that may prohibit gambling activity. Therefore, many tribes have opened casino operations on their lands.

PACHAKUTIK

In 1995, indigenous activists in Ecuador launched the Pachakutik Movement for Plurinational Unity (referred to as Pachakutik) to encourage the candidacies of indigenous people for political office. In the pan-Andean Quechua language, *pacha* means "time" or "land" and *kutik* means "a return." Hence, the word signifies change, rebirth, and transformation, in the sense of both a return in time and the coming of a new era.

Pachakutik emerged out of years of debate on the roles of indigenous peoples in electoral politics, including whether indigenous organizations should put forward their own candidates and issues or whether they should support sympathetic leftist parties. Pachakutik represented the emergence of a third option, a new political movement in which indigenous peoples and other sectors of Ecuador's popular movements organized together as equals in a joint project to achieve the common goals of a new and better world.

The movement opposed neoliberal economic policies that privatized public resources and functions and favored a more inclusive and participatory political system. Pachakutik's leaders spoke of four revolutions: ethical, socioeconomic, educational, and ecological.

Pachakutik was an explicit reversal of a policy adopted by the Confederación de Nacionalidades Indígenas del Ecuador (CONAIE, Confederation of Indigenous Nationalities of Ecuador), the country's primary indigenous organization, not to participate in elections, because neither the political system nor political parties functioned in a way that represented the people's interests. CONAIE emerged in the highlands in 1986 as an anti-electoral political force in opposition to existing political parties, whereas Pachakutik emerged out of the Amazon among activists who were much more willing to engage in party politics.

In August 1995, Amazonian activists, such as CONAIE President Luis Macas, unilaterally announced the formation of an indigenous political movement called Pachakutik. Members of Pachakutik quickly merged their efforts with highland activists, who had created a parallel political movement called Plurinational Unity.

Pachakutik realized mixed results in electoral contests. In 1996, it allied with journalist Freddy Ehlers, who came in third in the presidential race. Macas, however, won a post as a national deputy, becoming the first indigenous person elected to a countrywide office in Ecuador. In 2002, Pachakutik supported Lucio Gutiérrez, who won the presidency. In exchange, Macas was named minister of agriculture, and another longtime leader, Nina Pacari, assumed the head of foreign affairs until half a year later, when Pachakutik broke with Gutiérrez over his neoliberal economic policies.

This experience made indigenous activists more cautious about allying with people outside their movement. As a result, four years later, Pachakutik remained in opposition to the more sympathetic government of Rafael Correa. Although largely excluded from national power and averaging about 10 percent of the vote in Congress, Pachakutik realized substantially more success in local contests within indigenous communities.

Marc Becker

In 1988, Congress passed the Indian Gaming Regulatory Act, which manages the tribal–state relationship with respect to gambling. Approximately 400 Native American gambling properties annually generate $18.5 billion in revenues. While most of this money is used by the tribes for education, infrastructure, and expansion of services for tribal members, much of it also is directed toward increased political participation by tribes at the state and federal levels. Yet it is the tribe—not individual Indians—that is participating.

This participation includes hiring lobbyists in Washington, D.C., to look after tribal interests in Congress and the executive branch, in the state capitals, and in financial centers. Political participation also comes in the form of large donations to candidates in local and federal elections who are favorable to the tribe. In this way, the Native American peoples of the United States have been able to overcome some of the structural barriers to political participation that are arrayed against them.

Electronic Communication

With the emergence of the Internet and electronic social and political networking capabilities, tribes and individual native people have been better equipped to get out their political message in a cost-efficient manner that reaches a maximum audience. While many indigenous people maintain television and radio stations as well as newspapers in places where these are not limited or prohibited by the central government, such modes of communication customarily have been directed toward tribal members and the native community. Thus, political views were not regularly or systematically externalized. Now, native peoples can beam their political message around the globe, and researchers as well as policy makers easily can find out what native people think about political issues that affect them.

An increasing number of indigenous peoples maintain their own Web sites, outlining their historical perspectives, describing current events and issues, and discussing ongoing political and social movements related to their community. Many scholars regard the Internet and its accompanying electronic revolution as a great leveler in society across cultures and socioeconomic classes. If this is true, then indigenous people will only benefit from the revolution by making known their plight and their views.

International Representation

Despite significant obstacles to political participation within their nation-states, indigenous people have a forum on the international level within the United Nations (UN) in which to raise their concerns. Established in 2002, the Permanent Forum on Indigenous Issues (PFII) is an advisory body to the UN Economic and Social Council. According to its mandate, the PFII undertakes the following tasks: (1) provide expert advice and recommendations on indigenous issues to the council, as well as to programs, funds, and agencies of the United Nations, through the council; (2) raise awareness and promote the integration and coordination of activities related to indigenous issues within the UN system; and (3) prepare and disseminate information on indigenous issues.

The PFII was instrumental in the adoption of the Declaration on the Rights of Indigenous Peoples (UNDRIP) by the UN General Assembly on September 13, 2007. The declaration passed by a vote of 143–4 (Australia, Canada, New Zealand, and the United States opposed the measure), with eleven abstentions. Interestingly, the four states that initially voted against the declaration are home to some of the largest indigenous populations; all four have since reversed their positions. Article 5 of UNDRIP recognizes the right of political participation: "Indigenous peoples have the right to maintain and strengthen their distinct political, legal, economic, social and cultural institutions, while retaining their right to participate fully, if they so choose, in the political, economic, social and cultural life of the State."

Another informal yet vital function of the PFII is to serve as a nexus for networks of indigenous peoples to interact with and strengthen one another. So, for example, while the Maya of Guatemala, Uighurs of Western China, Roma of Central Europe, and Maori of New Zealand each have their own political and social movement networks, the PFII provides a common forum for these individualized networks to come together—sharing valuable strategies and tactics for increasing political participation and impact.

Importance of Political Participation

Indigenous peoples traditionally did not recognize participation in the political processes of their host states as important. So long as they controlled their internal affairs and were left alone, they had little interest in the politics of the dominant society.

However, as assimilation and economic integration occurred with almost every native group in almost every larger state, the crisis of disappearing cultures became apparent. Consequently, most indigenous peoples now recognize the importance of participation in the political processes of the dominant societies in which they live in order to protect their cultural heritage and preserve the existence of their societies.

Michael J. Kelly

See also: Groups: North America—Navajo. Groups: South Asia and Middle East—Kurds. Countries—Australia; Canada; Iraq; United States. Issues—Colonialism; Indigenous Peoples and the United Nations; United Nations Declaration.

Further Reading

Cleary, Edward L., and Timothy J. Steigenga. *Resurgent Voices in Latin America: Indigenous Peoples, Political Mobilization, and Religious Change.* New Brunswick, NJ: Rutgers University Press, 2004.

Magallanes, Catherine Iorns. "Dedicated Parliamentary Seats for Indigenous Peoples." *Murdoch University Electronic Journal of Law* 10:4 (December 2003), https://elaw.murdoch.edu.au.

Mason, W. Dale. *Indian Gaming: Tribal Sovereignty and American Politics.* Norman: University of Oklahoma Press, 2000.

Richardson, Benjamin J., Shin Imai, and Kent McNeil, eds. *Indigenous Peoples and the Law: Comparative and Critical Perspectives.* Portland, OR: Hart, 2009.

Sokolow, Gary, Jerry Stubben, and Raymond Smith. *Native Americans and Political Participation.* Santa Barbara, CA: ABC-CLIO, 2005.

Witmer, Richard, and Frederick Boehmke. "American Indian Political Incorporation in the Post-Indian Gaming Regulatory Act Era." *Social Science Journal* 44:1 (2007): 127–145.

Poverty

In the twenty-first century, native peoples are disproportionately represented on most indices of poverty throughout the world. From the poorest countries to the wealthiest, indigenous peoples commonly occupy the bottom rung of the socioeconomic ladder. Native poverty is a relatively recent phenomenon that can be traced to the historical processes of imperialism and conquest wrought by European powers, internal colonialism, ethnic cleansing, and social marginalization, as well as industrialization, globalization, and the uneven distribution of resources.

Indigenous people constitute just 4 percent of the world's total population, but they represent 10 percent of the global impoverished population. Asia is home to the vast majority of native people who are impoverished, representing approximately 60 percent to 70 percent of the worldwide total. Africa has about 17 percent of the global indigenous poor, while Latin America has about 18 percent. Overall, one out of every three indigenous people today lives in poverty.

Developing nations with indigenous populations vary significantly with respect to the share of native peoples who are impoverished, ranging from 5 percent in China to more than 50 percent in many other countries and reaching as high as 81 percent in Mexico and 85 percent in the Democratic Republic of Congo. In Latin America, the overall poverty rate averages 13 percent, while for indigenous peoples it is 30 percent. In the United States, the officially reported poverty rate on Indian reservations in 2010 was 28.4 percent compared to the national rate of 15.1 percent.

Factors That Explain Indigenous Poverty

A number of social factors explain indigenous poverty. Native peoples generally find themselves marginalized from mainstream society on a variety of levels. First, many have language, culture, and belief systems that are distinct from the rest of society. Second, within their home countries, they usually are an ethnic minority, and their political participation, especially at the national level, lags behind that of the rest of society. Third, native peoples tend to identify more closely with their community than with the nation. Fourth, they often are geographically removed from the centers of economic activity; therefore economic growth does not affect them in the same way as the rest of the population, and they frequently are beyond the reach of programs, either state or nongovernmental, designed to foster growth or development. Finally, in many instances, native peoples come from precolonial societies and have had to overcome the legacy of conquest, colonization, and violence.

Poverty is not the exclusive condition of the indigenes of poor nations. Even in the wealthiest nations, such as Australia, Canada, New Zealand, and the United States, poverty rates among native peoples far outpace those of the general population. In addition to low income levels that fail to meet a certain threshold for survival, indigenous peoples rate poorly on several quality-of-life indices.

To assess global development and poverty, the United Nations and the World Bank employ the Millennium Development Goal (MDG) Indicators, a set of sixty statistics that measure progress toward meeting international goals for development, health, education, and environmental sustainability. These baseline measures include mortality rates for children under the age of five (referred to as under-five mortality), access to clean water, adequate nutrition, literacy, and net primary school enrollment.

Across Asia, indigenous peoples rank behind the national averages on several of the MDG Indicators. In India, under-five mortality and male literacy rates among Scheduled Tribes (an official designation for the country's indigenous tribes) trail the average of the rest of society. In Laos and Vietnam, the Hmong have the lowest female literacy rates. The Hill Tribes in Thailand; the Kammu and Leu in Laos; and the Ba Na, Hmong, and Muong peoples of Vietnam have the worst access to adequate water resources in the region.

In Latin America, native peoples rank lowest on the MDG Indicators across the board. Infant mortality rates and cases of child malnutrition, for example, are highest among Quechua speakers in Bolivia and Peru and the Mam in Guatemala compared to other national groups. Female illiteracy is most prominent in Peru among Quechua speakers.

In Africa, under-five mortality rates are highest among West African groups, such as the Fulani and Tuareg. Whereas the Ethiopian and Maasai native groups have the lowest under-five morality rates, they also have the worst access to adequate water sources. Education indices are also lower among indigenous peoples, even among those with higher rates of literacy, as in Namibia.

In the United States, 36 percent of Native American families with two children under the age of eighteen who reside on reservations live below the poverty line (the poverty threshold in 2011 was $22,350 for a family of four), compared to 9.2 percent of families nationwide. Some reservations have even higher poverty rates, such as the San Carlos Reservation in Arizona (55.3 percent) and the Pine Ridge Reservation in South Dakota (50.8 percent).

The period from 1995 to 2004 was declared the Decade of Indigenous People by the United Nations. Despite the fanfare and global attention paid to indigenous peoples, the decade brought little progress with respect to lifting native peoples out of poverty. In Latin America, of the five countries with significant indigenous populations—Bolivia, Ecuador, Guatemala, Mexico, and Peru—only Guatemala saw a reduction in poverty among its native peoples. However, even those improvements proceeded at a slower pace than among nonindigenous sectors.

The decade also revealed that indigenous people often are far removed from changes that occur within the broader, national economy. In Ecuador and Peru, for example, both countries saw an increase in poverty nationwide from 1995 to 2004. However, this jump in overall poverty was not matched by comparable changes in poverty rates among indigenes. Moreover, the poverty gap (the average income or economic resources needed by indigenous people to reach the poverty line) not only is larger for the indigenous poor than the nonindigenous poor, but it also has widened in all countries with indigenous populations, including China and Vietnam.

Education

In terms of education, the twenty-first century brought increased access to schooling for indigenous populations.

However, the same was true for the rest of society, meaning that the education gap did not change substantially. In India, while 60 percent of nonindigenous people attend secondary school, only 40 percent of indigenous people (that is, members of Scheduled Tribes) do so. The difference is about the same as it was in the 1940s. In Africa, access to and achievement in education has improved overall. Nevertheless, the gap between those who have gone to school and those who have never attended has become more pronounced. This is especially true of native women in Africa. Likewise, in rural Laos, 34 percent of non–Lao Tai women have never attended school—twice the percentage of non–Lao Tai men and almost six times that of Lao Tai women.

In sub-Saharan Africa, of the 23 million girls who are not in school, three-quarters are from indigenous groups; similarly, South Asia has a comparable number of females who are not in school, of whom two-thirds are from indigenous groups. In the Middle East, of the 5 million girls who are not enrolled in school, 90 percent are indigenous females, while in Latin America, of the 1.5 million girls out of school, almost all are from indigenous groups.

In Latin American countries with significant indigenous populations, the education gap between indigenous and nonindigenous youths (over age fifteen) is pronounced, ranging from an average of 6.4 years of schooling (2.3 fewer years than nonindigenes) in Peru to 5.9 years of schooling (3.7 fewer years than nonindigenes) in Bolivia. Guatemala has the lowest level of indigenous education at 3.5 years of schooling per student, as compared to 6.3 years for nonindigenes. Initiatives targeting indigenous education have made some progress, as governmental and nongovernmental efforts in the 1990s helped shrink the gap. In Mexico, efforts to address native education over the last three decades have reduced the gap between indigenous and nonindigenous education by approximately 66 percent.

Even where education is made more available, indigenous schools are plagued by high rates of failure, repetition, and dropping out. Results on regional and international standardized tests and national school tests during the 2000s indicate lower scores on reading and math exams for indigenous students. In Latin America, the performance gap between indigenous and nonindigenous students is greatest in Peru and smallest in Mexico.

This problem is compounded by the fact that indigenous children continue to work while in school much more frequently than nonindigenous children. This reflects one of the foremost problems in developing policy that places education at the center of poverty reduction reforms. For rural native communities, cultural norms may include child labor, as children play a key role in the family economy. The requirement that families send their children to school removes their labor from the family economy and also incurs additional expenses such as transportation, uniforms and shoes, and school supplies. Therefore, many indigenous people consider education an expensive luxury, entailing out-of-pocket expenses that they cannot afford.

Another problem facing the indigenous population is limited and uneven access to bilingual education programs. A foremost complaint among native peoples is that they have little say in the development of the educational services provided to them. In Latin America, Mexico is a notable exception, as compensatory education programs include native peoples in the management of schools and learning processes.

Gap in Education Returns and Earnings

More education, however, does not automatically translate into greater earnings for indigenous peoples. In terms of returns on education, indigenous people generally earn about 40 percent less than nonindigenous peoples for each additional year of education.

In Bolivia, each additional year of schooling results in a 9 percent increase in earnings for nonindigenous people, while in Mexico, the number is 10 percent. However, in the indigenous sector, each additional year of schooling increases earnings by only 6 percent in Bolivia and 8 percent in Mexico. Peru is the exception to the rule, as it is the only indigenous country to register greater earnings per additional year of schooling for indigenous people compared to nonindigenous people (13 percent compared to 12 percent).

Whereas the gap between education returns at the secondary level is slight, the gap in higher education is significant. In Ecuador, for example, the average return for each year of undergraduate schooling is 7 percent for indigenous people and 8 percent for nonindigenous people. For those who completed higher education, the earnings gain is 15 percent for nonindigenous people, compared to a mere 9 percent for indigenous workers.

While indigenous peoples often are at a disadvantage because of inadequate education and training, in Latin America and elsewhere, indigenous people often remain disadvantaged in the labor market even when they have the same training as nonindigenous people. In fact, whereas about half of the earnings differential can be attributed to better human capital (education, training, and abilities), the other half remains unaccounted for, indicating that discrimination may play a role in compensation disparities. From the 1990s to 2004, while the unexplained earnings gap among males in Ecuador and Peru increased, in Bolivia, Guatemala, and Mexico, the gap decreased.

The situation is gradually improving in other nations as well: In the late 1980s, the earnings gap between indigenous and nonindigenous peoples in Mexico was approximately one-third; by the early 2000s, it was closer to one-fourth. Those victimized by the earnings gap tend to be young, with at least a secondary education and employed in the nonagricultural sector. This is a concern for policy makers who trumpet education as the key to escaping poverty and promoting development. In Asia, many indigenous peoples have found education to be a stepping-stone out of poverty. Yet many native people in Asia still earn significantly less than nonindigenous people and suffer from labor market discrimination.

Health Care

The last two decades have seen significant advances in health care that have improved living conditions for the general population. However, native peoples continue to experience health deficits. Not only are indigenous people more likely to suffer from poor health, even though many diseases they suffer from are preventable, they also are less likely to receive medical attention.

For example, in India and Vietnam, where considerable inroads have been made to reduce poverty, many health programs do not cover indigenous peoples. Whereas most indigenous peoples have been vaccinated against tuberculosis, the vast majority do not receive vaccinations for diphtheria, pertussis, tetanus, measles, and polio. Only about one-third of the indigenous people in India and Vietnam are vaccinated against all diseases.

Native peoples have uneven access to services and infrastructure at best. In Vietnam, for example, indigenous and nonindigenous peoples have equal access to electricity and the Internet; however, only 5 percent of ethnic minorities (a group that includes indigenous people) have access to adequate water supplies, compared to 25 percent of nonindigenous peoples. Moreover, ethnic minorities are less likely to have sanitation services and are more likely to live in temporary housing.

Indigenous people in Latin America, particularly women and children, also have limited access to basic health services. Health indicators, such as maternal mortality, in-hospital births, and vaccination coverage, are worse for indigenous peoples than for the nonindigenous population. Among all Latin American nations, health insurance coverage fails to reach 50 percent of the population, and the figures are much lower for indigenous populations. The percentages of the indigenous populations in Guatemala and Mexico with health insurance coverage at the turn of the twenty-first century were 5 percent and 17 percent, respectively; conversely, for the nonindigenous population, the percentages with health insurance in the same countries were 18 percent and 43 percent, respectively. In Ecuador and Peru, however, indigenous rates of health insurance were comparable to those of nonindigenous society; coverage in Ecuador for both was 12 percent, while in Peru, 47 percent of non-indigenes had health insurance compared to 41 percent of indigenes.

Another health concern for policy makers is malnutrition. In all countries with indigenous people, children disproportionately suffer from malnutrition compared to nonindigenous children. This is true even in countries where general malnutrition rates are low, such as Mexico.

Malnutrition also is responsible for the stunting (reduced growth rate) of indigenous children. In Mexico, indigenous children are almost three times more likely to experience stunting as nonindigenous children. In Ecuador, chronic malnutrition rates for indigenous peoples are double those of nonindigenous peoples; consequently, their children are twice as likely to have stunted development as compared to their nonindigenous counterparts. In Guatemala, the rate of stunting for the entire population is 44 percent; however, it is almost 60 percent for the indigenous population, about twice the figure recorded for nonindigenous children.

The derivative effects of malnutrition also are manifest in other indices of poverty. High rates of malnutrition among women produce high infant mortality rates as well as increased vulnerability to disease. Another consequence is low academic achievement.

Poverty Reduction

Poverty reduction programs have been implemented in all Latin American countries, with varying degrees of success. This is particularly true of efforts to assist the poor with school supplies and school nutrition. However, many programs do not specifically target the indigenous poor, despite their overwhelming need. And economic policies focused on reducing poverty for the general population do not guarantee comparable reductions in poverty for native peoples. Concomitant with general antipoverty initiatives, programs targeted directly at the indigenous population are also necessary.

In Guatemala, four out of five programs barely favor indigenous people, while the other favors nonindigenous people. In Peru, only one major school program has a higher incidence among indigenous people, while the rest favor nonindigenous people. In Mexico, on the other hand, rural poverty programs strongly favor indigenous families.

Economic growth in China and other Asian countries has translated into improved conditions for their native populations. In China, the percentage of people living below the World Bank's poverty line has dropped from 85 percent in 1981 to 15.9 percent in 2008. Moreover, although China is home to nearly 20 percent of the world's population, it has only 5 percent of all impoverished indigenous peoples in the world. Other countries that have made significant strides in reducing poverty among natives include India and Vietnam.

Asia's success in achieving sustainable economic growth has allowed those countries to implement poverty reduction strategies that have afforded native peoples better health, education, and earning opportunities. Therefore, in Asia, more social programs have been implemented to benefit indigenous populations than in most other regions.

In Vietnam, for example, native peoples receive a higher percentage of preferential credit, free health care, tuition exemptions and reductions, and agricultural, forestry, and aquaculture support. In India, indigenous people are more likely to benefit from the Integrated Child Development Services program, and they often are the beneficiaries of the National Rural Employment Scheme. In China, urban indigenes such as the Hui and Manchu have benefited from a variety of social programs. Moreover, China, like India, has implemented policies designed to benefit indigenous people exclusively; such policies include easing access to political office, looser fertility restrictions (as opposed to China's famous one child policy), and affirmative action measures that have increased indigenous matriculations at colleges and universities and made available education subsidies.

Efforts to reduce indigenous poverty have been undertaken at various levels, from constitutional and legislative (reforms), to greater political representation, to greater social spending and support for programs such as bilingual education and tailored health care programs. Over the last two decades, several countries have tailored health care programs to the specific conditions and cultures of indigenous peoples. For example, some have targeted the indigenous poor with direct cash payments to families in exchange for keeping children in school and obtaining basic health coverage. In Ecuador, the government has experimented with implementing national health services that offer traditional as well as modern treatments.

The state also has attempted to improve education with the creation of more high schools and outreach programs to indigenous communities, including extension learning services.

In Mexico, the program Oportunidades (Opportunities) has helped indigenous people overcome some of the obstacles imposed by poverty by reducing the opportunity costs (such as school supplies) and has fostered the productive potential of indigenous children through education and training. In addition to producing sharp upturns in schooling attainment, Oportunidades also has pushed initiatives to improve indigenous health and nutrition while reducing short-term poverty.

Reforms alone, however, have not brought about a reduction in poverty. Policy makers also must address discrimination. In Latin America, more so than in other regions, labor market discrimination is high and poses a challenge to reducing indigenous poverty levels. Until Latin American governments address labor market discrimination and earnings disparities, reform efforts to reduce poverty will be only partially successful at best.

Antipoverty initiatives in Australia, Canada, New Zealand, and the United States have been undertaken to address the demands for self-determination among native populations. However, the results have been mixed. Perhaps the most successful efforts made by federal governments to alleviate indigenous poverty include acknowledging indigenous rights to and facilitating self-representation.

Research conducted over the last decade by sociologist Stephen Cornell found a correlation between indigenous self-government and reduced incidences of poverty among Native American groups in the United States. Central to Cornell's argument is that state bureaucrats who make decisions on behalf of indigenous people have no stake in the outcome of their decisions. Moreover, there is little accountability for any mistakes made. However, those who have a vested interest in the well-being of the society and the economy—indigenous peoples themselves—are more likely to make the best decisions.

Despite efforts to improve the situation of indigenous people around the world, the poverty gap between indigenous and nonindigenous peoples, for the most part, has persisted and even widened. Whereas geography, topography, the environment, and climate are sometimes to blame for the lack of economic development in certain regions—there are many natural impediments to infrastructure—the main culprits for the persistence of native poverty are predatory national and multinational corporations and indifferent or ineffective nation-states. On one hand, extractive industries, from mineral and hydraulic to petroleum and gas, have exploited lands and political cultures where the rule of law is weak, particularly with regard to indigenous people. On the other hand, nation-states often have failed to implement appropriate social welfare programs that target indigenous populations in order to alleviate the conditions of poverty or that would build human capital through investments in health and education. Moreover, nation-states have not fostered cultures of self-determination and economic independence, which are instrumental in delivering indigenous peoples out of poverty in some countries.

Kenneth Kincaid

See also: *Issues*—Colonialism; Education; Indigenous Peoples and the United Nations; Industrial Development.

Further Reading

Cornell, Stephen. *Indigenous Peoples, Poverty and Self-Determination in Australia, New Zealand, Canada and the United States.* Joint Occasional Papers on Native Affairs (JOPNA No. 2006-02). Tucson, AZ: Native Peoples Institute for Leadership, 2006.

De la Peña, Guillermo. "Social and Cultural Policies Toward Indigenous Peoples: Perspectives from Latin America." *Annual Review of Anthropology* 34 (2005): 717–739.

Eversole, Robyn, John-Andrew McNeish, and Alberto D. Cimadamore, eds. *Indigenous Peoples and Poverty: An International Perspective.* London: Zed, 2006.

Gafar, John. "Income Distribution, Inequality, and Poverty During Economic Reforms in Guyana." *Journal of Developing Areas* 38:1 (Autumn 2004): 55–77.

Hall, Gillette, and Harry Anthony Patrinos, eds. *Indigenous Peoples, Poverty, and Development.* New York: Cambridge University Press, 2012.

———, eds. *Indigenous Peoples, Poverty, and Human Development in Latin America.* New York: Palgrave Macmillan, 2006.

Harmon, Alexandra. *Rich Indians: Native People and the Problem of Wealth in American History.* Chapel Hill: University of North Carolina Press, 2010.

Perreault, Thomas. "Social Capital, Development, and Indigenous Politics in Ecuadorian Amazonia." *Geographical Review* 93:3 (July 2003): 328–349.

Rao, K. Nageswara. *Poverty in India: Global and Regional Dimensions.* New Delhi, India: Deep & Deep, 2005.

Sandefur, Gary D., and National Research Council. *Changing Numbers, Changing Needs: American Indian Demography and Public Health.* Washington, DC: National Academy Press, 1996.

Yapa, Lakshman. "The Poverty Discourse and the Poor in Sri Lanka." *Transactions of the Institute of British Geographers,* new series, 23:1 (1998): 95–115.

Racism

The meanings of the terms *race* and *racism* have varied throughout history, with shifts in meaning often coinciding with periods of significant change in colonial and global relations. During such times, the meaning and interpretation of a concept such as race may change to fit the current political or cultural situation, a process that is referred to as "racial formation."

Racial formation is the theory that ideas about group identity are an outgrowth of the social context of a time. Race is not an objective fact, but rather an idea that is socially constructed. This does not mean that there are not important physical and cultural differences among peoples. At the same time, ethnic differentiation should not lead to racial domination, whereby differences among peoples become the basis for social stratification and the suppression of groups that are deemed inferior. Nevertheless, the concepts of race, racial prejudice, and discrimination often coexist with the rise of powerful states, the legacy of colonialism, and the ideological subordination of indigenous peoples. Furthermore, racism can be viewed through psychological, sociological, and sociopolitical lenses. Each of these approaches results in different perspectives, especially for indigenous peoples in the modern world.

Once they arrived in the New World, European empires called their invasion and seizure of native lands "discovery," and they formed early notions of race and what they called "savagery" without regard for the societies that they encountered and conquered. Thus, sociohistorical views of native peoples must include these histories of conquest, racial stratification, at times genocide, and, perhaps most important, the effects on the culture and societies of native groups. Similar processes occurred in virtually all encounters between Europeans and native people, although each encounter was shaped by the specific groups that came into contact and the specific traditions of each native people.

The existence of "race-like" conceptions in earlier empires and in other areas demonstrates that, contrary to some popular beliefs, racism was not solely a European invention. But equally clearly, it became most fully developed in European colonies and carried into the laws and customs of the succeeding independent states.

Racial Construction and Conquest (1492–1620)

The initial development of race as a concept applied to indigenous Americans became significant shortly after 1492. Even though the term *race* was not used, the idea lurked below the surface of many discussions about the rights and even the humanity of the natives that took place within what were considered *civilized* nations. Many labeled native peoples in Africa and the Americas *savages* and considered them *un-Christian* and *uncivilized,* terms that were used interchangeably.

This usage appears in discussions of the Taino-Arawak peoples living on the island of Hispaniola, and it is typical of the initial stages of European conquest. Upon his return to Spain, Christopher Columbus took with him a few Taino-Arawak individuals to demonstrate to the king and queen the existence of the *Indios*; the natives then were sold in the slave markets of Seville. Thus, during Columbus's time, race began to be reconceptualized and socially constructed as referring to a person's complexion rather than to his or her culture or ethnonational identity, and the indigenous people of the Americas became identified by their race.

As a result of Columbus's actions, including enslavement, and the spread of new diseases to which the native peoples had no immunity, the Taino-Arawak population was decimated in the following years. Many other Spanish and other Europeans followed Columbus's lead, resulting in a further reduction of the native population. As a result of the steep decline in the native workforce, the Spanish began to import blacks from Africa. They became the first race-based slaves imported into the Americas. Thus, the social construction of race is intimately connected to the genocide of the Taino-Arawak by 1540 and the creation of the world's first race-based slave population.

Similarly, within a few decades, Spanish explorer Hernán Cortés and his military force conquered the Aztec people, reducing them and all indigenous peoples in Mexico to the lowered status of Indian, even though they once had ruled one of the world's great empires. Skin tone, in addition to vast cultural differences, allowed the dominating groups to gain instant and permanent recognition of their status by virtue of race. In this way, the concept of the savage came to connote racial distinctions that were inescapable and lifelong, and the conquistadores and their descendants came to hold a permanent elite status over the native population. The effect on the native peoples in the Americas was always the same—either genocidal destruction or racial subordination with an attendant loss of culture and, more significantly, a loss of sovereignty and freedom.

The racial concepts that were in currency at that time differed importantly from those in common use in the twenty-first century. Indios were considered to be a lower race of people, partially enslaved, and killed in large numbers; though the Spanish definition of American natives was problematic, interbreeding and intermarriage further complicated matters. As Bartolomé de las Casas and others decried brutalization of the indigenous peoples in debates with European theorists of the Catholic Church, colonists already had begun replacing Native American slaves with Africans. By the 1550s and 1560s, Las Casas and other philosopher-priests of the time regretted supporting the enslavement of black Africans to replace the indigenous Arawak. But at least two trajectories of racial formation already had begun during this time period: one from the conquest of native peoples and the other from the enslavement of blacks.

Thus, millions of peoples and hundreds of societies—ranging from the relatively egalitarian Taino-Arawak peoples to the Aztec Empire—were reduced to a single racial category: Indio, or Indian in English. This same transformation extended throughout Central and South America, including the great Inca Empire in the Andes Mountains, the Calusa on the Florida Peninsula, and indigenous peoples throughout North America.

The transformation of racial distinctions into clear divisions within social institutions was considerably more ambiguous in the Caribbean colonies dominated by Spain and France than in the system that the English developed to subjugate the Irish and later replicated in their American colonies. The so-called savage tribes and indigenous chieftains of Ireland systematically were excluded from English social institutions because of their religion and cultural origin. When the English carried this system into their colonies in the Americas, they applied their concept of race to the Native Americans and subsequently to blacks, defining those races as subhuman, savage, and uncivilized. This transformation subsumed local identities and indigenous ethnonational distinctions under one category—race. Over centuries, the English institutionalized and hardened their racial categories to include Indian, black, and, later, a concept of the white race. These concepts can be seen in contemporary constructs of race and racism.

Racial Formation in the Americas (1600s–1900)

The first major English colonies in the Americas demonstrate the evolution of such racial distinctions, beginning with the Jamestown settlement in Virginia in 1607 and the Plymouth settlements in Massachusetts after 1620. Both English settlements tried to befriend the local native communities in order to get food and supplies, although they also had some conflicts, usually over land and leadership. These early colonists reported that the so-called savages were much healthier than the colonists, and many observers noted that native homes were clean and well maintained. Such observations underscored the gap between the poverty of many of the English settlers and the prosperous conditions of the indigenous peoples.

As more colonists migrated into the region, settlements expanded and armed conflicts with native tribes erupted. There were occasional pauses following agreements and treaties, but only until both colonies ultimately broke their treaties, with the Powhatan and Wampanoag

people, respectively. They justified this on the grounds that the natives were neither civilized nor Christian and thus could not enter into agreements with civilized peoples. Both cases set a precedent for future encounters, with high percentages of the native population eliminated by warfare, disease, and enslavement.

The grouping of diverse native peoples as Indians underpinned the settlers' political philosophy. Given the relative health and well-being of the indigenous peoples in what became New England, charges of "savagery," "brutality," and "lack of civilization" were actually rationalizations, not causes, for racialization and the elimination of the native population. Similarly, the supposed "inferiority" of black Africans became a rationalization for enslavement. Rationalizations for slavery, displacement, and murder were necessary, because such treatment of humans was considered immoral in all Christian religions.

When English colonists in Virginia first bought and kept African slaves around 1619, they simply adapted existing systems of race-based slavery to their own knowledge of how to dominate subordinated peoples through laws in their existing social institutions. Thereafter, race became immutable and permanently stratifying, precisely because of the classification of different races for different purposes: conquest and elimination for American natives; enslavement and subordination for the native Africans, now called Negros or blacks; and supremacy and cultural domination for those people first considered Christian, Anglo, and then gradually white—that is, of European descent.

The United States inherited this system, at least in its agricultural economies in the southern and middle colonies. After independence from England, these racialized categories became "facts" that were enshrined in the U.S. Constitution as part of the "Three-Fifths Compromise," which allowed states to count slaves as three-fifths of a person in reckoning their population for purposes of proportional representation, and in regulation about "intercourse" (that is, commercial exchange) with natives, thus defining native peoples as aliens in their own lands. In fact, the new republic would replicate central institutional features and social engines for constructing and maintaining systems of domination and perpetual stratification, many of which had been developed in Ireland. These were laws governing property, land holdings, inheritance, education, political participation, exclusion from some forms of legal protections, control of the military and police forces, taxation, trade, language, religion, and family systems. The last-named area was especially onerous for indigenous peoples with traditionally matrilineal societies (tracing descent through the female line) who were viewed as immoral, as they did not follow European patrilinality (tracing descent through the male line).

Under race-based slavery, African natives had all of these spheres of their lives either highly regulated or completely denied to them. Indians were a more complex group to control, as many tribes remained strong and thus could resist domination and maintain their own social systems—at least for a time. However, these indigenous institutions were under constant assault.

Many treaties required legal reinterpretation of existing land tenure and socioeconomic relations that were formed through the simple expedient of denying the rights of all indigenous peoples in the new country, even though it was built on the very land that they once controlled.

The central social features of racial domination in the first years of the United States were built around a number of foundations. The most obvious and powerful feature that overlapped all others was the construction of laws, social policies, and legal practices that maximized and enforced the deep-set stratification and race-based inequality that underpinned the entire system. Also, the controlling systems of racism were built over, around, and for social institutions that separated white Christian immigrant Americans from black slaves and Indian peoples. Early racial purity rules, especially in the English colonies, excluded nonwhites, hardening the racial rules for native Africans and underpinning "blood" descent for Native Americans. These rules did not acknowledge national origin and typically refused full citizenship to nonwhites. Instead, all Indian peoples were marked for elimination or assimilation, and treaties with them often were repealed as soon as the external threat was gone.

These three forms continued to evolve and take shape under the U.S. government from the seventeenth until mid-nineteenth century. Purity for whites was defined mostly as Anglo and Christian heritage at first. The hardening of racial rules for native Africans—meaning that a person was considered black if he or she had even one black ancestor, regardless of skin tone—occurred during the late 1600s and early 1700s. This notion was fixed formally in U.S. laws and court decisions throughout the nineteenth and into the twentieth century. Indians had existed as firm racial category since 1492, yet all treaties and agreements were made with specific native groups, which led to further division in the mid-nineteenth century between "full bloods" and "mixed bloods." By the twentieth century, this had developed into a complex set of "blood quantum" rules.

The formations for all three racial categories became complete in the United States in the early twentieth century. However, the scientific underpinnings of the races already had been classified during the late eighteenth century by German anthropologist Johann Blumenbach, defended by philosopher Immanuel Kant, and utilized by statesman Thomas Jefferson, outlining clear racial hierarchies that placed whites at the top.

Differences in the racialization of blacks and Indians were rooted in the social and economic needs of the colonies and, later, the independent United States. The continuing need to replace African slaves, especially after the transatlantic slave trade was halted by the British in the early nineteenth century, led to a racial classification system that maximized the number of people who legally could be enslaved.

On the other hand, the desire to minimize native claims to land led to a racial classification system than served to minimize the number of people who legally could claim Indian status. U.S. law required that in order to claim Indian status, a person had to have one-quarter Indian blood—that is, one grandparent who was a full blood or pure Indian, or two great-grandparents who were full-blood Indians.

Global Racism Against Native Peoples

Analogous processes took place throughout the world in other empires. Notions of race and the "other" percolated within the ideologies of states. However, few were well defined or officially espoused, except as they were linked to religious elites, who saw their enemies as "uncivilized" and often as "savage," especially with regard to indigenous concepts of their god or gods. In 1492, Spain, which only recently had driven the Moors out of the Iberian Peninsula, still was using the Inquisition to purge itself of the influences of non-Christian Jews and Muslims. Thus, the seeds of institutionalized racism were present in many places.

Racism was practiced globally in much more fluid situations, with tiered systems in Mexico and elsewhere in Latin America, including complicated but less institutionalized forms of racism in Brazil and in some of the Caribbean islands, though always with indigenous people at the bottom of the hierarchy. The colonization of "people of color" and "third-world nations" further embedded racism as a primary means of stratification throughout the twentieth century.

Tribal peoples and tribalism became an excuse for these racial divisions, making for very complex forms of racism in places such as South Africa under the apartheid system. In British colonies such as New Zealand, the suppression of the tribal Maori was riddled with racist implications based on skin color, as the indigenous people were called black. In Australia, deeply racist systems of prejudice against indigenous Aboriginals were marked by intense discrimination based on race and against indigenous peoples. Native peoples such as the *adivasi* people of South Asia were bound by tributary relationships to more powerful kingdoms and early states.

Racism has been identified as a central construct for suppression and discrimination in a wide variety of situations—for example, against Palestinians in Israel and Bedouins in the Middle East; against Kurds in Iran, Iraq, and Turkey; against indigenous peoples in Southeast Asia, such as Malaysia, Thailand, and Vietnam; against the Miao people in southern China; against the Tatars in central Russia; against the Pashtun and other peoples in Afghanistan and Pakistan; and in such varied situations as the Ainu in Japan or the Sami in Scandinavia. All of these forms of racism have been the result of, or associated with, the building of states or wealth. Today, racism has contributed to social struggles over stereotypes in educational curricula, historical representations in higher education, and even in mascots and team names in professional sports.

Finally, the social and economic bases for racial categories continue today in complex debates over the definition of *indigenous*. The term has become politicized and, in some places, racialized, as being defined as indigenous may open or close legal, political, civic, social, or cultural opportunities. Racial formation is not a completed process, nor are structures of racism. They continue today, especially for indigenous peoples.

James V. Fenelon and Thomas D. Hall

See also: *Countries*—United States. *Issues*—Colonialism; Genocide; Social Customs.

Further Reading

Berkhofer, Robert F. *The White Man's Indian: The History of an Idea from Columbus to the Present.* New York: Alfred A. Knopf, 1978.

Diamond, Jared. *Guns, Germs, and Steel: The Fates of Human Societies.* New York: W.W. Norton, 1997.

Dippie, Brian W. *The Vanishing American: White Attitudes and U.S. Indian Policy.* Middletown, CT: Wesleyan University Press, 1982.

Fenelon, James V. "Dual Sovereignty of Native Nations, the United States, and Traditionalists." *Humboldt Journal of Social Relations* 27:1 (2002): 106–145.

Fredrickson, George M. *Racism: A Short History.* Princeton, NJ: Princeton University Press, 2002.

Hannaford, Ivan. *Race: The History of an Idea in the West.* Baltimore: Johns Hopkins University Press, 1996.

Jennings, Francis. *The Invasion of America: Indians, Colonialism, and the Cant of Conquest.* New York: W.W. Norton, 1975.

Mann, Charles C. *1491: New Revelations of the Americas Before Columbus.* New York: Alfred A. Knopf, 2005.

Montagu, Ashley. *Man's Most Dangerous Myth: The Fallacy of Race.* 6th ed. Walnut Creek, CA: AltaMira, 1997.

Russell, James W. *Class and Race Formation in North America.* Toronto, Canada: University of Toronto Press, 2009.

Thornton, Russell. *American Indian Holocaust and Survival: A Population History Since 1492.* Norman: University of Oklahoma Press, 1987.

Reemerging People Groups

The last years of the twentieth century witnessed the reemergence of the world's native peoples. Whereas early twentieth-century conversations about indigenous peoples often were predicated on a belief in their inevitable disappearance or integration into mainstream society, today, native peoples number more than 300 million (estimates range between 300 million and 500 million), and they are viewed as permanent members of the global community, with rights corresponding to their status as first peoples.

This revival is evident on several fronts, from demographic growth, local organizing, national political participation, and international representation to cultural retention, territorial recovery, achieving human rights, and the emergence of plurinational states and native peoples with political autonomy. All of this has happened in spite of increased efforts by government entities and private interests to expropriate native lands and resources for development projects that threaten indigenous cultures. More than ever before, native peoples have a renewed sense of pride in their heritage and a determination to right the wrongs of the past in anticipation of a better future.

There are several explanations for this resurgence. Foremost among them is the response by native peoples to the Columbus Quincentennial in 1992. Anticipation of the five-hundredth anniversary of the arrival of Christopher Columbus to the New World precipitated a global buzz over how to commemorate this historic event. While the United States and other nations congratulated Spain and Italy for this achievement, native peoples did not share in the celebration of Columbus. Indeed, the indigenous people of the world used the Quincentennial event to organize, protest, publish, and gain increased recognition of their grievances and demands.

The 1990s and 2000s catapulted native peoples into global public consciousness. The decade witnessed a series of insurrections in Ecuador, led by the Confederación de Nacionalidades Indígenas del Ecuador (Confederation of Indigenous Nationalities of Ecuador), culminating in the ouster of that nation's president in 2000. The Maya-based Ejército Zapatista de Liberación Nacional

(Zapatista National Liberation Army) emerged from the Lacandon forest on January 1, 1994—the day that the North American Free Trade Agreement was to take effect—and took control of several cities and towns in the southeastern part of Mexico.

In 1992, Rigoberta Menchu, a Quiché human rights activist, became the first indigenous person to win the Nobel Peace Prize. The decade also saw the first indigenous head of state, when Bolivian Vice President Victor Hugo Cardenas, an Aymara Indian, temporarily assumed the charge in 1994. South African rights activist Nelson Mandela, of Khoisan ancestry, was elected president in that country's first fully democratic election in 1994. Mandela, though not the first African to be elected chief executive, was emblematic of the gains made by native peoples in one of the last bastions of colonialism.

In 2005, Evo Morales was elected president of Bolivia. A coca confederation organizer of Aymara ethnicity and socialist politics, Morales took 53 percent of the vote. In a referendum two years later to determine whether he would stay in office, he won two-thirds of the ballots, and in 2009, he was reelected with 63 percent. In Australia that same year, Mick Dodson, a Yururu, was named Australian of the Year for his work on land reform, civil rights, and attempting to create a more culturally inclusive climate.

These individuals and organizations owe their success to the evolution of an indigenous rights movement that was fifty years in the making and that is at once local and international, indigenous and nonindigenous. The international climate after World War II, coupled with the ability of indigenous people to project local grievances at the persistence of systematic colonialism, proved useful in creating powerful networks of global alliances while growing local movements to national and international dimensions.

Significant in the reemergence of the Indian has been an increasingly global society, which is at once more exploitative of indigenous lands and people than ever before and more intent on recognizing the human rights of all of the Earth's subjects. It is clear that since the 1940s, the concerns of native peoples have found a more receptive international audience than in the past. Moreover, the global human rights movements aided the worldwide indigenous rights movements of the 1970s.

Creation of International Forums for the Discussion of Native Issues

The aftermath of World War II saw the creation of the United Nations (UN). This international organization, established in 1945 by the victorious Allied nations, had as one of its mandates the mediation of international conflicts. The UN's Universal Declaration of Human Rights (1948) rejected the almost universally popular notions of cultural and biological superiority that placed some peoples (usually of European ancestry) in positions of power over others (usually of non-European lineage). It asserted that all people had the right to certain basic and fundamental rights. In addition to its pronouncements against race and ethnic hatred, it defined genocide and made it illegal.

The rhetoric of equality and liberation that emerged from the UN resonated among those who were subjugated by more powerful forces and inspired action. Decolonization and national liberation movements of the 1950s and 1960s in Africa, Asia, Latin America, and the Middle East championed self-rule and resulted in the creation of new states headed by formerly subject peoples.

For native peoples, the demise of European colonialism at the hands of organized insurgent forces was encouraging as they began to envision their own struggles for liberation. Moreover, the discourse of decolonization and antiracism that emerged from the national liberation movement was adopted by new indigenous organizations. Finally, indigenous leaders recognized that the criticism of European colonization that came from nations with indigenous populations was hypocritical and just as easily could be applied to their own practices of internal colonization.

As the international community became more committed to ethnic and human rights, national and local politics also became more receptive to indigenous claims. Whereas the demands of indigenous movements of the early twentieth century often fell on deaf ears, the movements of the 1960s and 1970s made claims that resonated nationally and internationally. Moreover, the rights movements that radicalized this era, from civil to environmental, and the more aggressive tactics that they employed inspired a new generation of indigenous activists and organizations that rejected the accommodationism of earlier leaders.

Rise of Ethnic Nationalism and Indigenous Rights Movements

Central to the indigenous rights movement was a philosophy of ethnic nationalism—a belief that native peoples should lead their own movement and put forth their own demands. For native peoples, one of the main challenges in organizing was creating an indigenous agenda distinct from that of the political left. Because the two had much in common, it was imperative for native peoples to emphasize their heritage and culture as much as economic concerns. Thus, early indigenous organizing focused on education, language rights, artisanal production, agricultural practices, hunting and fishing, resource management, land tenure, transportation, and treaty fulfillment.

Episodes of local unrest that led to more formidable organizing included the 1961 mobilization of the northern Alaskan Inupiat people after the arrests of several tribesmen for illegal duck hunting; the 1966 Gurindji cattle workers' strike in Australia; the 1978 firestorm over plans to build a golf course on Maori land in New Zealand; the 1979 protests of the Sami people in Norway and Sweden over the construction of a hydroelectric dam; and a series of protests in 1987 over logging by the Penan of Brunei and Malaysia. As local indigenous groups protested, they employed mass media to get their message out. As more people sympathized with the indigenous victims in these instances and looked for ways to help, what was once a small local protest evolved into regional or national organizations.

The evolution of the movement fostered reflection among native peoples, who began to view their problems in the context of global patterns created by capitalism, industrialization, and colonialism that required pan-indigenous organization. For native peoples, this represented political maturation as they recognized that their oppression was historically, culturally, and economically rooted. Indigenous peoples conceptualized themselves as the "fourth world," corresponding to their marginalized and stateless status.

In 1964, for example, Ecuador's Shuar people formed the Shuar Federation to protect lands that were being taken by mestizo colonists. In 1971, native Colombian leaders created the Indigenous Regional Council of the Cauca to recover rights to lands that had been lost and to strengthen local governance. In both cases, the organizations addressed cultural issues as well.

In time, indigenous organizations became larger, and the call for indigenous organization and rights reverberated throughout the Americas. In 1973, four indigenous organizations in La Paz, Bolivia, crafted the Manifesto of Tiawanaku. The document asserted that nation-states were indebted to their indigenous population as the basis of the country's national identity and that native people should have jurisdiction over their own cultural institutions. The 1974 Dene Declaration stated that the government of Canada was not the government of the Dene people. In 1977, the Nishnawbe-Aski of central Canada declared to the Ontario provincial government that the era of cultural genocide was over and that they vowed to resist future exploitation.

In New Zealand, the 1970s saw the resurgence of the Maori people. After experiencing significant population growth and increased urbanization, the Maori formed the political organization Nga Tamatoa (The Warriors) and participated in a number of public protests over the next two decades. The Maori also took advantage of new laws governing parliamentary proportionality to increase their participation in national politics. Perhaps the most significant aspect of the Maori cultural revival was the reintroduction of the Maori language in preschools and grade schools and the inclusion of other aspects of Maori traditions and cultural practices in school curricula.

In 1968, the American Indian Movement (AIM) was founded. Led by indigenous activists, it attempted to address issues critical to Native Americans, including inadequate housing, poverty, treaty disputes, and abuse by local law enforcement. The movement garnered national and international attention through several spectacular protests. In late 1969, for example, several AIM members claimed the island of Alcatraz, the former home of the famous federal prison, which had been deserted five years earlier; they based their claim on a treaty that recognized all abandoned federal lands as belonging to Indian peoples. Other events of note include the 1971 Trail of Broken Treaties rally in Washington, D.C., when AIM activists occupied the federal Bureau of Indian Affairs headquarters and submitted a list of twenty demands to the government, including the return of indigenous sovereignty. However, the episode that attracted the attention of the world for seventy-one days was the standoff between AIM activists and federal agents at Wounded Knee, South Dakota, resulting in the deaths of two AIM members. Tensions remained high for the next two years when another battle ensued at the Pine Ridge Reservation, resulting in the deaths of two Federal Bureau of Investigation agents and a questionable conviction and prison sentence for AIM activist Leonard Peltier. Peltier's case resonated with native peoples throughout the world, who viewed it as representative of their own past of violence and injustice.

The American Indian Movement had a significant influence on indigenous rights movements in other English-speaking nations, such as Australia, Canada, and New Zealand. By the mid-1970s, there was considerable interaction among native peoples. In 1975, after a meeting in Porter Alberni, British Colombia, Canada, native leaders from throughout the Americas, Oceania, and Scandinavia established the World Council of Indigenous Peoples (WCIP). The purpose of the WCIP was to provide international representation for indigenous peoples in matters relating to economic, social, cultural, and political rights, as well as territorial and resource retention. As an organization with UN observer status, the WCIP called for the international body to formulate a Declaration on the Rights of Indigenous Peoples, a draft of which finally was completed in 1992.

Other regional, continental, and international associations that emerged in the 1970s and 1980s were the International Indian Treaty Council (1974), the Inuit Circumpolar Conference (1977), and the Consejo Indio de Sud America (Indian Council of South America, 1980). Formed to raise the profile of indigenous issues, these organizations brought together indigenous and nonindigenous people alike.

Growth of Indigenous Organizations in the 1980s and 1990s

The 1980s saw an increase in indigenous organizations throughout the world as many were established and developed more of a regional and national focus. Examples include the Coordinadora de las Organizaciones Indígenas de la Cuenca Amazónica (Coordinator of Indigenous Nationalities of the Amazon Basin), which became the umbrella organization for other Amazonian groups. Indeed, this period saw more indigenous organization in the Amazon than in any other region in the Americas. A key concern of the protesters was the increasing presence in the forests of state agencies, colonists, oil and mining companies, hydroelectric projects, and other outside interest groups.

In Brazil, for example, forty-eight indigenous organizations formed in the 1980s. They were so influential in their protests that they were able to gain significant territorial concessions from the state; even more important, they achieved recognition of their collective rights and their rights to indigenous culture, such as language and beliefs, in the country's new constitution. This pattern would play out in other parts of Latin America as well, such as Bolivia, Colombia, Ecuador, and Nicaragua. For native peoples, the primary objective in dealing with the state has been to gain legal recognition of the country's pluricultural population and, as a consequence, achieve the same rights for native peoples as non-natives. In Nicaragua (as well as in Canada and the United States), however, the principal demands of native peoples have been greater self-determination, self-government, and degrees of autonomy.

In other regions, new indigenous associations also were created, such as the Association of the Numerically Small Peoples of the North (1990s) and the Working Group of Indigenous Minorities in Southern Africa (1997). For native peoples, the Columbus Quincentennial provided disparate groups with the opportunity to share experiences and develop global networks of solidarity and assistance.

International Conferences and the United Nations

In 1990, the First Continental Conference on 500 Years of Indian Resistance convened in the Ecuadorian Andes. The event brought together indigenous peoples from across the Americas to share with one another the challenges that they faced in the twentieth century, particularly those related to environmental destruction and cultural dissolution, and the ways in which they resisted outright destruction or assimilation by modern states.

The UN has taken up the cause of indigenous peoples in a variety of ways. In the 1950s, it asked the International Labour Organization (ILO) to prepare a convention that addressed relations between nations and their aboriginal populations. The result was Convention 107 in 1957. Its approach was integrationist, mandating that signatories take responsibility for promoting the assimilation of native peoples into mainstream society by providing social services and assistance, including improved education and better health care. Thirty years later, the ILO revised the outdated convention, whose assimilationist tenor had become inconsistent with contemporary attitudes on self-determination. In 1989, the ILO devised Convention 169, which recognized indigenous and tribal peoples as permanent societies that had rights to self-rule.

The decision to take up indigenous issues at the UN began at the UN Human Rights Center in Geneva, which suggested the creation of the Sub-Commission on Prevention of Discrimination and Protection of Minorities to study the suitability of addressing discrimination against indigenous peoples under the auspices of the UN. Following a favorable decision, the body became a permanent commission. One of the first challenges that it tackled was developing a working definition of "indigenous" and a summary of the legitimate rights and responsibilities of indigenous peoples within nation-states.

In 2007, the UN General Assembly adopted the Declaration on the Rights of Indigenous Peoples. The document had strong sovereigntist overtones and recognized collective rights, indigenous self-determination, and degrees of autonomy among its forty-six articles, and it gained the support of most indigenous organizations in the world. In the General Assembly, the vote was 143 in favor and 4 opposed, with 11 countries abstaining. The four nations that opposed the declaration (Australia, Canada, New Zealand, and the United States) continued to maintain that they had valid concerns, but all have voiced their approval of the declaration since that time. Nevertheless, the declaration does not exist in international law and has no official standing before any legal tribunal at the national or international level.

The UN has created three different bodies charged with indigenous affairs. These include the Expert Mechanism on the Rights of Indigenous Peoples, the Special Rapporteur on the situation of human rights and fundamental freedoms of indigenous peoples, and the Permanent Forum on Indigenous Issues. The last-named forum was a decade in the making when it became an official agency by UN resolution in 2000. Its purpose is to serve as an advisory board to the UN Economic and Social Council, and its specific charges are to provide expert advice and recommendations on indigenous people, to raise awareness and promote the integration of coordination of activities related to indigenous peoples, and to prepare and disseminate related information. In addition, the UN has attempted to increase awareness of native peoples by declaring the ten-year periods from 1995 to 2004 and 2005 to 2014 as the Decades of the World's Indigenous Peoples, and August 9 as the International Day of the World's Indigenous Peoples.

Nongovernmental organizations also have played leading roles in addressing the concerns of and promoting opportunities for native people. Unlike the paternalistic organizations of previous generations, the indigenous rights organizations of the last half decade take their orders from the indigenous peoples themselves. Their primarily goal is to provide assistance to native peoples who otherwise would have difficulty getting national and international attention.

Many organizations have been created specifically to promote and defend indigenous rights. Some of these include the International Work Group for Indigenous Affairs (IWGIA, 1968), Survival International (1969), and the Society for Threatened People (1970). The Denmark-based IWGIA, in particular, deserves attention for its close relation with indigenous groups. Other such organizations include Cultural Survival, founded in 1972, which has dedicated itself to defending the human rights of native peoples.

Amnesty International also has served native peoples as part of its general reporting of human rights violations and its monitoring of the treatment of indigenous prisoners by national governments. Environmental groups such as the World Rainforest Movement and Greenpeace have joined indigenous organizations in protesting development projects that are both ecologically and culturally destructive.

Era of Globalization

The United States' emergence as a global power following World War II allowed the country to penetrate lands and markets to which Americans previously had no access. Areas that had been ignored by nonindigenous peoples suddenly were under assault by miners, land speculators, engineers, and developers. These agents of "economic progress" sometimes attempted to pacify the native peoples by sending in missionaries ahead of time to proselytize and convert. Native peoples found their ways of life under assault, threatening both their belief systems and their landholdings.

Indigenous responses to such incursions varied from acceptance to violent resistance. The Huaorani, an Amazonian people, for example, rebuffed efforts by missionaries to pacify them through conversion in anticipation of the arrival of oil companies. These actions served to consolidate an indigenous identity. Similarly, Catholic missions that set up catechism programs among indigenous populations in many parts of the world discovered that biblical lessons emphasizing social justice, equality, and self-defense became cornerstones for indigenous rights movements, as occurred in Guatemala and highland Ecuador in the 1980s and 1990s. By the 1980s, some churches had abandoned the cultural biases of the past and began supporting indigenous peoples.

Liberal reforms throughout the world have worked to decentralize politics and economics in country after country. On one hand, this has allowed foreign interests to establish a presence in these countries. On the other hand, the absence of state institutions and agencies has served as an impetus for indigenous peoples to call for greater autonomy.

Furthermore, free trade agreements have subordinated national law to World Trade Organization agreements. Native peoples all over the world have seen their patrimony reduced as their lands have been appropriated and resold to foreign developers. The World Social Forum has challenged these "free trade" practices and, in doing so, has attracted support from critics of capitalism as well as indigenous leaders throughout the world. In the Americas, the Zapatistas have called free trade into question, while also basing their movement on the equality of all people and ethnicities. On January 1, 1994, thousands of Zapatista Maya emerged from the Lacandon forest and took over towns and cities in southern Mexico.

Indigenous organization in the era of globalization has transformed native leadership. In addition to traditional spiritual and political leaders, indigenous organizations today also rely on a new generation of leaders who are able to synthesize traditional knowledge with modern technology. Consequently, many of the world's new indigenous leaders have one foot in tradition and the other in modernity. To meet these demands, many organizations have created schools, agencies, and institutes to provide learning and research opportunities for the new generation of indigenous leaders, such as the Center for World Indigenous Studies' Fourth World Institute.

Perhaps one of the most important developments in the last twenty years has been the emergence of indigenous internationalism. As borders have become more fluid and travel and communication have become accessible to more people, native peoples throughout the world have established networks of mutual support and shared information. Acknowledging that there are many different indigenous peoples in the world, with each group having its own unique identity, they also recognize commonalities in their native identities, including their marginalized social status. Another is their identity as first peoples with rights that correspond to that status.

In addition to the efforts by international organizations, many nation-states also took up the charge to improve standards of living for their citizens. National budgets for education, health care, and housing were designed to aid those who were most marginalized in society, including tribal peoples. However, such programs tended to be geared toward assimilation and often created new problems for native peoples.

At the same time, native peoples also have been able to use their organizations and their international contacts to secure new legal standings. For example, the last four decades have seen a number of treaties modified and agreements signed between nation-states and indigenous people. In 1999, the Inuit Tapirisat/Nunavut Agreement created the first indigenous-dominated political jurisdiction in North America, the territory of Nunavut in Canada. It also provided extensive power of self-government, sizable land allocations, and revenue sharing for the native peoples, as well as the recognition of native resource rights. Recent decades also have seen the ratification of new constitutions that recognize indigenous autonomy, plurinational states, and collective rights.

Through the UN, the World Court, and other international agencies, minority groups have had new opportunities to present their cause to nonpartisan arbiters and to seek support for fair and just resolution of their demands. However, the power of these bodies is persuasion, as they have little legal power.

National court cases, however, have created legal precedents that often have been cited as indigenous peoples and organizations demand more rights. For example, cases involving harvesting rights, territorial protections, and salmon fishing have established legal precedents in countries where the cases were heard, and they have been cited in subsequent cases when tribal sovereignty and the establishment of tribal governments were in question. As a result, laws have emerged as cornerstones of indigenous protest and activism in various countries, especially in those with Western legal traditions.

Indigenous people have been able to exploit the media and sway public opinion in their favor in order to get intransigent governments to negotiate with them. They have been able to do so by utilizing a vast network of activists, supporters, and political and advocacy organizations. The use of the Internet and social media has given indigenous peoples even more power in dealing with the state and state actors. International allies, such as Survivor International and the IWGIA,

often are called on to develop petitions, process mailings, write letters and stories, provide resources, and organize lecture tours.

The reemergence of native peoples has put indigenous concerns on the international agenda. It also has succeeded in getting acknowledgment of land and resource rights, as well as recognition of some political demands. For example, the Scandinavian governments appear sincere in their support of Sami culture and language. The creation of the new territory of the Nunavut by the Canadian government in April 1999 gave the Inuit of the eastern Arctic region political control over a huge territory and a high level of self-government. Denmark's acceptance of Greenland's autonomy has empowered the Inuit people in that land. In Japan, the government finally has acknowledged the cultural existence of Ainu. Moreover, the international indigenous movement has become very successful in shaming countries, especially those in the West, and has pressured governments to take into account indigenous concerns and priorities prior to launching developmental or infrastructural projects.

Kenneth Kincaid

See also: *Groups: Central and South America*—Maya. *Countries*—Bolivia. *Issues*—Colonialism; Indigenous Peoples and the United Nations; Self-Determination.

Further Reading

Anaya, S. James. *Indigenous Peoples in International Law.* New York: Oxford University Press, 2004.

Banks, Dennis, with Richard Erdoes. *Ojibwa Warrior: Dennis Banks and the Rise of the American Indian Movement.* Norman: University of Oklahoma Press, 2004.

Becker, Marc. ¡*Pachakutik!: Indigenous Movements and Electoral Politics in Ecuador.* New York: Rowman & Littlefield, 2010.

Burger, Julian. *Report from the Frontier: The State of the World's Indigenous Peoples.* London: Zed, 1987.

Cornell, Stephen. *The Return of the Native: American Indian Political Resurgence.* New York: Oxford University Press, 1988.

Gutmann, Amy, ed. *Multiculturalism: Examining the Politics of Recognition.* Princeton, NJ: Princeton University Press, 1994.

Hodgson, Dorothy L. "Introduction: Comparative Perspectives on the Indigenous Rights Movement in Africa and the Americas." *American Anthropologist* 104:4 (December 2002): 1037–1049.

Langer, Erick D., and Elena Muñoz. *Contemporary Indigenous Movements in Latin America.* Wilmington, DE: Scholarly Resources, 2003.

Maybury-Lewis, David, and Theodore Macdonald, eds. *Indigenous Peoples, Ethnic Groups, and the State.* Boston: Allyn and Bacon, 2002.

Sivak, Martín. *Evo Morales: The Extraordinary Rise of the First Indigenous President of Bolivia.* New York: Palgrave Macmillan, 2010.

Wearne, Phillip. *Return of the Indian: Conquest and Revival in the Americas.* Philadelphia: Temple University Press, 1996.

Wylie, Alison. "Rethinking the Quincentennial: Consequences for Past and Present." *American Antiquity* 57:4 (October 1992): 591–594.

Religion (Indigenous)

The category of native religions is vast, covering eons of time and the entire Earth, just as native people have. Each cultural group had (and has) its own approach to reality, shaped by its era, surrounding cultures, and geography. Native religions, considered altogether, constitute the sixth-largest religious tradition in the world. They are found on every continent and in countless expressions.

However, it is difficult to discuss these belief systems as religions. For most native peoples, "religion" is different from the Western conception of a social structure that is defined by dogma, authority, and hierarchy; rather, their religion is more simply a belief system that is integrated with their way of life. It influences nearly everything that native traditional religionists—that is, those who adhere to native religious traditions—do in their daily lives.

Further complicating matters, such religions are not static—people and their beliefs change. Sometimes, change is brought about by a change in lifeways, such as a new food source or having to move to a new location, perhaps due to famine or drought. Other times, change might be brought on by an encounter with colonialism, as the dominant religion of the colonizing culture often has a profound effect on native religious systems.

Most studies of native spiritualities to date have been written by Western scholars and based on European primary sources. Although such a written record is vitally important, it must be kept in mind that these records cannot be used to explain native belief systems, just as native perspectives cannot fully explain Western cultures. The written record, therefore, must be examined carefully for bias, as Western chroniclers may have imposed their own religious assumptions on what they saw and recorded.

For instance, practically all of the European primary sources insist that native people "worshipped" a supreme being of some sort, which the chroniclers describe in terms of their own god. But in fact, there is no concept of worship or of a single "Great Spirit" in any authentic Native American tradition, as worship and monotheism imply hierarchies, an idea that is out of sync with the more egalitarian model of Native American traditions.

Imposing a Western perspective assumes the normativity of the Christian European universe. Thus, such Western terms often do not apply to native religions in other parts of the world as well.

Diversity of Expression

Attempting to apply a spiritual hierarchy to native religions does those faiths a disservice by examining them through an exclusively European American lens and by

Quechua *(left)* and Aymara *(right)* shamans meet at a New Year celebration in Bolivia. The figure of a shaman—a priest or medicine man who employs magic or esoteric knowledge to invoke the spirit world—is a common feature of indigenous religions everywhere. *(Aizar Raldes/AFP/ Getty Images)*

discounting the great diversity of belief systems found among native peoples. If one looks at the sheer number of belief systems, there are many more native religious systems than there are global religions found in dominant cultures.

These native religious systems are remarkable for their diversity. Even within culturally related groups, such as the Cheyenne, Sioux, and other tribes of the North American Great Plains, there may be similarities, but these are only on the surface, useful for making general assessments. Like so many other topics pertaining to native peoples, religions are difficult to generalize—but that is not the intent here. Rather, by looking at the roles that religion plays in the lives of native peoples and in their interactions with dominant cultures, similarities in experiences between native groups and their beliefs can be examined.

Native peoples do not so much have religion as democratically shared spiritual approaches. One commonality among them is the idea that "the sacred" pervades all space, both physical and metaphysical. Thus, native spirituality is a way of life, in constant enactment, a moment-by-moment recognition and protection of everything that exists in the universe. Adherents of native religions do not set aside two hours on Sunday morning or Saturday evening to attend ceremonies or services, while living the rest of the week without reference to the sacred. Rather, they seek to integrate spirituality into their lives every day, taking time to acknowledge the renewal of the sacred that constantly is occurring. Such activities engage with the spiritual forces surrounding the person or community so as to maintain or restore balance.

Where hierarchies do exist, such as among the Aztec, they are not the same as European notions of hierarchy. For instance, Aztec nobles, rather than peasants, inflicted pain on themselves, regularly and painfully letting their own blood in spirit-feeding rituals. Similarly, when human sacrifice took place—not nearly as often as Westerners might believe—people of the highest, not the lowest, social status were dispatched. By contrast, in Europe, the law declared that it was better for a commoner to suffer injury than for an aristocrat to suffer inconvenience.

These types of native belief systems are everywhere in the world. Many have very few "adherents," and thus they escape the gaze of missionaries who may seek to convert the people or that of academics who wish to study them. Many such belief systems, like global religions, have evolved over the centuries, changing as a result of contact with other peoples.

Some religious beliefs and rituals even have escaped the bounds of their tribal beginnings to take on a global role, as native peoples have become more visible in recent decades. Examples of this are the Australian Aboriginal didgeridoo (wind instrument) players, American Indian peoples playing drums for largely non-Indian audiences at powwows and other events, and New Zealand Maori *tohunga* (community religious experts) purifying auditoriums before Maori opera singers perform.

In addition, native musical styles, often a form of religious expression, have pervaded popular music. For instance, this can be heard in the music of Robbie Robertson, a Mohawk musician who rose to fame during the 1960s and 1970s as the front man for the popular group the Band.

The Divine and the Environment

The number of deities in native religions varies widely. Some belief systems are monotheistic, with one god that is the focus. More often, however, native religions encompass many divinities. In West Africa, groups such as the Yoruba believe in a pantheon of deities, most of whom are associated with the natural world or everyday life. Some once were humans and now are venerated as ancestors. Others function as intermediaries, mediating between the people and a supreme creator god, who does not make regular contact with humans. Among the Yoruba, these deities are represented in statues and other images made of metal or wood, and they are associated with the sea, weather, and other elements of the natural world. This connection between the ecosystem and the divine is not exclusive to the Yoruba or to native religions in general. Rather, it illustrates an important commonality among native religions: a close association with the natural environment.

In fact, many native religions emphasize the interconnectedness of the environment, the people, and the divine. For example, for the Maori of New Zealand, all things have a rhythm and a form, and these are interwoven to form the whole of the universe. The term *wheiao*, meaning "between two opposite states," is used to describe the transitory nature of things and people in the world. For example, light cannot be understood without reference to darkness.

Similarly, the Navajo of the United States express the idea of *hózhó*, meaning "balance" or "beauty." The term is used to express beauty, but also a harmony or balance between two extremes. For the Navajo, although this idea applies to particular things or ideas, it also is generalized to express the proper balance between society and the universe.

Native spiritualities often are tied to geography rather than houses of worship. The spirits of a particular place are paramount, and thus meaningful ceremonies, stories, and rituals may revolve around a specific physical location. Because people interact with the spirits of a particular place, ceremonies cannot be transported to other places, as this would result in chaos. For example, it is believed that attempting to perform a desert ceremony in a well-watered place would precipitate disaster, as the spirits of the watered place would not be able to make sense of the desert. Consequently, traditionalists are leery of adapting the ceremonies of one place to the uses of another and of allowing people with no knowledge of their ceremonies' sacred spaces to take part. Thus, outsiders usually are not welcome at Native American sacred ceremonies, such as Sun Dances, Midwinter Ceremonies, or Kachina Dances.

Many native religious conceptions, especially Native American religions, view the natural environment and the people's connections with it in terms of paired, complementary elements—conventionally expressed as "twins"—that explain the cosmos. The primary cosmic pair, which all others mirror, is called blood and breath, or sometimes water and air, although Western anthro-

pologists often refer to these elements as Earth and sky. A variety of beliefs are derived from these independent yet interdependent halves.

These beliefs are expressed through rituals, especially those focusing on water (Earth) and fire (sky); ceremonies, especially those featuring song (sky) and dance (Earth); and practices, which often incorporate Earth elements such as water, caves, and herbs or sky elements such as mountains, trees, and fire. Conceptually, these pairs form binaries, so that each alone is one-half, not one. Two halves—that is, both Earth and sky—are required to form the reality that we all inhabit. Thus, any attempt to wrench apart a pair—to consider just one half in isolation—necessarily misapprehends the concept. Fire must be seen in concert with water; field necessarily implies forest, and vice versa; and man cannot exist without a matching female.

This binary cosmos is replicated in native culture. For instance, native societies may be organized into matrilineal clans, which are divided into their natural

DIEGO DE LANDA

Diego de Landa, a Spanish Franciscan priest and bishop of Yucatán, is both credited with recording key accounts of Yucatán's preconquest Maya civilization and blamed for destroying an entire corpus of Maya writing. Landa was vilified as an overbearing and abusive cleric who directed the 1562 auto-da-fé at Maní, an inquisition that caused the deaths of hundreds of Maya as a result of torture or mass suicide, as well as the destruction of twenty-seven codices (folding scrolls written in Maya hieroglyphics on deer hide or bark).

Nevertheless, Maya scholars continue to cite Landa's *Relación de Las Cosas de Yucatán* (*On the Things of Yucatán*, 1566) as a key source for understanding the nuances of the Maya language. His alphabet enabled epigraphers to decipher the Maya hieroglyphics that were used in the surviving codices and inscribed on monuments of the Classic Period (200–900 C.E.).

Born in 1524 in Cifuentes, Spain, Landa entered the Franciscan order at age seventeen. In 1549, he departed for Yucatán, where the Franciscans wielded unparalleled secular and religious power. He dedicated himself to proselytizing the Maya. To better communicate with the native people and to train indigenous assistants, he studied the Maya writing system and recorded native informants' descriptions of the pre-Columbian past, observations that he included in his *Relación*.

Landa's missionary optimism turned to anger, however, when he discovered evidence of "idolatry"—that is, the persistence of pre-Columbian religious practices—which was rumored to include human sacrifice. From

1562 until 1563, he headed a campaign to wipe out idolatry.

The campaign's signal event was the 1562 auto-da-fé. Francisco de Toral, a fellow Franciscan, arrived in 1563 as bishop of the province and began his own investigation. Toral determined that Landa had overreached his authority by taking on the role of inquisitor, whipping the Maya people, and using torture in interrogations in defiance of royal prohibitions. By the end of 1563, Landa had resigned and returned to Spain to face charges of usurpation of inquisitorial authority.

The extent of Maya opposition to Landa remains unclear. At least seven letters written in the Yucatec Maya language to Spanish King Philip II in 1567 praised Landa and pleaded for his return. Close similarities in the language used in the letters prompted suspicions that Franciscans or native assistants under duress had written the letters using a formula. A later letter signed by four Maya leaders made additional complaints about the Franciscans' abuses and alleged that the friars had coerced signatures from their leaders on letters they had not written. Questions about the accuracy of Landa's accusations regarding idolatry also remain unresolved. Especially controversial were the allegations of human sacrifice.

For Landa, his removal was only a temporary setback. After successfully defending himself in Spain, he returned to Yucatán in 1573 in a more elevated position, spending the last years of his life there serving as bishop. He died in 1579.

Mark W. Lentz

halves. For instance, a wind half (sky) may be matched by a river half (Earth), with clans arrayed in each half, called moieties or phratries by anthropologists. Any number of lineages or clans may exist in either half. People are required to choose marriage partners from the complementary clan half. Marrying within one's clan half (not just within one's clan) is considered incest. Thus, if a person belongs to the Turtle (Earth) half, he or she must marry within the Wolf (sky) half. Nations may name their clan halves differently, but all are based on the binary of Earth and sky. Grasping the complementary nature of Earth and sky is key to understanding many native spiritualities, as the interactive twinship produces one cosmos.

These binaries of traditional thought are crucial to grasping native culture, from the architecture of Chechen Itza, to the Maya pyramid in Mexico's Yucatán, to the east–west doors of the Iroquoian longhouse in the American Northeast and southern Canada. Once the centrality of complementary structures is understood, it becomes clear, for instance, that the focal point of Chechen Itza is not its ceremonial pyramid, but the relationship between the artificial mountain and the Sacred Cenote (sink hole) 985 feet (300 meters) north (in the death direction) of the pyramid. Water walking (sacrificing to water) is an earth medicine, whereas air walking (climbing pyramids) is a sky medicine. The two must be in balance to ensure the life of the community.

The sort of earth writing exemplified at Chechen Itza bespeaks an ancient native practice that provides a ceremonial space using the full complement of the twinned halves of the cosmos. Thus, the Inca city of Cuzco, Peru, is laid out in the shape of a puma. This arrangement places a sacred animal, the female (or Earth) medicine of the puma, at a mountainous height, which is associated with male (sky) medicine, completing the pair. By the same token, the ancient city of Teotihuacan replicated the solar system (sky) in stone (Earth), forming a powerful complement of medicine at that place in Mexico.

Relationships with the Divine

Although some native religions venerate a number of deities, and others a supreme being or creator god, there is great diversity in how these deities interact with humans and vice versa. While many African religions see the creator god as all-powerful, that god is viewed as distant from humans, refraining from providing assistance when help in this world is needed. Often, that role is filled by the spirits of ancestors or lower deities, such as those representing natural phenomena or animal spirits. Those gods can be accessed directly or with the assistance of medicine men and women, who serve as religious specialists for many native villages.

In the Americas, a common belief in native spirituality is that those of the highest status and the most talent have the greatest responsibility for sacrifice. People gain respect by giving, not by acquiring—thus the most revered among holy elders are the poorest people in the community. The gift economies common to native cultures ensure that, just as the holy elders give for the people, the people give for the elders, so that the holy people at once possess the least but have access to the most that the culture has to offer. The key here is that the holy person works for the community, not for the self.

Prayer and ritual require that everyone take responsibility, realizing that taking in one respect might create an imbalance in another. This is one reason that most traditionalists shy away from specific requests and stick to thanksgiving: Creating an imbalance with a selfish act of petition could result in untoward consequences. Asking for health for one person might cast sickness on a well person somewhere else. Furthermore, if petitions are made, they must benefit the entire community, not just one person. Any requests for help from the spirits, such as the taking of food through farming or hunting, must be matched with a gift in return.

Native Religions in Combination with Major World Religions

Even in places where native religions have been over-formed by major world religions as a result of colonialism and missionary efforts, elements of the native religions have persisted. Often, a syncretic form of religion emerges that combines aspects of both native and world religions, such as Santeria (a mix of Catholic, Caribbean, and West African beliefs) in the Caribbean and Caribbean émigré communities in North America.

Sometimes, native rituals and ideas persist as a substratum of a syncretic form of a mainline religion. One example is the interaction between native religions and Roman Catholicism in Central and South America. There, the native peoples were forced to convert to Catholicism when the Spanish invaded. However, as the Spanish destroyed native religious sites, they still remained in use, as the conquerors often built Catholic churches on the same holy spots. This remembrance of native beliefs within Catholicism encouraged the blending of Catholic and native religious practices.

One of the best-known examples of this is the so-called patroness of the Americas, Our Lady of Guadalupe. This apparition of the Virgin Mary appeared to a Nahuatl man named Juan Diego in 1531, and she soon became a symbol of Latin American Catholicism. The shrine built to the Virgin Mary was constructed on a Nahuatl religious site, and when Mexico declared independence from Spain, Mexican troops fought under the banner of Guadalupe, a symbol of the Americas' break from European domination. In 1990, Pope John Paul II announced the beatification of Juan Diego, declaring him the "protector and advocate of the indigenous peoples."

In Brazil, the situation is even more complicated, as native traditions have interacted and blended not only with Catholicism, but also with native African traditions brought by slaves. As a result of syncretism with African religions such as Macumba, people began to identify the Catholic saints with gods in the African pantheon. At times, world religions have initiated reform movements, such as Wahhabism within Islam (established to rid North African Islam of the influence of Sufism), to combat this blending and to restore the "pure" form of the conquering religion.

Modern Threats

As so many native religions are tied to the land and language of the people, colonialism, followed by industrialization and urbanization, and then by globalization, all have posed a series of threats to these groups. Therefore, many native religionists have resisted such incursions into their cultures. But this resistance can only go so far when modern world cultures desire the resources of the lands on which native groups reside and other infringements on traditional lands, particularly sacred places, occur.

In places ranging from India to China to the United States, the construction of large hydroelectric dams has inundated many religious sites. Simple urban and industrial development desecrates the lands used by many groups as final resting places for their ancestors. In addition, academics have taken artifacts from many groups and robbed them of their power, instead housing them in museums. In the United States, at least, some remediation has begun since passage of the Native American Graves Protection and Repatriation Act in 1990. Similar recognition and repatriation is occurring in other nations around the world.

At the same time, the globalization of industry and the worldwide search for resources has threatened native religions in diverse locations such as the Amazon Rain Forest, where many of the world's hardwoods are harvested, and the Arctic areas of northern Alaska, where large oil reserves await exploitation by multinational conglomerates. As a result, many native traditional religionists have struck alliances with environmental groups, but even that contact means change for those who hold to native beliefs. However, change is a constant, even

within the perceived ancient belief systems held by native peoples worldwide.

Barbara Alice Mann and Steven L. Danver

See also: Issues—Colonialism; Globalization; Missionary Activities; Social Customs.

Further Reading

Apfel-Marglin, Frédérique, and Stephen A. Marglin, eds. *Decolonizing Knowledge: From Development to Dialogue.* New York: Oxford University Press, 1996.

Brokensha, David W., D.M. Warren, and Oswald Werner, eds. *Indigenous Knowledge Systems and Development.* Washington, DC: University Press of America, 1980.

Clarkson, Linda, Vern Morrissette, and Gabriel Regallet. *Our Responsibility to the Seventh Generation: Indigenous Peoples and Sustainable Development.* Winnipeg, Canada: International Institute for Sustainable Development, 1992.

Deloria, Vine, Jr. *For This Land: Writings on Religion in America.* New York: Routledge, 1999.

———. *God Is Red: A Native View of Religion.* 2nd ed. Golden, CO: North American Press, 1992.

Devi Khumbongmayum, Ashalata, M.L. Khan, and R.S. Tripathi. "Sacred Groves of Manipur, Northeast India: Biodiversity Value, Status and Strategies for Their Conservation." *Biodiversity and Conservation* 14:7 (2005): 1541–1582.

Grinde, Donald A., Jr., and Bruce E. Johansen. *Ecocide of Native America: Environmental Destruction of Indian Lands and Peoples.* Santa Fe, NM: Clear Light, 1995.

Harvey, Graham, ed. *Indigenous Religions: A Companion.* New York: Cassell, 2000.

———. "Sacred Places in the Construction of Indigenous Environmentalism." *Ecotheology* 7:1 (2002): 60–73.

Magesa, Laurenti. *African Religion: The Moral Traditions of Abundant Life.* New York: Orbis, 1997.

Seaman, Gary, and Jane S. Day, eds. *Ancient Traditions: Shamanism in Central Asia and the Americas.* Niwot: University Press of Colorado, 1994.

Sullivan, Lawrence E., ed. *Native Religions and Cultures of North America: Anthropology of the Sacred.* New York: Continuum, 2003.

Tinker, George E. *American Indian Liberation: A Theology of Sovereignty.* New York: Orbis, 2008.

Relocation

The relocation of ethnic groups or indigenous peoples, sometimes termed "forced migration," is not new to the modern era but has a long and varied history. Most often, relocation has been the result of conflict. As a conflict progressed or a war was lost, a group moved, relinquishing their lands to the stronger party.

Initially, the idea of "enforced relocation" was rooted in this process, as groups of people were moved off their traditional homelands for economic or military purposes. A modern example of this is the Spanish mission farms in Mexico and the American Southwest. As colonization progressed in Africa, the Americas, and South Asia, relocation had more disastrous implications.

Another form of relocation, termed "benign" relocation, refers to the movement of groups that is not the overt result of a government policy or military conflict. Economics, climate change, and disease all may prompt people to leave their homelands for a new region in order to have access to better economic and environmental opportunities.

Histories of Relocation

As European governments established colonies in the Americas, they argued that the land needed to be freed from native use to make way for new settlers, who would use the land in a more efficient and scientific manner. After a series of military campaigns during the nineteenth century, Native American tribes were moved onto reservations—often removed from their traditional hunting or spiritual grounds—managed by the federal Bureau of Indian Affairs.

In the United States, one of the most enduring historical images of native removal is the infamous "Trail of Tears" in 1838. Cherokee Indians, originally living in the Carolinas, Georgia, and eastern Tennessee, were removed to territories west of the Mississippi River under the Indian Removal Act of 1830, by which President Andrew Jackson ordered Indian lands open to settlement and commerce. Today, the Cherokee reside in reservations in North Carolina and Oklahoma, as well as off-reservation in California and other states, and thrive economically from various moneymaking ventures, including a booming casino industry.

In Africa, relocations occurred in much the same way, but often with the goal of creating an export-based

TRAIL OF TEARS

On May 28, 1830, the U.S. Congress passed the Indian Removal Act, which authorized the exchange of Indian homelands in the East for new territories west of the Mississippi River. Under this law, the so-called Five Civilized Tribes (Cherokee, Chickasaw, Choctaw, Creek, and Seminole) were removed from their ancestral lands between 1830 and 1839. The Cherokee, the last group to be removed, referred to their march to Indian Territory (present-day Oklahoma) as *Nunna daul Isunyi,* or the Trail of Tears.

By the 1830s, the Cherokee had adopted a policy of assimilation in an effort to coexist with their non-Indian neighbors: They had ratified a constitution with a bicameral legislature, created a written alphabet, published a bilingual newspaper, founded a well-established public school system, and engaged in cash crop agriculture. Instead of supporting these efforts, most white settlers felt threatened by the Cherokee's ability to adapt.

As the demand for land among non-Indian settlers and the U.S. government grew and pressure to give up their homelands increased, some Cherokee saw relocation as their only means of survival. In 1835, Cherokee leader Major Ridge, his son John Ridge, his nephews Elias Boudinot and Stand Watie, along with minority of Cherokee, gathered at New Echota, Georgia, to negotiate the arrangement with the U.S. government.

The treaty party, whose members were mostly from wealthy, assimilated families, signed the Treaty of New Echota, which stipulated that the Cherokee would cede to the United States their ancestral homeland east of the Mississippi River in exchange for lands to the west in Indian Territory and a payment of $5 million. While a small minority of Cherokee accepted the New Echota agreement, Principal Chief John Ross and a majority of Cherokee protested the treaty. Nevertheless, the U.S. Senate ratified the treaty in May 1836, giving the Cherokee two years to prepare for their move west.

In 1838, after the deadline for the voluntary move to Indian Territory had passed, General Winfield Scott rounded up approximately 17,000 Cherokee and placed them in temporary camps. Approximately 5,000 Cherokee were immediately moved to Indian Territory, but the remaining members were held in camps until the end of summer 1838. Even before they left the camps, some 3,000 Cherokee died as a result of malnutrition and disease. Another 1,000 died during the 800-mile (1,300-kilometer) forced march from starvation, disease, and extreme cold.

By March 1839, the survivors had reached their new home in Indian Territory. But the traumatic experience of the Trail of Tears was not over, as the Cherokee had to adapt to life in an alien environment. Food remained scarce, and they continued to be ravaged by disease. Many died soon after their arrival at what was to be their new home.

Azusa Ono

economy. The British removal of indigenous people in Kenya serves as an example of colonial removal policies in Africa. As Great Britain solidified control over its East African protectorate in the late nineteenth century, the empire began to remove the native peoples from Kenya's Central Highlands—a region that was particularly suited to large-scale agriculture and livestock programs. The colonial government created a situation that only confirmed prejudices about how indigenous groups "misused" the land, as it attempted to restructure the native peoples' traditional livelihoods, particularly methods of livestock management that groups such as the Maasai had established over centuries. As the indigenous people were pushed into other ethnic regions and the land became overburdened, they suffered from famine, disease, and denigration of their culture and social structure. Today, the Maasai continue to be impoverished and seek to regain their homelands.

The post–Cold War era (perhaps more so than the post–World War II era) has resculpted what "relocation" means and how it is practiced in many ways. In general, there has been a rise in relocation as a result of rampant warfare and ethnic conflict—Sudanese refugees or victims of the South African apartheid regime come to mind.

In addition, as the twentieth century gave way to the twenty-first century, there has been a rise in what journalist Mark Dowie calls "conservation refugees": native people removed from their traditional homelands as those regions are made into wilderness or conservation refuges. This is nothing new, but, Dowie points out, the practice has become the norm in this era of conservation.

A related practice is "ecological relocation": relocation of native peoples attributable to environmental concerns. Again, this type of relocation has occurred for centuries, but the issue seems to be exacerbated by modern-day concerns regarding global warming and environmental stability in ecologically fragile regions.

Results of Relocation

The effects of relocation are largely negative. Often when a group is moved, traditional social institutions come under intense pressure: Elders no longer are afforded the same status as before, traditional gender roles are no longer maintained, education systems break down, and health systems based on traditional lifeways dissolve.

Generally speaking, the economic fortunes of a relocated group decline over a prolonged period of time. (In rare cases—such as Native American casinos—the economic fortunes of a group improve, but not initially.) Often when a group moves, their new land cannot adequately support their former way of life—whether that be agriculture, subsistence hunting, or a nomadic existence based on animal husbandry. Relocation also removes

indigenous groups from sacred places; this issue arose during the Vietnam War (1954–1975), when American and French forces attempted to relocate local peoples. This, combined with the upheaval of social institutions, can lead to a number of problems.

High crime and a spike in socially transmitted diseases (such as influenza, tuberculosis, and sexually transmitted diseases) quickly emerge, further harming the ability of the relocated group to thrive economically. This is seen most often as nomadic groups are resettled—the Kham nomads in central China, for instance, resettled both of their own choice and under government development programs, have been pushed into what can be termed "fringe villages." These are villages attached to major population centers that give the newly settled pastoralists access to a mode of living previously unknown and unprepared for, paving the way for sharp increases in crime (these villages are often called "crime schools"), chronic unemployment, rampant alcoholism, and the spread of disease.

Relocated groups often are bereft of adequate education systems—either because of the breakdown of the traditional system or the government's inability or reluctance to provide enough support (such as money, buildings, and teachers). Thus, there is a lack of the kind of training that would allow newly urbanized groups to thrive in their new environment. This prevents large segments of the population from moving freely in their new society, trapping the group into fringe status.

Another negative result of relocation is language loss. This is especially evident when recent relocations are examined—often a group is placed in a situation in which their traditional language is not valued or used, alienating the older generation, which has limited access to education to learn the new language. Young people see that their traditional language is of little economic value in the marketplace, and they are placed in the position of having to learn the new language to the exclusion of their native tongue. Within three generations, a group of people that has been relocated without adequate means to adapt and preserve their language is in danger of losing their ability to communicate in the language of their ancestors, losing important connections to and understanding of their culture.

As a group loses its ability to communicate, it also loses its traditional ecological knowledge, as occurred with the Cherokee in Oklahoma. How a group understands and relates to the environmental system in which it lives is bound up in their language and culture. As language and connection to their culture are lost, the group loses their ability to live in nature, leaving the people bereft of an understanding of human–environment relationships.

A final problem is the relationship between a relocated group and the government. Often groups are promised some type of aid by the government—specialized education, free or discounted health care, and some type of remittance—for land, herds, or other resources left behind or taken. Often these promises are fulfilled only marginally, or, at worst, they are empty.

Historically it is easy to see where this has happened. For instance, the United States, in its efforts to relocate the Sioux in South Dakota, promised education and, in later years, economic assistance for community development initiatives. However, the U.S. government failed to adequately fulfill these promises, leaving communities economically depressed for generations.

The initial promise of education and job training sometimes is fulfilled partially, but then the people are left to their own devices in a rapidly modernizing world, effectively keeping them on the fringes of society. Among many African and Tibetan groups, for example, the relationship with the government is tenuous. While there is improving access to education and an increase in access to economic opportunities, this comes at a hefty price. Schools, especially high schools and universities, often conduct classes in the national language (French, for example), again pushing the younger generation away from their native language and culture.

Relocation is a varied experience. Overall, however, the impacts on the lives of indigenous peoples tend to be predominantly negative. As water sources become scarce, land degradation continues, and economic opportunities shift and fade, the current trend seems to point to more benign relocations, in which moving constitutes a movement toward a potentially better future.

Jared Phillips

See also: Groups, North America—Cherokee. Issues   Industrial Development; Social Customs; Urbanization.

Further Reading

Betts, Alexander. *Forced Migration and Global Politics.* Malden, MA: Wiley-Blackwell, 2009.

Dowie, Mark. *Conservation Refugees: The Hundred-Year Struggle Between Global Conservation and Native Peoples.* Cambridge, MA: MIT Press, 2009.

Hopkins, A.G., ed. *Globalization in World History.* New York: W.W. Norton, 2002.

Jentoft, Svein, Henry Minde, and Ragnar Nilsen, eds. *Indigenous Peoples: Resource Management and Global Rights.* Delft, Netherlands: Eburon, 2003.

Scott, James C. *Seeing Like a State: How Certain Schemes to Improve the Human Condition Have Failed.* New Haven, CT: Yale University Press, 1998.

Repatriation

Repatriation is the act of returning an individual or cultural possessions back to the person's or items' original place or people of origin. Social scientists have argued that return to the area of removal or origin is insufficient without an acknowledgment that control of the disposition of exhumed human remains and cultural items, often long removed from their geographic site, belongs to the people from whom separation occurred.

The process of return is made even more complex when there are no systems in place to determine who should receive repatriation and when groups have no organizational capacity to make claims and pursue ownership. Once the issue of control is resolved, native people with the right of possession determine disposition of human remains and cultural items, whether this entails reburial or loan to museums. Although repatriation is an international issue and has been acknowledged as such by museums and indigenous groups around the world, as well as by the United Nations (UN), it was the development of law regarding repatriation in the United States that became the model that other nations would eventually, hesitatingly begin to follow.

History of Repatriation in the United States

Over the past century, the United States has been a leader in repatriation legislation. Since 1906, the U.S. government has had management authority over the cultural and scientific resources under its jurisdiction. The Antiquities Act of that year, and later the Archaeological Resources Protection Act of 1979, established permitting authority for the recovery of scientific data on federal lands and Indian territories. Under these laws, any items removed from the ground—such as human remains and burial artifacts—were to remain under the U.S. government's control and be stored in government and university repositories.

Attempts by Native American tribes to reclaim the remains of their ancestors and tribal property proved unsuccessful. For example, when the Onondaga Nation filed suit in 1899 to retrieve several wampum belts held by the New York State Museum—items with significant value to the state's Iroquois tribes—the court rejected their claim, arguing that the Onondaga had no enforceable property rights to the items.

By the late twentieth century, however, the U.S. government had come to recognize that Native American culture merited respect and protection on an official basis. In 1978, the U.S. Congress passed the American Indian Religious Freedom Act, which aimed to protect and preserve the religious rights and cultural practices of native groups. In 1986, the board of directors of the New York State Museum voted to return the wampum belts to the Onondaga.

Ten years later, in 1996, President Bill Clinton issued an executive order on Indian sacred sites, directing federal agencies to allow Native Americans to practice traditional ceremonies at sites located on federal property. The National Historic Preservation Act of 1966 was amended, most recently in 2006, to recognize traditional cultural places meriting a listing on the National Register of Historic Places and to establish Tribal Historic Preservation Officers who would replace state authorities on tribal lands.

Specific legislation to address repatriation and the cultural property rights of Native Americans included the Native American Graves Protection and Repatriation Act (NAGPRA) of 1990, which established a model for the repatriation process. The NAGPRA encompasses property law, Indian law, human rights law, and administrative process. First, the act grants tribes and Native Americans Fifth Amendment property rights. The law recognizes that although human remains are not legally considered property and thus cannot be owned under common law, descendants have an obligation and a right to direct the disposition of their ancestors. Under the NAGPRA, funerary objects, sacred objects, and collectively owned, inalienable objects of cultural patrimony that previously were removed from tribes and Native American individuals without their permission and are held by federal agencies and museums receiving federal funds must be returned to the claimants. If the museum has a lawful chain of ownership and transfer for the item, it may assert its right of possession to refuse repatriation.

Under the NAGPRA, only lineal descendants and federally recognized tribes or Native Hawaiian organizations have standing to make repatriation claims. For newly exhumed burials and items protected by the NAGPRA that are located on federal or Indian land, claimants are prioritized as follows: lineal descendants; tribal land owners regardless of their cultural relationship; culturally affiliated, federally recognized tribes and Native Hawaiian organizations on federal land; and finally, federally recognized tribes or Native Hawaiian organizations that are the aboriginal occupants of an area, regardless of cultural affiliation, unless another group with standing has a stronger claim of relationship. There is no time limit for claims that are brought to establish the title to human remains of descendants or to cultural property.

The NAGPRA establishes separate processes for the repatriation of Native American and Native Hawaiian human remains and cultural items currently held in museum and federal collections and for those remains and items excavated on federal or Indian lands after 1990. New finds do not require repatriation, as they are not assumed to be the property of the United States; rather, Indian owners are to be determined immediately. Thus, permission for the study of new finds rests with the appropriate tribe.

The NAGPRA repatriation process requires museums, federal agencies, and other institutions with collections of Native American artifacts to compile an inventory of human remains, identified by cultural affiliation whenever possible, and to indicate which funerary objects are associated with those remains. Other cultural items generally are described in a summary. These documents make public the location of the repository so that tribes may assert their rights to human remains and make claims for the repatriation of cultural items belonging to them. Repositories—defined in the NAGPRA as museums that receive federal funds and have collections of Native American human remains and/or cultural items—must publish notices of their inventory in the *Federal Register,* thereby establishing the right of tribes to request the return of an ancestor's remains. The tribe, in turn, publishes a notice of intent to repatriate, which expresses the agreement between the repository and the tribe to transfer control of the objects. In each case, the notice provides information to other parties that may have competing claims.

In addition to the NAGPRA, Congress addressed repatriation in 1989, when it authorized the establishment of the National Museum of the American Indian, requiring the Smithsonian Institution to comply with repatriation to tribes. The Smithsonian is a federation of museums that includes the Native American cultural collections within its National Museum of Natural History; although the Smithsonian does not comply with the NAGPRA, its own repatriation rules set forth a parallel process to the NAGPRA.

International Repatriation

Human remains and cultural items taken to other nations also may be repatriated under international law, such as the Convention for the Protection of Cultural Property in the Event of Armed Conflict (1954) and the Hague Conventions of 1899 and 1907. The peacetime pronouncements of the UN Educational, Scientific and Cultural Organization provide for access to scientific study and protection of cultural property rights, including those of intangible property, ceremony, and natural resources of native peoples worldwide.

In 2004, Great Britain acknowledged the obligation to repatriate human remains with an act of Parliament, which follows the same basic form as the NAGPRA. Other pieces of legislation that follow British common law are the Antiquities Act of New Zealand (1975) and the Aboriginal and Torres Strait Islander Heritage Protection Act (1984) of Australia. Both laws acknowledge repatriation as a basic human right to the direct disposition of the dead, including funerary objects, and to take control of inalienable objects of culture.

In 2010, Hawaiian ancestral bones and funerary objects were successfully repatriated from the Maidstone Museum in Kent, England. The next year, a Hawaiian named Hui Mālama was able to obtain the return of an ancestral skull from the Hunterian Museum at the Royal College of Surgeons in London. However, efforts at repatriating items held by the British Museum, from various Native American artifacts to the so-called Elgin Marbles from the Greek Parthanon, have been less successful.

However, the idea of repatriation gained the status of a UN declaration, when in 2007 the UN General Assembly adopted the UN Declaration on the Rights of Indigenous Peoples (UNDRIP). In Article 12, it asserts that "States shall seek to enable the access and/or repatriation of ceremonial objects and human remains in their possession through fair, transparent and effective mechanisms developed in conjunction with Indigenous Peoples concerned." With the acceptance of UNDRIP by the last of the world's nations in 2010, repatriation has become an international priority.

Sherry Hutt

See also: Countries—United States. Issues—International Policy; United Nations Declaration.

Further Reading

Bowman, Margaret B. "The Reburial of Native American Skeletal Remains: Approaches to Resolution of a Conflict." *Harvard Environmental Law Review* 13:1 (1989): 147–208.

Cassman, Vicki, Nancy Ogegaard, and Joseph Powell, eds. *Human Remains: Guide for Museums and Academic Institutions.* Lanham, MD: AltaMira, 2007.

Echo-Hawk, Walter. "Museum Rights vs. Indian Rights: Guidelines for Assessing Competing Legal Interests in Native American Resources." *New York University Review of Law and Social Change* 14:2 (1986): 437–453.

McKeown, C. Timothy, and Sherry Hutt. "In the Smaller Scope of Conscience: The Native American Graves Protection and Repatriation Act Twelve Years After." *UCLA Journal of Environmental Law and Policy* 21:2 (2002/2003): 153–212.

Revitalization

With respect to indigenous peoples, revitalization refers to resisting, rebuilding, or adapting to the forces of colonialism, racism, globalization, and all attempts at coerced assimilation or adoption of the customs of dominant states. For some historians, the concept of revitalization undercuts the notion of indigenous identity. Most present-day scholars, however, agree that this view stems from a legacy of narrow anthropological and historical studies—soundly rejected in all of the social sciences today—that indigenous peoples were static until contact with Europeans or with other states or civilizations.

It is now well understood that all societies change over time—some slowly, some quickly; some voluntarily, some under coercion; some through their own invention, some through the adoption of customs and practices of other societies; and some intentionally, some accidentally. In situations in which new practices are adopted from other societies, those practices almost always are modified in ways that make them compatible with older values and beliefs, although those, too, change over time.

Social Change and Revitalization

For indigenous peoples, there are at least four key issues in societal change. First, there is the issue of autonomy, that is, having local control and say in all changes. Second, there is the issue of maintaining continuity with older traditions; this is a concern for all societies, but it is especially acute for peoples that have been subjected to many forced changes over recent centuries. A third collection of issues, a result of past forced changes, consists of efforts to recover lost or, more often, submerged or hidden traditions. Fourth, and a key component, is the issue of maintaining a distinctive identity and remaining indigenous. Combined, these issues and efforts to address them are what social scientists mean by the term *revitalization*.

A relevant example of revitalization is the Ghost Dance movement of the 1870s and 1890s, a spiritual dance ritual that started in the Far West and spread across the northern areas of the United States to the Great Plains. The 1890 Ghost Dance attempted to revive traditional Native American spirituality linked to community. Some Western and Northern native nations created completely new ways for cultural autonomy, while others merged traditional practices into new forms. This process created change in both the Ghost Dance ritual and the native culture that integrated it.

Europeans often spread Christianity and their own culture coercively—at times, violently, and at other times, through economic pressure. Many indigenous populations adopted Christianity, at least overtly, and attempted to incorporate some traditional practices into the new religion. Often, however, Christian practices were masked versions of "culturicide" and led to the banning of traditional ceremonies. Also, the spread of Christianity in the name of civilization caused conflicts with indigenous knowledge of the world structured around solstice and equinox observations and seasonal celebrations.

Indigenous peoples in the Americas were not the only ones to resist the replacement of their traditional religions, cultural expressions, and indigenous knowledge through revitalization. So, too, did many Arab peoples, who revived forms of Islam to resist European interlopers in North Africa and the Middle East from the early nineteenth through mid-twentieth centuries.

A late twentieth-century example of revitalization in the United States results from the spread of gaming among Indian nations; although most gaming operations have not generated extensive wealth, these revenue streams have supported cultural revitalization efforts. Some Indian nations used contested notions of sovereignty to develop high-stakes bingo and gaming operations. The wealth generated by casinos enabled some groups to gain sufficient capital to better build their own schools, hospitals, and businesses. It also facilitated local control of schools and tribal colleges, which helped residents sustain and promote local customs, religion, and language. Some nations that raised sufficient wealth from casinos used the money to promote scholarship about native peoples and to support Native American studies programs at public and private colleges. In a few cases, Indian nations donated funds to local governments to support local educational systems. Casinos also employ significant numbers of non-Indians, promoting general economic development.

Cultural Syncretism

Revitalization also may take the form of syncretic religions that mix aspects of traditional religions with Christian practices. Some well-known examples are the Sun Dance practices of many Plains and Western Native American groups, the Longhouse religion of the Iroquois, the Ghost Dance developed in present-day Nevada and practiced widely throughout the West, and the Native American Church (also known as the Peyote religion). Less well known are the Pai Marire and Ringatu religious movements among the Maori people of New Zealand in the late nineteenth century.

Often, these religious movements are seen as forms of resistance. They share many common aspects: emphasis on good behavior and obedience to laws, including traditional practices, hard work, and care for others. If practiced well and faithfully, the belief is that the old order will be restored. Research has shown that they do work when not overtly suppressed. By following the new practices, demoralized communities and individuals rebuild and revitalize the community. Such revitalized communities are not precisely the same as the older society. However, these communities change in ways that work with their traditions, and they do so voluntarily.

Sometimes, when efforts have been made by governments and other native groups to reject a particular group's claim to indigeneity, the effect has been the opposite—the revival and revitalization of what were perceived as long-lost traditions. Closer examination often shows that such traditions were not "lost" but rather were submerged and hidden by a veneer of assimilation. For instance, in many parts of Latin America, indigenous religious practices and rituals were, and still are, conducted as if they were celebrations of saints' days. By adapting this form of expression, indigenous groups avoided drawing opprobrium from the local priest or hostile elites.

There are many examples of these different types of revitalization movements in various parts of the world. In North America, such movements have taken place among the Lakota, Navajo, and Wampanoag peoples. In Latin America, Mexico's Zapatista movement and movements among the Mapuche, Guarani, and Miskito peoples have demonstrated revitalization traits. Changes among the Adevasi in India, the Maori in New Zealand, the Kurds in Iraq and Iran, and the Pashtun in Pakistan and Afghanistan, as well as many other cases, have included systems of decision making, economic distribution, land tenure, and community relations that qualify as revitalization movements and also have the impact of expressing native resistance to the globalized world system.

James V. Fenelon and Thomas D. Hall

See also: Issues—Missionary Activities; Religion (Indigenous); Self-Determination; Social Customs.

Further Reading

Hall, Thomas D., and James V. Fenelon. *Indigenous Peoples and Globalization: Resistance and Revitalization.* Boulder, CO: Paradigm, 2009.

Hämäläinen, Pekka. *The Comanche Empire.* New Haven, CT: Yale University Press, 2008.

Mullis, Angela, and David Kamper, eds. *Indian Gaming: Who Wins?* Los Angeles: University of California, American Indian Studies Center, 2000.

Roe, Frank G. *The Indian and the Horse.* Norman: University of Oklahoma Press, 1955.

Thornton, Russell. *We Shall Live Again: The 1870 and 1890 Ghost Dance Movements as Demographic Revitalization.* New York: Cambridge University Press, 1986.

Wallace, Anthony F.C. "Revitalization Movements." *American Anthropologist* 58 (1956): 264–281.

Wolf, Eric R. *Europe and the People Without History.* Berkeley: University of California Press, 1982.

Revolts

Indigenous people are those who have a historical, natural, and organic bond to a particular region, either real or imagined. Essentially, they are the first to establish and maintain residence in an area for a long period of time and, over that period, establish a physical and psychological bond with the land. Over the course of their existence, indigenous people create their own culture, religion, gender identifications, social order, economic system, and political structure. For example, the Aborigines of Australia have inhabited that continent for at least 40,000 years, creating particular systems of human interaction and organization. The native peoples of North America have resided there for between 12,000 and 24,000 years, creating their own cultural customs.

Throughout history, indigenous peoples across the globe have been migratory, putting them in conflict with other groups. The ancient Roman Empire, for example, was fractured by conflicts with indigenous groups in Asia and Europe, including the Huns, the Visigoths, and others. Inevitably, as other groups attempted to appropriate the lands and resources of indigenous peoples, conflict ensued. Despite the resistance of native peoples to such control by empires and incursions on their traditional lands, inevitably the stronger group dominated.

In cases where one people was able to accumulate enough power to overtake other peoples, the dominant group usually created new political, social, economic, and cultural institutions that usurped and threatened to destroy indigenous ways of life. As a result, indigenous peoples often revolted against such domination.

European Imperialism and Indigenous Responses

During the course of the nineteenth century, European states sought to spread their culture and political order through means of proselytization, exploitation, and military imperialization to feed their industrializing societies. The economic and political systems of various regions became dependent on Western capital and exports.

African and Asian indigenous societies faced the technology and military might of these expanding European empires. Central and South American indigenous cultures, afflicted by European colonial expansion from the sixteenth to the eighteenth centuries, were dominated by wealthy landed elites who developed an export economy by providing raw materials to the industrialized nation-states of Western Europe and the United States.

The indigenous people of these regions, typically restricted to agricultural lifestyles and poverty, increasingly were pushed off their land by indigenous and foreign elites. This exacerbated tensions between social classes, leading to uprisings by the turn of the nineteenth century, especially in South and Southeast Asia and, later, Africa.

For example, India, dominated by British elites as well as by Indian elites educated in the West, experienced the Sepoy Rebellion of 1857. Muslim and Hindu soldiers (called sepoys) serving in the army of the British East India Company were issued Enfield rifles whose gunpowder cartridges were doused with pig or cow tallow so that they were easier to open with the teeth. This was considered sacrilege to both Hindus and Muslims. Rumors also spread that the British had poisoned wells with pig and cow tallow in an effort to force Hindus and Muslims to convert to Christianity. A massive and bloody indigenous rebellion ensued as a result of the British lack of respect for the traditional religious values of their Hindu and Muslim Indian subjects. The British violently put down the uprising, and it ended in the massacre of hundreds of thousands of Indian and British men, women, and children.

Another example of indigenous revolt against European imperial control took place at the turn of the nineteenth century in southwestern Africa. German control of present-day Namibia was marked by brutality against the native Herero and Nama peoples. White German settlers increasingly pushed indigenous peoples from their land, seizing not only the most arable land but water supplies as well. Two decades of German rule saw countless incidences of rapes, forced labor, and, ultimately, deaths inflicted by the German authorities. Tensions between the Germans and the Herero people reached a crescendo in 1904, when the Herero ravaged German settlements, killing more than 100 German settlers. The Germans responded by herding some 24,000 Herero men, women, and children into the Kalahari Desert. A large majority were killed, and the remaining indigenous peoples were sent to German labor camps.

Twentieth Century

Nationalism and indigenous identity were key aspects of the 1919 Treaty of Versailles ending World War I, which aimed to create nation-states in Europe based on ethnic identity. American President Woodrow Wilson labeled this "self-determination."

Hence, the new nation-states of Czechoslovakia, Poland, and Yugoslavia, among others, were carved out of the former Austrian, German, and Ottoman empires. However, these nation-states remained sites of ethnic tension, as still more groups were merged into a conglomeration with other ethnicities. Moreover, the concept of nationalism was more pronounced by the turn of the century, using language and ethnicity as agents of unification as state power became more centralized.

The plight of ethnic groups became more evident in the early twentieth century with the advent of new and widespread media technologies, including radio and film. For example, the Olympic Games, seen by millions of people around the world, encouraged not only national rivalry and competition but also feelings of ethnic unity and disdain for other groups.

Other indigenous movements, such as the *indigenismo* movement in Central and South America, which called for the reclamation of traditional cultures, spawned revolutions, as in Mexico from 1910 to 1920. Following World War II, postcolonial movements began in Africa and Southeast Asia, leading to the eventual independence of numerous nation-states, as well as more indigenous revolts in both regions.

Groups such as the Irish Republican Army in Ireland, Euskadi Ta Askatasuna (Basque Homeland and Freedom) in Spain, the Liberation Tigers of Tamil Eelam in Sri Lanka, and the National Liberation Front in Algeria were willing to commit terrorist acts against their European oppressors in an effort to gain independence. Such acts

FERNANDO DAQUILEMA

"We find ourselves threatened by all the Indian masses," wrote Dario Latorre of Sicalpa, Ecuador, to Chimborazo provincial officials on December 19, 1871.

A day earlier, indigenous peoples in Cacha had attacked and killed tithe collector Rudecindo Rivera. The uprising quickly spread to the villages of Cajabamba, Punín, and Sicalpa. The rebels purportedly crowned a young Indian man named Fernando Daquilema as their king, and the uprising has been known by his name ever since.

Provincial and central government officials immediately sent armed forces into the area, and the rebellion came to an end on December 24. Government officials identified approximately fifty to sixty Indian men and women as instigators of the revolt and punished them severely: They executed a few key leaders, including Daquilema; other male leaders had to work on public works projects for several years, while female leaders received prison sentences.

Interpretations of the Daquilema revolt have changed significantly over time. For decades, Ecuadorian elites regarded the rebellion as evidence of savagery lurking under the highland Indians' timid façade, and they described the rebels as gleefully destroying property and drinking *chicha* (corn beer) out of victims' skulls. According to some writers, Indian women were the most savage of all, particularly Manuela León, whom they described as a madwoman with an insatiable hunger for violence. They claimed that the greatest atrocities of the uprising had occurred at León's urging. According to historians and social scientists, however, such descriptions reflected elite Ecuadorians' fears and prejudices rather than the rebels' actions or motives.

In reality, the Daquilema revolt was part of a spectrum of indigenous strategies aimed at limiting the negative impacts of late nineteenth-century state formation. Indigenous peoples typically used the court system to address their grievances about unfair authorities or taxes, but when peaceful means failed, they sometimes resorted to violence. Such uprisings often were successful in garnering temporary relief from burdens. After the Daquilema revolt, for example, tax collection was postponed, later taxes were reduced, and the minister of the interior formally prohibited tax collectors from abusing Indians.

Indigenous women's participation and leadership in the event likewise has undergone reevaluation. Many historians have noted that women in indigenous communities enjoyed central roles in agriculture, trade, and cultural events. Although women typically were absent from legal forms of community defense because of state officials' preference for male participants in the court system, the extralegal domain of rebellion allowed indigenous women to play a central role in defense of the community that reflected their crucial contributions to its life and culture.

Today, Ecuadorian indigenous activists look back on the Daquilema revolt as part of a centuries-long heritage of indigenous resistance against interethnic exploitation. And indigenous women take particular pride in the central role that their predecessors played in such events.

Erin E. O'Connor

were broadcast widely, as television coverage brought the plight of these groups to a global audience.

By the 1990s, with the fall of the Soviet Union and the end of the Cold War, ethnic crises began to erupt in the Balkans. Ethnic groups in Yugoslavia fought for independence, leading to the fracturing of that country into ethnically specific nation-states. The Caucasus region of southern Russia witnessed rebellion and terrorist acts as well, as Chechens sought independence from Russia. Palestinian intifadas against Israel in the 1980s and 1990s and terrorist bombings in the 2000s led to thousands of deaths. The Kurdish people of northern Iraq, long seeking an independent state, had their villages attacked with poison gas by Saddam Hussein's air forces in 1988; they gained a measure of autonomy following the U.S. invasion of Iraq in 2003, though tensions continue in the post-Saddam era.

Shane R. Tomashot

See also: Issues—Colonialism; Self-Determination; Violence and Warfare.

Further Reading

Anderson, Liam, and Gareth Stansfield. *The Future of Iraq: Dictatorship, Democracy or Division?* New York: Palgrave Macmillan, 2005.

Hobsbawm, Eric J. *Nations and Nationalism Since 1780: Programme, Myth, Reality.* New York: Cambridge University Press, 1990.

Horowitz, Donald L. *Ethnic Groups in Conflict.* Los Angeles: University of California Press, 1985.

Judah, Tim. *Kosovo: What Everyone Needs to Know.* New York: Oxford University Press, 2008.

Reader, John. *Africa: A Biography of the Continent.* London: Alfred A. Knopf, 1997.

Smith, Charles D. *Palestine and the Arab-Israeli Conflict: A History with Documents.* 7th ed. Boston: Bedford/St. Martin's, 2010.

Sacred Sites

For native peoples of the world, certain local landscapes, geographies, and structures are imbued with special significance, often cosmological, that makes them sacred. Not only are these places central to indigenous peoples' worldviews, but they also often contain elements that are life sustaining, such as water. Many of these places are awe inspiring and attract nonindigenous visitors from near and far. Some sites are man-made or were introduced by non-natives and, over time, have been accepted by native peoples as part of their sacred universe.

Geographic Features: Mountains, Hills, and Volcanoes

Sacred mountains, large hills, and volcanoes dominate native cosmologies. Highland areas serve as a place for native peoples to interact with the heavens. They often have historic value as the sites of legendary cities or transcendental events, may be valued as the abodes of legendary figures and deities, or may be viewed as constituent parts of a living world. Areas that are associated with healing also are regarded as sacred.

Native followers of Jainism in India revere five sacred mountains as sites where their Tirthankaras (those who have achieved enlightenment) and other holy people attained nirvana. In Sri Lanka, well before followers of Hinduism, Buddhism, Islam, or Christianity began worshipping Sri Pada (Adam's Peak), the indigenous Vedda were doing so and christened the mountain Samanala Kanda, choosing its name from one of the four guardian deities of the island.

Also in Sri Lanka, Mihintale is viewed as a sacred mountain, as it was here that Buddhism first was introduced to the island. Locals in India view Arunachala Hill as a representation of knowledge and a sacred healing place, particularly for addressing illnesses related to the lungs and female infertility. In what is now Honshu, Japan, for more than 1,500 years, native peoples have visited the area where the sacred mountain Nantai-san and the sacred lake Chuzenji come together to form the town of Nikko.

In the Andes of South America, mountains and volcanoes are two of many types of native sacred spaces, called *huacas,* that influence the everyday lives of indigenous people. In addition to mountains, huacas also can take the form of valleys, streams, lakes, and rock formations.

Mountains are the domains of *apus* (powerful spirits of the sacred mountain) or masculine spirits. Aymara and Quechua speakers today often ask the mountain spirits for protection or assistance during incantations. Mountains also are viewed as the dwelling places of deities that control the weather and thus the fertility of the land. The Andean highlands are venerated as the sites of ethnogenesis and as the link between the three spheres of the Underground, Earth, and Sky.

In Peru, Machu Picchu (meaning "old peak" in Quechua), considered one of the most sacred places in the Andean world, was used by the Inca in the fifteenth century as a royal estate and a field station to experiment with crop cultivation. As a city, it is extraordinary for the architecture and stone masonry of its buildings. Machu Picchu also functioned as an astronomical observatory. The Intihuatana stone (meaning "the place to which the sun is tied") wrongfully has been identified as a sundial.

Rather, most archaeologists today consider it to be a sacred compass, with its most prominent features aligning perfectly with the cardinal directions and the sacred mountains in the background.

Mexico is endowed with several sacred mountains. Near the capital of Mexico City rise Popocatepetl (meaning "smoking mountain" in Nahuatl) and Iztaccihuatl ("sleeping lady" or "white lady"). Both volcanoes rise to approximately 17,000 feet (5,400 meters) above sea level. Archaeological evidence indicates that these mountains were stages for important religious ceremonies among the Aztec and their predecessors.

These mountains are known best for the legend that surrounds them. According to one account, the warrior Popocatepetl was in love with the princess Iztaccihuatl and went to her father to ask for her hand in marriage. The king approved, but only on the condition that Popocatepetl defeat one of his rival tribes in battle. Although Popocatepetl was victorious, the feat took him much longer than he anticipated, and during his absence, a rival suitor misled Iztaccihuatl into believing that Popocatepetl had been killed in battle. Upon hearing this news, Iztaccihuatl died of grief. When Popocatepetl returned to find his love dead, he took her body and placed it atop a local mountain range that resembled the form of a sleeping woman. Popocatepetl then scaled the neighboring mountain to assume an eternal vigil over his lost love.

For centuries, groups native to the island of Jeju-do in South Korea have viewed the Halla-san volcano as sacred—a bridge between heaven and Earth. Also sacred are the forests leading up to the mountain, referred to as the Yonghsil, meaning "enchanted place wilderness." At the base of Halla-san is Sanbangsa, a cave temple that was sacred to the indigenous people prior to the arrival of Buddhism.

The ancient Chinese regarded mountains as sacred, as they believed that the mountains physically supported the heavens. Mountains also were viewed as the dwellings of nature spirits that created powerful storms and life-giving rain. Tai Shan has been venerated by the Chinese as a sacred peak since at least the third millennium B.C.E. It was considered the son of the Emperor of Heaven. It not only looked after humans but also served as a medium for people to speak to God.

In southwestern Tibet soars Mount Kailash at 22,027 feet (6,714 meters). It is sacred to four religions. Hindus believe it to be the abode of Shiva. Jains call the mountain Astapada, believing it to be the place where the first of the twenty-four Tirthankaras attained liberation. Followers of the pre-Buddhist shamanistic religion called B'on refer to the mountain as Yundrung Gu Tse and believe it to be the home of the sky goddess Sipaimen. Tibetan Buddhists call the mountain Kang Rinpoche, meaning "precious one of glacial snow." The creation myths of these religions sometimes refer to Mount Kailash as the mythical Mount Meru.

In Bali, tall volcanoes bisecting the island into northern and southern halves are considered sacred to different groups of people. For Bali's indigenous population inhabiting the jungles around Lake Batur, the mountain Gunung Batur is the most revered. Central to their belief is the power of the goddess of the lake, Dewi Danu, who provides the natural springs at the base and the lower elevations of Mount Batur.

In Hawaii, native peoples have revered the Haleakala (meaning "house of the sun") Crater since at least 800 C.E. According to Polynesian legend, the volcano was given this name when the demigod Maui captured the sun, forcing it to slow its trajectory across the sky so that people could enjoy more daylight. To this day, native peoples build small temples and altars within the volcano.

In New Mexico, a volcanic plume reaching 1,700 feet (518 meters) tall protrudes from the Earth's surface. Known by the name Shiprock or Tse Bi dahi, "rock with wings," it owes its name to an ancient Navajo myth. According to the tale, the Navajo were fleeing a warlike tribe across a narrow sea when they found themselves in a desert. Shamanic leaders invoked the Great Spirit for help. Immediately, the ground shook and then rose from beneath their feet to become an enormous bird. The Navajo held tight to the bird as it flew south for an entire day before settling at dusk at the place where Shiprock now stands. Today, the site is a pilgrimage destination for young indigenous men and women engaged in solitary vision quests.

In Mali, dotting the cliffs of the Bandiagara region are shrines created by the ancestors of the present-day Dogon people to commemorate the encounters of their forefathers with ancestors and spirits during their migration from their original homelands. In accordance with Binu, one of three principal cults of the Dogon, these shrines were created to house the spirits of the ancestors who lived in the era prior to the appearance of death among humans.

Caves, both man-made and natural, also are considered hallowed ground by indigenous peoples throughout the world. The Ellora and Ajanta man-made caves in central India were carved in the sides of basalt cliffs. Near the Ajanta caves are magnificent waterfalls. The Ellora caves became a holy shrine for Buddhists and were noted for the paintings that adorned the inner walls. The Ajanta, which were built later, were holy to Buddhists, Hindus, and Jains and decorated with elaborate sculptures.

For hundreds of years, the mountains, caves, and woodlands of the Black Hills in Wyoming and South Dakota have constituted part of the sacred universe of the

Bear Butte, in western South Dakota, has been listed as one of the most endangered historic places in the United States. Considered sacred ground by Native American tribes, the site is targeted for wind and oil energy development. *(M. Spencer Green/AP Images)*

Plains Indians. One sacred mountain, Bear Butte (Mato Paha to the Sioux), is regarded as the site where the Sioux Nation was born. The Cheyenne view the mountain as the dwelling of their creator. Other sacred mountains include Harney's Peak and Devil's Tower.

Water Features: Lakes, Rivers, and Waterfalls

Lakes, rivers, springs, waterfalls, and other bodies of water tend to be viewed as sacred by indigenous people. In Pushkar, India, for example, the lake that bears the town's name is revered by the townspeople, as it is believed to have been created by Lord Brahma 60,000 years ago. Pilgrims travel to Pushkar to purify and heal themselves physically and spiritually in the area ghats, or sacred baths.

Similarly, the Maya and their descendants revere underground wells, or cenotes, as they are valued as the source of spring water and the entrance to the underworld—the domain of Xibalba, the god of darkness. Cenotes have been sites of sacrifice and other forms of reverence, as indicated by discoveries of altars and other human artifacts.

Indigenous peoples of the lowlands also tend to understand sacred space in relation to their geography, in particular such features as rivers and waterfalls. In the Amazon, for example, where the indigenous people are animistic, many of the important geographic landmarks have an animal avatar. The Amazon is part of the living landscape and often associated with snakes and serpents.

Lakes usually figure prominently in the creation myths of indigenous peoples. In the Andean highlands between modern-day Peru and Bolivia, Aymara and Quechua speakers view Lake Titicaca as the site where the creator Wiracocha created the sun, moon, Earth, and people. Near Lake Titicaca are the majestic peaks of Ancohuma and Illampu. Archaeological evidence indicates that these summits have been the site of religious rituals designed to placate or appease the gods in exchange for essential rain. Watching over these mountains are condors, regarded as messengers of mountain spirits.

The waters of some lakes are believed to contain mystical properties that, when the water is consumed, facilitate spiritual fulfillment. Amritsar Lake in India, whose name means "pool of ambrosial nectar," has waters that are considered suitable for gods. When consumed by humans, these waters are said to produce moments of euphoria and enlightenment.

Celestial Bodies and Seasonal Sites

Celestial bodies are of special significance to indigenous peoples. Traditionally, indigenous peoples created monuments or temples at sites that allowed them to observe or experience powers associated with the cosmos.

The Maya, for example, paid special attention to the movements of Venus as well as the planetary constellations. Many of their most sacred places were coordinated with the heavens in mind. Similarly, in the Andes, temples correspond to constellations.

In Cambodia, the Angkor temple complex was created by the Khmer civilization as a shrine for the human remains and deified spirit of King Suryavarman in the twelfth century. Central to this complex is a massive five-tower temple representation of the fabled five peaks of Mount Meru. The layout of Angkor was based on favorable astronomical alignments. The intricately detailed engravings covering almost all of the surfaces of the stone give the impression of movement within the stone.

A man-made structure, estimated to be more than 700 years old, that is considered sacred to the native peoples of the Great Plains is the Great Medicine Wheel, located in the Bighorn Mountains in Wyoming. Created of rocks, this structure is formed by an 80-foot (24-meter) circle, a cairn in the center, and twenty-eight spokes that radiate from the center. For many indigenous people, wheels were viewed as sacred because they were at once ritual places and functioned to determine the seasons, as the spokes that radiated out aligned with solstice lines.

Built around 3,000 B.C. in Wiltshire, England, Stonehenge is a huge monument that celebrates the relationship between the sun and the seasons. This construction of massive stones, or megaliths, was configured to align with the east and oriented to the rising of the sun on the summer solstice, the longest day of the year. Historians believe the native builders designed Stonehenge as a worship site and also as an astronomical calendar to track the movements of the stars and the passing of the seasons. Similar sites exist in other locations around the world, for example at the ruins of the American Indian city of Cahokia, in present-day Illinois. Nicknamed "Woodhenge," it was a circular arrangement of logs that served a comparable function in terms of the astronomical calendar.

Sacred Geographies

Many indigenous groups regard their geography as sacred. Indigenous Australians believe that their land was created by ancestral beings who, during a mythical period known as Dreamtime, assumed animal and human forms and wandered across the Earth, singing and creating geographic formations. After the Dreamtime cycle was completed and the Earth hardened, the ancestors turned into bodies of water and unique landforms such as Uluru (Ayers Rock) and Kata Tjuta (Olgas).

Today, Australian Aborigines make yearly journeys called walkabouts along the traditional paths or song lines of their ancestral totemic spirits. As they walk these trails, they sing and recount the myths of Dreamtime. Upon arriving at the sacred sites where the mythical beings of the Dreamtime dwelt, the Aborigines perform rituals to invoke the *kurunba,* or spirit power of the place, which can be used for the benefit of the tribe or the health of the surrounding lands. Aborigines view walkabouts along the song lines as a way to support and regenerate the spirits of the living Earth and to experience a living memory of their ancestral Dreamtime heritage.

Part of Buddhist sacred geography is the ancient Bodh Gaya (Bodhi) tree. Located in Bihar State in India and often visited by monks, it is the place where Siddhartha Gautama, or the Buddha, attained ultimate spiritual enlightenment.

In North Africa, Ethiopians (or Abyssinians) regard the area surrounding the city of Aksum as sacred. According to Abyssinian lore, evil spirits inhabited Aksum, until the day that God descended upon the region, arriving at the sacred hill of Makada Egzi, and spread dust over the swamps to dry them up. Not only did this get rid of the evil spirits, but it also imbued the region with magical powers. In the fourth century, Aksum became a Christian kingdom. Since then, temples and other shrines have been created in homage to the site.

A significant part of indigenous cosmologies is gendered sacred space. In the Andes, for example, mountains, valleys, and lakes either are masculine or feminine. As part of the Andean constellation of sacred spaces, regions that provide a visual alignment of masculine and feminine sacred entities together as one are considered supremely sacred. The ancient Otavalo established their kingdom where they did because of the visual alignment of the sacred lake Imbacocha and the sacred mountain Imbabura. Today's indigenous communities around the lake continue to revere the lake, the mountain, and the unity of the two huacas. Similarly, the Srisailam Temple complex located near Rishabhagiri Hill along the banks of the sacred Krishna River in Andhra Pradesh, India, is home to major god and goddess shrines at the same location, making Srisailam an extremely holy site.

Some cities have so many sacred shrines or are so centrally important to regional cosmologies that they, too, are considered sacred. Cuzco in highland Peru was laid out in the form of a puma, with several of its contours representing sacred space. Varanasi in India also is considered sacred because of the hundreds of shrines that exist in the city and its proximity to the sacred Ganges River, which is considered the fluid medium of Shiva's divine existence. Varanasi is one of seven sacred cities in India; it is believed that those who die within its boundaries are liberated from the cycle of reincarnation and go on to achieve nirvana.

In the Pacific Ocean, 2,200 miles (3,540 kilometers) off the coast of Chile, is Rapa Nui or Easter Island. Its oldest name is Te Pito o Te Henua, meaning "center of the world." The island is best known for its large stone statues, called *moai*. Averaging 15 feet (4.5 meters) in height and weighing 14 tons (12.7 metric tons), they are carved from stone of the Rano Raraku volcano. Almost 300 of these statues have been discovered, and they sit on platforms called *ahu.* The creators of the moai were of Polynesian descent. In accordance with their religious views, they considered the moais, once carved and charged with a spiritual essence called *maná,* to be extremely sacred.

Challenges: Preservation and Industrial Development

Indigenous sacred sites today are under assault. Extractive industries often target lands that are the territories of indigenous people. This decision often is based on opinions that regard the interests and rights of native peoples as secondary to those of the rights of profit.

In Cajamarca, Peru, for example, in 2004, the U.S.-owned mining company Newmont attempted to usurp control of the Andean sacred mountain Cerro Quilish in order to extract gold dust. For the native highlanders, this mountain is an important source of water, and they regard it as a deity (huaca) that provides the people with this vital substance. Native peoples responded to this threat by mobilizing to protest this intrusion. Indigenous actions were successful in rebuffing the plans of the gold company and, in so doing, preserving their sacred space.

Kenneth Kincaid

See also: Issues—Land Rights; Religion (Indigenous); Social Customs.

Further Reading

Blain, Jenny, and Robert Wallis. *Sacred Sites, Contested Rites/ Rights: Pagan Engagements with Archaeological Monuments.* Eastbourne, UK: Sussex Academic Press, 2007.

Gelder, Kenneth Douglas, and Jane Margaret Jacobs. *Uncanny Australia: Sacredness and Identity in a Postcolonial Nation.* Melbourne, Australia: Melbourne University Press, 1998.

Johnston, Alison M. *Is the Sacred for Sale?: Tourism and Indigenous Peoples.* London: Earthscan, 2006.

Verschuuren, Bas, Robert Wild, Jeffrey A. McNeely, and Gonzalo Oviedo, eds. *Sacred Natural Sites: Conserving Nature and Culture.* London: Earthscan, 2010.

Versluis, Arthur. *Sacred Earth: The Spiritual Landscape of Native America.* Rochester, VT: Inner Traditions, 1992.

Self-Determination

Self-determination is a process by which a group of people that are united by national consciousness choose their own government without external compulsion. The term can denote the complete and territorial sovereignty of a state, or it can describe varying degrees of political autonomy from a parent state. At the simplest level, self-determination is the right of a group of people to control how they are governed.

Self-determination, as a principle, evolved out of nationalism and anticolonialism that emerged at the time of the French and American revolutions in the eighteenth century. During each of these political uprisings, people asserted the right to form their own state and to choose their own government.

It was not until World War I, however, that self-determination gained recognition as a political principle. Influenced by U.S. President Woodrow Wilson, the Allies accepted self-determination as a peaceful aim. The Paris Peace Treaties (1947) actively reconstituted the frontiers of Eastern Europe so that various states could rule themselves. The victorious Allies—France, Great Britain, and the United States—dismantled the Austro-Hungarian, German, and Ottoman empires to create a number of new states, including Czechoslovakia and Yugoslavia (initially called the Kingdom of Serbs, Croats, and Slovenes). The principle of self-determination was not applied evenly, however, and many of these new states comprised different ethnicities, with a majority group dominating the operation of the state.

Self-determination evolved further in the aftermath of World War II. In 1945, the United Nations (UN) was founded to provide a platform for international dialogue. One of the UN's principal goals was to facilitate self-determination among the subject peoples of the European empires. It defined self-determination as (1) the right of a state to choose its political, economic, and sociocultural systems, and (2) the right of a people to constitute themselves in a state or to freely determine their association with an existing state.

The right to self-determination is a fundamental principle of international law. It is enshrined in Article 1 of the Charter of the United Nations; in Article 1 of the

International Covenant on Economic, Social and Cultural Rights; and Article 1 of the International Covenant on Civil and Political Rights. Significantly, the last-named agreement provides for the right of peoples to self-determination, in addition to the right of ethnic, religious, or linguistic minorities to enjoy their own culture, practice their own religion, and use their own language.

The UN continues to work on raising international awareness of the right to self-determination. Since that body was founded, indigenous peoples have used the UN—and the rights language that it created—to challenge government policy. Indeed, the UN has provided indigenous leaders with a political space in which to advance their claims.

Indigenous Self-Determination in Practice

When used in reference to indigenous peoples, self-determination implies the right to participate in the democratic process of governance and to influence one's future—politically, socially, and culturally—within the existing (often nonindigenous) government framework. Examining the achievements toward aboriginal self-determination to date requires considering gains in ethnopolitical rights, particularly how indigenous peoples have exercised those rights to protect their interests.

Political scientist Will Kymlicka offers one way of understanding group rights, proposing three basic sets of rights: (1) rights of self-government, (2) polyethnic rights, and (3) rights of special representation. What follows is an examination of how these rights are reflected in different models of self-determination in indigenous territories in Canada, the United States, and Norway.

Self-Government

The right of self-government permits a group of people to have greater political autonomy or territorial jurisdiction. An autonomous institution is one that is able to regulate its own affairs.

In Canada, the Inuit achieved relative autonomy with the establishment of the federal territory of Nunavut (meaning "our land" in the Inuktitut language) in April 1999. Nunavut encompasses Inuit lands and the northern portions of the High Arctic islands, an expanse of more than 746,000 square miles (1.9 million square kilometers).

Demands for Inuit self-government were spurred by federal interference in the region. During World War II, Allied forces used the Canadian Arctic as a military base. In 1955, Canada and the United States partnered to construct the Distant Early Warning Line, a radar chain designed to warn Canadians and Americans of an anticipated Soviet attack. Once established, such military operations increased non-Inuit settlement in Nunavut (at that time, part of the Northwest Territories). Also in 1955, the North Rankin Nickel Mines developed extractive industry in Rankin Inlet.

As a result of increased non-Inuit presence in the Canadian Arctic, the federal government established a settlement at Itivia, a half mile (0.8 kilometers) from the mine. At the same time, the Canadian government interfered in the lives of the Inuit residents by encouraging indigenous peoples to abandon their nomadic lifestyle and settle in government-built communities. Many Inuit believe that such federal interference during the postwar era accelerated cultural changes and language loss. The Inuit envisioned self-government as a way to regain control over the management of matters that directly affected them and to help preserve their cultural identity.

Influenced by the civil rights movement in the United States, the Inuit Tapirisat of Canada proposed the creation of Nunavut as part of a comprehensive settlement of Inuit claims in the Northwest Territories in 1976. A few years later, the Legislative Assembly of the Northwest Territories voted in favor of dividing the territory. In 1999, the Nunavut Act, establishing Nunavut as a distinct political and geographic entity, was adopted by the Canadian Parliament and received royal assent.

During negotiations over the Nunavut Act, Inuit representatives demanded self-government. According to Thomas Suluk, one of several chief negotiators, federal representatives urged the Inuit to "eliminate this nativeness, this separateness, because it doesn't have a snowball's chance in hell of making it." Nevertheless, the result of the negotiations was a public government in which Inuit participation in regional affairs is determined by the voting majority. As a result, self-government is de facto—originating from voting demographics—rather than de jure.

Politically, Nunavut has its own legislative assembly, which has powers equivalent to those of any other federal territory, and its own supreme court. There are no political parties, and candidates run as individuals. The reigning consensus government, whereby decisions are made by majority agreement, is said to reflect Inuit cultural values. Self-determination in Nunavut is imperfect, however, as Inuit decision making is conditional. During the early stages, the Nunavut Implementation Committee—a federal advisory agency—profoundly influenced administrative operations.

Furthermore, as Nunavut is a public government, Inuit control is premised on the existence of an Inuit majority. While Nunavut is celebrated in Canadian textbooks as "the first full territory to be governed and administered by Aboriginal people," federal restrictions limit Inuit control over the territory's affairs.

Still, the creation of Nunavut is a step toward self-determination. Through public government, the Inuit are equipped to counterbalance the power of the non-Inuit nation-state in which they reside.

Polyethnic Rights

As a general rule, polyethnic rights protect the freedom to practice one's own culture—particularly language and traditional land use. However, polyethnic rights also may include food sovereignty, that is, "the right of Peoples to define their own policies and strategies for sustainable production, distribution, and consumption of food, with respect for their own cultures and their own systems of managing natural resources," as outlined in the 2002 Declaration of Atitlan, the First Indigenous Peoples' Global Consultation on the right to food and food security.

Among the polyethnic rights extended to indigenous peoples (and immigrants), Kymlicka argues that governments should create and/or extend affirmative action policies and public funding for cultural practices to minority groups. And yet, he argues, polyethnic rights are not absolute or permanent, and the exercise of polyethnic rights depends on the culture of the minority group.

In the United States, nonindigenous education once operated as "the handmaiden to assimilation." American bureaucrats and educators believed that Western education—ranging from learning English to participating in European style games—would offer Indians a free and equal chance to participate in American society. While Congress first authorized an annual stipend for a "civilization" program for the "aborigines" in 1808, European-style schools operated on American soil as early as 1492. The Jesuits established missionary schools during the early days of European settlement to educate natives in the Spanish language, the principles of industry, and the tenets of Catholicism.

Mission schools, later known as industrial schools, were designed to "civilize" America's indigenous population. Federal and church administrators labored under the assumption that native cultures countered American sociocultural values and therefore were unworthy of perpetuation. Given that mission schooling aimed to Westernize native students, lessons rarely had an academic focus. Instead, the curriculum revolved around topics such as hygiene or Christian piety. To expedite the process, federal officials forcefully separated native children from their parents and boarded them at schools throughout the year.

In the 1950s and 1960s, indigenous communities across the United States were influenced by the civil rights movement. Indigenous activists looked to education as a means to think about self-determination and to preserve native languages and traditions. In response to political pressure, the U.S. Senate Special Subcommittee on Indian Education was established to study Native American education. In 1969, the so-called Kennedy Report was released, claiming that native education in the United States was a "national tragedy." It became apparent that Western education systems were not adequately serving indigenous students.

As early as 1967, native parents from Rocky Boy, Montana, expressed their dissatisfaction with the non-native education system. Their children were bussed into town, attending school in the nearby Havre district, and they wanted a separate elementary school district composed of land on the reservation. They petitioned the county superintendent to realign the school district boundaries. The petition was declined.

It was not until 1970 that an independent public school was approved by the county superintendent and the state superintendent of public education. As a result of public pressure, the community gained Rocky Boy Elementary School. In the words of school board chairman Dorothy Small, Indian-controlled education at Rocky Boy allowed for an "emphasis on individual instruction, heavy reliance on Cree-speaking teacher aides, attention to Cree language and culture," and attempts to create teaching materials in Cree.

Residents of Rocky Boy achieved relative self-determination by exercising their polyethnic rights—the right to education. The benefits of self-determined education at Rocky Boy include, but are not limited to, decreased bussing distances, increased parental involvement, and access to a bilingual, culturally responsive curriculum. Perhaps more important, self-determined education reaffirms the importance of indigenous values.

Arguably, the Kennedy Report ushered in an era of self-determined education in the United States, facilitating the establishment of other tribally run schools. In 1972, the Indian Education Act created funding for special programs for Indian children in reservation schools. The legislation also encouraged the growth of community-run schools. In 1975, the Indian Self-Determination and Education Assistance Act was passed, increasing the involvement of Native Americans in educational programming. It transferred government control of Indian programs to Indian people, making Native Americans responsible for the planning, implementation, and administration of their own schools.

Established more than thirty years ago, Rocky Boy's public school remains in operation today and has expanded to include a high school. The success of self-determined education is exemplified by demand. In 2009,

Rocky Boy Superintendent Voyd St. Pierre announced, "We need to develop a concrete growth plan. The need is definitely here."

Special Representation Rights

The term "special representation" denotes the right of indigenous peoples to participate in and to shape a system of government. In Norway, for example, the indigenous Sami people achieved relative self-determination through the establishment of the Sami Parliament.

Norway's northward expansion, beginning in the sixteenth century, made the Sami an ethnic minority in their own lands. Nordic expansion also weakened Sami political power, as Nordic states drew national boundaries irrespective of indigenous systems of land use. To date, there are no reserves in Norway (nor are there aboriginal land claims). The Sami push for a parliament demanded recognition of indigenous presence on the land, not the annexation of the land to indigenous peoples.

The movement toward special representation rights resulted from conflict between indigenous and nonindigenous peoples over the damming of the Alta-Kautokeino River. In 1978, the Norwegian Water Resources and Energy Directorate announced a hydroelectric project that would inundate the Sami village of Maze. By 1979, protest had turned to civil disobedience as the Sami halted construction.

As a result of the controversy, the Norwegian government hosted meetings with a Sami delegation. Out of these meetings, the Sami Rights Committee was born. In 1985, the Rights Committee proposed the Sami Act. Approved by the Norwegian state, the act allowed for the establishment of the Sami Parliament, which opened in 1989. It hosts forty-three Sami representatives who are elected by direct vote every four years.

While the Sami Parliament acts as an advisory council to the Norwegian government, it does not constitute an order of government with jurisdiction over Sami territories. It does work on political issues that are deemed relevant to the indigenous peoples of Norway. Problematically, consultation depends on whether central decisions are believed to affect Sami interests. Since its establishment, the Norwegian government has granted the Sami Parliament the following rights:

1. Management of grant monies for Sami organizations (1989).
2. Responsibility for language development (1992).
3. Management of Sami culture and monies from the Norwegian Council of Cultural Affairs (1993).
4. Protection of Cultural Heritage Sites (1994).

The Sami Parliament is subject to a number of limitations: It lacks a clear constitutional position; it is not an independent body, but relies on the Norwegian state for funding; and it acts primarily as a referral body for the Norwegian state. In spite of these restrictions, the Sami successfully have navigated the political limits of long-established colonial rule to ensure indigenous participation in state affairs.

Indigenous Self-Determination: A State Threat?

Marie Léger, coordinator of the Rights of Indigenous Peoples Programme for the Canadian organization Rights & Democracy, indicated in 2002 that many states raise at least one of the following questions about indigenous self-determination:

1. How does the implementation of self-determination affect the territorial integrity of states?
2. How can self-determination be exercised within the framework of existing states?
3. How can a state accommodate a group's right to self-determination when its territory is occupied by different indigenous peoples who may wish to exercise their right to self-determination in different ways?

Indigenous demands for self-determination often create a culture of fear—fear that nonindigenous states will lose control over resources and be forced to cede valuable territories to minority groups. What is at stake is the federal government's ability to exercise sovereignty over territories that technically belong to the state but have a substantial indigenous presence. One issue, among many, is the state's economic stability. Does the federal government, for instance, retain the right to extract natural resources without indigenous consent?

Critics of self-determination propose that it leads to social chaos and endless fragmentation. Indian political commentator and human rights activist Balraj Puri argues that ethnic identities evolve, and that minority groups are socially constructed. He fears that minority groups will multiply over time. Puri writes, "emerging identities may seek self-determination and separate identity within every nation." If the state recognizes the right to self-determination of one minority group, must it recognize the right to self-determination for all groups? American foreign-policy analyst Strobe Talbot expresses similar concerns: "If this concept [of self-determination] is carried to an extreme, it means every one of the thousands of nationalities on the earth should have its own state."

It is the desire for "national unity" that led Australia

to reject indigenous peoples' rights to self-determination during 2002 UN negotiations working toward an international statement of indigenous rights. Under the advice of Indigenous Affairs Minister Philip Ruddock, the Australian cabinet proposed "self-management" by Aborigines instead of "self-determination."

As a spokesman for Minister Ruddock explained, "Our position is that we're not comfortable with the word because it implies separateness and a separate sovereignty." Acceptable to Australia, and conducive to social stability, was the delegation of administrative tasks and responsibilities to Aborigines. Justification of the self-management position originated from the ambiguity surrounding self-determination. Elaborating on Minister Ruddock's position, his spokesperson explained, "there's certainly no agreement on the use of the phrase 'self-determination.'" New Zealand supported Australia's "self-management" position.

Critics of the state position correlate opposition to self-determination with latent racism. In the words of James Davis, the first principal of Rocky Boy Elementary School, "When Whites and other affluent societies demand community control, it has been regarded as logical, normal, and appropriate, but once . . . a minority group begins to talk about control, people begin to see some dark and devious plot being constructed by militants and revolutionaries."

In reference to North America, historian Samuel R. Cook has argued that federal policy makers seemingly endorse indigenous rights while maintaining racial hierarchies. He suggests that self-determination is injected into legislation, policy statements, and opinions with "random fervor." Self-determination in North America, it seems, is more of a "magical incantation which, by its mere utterance, will render a policy perfect" than a political solution. Fear of the subaltern has resulted in piecemeal applications of indigenous rights and thus has maintained hierarchies that it seeks to modify.

Demanding Recognition

Building on the work of Nunavut, Rocky Boy Elementary School, and the Sami Parliament, the following institutions continue to work toward a self-determined future for indigenous peoples:

International Centre for Human Rights and Democratic Development: Established by the Canadian Parliament in 1988, this group works with governments to promote indigenous rights. Through the consultation process and submitting testimony to the UN Center for Human Rights, the center seeks to redress grievances and to promote and increase awareness of indigenous rights worldwide.

International Indian Treaty Council (IITC): Founded in 1974, the IITC grew out of the civil rights movement in the United States, and it has worked toward developing an international setting in which to address indigenous rights. The council was responsible for the development of a permanent forum for indigenous peoples within the UN and also submits testimony to the UN Center for Human Rights.

National Congress of American Indians (NCAI), United States: Founded in 1944 in response to postwar termination and assimilation policies, the NCAI seeks to protect sovereign and treaty rights. While recognizing tribal differences, it utilizes transnational unity and coordinated decision making to achieve federal recognition, monitors federal policy, and seeks to inform federal decisions affecting Native Americans.

Assembly of First Nations, Canada (AFN): Formed in 1985, the AFN is a national organization that represents First Nations (indigenous) citizens in Canada with the goal of protecting sovereign and treaty rights. Despite federal rejections of the right to self-government, the AFN works with Canada's existing government to protect indigenous interests and to harness available power to influence First Nations affairs.

Despite state obstacles and limited gains, indigenous peoples across the globe continue to pressure governments to recognize their right to self-determination. For many, self-determination means the freedom to live well, according to one's own cultural values and beliefs. Self-determination also is associated with indigenous peoples' right to participate in decisions affecting them. The possibility of direct change frequently is linked to survival.

For indigenous peoples, the reality of the exercise of the right to self-determination is clear: Few, if any, seek full independence or full autonomy as a nation-state. What is desired is an institutional framework that will safeguard indigenous identities and recognize indigenous peoples as equally contributing members of society.

Brittany Luby

See also: Issues—Indigenous Governments; Indigenous Peoples and the United Nations; International Policy; Political Participation.

Further Reading
Alfred, Taiaiake. *Wasáse: Indigenous Pathways of Action and Freedom.* Peterborough, Canada: Broadview, 2005.
Banting, Keith, and Will Kymlicka, eds. *Multiculturalism and the Welfare State: Recognition and Redistribution in Contemporary Democracies.* New York: Oxford University Press, 2006.

Buchanan, Allan. *Justice, Legitimacy, and Self-Determination: Moral Foundations for International Law.* New York: Oxford University Press, 2003.

Cirkovic, Elena. "Self-Determination and Indigenous Peoples in International Law." *American Indian Law Review* 31:2 (2007): 375–399.

Deloria, Vine, Jr., and Daniel Wildcat. *Power and Place: Indian Education in America.* Golden, CO: Fulcrum, 2001.

Hale, Lorraine. *Native American Education: A Reference Handbook.* Santa Barbara, CA: ABC-CLIO, 2002.

Kymlicka, Will. *Finding Our Way: Rethinking Ethnocultural Relations in Canada.* Toronto, Canada: Oxford University Press, 1998.

———. *Multicultural Citizenship: A Liberal Theory of Minority Rights.* Oxford, UK: Clarendon, 1995.

Nortext Multimedia Incorporated and Nunavut Tunngavik Incorporated. *Nunavut '99: Changing the Map of Canada.* Iqaluit, Canada: Nortext, 1999.

Poelzer, Greg. "Indigenous Rights and Self-Determination: Models and Options." In *Introduction to the Circumpolar World.* Saskatoon, Canada: University of Saskatchewan, 2005.

Puri, Balraj. "Sovereignty, Territorial Integrity and Right of Self-Determination." *Economic and Political Weekly,* January 27, 2001, 263–264.

Sámediggi. The Sami Parliament. www.samediggi.no.

Social Customs

Native peoples, generally speaking, have unique customs that have evolved over time and reflect ways of understanding the natural world, social relations, and the cosmological forces that govern life. Globalization, colonization, evangelization, and the mass media have eroded many cultural practices as native peoples increasingly have accepted Western culture. Nevertheless, native peoples adhere to a variety of traditional customs and practices dealing with many aspects of life.

Native peoples often use rituals as a way of coping with illness. The Guahibo people of Colombia, for example, represent the attitudes of many indigenous peoples, responding to illness with social empathy. Rather than isolating those who are sick, the Guahibo accompany them through their illness in the hope that their presence will alleviate suffering and improve the spirits of the sick so that he or she might recover faster. Such rituals are observed not only for the benefit of the individual who is ill, but also for the emotional health of and immunity-boosting benefits to the entire group.

Many native groups have made the retention of such cultural rites one of their key priorities in the twenty-first century, and they adhere to a variety of traditional customs and practices in many areas. Some social customs are related to transitional rituals that mark rites of passage for group members, such as birth, the transition to adulthood, marriage and courtship, and death. Others are community rituals that focus on religious practices and interaction with the spirit world, relationships within the community, and important times during a group's annual cycle. Though none of these are universal to all native groups, they are common and form the basis for comparative analysis.

Transitional Customs: Birth

Birth ceremonies vary widely among the world's indigenous peoples. The !Kung (sometimes referred to as Bushmen), a hunter-gather society in the Kalahari Desert region of Angola, Botswana, and Namibia, practice unassisted childbirth, believing that the Earth is the first mother and therefore should play the role of midwife. When a woman is about to give birth, she leaves her village, walking up to a mile away, and delivers her child into a small leaf-lined deposit that she has dug into the sand. She delivers the placenta and lays it next to the child; the mother then covers both with a large leaf and informs the village women of the birth. The women join the mother and perform a ritual that welcomes the newborn.

For the Quiché people of Guatemala, when a woman goes into labor, the father, the village leaders, and the couple's parents are present to receive the child into the community. After birth, the placenta, which is considered the baby's "companion," is burned at a special time of day. It is customary for the mother and child to be left alone for eight days after birth and to have limited contact with those who visit to bring them food and gifts. During those eight days, the community assumes full responsibility for the financial and social affairs of the family. At the end of this period, the mother and child are joined by the rest of the family. In a special ceremony, community members begin the process of integrating the child into the community and the Quiché universe. A communal lunch is held, and a candle is lit to symbolize the baby's link to the community as well as elements of the universe, such as earth, water, and sun.

Transitional Customs: Marriage and Courtship

For native peoples, marriage practices and customs are diverse. Among the Aborigines of Australia, polygamy is common, as a man may take several wives. Women, however, may have only one husband at a time. They live together as a family that includes all wives, children, and sometimes in-laws. Traditionally, it was not uncommon for a man to have two to four wives, or even several more; today, however, many men follow the Western practice of having only one wife. Another element of Aboriginal custom is in-law avoidance, whereby direct communication with one's mother-in-law is socially taboo; this is true for both men and women. Communication takes place through a third party.

In South India, the Yerukala people have adopted some Western traditions. Before 1947, when India achieved independence from Great Britain, marriage was the product of negotiation and economic exchanges, and polygamy frequently was practiced. Today, polygamy still is permitted, though it occurs rarely. Arranged marriages still are practiced.

In northern Nepal, Tibetans practice fraternal polyandry, whereby all brothers marry a single wife. In these relations, the younger brothers typically defer authority to the eldest. However, all brothers are required equally to work to support the family, and all participate as sexual partners. All of the offspring of the combined marriage are viewed equally by the fathers. Men are allowed to abandon this relationship and practice monogamy, but the children remain with the polyandrous family. This relationship is thought to avoid inheritance conflicts and division of estates.

Among the Cherokee in the United States, some marriage customs are unique to each clan. Clans are matrilineal, and marriage within one's own clan is prohibited. In the Cherokee world, space often is considered sacred, and the location of a wedding is blessed for one week prior to the ceremony. At the wedding ceremony, the bride is represented by her mother and oldest brother, and the groom is accompanied by his mother. The marriage rite includes a gathering at the sacred fire of the man and woman, a blessing by the priest, Cherokee songs, and the cloaking of the bride and groom in blue blankets, which are replaced by a single white blanket once they are declared husband and wife.

In hunter-gatherer societies such as the !Kung, the ability to hunt determines one's prospects for marriage. When a male returns after his first kill, his status as a marriage partner increases. Indeed, a man's ability to get along with his in-laws and to provide them with meat are considered the most important qualities in being selected by parents as a daughter's marriage partner.

In Quiché society, propriety is extremely important, and inappropriate or public courting is viewed as a lack of respect for one's ancestors and parents. Women have the right to ignore, reject, and even insult men who make advances publicly or without the permission of their

KHIPUS

According to archaeological evidence, the Inca, the largest pre-Columbian civilization in South America when the Spanish arrived in the sixteenth century, neither kept nor left behind any written records. They did, however, leave *khipus* (also spelled *quipus*), knotted, colored, and twisted textile strings that are believed to have served as the main record-keeping device of the largest state in the ancient New World.

From the early Spanish chronicles in the work of anthropologist Leland Locke in 1923 until the early twenty-first century, khipus were considered the principal numerical "bookkeeping" devices used by the Inca's imperial bureaucracy, which extended 3,000 miles (4,828 kilometers) from present-day Colombia south to central Chile. Employing a base-10 recording system and an elaborate procedure of checks and balances, the khipus were used by Inca accountants, called *Quipucamayocs,* to keep track of the resources of the vast empire. Some researchers, however, have speculated that the information recorded in the khipus might not be solely numerical.

In the late 1990s, anthropologist Gary Urton and his research team at Harvard University began to study some of the approximately 600 extant khipus in state and private collections. In 2005, they reported the first

evidence of non-numeric information embedded in seven khipus from Puruchuco, an Inca palace and administrative center on the coast of Peru. This information appeared to include stories and other narratives of historical events within the complex symbology of strings and knots contained in the khipus.

Working with an interdisciplinary team, including cryptographers, Urton found seven additional bits of binary information that seemed to signal narratives included in them. His team also discovered that the knots in the khipus contain a variety of pattern-finding algorithms and thousands of repeated knot sequences that suggest words or phrases.

The work of Guamán Poma de Ayala in 1615 and other early colonial documents recorded by Spanish travelers, conquistadores, and administrators, in addition to subsequent archaeological studies, attest that khipus were used for keeping records and sending messages via runners throughout the empire. And the growing evidence supported by Urton's research shows that the khipus apparently do preserve more than numeric sequences. Still, the deciphering of the information to be found in the khipus remains an ongoing task.

Patricio R. Ortiz

parents. According to Quiché social custom, marriage encompasses four steps. The first is the "open door," in which the young man and his parents visit the home of the young woman's family. The family of the girl decides whether to accept the suitor. If rejected, the young man may return a second time with his family or others who can vouch for him. This may go on until one side either abandons hope or relents. If the family opens their door to the suitor, the woman still reserves the right to reject him. Respect is extremely important in these deliberations, and it is common for a suitor and his family to kneel while awaiting the opening of the door. The second step is a celebration during which the preparations for the wedding begin to take place, and a commitment is made by the bride-to-be to honor her grandmother and the traditions of the ancestors. The third step is a ceremony in which the young man and woman make vows to each other before the community elders. The fourth ritual is the farewell ceremony, or *despedida,* in which the bride says goodbye to her parents' house, and in some cases her community, and begins a new life with her husband.

Community Customs: Religious Observance

In the Andean valley of Sinakara, Peru, in early June, at the full moon prior to the Feast of Corpus Christi (the Thursday before Easter on the Catholic calendar), thousands of Quechua pilgrims converge on Qollqepunku, the highest point in the valley and one of the region's three principal *apus,* or mountain spirits. These large groups, self-identified as *naciones* (nations), include financial sponsors, ritual leaders, dancers, and an entourage of others. Each group carries its own idol of the Señor de Qoyllur Rit'i, which is derived from an eighteenth-century encounter between a Quechua boy and a mestizo boy in which the mestizo was transformed into a bush bearing the image of Jesus Christ on the cross and the native boy fell dead on the spot. The custom is intended to appease Qollqepunku, a shaman who takes care of the people's health and whose medicine is the water from glacier ice. As selected Quechua climb higher to the glacial peaks, they break off large chunks of ice to distribute among the other pilgrims. After three days, the Quechua pilgrims set off for their villages, dancing and parading single file down the steep mountains with their prized ice.

In examples of celebrations by particular ethnic groups, elements of ritual dance can be seen. For example, among the Qolla (mestizo dancers) and Ukuku (trickster dancers), it is customary to dance ritual combats, taking turns whipping each other's legs. This is part of a tradition of ritual fighting called *tinku* in Quechua, in which

men and women from different communities engage each other, create a circle, while they dance and chant and urge combatants on as they fight one another. As the celebrants of Qoyllur Rit'i traverse the mountains, they chew the sacred coca leaf.

Community Customs: Interpersonal Relations

In the Andean highlands, coca chewing is practiced to provide one with energy, to dull the pangs of hunger, or to relieve the symptoms of altitude sickness. But it is also an important social custom that unites fellow chewers and the sacred deities. In the Andes, coca is the medium by which people interact. When one is invited to chew coca, it is an offer of social intercourse. When friends or family members encounter each other in a public space or when coworkers begin a task, they share coca. Coca chewing takes place at the end of the day after meals and during morning and afternoon breaks.

When Andeans gather to chew coca, they first offer a cluster of coca leaves, called a *k'intu.* The etiquette of sharing varies by region. In Sonqo, for example, coca bundles are extended with the right hand. In more formal situations, the k'intu is offered with both hands. Acceptance of the k'intu implies an acceptance of the terms of a social obligation. Prior to chewing the leaves, one blows on the leaves while waving them in front of the mouth and utters invocations to the earth, to sacred spaces, to the *ayllu* (clan), and to one's ancestors. Rejection of the k'intu also implies a rejection of social invitation or responsibility and may be viewed as an act of hostility.

Community Customs: Conflict Resolution

Finally, indigenous peoples have many ways of dealing with conflict or tension. For example, among indigenous Canadians, situations that cause anxiety provoke withdrawal, especially when engaging with outsiders. Demonstrations of anger and grief are repressed in public situations. Many abide by an ethic of noninterference as they refrain from passing judgment or imposing their ideas on others.

Ethnographic studies have focused extensively on endemic warfare between the Amazonian tribes, such as the Jívaro's wars of extermination or the Yanomami, who practice a ritualistic escalation of violence before engaging in all-out war. However, conflict resolution within an ethnic group sheds light on interesting practices.

In Australia, Aborigines engage in highly disciplined, ritual conflict as a way of mediating social tensions and creating social space. Brandishing knives, they are allowed to cut and stab their opponent only on the arms and back. When the fighting stops, the elders inspect the wounds and declare a winner. Then, to demonstrate equality, the winner is subjected to the same wounds that he inflicted on his opponent.

Among the !Kung in Botswana, conflict resolution is achieved through extensive talking, which includes banter, argument, and verbal abuse that often becomes extremely personal. However, as tensions arise and the verbal assaults become more pointed, the possibility of resolution through humorous quips increases, and laughter brings the sides back together.

Protection of Social Customs

Although these specific rituals are not observed by all native groups, many native peoples, such as the Quiché in Guatemala, are secretive about aspects of their culture and selective about what they share with people who are not members of their group. This is partly a defense mechanism and a sign of respect for previous generations. By refusing to disclose information about their culture, native peoples safeguard it from outside manipulation and efforts to eradicate it.

As previous generations were more inclined to share information with outsiders and often were victimized by this openness, many contemporary indigenous peoples, in recognition of that misplaced trust, frequently shun conversations that seem to pry or reveal only that which the community authorizes. For example, among some of the Pueblo in New Mexico, feast days and other community customs may be attended by non-natives, but only with the permission of the tribe.

Native peoples have learned through bitter experience the importance of protecting their social customs. In so doing, they hope to maintain those customs that have sustained their people for centuries.

Kenneth Kincaid

See also: Issues—Anthropology; Assimilation; Reemerging People Groups; Social Discrimination.

Further Reading

Allen, Catherine J. *The Hold Life Has: Coca and Cultural Identity in an Andean Community.* Washington, DC: Smithsonian Books, 2002.

Chagnon, Napoleon A. *Yanomamo.* 6th ed. Independence, KY: Wadsworth, 2012.

Dettwyler, Katherine A. *Dancing Skeletons: Life and Death in West Africa.* Long Grove, IL: Waveland, 1993.

Garrett, J.T., and Michael Tlanusta Garrett. *The Cherokee Full Circle: A Practical Guide to Sacred Ceremonies and Traditions.* Rochester, VT: Bear & Company, 2002.

Goettner-Abendroth, Heide. *Matriarchal Societies: Studies on Indigenous Cultures Across the Globe.* New York: Peter Lang, 2012.

Lee, Richard B. *The !Kung San: Men, Women, and Work in a Foraging Society.* Cambridge, UK: Cambridge University Press, 1979.

McNight, David. *Going the Whiteman's Way: Kinship and Marriage among Australian Aborigines.* London: Ashgate, 2004.

Menchú, Rigoberta. *I Rigoberta Menchú, An Indian Woman in Guatemala.* Ed. Elisabeth Burgos-Debray. Trans. Ann Wright. London: Verso, 1984.

Mines, Diane P., and Sarah E. Lamb. *Everyday Life in South Asia.* 2nd ed. Bloomington: Indiana University Press, 2010.

Orlove, Ben. *Lines in the Water: Nature and Culture at Lake Titicaca.* Berkeley: University of California Press, 2002.

Shostak, Marjorie. *Nisa: The Life and Worlds of a !Kung Woman.* Cambridge, MA: Harvard University Press, 2000.

Turnbull, Colin M. *The Forest People.* New York: Touchstone, 1987.

Social Discrimination

Social discrimination refers to the unfair treatment of a person or group of people based on race, class, religion, culture, language, or another socially defined category. Discrimination manifests in a variety of ways, but all forms are characterized by some manner of exclusion, segregation, or prohibition. Indigenous peoples have been the victims of social discrimination since Europeans began colonizing Africa, the Americas, Asia, and Oceania. Around the world, indigenous peoples experience pressure to assimilate into the dominant culture, a lack of political rights and power, and restrictions on their cultural practices and language. The long-term continuation of these circumstances often results in political conflict and civil war.

In nearly all circumstances, from the outset, indigenous peoples were discriminated against by European and later American authorities who refused to acknowledge their legal rights to land and used force to take control of indigenous land and resources. Indigenous people were classified as "uncivilized," and their land was claimed as *terra nullius,* or "no man's land"—that is, colonizers believed that the land belonged to no one, thereby justifying their forcible dispossession of these lands from indigenous people.

The stage was set for social discrimination in the newly colonized lands by two papal bulls (that is, written communications from the pope) issued during the fifteenth century. In 1452, *Romanus Pontifex,* written by Pope Nicholas V to King Afonso V of Portugal, set Christians around the world in a state of conflict with all non-Christians, justifying the conquest and colonization of non-Christian lands. In 1493, Pope Alexander VI responded to the "discovery" of the New World in the bull *Inter Caetera,* which divided the new lands between the Catholic powers of Spain and Portugal, calling on those nations to subjugate and convert the indigenous peoples to Christianity. Although indigenous people have asked the Vatican to revoke these bulls, successive popes have refused to honor that request.

The colonization of the world that followed, and the imposition of European will in numerous settings, resulted in discrimination, including forced relocation, the spread of disease (sometimes intentionally), starvation, open warfare, and—even where indigenous people were allowed to live—the suppression of their lifeways, cultural expressions, and religious beliefs.

Were such events to happen today, terms such as *genocide* or *ethnic cleansing* might be applied, but at the time, and in almost every situation, both policies and laws were in place to justify social discrimination against native peoples. The Doctrine of Discovery (based in U.S. law and the Supreme Court case *Johnson v. M'Intosh,* 1823) and the legal doctrine of terra nullius gave European and American colonizers the legal right to subjugate indigenous groups around the world.

Indigenous Lands

One of the most important and widespread forms of social discrimination around the world has been the application of the doctrine of terra nullius by colonizing countries, which has had a profound effect on indigenous peoples throughout the world. The concept of terra nullius, derived from the Latin phrase "no man's land," was an integral part of international law in the eighteenth and nineteenth centuries. The doctrine of terra nullius was built on the premise that a territory could be obtained by right of discovery if it was found to be unoccupied—in other words, vacant land. Thus, a country could claim sovereignty over a territory if it was found to be uninhabited; however, the way "occupation" was defined was determined by a set of criteria amounting to qualification and legitimate use of land.

Expressions of this idea can be seen in multiple contexts, including Australia and North America, where settlers spoke of "virgin wilderness." In some cases, imperial powers determined that even though indigenous peoples were living in an area, their occupation was not "legitimate" occupation or legal ownership and thus failed to meet European standards. This was the case in Canada, the western Sahara Desert, and Australia, where the concept of terra nullius was used by imperial powers to take over the lands of indigenous peoples by claiming that these lands were not being used in a "civilized" way. The imperial powers maintained that there was no government, agriculture, industry, economy, trade, religion, or social organization that constituted a "developed" culture.

In this way, the doctrine of terra nullius grossly discriminated against some indigenous societies and served the imperial powers as a means of acquiring foreign lands and expediting colonial expansion without the need to negotiate with indigenous peoples for land rights. The colonizers simply assumed sovereignty over a territory by right of discovery, annulling any legal status of land tenure held by an indigenous group.

Sovereignty over land inhabited by indigenous peoples can be established in three ways: by conquest, concession, or claiming right of discovery. When lands were taken by conquest or concession, an imperial power recognized that an indigenous people had a legal interest in the land that amounted to a form of proprietary right such as native title.

This was the case in some territories that were acquired in the United States, where authorities entered into treaties with indigenous peoples because they were seen as sedentary and living in villages, cultivating the land in gardens. However, among allegedly nomadic indigenous groups such as those in the western Sahara, the Spanish claimed the land as terra nullius, despite the presence of an indigenous population, by claiming the right of discovery without treaty.

The British and French acquired parts of Canada in a similar way, and when Australia was colonized by the British in 1788, it was determined that Australian Aborigines had no legal land tenure because they were not using land effectively. The use of terra nullius was strongly influenced in Australia by reports provided to the English House of Commons by two British explorers, James Cook and Joseph Banks, who had been given instructions to acquire land on behalf of the Crown "with the Consent of the Natives . . . in the Name of the King of Great Britain."

Australia

The HMS *Endeavour* under Cook's command reached the eastern coast of Australia in April 1770 and took possession of the region in the name of England's King George III on October 22. Cook and Banks recorded in their respective logbooks and journals observations of the Australian Aborigines along the eastern coast of Australia, characterizing the people as "naked savages" living in an uncivilized state who were nomadic with no fixed abodes. In Cook's words, they lived "in the pure state of Nature, the Industry of Man having had nothing to do with any part of it." Banks wrote that "a house was . . . nothing but a hollow shelter about 3 or 4 feet deep covered with bark . . . naked savages." Although Cook's instructions were to acquire land "with the consent of the natives," he simply claimed the eastern coast of Australia as terra nullius and by right of discovery.

Based on the information provided by Cook and Banks, the British government decided to colonize Australia without seeking a treaty with the indigenous population and assumed sovereignty and control of the indigenous land and resources by military force. Although the first governor of the colony at New South Wales was issued instructions regarding the Australian Aborigines that directed him "to conciliate their affections, enjoining all our subjects to live in amity and kindness with them," there was no recognition of their proprietary rights to land. As the British expanded their influence in the colony, the Aboriginal people were removed forcibly from their traditional lands.

John Batman, a pioneer in southern Australia, attempted to negotiate a treaty to purchase land from the Aborigines in 1835, but he was thwarted by colonial authorities. Governor Richard Bourke refused to recognize Batman's treaty and consequently issued a proclamation that effectively sealed terra nullius regarding Aboriginal land rights.

A similar proclamation was issued in Canada by the British in 1763 following military encounters with that country's First Nations, reinforcing terra nullius. As in Australia, the rights of indigenous peoples to hunt and fish were recognized, but they had no legal entitlement to land. As such, they could not negotiate the sale of the lands or receive compensation for them.

Throughout the nineteenth century, military interventions forced indigenous peoples off their traditional lands, resulting in undisclosed numbers of casualties. In Australia in 1838, the Myall Creek Massacre resulted in the execution of seven colonists for atrocities committed against indigenous peoples. Decades of violent frontier battles followed between British colonial forces and Australian Aborigines, culminating in the surrender of traditional indigenous lands and the dispossession of the original occupants. In 1883, the Aboriginal Protection Board was established to oversee the welfare of indigenous Australians, leading to the establishment of government- and church-owned missions and reservations.

In 1901, Australia formed a federation, and the new Australian government passed a constitution that excluded Australian Aborigines from the general population census, stating that "in reckoning the numbers of people . . . Aboriginal natives shall not be counted." Indigenous Australians were not only excluded from family endowment, voting, pensions, public health care, and employment in postal and armed services, but also from owning land.

In January 1972, a few indigenous men protesting for land rights raised a beach umbrella outside Parliament House in the capital of Canberra. The site became known as the Aboriginal Tent Embassy, and in the following months, it attracted hundreds of supporters who camped in tents on the lawn outside Parliament. Violence between campers and police was captured by television film crews, which broadcast footage of the police brutality to a national audience. The Aboriginal Tent Embassy celebrated its fortieth anniversary on January 26, 2012; for the past forty years, the site has been the focal point for protests for land rights and Aboriginal sovereignty.

In 1992, the native title interests of indigenous Australians were validated in a protracted legal case that became known as the *Mabo* decision. Indigenous Australians celebrated the Australian High Court's recognition of their native title rights to land. The judgment overturned the notion of terra nullius, which had been applied to the indigenous peoples of Australia regarding land rights. This decision had enormous implications, for it meant that from the first permanent occupation in 1788, indigenous Australians had been denied legitimate rights to their lands and waterways.

Africa

Indigenous peoples in Africa have faced marginalization from the dominant societies of which they are a part. Their desire to have their communal and human rights recognized and to live their traditional lifeways in places such as Africa's equatorial rain forests, mountain ranges, Rift Valley, or the deserts of the Kalahari and Sahara has placed them squarely in the way of development in those regions. Although indigenous peoples in African nations have strived to keep their cultures, languages, and lifeways alive, many of them have faced discrimination; economic, political, and social marginalization; and extreme poverty. The resulting social problems have included malnutrition, disease, alcoholism, drug abuse, and suicide.

In Central Africa, the Pygmies or forest peoples have had their indigenous cultures threatened by logging, agricultural use of land, and civil war. In addition, government policies designed to protect endangered species and environments often have the effect of changing the lifeways of groups such as the Pygmies, preventing them from engaging in hunting and other practices that have sustained their people for millennia. Such policies often are necessitated by the overuse of natural resources by nonindigenous peoples.

On the East African savannah, peoples such as the Maasai and Samburu are dealing with the imposition of nonindigenous farming on their lands, making their seminomadic herding culture unsustainable. In southern Africa, the San people (commonly known as Bushmen) have seen their traditional territories bought by white farmers as well as other Africans, forcing them out of their traditional lifeways. These factors often cause indigenous peoples to abandon their traditional cultures altogether, moving to urban areas and cities to find menial jobs in order to survive.

United States

In North America, the 10 million to 15 million indigenous peoples occupying the continent when Europeans arrived in the early seventeenth century were reduced by military, political, and social actions to approximately 300,000 by the end of the nineteenth century. Those native peoples that remained faced intense pressure to adopt the social mores, customs, and lifeways of the dominant non-native society. The pressure exerted by European and later American and Canadian settlers started with a familiar theme—pressure to acquire the vast lands held by native peoples.

American Indian land law and the concept of limited tribal sovereignty were established early in American history by U.S. Supreme Court decisions issued under Chief Justice John Marshall. In *Cherokee Nation v. Georgia* (1831), the Court declared that the Cherokee tribe constituted a "domestic dependent nation" whose members were to be considered wards of the United States and whose rights were to be protected by the federal government. The next year, in *Worcester v. Georgia,* the Marshall Court declared that "Indian nations had always been considered as distinct, independent political communities, retaining their original natural rights, as the undisputed possessors of the soil," asserting that terra nullius did not apply. However, President Andrew Jackson ignored the Court's decision confirming Cherokee land rights and forced the Cherokee across the infamous Trail of Tears to Indian Territory in present-day Oklahoma.

The Marshall Court's opinions in these cases have been cited throughout American history as setting a precedent for confirming tribal land rights. That standard was tested later in the nineteenth century by federal actions aimed at forcing the assimilation of American Indian peoples. Federal policy, as set out in the Dawes Act of 1887 (also known as the General Allotment Act), did away with the tribes' communal land base through the distribution of 160-acre (65-hectare) parcels of reservation land to individuals. The breakup of lands, the diminution of sovereignty, and the forced assimilation of Indian peoples formed the basis of American Indian policy until the 1930s.

This negative view of Indian land rights and tribal sovereignty would not be challenged in any meaningful way until the 1920s, when reformer John Collier was appointed as commissioner of Indian affairs by President Franklin D. Roosevelt. In 1928, the so-called Meriam Report outlined the deficiencies of American Indian policy, focusing on the Dawes Act. In 1934, the Indian Reorganization Act was passed, to secure certain land rights and local self-government for Native Americans. Collier dismantled the prior system of Indian management and the social discrimination that went along with it and, through the passage of the act, established a new system that provided more protection and self-determination for the tribes.

Although native tribes would face the disastrous "termination" policy of the 1950s, which sought to force American Indian peoples to assimilate into American society, greater self-determination finally would come with the Indian Self-Determination and Education Assistance Act of 1975. However, despite all of the progress that has been made, social ills such as poverty, alcoholism, poor health care, poor educational facilities, and a lack of economic opportunities still remain on Indian reservations in the United States.

Latin America

In Latin America, social discrimination followed different paths but achieved similar results. In Central and South America, similar efforts were made to separate indigenous people from their lands. Often, these efforts were based on racial considerations, similar to the justifications of terra nullius in other parts of the world, and had the same results, with massive losses to the indigenous people in terms of land, sovereignty, and culture.

As elsewhere, such changes frequently led to poverty. In Mexico, it is estimated that some 80 percent of the nation's indigenous peoples live in extreme poverty. Poor health conditions and limited access to health care are also common problems. Throughout Latin America, many indigenous peoples cannot write in Spanish, which has created inequality in the political process, as ballots and voter information are often available only in Spanish. Illiteracy also leads to discrimination in employment opportunities.

In Argentina, along with a persistent land rights problem, issues of maintaining cultural and linguistic forms have dominated. The smaller size of the indigenous population in that country (estimates range from 450,000 to 1.5 million) means that they are easier for the dominant society to ignore. Social discrimination ranges from the aforementioned factors to the use of colloquial derogatory expressions such as *hablo como un indio* (I'm speaking like an Indian), which is used to describe a person undertaking an unintelligent or ill-advised action.

In Latin America, indigenous peoples often have taken direct action to influence the factors leading to social discrimination and poverty. As oppression against indigenous peoples has taken many forms, there are many forms of response. Everyday forms of resistance have ranged from work slowdowns or breaking tools to legal action, small-scale rebellions, labor strikes, and full-scale revolts.

The effects of long-term social discrimination were seen vividly in the Mexican state of Chiapas, where a rebellion on behalf of indigenous people began in 1994, led by the Ejército Zapatista de Liberación Nacional (Zapatista National Liberation Army). Although outright hostilities ended in 1995, the Zapatistas continue their activities, creating town governments that are more or less independent of the Mexican federal government and holding nonviolent protests in support of indigenous rights.

Asia

Discrimination against the indigenous cultures of Asian nations historically has been very much a part of the dominant cultures of the nations in question. For example, in northwestern Bangladesh, social discrimination has taken the form of restaurants and tea stalls refusing to serve food or drink to indigenous peoples.

Across Asia, indigenous peoples have had to deal with a lack of access to health care and social services and poor educational opportunities. In India, 65 percent of the population is literate, whereas among indigenous groups, the rate varies from 35 percent to 55 percent. The figures are even worse for indigenous women, sometimes lower than 25 percent.

Social discrimination and limited educational opportunities have led to the relegation of indigenous peoples to low-paid, unskilled jobs. In China, the fifty-five recognized indigenous groups account for less than 9 percent of the population but more than 40 percent of those living in poverty. In Vietnam, the 14 percent of the population that is indigenous accounts for 30 percent of those in poverty. In Thailand, 1 million members of the Hill Tribes earn less than $100 U.S. per capita annually.

Land rights are a concern in Asia. For example, in Malaysia, where indigenous peoples make up approximately 12 percent of the population, indigenous groups have been discriminated against for failing to give up their lands for natural resource exploitation. The Orang Asli of the Malay Peninsula, the Dayak of Sarawak, and the Anak Negeri of Sabah all have pursued litigation to stop the government and multinational corporations from confiscating their lands for projects from which these groups will receive little or no benefit.

Some who opposed logging, dam building, and other actions on their lands have faced arrest, torture, and death. For example, in December 2007, a Penan village chief who resisted in Sarawak was found dead in the jungle, with evidence that he had been assaulted. Outsiders who sought to investigate such atrocities were not allowed to enter the province. The Malaysian government has faced condemnation from the United Nations Human Rights Council as a result.

Europe

In Europe, groups such as the Basques, Occitans, and Roma (Gypsies) still experience discrimination and marginalization. According to some Basques, the Spanish government overtaxes them, and government authorities monitor their activities closely, creating resentment against discriminatory policies.

Like other indigenous groups around the world, the Roma community long has dealt with discrimination throughout Europe and still does today. Inadequate education, employment, health care, and housing plague the Roma in many nations across Europe. The Roma have been the victims of racist demonstrations in the Czech Republic, where Romani children have been relegated to schools for the mentally disabled, despite a ruling in the European Court of Human Rights in November 2007. In May 2007, the Roma, along with the Sinti, were singled out for attention by the police across Italy, solely on the basis of their indigenous identity. Their transnational status makes citizenship problematic, which leads to a lack of social resources, and the transitory nature of their residences has led to evictions from temporary housing across Europe. In Hungary in 2008, there were sixteen documented incidents of violence against Romani homes, and at least four people were killed.

Effects of Social Discrimination

Although indigenous peoples from government-recognized groups make up approximately 5 percent of the world's population, they account for 15 percent of those living in poverty. The doctrine of terra nullius served the imperial powers as a pathway to take control of the lands occupied by indigenous peoples without negotiating a treaty that would have bestowed land rights to the original occupants. Through the succession of global imperialism, vast tracts of land and numerous waterways have been taken over by countries with no regard for the rights of indigenous peoples.

Indigenous people worldwide have been dispossessed of their land and deprived of their cultures. They often have been given little opportunity to better their lives or participate in decision making related to their welfare. As a result of such social discrimination, many indigenous groups have to depend on the very local and national governments that have discriminated against them for protection and preservation of their ways of life.

Greg Blyton and Steven L. Danver

See also: Issues—Colonialism; Land Rights; Political Discrimination; Self-Determination.

Further Reading

Asian Indigenous and Tribal Peoples Network. *Malaysia: Extinguishing Indigenous Peoples Rights.* New Delhi, India: Asian Indigenous and Tribal Peoples Network, 2008.

Austin-Broos, Diane, and Gaynor Macdonald, eds. *Culture, Economy and Governance in Aboriginal Australia: Proceedings of a Workshop of the Academy of the Social Sciences in Australia Held at the University of Sydney, 30 November–1 December 2004.* Sydney, Australia: Sydney University Press, 2005.

Chakma, Suhas, and Marianne Jensen, eds. *Racism Against Indigenous Peoples.* Copenhagen, Denmark: International Work Group for Indigenous Affairs, 2001.

Conversi, Daniele. *The Basques, the Catalans and Spain: Alternative Routes to Nationalist Mobilisation.* Reno: University of Nevada Press, 1997.

Deloria, Vine, Jr., and Clifford M. Lytle. *The Nations Within: The Past and Future of American Indian Sovereignty.* Austin: University of Texas Press, 1984.

Dowling, John Malcolm, and Yap Chin-Fang. *Chronic Poverty in Asia: Causes, Consequences, and Policies.* Hackensack, NJ: World Scientific, 2009.

Edwards, Philip, ed. *James Cook: The Journals.* Victoria, Australia: Penguin, 2003.

Kapaeeng Foundation: A Human Rights Organisation for Indigenous Peoples of Bangladesh. www.kapaeeng.org.

Langer, Erick D., and Elena Muñoz, eds. *Contemporary Indigenous Movements in Latin America.* Wilmington, DE: Scholarly Resources, 2003.

Minority Rights Group International. www.minorityrights.org.

Thornberry, Patrick. *Indigenous Peoples and Human Rights.* Huntington, NY: Juris, 2002.

Westra, Laura. *International Justice and the Rights of Indigenous Peoples: International and Domestic Legal Perspectives.* Sterling, VA: Earthscan, 2008.

Sustainable Development

Since the late twentieth century, there has been widespread recognition of the negative impacts of industrialization and globalization on local, regional, and global environments. Much of that attention has focused on environmental pollution in the industrial and developed regions of Europe and North America, the conservation of natural areas deemed to be of critical ecological importance such as tropical rain forests, and the causes and impacts of global climate change. Whereas industrialized countries have enacted environmental laws and regulations to limit pollution and to protect natural environments, developing countries, for the most part, have not done so. Further, developing countries have voiced concern over the promotion of economic growth at the expense of the natural environment and the livelihood and culture of impoverished populations.

Native peoples are especially susceptible to the environmental effects of unmanaged and unchecked industrial development, and they have suffered more than they have benefited from the expansion of the global economy. Many large transnational corporations and national governments have sought to exploit the natural resources found on native lands. The list of environmentally destructive activities includes mining, oil exploration and development, plantation-style agriculture, dam construction, logging, and tourism development. These activities have had negative impacts on native lands and threaten native traditional livelihood systems, economic development, community health, social structure, and native cultural traditions.

Defining Sustainable Development and International Forum

Beginning in the 1970s, the United Nations convened a series of international conferences to tackle the environmental problems associated with industrialization and unmanaged economic growth and, at the same time, to promote growth and economic development in less developed regions of the world. By the 1980s, the concept of "sustainable development" had emerged from this process; it was envisioned as a solution to the dilemma of promoting economic development without harming and degrading the environment.

In 1987, the World Commission on Environment and Development—also known as the Brundtland Commission, for chair Gro Harlem Bruntland of Norway—issued a report in which it defined sustainable development as "meet[ing] the needs of the present without compromising the ability of future generations to meet their own needs." Since then, sustainable development has been defined as a process that seeks to achieve a balance among three elements: economic development, environmental protection, and social development. In practice, sustainability has come to mean economic development that does not threaten the environment and that promotes social equity within and between generations.

Since 1987, the United Nations has convened two major international conferences on development and the environment—in Rio de Janeiro, Brazil (Earth Summit), in 1992 and in Johannesburg, South Africa (World Summit on Sustainable Development), in 2002—to debate, discuss, and promote the implementation of sustainable development policies. The official proclamations and policy statements resulting from these meetings recognize native peoples as important participants in sustainable development, and they urge national governments and multilateral funding agencies (such as the World Bank) to recognize and enhance the capacities of native peoples to develop and implement sustainable development plans.

Previously, native peoples held their own meetings and issued their own "declarations" concerning their rights to their lands and territories and economic and natural resource development on those lands. For example, prior to the World Summit on Sustainable Development, more than 300 native leaders met in Kimberley, South Africa, for the Indigenous Peoples International Summit on Sustainable Development. At the end of their meeting, they issued the Kimberley Declaration, which laid out a vision of indigenous sustainable development based on native self-determination and native peoples' spiritual and cultural relationship with the environment. The declaration called for the inclusion of native peoples in the implementation of national and international sustainable development plans.

Despite the recognition of native roles, capacities, and responsibilities in sustainable development at the international level, indigenous peoples continue to face many obstacles to sustainable development. These challenges include the environmentally destructive practices of much corporate and state-sponsored development and a mind-set that devalues native traditional livelihood systems (such as hunting and gathering, pastoralism, and shifting agriculture) and cultural traditions and denies native peoples' political sovereignty over their territory.

Sustainable Development and Native Peoples: Definition and Critical Issues

Native peoples' definitions of sustainable development differ from those put forward by the Brundtland Commission and by non-native development discourse since the late 1980s. Native concepts of sustainable development are based in the specific historical and cultural development of native communities.

Native peoples always have been productive, developing systems of livelihood that seek to reduce poverty and improve the material economic conditions of their communities. At the same time, native communities rooted in place developed very detailed knowledge of their natural environment. Their use of natural resources often differed in type and scale from that of modern industrial society.

This does not mean that native economic activities have no environmental impact. Indeed, native agricultural practices, hunting and gathering, and other activities resulted in changes to the environment—but the scale of environmental change was vastly different than that created by urban-based industrial societies. Like the Brundtland Commission, native peoples evaluate the sustainable use of their lands and resources in terms of the effects of development on future generations. It is common to hear Native Americans, for example, talk about the "seventh generation" (that is, the seventh generation yet to come, an idea inspired by the Iroquois) when discussing and defining sustainable development.

Perhaps what most distinguishes native sustainable development is the prominent role of noneconomic values and cultural traditions in setting limits on economic activities and preventing the misuse of natural resources. Land and nature are not considered inanimate resources to be used solely for profit and economic gain. Rather, many native peoples have spiritual and cultural links to the land and nature. Nonhuman nature is not subordinate to humans, they believe, and it deserves respect and protection. These cosmological and spiritual value systems impose limits on what can and cannot be done to or with the natural world.

Native identity is rooted in homelands and in connection to the plants, animals, and other aspects of their natural environment. Thus, native sustainable development may be defined as culturally appropriate development. Some refer to the influence of noneconomic native values or worldviews in shaping economic development on American Indian reservations as "native" or "tribal" capitalism. As a result, native sustainable development involves a mixture of modernity and tradition and integrates market-based activities with traditional subsistence activities.

One of the major challenges that native peoples face in developing and implementing sustainable development plans is a lack of sovereignty or political control over their territories, lands, and natural resources. The territorial rights of native peoples often are denied and opposed by governments and corporations. Native peoples have been excluded from decision-making processes that may affect their communities.

A critical issue for the implementation of native sustainable development is the recognition of native peoples' political rights to territory and their inclusion in economic and environmental management. Some native communities in the Arctic regions, for instance, have successfully gained recognition of their territorial rights, and in some cases, "comanagement" regimes have been created, whereby environmental management and development are administered jointly by native communities and non-native governmental entities.

Case Study of Native Sustainable Development: The Menominee Indian Tribe

The Menominee tribe of northeastern Wisconsin and the Upper Peninsula of Michigan provide an example of native sustainable development. Before and after contact with Europeans, the Menominee maintained an economy and culture that was rooted in the diverse plant and animal communities of the mixed deciduous and coniferous forests of the western Great Lakes region. Even though they lost much of their traditional territory through colonization and pressures to adopt agriculture, they retain a reservation that today encompasses one of the most sustainably managed forests in North America, and they maintain a cultural identity based in living in and with the forest.

Since the early twentieth century, the Menominee forest has seen intensive logging. The tribe uses the forest to provide for the needs of the community. Logging and the processing of forest products in a Menominee-owned sawmill provide employment and income to tribal members. The forest also is used by the Menominee for hunting, fishing, and gathering. Despite the amount of logging, the timber volume of the forest has increased compared to other forests of the region, and the forest maintains a healthy, diverse ecosystem.

The Menominee have been able to create an ecologically healthy and economically productive forest through an ethic of sustainability that strives to balance economic needs, protection (even enhancement) of the forest ecosystem, and maintenance of the cultural traditions and practices of the community. Unlike other forests, economic needs and the market for forest products do not determine the management of the Menominee forest. Instead, scientific forest principles, a cultural awareness of the necessity of maintaining the forest for future generations, and an ecosystem-based worldview shape harvesting and forest management decisions. The Menominee use scientific forest management techniques to inventory timber stands and monitor forest health in order to determine which trees and what volume of trees should be harvested.

The Menominee view themselves as people of the forest, not as separate from it. Without the forest, the Menominee would lose not only a source of income, but also their identity. The forest is not only an ecosystem needing management, but also a spiritual place requiring protection. Because of their success in balancing the economic, environmental, and cultural needs of their community and creating one of the most sustainable managed forests, the Menominee Sustainability Ethic has become a model for indigenous and nonindigenous peoples around the world.

Steven E. Silvern

See also: Issues—Agriculture; Ecosystem Management; Indigenous Peoples and the United Nations; Industrial Development; Land Rights.

Further Reading

Davis, Thomas. *Sustaining the Forest, the People, and the Spirit.* Albany: State University of New York Press, 2000.

Edwards, Andrew. *The Sustainability Revolution.* Gabriola Island, Canada: New Society, 2005.

Hosmer, Brian, and Colleen O'Neill, eds. *Native Pathways: American Indian Culture and Economic Development in the Twentieth Century.* Boulder: University of Colorado Press, 2004.

International Work Group for Indigenous Affairs. www.iwgia.org.

Jentoft, Svein, Henry Minde, and Rangar Nilsen. *Indigenous Peoples: Resource Management and Global Rights.* Delft, Netherlands: Eburon, 2003.

Reed, Richard K. *Forest Dwellers, Forest Protectors: Indigenous Models for International Development.* 2nd ed. Upper Saddle River, NJ: Prentice Hall, 2009.

Smith, Dean Howard. *Modern Tribal Development: Paths to Self-Sufficiency and Cultural Integrity in Indian Country.* Walnut Creek, CA: AltaMira, 2000.

United Nations. *State of the World's Indigenous Peoples.* New York: United Nations, 2009.

United Nations Declaration

The United Nations (UN) Declaration on the Rights of Indigenous Peoples was adopted by the UN General Assembly on September 13, 2007. The declaration aims to prevent human rights abuses against indigenous peoples by establishing fundamental individual and collective rights for indigenous peoples of all ages and by acting as a safeguard against marginalization and discrimination.

This comprehensive document contains forty-six articles that outline the political, economic, social, cultural, and environmental rights of indigenous peoples worldwide, addressing matters such as identity, language, landownership, education, and employment. The declaration emphasizes the rights of indigenous peoples to preserve and develop their institutions, traditions, and cultures in accordance with their own unique aspirations and needs. It also outlines governance recommendations for states to prevent unfair treatment and to promote the welfare and future of indigenous peoples.

Since the 1970s, the United Nations increasingly has become a forum for advocating the rights of indigenous peoples around the world. American and Canadian Iroquois leaders as well as Maori leaders from New Zealand have addressed the international body.

In 1971, the *Study on the Problem of Discrimination Against Indigenous Populations* was launched, led by José R. Martínez Cobo, the special rapporteur for the Sub-Commission on Prevention of Discrimination and Protection of Minorities. The study highlighted the discrimination and marginalization faced by indigenous peoples worldwide. As a result of the study's findings, a Working Group on Indigenous Populations, chaired by Chief Ted Moses of the Grand Council of the Crees in Canada, was established in 1982 by the UN Economic and Social Council.

Members of the working group were tasked with developing a set of basic human rights standards to protect indigenous peoples. In response, they conceived of a declaration that would outline the rights of indigenous peoples and submitted a draft to the Sub-Commission on Prevention of Discrimination and Protection of Minorities in 1993. The draft was approved in 1994 and subsequently was submitted to the UN Commission on Human Rights for further consideration. The draft sparked discussion of some of its core provisions, including control over natural resources on the traditional lands of indigenous peoples and the right to self-determination.

A second open-ended intersessional working group was established in 1995 to examine and elaborate the terms of the draft declaration. A final draft of the declaration was expected to be submitted to the General Assembly during the International Decade of the World's Indigenous People (1995–2004). During this period, the working group met annually and received regular input from indigenous peoples and from nonprofit organizations such as the International Indian Treaty Council; however, it failed to reach a consensus by the end of 2004. Some accused powerful nations such as the United States of undermining the group's efforts.

The Commission on Human Rights extended the working group's mandate into the Second International Decade of the World's Indigenous Peoples (2005–2015) and pressed the body to present a final draft as soon as possible. During the working group's eleventh session in 2006, Chairman Luis-Enrique Chávez of Peru prepared a final draft of the declaration based on compilations of proposals and input from previous discussions. This final draft was submitted to the UN Human Rights Council, the successor to the Commission on Human Rights. At its inaugural session on June 29, 2006, the council adopted the draft declaration with thirty member states in favor, two against, twelve abstentions, and three absentees.

Following its approval by the Human Rights Council, the draft declaration was submitted to the Social, Humanitarian and Cultural Affairs Committee of the General Assembly in November 2006. The African Group of States, the UN's largest regional group with fifty-four member states, called for a delay in the voting process to allow for further consultation. Additional amendments were made to the draft, and the General Assembly finally voted on the adoption of the revised declaration on September 13, 2007. The Declaration on the Rights of Indigenous Peoples was adopted with 144 states voting in its favor, four voting against, eleven abstaining, and thirty-four absent from the vote.

The four member states that voted against the declaration were Australia, Canada, New Zealand, and the United States. All four nations since have reversed their decisions and endorsed the declaration.

Australia initially rejected the declaration because of a number of concerns relating to self-determination, lands and resources, intellectual property, third-party rights, customary law, the status of the declaration, and free, prior, and informed consent. Under the leadership of Prime Minister Kevin Rudd, the Australian government changed its position and formally endorsed the declaration on April 3, 2009.

New Zealand stated that it was in agreement with the aspirations of the declaration but objected to certain provisions that were considered incompatible with the country's constitutional and legal system (Article 26 on resources and lands, Article 28 on redress, and Articles 19 and 32 on the right of veto over the government). On April 19, 2010, Minister of Māori Affairs Pita Sharples announced that New Zealand would support the declaration.

Canada also supported the spirit of the declaration but opposed articles pertaining to landownership and free, prior, and informed consent. On November 12, 2010, Prime Minister Stephen Harper reversed Canada's position and officially endorsed the declaration.

The United States shared many of the same concerns and expressed reservations about the declaration's failure to provide a clear definition of "indigenous peoples." Nevertheless, President Barack Obama announced during the second White House Tribal Conference on December 16, 2010, that the United States would endorse the declaration.

Although the declaration is not a legally binding document under international law, it is the most comprehensive and universal statement to date on the rights of indigenous peoples, and thus it represents a milestone for indigenous peoples at the international level. UN Secretary-General Ban Ki-moon described the adoption of the declaration as a "historic moment" and praised the document for providing leadership to help nations form better relationships with their indigenous populations.

Some nations, such as Bolivia, have incorporated the declaration's terms into their constitutions and national laws. Other organizations, such as the African Commission on Human and Peoples' Rights and the Organization of American States, are using the declaration as a point of reference when drafting regional declarations on human rights. The implementation of the declaration also is being enforced through the commitment and work of the UN's Office of the High Commissioner for Human Rights.

Leaders such as U.S. President Barack Obama have expressed their desire to see this historic human rights instrument serve as a vital safeguard against the marginalization and discrimination of the more than 370 million indigenous peoples around the world. Ultimately, it is hoped that this measure will contribute to the elimination of human rights violations globally.

Janelle Teng

See also: Issues—Globalization; Indigenous Identity; Indigenous Peoples and the United Nations; International Policy; Land Rights.

Further Reading

Allen, Stephen, and Alexandra Xanthaki. *Reflections on the UN Declaration on the Rights of Indigenous Peoples.* Oxford, UK: Hart, 2012.

Charters, Claire, and Rodolfo Stavenhagen, eds. *Making the Declaration Work: The United Nations Declaration on the Rights of Indigenous Peoples.* Copenhagen, Denmark: International Work Group for Indigenous Affairs, 2009.

Claude, Richard Pierre, and Burns H. Weston, eds. *Human Rights in the World Community: Issues and Action.* Philadelphia: University of Pennsylvania Press, 2006.

Roulet, Florencia. *Human Rights and Indigenous Peoples: A Handbook on the UN System.* Copenhagen, Denmark: International Work Group for Indigenous Affairs, 1999.

Urbanization

During the twentieth century, scholars, government officials, nongovernmental organizations, native nongovernmental organizations, and the media documented the urban experience of indigenous people across the world. In North America, some social science researchers focused their attention on the dynamics and complexities of living in urban centers, while others examined the process of moving back and forth between reserves and urban areas.

In 2004, scholar Regina Darnell described these experiences as remnants of nomadic culture, whereby indigenous people continue to follow a mobile pattern while improving their quality of life. Her work underscored that we cannot think of indigenous populations as residing "permanently" in any urban area, as their residential patterns are complex and may persist anywhere from a couple of months to decades.

The continuing migration of indigenous peoples to urban areas is a documented reality around the globe. This acknowledgment is fundamental to indigenous peoples' politics, in part due to the myriad attempts by governments to assimilate or eliminate them. Traditional modes of subsistence—hunting, gathering, trapping, and fishing—no longer serve many indigenous people living in urban areas. Rather, they have had to develop new skills that are needed for survival in settings far different from their former reservation or other rural environment.

Migration and Initial Contact

Immigration is almost always difficult, and it is even more so for indigenous peoples leaving reservations or other rural regions to move to cities in Canada and the United States. Many have migrated to cities even though they know only one person, such as a family member, acquaintance, or friend. From there, their social network begins to intertwine with multiple individuals and organizations. Similar stories have been documented for Mexicans who immigrate to the United States. Typically, their first contact provides them with the shelter and guidance they need while they get used to the city's dynamics.

The second contact for indigenous people dwelling in urban centers often is a staff member of a social support organization. Knowing someone in a native or a nonnative organization can be crucial for establishing social networks and gaining access to the pool of services that are available to indigenous people.

A significant number of indigenous peoples seek out the employment and literacy services offered by native nongovernmental organizations. In some cases, learning initiatives may not only strive to teach English, math, and other subjects, but also indigenous knowledge and traditions. For instance, some literacy courses begin with a smudging ceremony—burning certain herbs to clear away negative thoughts and energies—and teach participants about the medicine wheel, dream catchers, and other traditions.

Challenges and Experiences

Indigenous people are documented as consistently experiencing high rates of victimization and substandard education in the Canadian educational system in urban centers. This reflects a persistent pattern of racist and bullying practices inflicted on indigenous students. In addition, it indicates an overall lack of support among teachers for indigenous students who fall behind the required level of achievement. The rejection and alienation that indigenous students may feel from classmates and teachers reflect a lack of direct support from school systems.

Racism also is present on the streets, as ethnic slurs may be used by residents to refer to their indigenous counterparts in public spaces. Statements such as "slow Indian," "lazy or drunk Indian," and "homeless Indian" still prevail within the discourse of mainstream society.

However, many native organizations are working to reduce racism and the social and educational gap between native and non-native population. For instance, in London, Ontario, the N'Amerind Friendship Centre and Nokee Kwe, two urban-based centers focused on helping native immigrants, have undertaken educational and social awareness work aimed at building respect, a better understanding of, and more support for indigenous peoples living among the non-native population. Community members also are working toward such goals, including sharing information on native issues and traditions, such as Dan Smoke Asayenes (a Seneca) and his wife Mary Lou Smoke-Kwe (an Ojibwa), who since 1991 have hosted a radio news magazine called Smoke Signals First Nations Radio on CHRW Radio Western.

Unemployment is one of the major challenges faced by indigenous peoples who move to urban areas. Most government programs fund multiple educational strategies, partnerships, and apprenticeships, all with the purpose of transitioning indigenous peoples into the labor market. Many native nongovernmental organizations offer services such as job referrals, job search assistance, apprenticeships, schooling, and skills training to prepare their indigenous clientele for meaningful employment.

Finally, the lack of proper housing and/or affordable housing is another problem that many indigenous people face in the metropolis. Most rental properties, if affordable, are in need of major upgrades and repairs. Native housing networks report that many single women with children are living in poverty. This situation is not changing rapidly, and more efforts among government officials, housing authorities and property owners, and native representatives are needed to address the higher demand and the needs of such urban residents.

Indigenous people experience urban life as a process of change in which multiple and contradictory strategies intertwine with aspects of their traditional lifeways. Because they live among a non-native urban population, social scientists maintain that it is important that they take advantage of available resources, such as native nongovernmental organizations, as well as applicable government programs. At the same time, they also undertake the challenge of surviving in a different and sometimes aggressive environment that requires personal fortitude, action, and change. Thus, indigenous peoples undergoing the process of urbanization, as in other contexts, are constantly in search of a more productive and healthy life and future.

María Cristina Manzano-Munguía

See also: *Issues*—Assimilation; Globalization; Relocation; Social Customs.

Further Reading

Clark, A. Kim, and Marc Becker, eds. *Highland Indians and the State in Modern Ecuador.* Pittsburgh, PA: University of Pittsburgh Press, 2007.

Fixico, Donald. *The Urban Indian Experience in America.* Albuquerque: University of New Mexico Press, 2000.

Jackson, Deborah. *Our Elders Lived It: American Indian Identity in the City.* DeKalb: Northern Illinois University Press, 2002.

Krouse, Susan Applegate, and Heather A. Howard. *Keeping the Campfires Going: Native Women's Activism in Urban Communities.* Lincoln: University of Nebraska Press, 2009.

Royal Commission on Aboriginal Peoples Report. Vol. 4. *Perspectives and Realities.* Ottawa, Canada: Canada Communication Group, 1996.

Sanderson, Frances, and Heather Howard-Bobiwash. *The Meeting Place: Aboriginal Life in Toronto.* Toronto, Canada: Native Canadian Centre of Toronto, 1997.

Violence and Warfare

Since antiquity, every society has developed complex ideas about violence: when it is appropriate to use violence, what sorts of violence are acceptable to use, and the social and legal ramifications of its use. Indigenous societies are no exception to this rule. Both intergroup and intragroup violence have been facts of life in the world's indigenous communities.

Each community has its own rules governing the use of violence and means in place to punish those who break the rules. This is true even in societies in which laws are not written down; individuals can be punished for acts that the community deems too violent or of an offending nature. Ideas about violence are closely tied to a community's worldview, including gender roles and religious beliefs, and each native group has its own distinct culture of violence.

Warfare, defined as armed conflict between distinct groups of people, is one of the few nearly universal human activities. Indigenous people throughout the world engaged in warfare long before they were colonized by outsiders. Colonization, regardless of when it occurred, also was accompanied by acts of violence and warfare, even though the scale generally was somewhat smaller than modern warfare. Occasionally, colonized indigenous populations engaged in warfare that resulted in their liberation.

When discussing the subject of warfare, social scientists maintain that it is essential to refrain from casting human societies as "primitive" or "advanced." Such terms and the attendant tendency to portray indigenous societies as especially warlike have been used in the past to justify what today might be termed crimes against humanity. It is equally important to avoid casting the precolonial era as peaceful and harmonious. Human societies around the world practiced long-distance trade, engaged in complicated diplomacy, and went to war against one another long before Europeans came to dominate large swaths of the globe.

Intertribal Warfare

In native North America, both oral traditions and physical evidence document the occasional occurrence of large-scale intergroup violence. For example, a group of Creek (or Muscogee) Indians in the Southeast related a story to English colonizers in the 1730s in which several Creek towns went to war to determine which was the oldest or most powerful. Excavations at Crow Creek in South Dakota unearthed evidence of a town taken by surprise and nearly wiped off the map—almost 500 skeletons appear to have been hastily buried in a pit. Though such large-scale assaults occurred, they were comparatively rare prior to the arrival of Europeans.

In many places, warfare was associated closely with spiritual practice and masculinity. The Mississippian-era (ca. 1000–1550 C.E.) chiefdoms of the American Southeast took part in a combination of rare high-stakes pitched battles and more frequent small-scale raids and skirmishes. Fighting men engaged in elaborate rituals to prepare for combat, purifying themselves and avoiding contamination, and artwork of the period depicts acts of violence, either spiritual or physical. The causes of warfare between communities were many: Trade, territorial aggrandizement, and religion are among the most significant. Warfare between peoples before colonization was a fact of life, though it was hardly endemic, and most places in the world were not characterized by either an absence or an overabundance of warfare.

Colonial Warfare

In the late fifteenth and early sixteenth centuries, Europeans began, tentatively at first, to claim and colonize territories outside Europe. Although violence always had been a part of existence, Europeans introduced new forms of violence, using it as a means of conquest, leading to countless deaths. As the precolonial examples demonstrate, violence was not a new phenomenon when Europeans arrived in the Americas. However, warfare in most native cultures did not include the wholesale slaughter of women and children, whereas warfare as waged by the Europeans often did.

Societies that were incapable of resisting the Europeans militarily quickly found their polities eradicated and their people killed or enslaved (the Taino of the Carib-

The robed Kamajor warriors of Sierra Leone are believed to possess magical powers, granted by a priestess and enhanced by traditional herbs. The rules of violence and warfare are as deeply rooted, varied, and complex as human societies throughout history. *(Daimon Xanthopoulos/Gamma-Rapho/Getty Images)*

bean and the Guanche of the Canary Islands were early victims). Many native commentators, and even a handful of Europeans, commented on the level of violent deaths that Europeans introduced into the places they colonized. For a long time, it was fashionable to write about this sort of colonizing violence as a particularly Iberian (Spanish and Portuguese) trait, and a "Black Legend" developed around the violent Spanish invasion of the Americas. Of course, all of the colonizing powers were capable of committing acts of great violence. Witness the French attempt to erase the Fox Indians in the North American Midwest in the 1730s, or the English destruction of a Pequot town on the Mystic River in 1637. A toxic combination of religious, economic, and nationalist motives drove Europeans into the wider world, and they brought warfare nearly everywhere they went.

The Spanish invasion of North America in the early sixteenth century provides another key example. As with most of the indigenous populations of the Americas, the city-states of Mexico's Central Valley experienced periodic but not sustained warfare. The peoples there had gone to war at times in the past, practicing elaborate ceremonies intended to ensure success in combat. Just before the Spanish invasion, the "Triple Alliance" (Aztec Empire) had come to dominate the region. The Aztec hold on power was not complete, however. The Triple Alliance had attempted, and failed, to subjugate the state of Tlaxcala, for instance.

When a small Spanish army under the leadership of Hernán Cortés arrived in the 1510s, it was able to take advantage of several factors to conquer the Aztec. A smallpox epidemic weakened the Aztec's ability to resist the Spanish. At the same time, the Spanish relied on shocking levels of violence, including mass killings and the use of war dogs, to terrorize their enemies. Most important, though, the Spanish who marched toward the Aztec capital at Tenochtitlán were not alone. They recruited thousands of allies, some from tributary states and others from states that had not been conquered by the Aztec, such as the Tlaxcalan, to aid their expedition. Ultimately, European success in warfare brought thousands of indigenous communities, and millions of people, under European control in the era of colonization, which lasted in some areas through the 1970s, if it ever ended at all.

Revolution and Postcolonial Warfare

Warfare also could play a role in the overthrow of colonial rule. Colonized people rarely were capable of mounting direct assaults on colonizers, and the cost of violent resistance to colonialism was quite high, but guerrilla warfare proved effective at ending colonial rule in some instances. In Algeria, beginning in 1955, a group calling itself the Front de Libération Nationale (FLN, National Liberation Front) began a guerrilla war against the French. The onset of violence was particularly surprising to the French, as Algeria had been perceived as a stable, tranquil part of the French Empire—indeed, it was quite "French" by their standards, and about a third of the colony's population was of European descent. Still, French administrative practices had created a wide chasm between the minority French population and the colony's millions of Muslims.

The French military campaign to suppress the uprising was brutal, and the FLN responded with brutal tactics of its own. When the French sent 100,000 soldiers to reinforce their colonial rule (and to avoid a repeat of the humiliating loss of Vietnam), the FLN began to target civilians, which it studiously had avoided in the first stage of the conflict. This, in turn, prompted French soldiers to use water torture and electric shock to force the rebels to cooperate. Eventually, more than 500,000 French soldiers were deployed to Algeria, but support for the war among the French proved divisive and it was questionable whether the conflict was winnable. In the end, the French government was forced to negotiate the end of colonial rule in Algeria. The cost in human lives was great: Estimates run from 300,000 to 1 million casualties.

Warfare was present before the era of colonization, it was integral to Europe's expansion into the New World, and, in some places, it helped bring an end to colonial rule. However, the stereotype that indigenous people are somehow "warlike" and that their societies are especially bloodthirsty or militaristic, though popular in mythology, does not ring true in most cases. More often fighting wars over land that were instigated by other tribes or colonial powers, indigenous groups reacted like any group of people whose land is invaded by outsiders, with warfare as the most common outcome.

Matthew Jennings

See also: *Issues*—Colonialism; Land Rights; Military Service; Revolts.

Further Reading
Jennings, Matthew. *New Worlds of Violence: Cultures and Conquests in the Early American Southeast.* Knoxville: University of Tennessee Press, 2011.
Prashad, Vijay. *The Darker Nations: A People's History of the Third World.* New York: New Press, 2008.
Restall, Matthew. *The Seven Myths of the Spanish Conquest.* New York: Oxford University Press, 2004.

Water Rights

Indigenous people around the world depend on water for their livelihood, agriculture, cultural traditions, and religious and spiritual practices. Contemporary water rights for indigenous communities have built on traditional systems of water use and have evolved within the complex legal systems of postcolonial states.

Because water is a continually moving resource, water rights are notoriously difficult to define. Water rights are defined in terms of the right to use water but also imply operational rights, as well as decision-making rights in the management of water resources: *Who* can use *how much* water from *what source* and for *what purpose.* Given the many different uses for water and the many forms in which it exists—waterways, lakes, streams, underground reservoirs—water rights regimes are complex and diverge from one place to the other.

In Africa, Asia, and Europe, water rights intrinsically are attached to land and passed along with the title to land. By contrast, in regions where there is intense competition over water—such as that between native and non-native communities, between urban and rural areas, and between industry and agriculture—as in well-publicized cases in Australia, Chile, and the Western United States, decision makers consider ways of separating water rights from land rights. Regardless of how the governance framework is regulated, effective water rights require active management of the resource. Given these complexities, as well as the increasing scarcity of water and competition from its use, water rights are a frequent source of conflict, both legal and physical.

Sources of Indigenous Water Rights

Competition over water use between indigenous and nonindigenous communities in the arid Western United States has resulted in much litigation. Native American water rights were outlined by the courts at the turn of the twentieth century in response to a dispute between the Assiniboine and Gros Ventre peoples of the Fort Belknap Indian Reservation in north-central Montana. During the dry season, settlers upriver diverted all of the water from the Milk River, so that none was allowed to reach the reservation. In its 1908 ruling in *Winters v. United States,* the U.S. Supreme Court handed down what came to be known as the *Winters* doctrine, asserting that the federal government owned the land and water on Native American reservations and therefore was responsible for the natives and for helping them make good use of their water.

The *Winters* doctrine protected an inchoate future use of water for native peoples and established a water rights precedent that still is followed throughout the United States. The hard political and socio-economic realities of nonindigenous development, however, have dramatically limited the real implementation of these reserved rights. In reality, such issues have impacted the actual dispersion of water, and most significant investments have gone into supplying water for non-native agriculture rather than for use by the native peoples.

Water rights also derive from sources besides government. There are many examples of customary law (which changes over time) that are backed by local authority and social norms. The *acequia* system in Spain and its former colonies in the Americas, particularly in the Andean region of South America, northern Mexico, and the Southwestern United States, is an example of a community-run ditch irrigation system in which local associations govern water users' usage according to local precedents and traditions. In such traditional systems, water rights come with corresponding duties that apply to the rights holder—usually the duty to use the water and dispose of waters in a certain manner and to provide money, labor, or other needed resources to maintain the water supply.

Sometimes, customary law that is devised to fit a new situation becomes institutionalized, such as in the doctrine of prior appropriation, which governs water law in the Western United States. This system was devised by local farmers to make use of the region's scarce water supply, and it became law when constitutions were written for states newly admitted to the Union, such as California and Colorado.

Water rights have been the source of much political conflict in Central and South America, where the traditional authority of indigenous and peasant organizations over water and other natural resources has been denied, their rights to use water increasingly restricted, and their control over related decision-making processes undermined by state authorities. The right to water became a politically salient issue in the wake of neoliberal reforms in nations such as Bolivia and Chile during the 1980s and 1990s. In the past two decades, international institutions such as the World Bank have heralded the Chilean experiment with water markets as an example for other countries to follow.

The experiment began in 1981 when a new water law in Chile established a system of market trading in water rights, stipulating that the right to use water was a tradable good to be registered by the state. Unregistered rights were auctioned off to the highest bidder. Most indigenous communities, however, were unaware of the requirement to register their centuries-old customary claims to water. Communities that tried to register their water rights often were told that no further rights could be granted, because all of the resources already had been allocated, mostly to large landowners and power-generating and mining companies.

Similar models have been proposed and defeated in countries such as Bolivia and Ecuador, where there have been massive uprisings against government proposals to marketize water resources. In these two countries, which have the highest shares of indigenous populations in South America, the traditional struggle for equal land distribution has been accompanied or replaced by collective claims for more equal water distribution, as well as demands for autonomy and respect for local cultural practices. Well-organized indigenous and peasant organizations have put pro-indigenous reforms on the national policy agenda.

In Ecuador, indigenous cultural and social rights and representation of indigenous users have been recognized within the institutional framework for water management and by constitutional reforms in 1998 and 2007. Following the so-called Water War in Bolivia in April 2000, during which the people of the city of Cochabamba rose up in protest against the privatization of a local water utility and the government's privatization law, a new process of water reforms moved toward recognizing the concerns of indigenous and peasant groups. New irrigation bylaws and drinking water laws passed in 2004 recognize the uses and customs of indigenous peoples, and the 2009 constitution that established Bolivia as a plurinational state recognizes the human right to water.

Indigenous Rights to Water in International Law

In 2002, the United Nations Committee on Economic, Social and Cultural Rights, the body that interprets the International Covenant on Economic, Social and Cultural Rights, made specific mention of indigenous peoples in its statements about water rights. The committee declared that an individual or group may not "be deprived of its means of subsistence" and that states have a duty to ensure "that there is adequate access to water for subsistence farming and for securing the livelihoods of indigenous peoples." The committee also mandated that states pay special attention to communities that have faced historical difficulties in exercising their right to water. In particular, states should ensure that "indigenous peoples' access to water resources on their ancestral lands is protected from encroachment and unlawful pollution. States should provide resources for indigenous peoples to design, deliver, and control their access to water."

On July 28, 2010, the United Nations General Assembly adopted Resolution 10967, recognizing water as a basic human right and declaring that "the right to safe and clean drinking water and sanitation as a human right that is essential for the full enjoyment of life and all human rights." Each citizen enjoys these rights without discrimination of any kind, but, unlike previous statements by the Committee on Economic, Social and Cultural Rights, the resolution makes no specific reference to the indigenous right to water. Historians and scholars have said that they trust the resolution will provide a legal resource for indigenous peoples in national litigation, such as the San people (also known as the Khwe or Bushmen) of the Kalahari Desert, whose right to drill wells in their traditional territory was denied by the Supreme Court of Botswana in 2010.

Indigenous peoples seldom have been recognized as important players in water-related policy decisions, and weak political organization at the international level has restricted their ability to promote their water interests in the policy arena. Thanks to decades of indigenous activism by groups such as the Mni Sose Intertribal Water Rights Coalition in the Missouri River Basin in the United States and the Water for Food Movement in South Africa, as well as countless individuals around the world, the policy climate is now more open, and it has shifted in favor of including indigenous representatives as stakeholders in the policy dialogue about water rights.

These lobbying efforts have been recognized by international bodies, such as the World Commission on Dams, which in its 2000 report recognized the principle of "free and informed consent." This recognition has helped legitimize discussion within the development community about indigenous land and water rights as a topic that should concern society as a whole. The World Water Forum in Kyoto in 2003, which also invited the participation of indigenous peoples, resulted in the signing of the Indigenous Peoples Kyoto Declaration, which laid out the attitudes toward water held by many indigenous groups and their right to self-determination in the care and use of such resources.

While progress has been made on the international front, the concerns of indigenous people for protecting their waters can be met only partly through legal safeguards. As the struggle for water against non-native development in the Western United States suggests, the destruction of sacred waters and the demise of traditional knowledge are occurring well within legal frameworks. Often no laws are broken, and yet water heritage is being lost.

The external policy environment has become more favorable to indigenous interests, and there is growing awareness about the value of preserving indigenous knowledge and water heritage. Nevertheless, the struggle to preserve native peoples' rights to water is as complex as the struggle to control the implementation and impact of development itself.

Susan Spronk

See also: Issues—Indigenous Governments; Industrial Development; Land Rights; Self-Determination.

Further Reading

Boelens, Rutgerd, David Getches, and Armando Guevara-Gil, eds. *Out of the Mainstream: Water Rights, Politics and Identity.* Washington, DC: Earthscan, 2010.

Danver, Steven L., and John R. Burch, eds. *Encyclopedia of Water Politics and Policy in the United States.* Washington, DC: CQ, 2010.

Indigenous Peoples' Kyoto Water Declaration. Kyoto, Japan: Third World Water Forum, 2003.

McLean, Jess. "Water Injustices and Potential Remedies in Indigenous Rural Contexts: A Water Justice Analysis." *Environmentalist* 27:1 (March 2007): 25–38.

Shurts, John. *Indian Reserved Water Rights: The Winters Doctrine in Its Social and Legal Context, 1880s–1930s.* Norman: University of Oklahoma Press, 2000.

Women's Rights

The topic of women's rights within native communities necessitates a multipart discussion. First, it is important to discuss women's roles and responsibilities in native cultures before the onset of colonialism. In most cases, native cultures were vastly different from the colonial cultures that arrived in the lands inhabited by native peoples from the fourteenth through the nineteenth centuries. Next, the loss of those roles as a result of the colonial experience must be addressed. With that loss, women's roles became "rights" that needed to be regained. Finally, as colonialism ended and the push for human rights began in the twentieth century (continuing into the twenty-first century), a reassertion of rights gradually took place, with profound implications for native women.

In considering the status of women, scholars and the public often look at the tasks or functions performed by women and assume that work is viewed and valued similarly across all cultures. The operative consideration, however, is how a task is socially constructed. For white women, farming and carrying heavy loads was an indication of their oppressed status. Having no property of their own, they worked hard for someone else. Native women, when doing the exact same work, viewed their tasks as part of their responsibility as stewards of the land and workers who had authority over the land. Lakota women, for instance, owned the tepees that they put up and took down. This often was misunderstood by European and American observers, who labeled native women "beasts of burden," believing that they were under the control of men, like white women. Native men, on the other hand, were shocked by the disrespect that white men showed to their women.

The term *women's rights* may be a misnomer for the position that native women occupied before European contact. The concept of rights is based on deprivation. But in many native societies throughout the world, women did not have "rights"; rather, they lived in a state of equality. Men and women had different responsibilities, but neither was viewed as more important or had power over the other. Gender balance best describes relations between men and women in native societies before the onset of colonialism.

Women played many roles in the domestic, economic, religious, and political lives of their peoples. Certainly, men's and women's roles differed, but in nearly all indigenous cultures, the roles of men and women were complementary. Women often were in charge of domestic life. In many West African cultures, in the Aztec and Maya cultures of Central and South America, and in the Iroquois culture of North America, this went hand in hand with their role as child bearers. Within this role, women did more than simply maintain the home for men; they also acted as the keepers of the culture, transmitting it from one generation to the next.

Native Women and Native Societies: The Iroquois

The most-studied North American native nation in regard to women's rights is the Iroquois, the French name for the confederation of tribes also known as the Haudenosaunee. Other Native American nations with similar gender patterns include the Cherokee (Tsalagi or Aniyvwiyai) and the Navajo (Dine), both of which trace descent through the female line.

Establishing a measurement by which to determine the presence of women's rights runs the risk of cultural bias. Observers typically have looked for political rights within a male hierarchical system of authority. What they have seen, then, is native women sitting silently in the background as men sit in council, vocal and visible. Casual visitors often assumed that this meant the women had no political voice.

From the time of contact, however, missionaries, traders, visitors, and scholars documented the reciprocal gender system of checks and balances established by the

Iroquois. Clan mothers nominated the chiefs (sachem) and held them in position. Consensus decision making was done through women's and men's councils. The women held responsibility for the land and peace. Clan mothers, chiefs, and faith keepers were not leaders of the people; they were led *by* the people. In an upside-down pyramid of authority, the power of the people funneled down to those who carried out their wishes. Everyone was equally important.

Representation in the political system traditionally was based on the clan family rather than geographic area. In a matrilineal society such as the Iroquois, the children followed the mother's line and were born into their mother's clan.

Within North American Iroquois society, because the women raised the children, the clan mothers could—and still do today—groom their male children to assume responsibility when and if they were installed as chief. Holding the horns, the symbol of authority of the sachem (paramount chief), naturally fell to the women. When a standing chief passed on, the horns would be returned to the female representative of the clan—the clan mother—until she nominated the next representative. Everyone in the clan had a voice in approving her nomination. Once in place, she would sit with the chief and counsel him in his decisions. In a well-established protocol, she had the responsibility to warn him if he did not heed her and follow the will of the people. After the third warning, she could remove the chief from office, in a rare moment of imbalance in the social order. This system still continues among the traditional Iroquois.

Iroquois women had the moral and practical authority to stop war. Because warriors owed their allegiance to their clans and not to their nations or communities, they, like the chiefs, followed the women's wisdom. The women of the clan provided the warriors with supplies, including food (primarily charred corn pounded into meal and sweetened with maple sugar) and moccasins. If they did not want the men to go to war, they could withhold such supplies. The women, and not the council, also decided on the treatment of prisoners taken in war, determining whether they should be killed or adopted into the clan to replace members who had been lost. Because women had responsibility for the land, they also had a voice in early treaties and negotiations for the sale of land.

While land and commodities were held in common, each person had his or her own personal property. Native men owned ponies and other personal possessions, while women possessed their own horses and dogs, the longhouse or tepee, and everything needed to run the household. Children, too, owned their own articles, as no property was held in common by the family. Each could do what he or she wished with his or her own possessions. This type of egalitarian perspective on landownership and possessions was not unique to the Iroquois, as many other groups in North America and elsewhere, such as the Jomon in Japan, held land in common and passed what personal possessions they had down through the female line.

Central to women's authority was their birthing responsibility. Because everything that humans needed to survive was provided by the Earth, and women gave birth, theirs was the sacred responsibility to bring forth life from the soil. The connection between women as mothers and Mother Earth was so complete that the Iroquois, to this day, refer to the generations to come as "the faces still in the ground." Women and Mother Earth are one—givers of life—as expressed in the thanksgiving address, an ancient form of prayer made by Iroquois elders before and after an important event.

In the Iroquois creation story, the first woman, who had fallen from the sky world, buried her daughter and planted in her grave the plants and leaves that she had grabbed in an attempt to break her fall. From these plants grew corn, beans, and squash above her daughter's head. Sacred tobacco, used to send greetings to the creator, grew from her heart. Medicine plants, such as strawberries, that could be used to cure sickness, grew at her feet. Because she had become one with the Earth, the Earth itself is referred as "Our Mother." It was believed that the Earth would not bear foods unless cultivated by women.

In North and South America, women developed agriculture, working together on communally held land. Though the work was hard, they sang and talked in their work parties as they planted, often in mounds. The staple crops were corn, beans, and squash. The effectiveness of the women's farming is attested by the fact that Iroquois women generally had two to three years' surplus of dried food stored in underground caches.

Women had the responsibility of both producing and controlling the distribution of staple foods. Men hunted and brought the animals that they killed to the women to clean, distribute, and cook. Women's responsibility for creating life, from their bodies and from the soil, and managing the people's sustenance balanced the men's responsibility for providing meat, governing, and diplomacy. The underpinning of women's authority rested in their ability to give or withhold life in the form of birth and food. Ceremonies were connected to the land and agriculture, and so their timing—the planting of the corn, the harvest, and so on—was determined by women.

The abuse of women and children was rare among native nations because of the way in which they organized their societies and legal institutions. Matrilocal residence discouraged a man from treating his wife disrespectfully.

The all-female village of Umoja in northern Kenya provides refuge for women and girls who have been abandoned by their husbands or are running from abuse, early marriage, or female genital mutilation—dangers faced by native women in many societies. *(Kitra Cahana/ Getty Images)*

Knowing that such behavior would not be tolerated and that he would be put out of the household immediately strengthened the sanctions against spousal abuse. More important, the powerful tradition of women as the holders of life and death underpinned a social order in which rape was unthinkable. When violent crimes against women did occur, under native justice, they were dealt with harshly by banishment or death.

The woman's male clan members ensured her safety and well-being, taking action against any who committed an act against her. When non-native law replaced native justice, native women lost their protections against physical and sexual violence. For example, under U.S. law, a woman's relatives might be punished for assault, while her assailant walked free.

It may never be ascertained how widespread Iroquois women's traditional social and political equality actually was in practice, as the institutional structures that created and sustained it came under attack from the first moment of contact. And, of course, the Iroquois experience was different from that of other tribes in North America, as well as that of native peoples in other locations around the world.

The Colonial Experience and the Loss of Rights

The colonial mind-set regarding gender roles stretches far back into antiquity. The roots of what would become Western Christian patriarchy originated in the ancient Middle East, where women occupied a subservient position in a number of early cultures. When the colonizers (primarily the English, Spanish, French, Dutch, Russians, and, later, Americans) brought this tradition with them to Africa, the Americas, and Asia, they influenced the balance of gender roles in many native cultures.

At a meeting of the International Council of Women in 1888, social scientist and suffragist Alice Fletcher spoke about of how women's political authority increasingly was being eroded as native peoples faced forced assimilation under the U.S. government's "Christianize and Civilize" policy toward native people. Children taken from their homes to boarding schools far away were forced to reject their native beliefs and practices and incorporate Western Christian principles into their lives. Such principles were those of a society in which women held a secondary position. In the United States, women could not vote, hold political office, serve on juries, or act with a political voice of authority in any but those states where suffragists had organized and, in small victories, changed local laws.

Women of the Dakota, Lakota, Omaha, Winnebago, and other American Indian tribes feared the loss of their rights as their nations lost sovereignty under U.S. law. European American laws and customs were replacing their system of gender equality. At the same time, a movement was under way among white and African American women to change hearts, minds, and laws to win equality.

As wheat—cultivated by men—replaced the indigenous diet of corn, beans, and squash—crops traditionally cultivated by women—and as communal lands were divided into privately owned parcels, native women lost their economic grounding. Accompanied by forced Christianization, which took the sacred from Mother Earth and placed it in the hands of a male sky god, the connection between women and Earth was threatened and, in some cases, broken.

What had been an egalitarian culture before contact was subsumed by colonial cultures, with dramatic results for native peoples around the world in general and for native women in particular. Within the colonists' worldview, native women faced double discrimination, first on the basis of their native identity and then on the basis of their gender. Male colonists dominated the European colonial world, and women were literally nonpersons before the law in many locations. Discrimination against native women also began to come from within native women's own communities. As some native men decided that the only way forward was to assimilate with the new, dominant culture, they often disregarded their egalitarian culture in exchange for the benefits of fitting in with Christian civilization.

Even when men retained their native beliefs regarding gender roles, the integration of communities into the colonial power structure often meant a weakening of the status of native women. Women suffered higher rates of violence against them, preventable diseases, and economic discrimination. Maternal mortality rates were much higher among native women than among non-natives. In addition, native women who were unfortunate enough to be captured by non-natives during warfare often faced sexual violence or were trafficked into a life of sexual subservience.

Native women did not speak of "rights" before contact, because there was no such concept. Equality was simply the way society functioned in most cases. Talk of "rights" (whether natural rights, human rights, or civil rights) implies a denial of something that should be the case. With the onset of colonialism, native women's rights quickly were defined and denied. As the colonial experience progressed, native women began to define those rights and identify the violations they saw. These included the denial of participation in political and social decision making, the denial of economic control over their lives and work products, the denial of the right to own and control land, and the denial of access to education. The denial of these and other rights outlived the colonial era, which came to an end by the mid-twentieth century. The story of the modern era, since World War II, has been defined by the assertion of rights by populations that have been denied them.

Reassertion of Native Women's Rights

Beginning in the 1960s, a number of native rights movements sprung up around the world. From the Red Power movement in the United States, to the Sami Rights Committee in Norway, to the Indigenous Peoples of Africa Coordinating Committee in Zimbabwe, native peoples began to reassert their identity and reclaim cultures that long had been suppressed under colonial rule. In this milieu, native women began the long process of reclaiming their place in their cultures.

As native scholars, trained in the tools of Western scholarship and immersed in their native traditions, emerged during the second half of the twentieth century and the early twenty-first century, they began to transform knowledge and provide evidence of widespread gender balance in native nations. At the same time, the disciplines of anthropology, archaeology, and history began to examine cultural and gender biases that have brought Western assumptions to such evidence and tainted the scholarship of their professions.

Rights for native people in general and for women in particular are closely tied. Women cannot gain their true place in native cultures unless those cultures have the right to self-determination. And native cultures remain incomplete unless women are respected alongside men, fulfilling their functions in native societies.

In the United States, some native women describe their position as being "sovereign women in a sovereign nation." If a nation is not recognized as sovereign, there is no sovereignty for anyone in that nation. If a political power that does not recognize or practice gender balance gains cultural control, the institutional underpinnings of that balance are threatened.

This is borne out by the history of physical and cultural discrimination practiced against native nations of the world. Only when both native and non-native societies come to terms with that history, acknowledge what has been lost, and rebuild a new ethic of racial and gender equality can Native American women's history and rights, along with those of all their people, be put into the proper perspective.

Sally Roesch Wagner and Steven L. Danver

See also: *Issues*—Colonialism; Political Participation; Social Customs.

Further Reading

Allen, Paula Gunn. *The Sacred Hoop: Recovering the Feminine in American Indian Traditions.* Boston: Beacon, 1986.

Green, Joyce, ed. *Making Space for Indigenous Feminism.* New York: Zed, 2007.

Green, Rayna. *Women in American Indian Society.* New York: Chelsea House, 1992.

Hepburn, Stephanie, and Rita J. Simon. *Women's Roles and Statuses the World Over.* Lanham, MD: Lexington, 2006.

Kellogg, Susan. *Weaving the Past: A History of Latin America's Indigenous Women from the Prehistoric Period to the Present.* New York: Oxford University Press, 2005.

Mihesuah, Devon Abbott. *Indigenous American Women: Decolonization, Empowerment, Activism.* Lincoln: University of Nebraska Press, 2003.

Moreton-Robinson, Aileen. *Talkin' Up to the White Woman: Aboriginal Women and Feminism.* St. Lucia, Australia: University of Queensland Press, 2000.

Purdue, Theda. *Cherokee Women: Gender and Culture Change, 1700–1835.* Lincoln: University of Nebraska Press, 1998.

Suzack, Cheryl, Shari M. Huhndorf, Jeanne Perrault, and Jean Barman, eds. *Indigenous Women and Feminism: Politics, Activism, Culture.* Vancouver, Canada: University of British Columbia Press, 2010.

Wagner, Sally Roesch. "The Indigenous Roots of United States Feminism." In *Feminist Politics, Activism and Vision: Local and Global Challenge,* ed. Luciana Ricciutelli, Angela Miles, and Margaret H. McFadden. New York: Zed, 2004.

———. *Sisters in Spirit: The Haudenosaunee (Iroquois) Influence on Woman's Rights.* Summertown, TN: Native Voices, 2001.

Youth

Indigenous youth around the world face the challenge of reclaiming the traditional knowledge and land of their people, as well as reviving, sustaining, and strengthening their indigenous identities, languages, and cultures. They live in a time when traditional lifeways are intersecting with ongoing changes in their environment, modern-day commerce and technology, and society as a whole. The lives of indigenous youth around the world are best characterized by their shifting conditions, complexities, challenges, and accomplishments.

Many indigenous youth lead a transnational existence, meaning that they belong to communities that span the borders of modern nation-states, creating both jurisdictional and cultural problems within the host nations. At the same time, indigenous youth movements across the globe are engaging in political activism in ways not seen before. One example is the use of information technology to mobilize indigenous people and resources for political changes in local contexts, which often have far broader implications.

Native organizations and other gathering places provide a variety of social, health, healing, employment, housing, training, and educational services to indigenous youth. These sites give continuity to indigenous worldviews and traditions through activities tailored to indigenous youth, including youth conferences, workshops, and social outings; powwows and other traditional gatherings; elders' teachings, prayers, and conferences; and classes in such traditional crafts as beading, carving, or weaving. Other native groups may blend the application of traditional knowledge and healing practices with modern medicine.

Another area of growing interest among indigenous youth is traditional diet—hunting and fishing the animals that were hunted by their ancestors and growing the crops traditionally cultivated by their people. At the same time, elders are being approached by youth who wish to learn about indigenous values, knowledge, traditions, languages, histories, and identities. These learning experiences build long-lasting bonds of respect, enhance cultural identity and continuity, and contribute significantly to the indigenous community.

There is an increasing number of talented young indigenous artists and performers whose work gives expression to their indigenous ancestry and identity. Some use their talent and voice to contest poverty, violence, racism, and experiences of social, economic, political, and cultural exclusion. In urban and reserve areas, these expressions might take shape as graffiti art, gang activity, or hip-hop music. Others emphasize their gay or lesbian identity, exalt tribal feminism, or plead for gender equity through artistic displays, letters, songs, and plays. These are only a few examples of a subversive indigenous youth culture.

Still, the challenge of earning respect and enjoying an average quality of life represents an ongoing battle. For instance, as recently as February 2012, a teacher from a Wisconsin Catholic school punished a twelve-year-old student for speaking her indigenous Menominee language, demonstrating what remains a frustrating and disturbing reality for indigenous youth. To complicate the matter, indigenous youth in urban and reserve settings face intergenerational problems of unequal access to higher education, a lack of employment, substance abuse, crime and imprisonment, depression, and suicide. As a result of such struggles, many young people move back and forth from urban centers to their communities or reserves (even moving across international borders), seeking the best of both indigenous and nonindigenous cultures.

Since the mid-twentieth century, a variety of special-interest (and often short-lived) youth groups around the world have fought for the rights of indigenous peoples. These have included the Canadian Indian Youth Council (1960s); the Saskatchewan Native Youth Group (1970s), also of Canada; and Amigos de las Americas (founded in 1965 as Amigos de Honduras), which reaches indigenous youth and adults in Brazil, Costa Rica, Colombia, Ecuador, Nicaragua, and Mexico. The Asia Pacific Indigenous Youth Network, an alliance of indigenous youth organizations in Asia and the Pacific, works to promote and defend the rights of indigenous peoples. Similarly, the Aboriginal Youth Network, an online community formed in Edmonton, Alberta, was created to address social and health issues among Aboriginal youth in Canada.

Despite their experiences of oppression, racism, and poverty, the younger generation represents the future and driving force for many indigenous nations, communities, and countries,. A good example is Lynn "Nay" Valbuena, who was appointed housing commissioner for California's San Manuel band of Serrano Mission Indians at the age of twenty; since then, her work for the betterment of Indian nations has been an ongoing battle. She has been a delegate to the National Congress of American Indians for twenty-one years and served as chairwoman of the Tribal Alliance of Sovereign Indian Nations for sixteen years. In 2012, she won the American Indian Leadership Award from the National Center for American Indian Enterprise Development, stating, "[t]here is still a lot to be done in Indian country, but I am happy to see where we are at today."

María Cristina Manzano-Munguía

See also: Issues—Political Participation; Self-Determination; Social Customs.

Further Reading

Abu-Saad, Ismael, and Duane Champagne. *Indigenous Education and Empowerment: International Perspectives.* Lanham, MD: AltaMira, 2006.

Alfred, Taiaiake. *Wasáse: Indigenous Pathways of Action and Freedom.* Peterborough, Canada: Broadview, 2005.

Alfred, Taiaiake, Brock Pitawanakwat, and Jackie Price. *The Meaning of Political Participation for Indigenous Youth: Charting the Course for Youth Civic and Political Participation.* Ottawa, Canada: Canadian Policy Research Networks, 2007.

Darnell, Regna, and María Cristina Manzano-Munguía. "Nomadic Legacies and Urban Algonquian Residence." In *Proceedings of the 36th Algonquian Conference,* ed. H.C. Wolfart. Winnipeg, Canada: University of Manitoba Press, 2005.

Manzano-Munguía, María Cristina. "Conceptualizing Native Non-Government Organizations in Canada: An Ethnographic Approach." *International Journal of Interdisciplinary Social Sciences* 2:1 (2007): 449–459.

Proulx, Craig. "Aboriginal Hip Hoppers: Representin' Aboriginality in Cosmopolitan Worlds." In *Indigenous Cosmopolitans: Transnational and Transcultural Indigeneity in the Twenty-First Century,* ed. Maximilian C. Forte. New York: Peter Lang, 2010.

Documents

Indigenous and Tribal Populations Convention (International Labour Organization Convention 107; 1957)

The General Conference of the International Labour Organisation

Having been convened at Geneva by the Governing Body of the International Labour Office, and having met in its Fortieth Session on 5 June 1957, and

Having decided upon the adoption of certain proposals with regard to the protection and integration of indigenous and other tribal and semi-tribal populations in independent countries, which is the sixth item on the agenda of the session, and

Having determined that these proposals shall take the form of an international Convention, and

Considering that the Declaration of Philadelphia affirms that all human beings have the right to pursue both their material well-being and their spiritual development in conditions of freedom and dignity, of economic security and equal opportunity, and

Considering that there exist in various independent countries indigenous and other tribal and semi-tribal populations which are not yet integrated into the national community and whose social, economic or cultural situation hinders them from benefiting fully from the rights and advantages enjoyed by other elements of the population, and

Considering it desirable both for humanitarian reasons and in the interest of the countries concerned to promote continued action to improve the living and working conditions of these populations by simultaneous action in respect of all the factors which have hitherto prevented them from sharing fully in the progress of the national community of which they form part, and

Considering that the adoption of general international standards on the subject will facilitate action to assure the protection of the populations concerned, their progressive integration into their respective national communities, and the improvement of their living and working conditions, and

Noting that these standards have been framed with the co-operation of the United Nations, the Food and Agriculture Organisation of the United Nations, the United Nations Educational, Scientific and Cultural Organisation and the World Health Organisation, at appropriate levels and in their respective fields, and that it is proposed to seek their continuing co-operation in promoting and securing the application of these standards,

adopts this twenty-sixth day of June of the year one thousand nine hundred and fifty-seven the following Convention, which may be cited as the Indigenous and Tribal Populations Convention, 1957:

PART I. GENERAL POLICY

Article 1
1. This Convention applies to—

(a) members of tribal or semi-tribal populations in independent countries whose social and economic conditions are at a less advanced stage than the stage reached by the other sections of the national community, and whose status is regulated wholly or partially by their own customs or traditions or by special laws or regulations;

(b) members of tribal or semi-tribal populations in independent countries which are regarded as indigenous on account of their descent from the populations which inhabited the country, or a geographical region to which the country belongs, at the time of conquest or colonisation and which, irrespective of their legal status, live more in conformity with the social, economic and cultural institutions of that time than with the institutions of the nation to which they belong.

2. For the purposes of this Convention, the term *semi-tribal* includes groups and persons who, although they are in the process of losing their tribal characteristics, are not yet integrated into the national community.

3. The indigenous and other tribal or semi-tribal populations mentioned in paragraphs 1 and 2 of this Article are referred to hereinafter as "the populations concerned."

Article 2
1. Governments shall have the primary responsibility for developing co-ordinated and systematic action for the protection of the populations concerned and their progressive integration into the life of their respective countries.

2. Such action shall include measures for—

(a) enabling the said populations to benefit on an equal footing from the rights and opportunities which national laws or regulations grant to the other elements of the population;

(b) promoting the social, economic and cultural development of these populations and raising their standard of living;

(c) creating possibilities of national integration to the exclusion of measures tending towards the artificial assimilation of these populations.

3. The primary objective of all such action shall be the fostering of individual dignity, and the advancement of individual usefulness and initiative.

4. Recourse to force or coercion as a means of promoting the integration of these populations into the national community shall be excluded.

Article 3
1. So long as the social, economic and cultural conditions of the populations concerned prevent them from enjoying the benefits of the general laws of the country to which they belong, special measures shall be adopted for the protection of the institutions, persons, property and labour of these populations.

2. Care shall be taken to ensure that such special measures of protection—

(a) are not used as a means of creating or prolonging a state of segregation; and

(b) will be continued only so long as there is need for special protection and only to the extent that such protection is necessary.

3. Enjoyment of the general rights of citizenship, without discrimination, shall not be prejudiced in any way by such special measures of protection.

Article 4
In applying the provisions of this Convention relating to the integration of the populations concerned—

(a) due account shall be taken of the cultural and religious values and of the forms of social control existing among these populations, and of the nature of the problems which face them both as groups and as individuals when they undergo social and economic change;

(b) the danger involved in disrupting the values and institutions of the said populations unless they can be replaced by appropriate substitutes which the groups concerned are willing to accept shall be recognised;

(c) policies aimed at mitigating the difficulties experienced by these populations in adjusting themselves to new conditions of life and work shall be adopted.

Article 5
In applying the provisions of this Convention relating to the protection and integration of the populations concerned, governments shall—

(a) seek the collaboration of these populations and of their representatives;

(b) provide these populations with opportunities for the full development of their initiative;

(c) stimulate by all possible means the development among these populations of civil liberties and the establishment of or participation in elective institutions.

Article 6
The improvement of the conditions of life and work and level of education of the populations concerned shall be given high priority in plans for the over-all economic development of areas inhabited by these populations. Special projects for economic development of the areas in question shall also be so designed as to promote such improvement.

Article 7
1. In defining the rights and duties of the populations concerned regard shall be had to their customary laws.

2. These populations shall be allowed to retain their own customs and institutions where these are not incompatible with the national legal system or the objectives of integration programmes.

3. The application of the preceding paragraphs of this Article shall not prevent members of these populations from exercising, according to their individual capacity, the rights granted to all citizens and from assuming the corresponding duties.

Article 8
To the extent consistent with the interests of the national community and with the national legal system—

(a) the methods of social control practised by the populations concerned shall be used as far as possible for dealing with crimes or offences committed by members of these populations;

(b) where use of such methods of social control is not feasible, the customs of these populations in regard to penal matters shall be borne in mind by the authorities and courts dealing with such cases.

Article 9
Except in cases prescribed by law for all citizens the exaction from the members of the populations concerned of compulsory personal services in any form, whether paid or unpaid, shall be prohibited and punishable by law.

Article 10
1. Persons belonging to the populations concerned shall be specially safeguarded against the improper application of preventive detention and shall be able to take legal proceedings for the effective protection of their fundamental rights.

2. In imposing penalties laid down by general law on members of these populations account shall be taken of the degree of cultural development of the populations concerned.

3. Preference shall be given to methods of rehabilitation rather than confinement in prison.

PART II. LAND

Article 11
The right of ownership, collective or individual, of the members of the populations concerned over the lands which these populations traditionally occupy shall be recognised.

Article 12
1. The populations concerned shall not be removed without their free consent from their habitual territories except in accordance with national laws and regulations for reasons relating to national security, or in the interest of national economic development or of the health of the said populations.

2. When in such cases removal of these populations is necessary as an exceptional measure, they shall be provided with lands of quality at least equal to that of the lands previously occupied by them, suitable to provide for their present needs and future development. In cases where chances of alternative employment exist and where the populations concerned prefer to have compensation in money or in kind, they shall be so compensated under appropriate guarantees.

3. Persons thus removed shall be fully compensated for any resulting loss or injury.

Article 13
1. Procedures for the transmission of rights of ownership and use of land which are established by the customs of the populations concerned shall be respected, within the framework of national laws and regulations, in so far as they satisfy the needs of these populations and do not hinder their economic and social development.

2. Arrangements shall be made to prevent persons who are not members of the populations concerned from taking advantage of these customs or of lack of understanding of the laws on the part of the members of these populations to secure the ownership or use of the lands belonging to such members.

Article 14
National agrarian programmes shall secure to the populations concerned treatment equivalent to that accorded to other sections of the national community with regard to—

(a) the provision of more land for these populations when they have not the area necessary for providing the essentials of a normal existence, or for any possible increase in their numbers;

(b) the provision of the means required to promote the development of the lands which these populations already possess.

PART III. RECRUITMENT AND CONDITIONS OF EMPLOYMENT

Article 15

1. Each Member shall, within the framework of national laws and regulations, adopt special measures to ensure the effective protection with regard to recruitment and conditions of employment of workers belonging to the populations concerned so long as they are not in a position to enjoy the protection granted by law to workers in general.

2. Each Member shall do everything possible to prevent all discrimination between workers belonging to the populations concerned and other workers, in particular as regards—

(a) admission to employment, including skilled employment;

(b) equal remuneration for work of equal value;

(c) medical and social assistance, the prevention of employment injuries, workmen's compensation, industrial hygiene and housing;

(d) the right of association and freedom for all lawful trade union activities, and the right to conclude collective agreements with employers or employers' organisations.

PART IV. VOCATIONAL TRAINING, HANDICRAFTS AND RURAL INDUSTRIES

Article 16

Persons belonging to the populations concerned shall enjoy the same opportunities as other citizens in respect of vocational training facilities.

Article 17

1. Whenever programmes of vocational training of general application do not meet the special needs of persons belonging to the populations concerned governments shall provide special training facilities for such persons.

2. These special training facilities shall be based on a careful study of the economic environment, stage of cultural development and practical needs of the various occupational groups among the said populations; they shall, in particular enable the persons concerned to receive the training necessary for occupations for which these populations have traditionally shown aptitude.

3. These special training facilities shall be provided only so long as the stage of cultural development of the populations concerned requires them; with the advance of the process of integration they shall be replaced by the facilities provided for other citizens.

Article 18

1. Handicrafts and rural industries shall be encouraged as factors in the economic development of the populations concerned in a manner which will enable these populations to raise their standard of living and adjust themselves to modern methods of production and marketing.

2. Handicrafts and rural industries shall be developed in a manner which preserves the cultural heritage of these populations and improves their artistic values and particular modes of cultural expression.

PART V. SOCIAL SECURITY AND HEALTH

Article 19

Existing social security schemes shall be extended progressively, where practicable, to cover—

(a) wage earners belonging to the populations concerned;

(b) other persons belonging to these populations.

Article 20

1. Governments shall assume the responsibility for providing adequate health services for the populations concerned.

2. The organisation of such services shall be based on systematic studies of the social, economic and cultural conditions of the populations concerned.

3. The development of such services shall be co-ordinated with general measures of social, economic and cultural development.

PART VI. EDUCATION AND MEANS OF COMMUNICATION

Article 21

Measures shall be taken to ensure that members of the populations concerned have the opportunity to acquire education at all levels on an equal footing with the rest of the national community.

Article 22
1. Education programmes for the populations concerned shall be adapted, as regards methods and techniques, to the stage these populations have reached in the process of social, economic and cultural integration into the national community.

2. The formulation of such programmes shall normally be preceded by ethnological surveys.

Article 23
1. Children belonging to the populations concerned shall be taught to read and write in their mother tongue or, where this is not practicable, in the language most commonly used by the group to which they belong.

2. Provision shall be made for a progressive transition from the mother tongue or the vernacular language to the national language or to one of the official languages of the country.

3. Appropriate measures shall, as far as possible, be taken to preserve the mother tongue or the vernacular language.

Article 24
The imparting of general knowledge and skills that will help children to become integrated into the national community shall be an aim of primary education for the populations concerned.

Article 25
Educational measures shall be taken among other sections of the national community and particularly among those that are in most direct contact with the populations concerned with the object of eliminating prejudices that they may harbour in respect of these populations.

Article 26
1. Governments shall adopt measures, appropriate to the social and cultural characteristics of the populations concerned, to make known to them their rights and duties, especially in regard to labour and social welfare.

2. If necessary this shall be done by means of written translations and through the use of media of mass communication in the languages of these populations.

PART VII. ADMINISTRATION

Article 27
1. The governmental authority responsible for the matters covered in this Convention shall create or develop agencies to administer the programmes involved.

2. These programmes shall include—

(a) planning, co-ordination and execution of appropriate measures for the social, economic and cultural development of the populations concerned;

(b) proposing of legislative and other measures to the competent authorities;

(c) supervision of the application of these measures.

PART VIII. GENERAL PROVISIONS

Article 28
The nature and the scope of the measures to be taken to give effect to this Convention shall be determined in a flexible manner, having regard to the conditions characteristic of each country.

Article 29
The application of the provisions of this Convention shall not affect benefits conferred on the populations concerned in pursuance of other Conventions and Recommendations.

Article 30
The formal ratifications of this Convention shall be communicated to the Director-General of the International Labour Office for registration.

Article 31
1. This Convention shall be binding only upon those Members of the International Labour Organisation whose ratifications have been registered with the Director-General.

2. It shall come into force twelve months after the date on which the ratifications of two Members have been registered with the Director-General.

3. Thereafter, this Convention shall come into force for any Member twelve months after the date on which its ratifications has been registered.

Article 32
1. A Member which has ratified this Convention may denounce it after the expiration of ten years from the date on which the Convention first comes into force, by an act communicated to the Director-General of the International Labour Office for registration. Such denunciation shall not take effect until one year after the date on which it is registered.

2. Each Member which has ratified this Convention and which does not, within the year following the expiration of the period of ten years mentioned in the preceding paragraph, exercise the right of denunciation provided for in this Article, will be bound for another period of ten years and, thereafter, may denounce this Convention at the expiration of each period of ten years under the terms provided for in this Article.

Article 33
1. The Director-General of the International Labour Office shall notify all Members of the International Labour Organisation of the registration of all ratifications and denunciations communicated to him by the Members of the Organisation.

2. When notifying the Members of the Organisation of the registration of the second ratification communicated to him, the Director-General shall draw the attention of the Members of the Organisation to the date upon which the Convention will come into force.

Article 34
The Director-General of the International Labour Office shall communicate to the Secretary-General of the United Nations for registration in accordance with Article 102 of the Charter of the United Nations full particulars of all ratifications and acts of denunciation registered by him in accordance with the provisions of the preceding Articles.

Article 35
At such times as it may consider necessary the Governing Body of the International Labour Office shall present to the General Conference a report on the working of this Convention and shall examine the desirability of placing on the agenda of the Conference the question of its revision in whole or in part.

Article 36
1. Should the Conference adopt a new Convention revising this Convention in whole or in part, then, unless the new Convention otherwise provides:

a) the ratification by a Member of the new revising Convention shall ipso jure involve the immediate denunciation of this Convention, notwithstanding the provisions of Article 32 above, if and when the new revising Convention shall have come into force;

b) as from the date when the new revising Convention comes into force this Convention shall cease to be open to ratification by the Members.

2. This Convention shall in any case remain in force in its actual form and content for those Members which have ratified it but have not ratified the revising Convention.

Article 37
The English and French versions of the text of this Convention are equally authoritative.

Source: International Labour Organization, 2011.

Declaration of Indigenous Peoples of the World (1992)

We the Indigenous Peoples of the world, manifest our concern at this moment, when people from the whole planet are gathered here in Rio to discuss the direction of our lives, our planet Mother Earth and the future of our children and grandchildren. We manifest our concern because our voices, the voices of traditional peoples, are not being heard.

At this moment, the governments of the rich nations are discussing how to exert even more control over the less favored nations. The global community of colonial states has been meeting with each other as First, Second and Third World powers. All are recognized members of the United Nations. The Indigenous Nations are primarily considered Fourth World and are excluded. The Intent of the Earth Summit is to address the necessity of developing intergovernmental agreements and policies that shall move the global community of states into a sustainable yield relationship with the natural earth's resources and biospheres. All states should bind themselves to these agreements to protect the natural environment.

However, throughout this process, the Indigenous Nations have been totally excluded from the formal proceedings, except In very narrow occasions In which the appearances have been more window dressing than respect for the sovereignty of Indigenous Nations.

Indigenous Nations are in agreement. Our exclusion is colonial racism in all its institutional forms. The "State" governments that are significant participants In the Earth Summit process are the most powerful colonial governments in possession of Indigenous Lands, natural resources, territories and populations. To exclude Indigenous Nations helps assure those States' control of what they mutually classify as "domestic affairs." Their domestic policies, programs and governmental relationships with Indigenous Peoples result in our destruction. Statistics of the highest infant mortality, shortest life expectancy, poorest health, highest poverty and so on, are reflections of the Injustices against Indigenous Peoples by State governments and societies enriched by the illegal takings and thievery.

Indigenous Peoples demand:

- our territory and lands be protected from external invasion and exploitation;
- our air, water and lands must remain free from pollution, poison and other contaminants.
- our individual human rights and freedoms are protected;
- our rights to self-governance is guaranteed;
- our rights to self-determination protected;
- our traditional, ceremonial and spiritual sovereignty;
- our right to control and govern over all foreign persons that shall enter our territory;
- our sovereignty over our language and culture;
- our sovereign control over all economic development of our land, resources, territory and peoples;
- our protection of all our sacred sites and objects; the freedom from being downwind of environmentally damaging, or poisoning activities of foreign Individuals or corporations that impact the quality of air, water and lands;
- our forests be protected as we Indigenous Peoples have always protected our forests, the animals we hunt, our fish, our mountains and our PAJES (spiritual leaders) who live in the sacred places amildst our forests.
- that treaties, paid for by our people in land and blood, be honored by those nations which have prospered by these agreements.

HOWEVER, AND MOST IMPORTANTLY, Indigenous Nations want the integrity of our sovereignty respected. The Great Spirit has endowed the Indigenous Nations with the same rights as other member societies of the global community. The world must hear us. Not only have Indigenous Peoples been treated in token ways, but deliberate external influences have operated to divide us form one another. This "divide and conquer" ploy has come form many United Nation leaders.

We should like to tell you this moment that our Indigenous spiritual leaden an watching over and observing how your spirit moves. We ask respect for the depths of the earth, home of the fierce spirits which guarantee the protection of all the people and life forms of the planet.

We know this Earth Summit will sign the Fundamental Principles governing the destiny for the future (Agenda 21). We, Indigenous Peoples of the world, desire that this document be decisive in respecting the life of all the forest and Indigenous Peoples of the world.

June 7, 1992. Declaration #141 of the Global Forum. Rio de Janiero, Brazil.

Source: *We, Indigenous Peoples: A Compilation of Indigenous Peoples' Declarations.* Baguio City, Philippines: Tebtebba Foundation, 2005, pp. 209–211.

United Nations Declaration on the Rights of Indigenous Peoples (2007)

The General Assembly,

Guided by the purposes and principles of the Charter of the United Nations, and good faith in the fulfilment of the obligations assumed by States in accordance with the Charter,

Affirming that indigenous peoples are equal to all other peoples, while recognizing the right of all peoples to be different, to consider themselves different, and to be respected as such,

Affirming also that all peoples contribute to the diversity and richness of civilizations and cultures, which constitute the common heritage of humankind,

Affirming further that all doctrines, policies and practices based on or advocating superiority of peoples or individuals on the basis of national origin or racial, religious, ethnic or cultural differences are racist, scientifically false, legally invalid, morally condemnable and socially unjust,

Reaffirming that indigenous peoples, in the exercise of their rights, should be free from discrimination of any kind,

Concerned that indigenous peoples have suffered from historic injustices as a result of, inter alia, their colonization and dispossession of their lands, territories and resources, thus preventing them from exercising, in particular, their right to development in accordance with their own needs and interests,

Recognizing the urgent need to respect and promote the inherent rights of indigenous peoples which derive from their political, economic and social structures and from their cultures, spiritual traditions, histories and philosophies, especially their rights to their lands, territories and resources,

Recognizing also the urgent need to respect and promote the rights of indigenous peoples affirmed in treaties, agreements and other constructive arrangements with States,

Welcoming the fact that indigenous peoples are organizing themselves for political, economic, social and cultural enhancement and in order to bring to an end all forms of discrimination and oppression wherever they occur,

Convinced that control by indigenous peoples over developments affecting them and their lands, territories and resources will enable them to maintain and strengthen their institutions, cultures and traditions, and to promote their development in accordance with their aspirations and needs,

Recognizing that respect for indigenous knowledge, cultures and traditional practices contributes to sustainable and equitable development and proper management of the environment,

Emphasizing the contribution of the demilitarization of the lands and territories of indigenous peoples to peace, economic and social progress and development, understanding and friendly relations among nations and peoples of the world,

Recognizing in particular the right of indigenous families and communities to retain shared responsibility for the upbringing, training, education and well-being of their children, consistent with the rights of the child,

Considering that the rights affirmed in treaties, agreements and other constructive arrangements between States and indigenous peoples are, in some situations, matters of international concern, interest, responsibility and character,

Considering also that treaties, agreements and other constructive arrangements, and the relationship they represent, are the basis for a strengthened partnership between indigenous peoples and States,

Acknowledging that the Charter of the United Nations, the International Covenant on Economic, Social and Cultural Rights and the International Covenant on Civil and Political Rights, as well as the Vienna Declaration and Programme of Action, affirm the fundamental importance of the right to self-determination of all peoples, by virtue of which they freely determine their political status and freely pursue their economic, social and cultural development,

Bearing in mind that nothing in this Declaration may be used to deny any peoples their right to self-determination, exercised in conformity with international law,

Convinced that the recognition of the rights of indigenous peoples in this Declaration will enhance harmonious and cooperative relations between the State and indigenous peoples, based on principles of justice, democracy, respect for human rights, non-discrimination and good faith,

Encouraging States to comply with and effectively implement all their obligations as they apply to indigenous peoples under international instruments, in particular those related to human rights, in consultation and cooperation with the peoples concerned,

Emphasizing that the United Nations has an important and continuing role to play in promoting and protecting the rights of indigenous peoples,

Believing that this Declaration is a further important step forward for the recognition, promotion and protection of the rights and freedoms of indigenous peoples and in the development of relevant activities of the United Nations system in this field,

Recognizing and reaffirming that indigenous individuals are entitled without discrimination to all human rights recognized in international law, and that indigenous peoples possess collective rights which are indispensable for their existence, well-being and integral development as peoples,

Recognizing that the situation of indigenous peoples varies from region to region and from country to country and that the significance of national and regional particularities and various historical and cultural backgrounds should be taken into consideration,

Solemnly proclaims the following United Nations Declaration on the Rights of Indigenous Peoples as a standard of achievement to be pursued in a spirit of partnership and mutual respect:

Article 1

Indigenous peoples have the right to the full enjoyment, as a collective or as individuals, of all human rights and fundamental freedoms as recognized in the Charter of the United Nations, the Universal Declaration of Human Rights and international human rights law.

Article 2

Indigenous peoples and individuals are free and equal to all other peoples and individuals and have the right to be free from any kind of discrimination, in the exercise of their rights, in particular that based on their indigenous origin or identity.

Article 3

Indigenous peoples have the right to self-determination. By virtue of that right they freely determine their political status and freely pursue their economic, social and cultural development.

Article 4

Indigenous peoples, in exercising their right to self-determination, have the right to autonomy or self-government in matters relating to their internal and local affairs, as well as ways and means for financing their autonomous functions.

Article 5

Indigenous peoples have the right to maintain and strengthen their distinct political, legal, economic, social and cultural institutions, while retaining their right to participate fully, if they so choose, in the political, economic, social and cultural life of the State.

Article 6

Every indigenous individual has the right to a nationality.

Article 7

1. Indigenous individuals have the rights to life, physical and mental integrity, liberty and security of person.

2. Indigenous peoples have the collective right to live in freedom, peace and security as distinct peoples and shall not be subjected to any act of genocide or any other act of violence, including forcibly removing children of the group to another group.

Article 8

1. Indigenous peoples and individuals have the right not to be subjected to forced assimilation or destruction of their culture.

2. States shall provide effective mechanisms for prevention of, and redress for:

(a) Any action which has the aim or effect of depriving them of their integrity as distinct peoples, or of their cultural values or ethnic identities;

(b) Any action which has the aim or effect of dispossessing them of their lands, territories or resources;

(c) Any form of forced population transfer which has the aim or effect of violating or undermining any of their rights;

(d) Any form of forced assimilation or integration;

(e) Any form of propaganda designed to promote or incite racial or ethnic discrimination directed against them.

Article 9

Indigenous peoples and individuals have the right to belong to an indigenous community or nation, in accordance with the traditions and customs of the community or nation concerned. No discrimination of any kind may arise from the exercise of such a right.

Article 10

Indigenous peoples shall not be forcibly removed from their lands or territories. No relocation shall take place without the free, prior and informed consent of the indigenous peoples concerned and after agreement on just and fair compensation and, where possible, with the option of return.

Article 11

1. Indigenous peoples have the right to practise and revitalize their cultural traditions and customs. This includes the right to maintain, protect and develop the past, present and future manifestations of their cultures, such as archaeological and historical sites, artefacts, designs, ceremonies, technologies and visual and performing arts and literature.

2. States shall provide redress through effective mechanisms, which may include restitution, developed in conjunction with indigenous peoples, with respect to their cultural, intellectual, religious and spiritual property taken without their free, prior and informed consent or in violation of their laws, traditions and customs.

Article 12

1. Indigenous peoples have the right to manifest, prac-

tise, develop and teach their spiritual and religious traditions, customs and ceremonies; the right to maintain, protect, and have access in privacy to their religious and cultural sites; the right to the use and control of their ceremonial objects; and the right to the repatriation of their human remains.

2. States shall seek to enable the access and/or repatriation of ceremonial objects and human remains in their possession through fair, transparent and effective mechanisms developed in conjunction with indigenous peoples concerned.

Article 13
1. Indigenous peoples have the right to revitalize, use, develop and transmit to future generations their histories, languages, oral traditions, philosophies, writing systems and literatures, and to designate and retain their own names for communities, places and persons.

2. States shall take effective measures to ensure that this right is protected and also to ensure that indigenous peoples can understand and be understood in political, legal and administrative proceedings, where necessary through the provision of interpretation or by other appropriate means.

Article 14
1. Indigenous peoples have the right to establish and control their educational systems and institutions providing education in their own languages, in a manner appropriate to their cultural methods of teaching and learning.

2. Indigenous individuals, particularly children, have the right to all levels and forms of education of the State without discrimination.

3. States shall, in conjunction with indigenous peoples, take effective measures, in order for indigenous individuals, particularly children, including those living outside their communities, to have access, when possible, to an education in their own culture and provided in their own language.

Article 15
1. Indigenous peoples have the right to the dignity and diversity of their cultures, traditions, histories and aspirations which shall be appropriately reflected in education and public information.

2. States shall take effective measures, in consultation and cooperation with the indigenous peoples concerned, to

combat prejudice and eliminate discrimination and to promote tolerance, understanding and good relations among indigenous peoples and all other segments of society.

Article 16
1. Indigenous peoples have the right to establish their own media in their own languages and to have access to all forms of non-indigenous media without discrimination.

2. States shall take effective measures to ensure that State-owned media duly reflect indigenous cultural diversity. States, without prejudice to ensuring full freedom of expression, should encourage privately owned media to adequately reflect indigenous cultural diversity.

Article 17
1. Indigenous individuals and peoples have the right to enjoy fully all rights established under applicable international and domestic labour law.

2. States shall in consultation and cooperation with indigenous peoples take specific measures to protect indigenous children from economic exploitation and from performing any work that is likely to be hazardous or to interfere with the child's education, or to be harmful to the child's health or physical, mental, spiritual, moral or social development, taking into account their special vulnerability and the importance of education for their empowerment.

3. Indigenous individuals have the right not to be subjected to any discriminatory conditions of labour and, inter alia, employment or salary.

Article 18
Indigenous peoples have the right to participate in decision-making in matters which would affect their rights, through representatives chosen by themselves in accordance with their own procedures, as well as to maintain and develop their own indigenous decision-making institutions.

Article 19
States shall consult and cooperate in good faith with the indigenous peoples concerned through their own representative institutions in order to obtain their free, prior and informed consent before adopting and implementing legislative or administrative measures that may affect them.

Article 20
1. Indigenous peoples have the right to maintain and

develop their political, economic and social systems or institutions, to be secure in the enjoyment of their own means of subsistence and development, and to engage freely in all their traditional and other economic activities.

2. Indigenous peoples deprived of their means of subsistence and development are entitled to just and fair redress.

Article 21
1. Indigenous peoples have the right, without discrimination, to the improvement of their economic and social conditions, including, inter alia, in the areas of education, employment, vocational training and retraining, housing, sanitation, health and social security.

2. States shall take effective measures and, where appropriate, special measures to ensure continuing improvement of their economic and social conditions. Particular attention shall be paid to the rights and special needs of indigenous elders, women, youth, children and persons with disabilities.

Article 22
1. Particular attention shall be paid to the rights and special needs of indigenous elders, women, youth, children and persons with disabilities in the implementation of this Declaration.

2. States shall take measures, in conjunction with indigenous peoples, to ensure that indigenous women and children enjoy the full protection and guarantees against all forms of violence and discrimination.

Article 23
Indigenous peoples have the right to determine and develop priorities and strategies for exercising their right to development. In particular, indigenous peoples have the right to be actively involved in developing and determining health, housing and other economic and social programmes affecting them and, as far as possible, to administer such programmes through their own institutions.

Article 24
1. Indigenous peoples have the right to their traditional medicines and to maintain their health practices, including the conservation of their vital medicinal plants, animals and minerals. Indigenous individuals also have the right to access, without any discrimination, to all social and health services.

2. Indigenous individuals have an equal right to the enjoyment of the highest attainable standard of physical and mental health. States shall take the necessary steps with a view to achieving progressively the full realization of this right.

Article 25
Indigenous peoples have the right to maintain and strengthen their distinctive spiritual relationship with their traditionally owned or otherwise occupied and used lands, territories, waters and coastal seas and other resources and to uphold their responsibilities to future generations in this regard.

Article 26
1. Indigenous peoples have the right to the lands, territories and resources which they have traditionally owned, occupied or otherwise used or acquired.

2. Indigenous peoples have the right to own, use, develop and control the lands, territories and resources that they possess by reason of traditional ownership or other traditional occupation or use, as well as those which they have otherwise acquired.

3. States shall give legal recognition and protection to these lands, territories and resources. Such recognition shall be conducted with due respect to the customs, traditions and land tenure systems of the indigenous peoples concerned.

Article 27
States shall establish and implement, in conjunction with indigenous peoples concerned, a fair, independent, impartial, open and transparent process, giving due recognition to indigenous peoples' laws, traditions, customs and land tenure systems, to recognize and adjudicate the rights of indigenous peoples pertaining to their lands, territories and resources, including those which were traditionally owned or otherwise occupied or used. Indigenous peoples shall have the right to participate in this process.

Article 28
1. Indigenous peoples have the right to redress, by means that can include restitution or, when this is not possible, just, fair and equitable compensation, for the lands, territories and resources which they have traditionally owned or otherwise occupied or used, and which have been confiscated, taken, occupied, used or damaged without their free, prior and informed consent.

2. Unless otherwise freely agreed upon by the peoples

concerned, compensation shall take the form of lands, territories and resources equal in quality, size and legal status or of monetary compensation or other appropriate redress.

Article 29
1. Indigenous peoples have the right to the conservation and protection of the environment and the productive capacity of their lands or territories and resources. States shall establish and implement assistance programmes for indigenous peoples for such conservation and protection, without discrimination.

2. States shall take effective measures to ensure that no storage or disposal of hazardous materials shall take place in the lands or territories of indigenous peoples without their free, prior and informed consent.

3. States shall also take effective measures to ensure, as needed, that programmes for monitoring, maintaining and restoring the health of indigenous peoples, as developed and implemented by the peoples affected by such materials, are duly implemented.

Article 30
1. Military activities shall not take place in the lands or territories of indigenous peoples, unless justified by a relevant public interest or otherwise freely agreed with or requested by the indigenous peoples concerned.

2. States shall undertake effective consultations with the indigenous peoples concerned, through appropriate procedures and in particular through their representative institutions, prior to using their lands or territories for military activities.

Article 31
1. Indigenous peoples have the right to maintain, control, protect and develop their cultural heritage, traditional knowledge and traditional cultural expressions, as well as the manifestations of their sciences, technologies and cultures, including human and genetic resources, seeds, medicines, knowledge of the properties of fauna and flora, oral traditions, literatures, designs, sports and traditional games and visual and performing arts. They also have the right to maintain, control, protect and develop their intellectual property over such cultural heritage, traditional knowledge, and traditional cultural expressions.

2. In conjunction with indigenous peoples, States shall take effective measures to recognize and protect the exercise of these rights.

Article 32
1. Indigenous peoples have the right to determine and develop priorities and strategies for the development or use of their lands or territories and other resources.

2. States shall consult and cooperate in good faith with the indigenous peoples concerned through their own representative institutions in order to obtain their free and informed consent prior to the approval of any project affecting their lands or territories and other resources, particularly in connection with the development, utilization or exploitation of mineral, water or other resources.

3. States shall provide effective mechanisms for just and fair redress for any such activities, and appropriate measures shall be taken to mitigate adverse environmental, economic, social, cultural or spiritual impact.

Article 33
1. Indigenous peoples have the right to determine their own identity or membership in accordance with their customs and traditions. This does not impair the right of indigenous individuals to obtain citizenship of the States in which they live.

2. Indigenous peoples have the right to determine the structures and to select the membership of their institutions in accordance with their own procedures.

Article 34
Indigenous peoples have the right to promote, develop and maintain their institutional structures and their distinctive customs, spirituality, traditions, procedures, practices and, in the cases where they exist, juridical systems or customs, in accordance with international human rights standards.

Article 35
Indigenous peoples have the right to determine the responsibilities of individuals to their communities.

Article 36
1. Indigenous peoples, in particular those divided by international borders, have the right to maintain and develop contacts, relations and cooperation, including activities for spiritual, cultural, political, economic and social purposes, with their own members as well as other peoples across borders.

2. States, in consultation and cooperation with indigenous peoples, shall take effective measures to facilitate the exercise and ensure the implementation of this right.

Article 37

1. Indigenous peoples have the right to the recognition, observance and enforcement of treaties, agreements and other constructive arrangements concluded with States or their successors and to have States honour and respect such treaties, agreements and other constructive arrangements.

2. Nothing in this Declaration may be interpreted as diminishing or eliminating the rights of indigenous peoples contained in treaties, agreements and other constructive arrangements.

Article 38

States, in consultation and cooperation with indigenous peoples, shall take the appropriate measures, including legislative measures, to achieve the ends of this Declaration.

Article 39

Indigenous peoples have the right to have access to financial and technical assistance from States and through international cooperation, for the enjoyment of the rights contained in this Declaration.

Article 40

Indigenous peoples have the right to access to and prompt decision through just and fair procedures for the resolution of conflicts and disputes with States or other parties, as well as to effective remedies for all infringements of their individual and collective rights. Such a decision shall give due consideration to the customs, traditions, rules and legal systems of the indigenous peoples concerned and international human rights.

Article 41

The organs and specialized agencies of the United Nations system and other intergovernmental organizations shall contribute to the full realization of the provisions of this Declaration through the mobilization, inter alia, of financial cooperation and technical assistance. Ways and means of ensuring participation of indigenous peoples on issues affecting them shall be established.

Article 42

The United Nations, its bodies, including the Permanent Forum on Indigenous Issues, and specialized agencies, including at the country level, and States shall promote respect for and full application of the provisions of this Declaration and follow up the effectiveness of this Declaration.

Article 43

The rights recognized herein constitute the minimum standards for the survival, dignity and well-being of the indigenous peoples of the world.

Article 44

All the rights and freedoms recognized herein are equally guaranteed to male and female indigenous individuals.

Article 45

Nothing in this Declaration may be construed as diminishing or extinguishing the rights indigenous peoples have now or may acquire in the future.

Article 46

1. Nothing in this Declaration may be interpreted as implying for any State, people, group or person any right to engage in any activity or to perform any act contrary to the Charter of the United Nations or construed as authorizing or encouraging any action which would dismember or impair, totally or in part, the territorial integrity or political unity of sovereign and independent States.

2. In the exercise of the rights enunciated in the present Declaration, human rights and fundamental freedoms of all shall be respected. The exercise of the rights set forth in this Declaration shall be subject only to such limitations as are determined by law and in accordance with international human rights obligations. Any such limitations shall be non-discriminatory and strictly necessary solely for the purpose of securing due recognition and respect for the rights and freedoms of others and for meeting the just and most compelling requirements of a democratic society.

3. The provisions set forth in this Declaration shall be interpreted in accordance with the principles of justice, democracy, respect for human rights, equality, non-discrimination, good governance and good faith.

Source: United Nations, General Assembly, 2007.

Bibliography

Books

Abazov, Rafis. *Cultures of the World: Tajikistan.* New York: Benchmark, 2006.

Abdullahi, Mohamed Diriye. *Culture and Customs of Somalia.* Westport, CT: Greenwood, 2001.

Abols, Guntars. *Contribution of History to Latvian Identity.* Riga, Latvia: Nacionalais Apgads, 2003.

Abrams, H. Leon. *The Mixtec People: A Glance at Their Background, Their Condition a Quarter of a Century Ago, and Their Position Today.* Greeley: University of Northern Colorado, Museum of Anthropology, 1984.

Abun-Nasr, Jamil M. *A History of the Maghrib.* Cambridge, UK: Cambridge University Press, 1971.

Abu-Saad, Ismael, and Duane Champagne. *Indigenous Education and Empowerment: International Perspectives.* Lanham, MD: AltaMira, 2006.

Adekunle, Julius O. *Culture and Customs of Rwanda.* Westport, CT: Greenwood, 2007.

Afigbo, A.E. *Ropes of Sand: Studies in Igbo History and Culture.* New York: Oxford University Press, 1981.

Alfred, Taiaiake. *Wasáse: Indigenous Pathways of Action and Freedom.* Peterborough, Canada: Broadview, 2005.

Alfred, Taiaiake, Brock Pitawanakwat, and Jackie Price. *The Meaning of Political Participation for Indigenous Youth: Charting the Course for Youth Civic and Political Participation.* Ottawa, Canada: Canadian Policy Research Networks, 2007.

Alia, Valerie. *Names and Nunavut: Culture and Identity in the Inuit Homeland.* New York: Berghahn, 2006.

Allen, James de Vere. *Swahili Origins: Swahili Culture and the Shungwaya Phenomenon.* London: James Currey, 1993.

Allen, Matthew. *Identity and Resistance in Okinawa.* Lanham, MD: Rowman & Littlefield, 2002.

Allen, Philip M. *Madagascar: Conflicts of Authority in the Great Island.* Boulder, CO: Westview, 1995.

Anaya, S. James. *Indigenous Peoples in International Law.* New York: Oxford University Press, 2004.

Andersen, Peter B. *Santals: Glimpses of Culture and Identity.* Bhubaneswar, India: National Institute of Social Work and Social Sciences, 2002.

Anderson, Gary Clayton. *Sitting Bull and the Paradox of Lakota Nationhood.* New York: Longman, 2007.

Anson, Bert. *The Miami Indians.* Norman: University of Oklahoma Press, 1970.

Anthropological Survey of India. *India, Scheduled Tribes.* Kolkata, India: National Government, 2000.

Asch, Michael, ed. *Aboriginal and Treaty Rights in Canada: Essays on Law, Equality, and Respect for Difference.* Vancouver, Canada: University of British Columbia Press, 2002.

Asian Indigenous and Tribal Peoples Network. *Malaysia: Extinguishing Indigenous Peoples Rights.* New Delhi, India: Asian Indigenous and Tribal Peoples Network, 2008.

Astren, Fred. *Karaite Judaism and Historical Understanding.* Columbia: University of South Carolina Press, 2004.

Atkinson, James R. *Splendid Land, Splendid People: The Chickasaw Indians to Removal.* Tuscaloosa: University of Alabama Press, 2003.

Atreya, Harka Bahadur Chhetri. *The Bodos in Assam: A Socio-Cultural Study.* Kolkata, India: Towards Freedom, 2007.

Attwood, Bain. *Telling the Truth About Aboriginal History.* Sydney, Australia: Allen & Unwin, 1994.

Axtell, James. *The European and the Indian: Essays in the Ethnohistory of Colonial North America.* New York: Oxford University Press, 1981.

Ayot, Henry Okello. *A History of the Luo Abasuba of Western Kenya.* Nairobi, Kenya: Kenya Literature Bureau, 1979.

Aziz, Mahir A. *The Kurds of Iraq: Ethnonationalism and National Identity in Iraqi Kurdistan.* New York: I.B. Tauris, 2011.

Azuonye, Chukwuma. *Dogon.* New York: Rosen, 1996.

Bacquart, Jean-Baptiste. *The Tribal Arts of Africa.* New York: Thames & Hudson, 1998.

Bage, Mary G. *Tribal Knowledge System: Studies on the Kharia and Kisan Tribes of Odisha.* Bhubaneswar, India: Academy of Tribal Languages and Culture, 2010.

Bailey, Garrick, and Roberta Glenn Bailey. *A History of the Navajos: The Reservation Years.* Santa Fe, NM: School of American Research Press, 1986.

Baird, W. David. *The Osage People.* Phoenix, AZ: Indian Tribal Series, 1972.

Banks, Dennis, with Richard Erdoes. *Ojibwa Warrior: Dennis Banks and the Rise of the American Indian Movement.* Norman: University of Oklahoma Press, 2004.

Bareh, Hamlet. *The History and Culture of the Khasi People.* Delhi, India: Spectrum, 1997.

Barker, Graeme, and Tom Rasmussen. *The Etruscans.* Malden, MA: Blackwell, 1998.

Barker, Jonathan. *Rural Communities Under Stress: Peasant Farmers and the State in Africa.* New York: Cambridge University Press, 1989.

Barnard, Alan. *Hunters and Herders of Southern Africa: A Comparative Ethnography of the Khoisan Peoples.* Cambridge, UK: Cambridge University Press, 1992.

Barnard, Alan, and Justin Kenrick, eds. *Africa's Indigenous Peoples: "First Peoples" or "Marginalized Minorities"?* Edinburgh, UK: Centre for African Studies, University of Edinburgh, 2001.

Barnes, Gina Lee. *State Formation in Korea: Historical and Archaeological Perspectives.* London: Psychology Press, 2001.

Bartholomeusz, Tessa J., and Chandra R. de Silva. *Buddhist Fundamentalism and Minority Identities in Sri Lanka.* Albany: State University of New York Press, 1998.

Barzini, Luigi. *The Italians.* New York: Touchstone, 1996.

Bass, Althea. *Cherokee Messenger.* Norman: University of Oklahoma Press, 1996.

Bassman, Theda. *Treasures of the Hopi.* Flagstaff, AZ: Northland, 1997.

Basso, Keith, H. *Wisdom Sits in Places: Landscape and Language Among the Western Apache.* Albuquerque: University of New Mexico Press, 1996.

Bastien, Betty. *Blackfoot Ways of Knowing: The Worldview of the Siksikaitsitapi.* Ed. Jürgen W. Kremer. Calgary, Canada: University of Calgary Press, 2004.

Bateman, Roy. *Eritrea: Even the Stones Are Burning.* Trenton, NJ: Red Sea, 1998.

Baudesson, Henry. *Indo-China and Its Primitive People.* Trans. E. Appleby Holt. Bangkok, Thailand: White Lotus, 1997.

Baxter, P.T.W., Jan Hultin, and Alessandro Triulzi. *Being and Becoming Oromo: Historical and Anthropological Enquiries.* Lawrenceville, NJ: Red Sea, 1996.

Bayer, Laura, with Floyd Montoya and the Pueblo of Santa Ana. *Santa Ana: The People, the Pueblo, and the History of Tamaya.* Albuquerque: University of New Mexico Press, 1994.

Beach, D.N. *The Shona and Zimbabwe, 900–1850: An Outline of Shona History.* New York: Africana, 1980.

Beck, David R.M. *Siege and Survival: History of the Menominee Indians, 1634–1856.* Lincoln: University of Nebraska Press, 2002.

Becker, Marc. *¡Pachakutik!: Indigenous Movements and Electoral Politics in Ecuador.* New York: Rowman & Littlefield, 2010.

Beckwith, Christopher I. *Empires of the Silk Road: A History of Central Eurasia from the Bronze Age to the Present.* Princeton, NJ: Princeton University Press, 2009.

Bedford, Stuart, Christophe Sand, and Sean P. Connaughton, eds. *Oceanic Explorations: Lapita and Western Pacific Settlement.* Canberra, Australia: Australian National University E-Press, 2007.

Behera, Bijay K. *Tribal Culture, Modernisation, and Development: A Study of Kondh Tribe.* New Delhi, India: Khama, 1996.

Behera, Deepak Kumar, and Georg Pfeffer. *Contemporary Society: Tribal Studies.* Vol. 4, *Social Realities.* New Delhi, India: Concept, 1999.

———. *Contemporary Society: Tribal Studies.* Vol. 6, *Tribal Situation in India.* New Delhi, India: Concept, 2005.

Belich, James. *Making Peoples: A History of the New Zealanders from Polynesian Settlement to the End of the Nineteenth Century.* Honolulu: University of Hawaii Press, 2002.

Benedek, Emily. *The Wind Won't Know Me: A History of the Navajo–Hopi Land Dispute.* New York: Alfred A. Knopf, 1992.

Bennigsen, Alexandre, and S. Enders Wimbush. *Muslims of the Soviet Empire: A Guide.* Bloomington: Indiana University Press, 1986.

Bera, Gautam K., and Nishi Bera. *Echoes from the Hillocks: A Compendium on the Tribes of Tripura.* Agartala, India: Tripura Bani Prakashani, 2009.

Berthrong, Donald J. *The Cheyenne and Arapaho Ordeal: Reservation and Agency Life in the Indian Territory, 1875–1907.* Norman: University of Oklahoma Press, 1992.

Bertrand, Jacques. *Nationalism and Ethnic Conflict in Indonesia.* New York: Cambridge University Press, 2004.

Bessire, Aimée, and Mark Bessire. *Sukuma: The Heritage Library of African Peoples.* New York: Rosen, 1997.

Best, B. Jonathan. *A History of the Early South Korean Kingdom of Paekche.* Cambridge, MA: Harvard University Press, 2006.

Best, Elsdon. *The Maori.* Wellington, New Zealand: H.H. Tombs, 1924.

Bethrong, Donald. *The Southern Cheyennes.* Norman: University of Oklahoma Press, 1972.

Bhattacharjee, Prodip N. *The Garos of Tripura.* Agartala, India: Directorate of Research, 1992.

Bhengra, Ratnaker, C.R. Bijoy, and Shimreichon Luithui. *The Adivasis of India.* London: Minority Rights Group International, 1999.

Bianchi, Robert Steven. *Daily Life of the Nubians.* Westport, CT: Greenwood, 2004.

Biebuyck, Daniel P. *Lega Culture: Art, Initiation, and Moral Philosophy Among a Central African People.* Berkeley: University of California Press, 1973.

Bierhorst, John. *History and Mythology of the Aztecs: The Codex Chimalpopoca.* Tucson: University of Arizona Press, 1992.

Biesele, Megan, Robert K. Hitchcock, and Peter P. Schweitzer, eds. *Hunters and Gatherers in the Modern World: Conflict, Resistance, and Self-Determination.* Brooklyn, NY: Berghahn, 2000.

Bigart, Robert, and Clarence Woodcock, eds. *In the Name of the Salish and Kootenai Nation: The 1855 Hell Gate Treaty and the Origin of the Flathead Reservation.* Pablo, MT: Salish Kootenai College Press, 1996.

Biko, Adolfo Obiang. *Equatorial Guinea: From Spanish Colonialism to the Discovery of Oil.* Malabo, Equatorial Guinea: Monalige, 2000.

Binda, K.P., and Sharilyn Caillou, eds. *Aboriginal Education in Canada: A Study in Decolonization.* Mississauga, Canada: Canadian Educators' Press, 2001.

Blackhawk, Ned. *Violence over the Land: Indians and Empires in the Early American West.* Cambridge, MA: Harvard University Press, 2006.

Blaine, Martha Royce. *The Ioway Indians.* Norman: University of Oklahoma Press, 1995.

Blaser, Mario, Harvey A. Feit, and Glenn McRae, eds. *The Way of Development: Indigenous Peoples, Life Projects and Globalization.* London: Zed, 2004.

Blok, Josine H. *The Early Amazons: Modern and Ancient Perspectives on a Persistent Myth.* New York: Brill, 1995.

Blu, Karen I. *The Lumbee Problem: The Making of an American Indian People.* Rev. ed. Lincoln: University of Nebraska Press, 2001.

Blusse, Leonard, and Natalie Everts. *The Formosan Encounter: Notes on Formosa's Aboriginal Society: A Selection of Documents from Dutch Archival Sources.* Taipei, Taiwan: Shung Ye Museum of Formosan Aborigines, 2000.

Bøås, Morten, and Kevin C. Dunn, eds. *African Guerrillas: Raging Against the Machine.* Boulder, CO: Lynn Rienner, 2007.

Boehm, Christopher. *Montenegrin Social Organization and Values: Political Ethnography of a Refuge Area Tribal Adaptation.* New York: AMS, 1983.

Boelscher, Marianne. *The Curtain Within: Haida Social and Mythical Discourse.* Vancouver, Canada: University of British Columbia Press, 1988.

Bone, Robert M. *The Canadian North: Issues and Challenges.* New York: Oxford University Press, 2009.

Bonvillain, Nancy. *The Mohawk.* New York: Chelsea House, 1992.

Boremanse, Didier. *Hach Winik: The Lacandon Maya of Chiapas, Southern Mexico.* Albany, NY: Institute for Mesoamerican Studies, 1986.

Borofsky, Robert. *Yanomami: The Fierce Controversy and What We Might Learn from It.* Berkeley: University of California Press, 2005.

Boucher, Philip P. *Cannibal Encounters: Europeans and Island Caribs, 1492–1763.* Baltimore: Johns Hopkins University Press, 1992.

Bourne, Russell. *Gods of War, Gods of Peace: How the Meeting of Native and Colonial Religions Shaped Early America.* New York: Harcourt, 2002.

Bradbury, Mark. *Becoming Somaliland.* Bloomington: Indiana University Press, 2008.

Bradt, Hillary, and Austin Daniel. *Madagascar.* Guilford, CT: Globe Pequot, 2007.

Braimah, J.A., and Jack Goody. *Salaga: The Struggle for Power.* London: Longmans, 1967.

Bratenberg, Terje, Janne Hansen, and Henry Minde, eds. *Becoming Visible: Indigenous Peoples and Self-Government.* Trømso, Norway: University of Trømso, Centre for Sami Studies, 1995.

Brett, Michael, and Elizabeth Fentress. *The Berbers.* Oxford, UK: Blackwell, 1996.

Briones, Claudia, and Jose Luis Lanata, eds. *Living on the Edge: Contemporary Perspectives on the Native Peoples of Pampa, Patagonia, and Tierra del Fuego.* Westport, CT: Bergin & Garvey, 2002.

Briscoe, Gordon, and Len Smith, eds. *The Aboriginal Population Revisited: 70,000 Years to the Present.* Canberra, Australia: Aboriginal History, 2002.

Brock, Beverly. *The Nyiha of Mbozi.* Nairobi, Kenya: East African Publishing House, 1968.

Broome, Richard. *Aboriginal Australians: A History Since 1788.* 4th ed. Sydney, Australia: Allen & Unwin, 2010.

Brøsted, Jens, and Jens Dahl, eds. *Native Power: the Quest for Autonomy and Nationhood of Indigenous Peoples.* Bergen, Norway: Universitetsforlaget AS, 1985.

Brower, Barbara A., and Barbara Rose Johnston, eds. *Disappearing Peoples? Indigenous Groups and Ethnic Minorities in South and Central Asia.* Walnut Creek, CA: Left Coast, 2007.

Brown, Melissa J., ed. *Negotiating Ethnicities in China and Taiwan.* Berkeley: University of California Press, 1996.

Brysk, Alison. *From Tribal Village to Global Village: Indian Rights and International Relations in Latin America.* Stanford, CA: Stanford University Press, 2000.

Buechler, Hans C., and Judith-Maria Buechler. *The Bolivian Aymara.* New York: Holt, Reinhart and Winston, 1970.

Bulkan, Christopher Arif. *The Land Rights of Guyana's Indigenous Peoples.* Ottawa, Canada: Library and Archives of Canada, 2009.

Burgun, Michael. *Inuit.* Milwaukee, WI: Gareth Stevens, 2004.

Burger, Julian. *Report from the Frontier: The State of the World's Indigenous Peoples.* London: Zed, 1987.

Burke, Andrew, and Joe Cummings. *Laos.* London: Lonely Planet, 2007.

Burman, J.J. Roy. *Ethnography of a Denotified Tribe: The Laman Banjara.* New Delhi, India: Mittal, 2010.

Burnham, Philip. *The Gbaya.* New York: Rosen, 1997.

Burns, Louis F. *A History of the Osage People.* Tuscaloosa: University of Alabama Press, 2004.

Cal y Mayor, Aracely Burguete. *Indigenous Autonomy in Mexico.* Copenhagen, Denmark: International Work Group for Indigenous Affairs, 2000.

Calloway, Colin G. *The Shawnees and the War for America.* New York: Viking, 2007.

Campbell, Howard, Leigh Binford, Miguel Bartolomé, and Alicia Barabas, eds. *Zapotec Struggles: Histories, Politics and Representations from Juchitán, Oaxaca.* Trans. Nathaniel Tara. Washington, DC: Smithsonian Institution Press, 1993.

Campbell, Ian C. *Island Kingdom: Tonga, Ancient and Modern.* Christchurch, New Zealand: Canterbury University Press, 1992.

Carmack, Robert M. *Rebels of Highland Guatemala: The Quiché-Mayas of Momostenango.* Norman: University of Oklahoma Press, 1995.

Carrin-Bouez, Marine, and Harald Tambs-Lyche. *An Encounter of Peripheries: Santals, Missionaries, and Their Changing Worlds, 1867–1900.* New Delhi, India: Manohar, 2008.

Carter, Cecile Elkins. *Caddo Indians: Where We Come From.* Norman: University of Oklahoma Press, 1995.

Carter, William B. *Indian Alliances and the Spanish in the Southwest, 750–1750.* Norman: University of Oklahoma Press, 2009.

Cash, Joseph H., and Gerald W. Wolff. *The Ponca People.* Phoenix, AZ: Indian Tribal Series, 1975.

Chacko, Pariyaram M. *Tribal Communities and Social Change.* New Delhi, India: Sage, 2005.

Chakma, Suhas, and Marianne Jensen, eds. *Racism Against Indigenous Peoples.* Copenhagen, Denmark: International Work Group for Indigenous Affairs, 2001.

Chakraborty, Dilip Kumar. *The Great Andamanese, Struggling for Survival.* Kolkata, India: Seagull, 1990.

Champagne, Duane. *Social Change and Cultural Continuity Among Native Nations.* Lanham, MD: AltaMira, 2007.

Champagne, Duane, Karen Torjesen, and Susan Steiner, eds. *Indigenous People and the Modern State.* Walnut Creek, CA: AltaMira, 2005.

Chandra, Bipan, Aditya Mukherjee, and Mridula Mukherjee. *India After Independence, 1947–2000.* New Delhi, India: Penguin, 2000.

Charters, Claire, and Rodolfo Stavenhagen, eds. *Making the Declaration Work: The United Nations Declaration of the Rights of Indigenous Peoples.* Copenhagen, Denmark: International Work Group for Indigenous Affairs, 2009.

Chattopadhyay, Tapan. *Lepchas and Their Heritage.* Delhi, India: B.R., 1990.

Chatty, Dawn, ed. *Nomadic Societies in the Middle East and North Africa: Entering the 21st Century.* Leiden, Netherlands: Brill, 2006.

Chaudhuri, Sarit K., and Sucheta Sen Chaudhuri, eds. *Primitive Tribes in Contemporary India.* New Delhi, India: Mittal, 2005.

Chauvel, Richard, and Ikrar Nusa Bhakti. *The Papua Conflict: Jakarta's Perceptions and Policies.* Washington, DC: East-West Center Washington, 2004.

Chazée, Laurent. *The Peoples of Laos: Rural and Ethnic Diversities.* Bangkok, Thailand: White Lotus, 1999.

Cheema, Pervez Iqbal, and Maqsudul Hasan Nuri, eds. *Tribal Areas of Pakistan: Challenges and Responses.* Islamabad, Pakistan: Islamabad Policy Research Institute, 2005.

Chesterman, John. *Citizens Without Rights: Aborigines and Australian Citizenship.* New York: Cambridge University Press, 1996.

Chi, Jennifer Y., ed. *Wine, Worship, and Sacrifice: The Golden Graves of Ancient Vani.* Princeton, NJ: Princeton University Press, 2008.

Choudhury, Sujit. *The Bodos: Emergence and Assertion of an Ethnic Minority.* Shimla, India: Indian Institute of Advanced Study, 2007.

Christophory, Jul. *The Luxembourgers in Their Own Words.* Luxembourg: Self-published, 1978.

Churchill, Ward. *Struggle for the Land: Native North American Resistance to Genocide, Ecocide and Colonization.* San Francisco: City Lights, 2002.

Ćirković, Sima M. *The Serbs.* Trans. Vuk Tošić. Malden, MA: Blackwell, 2008.

Clark, A. Kim, and Marc Becker, eds. *Highland Indians and the State in Modern Ecuador.* Pittsburgh, PA: University of Pittsburgh Press, 2007.

Clark, Jerry E. *The Shawnee.* Lexington: University Press of Kentucky, 1993.

Clarkson, Linda, Vern Morrissette, and Gabriel Regallet. *Our Responsibility to the Seventh Generation: Indigenous Peoples and Sustainable Development.* Winnipeg, Canada: International Institute for Sustainable Development, 1992.

Clastres, Hélène. *The Land-Without-Evil: Tupi-Guaraní Prophetism.* Trans. Jacqueline Grenez Brovender. Urbana: University of Illinois Press, 1995.

Claude, Richard Pierre, and Burns H. Weston, eds. *Human Rights in the World Community: Issues and Action.* Philadelphia: University of Pennsylvania Press, 2006.

Cleary, Edward L., and Timothy J. Steigenga. *Resurgent Voices in Latin America: Indigenous Peoples, Political Mobilization, and Religious Change.* New Brunswick, NJ: Rutgers University Press, 2004.

Clendinnen, Inga. *Ambivalent Conquests: Maya and Spaniard in Yucatan, 1517–1570.* 2nd ed. New York: Cambridge University Press, 2003.

Clifton, James. *The Prairie People: Continuity and Change in Potawatomi Indian Culture, 1665–1965.* Lawrence: Regents Press of Kansas, 1977.

Coe, Michael D. *The Maya.* New York: Thames & Hudson, 1999.

———. *Mexico: From the Olmecs to the Aztecs.* 4th ed. London: Thames & Hudson, 2000.

Coel, Margaret. *Chief Left Hand: Southern Arapaho.* Norman: University of Oklahoma Press, 1988.

Cohen, David, and E.S. Atieno Odhiambo. *Siaya: The Historical Anthropology of an African Landscape.* London: James Currey, 1989.

Collins, Robert O. *A History of Modern Sudan.* New York: Cambridge University Press, 2008.

Collins, Roger. *The Spanish.* Malden, MA: Wiley, 2009.

Condominas, George. *We Have Eaten the Forest: The Story of a Montagnard Village in the Central Highlands of Vietnam.* Trans. Adrienne Foulke. New York: Kodansha America, 1994.

Conversi, Daniele. *The Basques, the Catalans and Spain: Alternative Routes to Nationalist Mobilisation.* Reno: University of Nevada Press, 1997.

Conzemius, Edward. *Ethnographical Survey of the Miskito and Suma Indians of Honduras and Nicaragua.* Bulletin No. 106. Washington, DC: American Bureau of Ethnology, 1932.

Cook, Sherburne F. *The Conflict Between the California Indian and White Civilization.* Berkeley: University of California Press, 1976.

Coombs, H.C. *Aboriginal Autonomy: Issues and Strategies.* New York: Cambridge University Press, 1995.

Cordell, Dennis D. *Dar al-Kuti and the Last Years of the Trans-Saharan Slave-Trade.* Madison: University of Wisconsin Press, 1984.

Corfield, Frank. *The Origins and Growth of Mau Mau.* Nairobi, Kenya: Government of Kenya, 1960.

Cornell, Stephen. *Indigenous Peoples, Poverty and Self-Determination in Australia, New Zealand, Canada and the United States.* Joint Occasional Papers on Native Affairs (JOPNA No. 2006 02). Tucson, AZ: Native Peoples Institute for Leadership, 2006.

Cotterill, R.S. *The Southern Indians: The Story of the Civilized Tribes Before Removal.* Norman: University of Oklahoma Press, 1954.

Crandall, David P. *The Place of Stunted Ironwood Trees: A Year in the Lives of the Cattle-Herding Himba of Namibia.* New York: Continuum, 2000.

Crossley, Pamela Kyle. *The Manchus.* Cambridge, MA: Blackwell, 1997.

Crow Dog, Mary, with Richard Erdoes. *Lakota Woman.* New York: HarperCollins, 1990.

Crum, Steven J. *The Road on Which We Came: A History of the Western Shoshone.* Salt Lake City: University of Utah Press, 1994.

Crumrine, N. Ross. *The Mayo Indians of Sonora: A People Who Refuse to Die.* Tucson: University of Arizona Press, 1977.

Curzon, R. *The Iranian Peoples of the Caucasus: A Handbook.* London: Routledge, 2001.

Cushman, H.B. *History of the Choctaw, Chickasaw and Natchez Indians.* Ed. Angie Debo. Norman: University of Oklahoma Press, 1999.

Daguan, Zhou. *A Record of Cambodia: The Land and Its People.* Trans. Peter Harris. Chiang Mai, Thailand: Silkworm, 2007.

Dalrymple, John Charles. *Ashanti and the Gold Coast and What We Know of It: A Sketch.* Stanford, CA: Stanford University Press, 1874.

Dalton, E.T. *Descriptive Ethnology of Bengal.* Kolkata, India: Government Printing, 1872.

Daniels, Harry W., ed. *The Forgotten People: Metis and Non-Status Indian Land Claims.* Ottawa, Canada: Native Council of Canada, 1979.

Das, Rajat K. *Tribalism and Beyond: Bodo (Boro), Garo, Khasi and Mizo Tribes of North East India.* Kolkata, India: Punthi Pustak, 2004.

Das, Sibir R. *Persistence and Change in Bhumia Culture.* Kolkata, India: Anthropological Survey of India, 2004.

Das Gupta, Malabika. *Class Formation Among the Mogs of Tripura.* Kolkata, India: Sujan, 1997.

Dasa, R.N., ed. *Art and Culture of the Juang.* Bhubaneswar, India: Orissa Lalit Kala Akademi, 1992.

Davis, Thomas. *Sustaining the Forest, the People, and the Spirit.* Albany: State University of New York Press, 2000.

De la Cadena, Marisol, and Orin Starn, eds. *Indigenous Experience Today.* New York: Berg, 2007.

Debo, Angie. *A History of the Indians of the United States.* Norman: University of Oklahoma Press, 1970.

Deloria, Vine, Jr., and Clifford M. Lytle. *The Nations Within: The Past and Future of American Indian Sovereignty.* Austin: University of Texas Press, 1984.

Deng, Francis Mading. *The Dinka of Sudan.* Rev. ed. Long Grove, IL: Waveland, 1984.

Denig, Edwin Thompson. *Five Indian Tribes of the Upper Missouri: Sioux, Arickaras, Assiniboines, Crees, Crows.* Norman: University of Oklahoma Press, 1975.

Deogaonkar, S.G. *The Gonds of Vidarbha.* New Delhi, India: Concept, 2007.

Deogaonkar, S.G., and S.S. Deogaonkar. *The Banjara.* New Delhi, India: Concept, 1992.

Dessaint, Alain Y. *Minorities of Southwest China: An Introduction to the Yi (Lolo) and Related Peoples.* New Haven, CT: Human Relations Area Files, 1980.

Devi, Premalata. *Social and Religious Institutions of Bodos.* Guwahati, India: Geophil, 2004.

Diakonova, Natalia, and Ektarina Romanova. *The Role of the Yakut Intelligentsia in the National Movement.* Sendai, Japan: Tohoku University, 2003.

Dial, Adolph L. *The Lumbee: Indians of North America.* New York: Chelsea, 1993.

Díaz Polanco, Héctor. *Indigenous Peoples in Latin America: The Quest for Self-Determination.* Trans. Lucia Rayas. Boulder, CO: Westview, 1997.

Dickason, Olive Patricia, and William Newbigging. *A Concise History of Canada's First Nations.* 2nd ed. Don Mills, Canada: Oxford University Press, 2010.

Dickson, Murray. *The Andaman Islanders.* London: Murray Dickson, 1992.

Dobyns, Henry F. *The Pima-Maricopa.* New York: Chelsea House, 1989.

Dobyns, Henry F., and Robert Eule. *The Walapai People.* Phoenix, AZ: Indian Tribal Series, 1976.

Donham, Donald, and Wendy James, eds. *The Southern Marches of Imperial Ethiopia: Essays in History and Social Anthropology.* Athens: Ohio University Press, 2002.

Dowd, Gregory Evans. *War Under Heaven: Pontiac, the Indian Nations, and the British Empire.* Baltimore: Johns Hopkins University Press, 2002.

Dowie, Mark. *Conservation Refugees: The Hundred-Year Conflict*

Between Global Conservation and Native Peoples. Cambridge, MA: MIT Press, 2009.

Dragnich, Alex N. *Serbs and Croats: The Struggle in Yugoslavia.* New York: Harcourt Brace Jovanovich, 1992.

Duffy, Kevin. *Children of the Forest.* New York: Dodd, Mead, 1984.

Dunbar-Ortiz, Roxanne. *Indians of the Americas: Human Rights and Self-Determination.* London: Zed, 1984.

Durrenberger, E. Paul, and Gísli Pálsson, eds. *The Anthropology of Iceland.* Iowa City: University of Iowa Press, 1989.

Eades, J.S. *The Yoruba Today.* New York: Cambridge University Press, 1980.

Early, John D., and John F. Peters. *The Xilixana Yanomami of the Amazon: History, Social Structure, and Population Dynamics.* Gainesville: University Press of Florida, 2000.

Edgar, Adrienne Lynn. *Tribal Nation: The Making of Soviet Turkmenistan.* Princeton, NJ: Princeton University Press, 2004.

Edmunds, R. David. *The Potawatomis: Keepers of the Fire.* Norman: University of Oklahoma Press, 1978.

Edwards, David N. *The Nubian Past: An Archaeology of the Sudan.* London: Routledge, 2004.

Edwards, William Howell. *An Introduction to Aboriginal Societies.* Wentworth Falls, Australia: Social Science Press, 1988.

Ekeh, Peter P., ed. *History of the Urhobo People of Niger Delta.* Buffalo, NY: Urhobo Historical Society, 2007.

Elkins, Caroline. *Imperial Reckoning: The Untold Story of Britain's Gulag in Kenya.* New York: Henry Holt, 2005.

Elliott, Mark C. *The Manchu Way: The Eight Banners and Ethnic Identity in Late Imperial China.* Stanford, CA: Stanford University Press, 2001.

Ellis, Donald, ed. *Tsimshian Treasures: The Remarkable Journey of the Dundas Collection.* Toronto, Canada: Douglas and McIntyre, 2007.

Emadi, Hafizullah. *Culture and Customs of Afghanistan.* Westport, CT: Greenwood, 2005.

Emmerson, Donald K., ed. *Indonesia Beyond Suharto: Polity, Economy, Society, Transition.* Armonk, NY: M.E. Sharpe, 1999.

Emmons, George Thornton. *The Tlingit Indians.* Seattle: University of Washington Press, 1991.

Endicott-West, Elizabeth. *Aspects of Khitan Liao and Mongolian Yuan Imperial Rule: A Comparative Perspective.* Los Angeles: Ethnographics, 1991.

Ens, Gerhard J. *Homeland to Hinterland: The Changing Worlds of the Red River Métis in the Nineteenth Century.* Toronto, Canada: University of Toronto Press, 1996.

Erickson, Kirstin C. *Yaqui Homeland and Homeplace: The Everyday Production of Ethnicity.* Tucson: University of Arizona Press, 2008.

Ethridge, Robbie Franklyn. *Creek Country: The Creek Indians and Their World.* Chapel Hill: University of North Carolina Press, 2003.

Euler, Robert C. *Grand Canyon Indians.* Dillon: Western Montana College Foundation, 1980.

Evans, W. McKee. *To Die Game: The Story of the Lowry Band, Indian Guerrillas of Reconstruction.* Baton Rouge: Louisiana State University Press, 1971.

Eversole, Robyn, John-Andrew McNeish, and Alberto D. Cimadamore, eds. *Indigenous Peoples and Poverty: An International Perspective.* London: Zed, 2006.

Ewen, Alexander, ed. *Voice of Indigenous Peoples: Native People Address the United Nations.* Santa Fe, NM: Clear Light, 1994.

Fabian, Stephen Michael. *Space-Time of the Bororo of Brazil.* Gainesville: University Press of Florida, 1992.

Falola, Toyin, ed. *Africa.* Vol. 2, *African Cultures and Societies Before 1885.* Durham, NC: Carolina Academic Press, 2000.

———, ed. *Africa.* Vol. 4, *The End of Colonial Rule: Nationalism and Decolonization.* Durham, NC: Carolina Academic Press, 2002.

Falola, Toyin, and Matt D. Childs, eds. *The Yoruba Diaspora in the Atlantic World.* Bloomington: Indiana University Press, 2004.

Falola, Toyin, and Ann Genova, eds. *Yoruba in Transition: History, Values, and Modernity.* Durham, NC: Carolina Academic Press, 2006.

Farris, Nancy M. *Maya Society Under Colonial Rule: The Collective Enterprise of Survival.* Princeton, NJ: Princeton University Press, 1984.

Farsoun, Samih K. *Culture and Customs of the Palestinians.* Westport, CT: Greenwood, 2004.

Faulk, Odie B., and Laura E. Faulk. *The Modoc.* New York: Chelsea House, 1988.

Feest, Christian F. *The Powhatan Tribes.* New York: Chelsea House, 1990.

Ferdon, Edwin N. *Early Tonga: As the Explorers Saw It, 1616–1810.* Tucson: University of Arizona Press, 1987.

Ferguson, R. Brian, and Neil L. Whitehead, eds. *War in the Tribal Zone: Expanding States and Indigenous Warfare.* Santa Fe, NM: School of American Research Press, 1992.

Fernández-Armesto, Felipe, ed. *The Times Guide to the Peoples of Europe.* London: Times Books, 1994.

Firth, Stewart. *New Guinea Under the Germans.* Carlton, Australia: Melbourne University Press, 1987.

Fischer, Christopher J. *Alsace to the Alsatians? Visions and Divisions of Alsatian Regionalism, 1870–1939.* New York: Berghahn, 2010.

Fischer, Edward F., and R. McKenna Brown, eds. *Maya Cultural Activism in Guatemala.* Austin: University of Texas Press, 1996.

Fisher, Angela, and Carol Beckwith. *Dinka: Legendary Cattle Keepers of the Sudan.* New York: Rizzoli, 2010.

Fixico, Donald L. *American Indians in a Modern World.* Lanham, MD: AltaMira, 2008.

Fleras, Augie, and John Leonard Elliott. *The "Nations Within": Aboriginal–State Relations in Canada, the United States, and New Zealand.* Toronto, Canada: Oxford University Press, 1992.

Fletcher, Richard. *Moorish Spain.* Los Angeles: University of California Press, 2006.

Flood, Josephine. *The Original Australians: Story of the Aboriginal People.* Sydney, Australia: Allen & Unwin, 2007.

Forsyth, James. *A History of the Peoples of Siberia: Russia's North Asian Colony 1581–1990.* New York: Cambridge University Press, 1994.

Forte, Maximilian C., ed. *Indigenous Resurgence in the Contemporary Caribbean: Amerindian Survival and Revival.* New York: Peter Lang, 2006.

Foster, Robert J., ed. *Nation Making: Emergent Identities in Postcolonial Melanesia.* Ann Arbor: University of Michigan Press, 1997.

Foster, Sally M. *Picts, Gaels and Scots.* London: B.T. Batsford, 2004.

Fowler, Loretta. *Tribal Sovereignty and the Historical Imagination: Cheyenne Arapaho Politics.* Lincoln: University of Nebraska Press, 2002.

Fox, Geoffrey. *The Land and People of Venezuela.* New York: HarperCollins, 1991.

Frank, Allen J. *Islamic Historiography and "Bulghar" Identity Among the Tatars and Bashkirs of Russia.* Leiden, Netherlands: Brill, 1998.

Frank, Andrew K. *The Seminole.* New York: Chelsea, 2010.

Frank, Mitch. *Understanding the Holy Land: Answering Questions About the Israeli-Palestinian Conflict.* New York: Viking, 2005.

Franke, Herbert, and Hok-lam Chan. *Studies on the Jurchens and the Chin Dynasty.* London: Ashgate, 1997.

Franklin, Simon, and Jonathan Shepard. *The Emergence of Rus, 750–1200.* New York: Longman, 1996.

Fraser, Angus. *The Gypsies.* Oxford, UK: Blackwell, 1992.

Frideres, James S. *Native Peoples in Canada: Contemporary Conflicts.* 3rd ed. Scarborough, UK: Prentice Hall, 1988.

Fuchs, Stephen. *The Gond and Bhumia of Eastern Mandla.* New Delhi, India: Reliance, 1991.

Gahlot, Sukhvir S., and Banshi Dhar. *Castes and Tribes of Rajasthan.* Jodhpur, India: Jain Brothers, 1989.

Gailey, Christine Ward. *Kinship to Kingship: Gender Hierarchy and State Formation in the Tongan Islands.* Austin: University of Texas Press, 1987.

Galliou, Patrick, and Michael Jones. *The Bretons.* Cambridge, MA: B. Blackwell, 1991.

Gangte, Priyadarshni M. *Customary Laws of Meitei and Mizo Societies of Manipur.* New Delhi, India: Akansha, 2008.

Gann, L.H., and Peter Duignan. *The Rulers of German Africa, 1884–1914.* Stanford, CA: Stanford University Press, 1977.

Ganson, Barbara. *The Guaraní Under Spanish Rule in the Rio de la Plata.* Stanford, CA: Stanford University Press, 2003.

García, María Elena. *Making Indigenous Citizens: Identities, Education, and Multicultural Activism in Peru.* Stanford, CA: Stanford University Press, 2005.

García-Alix, Lola. *The Permanent Forum on Indigenous Issues.* Copenhagen, Denmark: International Work Group for Indigenous Affairs, 2003.

Garvan, John M. *The Negritos of the Philippines.* Vienna, Austria: Wiener Beitrage zur Kulturgeschichte und Linguistik, 1964.

Gemie, Sharif. *Galicia: A Concise History.* Cardiff, UK: University of Wales Press, 2006.

Ghurye, G.S. *The Scheduled Tribes of India.* New Brunswick, NJ: Transaction, 1980.

Gifford, Edward W. *The Northeastern and Western Yavapai.* Berkeley: University of California Press, 1936.

———. *The Southeastern Yavapai.* Berkeley: University of California Press, 1932.

Goettner-Abendroth, Heide. *Matriarchal Societies: Studies on Indigenous Cultures Across the Globe.* New York: Peter Lang, 2012.

Golovnev, Andrei V., and Gail Osherenko. *Siberian Survival: The Nenets and Their Story.* Ithaca, NY: Cornell University Press, 1999.

Gomes, Mércio P. *The Indians and Brazil.* 3rd ed. Trans. John W. Moon. Gainesville: University Press of Florida, 2000.

Gonzalez, Nancie. *Sojourners of the Caribbean: Ethnogenesis and Ethnohistory of the Garífuna.* Urbana: University of Illinois Press, 1988.

Goodwin, Grenville. *The Social Organization of the Western Apache.* Chicago: University of Chicago Press, 1942.

Gordillo, Gastón. *Landscapes of Devils: Tensions of Place and Memory in the Argentinean Chaco.* Durham, NC: Duke University Press, 2004.

Gordon, Robert J. *The Bushman Myth: The Making of a Namibian Underclass.* Boulder, CO: Westview, 1992.

Gorenburg, Dmitry P. *Minority Ethnic Mobilization in the Russian Federation.* New York: Cambridge University Press, 2003.

Gorter, Durk, ed. *The Sociology of Frisian.* Berlin, Germany: Mouton de Gruyter, 1987.

Gosh, Danile P.S., Matilda Gabrielpillai, Philip Holden, and Gaik Cheng Khoo, eds. *Race and Multiculturalism in Malaysia and Singapore.* London: Taylor & Francis, 2009.

Gould, Jeffrey L. *To Die in This Way: Nicaraguan Indians and the Myth of Mestizaje, 1880–1965.* Durham, NC: Duke University Press, 1998.

Gow, David D. *Countering Development: Indigenous Modernity and the Moral Imagination.* Durham, NC: Duke University Press, 2008.

Gow, James, and Cathie Carmichael. *Slovenia and the Slovenes: A Small State and the New Europe.* Bloomington: Indiana University Press, 2000.

Granberg, William J. *People of the Maguey: The Otomí Indians of Mexico.* New York: Praeger, 1970.

Grandin, Greg. *The Blood of Guatemala: A History of Race and Nation.* Durham, NC: Duke University Press, 2000.

Grant, Glen. *Fornander's Ancient History of the Hawaiian People to the Times of Kamehameha I.* Honolulu, HI: Mutual, 1996.

Gray, Patty A. *The Predicament of Chukotka's Indigenous Movement: Post-Soviet Activism in the Russian Far North.* New York: Cambridge University Press, 2004.

Green, Joyce, ed. *Making Space for Indigenous Feminism.* New York: Zed, 2007.

Griffiths, Walter G. *The Kol Tribe of Central India.* Kolkata, India: Royal Asiatic Society of Bengal, 1993.

Grimble, Ian. *Scottish Clans and Tartans.* London: Octopus, 2004.

Grinde, Donald A., Jr., and Bruce E. Johansen. *Ecocide of Native America: Environmental Destruction of Indian Lands and Peoples.* Santa Fe, NM: Clear Light, 1995.

Grootaers, Jan-Lodewijk. *Ubangi: Art and Cultures from the African Heartland.* Brussels, Belgium: Mercatorfonds, 2007.

Guchinova, Elza-bair. *The Kalmyks: A Handbook.* Trans. David C. Lewis. New York: Routledge/Curzon, 2006.

Guerry, Vincent. *Life with the Baoulé.* Trans. Nora Hodges. Washington, DC: Three Continents, 1975.

Gungör, Harun, and Mustafa Argunsah. *The Gagauz: A Handbook.* London: Curzon, 2000.

Gupta, J.P. *The Customary Laws of the Munda and the Oraon.* Ranchi, India: Jharkhand Tribal Welfare Research Institute, 2002.

Gurr, Ted Robert. *Peoples Versus States: Minorities at Risk in the New Century.* Washington, DC: United States Institute of Peace Press, 2000.

Haetta, Odd Mathis. *The Sami: An Indigenous People of the Arctic.* Karasjok, Norway: Davvi Girji, 1996.

Hajong, B. *The Hajongs and Their Struggle.* Assam, India: Janata, 2002.

Hale, Charles R. *Resistance and Contradiction: Miskitu Indians and the Nicaraguan State, 1894–1987.* Stanford, CA: Stanford University Press, 1994.

Hall, Gillette, and Harry Anthony Patrinos, eds. *Indigenous Peoples, Poverty, and Development.* New York: Cambridge University Press, 2012.

Hall, Thomas D., and James V. Fenelon. *Indigenous Peoples and Globalization: Resistance and Revitalization.* Boulder, CO: Paradigm, 2009.

Hämäläinen, Pekka. *The Comanche Empire.* New Haven, CT: Yale University Press, 2008.

Hameso, Seyoum Y. *Ethnicity in Africa: Towards a Positive Approach.* Lincoln, NE: iUniverse, 2001.

Hammond-Tooke, W.D. *The Bantu-Speaking Peoples of Southern Africa.* London: Routledge, 1974.

Hanks, Jane Richardson, and Lucien Mason Hanks. *Tribes of the North Thailand Frontier.* New Haven, CT: Yale University Southeast Asia Studies, 2001.

Hardy, Grant, and Anne Behnke Kinney. *The Establishment of the Han Empire and Imperial China.* Westport, CT: Greenwood, 2005.

Harker, Santiago. *Wayuu: People of the Colombian Desert.* Bogotá, Colombia: Villegas Editores, 1998.

Harper, T.N. *The End of Empire and the Making of Malaya.* Cambridge, UK: Cambridge University Press, 2001.

Harrell, Stevan, ed. *Cultural Encounters on China's Ethnic Frontiers.* Seattle: University of Washington Press, 1995.

Harrison, Richard J. *Spain at the Dawn of History: Iberians, Phoenicians and Greeks.* London: Thames & Hudson, 1988.

Hart, David M. *Tribe and Society in Rural Morocco.* Portland, OR: Frank Cass, 2000.

Hasan, M., and Helal Mohiuddin. *Livelihoods of the Santals: Contemporary Change Dynamics.* Dhaka, Bangladesh: Center for Applied Social Studies, 2006.

Hauptman, Laurence M., and James D. Wherry, eds. *The Pequots in Southern New England: The Fall and Rise of an American Indian Nation.* Norman: University of Oklahoma Press, 1990.

Hayden, Tom, ed. *The Zapatista Reader.* New York: Thunder's Mouth, 2002.

Haywood, A.J. *Siberia: A Cultural History.* New York: Oxford University Press, 2010.

Heiberg, Marianne. *The Making of the Basque Nation.* Cambridge, UK: Cambridge University Press, 1989.

Heinen, H. Dieter. *Oko Warao: Marshland People of the Orinoco Delta.* Münster, Germany: Lit Verlag, 1988.

Helms, Mary. *Asang: Adaptations to Culture Contact in a Miskito Community.* Gainesville: University Press of Florida, 1971.

Hemming, John. *Red Gold: The Conquest of the Brazilian Indians.* Cambridge, MA: Harvard University Press, 1978.

Henson, Donald. *The Origins of the Anglo-Saxons.* Hockwold-cum-Wilton, UK: Anglo-Saxon Books, 2006.

Hickerson, Harold. *The Chippewa and Their Neighbors: A Study in Ethnohistory.* New York: Holt, Rinehart and Winston, 1970.

Hilton, Anne. *The Kingdom of the Kongo.* Oxford, UK: Clarendon, 1985.

Hilton, Tony E. Samuel, and Lazarus Lalsingh. *Banjara: A People in India.* Chennai, India: People India Research and Training Institute, 1999.

Hinton, Thomas B., and Phil C. Weigand. *Themes of Indigenous Acculturation in Northwest Mexico.* Tucson: University of Arizona Press, 1981.

Hitchcock, Richard, and Diana Vinding, eds. *Indigenous Peoples' Rights in Southern Africa.* Copenhagen, Denmark: International Work Group for Indigenous Affairs, 2004.

Hodgson, Dorothy L. *Once Intrepid Warriors: Gender, Ethnicity, and the Cultural Politics of Maasai Development.* Bloomington: Indiana University Press, 2001.

Hodson, T.C. *The Naga Tribes of Manipur.* London: Macmillan, 1911.

Hoffman, John. *The World of the Mundas.* New Delhi, India: Critical Quest, 2005.

Hoffman, Katherine E. *We Share Walls: Language, Land, and Gender in Berber.* Malden, MA: Blackwell, 2008.

Hoffman, Katherine E., and Susan Gilson Miller. *Berbers and Others: Beyond Tribe and Nation in the Maghrib.* Bloomington: Indiana University Press, 2010.

Holland, Clive. *Tyrol and Its People.* New York: James Pott & Co., 1909.

Horowitz, Donald L. *Ethnic Groups in Conflict.* Los Angeles: University of California Press, 1985.

Horton, Mark, and John Middleton. *The Swahili: The Social Landscape of a Mercantile Society.* Malden, MA: Blackwell, 2000.

Howard, James H. *The Ponca Tribe.* Lincoln: University of Nebraska Press, 1995.

———. *Shawnee! The Ceremonialism of a Native Indian Tribe and Its Cultural Background.* Athens: Ohio University Press, 1981.

Howe, James. *The Kuna Gathering: Contemporary Village Politics in Panama.* Austin: University of Texas Press, 1984.

———. *A People Who Would Not Kneel: Panama, the United States, and the San Blas Kuna.* Washington, DC: Smithsonian Institution, 1998.

Howe, K.R. *Where the Waves Fall: A New South Seas Islands History from First Settlement to Colonial Rule.* Honolulu: University of Hawaii Press, 1984.

Hudson, Charles. *The Southeastern Indians.* Knoxville: University of Tennessee Press, 1976.

Huertos Castillo, Beatrice. *Indigenous Peoples in Isolation in the Peruvian Amazon.* Copenhagen, Denmark: International Work Group for Indigenous Affairs, 2004.

Hulme, Peter. *Remnants of Conquest: The Island Caribs and Their Visitors, 1877–1998.* New York: Oxford University Press, 2000.

Hume, Martin A.S. *The Spanish People: Their Origin, Growth, and Influence.* New York: D. Appleton, 1901.

Humphrey, Caroline, and David Sneath. *The End of Nomadism? Society, State, and the Environment in Inner Asia.* Durham, NC: Duke University Press, 1999.

Humphreys, Andrews, and Krista Mits, eds. *The Red Book of the Peoples of the Russian Empire.* Tallinn, Estonia: NGO Red Book, 2001.

Hutchinson, John. *The Dynamics of Cultural Nationalism: The Gaelic Revival and the Creation of the Irish Nation State.* London: Allen & Unwin, 1987.

Hyde, George E. *The Pawnee Indians.* Norman: University of Oklahoma Press, 1988.

Ibrahim, Ferhad, and Gülistan Gürbey, eds. *The Kurdish Conflict in Turkey: Obstacles and Chances for Peace and Democracy.* New York: St. Martin's, 2000.

Ikime, Obaro. *Groundwork of Nigerian History.* Portsmouth, NH: Heinemann, 1985.

Isaac, Thomas. *Aboriginal and Treaty Rights in the Maritimes: The Marshall Decision and Beyond.* Saskatoon, Canada: Purich, 2001.

Issacson, Rupert. *The Healing Land: The Bushmen and the Kalahari.* New York: Grove, 2004.

Iverson, Peter. *We Are Still Here: American Indians in the Twentieth Century.* Wheeling, IL: Harlan Davidson, 1998.

Jacobs, Julian, with Alan MacFarlane and Sarah Harrison, and Anita Herle. *The Nagas: Hill Peoples of Northeast India: Society, Culture and the Colonial Encounters.* London: Thames & Hudson, 1990.

Jaimes, M. Annette, ed. *The State of Native America: Genocide, Colonization, and Resistance.* Boston: South End, 1992.

Jaimoukha, Amjad M. *The Chechens: A Handbook.* London: Psychology Press, 2005.

James, Harold. *A German Identity: 1770–1990.* London: Weidenfeld and Nicolson, 1989.

James, Harry C. *Pages from Hopi History.* Tucson: University of Arizona Press, 1974.

Jamir, Talitemjen, and A. Lanunungsang. *Naga Society and Culture: A Case Study of the Ao.* Mokokchung, India: Nagaland University, 2005.

Jaspan, M.A. *The Ili-Tonga Peoples of Northwestern Rhodesia.* London: International African Institute, 1953.

Jayasuriya, Shihan de Silva. *African Identity in Asia: Cultural Effects of Forced Migration.* Princeton, NJ: Markus Wiener, 2009.

Jena, Mihir K. *The Dongaria Kondh.* New Delhi, India: D.K. Printworld, 2002.

———. *The Kuttia Kondh.* New Delhi, India: D.K. Printworld, 2006.

Jenish, D'Arcy. *Indian Fall: The Last Days of the Plains Cree and the Blackfoot Confederacy.* Toronto, Canada: Penguin, 1999.

Jennings, Francis. *The Ambiguous Iroquois Empire: The Covenant Chain Confederation of Indian Tribes with English Colonies.* New York: W.W. Norton, 1984.

———. *The Invasion of America: Indians, Colonialism, and the Cant of Conquest.* New York: W.W. Norton, 1975.

Jensen, Gordon D., and Luh Ketut Suryani. *The Balinese People: A Reinvestigation of Character.* New York: Oxford University Press, 1992.

Jentoft, Svein, Henry Minde, and Ragnar Nilsen, eds. *Indigenous Peoples: Resource Management and Global Rights.* Delft, Netherlands: Eburon, 2003.

Jochelson, Waldemar. *History, Ethnology, and Anthropology of the Aleut.* Washington, DC: Carnegie Institution of Washington, 1933.

———. *The Yakut.* New York: American Museum of Natural History, 1933.

Johansen, Bruce E., and Barbara Alice Mann, eds. *Encyclopedia of the Haudenosaunee (Iroquois Confederacy).* Westport, CT: Greenwood, 2000.

Jones, Dorothy M. *Aleuts in Transition: A Comparison of Two Villages.* Seattle: University of Washington Press, 1976.

Jones, Grant D., ed. *Anthropology and History in Yucatán.* Austin: University of Texas Press, 1977.

Josephy, Alvin M., Jr. *The Nez Perce Indians and the Opening of the Northwest.* New York: Houghton Mifflin, 1997.

Kabamba, Nkamany. *Songye of the Democratic Republic of Congo: A Legacy to Remember.* Hallandale, FL: Aglob, 2004.

Kalgi, B.B. *The Scheduled Tribes in Transition: A Sociological Study of Gonds.* New Delhi, India: Classical, 2008.

Kambed, Bachoobhai Pitamber. *The History of Koli Tribe.* Gujarat, India: Talpoda Koli Community of Bhavnagar, 1981.

Kamei, Gangmumei. *A History of the Zeliangrong Nagas: From Makhel to Rani Gaidinliu.* Delhi, India: Spectrum, 2004.

Karp, Ivan. *Fields of Change Among the Iteso of Kenya.* London: Routledge, 2004.

Kasper, Martin. *Language and Culture of the Lusatian Sorbs Throughout Their History.* Berlin, Germany: Akademie-Verlag, 1987.

Kasten, Erich, ed. *Bicultural Education in the North: Ways of Preserving and Enhancing Indigenous Peoples' Languages and Traditional Knowledge.* Münster, Germany: Waxmann Verlag, 1998.

Kaup, Katherine Palmer. *Creating the Zhuang: Ethnic Politics in China.* Boulder, CO: Lynne Rienner, 2000.

Keeling, Richard. *Cry for Luck: Sacred Song and Speech Among the Yurok, Hupa, and Karok Indians of Northwestern California.* Berkeley: University of California Press, 1992.

Kennedy, John G. *The Tarahumara.* New York: Chelsea House, 1990.

Kenyatta, Jomo. *Facing Mount Kenya: The Tribal Life of the Gikuyu.* London: Secker and Warburg, 1938.

Kerr, George H. *Okinawa: The History of an Island People.* Rev. ed. Boston: Tuttle, 2000.

Khalidi, Rashid. *Palestinian Identity: The Construction of Modern National Consciousness.* New York: Columbia University Press, 2009.

Khan, M.Z., and Archana Dassi. *Road to Dignity: Socio-Economic Rehabilitation of Valmikis.* New Delhi, India: Concept, 1998.

Khodarkovsky, Michael. *Russia's Steppe Frontier: The Making of a Colonial Empire, 1500–1800.* Bloomington: Indiana University Press, 2004.

Kimmerling, Baruch, and Joel S. Migdal. *The Palestinian People: A History.* Rev. ed. Cambridge, MA: Harvard University Press, 2003.

King, Charles. *The Moldovans: Romania, Russia, and the Politics of Culture.* Stanford, CA: Hoover Institution Press, 2000.

King, Duane H., ed. *The Cherokee Indian Nation: A Troubled History.* Knoxville: University of Tennessee Press, 1979.

King, Michael. *Moriori: A People Rediscovered.* New York: Viking, 2000.

King, Victor T. *The Peoples of Borneo.* Oxford, UK: Blackwell, 1993.

Kirch, Patrick Vinton. *On the Road of the Winds: An Archaeological History of the Pacific Islands Before European Contact.* Berkeley: University of California Press, 2002.

Kircher, Ingrid A. *The Kanaks of New Caledonia.* London: Minority Rights Group, 1986.

Kirsch, Stuart. *Reverse Anthropology: Indigenous Analysis of Social and Environmental Relations in New Guinea.* Stanford, CA: Stanford University Press, 2006.

Knack, Martha C. *Boundaries Between: The Southern Paiutes, 1775–1995.* Lincoln: University of Nebraska Press, 2004.

Knight, Ian. *Zulu, 1816–1906.* Oxford, UK: Osprey, 1995.

Kolata, Alan L. *Valley of the Spirits: A Journey into the Lost Realm of the Aymara.* Hoboken, NJ: Wiley, 1996.

Kraft, Herbert C. *The Lenape: Archaeology, History, and Ethnography.* Newark: New Jersey Historical Society, 1986.

Kroeber, Alfred L. *The Arapaho.* Lincoln: University of Nebraska Press, 1983.

Kuiper, Kathleen, ed. *The Culture of India.* New York: Britannica Educational, 2011.

Kumar, Bachchan. *The Bhils: An Ethno-Historic Analysis.* Delhi, India: Sharada, 1997.

Kunstadter, Peter, ed. *Southeast Asian Tribes, Minorities, and Nations.* Princeton, NJ: Princeton University Press, 1967.

Laing, Lloyd, and Jenny Laing. *The Picts and the Scots.* Phoenix Mill, UK: Sutton, 1994.

Lallukka, Seppo. *The East Finnic Minorities in the Soviet Union: An Appraisal of the Erosive Trends.* Helsinki, Finland: Academia Scientiarum Fennica, 1990.

Lâm, Maivân Clech. *At the Edge of the State: Indigenous Peoples and Self-Determination.* Ardsley, NY: Transnational Publishers, 2000.

Lambert, Malcolm. *The Cathars.* Malden, MA: Blackwell, 1998.

Langer, Erick D., and Elena Muñoz, eds. *Contemporary Indigenous Movements in Latin America.* Wilmington, DE: Scholarly Resources, 2003.

Lansing, John Stephen. *The Balinese.* New York: Harcourt Brace, 1995.

Lapidus, Ira M. *A History of Islamic Societies.* New York: Cambridge University Press, 2002.

Latorre, Felipe A., and Dolores L. Latorre. *The Mexican Kickapoo Indians.* Mineola, NY: Dover, 1991.

Laughlin, William S. *Aleuts: Survivors of the Bering Land Bridge.* New York: Holt, Rinehart and Winston, 1980.

Lavender, David. *Let Me Be Free: The Nez Perce Tragedy.* New York: HarperCollins, 1992.

Lawrance, J.C.D. *The Iteso: Fifty Years of Change in a Nilo-Hamitic Tribe of Uganda.* London: Oxford University Press, 1957.

Lawson, Stephanie. *Tradition Versus Democracy in the South Pacific: Fiji, Tonga and Western Samoa.* Cambridge, UK: Cambridge University Press, 2008.

Lee, Richard B. *The Dobe !Kung.* New York: Holt, Rinehart and Winston, 1984.

———. *The !Kung San: Men, Women, and Work in a Foraging Society.* Cambridge, UK: Cambridge University Press, 1979.

Leepreecha, Prasit, Kwanchewan Buadaeng, and Don McCaskill, eds. *Integration, Marginalization and Resistance: Ethnic Minorities of the Greater Mekong Subregion.* Chiangmai, Thailand: Silkworm, 2008.

Lehtola, Veli-Pekka. *The Sámi People: Traditions in Transition.* Anchorage: University of Alaska Press, 2004.

Leis, Philip E. *Enculturation and Socialization in an Ijaw Village.* New York: Irvington, 1983.

Lekuton, Joseph Lemasolai, with Herman Viola. *Facing the Lion: Growing Up Maasai on the African Savanna.* Washington, DC: National Geographic Society, 2003.

Levy, Robert I. *Tahitians: Mind and Experience in the Society Islands.* Chicago: University of Chicago Press, 1973.

Lewis, Bernard. *The Multiple Identities of the Middle East.* New York: Schocken, 2001.

Lewis, Jerome. *Batwa Pygmies of the Great Lakes Region.* London: Minority Rights Group International, 2000.

Lewis, Paul W., and Elaine Lewis. *Peoples of the Golden Triangle: Six Tribes in Thailand.* New York: Thames & Hudson, 1984.

Lie, John. *Multiethnic Japan.* Cambridge, MA: Harvard University Press, 2001.

Loukacheva, Natalia. *The Arctic Promise: Legal and Political Autonomy of Greenland and Nunavut.* Toronto, Canada: University of Toronto Press, 2007.

Lowie, Robert H. *The Crow Indians.* Lincoln: University of Nebraska Press, 2004.

Lucas, Kintto. *We Will Not Dance on Our Grandparents' Tombs: Indigenous Uprisings in Ecuador.* London: Catholic Institute for International Relations, 2000.

Lussier, Antoine S. *Aspects of Canadian Metis History.* Ottawa, Canada: Department of Indian and Northern Affairs, 1985.

Lussier, Antoine S., and Bruce D. Sealey, eds. *The Other Natives: The Métis.* Winnipeg, Canada: Manitoba Métis Federation, 1978.

Lwanda, John Lloyd. *Kamuzu Banda of Malawi: A Study in Power, Promise, and Legacy.* Zomba, Malawi: Kachere, 2009.

Mabbett, Ian, and David Chandler. *The Khmers.* Malden, MA: Blackwell, 1995.

MacGaffey, Wyatt. *Kongo Political Culture.* Bloomington: Indiana University Press, 2000.

MacGonagle, Elizabeth. *Crafting Identity in Zimbabwe and Mozambique.* Rochester, NY: University of Rochester Press, 2007.

Mackenzie, Molly. *Turkish Athens: The Forgotten Centuries, 1456–1832.* Reading, UK: Ithaca, 1992.

Madsen, Brigham D. *The Northern Shoshoni.* Caldwell, ID: The Caxton Printers, 1980.

Maenchen-Helfen, J. Otto. *The World of the Huns: Studies in Their History and Culture.* Berkeley: University of California Press, 1973.

Magosci, Paul, ed. *The Aboriginal Peoples of Canada: A Short Introduction.* Toronto, Canada: University of Toronto Press, 2002.

Maier, F.G., and Vassos Karageorghis. *Paphos: History and Archaeology.* Nicosia, Cyprus: A.G. Leventis, 1984.

Mailhot, José. *In the Land of the Innu: The People of Sheshatshit.* St. John's, Canada: Memorial University of Newfoundland, 1997.

Mails, Thomas E. *The Hopi Survival Kit.* New York: Penguin, 1997.

Malkki, Liisa H. *Purity and Exile: Violence, Memory, and National Cosmology Among Hutu Refugees in Tanzania.* Chicago: University of Chicago Press, 1995.

Mallon, Florencia E. *Courage Tastes of Blood: The Mapuche Community of Nicolás Ailío and the Chilean State, 1906–2001.* Durham, NC: Duke University Press, 2005.

Maloba, Wunyabari O. *Mau Mau and Kenya: An Analysis of a Peasant Revolt.* Bloomington: Indiana University Press, 1998.

Mann, Charles C. *1491: New Revelations of the Americas Before Columbus.* New York: Alfred A. Knopf, 2005.

Mann, John W.W. *Sacajawea's People: The Lemhi Shoshones and the Salmon River Country.* Lincoln: University of Nebraska Press, 2004.

Manners, Robert A. *Havasupai Indians: An Ethnohistorical Report.* New York: Garland, 1974.

Marazov, Ivan, ed. *Ancient Gold: The Wealth of the Thracians.* New York: Harry N. Abrams, 1998.

Marcus, Joyce, and Kent V. Flannery. *Zapotec Civilization: How Urban Society Evolved in Mexico's Oaxaca Valley.* London: Thames & Hudson, 1996.

Marler, Joan, ed. *The Danube Script: Neo-Eneolithic Writing in Southeastern Europe.* Sebastopol, CA: Institute of Archaeomythology, 2008.

Martin, Henry Desmond. *The Mongol Wars with Hsi Hsia (1205–27).* London: Royal Asiatic Society of Great Britain and Ireland, 1942.

Marvin, Laurence W. *The Occitan War: A Military and Political History of the Albigensian Crusade, 1209–1218.* New York: Cambridge University Press, 2008.

Mason, W. Dale. *Indian Gaming: Tribal Sovereignty and American Politics.* Norman: University of Oklahoma Press, 2000.

Mawrie, Barnes L. *Introduction to Khasi Ethics.* Shillong, India: Don Bosco Center for Indigenous Cultures, 2005.

Maybury-Lewis, David, ed. *Dialectical Societies: The Gê and Bororo of Central Brazil.* Cambridge, MA: Harvard University Press, 1979.

———, ed. *The Politics of Ethnicity: Indigenous Peoples in Latin American States.* Cambridge, MA: Harvard University, David Rockefeller Center for Latin American Studies, 2002.

Maybury-Lewis, David, and James Howe. *The Indian Peoples of Paraguay: Their Plight and Their Prospects.* Cambridge, MA: Cultural Survival, 1980.

Maybury-Lewis, David, and Theodore Macdonald, eds. *Indigenous Peoples, Ethnic Groups, and the State.* Boston: Allyn and Bacon, 2002.

Maybury-Lewis, David, Theodore MacDonald, and Biorn Maybury-Lewis, eds. *Manifest Destinies and Indigenous Peoples.* Cambridge, MA: Harvard University Press, 2009.

Maynor, Malinda. *Lumbee Indians in the Jim Crow South.* Chapel Hill: University of North Carolina Press, 2010.

Mbaku, John Mukum. *Culture and Customs of Cameroon.* Westport, CT: Greenwood, 2005.

McAmis, Robert Day. *Malay Muslims: The History and Challenge of Resurgent Islam in Southeast Asia.* Grand Rapids, MI: William B. Eerdmans, 2002.

McCall, Lynne, and Rosalind Perry. *California's Chumash Indians.* San Luis Obispo, CA: EZ Nature Books, 1986.

McClanahan, Alexandra J., and Hallie L. Bissett. *Na'eda, Our Friends: A Guide to Alaska Native Corporations, Tribes, Cultures, ANCSA, and More.* Anchorage, AK: CIRI Foundation, 2003.

McKinnon, John, and Wanat Bhruksasri, eds. *Highlanders of Thailand.* New York: Oxford University Press, 1983.

McLester, L. Gordon, Laurence M. Hauptman, and Oneida History Conference Committee, eds. *The Oneida Indian Journey: From New York to Wisconsin, 1784–1860.* Madison: University of Wisconsin Press, 1999.

McLoughlin, William G. *Cherokees and Missionaries, 1789–1839.* Norman: University of Oklahoma Press, 1995.

McMillan, Alan D. *Native Peoples and Cultures of Canada.* Vancouver, Canada: Douglas & McIntyre, 1988.

McNab, D.T., and Ute Lischke, eds. *The Long Journey of Canada's Forgotten People: Studies in Métis History and Identities.* Waterloo, Canada: Wilfrid Laurier University Press, 2007.

McReynolds, Edwin C. *The Seminoles.* Norman: University of Oklahoma Press, 1957.

Meadows, William C. *Kiowa Ethnogeography.* Austin: University of Texas Press, 2008.

Medicine Crow, Joseph. *From the Heart of the Crow Country: The Crow Indians' Own Stories.* Lincoln: University of Nebraska Press, 2000.

Mehta, Prakash C. *Changing Face of Bhils.* Udaipur, India: Shiva, 1998.

Meir, Avinoam. *As Nomadism Ends: The Israeli Bedouin of the Negev.* Westview, CO: Boulder, 1997.

Menges, Karl H. *The Turkic Languages and Peoples: An Introduction to Turkic Studies.* 2nd ed. Wiesbaden, Germany: Harrassowitz, 1995.

Menis, Gian Carlo. *History of Friuli: The Formation of a People.* Pordenone, Italy: Grafiche Editoriali Artistiche Pordenonesi Spa, 1988.

Meyer, Roy W. *History of the Santee Sioux: United States Indian Policy on Trial.* Rev. ed. Lincoln: University of Nebraska Press, 1993.

Mezlekia, Nega. *Notes from the Hyena's Belly.* New York: Picador, 2000.

The Middle East: The History, the Culture, the Conflicts, the Faiths. New York: Time, 2006.

Middleton, John. *The World of the Swahili: An African Mercantile Civilization.* New Haven, CT: Yale University Press, 1992.

Miescher, Giorgio, and Dag Henrichsen, eds. *New Notes on Kaoko: The Northern Kunene Region (Namibia) in Texts and Photographs.* Basel, Switzerland: Basler Afrika Bibliographien, 2000.

Mihesuah, Devon Abbott. *Indigenous American Women: Decolonization, Empowerment, Activism.* Lincoln: University of Nebraska Press, 2003.

Miley, Misty. *An Introduction and Overview of the Situation of Indigenous Peoples in Burma.* Chiang Mai, Thailand: Indigenous Peoples Human Rights Defenders Network, 2008.

Miller, Bruce W. *Chumash: A Picture of Their World.* Los Osos, CA: Sand River, 1988.

Miller, Christopher L. *Prophetic Worlds: Indians and Whites on the Columbia Plateau.* Seattle: University of Washington Press, 2003.

Miller, David, Dennis J. Smith, Joseph R. McGeshick, James Shanley, and Caleb Shields. *The History of the Assiniboine and Sioux Tribes of the Fort Peck Indian Reservation, Montana, 1800–2000.* Helena: Montana Historical Society, 2008.

Miller, Elmer, ed. *Peoples of the Gran Chaco.* Westport, CT: Bergin & Garvey, 2001.

Miller, Mark E. *Forgotten Tribes: Unrecognized Indians and the Federal Acknowledgment Process.* Lincoln: University of Nebraska Press, 2004.

Milner, Anthony. *The Malays.* Oxford, UK: Wiley-Blackwell, 2011.

Minde, Henry, ed. *Indigenous Peoples: Self-Determination, Knowledge, Indigeneity.* Delft, Netherlands: Eburon Delft, 2008.

Minority Rights Group, ed. *Polar Peoples: Self-Determination and Development.* London: Minority Rights Publications, 1994.

Miriuki, Godfrey. *A History of the Kikuyu, 1500–1900.* Oxford, UK: Oxford University Press, 1974.

Mishra, Patit Paban. *A Contemporary History of Laos.* New Delhi, India: National Book Organisation, 1999.

———. *Laos: Land and Its People.* New Delhi, India: Indian Centre for Studies on Indochina, n.d.

Misra, K.K. *Social Structure and Change Among the Ho of Orissa.* Delhi, India: Giani, 1987.

Mitchell, J. Clyde. *The Yao Village: A Study in the Social Structure of a Malawian Tribe.* Manchester, UK: Manchester University Press, 1971.

Momin, Mignonette, and Milton S. Sangma. *Readings in History and Culture of the Garos: Essays in Honour of Milton S. Sangma.* New Delhi, India: Regency, 2003.

Monsutti, Alessandro. *War and Migration: Social Networks and Economic Strategies of the Hazaras of Afghanistan.* New York: Routledge, 2005.

Moore, Clive. *Kanaka: A History of Melanesian Mackay.* Port Moresby, Papua New Guinea: University of Papua New Guinea, 1985.

Moore, John. *The Cheyenne.* Hoboken, NJ: Wiley, 1999.

Morgan, David. *The Mongols.* Oxford, UK: Blackwell, 1986.

Morgan, Phillip Carroll. *Chickasaw Renaissance.* Ada, OK: Chickasaw Press, 2010.

Morris, Donald R. *The Washing of the Spears: The Rise and Fall of the Zulu Nation.* New York: Simon & Schuster, 1965.

Morrison, Dane, ed. *American Indian Studies.* New York: Peter Lang, 1997.

Morrison, Kenneth. *Montenegro: A Modern History.* London: I.B. Taurus, 2008.

Moseley, Christopher. *Livonian.* Munich, Germany: Lincom Europa, 2002.

Mousavi, Sayed Askar. *The Hazaras of Afghanistan: An Historical, Cultural and Political Study.* New York: St. Martin's, 1997.

Mueller, Gerald. *Defending Rama Indian Community Lands and the Southeastern Nicaragua Biosphere Reserve.* Edmonton, Canada: Four Directions Geographic Consulting, 2001.

Mukhopadhyay, Chandidas. *Kharia: The Victim of Social Stigma.* Kolkata, India: K.P. Bagchi, 1998.

Mukhopadhyay, Subrata K. *Chang: A Dying Folk-Art of the Lodha Tribes of Suharnarekha Basin.* Kolkata, India: Government of West Bengal, 2003.

Mullick, Bosu. *Indigenous Peoples in Urban Areas.* Copenhagen, Denmark: International Work Group for Indigenous Affairs, 2002.

Munoz, Paul Michel. *Early Kingdoms of the Indonesian Archipelago and the Malay Peninsula.* Barrington, IL: Continental Sales, 2006.

Munro-Hay, Stuart. *Aksum: A Civilization of Late Antiquity.* Edinburgh, UK: Edinburgh University Press, 1991.

Murrieta, Cynthia Radding. *Landscapes of Power and Identity: Comparative Histories in the Sonoran Desert and the Forests of Amazonia from Colony to Republic.* Durham, NC: Duke University Press, 2005.

Mwakikagile, Godfrey. *Ethnicity and National Identity in Uganda: The Land and Its People.* Scotts Valley, CA: Custom Books, 2009.

———. *Kenya: Identity of a Nation.* Pretoria, South Africa: New Africa, 2008.

———. *South Africa and Its People.* Pretoria, South Africa: New Africa, 2008.

Naga Hoho. *White Paper on Naga Integration.* Kohima, India: Naga Hoho, 2002.

Nagel, Joane. *American Indian Ethnic Renewal: Red Power and the Resurgence of Identity and Culture.* New York: Oxford University Press, 2009.

Nanda, Bikram N. *Contours of Continuity and Change: The Story of the Bonda Highlanders.* New Delhi, India: Sage, 1994.

Nayak, Radhakant, Barbara M. Boal, and Nabor Soreng. *The Juangs: A Handbook for Development.* New Delhi, India: Indian Social Institute, 1993.

Ndarubagiye, Léonce. *Burundi: The Origins of the Hutu–Tutsi Conflict.* Nairobi, Kenya: L. Ndarubagiye, 1996.

Ndege, George O. *Culture and Customs of Mozambique.* Westport, CT: Greenwood, 2007.

Ndukwe, Pat I. *Fulani.* New York: Rosen, 1996.

Nelson, Byron, and Laura Bayer. *Our Home Forever: A Hupa Tribal History.* Hoopa, CA: Hupa Tribe, 1978.

Nelson, Richard K. *The Athabaskans: People of the Boreal Forest.* Fairbanks: University of Alaska Museum, 1983.

Nettheim, Garth, Gary Meyers, and Donna Craig. *Indigenous Peoples and Governance Structures: A Comparative Analysis of Land and Resource Management Rights.* Canberra, Australia: Aboriginal Studies Press, 2002.

Newbury, Colin. *Tahiti Nui: Change and Survival in French Polynesia, 1767–1945.* Honolulu: University Press of Hawaii, 1980.

Nicol, George S. *Clans Map of Scotland.* Edinburgh, UK: Bartholomew, 1984.

Nieberding, Velma. *The History of Ottawa Country.* Miami, OK: Walsworth, 1983.

Nietschmann, Bernard. *The Unknown War: The Miskito Nation, Nicaragua, and the United States.* Lanham, MD: University Press of America, 1989.

Niezen, Ronald. *The Origins of Indigenism: Human Rights and the Politics of Identity.* Berkeley: University of California Press, 2003.

———. *The Rediscovered Self: Indigenous Identity and Cultural Justice.* Montreal, Canada: McGill-Queen's University Press, 2009.

Nimmo, H. Arlo. *The Sea People of Sulu: A Study of Social Change in the Philippines.* San Francisco: Chandler, 1972.

Nimuendajú, Curt. *The Tukuna.* Berkeley: University of California Press, 1952.

Nisan, Mordechai. *Minorities in the Middle East: A History of Struggle and Self Expression.* Jefferson, NC: McFarland, 2002.

Nordyke, Eleanor C. *The Peopling of Hawaii.* 2nd ed. Honolulu: University of Hawaii Press, 1989.

Norwich, John Julius. *Byzantium: The Apogee.* New York: Viking, 1991.

Noval-Morales, Daisy Y. *A Primer on the Negritos of the Philippines.* Manila, Phillipines: Philippine Business for Social Progress, 1979.

Núñez Astrain, Luis. *The Basques: Their Struggle for Independence.* Trans. Meic Stephens. Cardiff, UK: Welsh Academic Press, 1997.

Nurse, Derrick, and Thomas Spear. *The Swahili: Reconstructing the History and Language of an African Society, 800–1500.* Philadelphia: University of Pennsylvania Press, 1985.

Nuttall, Mark. *Protecting the Arctic: Indigenous Peoples and Cultural Survival.* Amsterdam, Netherlands: Harwood, 1998.

Nyati-Ramahobo, Lydia. *Minority Tribes in Botswana: The Politics of Recognition.* London: Minority Rights Group International, 2008.

O'Brien, Sharon. *American Indian Tribal Governments.* Norman: University of Oklahoma Press, 1993.

Ocholla-Ayayo, A.B.C. *The Luo Culture, A Reconstruction of the Material Culture Patterns of a Traditional African Society.* Wiesbaden, Germany: Steiner, 1980.

O'Connor, Mary I. *Descendants of the Totoliguoqui: Ethnicity and Economics in the Mayo Valley.* Berkeley: University of California Press, 1989.

Ogundiran, Akinwumi, ed. *Pre-Colonial Nigeria: Essays in Honor of Toyin Falola.* Trenton, NJ: Africa World, 2005.

Oinas, Felix. *The Karelians.* New Haven, CT: Human Relations Area Files, 1995.

Olcott, Martha. *The Kazakhs.* Stanford, CA: Hoover Institution Press, 1995.

Oliver, Douglas L. *Ancient Tahitian Society.* Honolulu: University Press of Hawaii, 1974.

Oliver, José R. *Caciques and Cemí Idols: The Web Spun by Taíno Rulers Between Hispaniola and Puerto Rico.* Tuscaloosa: University of Alabama Press, 2009.

Olson, Wallace M. *The Tlingit: An Introduction to Their Culture and History.* Akuke Bay, AK: Heritage Research, 2004.

Opler, Morris E. *An Apache Life-Way: The Economic, Social, and Religious Institutions of the Chiricahua Indians.* Chicago: University of Chicago Press, 1941.

Orange, Claudia. *The Treaty of Waitangi.* Wellington, New Zealand: Allen & Unwin, 1987.

Oraon, Prakash C. *Land and People of Jharkhand.* Ranchi, India: Jharkhand Tribal Welfare Research Institute, 2003.

O'Rourke, Shane. *The Cossacks.* Manchester, UK: Manchester University Press, 2007.

Oshomha, Imoagene. *The Hausa and Fulani of Northern Nigeria.* Ibadan, Nigeria: New-Era, 1990.

Ota, A.B. *Primitive Tribal Groups of Orissa.* Bhubaneswar, India: Scheduled Castes and Scheduled Tribes Research and Training Institute, 2008.

Ota, A.B., and Sarat C. Mohanty. *Bonda.* Bhubaneswar, India: Scheduled Castes and Scheduled Tribes Research and Training Institute, 2008.

O'Tailan, Jock. *Laos.* Bath, UK: Footprint, 2008.

Oyebade, Adebayo, ed. *The Foundations of Nigeria: Essays in Honor of Toyin Falola.* Trenton, NJ: Africa World Press, 2003.

Oyeneye, O.Y., and M.O. Shoremi, eds. *Nigerian Life and Culture.* Ogun, Nigeria: Ogun State University Press, 1985.

Padhy, Krushna S., and Purna C. Satapathy. *Tribal India.* New Delhi, India: Ashish, 1989.

Paine, Robert. *Herds of the Tundra: A Portrait of Saami Reindeer Pastoralism.* Washington, DC: Smithsonian Institution Press, 1994.

Palka, Joel W. *Unconquered Lacandon Maya.* Gainesville: University Press of Florida, 2005.

Pan, Christoph, Beate Sybille Pfeil, and Michael Geistlinger. *National Minorities in Europe.* West Lafayette, IN: Purdue University Press, 2004.

Panda, Nishakar. *Policies, Programmes, and Strategies for Tribal Development: A Critical Appraisal.* Delhi, India: Kalpaz, 2006.

Pankhrust, Richard. *The Ethiopians: A History.* Oxford, UK: Blackwell, 2001.

Parker, Arthur C. *An Analytical History of the Seneca Indians.* Rochester: New York State Archaeological Association, Lewis H. Morgan Chapter, 1926.

Parkin, Robrt. *The Munda of Central India: An Account of Their Social Organization.* New York: Oxford University Press, 1992.

Parris, Ronald G. *Hausa.* New York: Rosen, 1996.

Pati, R.N., and Jagannath Dash. *Tribes and Indigenous People of India: Problems and Prospects.* New Delhi, India: APH, 2002.

Patnaik, N. *The Kandha of Orissa.* Bhubaneswar, India: Scheduled Castes and Scheduled Tribes Research and Training Institute, 2006.

Pavitt, Nigel. *Turkana.* London: Harvill, 1997.

Pavy, Didier. *The Belgians.* Paris: Grasset, 1999.

Peers, Laura. *The Ojibwa of Western Canada, 1780 to 1870.* St. Paul: Minnesota Historical Society, 1994.

Peires, J.B. *The House of Phalo: The History of the Xhosa People in the Days of Their Independence.* Berkeley: University of California Press, 1983.

Peterson, Jacqueline Louise, and Jennifer Brown, eds. *The New Peoples: Being and Becoming Métis in North America.* Winnipeg, Canada: University of Manitoba Press, 1984.

Petridis, Constantine. *Art and Power in the Central African Savanna: Luba, Songye, Chokwe, Luluwa.* Cleveland, OH: Cleveland Museum of Art, 2008.

Pevar, Stephen L. *The Rights of Indians and Tribes: The Basic ACLU Guide to Indian and Tribal Rights.* 2nd ed. Carbondale: Southern Illinois University Press, 1992.

Pflüg, Melissa A. *Ritual and Myth in Odawa Revitalization: Reclaiming a Sovereign Place.* Norman: University of Oklahoma Press, 1998.

Phillips, Caroline, and Harry Allen, eds. *Bridging the Divide: Indigenous Communities and Archaeology into the 21st Century.* Walnut Creek, CA: Left Coast, 2010.

Pholsena, Vatthana. *Post-War Laos: The Politics of Culture, History, and Identity.* Ithaca, NY: Cornell University Press, 2006.

Plakans, Andrejs. *The Latvians: A Short History.* Stanford, CA: Hoover Institution Press, 1995.

Pluth, David, Sylvester Onyang, and Jeremy O'Kasick. *Karamoja: Uganda's Land of Warrior Nomads.* Stäfia, Switzerland: Little Wolf, 2007.

Poggo, Scopas Sekwat. *The First Sudanese Civil War: Africans, Arabs, and Israelis in the Southern Sudan, 1955–1972.* New York: St. Martin's, 2009.

Pool, David. *From Guerrillas to Government: The Eritrean People's Liberation Front.* Athens: Ohio University Press, 2001.

Popescu, Nicu. *Europe's Unrecognised Neighbours: The EU in Abkhazia and South Ossetia.* Brussels, Belgium: Centre for European Policy Studies, 2007.

Poruciuc, Adrian. *Prehistoric Roots of Romanian and Southeast European Traditions.* Ed. Joan Marler and Miriam Robbins Dexter. Sebastopol, CA: Institute of Archaeomythology, 2010.

Postero, Nancy Grey, and León Zamosc, eds. *The Struggle for Indigenous Rights in Latin America.* Portland, OR: Sussex Academic Press, 2004.

Prasad, R.N., and A.K. Agarwal. *Modernisation of the Mizo Society: Imperatives and Perspectives.* New Delhi, India: Mittal, 2003.

Prashad, Vijay. *The Darker Nations: A People's History of the Third World.* New York: New Press, 2008.

Prins, Harald E.L. *The Mi'kmaq: Resistance, Accommodation, and Cultural Survival.* Toronto, Canada: Harcourt Brace, 1996.

Prizel, Ilya. *National Identity and Foreign Policy: Nationalism and Leadership in Poland, Russia, and the Ukraine.* New York: Cambridge University Press, 1998.

Probst, Peter, and Gerd Spittler, eds. *Between Resistance and Expansion: Explorations of Local Vitality in Africa.* Münster, Germany: Lit, 2004.

Pugliese Carratelli, Giovanni, ed. *The Western Greeks: Classical Civilization in the Western Mediterranean.* London: Thames & Hudson, 1996.

Rabben, Linda. *Brazil's Indians and the Onslaught of Civilization: The Yanomami and the Kayapó.* Seattle: University of Washington Press, 2004.

Radcliffe-Brown, A.R. *The Andaman Islanders.* New York: Free Press, 1964.

Radin, Paul. *The Winnebago Tribe.* Lincoln: University of Nebraska Press, 1990.

Rafert, Stewart J. *The Miami Indians of Indiana: A Persistent People, 1654–1994.* Indianapolis: Indiana Historical Society, 1999.

Rahhal, Suleiman Musa. *The Right to Be Nuba: The Story of a Sudanese People's Struggle for Survival.* Trenton, NJ: Red Sea, 2001.

Rahman, Mizanur. *The Garos: Struggling to Survive in the Valley of Death.* Dhaka, India: Empowerment through Law of the Common People, 2006.

Rao, Vavilala S., and D.R. Krishna Patnaik. *Gadaba: The Language and the People.* Guntur, India: Soumya Sushama, 1992.

Ravuvu, Asesela. *Vaka i Taukei: The Fijian Way of Life.* Suva, Fiji: University of the South Pacific, 1983.

Rawls, James J. *Indians of California: The Changing Image.* Norman: University of Oklahoma Press, 1984.

Rear, Michael. *Intervention, Ethnic Conflict and State-Building in Iraq: A Paradigm for the Post-Colonial State.* New York: Routledge, 2008.

Reed, Nelson A. *The Caste War of Yucatán.* Stanford, CA: Stanford University Press, 2001.

Reed, Richard K. *Forest Dwellers, Forest Protectors: Indigenous Models for International Development.* 2nd ed. Upper Saddle River, NJ: Prentice Hall, 2009.

Reefe, Thomas. *The Rainbow and the Kings: A History of the Luba Empire to 1891.* Berkeley: University of California Press, 1981.

Reichel-Dolmatoff, Geraldo. *The Forest Within: The World View of the Tukano Amazonian Indians.* London: Themis, 1997.

Reinhardt, Akim D. *Ruling Pine Ridge: Oglala Lakota Politics from the IRA to Wounded Knee.* Lubbock: Texas Tech University Press, 2007.

Renshaw, John. *The Indians of the Paraguayan Chaco: Identity and Economy.* Lincoln: University of Nebraska Press, 2002.

Renton, David, David Seddon, and Leo Zeilig. *The Congo Plunder and Resistance.* New York: Zed, 2007.

Rhodes, Daniel. *Historical Archaeologies of Nineteenth-Century Colonial Tanzania: A Comparative Study.* Oxford, UK: Archaeopress.

Richardson, Benjamin J., Shin Imai, and Kent McNeil, eds. *Indigenous Peoples and the Law: Comparative and Critical Perspectives.* Portland, OR: Hart, 2009.

Richter, Daniel K. *The Ordeal of the Longhouse: The People of the Iroquois League in the Era of European Colonization.* Chapel Hill: University of North Carolina Press, 1992.

Rizvi, S.H.M., and Shibani Roy. *Garo (Achik) Tribe of Meghalaya.* Delhi, India: B.R., 2006.

———. *Khasi Tribe of Meghalaya.* Delhi, India: B.R., 2006.

———. *Mizo Tribes in North East India.* Delhi, India: B.R., 2006.

Roberts, Andrew D. *A History of the Bemba: Political Growth and Change in North-Eastern Zambia Before 1900.* Madison: University of Wisconsin Press, 1973.

Robinson, David. *Muslim Societies in African History.* Cambridge, UK: Cambridge University Press, 2004.

Robinson, David, and Douglas Smith. *Sources of the African Past: Case Studies of Five Nineteenth-Century African Societies.* New York: Africana, 1979.

Rodnick, David. *The Fort Belknap Assiniboine of Montana: A Study in Culture Change.* New York: AMS, 1978.

Romano, David. *The Kurdish Nationalist Movement: Opportunity, Mobilization, and Identity.* New York: Cambridge University Press, 2006.

Róna-Tas, András. *Chuvash Studies.* Budapest, Hungary: Akademiai Kiado, 1982.

Rorlich, Azade-Ayse. *The Volga Tatars: A Profile in National Resilience.* Stanford, CA: Hoover Institution Press, 1986.

Roscoe, John. *The Baganda.* London: Macmillan, 1911.

Ross, Eric S. *Culture and Customs of Senegal.* Westport, CT: Greenwood, 2008.

Rossabi, Morris. *Modern Mongolia: From Khans to Commissars to Capitalists.* Berkeley: University of California Press, 2005.

Roulet, Florencia. *Human Rights and Indigenous Peoples: A Handbook on the UN System.* Copenhagen, Denmark: International Work Group for Indigenous Affairs, 1999.

Rouse, Irving. *The Taínos: Rise and Decline of the People Who Greeted Columbus.* New Haven, CT: Yale University Press, 1992.

Roy, B.C., ed. *Tribals of Orissa.* Delhi, India: Gian, 1989.

Roy, D.C. *Dynamics of Social Formation Among the Lepchas.* New Delhi, India: Akansha, 2005.

Roy, Shibani. *Koli Culture: A Profile of the Culture of Talpad Vistar.* New Delhi, India: Cosmo, 1983.

Rubel, Paula G. *The Kalmyk Mongols.* New York: Routledge, 1997.

Ruby, Robert H., and John A. Brown. *Indians of the Pacific Northwest.* Norman: University of Oklahoma Press, 1988.

Ruland-Thorne, Kate. *The Yavapai: People of the Red Rocks, People of the Sun.* Sedona, AZ: Thorne, 1983.

Rus, Jan, Rosalva Aída Hernández Castillo, and Shanna L. Mattiace, eds. *Mayan Lives, Mayan Utopias: The Indigenous Peoples of Chiapas and the Zapatista Rebellion.* Lanham, MD: Rowman & Littlefield, 2003.

Russell, R.V. *The Tribes and Castes of the Central Provinces of India.* Vol. 4. New Delhi, India: Asian Educational Services, 1993.

Sachchidananda and R.R. Prasad, eds. *Encyclopaedic Profile of Indian Tribes.* New Delhi, India: Discovery, 1998.

Sachse, Frauke, ed. *Maya Ethnicity: The Construction of Ethnic Identity from Preclassic to Modern Times.* Markt Schwaben, Germany: Verlag Anton Saurwein, 2006.

Sahay, Kamal K. *Development of Gond Tribes in Modern Perspective: A Sociological Study.* New Delhi, India: Classical, 2005.

Sahu, Chaturbhuj. *Aspects of Tribal Studies.* New Delhi, India: Sarup & Sons, 2006.

Salamone, Frank A. *The Hausa of Nigeria.* Lanham, MD: University Press of America, 2010.

Salm, Steven J., and Toyin Falola. *Culture and Customs of Ghana.* Westport, CT: Greenwood, 2002.

Salvador, Mari Lyn. *The Art of Being Kuna: Layers of Meaning Among the Kuna of Panama.* Seattle: University of Washington Press, 1997.

Samek, Hana. *The Blackfoot Confederacy, 1880–1920: A Comparative Study of Canadian and U.S. Indian Policy.* Albuquerque: University of New Mexico Press, 1987.

Samson, Colin. *A Way of Life That Does Not Exist: Canada and the Extinguishment of the Innu.* St. John's, Canada: Institute of Social and Economic Research, 2003.

Sando, Joe S. *Pueblo Profiles: Cultural Identity Through Centuries of Change.* Santa Fe, NM: Clear Light, 1998.

Sarkar, Jayanta, and Jyotirmoy Chakraborty, eds. *Transition, Change and Transformation: Impacting the Tribes in India.* Kolkata, India: Anthropological Survey of India, 2003.

Sawyer, Suzana. *Crude Chronicles: Indigenous Politics, Multinational Oil, and Neoliberalism in Ecuador.* Durham, NC: Duke University Press, 2004.

Schaefer, Stacy B., and Peter T. Furst. *People of the Peyote: Huichol Indian History, Religion and Survival.* Albuquerque: University of New Mexico Press, 1996.

Schliesinger, Joachim. *Ethnic Groups of Laos: Sino-Tibetan Speaking People.* Bangkok, Thailand: White Lotus, 2004.

Schmal, John P. *Indigenous Mexico: A State-by-State Analysis.* Austin: Texas Education Agency, 2006.

Schuster, Helen H. *The Yakima.* New York: Chelsea House, 1990.

Schwerzel, Jeffrey, Shanti Tuinstra, and Juddha Prasad Vaidya. *The Lapcha of Nepal.* Kathmandu, India: Udaya, 2000.

Seaman, Gary, and Jane S. Day, eds. *Ancient Traditions: Shamanism in Central Asia and the Americas.* Niwot: University Press of Colorado, 1994.

Selbach, Christopher. *The Volga Tatars Under Russian Domination.* Norderstedt, Germany: GRIN Verlag, 2001.

Sellato, Bernard. *Innermost Borneo: Studies in Dayak Culture.* Singapore: Singapore University Press, 2002.

Selverston-Scher, Melina. *Ethnopolitics in Ecuador: Indigenous Rights and the Strengthening of Democracy.* Coral Gables, FL: North-South Center Press at the University of Miami, 2001.

Sen, Satadru. *Savagery and Colonialism in the Indian Ocean: Power, Pleasure and the Andaman Islanders.* New York: Routledge, 2010.

Sen, Sipra. *Tribes of Tripura: Description, Ethnology and Bibliography.* New Delhi, India: Gyan, 1993.

Sengupta, Anita. *The Formation of the Uzbek Nation-State: A Study in Transition.* Lanham, MD: Lexington, 2003.

Service, Elman R. *Spanish–Guarani Relations in Early Colonial Paraguay.* Westport, CT: Greenwood, 1971.

Shack, William. *The Gurage: A People of the Ensete Culture.* London: Oxford University Press, 1966.

Sharer, Robert, and Loa Traxler. *The Ancient Maya.* Stanford, CA: Stanford University Press, 2005.

Sharma, Anima. *Tribe in Transition: A Study of Thakur Gonds.* New Delhi, India: Mittal, 2005.

Sharma, R.K., and S.K. Tiwari. *Tribal History of Central India.* Vol. 3. New Delhi, India: Aryan, 2002.

Sharma, S.K. *Mizoram.* New Delhi, India: Mittal, 2006.

Shasi, S.S. *Tribes of Andhra Pradesh.* New Delhi, India: Anmol, 1997.

Shaw, Anna Moore. *A Pima Past.* Tucson: University of Arizona Press, 1974.

Sheehan, Patricia. *Cultures of the World: Côte d'Ivoire.* New York: Marshall Cavendish, 2000.

Sheridan, Thomas E., and Nancy J. Parezo, eds. *Paths of Life: American Indians of the Southwest and Northern Mexico.* Tucson: University of Arizona Press, 1996.

Shirokogorov, Sergei M. *Social Organization of the Northern Tungus.* New York: Garland, 1979.

Siddle, Richard. *Race, Resistance and the Ainu of Japan.* London: Routledge, 1996.

Sieder, Rachel, ed. *Multiculturalism in Latin America: Indigenous Rights, Diversity, and Democracy.* New York: Palgrave Macmillan, 2002.

Simeone, William E. *Rifles, Blankets, and Beads: Identity, History, and the Northern Athapaskan Potlatch.* Norman: University of Oklahoma Press, 2002.

Simmons, Virginia McConnell. *The Ute Indians of Utah, Colorado, and New Mexico.* Boulder: University Press of Colorado, 2000.

Singh, C.P. *The Ho Tribe of Singhbhum.* New Delhi, India: Classical, 1978.

Singh, K. Suresh, ed. *People of India.* Kolkata, India: Anthropological Survey of India, 2008.

Sinha, A.P. *Religious Life in Tribal India: A Case-Study of Dudh Kharia.* New Delhi, India: Classical, 1989.

Skinner, Elliot P. *The Mossi of Burkina Faso: Chiefs, Politicians, and Soldiers.* Prospect Heights, IL: Waveland, 1989.

Skrefsrud, L.O., and P.O. Bodding. *Traditions and Institutions of the Santals.* New Delhi, India: Gyan, 2001.

Slezkine, Yuri. *Arctic Mirrors: Russia and the Small Peoples of the North.* Ithaca, NY: Cornell University Press, 1994.

Smith, Claire, Heather Burke, and Graeme K. Ward, eds. *Indigenous Cultures in an Interconnected World.* St. Leonards, Australia: Allen & Unwin, 2000.

Smith, Dean Howard. *Modern Tribal Development: Paths to Self-Sufficiency and Cultural Integrity in Indian Country.* Walnut Creek, CA: AltaMira, 2000.

Smith, Donald B., and Edward S. Rogers, eds. *Aboriginal Ontario: Historical Perspectives on the First Nations.* Toronto, Canada: Dundurn, 1994.

Snow, Dean R. *The Iroquois.* Cambridge, MA: Blackwell, 1994.

Snyder, Timothy. *The Reconstruction of Nations: Poland, Ukraine, Lithuania, Belarus, 1569–1999.* New Haven, CT: Yale University Press, 2004.

Sokolow, Gary, Jerry Stubben, and Raymond Smith. *Native Americans and Political Participation.* Santa Barbara, CA: ABC-CLIO, 2005.

Spicer, Edward H. *The Yaquis: A Cultural History.* Tucson: University of Arizona Press, 1980.

Stahl, Ann Brower. *Making History in Banda: Anthropological Visions of Africa's Past.* New York: Cambridge University Press, 2004.

Stamm, Henry E. *People of the Wind River: The Eastern Shoshones, 1825–1900.* Norman: University of Oklahoma Press, 1999.

Staniland, Martin. *The Lions of Dagbon: Political Change in Northern Ghana.* Cambridge, UK: Cambridge University Press, 1975.

Stark-Arola, Laura. *Peasants, Pilgrims, and Sacred Promises: Ritual and the Supernatural in Orthodox Karelian Folk Religion.* Helsinki, Finland: Finnish Literature Society, 2002.

Stearns, Mary Lee. *Haida Culture in Custody.* Seattle: University of Washington Press, 1981.

Steckley, John. *Full Circle: Canada's First Nations.* Ed. Bryan David Cummins. Toronto, Canada: Prentice Hall, 2001.

Stephen, Lynn. *Zapotec Women: Gender, Class, and Ethnicity in Globalized Oaxaca.* Durham, NC: Duke University Press, 2005.

Stern, Pamela R. *A to Z of the Inuit.* Lanham, MD: Rowman & Littlefield, 2009.

Stern, Pamela R., and Lisa Stevenson, eds. *Critical Inuit Studies: An Anthology of Contemporary Arctic Ethnography.* Lincoln: University of Nebraska Press, 2006.

Stern, Theodore. *The Klamath Tribe: A People and Their Reservation.* Seattle: University of Washington Press, 1966.

Steward, Charles, ed. *Creolization: History, Ethnography, Theory.* Walnut Creek, CA: Left Coast, 2007.

Steward, Julian H., ed. *Handbook of South American Indians.* New York: Cooper Square, 1963.

Steward, Julian H., and Erminie Wheeler-Voegelin. *The Northern Paiute Indians.* New York: Garland, 1974.

Stewart, Omer C. *Ute Peyotism: A Study of a Cultural Complex.* Boulder: University of Colorado Press, 1948.

Stidsen, Sille, ed. *The Indigenous World 2007.* Copenhagen, Denmark: International Work Group for Indigenous Affairs, 2007.

Stockel, H. Henrietta. *Shame and Endurance: The Untold Story of the Chiricahua Apache Prisoners of War.* Tucson: University of Arizona Press, 2006.

Stone, Gerald. *The Smallest Slavonic Nation: The Sorbs of Lusatia.* London: Athlone, 1972.

Stonich, Susan C., ed. *Endangered Peoples of Latin America: Struggles to Survive and Thrive.* Westport, CT: Greenwood, 2001.

Strother, Zoë S. *Visions of Africa: Pende.* Milan, Italy: 5 Continents, 2008.

Stunnenberg, Petrus Walterus. *Entitled to Land: The Incorporation of the Paraguayan and Argentinean Gran Chaco and the Spatial Marginalization of the Indian People.* Fort Lauderdale, FL: Breitenbach, 1993.

Sullivan, Lawrence E., ed. *Native Religions and Cultures of North America: Anthropology of the Sacred.* New York: Continuum, 2003.

Surrallés, Alexandre, and Pedro García Hierro, eds. *The Land Within: Indigenous Territory and the Perception of the Environment.* Copenhagen, Denmark: International Work Group for Indigenous Affairs, 2005.

Suzack, Cheryl, Shari M. Huhndorf, Jeanne Perrault, and Jean Barman, eds. *Indigenous Women and Feminism: Politics, Activism, Culture.* Vancouver, Canada: University of British Columbia Press, 2010.

Suzman, James. *Minorities in Independent Namibia.* London: Minority Rights Group International, 2002.

Swanton, John R. *The Indians of the Southeastern United States.* Washington, DC: Smithsonian Institution, 1979.

Swinimer, Ciarunji Chesaina. *Pokot.* New York: Rosen, 1994.

Symington, D.F. *Hunters of the Plains: Assiniboine Indians.* Toronto, Canada: Ginn, 1972.

Syukri, Ibrahim. *History of the Malay Kingdom of Patani.* Athens: Ohio University Press, 1985.

Szporluk, Roman, ed. *National Identity and Ethnicity in Russia and the New States of Eurasia.* Armonk, NY: M.E. Sharpe, 1994.

Ta-chuan, Sun. *The Struggle for Renaissance: Taiwan's Indigenous Culture.* Taipei, Taiwan: Sinorama, 1995.

Taylor, Colin F. *The American Indian: The Indigenous People of North America.* London: Salamander, 2003.

Taylor, Jean Gelman. *Indonesia: Peoples and Histories.* New Haven, CT: Yale University Press, 2004.

Taylor, Philip. *Cham Muslims of the Mekong Delta: Place and Mobility in the Cosmopolitan Periphery.* Honolulu: University of Hawaii Press, 2007.

Tehranian, Majid, and B. Jeannie Lum, eds. *Globalization and Identity: Cultural Diversity, Religion, and Citizenship.* Piscataway, NJ: Transaction, 2006.

Terraciano, Kevin. *The Mixtecs of Colonial Oaxaca: Nudzahui History, Sixteenth Through Eighteenth Centuries.* Stanford, CA: Stanford University Press, 2001.

Thompson, Liz, and Simon Coate. *The Bhil of India.* Port Melbourne, Australia: Reed Library, 1997.

Thornberry, Patrick. *Indigenous Peoples and Human Rights.* Huntington, NY: Juris, 2002.

Townsend, Richard F. *The Aztecs.* Rev. ed. London: Thames & Hudson, 2000.

Tran Ky Phuong, and Bruce M. Lockhart, eds. *The Cham of Vietnam: History, Society, and Art.* Singapore: National University of Singapore Press, 2010.

Trask, R.L. *The History of Basque.* London: Routledge, 1997.

Trigger, Bruce G. *Natives and Newcomers: Canada's "Heroic Age" Reconsidered.* Montreal, Canada: McGill-Queen's University Press, 1986.

Trivedi, Mridula. *Towards Social Mobility: A Study of the Bhils of South Rajasthan.* Udaipur, India: Himanshu, 2007.

Tucker, Toba. *Haudenosaunee: Portraits of the Firekeepers, the Onondaga Nation.* Syracuse, NY: Syracuse University Press, 1999.

Turnbull, Colin M. *The Forest People.* New York: Touchstone, 1987.

Turner, George. *Samoa: A Hundred Years Ago and Long Before.* Teddington, UK: Echo Library, 2006.

United Nations. *State of the World's Indigenous Peoples.* New York: United Nations, 2009.

Urban, Greg, and Joel Sherzer, eds. *Nation-States and Indians in Latin America.* Austin: University of Texas Press, 1991.

Uzendoski, Michael. *The Napo Runa of Amazonian Ecuador.* Urbana: University of Illinois Press, 2005.

Vaggioli, Domenico Felice, and John Crockett. *The Maori: A History of the Earliest Inhabitants of New Zealand.* Lewiston, NY: Edwin Mellen, 2010.

Vail, Leroy, ed. *The Creation of Tribalism in Southern Africa.* Berkeley: University of California Press, 1991.

Vakhtin, Nikolai. *Native Peoples of the Russian Far North.* London: Minority Rights Group, 1992.

Valdez, Norberto. *Ethnicity, Class, and the Indigenous Struggle for Land in Guerrero, Mexico.* New York: Garland, 1998.

Van Cott, Donna Lee., ed. *Indigenous Peoples and Democracy in Latin America.* New York: St. Martin's, 1994.

———. *Radical Democracy in the Andes.* New York: Cambridge University Press, 2008.

Van der Post, Laurens. *The Lost World of the Kalahari.* New York: Harcourt Brace Jovanovich, 1977.

Vansina, Jan. *Antecedents to Modern Rwanda: The Nyiginya Kingdom.* Oxford, UK: James Currey, 2004.

———. *Being Colonized: The Kuba Experienced in Rural Congo, 1880–1960.* Madison: University of Wisconsin Press, 2010.

Varese, Steffano. *Salt of the Mountain: Campa Ashaninka History and Resistance in the Peruvian Jungle.* Norman: University of Oklahoma Press, 2002.

Velasco Ortiz, Laura. *Mixtec Transnational Identity.* Tucson: University of Arizona Press, 2005.

Vennum, Thomas, Jr. *Wild Rice and the Ojibway People.* St. Paul: Minnesota Historical Society, 1988.

Vickers, Miranda. *The Albanians: A Modern History.* 2nd ed. London: I.B. Tauris, 1997.

Vitebsky, Piers. *The Reindeer People: Living with Animals and Spirits in Siberia.* Boston: Houghton Mifflin, 2005.

Von Fürer-Haimendorf, Christoph, ed. *Tribes of India; The Struggle for Survival.* Berkeley: University of California Press, 1982.

Wadden, Marie. *Nitassinan: The Innu Struggle to Reclaim Their Homeland.* Vancouver, Canada: Douglas and McIntyre, 1991.

Wagner, Günter. *The Bantu of North Kavirondo.* Oxford, UK: Oxford University Press, 1949.

Walker, James R. *Lakota Society.* Ed. Raymond J. DeMallie. Lincoln: University of Nebraska Press, 1982.

Wallace, Anthony F.C. *The Death and Rebirth of the Seneca.* New York: Alfred A. Knopf, 1970.

Wallin, Theodore. *The Ngbaka of Northern Zaire.* Washington, DC: Library of Congress, 1973.

Warren, Kay B. *Indigenous Movements and Their Critics: Pan-Maya Activism in Guatemala.* Princeton, NJ: Princeton University Press, 1998.

———. *Indigenous Movements, Self-Representation, and the State in Latin America.* Austin: University of Texas Press, 2003.

Watson, Robert Mackezie. *History of Samoa.* 1918. Breinigsville, PA: BiblioBazaar, 2009.

Weaver, Muriel Porter. *The Aztecs, Maya, and Their Predecessors: Archaeology of Mesoamerica.* 3rd ed. San Diego, CA: Academic Press, 1993.

Weinberg, Bill. *Homage to Chiapas: The New Indigenous Struggles in Mexico.* New York: Verso, 2002.

Weiner, James F. *Mountain Papuans: Historical and Comparative Perspectives from New Guinea Fringe Highland Societies.* Ann Arbor: University of Michigan Press, 1988.

Weiss, Gerald. *Campa Cosmology: The World of a Forest Tribe in South America.* New York: American Museum of Natural History, 1975.

Weist, Tom. *A History of the Cheyenne People.* Billings, MT: Council for Indian Education, 2005.

Weller, R. Charles. *Rethinking Kazakh and Central Asian Nationhood: A Challenge to Prevailing Western Views.* Los Angeles: Asia Research Associates, 2006.

Were, Gideon S. *A History of the Abaluyia of Western Kenya, c. 1500–1930.* Nairobi, Kenya: East African Publishing House, 1967.

Wessendorf, Kathrin, ed. *The Indigenous World 2008.* Copenhagen, Denmark: International Work Group for Indigenous Affairs, 2008.

Westra, Laura. *International Justice and the Rights of Indigenous Peoples: International and Domestic Legal Perspectives.* Sterling, VA: Earthscan, 2008.

Whitecotton, Joseph W. *The Zapotecs: Princes, Priests and Peasants.* Norman: University of Oklahoma Press, 1977.

Whitten, Norman E., Jr., and Dorothea S. Whitten. *Puyo Runa: Imagery and Power in Modern Amazonia.* Urbana: University of Illinois Press, 2008.

Wijsen, Frans, and Ralph Tanner. *I Am Just a Sukuma: Globalization and Identity Construction in Northwest Tanzania.* New York: Rodopi, 2002.

Willis, Roy G. *The Fipa and Related Peoples of South-West Tanzania and North-East Zambia.* London: International African Institute, 1966.

Wilson, Samuel M., ed. *The Indigenous People of the Caribbean.* Gainesville: University Press of Florida, 1997.

Winstedt, Richard Olof, and Seong Chee Tam. *The Malays: A Cultural History.* Boulder, CO: Lynne Rienner, 1981.

Wolf, Eric R. *Europe and the People Without History.* Berkeley: University of California Press, 1982.

Wongtes, Sujit. *The Thai People and Culture.* Bangkok, Thailand: Public Relations Department, 2000.

Work, L. Susan. *The Seminole Nation of Oklahoma: A Legal History.* Norman: University of Oklahoma Press, 2010.

Wright, Bill, and E. John Gesick, Jr. *The Texas Kickapoo: Keepers of Tradition.* El Paso: Texas Western, 1996.

Wunder, John R. *The Kiowa.* New York: Chelsea House, 1989.

Yescas, Carlos. *Indigenous Routes: A Framework for Understanding Indigenous Migration.* Geneva, Switzerland: International Organization for Migration, 2008.

Zhongshu, Wang. *Han Civilization.* Trans. K.C. Chang et al. New Haven, CT: Yale University Press, 1982.

Web Sites

Alaska Native Collections, Smithsonian Institution. http://alaska.si.edu/cultures.asp

Assembly of First Nations. www.afn.ca

Black Mesa Indigenous Support. http://blackmesais.org

Center for Native Peoples and the Environment. www.esf.edu/nativepeoples

Center for World Indigenous Studies. http://cwis.org

Cultural Survival. www.culturalsurvival.org

Indian Law Resource Center. www.indianlaw.org

Indigenous Peoples Issues & Resources. http://indigenouspeoplesissues.com

Inter Press Service News Agency. www.ipsnews.net

International Fund for Agricultural Development, Indigenous Peoples. www.ifad.org/english/indigenous/index.htm

International Work Group for Indigenous Affairs. www.iwgia.org

Inuit Circumpolar Conference. www.inuit.org

Kapaeeng Foundation: A Human Rights Organisation for Indigenous Peoples of Bangladesh. www.kapaeeng.org

Métis Nation of Ontario. www.metisnation.org

Ministry of Amerindian Affairs, Guyana. www.amerindian.gov.gy

Minority Rights Group International. www.minorityrights.org

National Geographic Society, Enduring Voices Project. http://travel.nationalgeographic.com/travel/enduring-voices

Native Peoples Magazine. www.nativepeoples.com

Native Web, Resources for Indigenous Cultures around the World. www.nativeweb.com

Navajo Nation. www.navajo-nsn.gov

Newfoundland and Labrador Heritage. www.heritage.nf.ca

South African San Institute. www.san.org.za

Survival International. www.survivalinternational.org

Union of British Columbia Indian Chiefs. www.ubcic.bc.ca

United Nations Development Programme. www.undp.org

United Nations Office of the High Commissioner for Human Rights. www.ohchr.org

United Nations Permanent Forum on Indigenous Issues. http://social.un.org/index/IndigenousPeoples.aspx

Index

Page numbers in italics indicate illustrations; italic page numbers followed by t indicate tables.

Bafio (Gbaya leader), 1:33
Baganda, 1:18–19; 3:691, 692
Bagaza, Jean-Baptiste, 3:582
Baggara, 3:676
Bagisu, 1:19; 3:691
Bagratid dynasty, 2:262
Bagwere, 1:19
Bahā' Ullā, 3:626
Baha'i faith, 3:626
Baha'i Radio Project, 3:779
Bahamas, 2:487
   See also Taino
Bahasa Indonesia. See Indonesian
   language
Bah-kho-je. See Iowa people
Bahnar, 1:226
Bahrey (Amhara monk), 1:71
Bai, 3:590
Baiga, 2:524
Bainimarama, Voreqe "Frank," 3:613,
   614
Baishagu festival, 2:526
Baja California, Mexico, 3:641, 642, 785
BAJARAKA (Hill Tribe independence
   movement), 1:227
Bajau, 1:192–193
Bajuni, 1:84; 3:669, 670
Baka, 3:583
Bakassi Self-Determination Movement,
   3:583–584
Baker, Shirley, 3:687
Baki. See Lega
Bakiyev, Kurmanbek, 2:546
Balaguer, Joaquín, 3:604
Balangir District, Orissa, India, 2:524,
   540–541
Balbali, Makhluf al- (Muslim jurist),
   2:333
Balearic Islands, Spain, 3:674
Balega. See Lega
Balewa, Alhaji Abubarka Tafawa, 1:37
Bali (island), Indonesia, 1:194; 3:832
Balinese, 1:193–194
Balinese language, 1:193
Balkan Romani, 2:361
Balkan War, first (1912), 2:273, 320
Balkan War, second (1913), 2:273
Balkans, 2:255
   See also Albanians; Serbs
Ballplay, Tennessee, 2:415
Baloch, 2:513, 515, 516
Balochistan, Pakistan, 2:515
Baltic Germans, 2:339
Baltic languages, 2:338, 339, 340, 341
Baltic peoples, 3:665
   See also Estonians; Latvians;
      Lithuanians

Baltic-Finnic languages, 2:297–298
Baltic-Finnic people, 2:335–336
   See also Finns
Baluba Empire, 1:81
Baluba people, 1:56
Balubaale (religion), 1:18
Balún Canán (Castellanos), 1:166
Bamar language, 1:194
Bamileke, 1:7, 19–20; 3:583
Bamileke dialect continuum, 1:19–20
Bamiyan, Afghanistan, 2:532, 533
Bamiyan University, Afghanistan,
   2:533
Ban Ki-moon, 3:681, 852
Banda, 1:20–21
Banda, Hastings Kamuzu, 3:638
Banda Paroja. See Bonda
Bandapana Parab festival, 2:529
Banderas, Juan, 1:143, 172
Bandiagara Escarpment, Mali, 1:29
Bandiagara region, Mali, 3:832
Bangla language. See Bengali language
Bangladesh
   assimilation, 3:713
   climate change impact, 3:715–716
   formation, 2:513; 3:800
   industrial development, 3:757
   introduction, 2:513–514
   Kuki, 2:543
   languages, 2:514
   Magh, 2:549
   Mizo population, 2:551
   Munda, 2:552
   Pashtun minority, 2:559
   population, 2:513
   Santal, 2:560
   social discrimination, 3:847
   Sunni Muslims, 2:514
   tribes, 2:514
   See also Garo; Hajong
Baniwa, 3:579
Banjara (Lambadi), 2:518; 3:623
Banjuri. See Banjara
Banks, Dennis, 3:694
Banks, Joseph, 3:844–845
Bankura District, West Bengal, India,
   2:538
Bannock, 2:474, 486, 493
Bannock War (1878), 2:474, 493
Bantu language group
   Central African Republic, 3:588
   Hehe, 1:38
   Hutu, 1:39
   Kikuyu, 1:48
   Kinyamwezi, 1:67
   Kiswahili, 1:84
   Otjiherero, 1:39

Bantu language group (continued)
   Rundi, 1:73
   Sukuma, 1:83
   Zulu, 1:100
Bantu-speaking peoples
   Baganda, 1:18
   Bagwere, 1:19
   Bemba, 1:22
   in Cameroon, 3:583
   in Democratic Republic of the
      Congo, 3:599, 600
   environmental influences, 1:7
   expansion, 1:77
   forced assimilation, 3:711
   intermarriage with Pokot, 1:73
   in Kenya, 3:632, 633
   Luhya, 1:53
   in Madagascar, 3:636
   in Malawi, 3:637
   marriage laws, 1:19
   migrations, 1:5; 3:609
   in Mozambique, 3:644
   religion, 1:19
   Shona, 1:76–78
   in Somalia, 3:669, 670
   in Swahili heritage, 1:83, 84
   in Tanzania, 3:684
   in Uganda, 3:691
   Xhosa, 1:95
   Yombe, 1:97
   in Zambia, 3:699
"Bantustans" (self-governing
   territories), 1:64, 65, 88–89, 96
Banu Marin (Marinid dynasty), 3:643
Banu Umayyad clan, 3:680
Banyankole, 3:691, 740
Banyarwanda. See Tutsi
Banyoro, 3:691
Baqhdaida, Iraq, 2:517; 3:629
Barack Khan (White Horde), 2:536
Baranof, Alexander, 2:498
Barbareno. See Chumash
Barbary Coast, North Africa, 1:24
Barboncito (Navajo leader), 2:463
Barclay, Barry, 1:228
Bargarh District, Orissa, India, 2:524,
   550
Baring, Evelyn. See Cromer, Lord
Barito languages, 1:61
Barnwell, John, 2:445–446
Barons, Krišjānis, 2:338
Barras, Bruno, 3:794
Barre, Siad, 1:80
Barreiro, José, 3:599
Barreto, Francisco, 1:78
Barrett, Stephen Melvil, 2:405
Barrows, David, 3:664

Kayaes Matchitiwuk. *See* Menominee
Kayaking, 2:508
Kayambi, 1:129, 131
Kayan (Long Neck Karen), 3:639, 747
Kayapó, 1:110; 3:782
Kayi Turkmen, 2:566
Kayibanda, Grégoire, 1:92
Kayor, 1:94
Kazakh Autonomous Prefecture,
    China, 2:536
Kazakh khanate, 2:536
Kazakh language, 2:536
Kazakhs, 2:536–538
    in China, 3:590
    conflicts with Oyrat, 2:536, 546
    festivals, 2:537
    introduction, 1:183
    mistakenly called Kyrgyz, 2:545
    Mongolian influences, 1:226; 2:536
    Persian influences, 2:536
    religious history, 2:536
    Russian control, 2:536–537
Kazakhstan
    ethnic groups, 2:313, 384, 519, 536,
        545, 563; 3:618
    independence, 2:537
    population, 2:536
    Russian control, 2:537
    See also Altay; Armenians; Chechens;
        Chuvash; Kazakhs
Kazan khanate, 2:346, 367, 383, 519;
    3:665, 666
Kearny, Stephen W., 2:483
Kebra Nagast (Glory of the Kings), 1:15
Kechwa language, 1:174
Kede, 3:740
Keeler, W.W., 2:417
Keening, 3:772
Kefa kingdom, 1:79
Keino, Kip, 1:46
Kekchi Maya, 3:575, 785
Kekionga, Indiana, 2:452
Kennedy, John F., 2:315
Kennedy Report (1969), 3:837
Kente cloth, 1:17
Kenya, 3:631–633
    all-female village, 3:860
    colonial era, 1:54, 57; 3:632–633
    drought, 1:90; 3:632
    ethnic conflicts, 1:57–58
    ethnic groups, 3:632
    geography, 3:631
    history of the native people,
        3:632–633
    independence, 1:49, 55, 90
    indigenous policy, 3:633
    land rights, 3:633

Kenya *(continued)*
    languages, 1:9, 85; 3:632, 684, 769
    mining, 3:796
    politics and government, 1:55–56, 73
    population, 3:632
    Somalia peace talks, 3:670
    trade, 3:632
    water rights, 3:796
    women's rights, 3:860
    See also Borana; Dinka; Kalenjin;
        Kikuyu; Luhya; Luo; Maasai;
        Pokot; Swahili; Teso; Turkana
Kenya, Mount, Kenya, 1:6
Kenya National African Union, 1:55
Kenyah, 3:639
Kenyatta, Jomo, 1:49
Keokuk, Chief (Sac), 2:485
Keonjhar District, Orissa, India, 2:522,
    534, 541
Kepulauan Biak, Indonesia, 1:222
K'eq'chi Indians, 1:141
Kerala, India, 2:556; 3:623
Kerei (Kazakh khan), 2:536
Keresan Pueblo, 2:482
Kerlani Pashtun, 2:513
Keshena, Wisconsin, 2:447
Ket, 1:212, 235
Ketagalan, 3:683
Kettle Falls, Washington, 2:425
Khairun, sultan of Ternate, 3:624
Kham Tibetans, 3:725, 824
Khama, Ian, 3:579
Khamenci, Ayatollah, 3:627
Khammam District, Andhra Pradesh,
    India, 2:542–543
Khanda. *See* Khond
Khandayat Bhuinya, 2:522
Khangar, 2:550
Khanty, 3:795
Kharia, 2:533, 538; 3:784
Kharia language, 2:538
Kharijite Berbers, 3:688
Kharjites (Islamic sect), 3:688
Khasi, 2:514, 539; 3:623
Khasi Hills, Meghalaya, India, 2:539
Khasi language, 2:514, 539
Khasim Khan (Kazakh), 2:536
Khatulwar Gond, 2:530
Khazars, 2:334, 346
Kherai Puja festival, 2:526
Khieu Samphan, 1:198
Khipus, 3:841
Khitan, 1:209, 213; 2:545
    See also Liao
Khma people, 3:634
Khmelnytsky, Bohdan, 2:386
Khmer Angkor state, 3:594

Khmer Empire, 1:196; 3:775, 834
    See also Cambodians
Khmer Loeu. *See* Montagnards
Khmer Rouge, 1:196, 197–198; 3:594
Khoe language, 1:74
Khoikhoi, 3:711
Khoikhoi-speaking peoples, 3:646
Khoisan, 1:5; 3:632, 699, 813
Khoisan languages, 1:9; 3:671
Khoisan-speaking peoples, 3:684
Khomeini, Ayatollah, 2:544; 3:627
Khond, 2:539–540; 3:623
Khondmal region, India, 2:540
Khono, 1:226
Khrushchev, Nikita, 1:236; 2:537
Khurda Rebellion (1817), 3:623
Khwe. *See* San
Khyber Pakhtunkhwa region, Pakistan,
    2:532
Kialegee Tribal Town, 2:460
Kibaki, Mwai, 1:58
K'iche'. *See* Quiché
Kichwa, 1:129–133, 154, 175; 3:605,
    606, 796
Kichwa language, 1:130, 132, 155,
    174
Kickapoo, 2:394, 439–440, 485
Kicking Bear, 2:473
Kiel, Treaty of (1814), 2:292, 352,
    381; 3:679
Kiev, Ukraine, 2:366, 380, 386
Kievan Rus, 2:385; 3:665
Kiga. *See* Hutu
Kikuyu, 1:7, 48–49, 57–58, 85; 3:633
Kikuyu language, 1:48
Kilega language, 1:51
Kilimanjaro, Mount, Tanzania, 1:6
Kilivila language, 1:222
Kilivila-Louisiades languages, 1:222
Kiliwa, 3:785
Kiliwa language, 3:642
Kilwa (island), Tanzania, 3:685
Kim Pusik, 1:230
Kimambo, Isaria, 3:685
Kimberley, South Africa, 3:849
Kinbasket. *See* Shuswap
King, Michael, 1:228
King Philip (Metacom; Wampanoag),
    2:503
King Philip's War (1675–1676),
    2:403, 461, 477, 503
Kingdom of Serbs, Croats, and
    Slovenes, 2:269, 348, 374, 377
Kingman, Arizona, 2:436
Kings
    as deities, 1:52
    See also specific kings